0°
20°

Murmansk

Narvik

White Sea

Archangel

SWEDEN

FINLAND

Trondheim

NORWAY

Kronstadt

Bergen

Oslo

Leningrad

Stockholm

60°

*NORTH
SEA*

ESTONIA

BALTIC SEA

LATVIA

S O V I E T

DENMARK

LITHUANIA

Vilno

Minsk

Moscow

GREAT
BRITAIN

EIRE

NETH.

Berlin

EAST
PRUSSIA

Danzig

Warsaw

U N I O N

London

GERMANY

POLAND

Kiev

Kursk

BEL.

Prague

Dunkirk

CZECHOSLOVAKIA

Paris

Maginot
Line

Munich

Vienna

Stalingrad

FRANCE

SWITZ.

AUSTRIA

HUNGARY

English Channel

Vichy

Geneva

Ljubljana

ROMANIA

Milan

ITALY

Trieste

Belgrade

Yalta

Bordeaux

Toulon

YUGOSLAVIA

BULGARIA

BLACK SEA

Rome

Anzio

ALBANIA

Madrid

CORSICA

Salerno

GREECE

40°

PORTUGAL

SPAIN

SARDINIA

T U R K E Y

Teheran

M E D I T E R R A N E A N

SICILY

Athens

Adana

Algiers

Gibraltar

SPAN. MOROCCO

Tunis

CRETE

SYRIA

Casablanca

TUNISIA

S E A

LEBANON

Tripoli

Benghazi

Alexandria

PALESTINE

MOROCCO

Tobruk

Cairo

JORDAN

ALGERIA

El Alamein

*Suez
Canal*

SAUDI
ARABIA

Cyrenaica

Tripolitania

LIBYA

EGYPT

RED SEA

20°

FRENCH WEST AFRICA

ANGLO-EGYPTIAN
SUDAN

ERITREA

FRENCH
EQUATORIAL
AFRICA

GOLD
COAST

0°

NE

Takoradi

NIGERIA

ETHIOPIA

40°

20°

H. Faye

THE BIG THREE

THE BIG THREE

CHURCHILL
ROOSEVELT
AND STALIN
IN PEACE & WAR

ROBIN EDMONDS

W. W. NORTON & COMPANY · New York London

Lines from W. H. Auden's "Out on the Lawn I Lie in Bed"
are reprinted by kind permission of Princeton University
Press.

PRINTED IN THE UNITED STATES OF AMERICA

The text of this book is composed in Bembo,
Composition and manufacturing by the
Haddon Craftsmen Inc.
Book design by *Guenet Abraham.*

Library of Congress Cataloging-in-Publication Data

Edmonds, Robin.
The big three : Churchill, Roosevelt, and Stalin in peace and
war / Robin Edmonds.
p. cm.
Includes bibliographical references.
1. World War, 1939–1945—Diplomatic history.
2. Churchill, Winston, Sir, 1874-1965.   3. Roosevelt,
Franklin D. (Franklin Delano), 1882-1945.   4. Stalin,
Joseph, 1879-1953.   I. Title.
D749.E36   1990
940.53'2—dc20   90-6854

ISBN 0-393-02889-5
W.W. Norton & Company, Inc. , 500 Fifth Avenue,
New York, N.Y. 10110
W.W. Norton & Company, Ltd., 10 Coptic Street,
London WCIA IPU

2   3   4   5   6   7   8   9   0

FOR ENID

MARK ANTONY: . . . Therefore let our alliance be combin'd
Our best friends made and our best means stretched out
And let us presently go sit in Council,
How covert matters may be best disclos'd
And open perils surest answered.

OCTAVIUS CAESAR: Let us do so: for we are at the stake,
And bay'd about with many enemies
And some, that smile, have in their hearts, I fear,
Millions of mischiefs.

—Shakespeare, *Julius Caesar, Act IV: Sc. 1 (the end of the Triumvir scene)*

CONTENTS

LIST OF ILLUSTRATIONS

Photographs Follow Page 288

ILLUSTRATIONS

Churchill's birthday dinner party, Teheran, 30 November 1943.

"Rendezvous," David Low, cartoon, 20 September 1939.

"Now supposing we all try to go somewhere together," David Low, cartoon, 7 August 1942.

Winston Churchill, by Max Beerbohm, circa 1900.

Roosevelt reviewing the fleet, July 1938.

Franklin Roosevelt, by Leon Carlin, February 1934.

Stalin casting his vote in the Soviet election, 1937.

"Stalin's pipe," *Pravda*, cartoon, 25 February 1930.

"What, no chair for me?" David Low, cartoon, 30 September 1938.

"Britain's new defence," David Low, cartoon 5 October 1938.

"The Motherland—Mother calls!" poster.

"Women of Britain come into the factories," poster.

"Triumph over tyranny—Buy war bonds," poster.

The Big Three on the porch of the Soviet Legation, Teheran, December 1943.

The Big Three outside the Livadia Palace, Yalta, February 1945.

Roosevelt's last address to Congress, 1 March 1945

Churchill making his victory broadcast, May 1945.

Truman's final instruction to Stimson about the press release regarding the atomic bomb.

Attlee, Truman and Stalin at the Potsdam Conference, 1945.

Stalin's funeral bier, March 1953.

Churchill, aged 77, on board the *Williamsburg* with Truman.

MAPS

history may be most effectively reassessed: not too soon, when the events are still too close to the participants and not all the evidence can be assembled, but not too late, because those whose personal (though perhaps distorted) recollection of what happened may add an additional dimension, are no longer alive. In this particular case—the relationship between the "Big Three," as they came to be called during the Second World War—fifty years since the outbreak of the war seems the right interval. While the Cold War was at its height and for many years afterwards, historical vision was easily blurred. For a western historian it was tempting to attribute the defects of the post-war world to western ingenuousness or Soviet cunning in the 1940s, or to a mixture of the two; for an eastern historian the same applied in reverse. Simplistic views of this kind have become harder to sustain in the different political climate of today. On 20 January 1989 *Pravda* devoted six columns to an appreciation of Ronald Reagan; President Bush spoke, in his inaugural address on Capitol Hill, of "the new closeness with the Soviet Union," six weeks after President Gorbachev had—in New York—offered a partnership "to continue the dialogue" with the United States; and as this *annus mirabilis* went forward, it brought with it a tidal wave of political change in Eastern and Central Europe. Now that the era of "megaphone diplomacy"[2] has receded and the long-accepted premises of the East-West relationship are being reassessed, we may perhaps be spared the rhetoric that has coloured some historical work on both sides: selections of quotations from the past carefully tailored to suit almost any contemporary political prejudice. Today, moreover, Soviet willingness to apply *glasnost'* to the *belye pyatna* (blank spots) in Soviet history may also prompt a reexamination of some of the mythology that has become engrained in the national consciousness of the West.

Some distinguished forerunners[3] took 1941 as their point of departure. By the end of that year Britain, the Soviet Union and the United States were all three at war with Germany (and Britain and the United States also with Japan). At first sight this looks logical, because it tidies up the asymmetry of the different dates on which the three countries went to war. At the same time, it also tends to obscure the fact that the

PREFACE

This book tells a story of success and failure that has profoundly affected everyone living in the second half of the twentieth century, whether or not they lived through the Second World War. The international political[1] structure of the modern world, moreover, is directly linked to the way in which the relationship between Churchill, Roosevelt and Stalin evolved; how they reacted personally to each other; how they came to set their political sights for the post-war world as high as they did; and how this interplay between three men conducting a fight to the finish against common enemies across the world was followed, after the war had been won, by conflicting strains similar to those that brought the triumvirate of ancient Rome to an end.

Sooner or later an optimal moment arrives at which great events of

reasons for which each of them was in turn obliged to fight were completely different. Rather than pass over this distinction, this book follows another course: deepening the perspective to a point ten years before the Teheran Conference. The development of the wartime relationship between Churchill, Roosevelt and Stalin becomes more readily comprehensible if the historian begins by stepping back to 1933—the nadir of the Great Depression and the year in which Adolf Hitler assumed supreme power in Germany—and recalls where each of the three men stood at that time; and if he then goes on to examine the different ways in which they reacted to the tragic phantasmagoria of 1933–39. The opening chapters of this book, therefore, offer an account of the three men's ideas and policies during their separate, very different, approaches to a war that none of the three countries sought; indeed, all three governments went to extreme lengths in order not to become involved.

This approach obliges the historian to contend with another asymmetry—the prewar position of Churchill, who was out of office from 1929 until the outbreak of the Second World War, although this difficulty is lessened by the fact that in the political wilderness Churchill did not lead the life of a political hermit. A third asymmetry in this triangular relationship stems from the fact that the youngest member of the triumvirate died first—a month before the Second World War ended in Europe. Strictly speaking, therefore, the personal relationship between these three men ended on 12 April 1945. Partly because the Yalta Conference is impossible to understand in isolation from the Potsdam Conference that followed five months later, and partly because in the early months of his presidency Harry Truman pursued broadly Rooseveltian policies (stemming from decisions taken not only at Yalta, but also at Teheran, in 1943), the timespan of this study has been extended to the surrender of Japan, the last nation remaining at war with the Allies, in August 1945.

Whereas forty years ago one of the historian's most difficult problems was how to read between the lines of what was then known of the early 1940s, today it is how to read the story as a coherent whole. The analysis that this study offers will contain no dramatic revelations—the drama is all there already—but it may suggest some shifts of perspective that can modify our vision of the whole canvas. The historical balance was, for example, thrown out of kilter as long as the atomic dimension was treated almost as a side issue, whereas—as we now know—by the time the war ended it was uncomfortably near the heart of the matter.[4] The atomic gap in the historical evidence remained for nearly twenty years after the war. The *Ultra* secret (the cracking of the German *Enigma* high-grade cypher) was also closely guarded for a quarter of a century. Moreover, while the profusion of American and British governmental records of the whole of this period[5] has long been taken for granted, it is not generally realised how much Soviet primary material (for example, the volumes of the Soviet Government's wartime correspondence with the governments of Britain, France and the United States, published only in the 1980s) is now available. Many of these Soviet documents have not, at the time of writing, been translated from the Russian;[6] and to write this story without taking account of this material and of the historical reinterpretation currently being undertaken in the Soviet Union (of which Colonel-General Dmitrii Volkogonov's study of Stalin is a recent example) runs the risk of making it appear like an Anglo-American film with occasional Russian subtitles.[7]

The proportions of the labyrinth of historical material, both primary and secondary, relating to Churchill, Roosevelt and Stalin are now so vast that, for the student of this triangular relationship, the only sure guide through the labyrinth is to follow the footsteps of the three leaders, wherever they may lead him. If he chooses to follow this Ariadne's thread and clings to it, he must concentrate on whatever seems to be of greatest relevance to their relationship, even though this will oblige him, on his way through the labyrinth, to give no more than a passing glance at other, major figures and often to condense or even to omit altogether some events which, however significant they may be in another context, do not—for one reason or another—have a direct bearing on the subject of the Big Three. An example of such an omission in Part I of this book is the exact sequence of events in London in the second half of March 1939 and, both in London and in other capitals, during the final ten days* before the British and French declaration of war on Germany six months later, which is crucial for a study of the origins of the Second World War, but only indirectly relevant to the triangular relationship that is the theme of this book. In Parts II and III, moreover, although the strictly military history of the war forms their constant backdrop, it is for the most part recounted only in the barest outline; and within this outline pride of place has been given to the war in the western theatres, because for most of the time the conduct of the war in the Pacific and South-East Asian theatres did not directly affect the triangular relationship to nearly the same degree. (An exception is made at certain points, however, where the exact sequence of military events is so interwoven with the conduct of the principal actors that it has to be summarised separately—for example, in Chapters 6 and 7, both of which are introduced with a section describing the military setting.) For this deliberate choice of the rifle in preference to the scatter-gun, even though it involves some disadvantages, no further explanation will be offered in the text of the book.

A member of my generation writing about this period has an inevitable bias which he can never wholly eradicate; all he can do is try to clear his mind of cant and write about those years as dispassionately as he can. But he also has one advantage: that of being a living link in the long chain of witnesses of the words and actions of both the giants and the pygmies during those extraordinary decades. It is not only that he may recall what Churchill, Roosevelt, Stalin and others sounded like on the radio, although this is not unimportant. To cite an example from my own experience—I was one of those present in the audience to which Neville Chamberlain delivered his "Hitler missed the bus" speech in April 1940; no one who heard that disastrous address could doubt that, sooner or later, Chamberlain would have to leave 10 Downing Street. At the very moment when he was speaking, as soon

---

*Sequences vividly described by Donald Cameron Watt in his recently published *How War Came: the immediate origins of the Second World War 1938–1939*.

became apparent, German forces were—unbeknown to Chamberlain—already on their way to Norway. Nor could anyone of my generation who was politically conscious in the following month (I was president of the Oxford Union at the time) be surprised, as some historians have since seemed to be, that when it came to the crunch on 9–10 May, the preference shared by many—perhaps most—conservative members of Parliament for Halifax over Churchill, as Chamberlain's successor, was overcome by the sweep of events.

What then is the purpose of studying the relationship between Churchill, Roosevelt and Stalin during the final phase of what was, in Europe, a second Thirty Years' War, if the driving force of history is not the impact of individual decisions or individual ideas, but the horseless "snaffle and curb"[8] of the structural functionalist, or the *"longue durée"* of the social historian, or the fundamental dynamic of "the deeper transformations of world power" that is the core of a recent historical best-seller?[9] The argument about what President Kennedy once called the "mystery of ultimate decision"[10] goes back a long way. In Alexis de Tocqueville's lucid summary of the argument, he hedged his bets between "general causes" and "particular incidents."[11] In the same century, however, it was also well said that

> There are really only two ways of acquiring knowledge about human affairs: through the perception of the particular, or through abstraction; the latter is the method of philosophy, the former of history. There is no other way. . . . Still, this does not suffice; the historian must keep his eye on the universal aspect of things. He will have no preconceived ideas as does the philosopher; rather, while he reflects on the particular, the development of the world in general will become apparent to him.[12]

Anyone writing about Churchill, Roosevelt and Stalin in the latter half of the twentieth century ignores at his peril the influence exercised on the course of history by the underlying social, economic and scientific environment in which the triangular relationship between the leaders of the Grand Alliance came about in the 1940s. Nevertheless, the great decisions and the great discoveries of history—those that made the deepest impact on the lives of men—have, I suggest, usually been reached on the margin: whether the margin be military (the hairsbreadth that may separate victory from defeat in battle), political (the handful of votes cast one way or the other in an election, a Cabinet meeting or a parliamentary debate), or scientific (the, at first sight, small change in the way of looking at something that leads to a redefinition, whose effect may be to remodel the concept of the universe). In the history of nations, as in the lives of individuals, most major decisions begin by being marginal—in the original sense of this word (meaning "pertaining to a border or boundary," not in the contemporary usage, meaning "of minor significance"). Whatever the direction of the underlying momentum may be at a given moment, the individual may, by his decisions or his ideas, be able to retard it, to divert it into a new channel, to give it an additional thrust forwards, or even to break a completely new horizon. The horizon-breaker is the exception in history; and although Churchill, Roosevelt and Stalin were all exceptional men, none of them quite qualifies for this rare historical category. But some decisions, taken initially on the margin—as here defined—subsequently broaden their scope and end by encompassing a huge area of human activity. And such decisions are never of more critical importance than in time of war: a judgement that is amply substantiated by a study of the relationship between Churchill, Roosevelt and Stalin.

Ramsbury, Wiltshire

May 1990

ACKNOWLEDGEMENTS

This study represents the vision of a single pair of eyes.* But my vision has been broadened by that of many others, to whose help I am deeply indebted. For a start, there are three of them without whom the book would never have been written at all: Mr. Donald Lamm, president of W. W. Norton, whose suggestion it was that I should write it; Lord Bullock, who, although he may not have been aware of this when we first discussed the project, convinced me that I ought to try to carry it out; and my wife, who—the decision to

---

*It goes without saying that it does not express the views of the British Government. For the benefit of American readers, British rules require this disclaimer to be entered because in the summer of 1945 (while still in the Army) I began working in Vienna for the British Foreign Service.

make the attempt once taken—has, more than anyone else, made sure that the book was written. All three have read the typescript with patience and discernment. So, too, have General Sir David Fraser, Mr. Thomas C. Sorensen and Dr. Stephen White; the advice on military history that I have received from General Fraser and on American and Soviet political history from Mr. Sorensen and Dr. White respectively has been invaluable.

Some chapters have been read by Air Chief Marshal Sir John Aiken, Dr. David Gillard, Mr. Joseph C. Harsch, Sir William Hayter, Mr. Kym Isolani, Lieutenant-General Sir Ian Jacob, Sir Curtis Keeble, Professor Roger Louis, Sir Brooks Richards, Professor Arthur M. Schlesinger, Jr., Professor Gaddis Smith and Professor Christopher Thorne. Specific passages have been read by Mr. Austen Albu, Sir Richard Bayliss, Professor John Erickson, Dr. Martin Rossdale and Mr. Anthony Verrier. And on particular points I have consulted Mr. René Beerman, Lord Beloff, Lord Bridges, Sir Ashley and Lady Clarke, Mr. Robert Cooper, Mr. Ian Davies, the late Mr. Ivo Forde, Lord Franks, Dr. Terry Garrett, Dr. Martin Gilbert, Sir John Graham, Professor Sir Michael Howard, Rear-Admiral Sir Edmund Irving, Dr. Sergei Karaganov, the late Mr. Henryk Krzeczkowski, Lord Lansdowne, Mr. Peter Mackay, Dr. Evan Mawdsley, Mr. Geoffrey Murrell, Professor Alec Nove, Professor Robert O'Neill, Mr. John Pinder, Sir Frank Roberts, Professor Keith Robbins, Dr. O. A. Rzheshevsky, Lieutenant-Colonel Alan Shepperd, Dr. Harold Shukman, Professor Spiros Simitis, Professor V. Ya. Sipols, Professor Vladimir Trukhanovsky, Colonel-General Dmitrii Volkogonov, Professor Donald Watt and Mr. Samuel Wells, Jr. In addition I have been much assisted by the advice of Mr. Andrew Franklin (Publishing Director, Hamish Hamilton).

If there are any inadvertent omissions from this long list, I hope that my apologies will be accepted. From all their counsel I have greatly benefited; the defects that remain are my own. To single out any one name from the list would be invidious. Nevertheless, I cannot leave unrecorded the privilege, which I have been fortunate to enjoy, of several hours of discussion with the only surviving member of Churchill's personal staff during the Second World War, Lieutenant-General

Sir Ian Jacob, who attended all but one of Churchill's major wartime conferences. His iron memory and shrewd judgement (reinforced by the evidence of his wartime diary) combine to make conversation with him a fascinating experience for the historian.

Sir Curtis Keeble and Mr. Anthony Verrier have kindly allowed me to read, before publication, the typescripts of their books, respectively on Anglo-Soviet relations and on the assassination of Admiral Darlan. My especial thanks also go to four institutions without whom the research required by this book could not have been carried out. First, to the Leverhulme Trust for their generosity in awarding me a Leverhulme Research Fellowship. Secondly, as an Honorary Fellow of the Soviet and East European Studies Institute of Glasgow University, I have been able both to use the Institute's collection of Soviet material and to exchange ideas over the past two years with Professor William Wallace and his colleagues at the Institute and with members of the university departments of History and of Politics. At the Franklin D. Roosevelt Presidential Library at Hyde Park, New York, Dr. William Emerson and his staff have greatly facilitated my task during visits to that superb collection. Last—but by no means least—the unstinting help of Mrs. Nicole Gallimore and Miss Susan Boyde, the Chatham House Librarians, together with that of their colleagues, has converted into a pleasure what might otherwise have been drudgery. Others to whom I would like to express my thanks are the staff of the Public Record Office, Kew, and of the National Archives, Washington, D.C.; Dr. Juan Pablo Fusi, Director of the National Library of Spain; Dr. Benedict K. Zobrist, Director of the Harry Truman Library, Independence, Missouri; and the staffs of the Sterling Memorial Library at Yale University and of the Goethe Institute and the Spanish Institute in London. I am further grateful to the British Ambassador in Moscow, Sir Rodric Braithwaite, and to the Director of the Institute of Europe of the Soviet Academy of Sciences, Dr. Vitaly Zhurkin, for inviting me to give seminars in Moscow on the subject of this book. These visits enabled me to meet a wide range of Soviet writers interested in the same period of history, who significantly increased my understanding of its Soviet dimension.

Mr. Peter Grove prepared the maps on which most of those included in this book are based; Mr. Richard Aldous drafted the Selective Chronology of World War II; Mrs. Danese Dyer bore the brunt of decyphering my handwriting for the first eighteen months; Miss Laura Tatham stepped into the breach at some critical moments along the way; and Mrs. Carol Smith typed the whole of the second half of the book. The proofs have kindly been read, among others, by Sir Edgar Williams, with his customary rigour. To all of them I am extremely grateful.

I express my thanks to Lieutenant-General Sir Ian Jacob for permission to quote two passages from his diary; to the Borthwick Institute of Historical Research, York, for permission to quote from the entries of Lord Halifax's Secret Diary for 1 and 2 December 1941; to Yale University Library for permission to print portions of the Henry L. Stimson Diaries contained in the Henry L. Stimson Papers, Manuscripts and Archives, Yale University Library; and to the holders of the copyrights of the photographs reproduced in this book. All quotations from documents at the Public Record Office, Kew, in Crown copyright appear by permission of the Controller of Her Majesty's Stationery Office.

Finally, I have drawn on my own recollections of the 1930s and 1940s, generally without acknowledgement; an exception is the bizarre episode described on pp. 180–1, which might otherwise have appeared barely credible to the present-day reader.

THE BIG
THREE

WINSTON LEONARD SPENCER CHURCHILL

Born Blenheim Palace, Oxfordshire, 30 November 1874
Died London, 24 January 1965

FRANKLIN DELANO ROOSEVELT

Born Hyde Park, New York, 30 January 1882
Died Warm Springs, Georgia, 12 April 1945

JOSEPH VISSARIONOVICH STALIN

Born Gori, Georgia, 21 December 1879
Died Moscow, 5 March 1953

1

THE BIG THREE:

FIRST ENCOUNTER

We can see in the sky, for the first time, that
traditional symbol of hope, the rainbow.

—*Franklin Roosevelt, 30 November 1943*

On the last evening of November 1943 three formidable men dined together in an opulent house built in the mid-Victorian era, set in a compound of some sixteen acres in the centre of Teheran and then guarded by a brigade of British and Indian troops. After three days of gruelling discussion, they were celebrating Winston Churchill's sixty-ninth birthday, at the British Legation. Franklin Roosevelt sat on Churchill's right and Joseph Stalin on his left. The photograph taken of the three men, when the candles on the birthday cake had just been lit, shows Churchill in animated conversation with Stalin, whereas Roosevelt's expression looks bored; unlike Churchill and Stalin, he did not normally keep very late hours, and this dinner party lasted until two o'clock in the morning. It was Roosevelt, however, who—at his own request—proposed the Loyal Toast on this special occasion; and it was he who spoke the last words at the end of the dinner:

> We have proved here at Teheran that the varying ideals of our nations can come together in a harmonious whole, moving unitedly for the common good of ourselves and of the world. . . .[1]

Churchill toasted "Stalin the Great." Stalin toasted Churchill as his "great friend"; and he had earlier kissed the blade of the Sword of Honour presented to him by Churchill on behalf of King George VI, for the people of Stalingrad, where the city's German besiegers had themselves surrendered to the Red Army in February 1943.[2] This was not just the euphoria of the hour. In the words of the Declaration of the Three Powers signed the following day, the three leaders of the Grand Alliance parted, "friends in fact, in spirit and in purpose."[3] After reaching agreement on this resounding declaration, they left Teheran by air—Churchill and Roosevelt flying back to Cairo, where they had met immediately before the Teheran Conference and where they would now confer once again; Stalin, who disliked flying, only as far as Baku.[4]

Roosevelt and Stalin were both younger than Churchill, Roosevelt by just over seven years and Stalin by five. At the moment of this first encounter of the three leaders, the description of Churchill, as he had seemed to a fellow war correspondent on the sea voyage to South Africa forty-four years earlier,[5] was (with the major exception of his waistline) still recognisable: "slim, slightly reddish-haired, pale, lively, frequently plunging along the deck 'with neck out-thrust' as Browning fancied Napoleon." By his seventieth year the "neck out-thrust" had become Churchill's defiant bulldog look, although in repose his expression could also appear reflective and benign: witness the photograph taken of him on an historic occasion eighteen months after the Teheran Conference. He always ate and drank copiously and he was seldom without a cigar; but he never inhaled, lighting and relighting it until it was half done, when he threw it away. By now his cigar and his V-sign were symbols familiar throughout the world.[6]

Roosevelt was a handsome man. Six feet two inches in height, on the rare occasions when he stood upright he was about a head taller than Churchill and he towered over Stalin. Unlike Churchill,[7] Roosevelt dressed conventionally, except for his naval cape, which—like his cigarette-holder—had become his insignia. After poliomyelitis had left him crippled in 1921, he developed his shoulder and chest muscles to what he described at the time as Jack Dempsey proportions. His disability obliged him to watch his diet; the cocktails that he mixed himself consisted mainly of vermouth; and he swam regularly. Three years before the Teheran Conference his doctor, Admiral Ross McIntire, had found him in the best condition that he had observed for many years,[8] although a dramatic change was imminent by the time Roosevelt travelled to Teheran.

The best physical description of Stalin in his early sixties is one of his appearance at a meeting not long after the Teheran Conference:

> Stalin was in a marshal's uniform and soft boots, without any medals except a golden star—the Order of Hero of the Soviet Union, on the left side of his breast. . . . He toyed with his pipe, which bore the white dot of the English firm Dunhill.*
>
> He was of very small stature and ungainly build. His torso was short and narrow, while his legs and arms were too long. His left arm and shoulder seemed rather still. He had quite a large paunch, and his hair was sparse though his scalp was not completely bald. His face was white, with ruddy cheeks. . . . His teeth were black and irregular, turned inward. Not even his moustache was thick or firm. Still the head was not a bad one . . . with those yellow eyes and a mixture of sternness and mischief.[10]

Like Churchill at this stage of his life, Stalin took no exercise of any kind. Unlike Churchill, he drank mainly wine—from Georgia.

---

*The London firm of Alfred Dunhill (who also supplied Churchill's cigars) supplied Stalin with pipes—one of his few luxuries—from 1942 onwards.[9]

The Second World War made each of these three men in turn—first
Churchill, then Stalin and finally Roosevelt—a military as well as a
political leader. Strategically, all three of them had made monumental
mistakes in 1941. In 1942 each of them had shown tremendous resilience. By the end of 1943 their countries had won great victories, which
made it possible for the Big Three to spend four days in Teheran
planning the future course of the war and beginning to discuss the
shape of the post-war world. Within a fortnight after this first encounter, Churchill suffered pneumonia and a heart attack; in March 1944
Roosevelt's doctors diagnosed the disease that killed him before the
war ended; and in the spring of 1944 Stalin was on one occasion found
unconscious at his desk.[11] But they were physically, as well as politically, resilient men. They would meet once again, in the middle of the
winter of 1945, in an even more improbable place: the Crimea.

Each of these three men was a product of the era of the late nineteenth century. Each was also unique in the political forum of his own
country during the first half of the twentieth century. No one in
British political life of that period could be compared with Churchill;
no one in American politics with Roosevelt, from 1933 onwards; and
from an early date in the history of the Soviet Union, Stalin stood
alone. Although the wartime authority enjoyed by Churchill and
Roosevelt (the one as Prime Minister and Minister of Defence, the
other as President and Commander-in-Chief) was of a different order
from the power wielded by Stalin, their capacity to take global decisions when they met, halfway through the Second World War, was on
a scale not readily imaginable in a later age of regular summit meetings,
carefully prepared in advance by the senior members of multiple
bureaucracies: the modern "sherpa" teams, which in those days did not
exist. True, Churchill, Roosevelt and Stalin had their teams of advisers,
some of whom were outstanding men, but in a real sense they constituted the triumvirate of the Grand Alliance: three hardened negotiators, presiding at Teheran, in Churchill's words at the time, over the
greatest concentration of worldly power that had ever been seen in the
history of mankind.[12] They were the Big Three.

Their triangular correspondence had begun in the summer of 1941;

Churchill had visited Stalin in Moscow in 1942; while Churchill and Roosevelt had met more than once since their first conference, in August 1941. But when the opening plenary session of the Teheran Conference was held, on 28 November 1943, it was the first face-to-face encounter of the three leaders as a group. Above all, it was at Teheran that Roosevelt and Stalin met each other for the first time—and because Stalin had refused to travel further afield, this conference convened in the capital of Iran, traditionally one of the principal prizes in the "Great Game"[13] played by Britain and Russia, but for the past two years a country under Anglo-Soviet military occupation.

That three men as dissimilar as Churchill, Roosevelt and Stalin would agree at Teheran in 1943—as they would again at Yalta—"how covert matters may be best disclos'd/And open perils surest answered" would have seemed a laughable prospect a decade earlier, at the beginning of 1933. Of these three men, the first was then in the political wilderness; the second had only just been elected President of the United States; and the third was still engrossed in the process of collectivising the peasantry of the Soviet Union and converting his country into a major industrial power. Until nearly the end of 1933 the U.S. and Soviet governments still had no diplomatic relations with each other. Relations between the British and Soviet governments had been restored only in 1929, following a break of two years. And Churchill himself was widely regarded, with good reason, as the chief advocate of the Allies' unsuccessful military intervention in the Soviet Union in 1919.* As we can now see, a completely new dimension was added on 30 January 1933, when Adolf Hitler became Chancellor of Germany. Time then gradually ran out. During the six locust years that followed, Britain, the Soviet Union and the United States all bought time, to varying degrees and much of it at each other's expense—Britain and

---

*British troops had originally been sent to Archangel and Murmansk to guard Allied supply dumps against German forces after the Russian October Revolution, but subsequently the White (anti-Soviet) commanders in southern Russia and Siberia received substantial British support. A British force occupied Baku.

the Soviet Union very dearly, almost to the point of self-destruction. By contrast, by the end of 1941 the survival of the three countries depended on combining their alliance in almost exactly the words that Shakespeare puts into Mark Antony's mouth in the final lines of the triumvir scene in *Julius Caesar.*

That the relationship between the Big Three was, to begin with, paradoxical—like that between the triumvirs of ancient Rome, thrown together, in Shakespeare's words, "at the stake,/And bay'd about with many enemies"—is true. And since, in the event, the sanguine hopes of the Big Three for the post-war world were dashed, to many historians this failure—and the disillusionment that went with it—has seemed inevitable from the outset.[14] Yet it is also clear that, as the years of war went by and as Churchill, Roosevelt and Stalin were able to observe each other closely, they themselves came to see their alliance as something more. It became not merely an ephemeral relationship dictated by military necessity, but also a political relationship: the prelude to the establishment of a new international order. So widely was this view held at the time that, a few months after this first encounter of the Big Three at Teheran, it was possible for a distinguished American writer (who himself later coined the phrase "cold war") to assert, without much risk of contradiction, that "not since the unity of the ancient world was disrupted" had there been "so good a prospect of settled peace."[15]

PEACE

and WAR

2

RETROSPECT:

THREE PATHS

TO POWER

The only thing we have to fear is fear itself. . . .

—*Roosevelt, March 1933*

I have nothing to offer but blood, toil, tears
and sweat.

—*Winston Churchill, May 1940*

Brothers, sisters, I turn to you, my friends.

—*Joseph Stalin, July 1941*

"*T he whole world* is the tomb of famous men," wrote the historian of another Thirty Years' War, which tore the Greek world apart two and a half millennia ago.[1] By the time that the Big Three met at Teheran, however, all three of them were already legendary figures. Their roles in the Second World War were by no means the only reason for their fame. Long before the war began, anything that each of them said in public had been attentively listened to across the world. For they lived in the golden afternoon of political oratory: set-piece speeches, drafted and redrafted with elaborate care. Stalin's were of immense length, mainly addressed to Communist Party audiences; Churchill's were by no means short and, for the House of Commons—thanks to his remarkable memory—learned by heart;

Roosevelt's bring us nearest to the modern age.* It was Roosevelt who pioneered the use of the radio as a political medium, in the Fireside Chats with the American people which he began from the first week of his first term as President, and Churchill followed his example during the war.

Widely different though the oratorical styles of these three men were, each possessed a unique ability: at a moment of supreme challenge, to unite a people's endeavour behind his leadership. The three quotations in the epigraph to this chapter show them at their most compelling. Roosevelt began the solemn address that he delivered at his inauguration on Capitol Hill on 4 March 1933 by describing it as "a day of national consecration," and he went on to assert the firm belief:

> The only thing we have to fear is fear itself†—nameless, unreasoning, unjustified terror which paralyses needed efforts to convert retreat into advance. In every dark hour of our national life a leadership of frankness and vigor has met with that understanding and support of the people themselves which is essential to victory. I am convinced that you will again give that support to leadership in these critical days. . . .[2]

In the uncharacteristically short speech that Churchill made in the House of Commons, specially convened on 13 May 1940, to ask for a vote of confidence in the government that he had just formed (when it was still Chamberlain, who had resigned the premiership three days earlier, whom the Conservative Party members rose to cheer, rather than Churchill as he entered the Chamber), the sentence that preceded Churchill's declaration of policy was this: "I have nothing to offer but

---

*Speeches by all three of them can be heard on Edward R. Murrow and Fred W. Friendly's long-playing Columbia Masterworks record, ML4095, *I Can Hear It Now, 1933–1945* (produced by J. G. Gude).

†Between the words "is" and "fear itself" Roosevelt paused: a stroke of rhetorical brilliance. This phrase was added to the speech only in the final draft; and the phrase "a day of consecration" was added in longhand while Roosevelt was waiting in the Senate Committee Room.

blood, toil, tears and sweat." And he went on to define his government's policy as being to wage war with the aim of "victory . . . for without victory, there is no survival."*

Stalin's speech (also quoted in the epigraph to this chapter) is the one that he delivered by radio to the Soviet people at a moment when his back—and theirs—was right up to the wall, twelve days after the German onslaught on the Soviet Union. He began, not in the customary Communist Party manner, but with the words: "Brothers, sisters, I turn to you, my friends." He then made a personal appeal to the entire Soviet people for a relentless struggle against the enemy; any Soviet soil that had to be left to the invader must be scorched earth.[3] His appeal in 1941, like Churchill's in 1940 and Roosevelt's in 1933, evoked an overwhelming national response.

However disparate their formation and their outlook on the world, each of the three leaders had also accumulated a wealth of political experience and acumen, which they brought to their common task in the Second World War. By the time that they met in Teheran, Roosevelt had been in power for over a decade and Stalin for longer still. (True, by comparison with Churchill, neither of them was well travelled. But although Roosevelt had not set foot in Europe since 1918, he had travelled there often earlier in his life; and although Stalin had not been abroad since before the First World War—and during the Second World War he hardly ever left Moscow—he was well served, as we now know know from published Soviet documents, by a competent network of missions abroad, whose assessment of international events was for the most part accurate and usually free from ideological claptrap.) As for Churchill, his international experience spanned the century.

---

*On his way out afterwards he is said to have remarked to a friend: "That got the sods, didn't it?"[4]

Winston Churchill

Churchill's character, like that of Roosevelt and Stalin, does not lend itself to summary description. Not too much should be made of the fact that his mother was American. He was "half-American, but all British."[5] Far more important was the frequency of his visits to the United States; his earliest lecture tour there was made in 1900, when he was just twenty-six. The tour was gruelling—ten cities, including New York, Washington and Boston, in the first fortnight. He does not seem to have enjoyed his lecturing, but he met the current President, William McKinley, and in Albany, New York he dined with Theodore Roosevelt (soon to become President, after McKinley's assassination).[6] Churchill was one of the few European politicians of the period who knew the United States well.

As for Churchill's view of the Soviet Union, his dislike of communism was no greater than that of many of his political contemporaries on both sides of the Atlantic, even if it was more forcibly expressed, thanks to Churchillian eloquence: for example, "a pestilence more destructive of life than the Black Death or the Spotted Typhus." But it was matched by Churchill's knowledge of the potential of Soviet military power. Exceptionally for that period, Churchill was aware of the size of the German and Austro-Hungarian forces that had to be assembled in order to face the Russian Army in 1916—greater than those on the Western Front at the time. In the Preface to the volume of his *World Crisis* entitled *The Eastern Front,* published in 1931, he also recorded how he had thought at one time of calling this volume *The Forgotten Front;* and by the end of the book he reached the conclusion that "these terrible campaigns [on the Russian front, 1914–16] . . . constitute a prodigy no less astounding than the magnitude of her collapse thereafter."[7] The Red Army was underestimated in the West almost up to the end of 1941. By contrast, the gap between Churchill's view of Soviet military power and his definition of Soviet foreign policy eight years later—a riddle wrapped in a mystery inside an enigma—is not a very large one.[8] And one of his letters written at the age of twenty-two reveals an unusual understanding of a traditional objective of imperial Russian foreign policy: the Straits—"Russia must have Constantinople. . . . Seventy millions of people without a warm water port. Is it rational?"[9]

Superficially, Churchill could be caricatured—and he was by his country's enemies in the Second World War—as a luxury-loving grandee, born into a world of privilege far more representative of the century of his great ancestor, the Duke of Marlborough, than of his own. The evidence of his early life, including Churchill's own account, is abundant.[10] Born in Blenheim Palace (the Marlborough family home in Oxfordshire), he received the bare minimum of parental understanding; but he was extremely fortunate in his parents' choice of Mrs. Elizabeth Everest, who became his personal confidante for eighteen years, as his nanny. His formal education was unimpressive: after a poor performance at Harrow School, his father sent him to the Royal Military College, Sandhurst,* not because of the pleasure that the young Winston had taken in playing with his large collection of toy soldiers, but because he did not consider him up to the standards of the Bar. (What, one wonders, would a case conducted by Mr. Winston Churchill, KC, have been like?) Although he passed out of Sandhurst twentieth in a class of one hundred and thirty, he succeeded in entering it from Harrow only at his third attempt at the examination. In short, he was—intellectually—a late developer. It was not until he found himself with little or nothing to do as a cavalry subaltern in Bangalore that he began his voracious reading, devouring one by one—among other books—the volumes of Gibbon and Macaulay sent out to him by his mother.

As for his love of luxury, this, like the hospitality that he dispensed at his home, Chartwell Manor, between the wars, was largely financed by the ceaseless output of his pen. As early as January 1901 he could

---

*At that period the intellectually demanding route into the Army was the Royal Military Academy, Woolwich, where future gunner and sapper officers were trained, rather than Sandhurst, which trained for the infantry and cavalry. The two military colleges were not combined until half a century afterwards.

look back on total earnings of £10,000 over the preceding two years. His very first book, *The Story of the Malakand Field Force,* sold no fewer than 8,500 copies. It was to be followed over the next half century, among other works, by his biographies of his father, Randolph Churchill, and of Marlborough, his histories of the First World War and of the Second; his *History of the English Speaking Peoples* (completed after the Second World War); and a stream of newspaper articles. Churchill was in one sense a self-made man, who to a large extent educated himself and, especially in youth, sought out and created his own opportunities. The fact that he took part in the Sudanese campaign* at all—let alone in the British Army's last great cavalry charge, at the Battle of Omdurman in 1898—was entirely his own doing (his regiment was in India at the time). And one of his letters written from India contains the revealing passage: "Being in many ways a coward—particularly at school—there is no ambition I cherish so keenly as to gain a reputation for personal courage. . . ."[11]

In the following year Churchill resigned his commission; he stood, unsuccessfully, for Parliament in July 1899; and in September he was engaged by the *Morning Post* as special correspondent in South Africa, where the Boer War began on 12 October. On 15 November he was captured when Boer forces derailed the armoured train in which he was travelling. Imprisoned in Pretoria, he escaped four weeks later. Returning to Britain in July 1900, he was elected MP for Oldham on 1 October. In his maiden speech in the House of Commons he declared that, had he been a Boer, he hoped that he would be "fighting in the field."[13]

Churchill's political career, unlike that of Roosevelt and of Stalin, touched its lowest point in the 1930s. True, he had been a member of Parliament (with one gap of two years) since 1900, and—short of the premiership and the Foreign Office—he had held every high office in

---

*In this campaign an Anglo-Egyptian army commanded by General Kitchener recaptured Khartoum (which had been lost in 1885 to the Mahdist rebel forces, who had killed the British commander, General Gordon, on the steps of the Governor's Palace).[12]

government: the Board of Trade, the Home Office, the Admiralty, the War Office, the Colonial Office, and most recently, from 1924 to 1929, the Treasury. But in 1933 the conventional wisdom about Churchill was that, in spite of his long administrative experience, his unbounded energy, his personal courage and his brilliant pen, all of which were undoubted, politically he was "unsound." This epithet is deliberately put in quotation marks here because it was—and has long remained— Conservative Party shorthand for a man who cannot be relied upon not to rock the political boat. In the eyes of his critics, Churchill had earned this description more than once in the previous thirty years, notably by crossing the floor of the House of Commons in 1904, when he left the Conservative Party benches to join the Liberal Party. The other land-mark in Churchill's early career, which neither he himself nor his opponents ever forgot, was his advocacy of the ill-fated Dardanelles campaign in the First World War.*

In 1924, Churchill rejoined the Conservative Party. After leaving the equivalent of the Conservative Party Shadow Cabinet in 1931— the Conservatives were then in opposition—Churchill went on to supply his critics, both in his party and outside it, with further fuel, first by vigorously opposing his own party's reformist Government of India Bill right up to the day on which it finally became law, in 1935; and then in 1936, as a later chapter will relate, by a lonely intervention on behalf of King Edward VIII's lost cause on the eve of his abdication.[14] Thus not only Ramsay MacDonald but also both Conservative prime ministers† denied Churchill office in the 1930s, Neville Chamberlain relenting only on the eve of the outbreak of war. By then Churchill had suffered an eclipse far greater than the ostracism to which he was

---

*The Dardanelles campaign was approved by the British War Council in January 1915 as an outflanking operation, with the Gallipoli Peninsula as the immediate and Constantinople as the ultimate objective. The concept, strongly backed by Churchill, was good, but its execution was bad, ending in evacuation a year later. Churchill accepted more of the responsibility for this costly failure than he need have done.

†Untypically, between August 1931 and May 1940 Britain had six different cabinets and four prime ministers: see Appendix I.

subjected in 1915, following the failure of the Dardanelles campaign. In the event, when Churchill's supreme moment arrived in the summer of 1940, the very fact that he could not be held responsible for what had happened during his long absence from office and from the inner councils of his party proved to be one of his greatest strengths. At the time, however, in the words in which he later described his own chagrin at one of his many setbacks, this was not the first occasion on which he had received a blessing in what was at the time a most effective disguise.[15]

One of the most important dates in Churchill's life was 12 September 1908: the day on which he married Clementine Hozier. Throughout their long marriage, her loyalty to her husband never prevented her from offering him sound advice—she was a life-long Liberal—although he ignored it at some critical moments of his career. Moreover, some of the most succinct words about Churchill in his lifetime come from a letter written by his wife: "he has the supreme quality . . . the power, the imagination, the deadliness, to fight Germany."[16] Although written in 1915, this description applied with equal force twenty years later. It could also have been said of his two future colleagues in the Grand Alliance. On the other hand, there were two important respects, apart from his age, in which Churchill differed from both of them. He was the only one of the three who (as opposed to the very different experience of military administration) had personally commanded men in battle, not only as a subaltern at the turn of the century, but during the six months in 1915–16 when he temporarily left the political arena to take command of a battalion on the Western Front.* And, unlike Roosevelt, the quintessential pragmatist, and Stalin, the Marxist revolutionary, both of whom—for different reasons—looked towards the changes that the second half of the twentieth century would bring, Churchill believed in the maintenance of a specific world order. This belief was founded in his confidence in what Churchill described, in his

---

*When Churchill's political star waned, following the Dardanelles fiasco, he reverted to his original profession, at the age of forty-one.

life of Marlborough (with whom he had more than blood in common), as "the inherent sanity and vigour of the political conceptions sprung from the genius of the English race."[17]

Franklin Roosevelt

Roosevelt was the youngest member of the future triumvirate; he had just turned fifty-one when, on 4 March 1933, he delivered his first inaugural address on Capitol Hill. The first twenty-eight years of his life had been unremarkable. Unlike Churchill and Stalin, he did not plunge headlong into politics at the earliest opportunity; indeed, it could almost be said that political life came to Roosevelt by degrees. A placid upbringing as an only child, on the family estate at Hyde Park on the Hudson River, was followed by late entry (at the age of fourteen) into a small, exclusive private school at Groton, Massachusetts, whose headmaster's educational principles seem to an Englishman to have much in common with those of a headmaster of Rugby School famous earlier in the century (respectively, Endicott Peabody and Thomas Arnold). Academically, Roosevelt performed rather better at Groton than Churchill did at Harrow (his grades just rose to the B level). He himself wanted to enter Annapolis, but to please his parents, he went to Harvard, where he took the liberal arts course; his average there was a C. He did not take a master of arts degree, and his main distinction was that of editing the undergraduate daily newspaper, the *Crimson,* for which purpose he stayed on at Harvard for a fourth year.

A conventional beginning, combined with a comfortable inherited fortune, gave Roosevelt a patrician self-confidence, coupled with an old-fashioned country gentleman's sense of obligation towards, and concern for, those less privileged than himself. This attitude, however, suggested to his critics that he was looking down his nose at other people (it was indeed, in a literal sense, a habit of which he did not rid himself for many years—from his height, he tended to look over his pince-nez and straight over people's heads). Or perhaps, as he himself put it long afterwards, "I was an awfully mean cuss when I first went into politics."[18] This he did for the first time not on the national but on the local level, in 1910. In that year he was elected state senator in Dutchess County, a district of his home constituency in New York State which had been carried by the Democratic Party only once since the Civil War.

Roosevelt's three years at Columbia Law School, New York, which he entered after leaving Harvard, were undistinguished. His marriage in 1905 to his distant cousin, Eleanor, the niece of Theodore Roosevelt (who completed his second term as President in March 1909), would become a major political factor only many years afterwards. At the time of his marriage, Roosevelt admired his wife's Republican uncle, but his own father had been a Democrat. Before 1910, Roosevelt might have run for either party. It was the Democratic Party who approached him as their prospective candidate for Dutchess County, however; he accepted; and in his campaign then there was already a hint of the "President of all the people" a quarter of a century later.

Three years afterwards Roosevelt was offered federal office: the post of Assistant Secretary of the Navy, which he was later to describe—not quite accurately—as a position similar to Churchill's during the First World War.* His tenure of this office reveals something, though not a great deal, about the future President: his continuing love of the sea, his understanding of sea power, and also his regret that he did not receive permission to request a commission until the war was almost over. Indeed, he tried to persuade the Grotonian who was preparing a school memorial to those who had served in the war that his visit in 1918 to the Western Front, as Assistant Secretary, warranted his inclusion in the first division of those who were in the service. This visit took him through London, where he spoke briefly at a Gray's Inn dinner at which Churchill was present. In spite of Churchill's recollection, in his memoirs, of Roosevelt's "magnificent presence in all his youth and

---

*In the First World War, Churchill's opposite number was not Roosevelt, but Josephus Daniels, Secretary of the Navy, the only man under whom Roosevelt ever served. Another example of Roosevelt's tendency to exaggerate was his unhappy claim, in a speech delivered in 1920, that he had written the constitution of Haiti.

life of Marlborough (with whom he had more than blood in common), as "the inherent sanity and vigour of the political conceptions sprung from the genius of the English race."[17]

Franklin Roosevelt

Roosevelt was the youngest member of the future triumvirate; he had just turned fifty-one when, on 4 March 1933, he delivered his first inaugural address on Capitol Hill. The first twenty-eight years of his life had been unremarkable. Unlike Churchill and Stalin, he did not plunge headlong into politics at the earliest opportunity; indeed, it could almost be said that political life came to Roosevelt by degrees. A placid upbringing as an only child, on the family estate at Hyde Park on the Hudson River, was followed by late entry (at the age of fourteen) into a small, exclusive private school at Groton, Massachusetts, whose headmaster's educational principles seem to an Englishman to have much in common with those of a headmaster of Rugby School famous earlier in the century (respectively, Endicott Peabody and Thomas Arnold). Academically, Roosevelt performed rather better at Groton than Churchill did at Harrow (his grades just rose to the B level). He himself wanted to enter Annapolis, but to please his parents, he went to Harvard, where he took the liberal arts course; his average there was a C. He did not take a master of arts degree, and his main distinction was that of editing the undergraduate daily newspaper, the *Crimson,* for which purpose he stayed on at Harvard for a fourth year.

A conventional beginning, combined with a comfortable inherited fortune, gave Roosevelt a patrician self-confidence, coupled with an old-fashioned country gentleman's sense of obligation towards, and concern for, those less privileged than himself. This attitude, however, suggested to his critics that he was looking down his nose at other people (it was indeed, in a literal sense, a habit of which he did not rid himself for many years—from his height, he tended to look over his pince-nez and straight over people's heads). Or perhaps, as he himself put it long afterwards, "I was an awfully mean cuss when I first went into politics."[18] This he did for the first time not on the national but on the local level, in 1910. In that year he was elected state senator in Dutchess County, a district of his home constituency in New York State which had been carried by the Democratic Party only once since the Civil War.

Roosevelt's three years at Columbia Law School, New York, which he entered after leaving Harvard, were undistinguished. His marriage in 1905 to his distant cousin, Eleanor, the niece of Theodore Roosevelt (who completed his second term as President in March 1909), would become a major political factor only many years afterwards. At the time of his marriage, Roosevelt admired his wife's Republican uncle, but his own father had been a Democrat. Before 1910, Roosevelt might have run for either party. It was the Democratic Party who approached him as their prospective candidate for Dutchess County, however; he accepted; and in his campaign then there was already a hint of the "President of all the people" a quarter of a century later.

Three years afterwards Roosevelt was offered federal office: the post of Assistant Secretary of the Navy, which he was later to describe—not quite accurately—as a position similar to Churchill's during the First World War.* His tenure of this office reveals something, though not a great deal, about the future President: his continuing love of the sea, his understanding of sea power, and also his regret that he did not receive permission to request a commission until the war was almost over. Indeed, he tried to persuade the Grotonian who was preparing a school memorial to those who had served in the war that his visit in 1918 to the Western Front, as Assistant Secretary, warranted his inclusion in the first division of those who were in the service. This visit took him through London, where he spoke briefly at a Gray's Inn dinner at which Churchill was present. In spite of Churchill's recollection, in his memoirs, of Roosevelt's "magnificent presence in all his youth and

---

*In the First World War, Churchill's opposite number was not Roosevelt, but Josephus Daniels, Secretary of the Navy, the only man under whom Roosevelt ever served. Another example of Roosevelt's tendency to exaggerate was his unhappy claim, in a speech delivered in 1920, that he had written the constitution of Haiti.

strength," other evidence suggests both that he did not really recall their encounter and that, at the time, he did not greatly impress Roosevelt.[19] Conversely, although Roosevelt's energy and charm helped to make his Assistant Secretaryship of the Navy a success, and although these years in Washington* taught him much about the workings of the government of the United States, there were many close observers there for whom he was "a good fellow with rather a soft edge."[21] By 1920 Roosevelt's position in his party had become substantial enough to earn him nomination as Democratic vice-presidential candidate. In this election, support for the League of Nations was a central plank of the Democratic campaign, which ended in failure for the Democratic Party and years of American isolationism—a lesson that Roosevelt would never forget. In August 1921 poliomyelitis left Roosevelt virtually a cripple. It was then, at the age of thirty-nine, that the great period of his life began.

The specialist who looked after Roosevelt in New York for six weeks wrote: "He has such courage, such ambition, and yet at the same time such an extraordinarily sensitive emotional mechanism."[22] In the years that followed, his refusal to give in to the disease was matched by his determination—in which he was opposed by his forceful mother, but strongly supported by his wife—to stay in politics. His wife, with whom Roosevelt had long kept up the outward appearances of a normal relationship, gradually became his political eyes and ears. Very gradually, too, he came to terms with the fact that he would never walk again.[23] The convention that he was never to be seen being carried in public was strictly observed. And when he decided to contest an election—for the governorship of the state of New York—in 1928, he remarked that he counted on his friends to help him walk in, even if he could not "run" for office. (These friends then included the outgoing governor and Democratic presidential candidate, Al Smith—a

---

*It was also at the outset of these years that Roosevelt first met and fell in love with the beautiful Lucy Mercer, whom his wife had engaged as social secretary. (A southern Roman Catholic, she later married Winthrop Rutherfurd.)[20]

political alliance that broke down in 1931.) Roosevelt was elected governor of New York by a narrow margin of just over 25,000 votes. His victory in the next New York gubernatorial election, however, was on such a scale that the White House was in sight. In private, he now said: 'I believe I can be nominated for the Presidency in 1932."[24] By then (under a Republican President) the Great Depression had begun; and in 1932 Roosevelt's moment of opportunity did indeed arrive.

The necessary two-thirds majority of the votes cast by the delegates at the party convention that convened in Chicago on 27 June 1932 was not easily won. Roosevelt was only just nominated Democratic presidential candidate. As Churchill accurately observed in the essay "Roosevelt from Afar," included in his *Great Contemporaries:* "There was one moment when his nomination turned upon as little as the spin of a coin. When it fell there was no doubt whose head was stamped upon it."[25]

Instead of the normal practice of accepting the nomination later on, Roosevelt flew from Albany to Chicago to deliver his acceptance speech to the party convention straight away. At first the "New Deal"—the phrase which he originally used in this speech—had little content. His electoral campaign was far from radical. But its outcome "stamped" Roosevelt's head on the American coin unmistakably. Only six states voted for his Republican opponent (Hoover) and the Democratic Party won a majority in both Houses of Congress. Until Roosevelt reached the White House in March 1933, however, some of the shrewdest Americans were still uncertain what kind of President he would make. Herbert Hoover called him a "chameleon on plaid"; for Walter Lippmann he was an "amiable man with many philanthropic interests" who was "too eager to please,"[26] although Lippmann soon changed his mind; and even in 1934 Oliver Wendell Holmes' summing up was 'a second-class intellect, but a first-class temperament."[27]

As for Churchill, he inscribed the copy of his life of Marlborough, which he sent to Roosevelt six months after his First Hundred Days had already marked him out as one of the outstanding presidents in American history: "with earnest best wishes for the success of the greatest crusade of modern times."[28] The first known assessment of Roosevelt by Churchill is the essay referred to above. Published in the second year of his first term, this assessment was by no means one of unqualified praise. For example, Churchill expressed anxiety lest "forces are gathering under his shield which at a certain stage may thrust him into the background and take the lead themselves." Its final verdict was an open one:

> Will he succeed or will he fail? . . . succeed or fail, his impulse is one which . . . may well eclipse both the lurid flames of German Nordic national self-assertion and the baleful unnatural lights which are diffused from Soviet Russia.

That Churchill respected Roosevelt from the beginning of the 1930s is clear, although there is little sign of the relationship that would develop between the two men, as wartime leaders, ten years later. (There is no evidence, for example, that Roosevelt thought it worth his while to invite Churchill to visit him during the latter's lecture tour in the United States in 1932.) On the other hand, there were already then two interesting affinities between them. Both men had a strong element of the grand seigneur; Roosevelt's patrician attitude is paralleled by Churchill's magnanimity. Each, moreover, had to contend with a handicap. Roosevelt's was physical. His way of dealing with his affliction—as with political problems for which no immediate solution was in sight—was, as far as possible, to appear to ignore it; or, as his wife put it, "I never knew him to face life, or any problem that came up, with fear."[29] Only in the last weeks of his life, by which time he was a very sick man, did he address the Congress sitting down, remarking as he did so that it made things a lot easier for him not to have to carry ten pounds of steel around on the bottom of his legs: one of his very rare public references to his disability. Twelve years earlier, by contrast, he had managed, stiffly, to walk thirty-five yards to the Speaker's stand outside the Senate, where he delivered his inaugural speech standing up, his hands gripping the lectern.

Churchill's handicap, which he was able to contain until the last few years of his life (over which even the book published immediately after his death by his egregious physician drew a veil), consisted of periodic depression. That he suffered from bouts of what he himself called "Black Dog" is well attested.*[30] Since this is not a psycho-history, no attempt will be made to relate phases of this malady to those of Churchill's political career. A more important question is whether and, if so, to what extent and from what date, the political decisions of the third member of the future triumvirate—Stalin—were influenced by some form of mental illness. To this the answer is still largely guesswork. The author of the most recent Soviet study of Stalin lays stress on Stalin's moral responsibility for what he did throughout his life, but at one point he uses a different concept—"pathological cruelty."[32]

Joseph Stalin

By 1933, Stalin had held for eleven years what became in his hands—and long remained—the key office in the Soviet Union, that of General Secretary of the Soviet Communist Party.† Six weeks after Stalin's appointment as General Secretary, on 3 April 1922, Lenin suffered his first stroke. Before the end of the year he wrote a letter to the Party Congress, including the warning that Stalin "has concentrated immense power in his hands, and I am not certain he will always know how to make use of this power with sufficient caution." On 4 January 1923 Lenin added his prophetic postscript: "Stalin is too rough,‡ and this

---

*One of these may conceivably have accounted for the sad destruction of Graham Sutherland's portrait of Churchill. This portrait "weighed more and more on his mind during the months that followed its presentation in November 1954" (by both Houses of Parliament, to celebrate his eightieth birthday). It was revealed in 1978 that his wife had burned it within a year of the presentation. A photograph in the National Portrait Gallery, London, conveys some idea of what has been lost.[31]

†Then known as the Russian Communist Party (Bolsheviks). In 1925 its title became the All-Union Communist Party. Its modern title (not adopted until 1952) is used in this book: the Communist Party of the Soviet Union (CPSU).

‡*Stalin slishkom grub*—a word that is not easily translated in this context. It also means "rude" and "vulgar." The English edition of Roy Medvedev's *Let History Judge* even prefers to render it as "nasty."

defect becomes . . . intolerable for one who holds the office of General Secretary."[33] Yet it had been Lenin who in January 1912 had persuaded his party's Central Committee to coopt Stalin as a member; and it was in this year that Stalin also became a member of the Party's inner leadership within Russia, a fact that later enabled him, as its senior member on the spot, to assume the Party's leadership in Petrograd in 1917 pending Lenin's return from exile. The year 1912 was also the year of *Pravda*'s very first issue, carrying an editorial by Stalin (under his Georgian pseudonym "Koba"—Turkish for "the Fearless"). He was then thirty-two. Thus 1912 was a watershed in Stalin's political career. Just after this year ended Roosevelt was offered, and accepted, his first federal office; Churchill had been a member of the British Cabinet for four years.

Hard evidence of Stalin's earlier years is sparse. There can be little doubt that he was speaking of his own father when, half a century later, he wrote:

> Imagine a shoemaker who had a tiny workshop, but could not stand the competition of big businesses. The shoemaker closed his workshop and hired himself, say, to Adelkhanov, at the Tbilisi shoe factory. He came to Adelkhanov's factory not to remain a worker for ever but to save some money, to lay aside a small capital and then to reopen his own workshop. . . .[34]

It was near Tiflis (today Tbilisi) that Joseph was born in December 1879 to Georgian parents, Vissarion and Ekaterina Djugashvili, both of whom had themselves been born serfs. Joseph, the only one of four children to survive, suffered illnesses that left traces on him visible until the end of his life: smallpox and an infection of his left hand, which stiffened his arm at the elbow to such an extent that he was declared unfit for military service in the First World War. Joseph's father*

---

*Who, according to the most recent Soviet information, probably died much later than was long supposed—in 1909, not 1890.[35]

failed in his business attempt; and his mother, who earned money as a washerwoman, sent him to the eccesiastical school at Gori. After five years at this school, Joseph won a scholarship to the theological seminary at Tiflis (in the same year as Churchill passed out of Sandhurst). This was then virtually the sole institution of higher education in Georgia and a breeding ground of Georgian patriotism. Paradoxically, therefore, it was from a religious institution that the future Marxist ruler of Russia received his initiation into politics.

The politics were those of Georgia. The territory in the middle of which Djugashvili was born was a highly sensitive region of the Russian Empire. Its wildness, its turbulence and its geographical position— at the meeting point of the Russian and Ottoman empires and Iran—have invited a military comparison with the north-west frontier of India in the nineteenth century. But there were also two great differences: the mineral wealth of the Caucasus, and the fact that the Russians found allies there against Islam in two ancient Christian peoples, the Armenians and the Georgians. At the time of Djugashvili's birth, the Russian conquest of Georgia was still an event within living memory;* the gradual pacification of the Caucasus region was comparatively recent; and it was only four years after he was born that the completion of the railway linking Baku with Batum enabled oil to be exported—from then on, in rapidly increasing quantities.

It was in Georgian that Djugashvili's first poem was published, in the liberal periodical *Iberya* in 1895. His reading was wide, and his memory powerful. Here again there is a parallel with Churchill, but Djugashvili's superiors, unlike Churchill's in the Indian Army, confined him to the punishment cell for borrowing from the local library Victor Hugo's novels, which he read in Russian translations, as he also did Thackeray's *Vanity Fair*. (In later life, the Russian writers whom he read most and often quoted were Chekhov, Gogol and Saltykov-Shchedrin; and he is also said to have become familiar with Shakespeare, Heine, Balzac and Maupassant.)

---

*Georgia was finally annexed in 1801, Tiflis having been sacked by Persian invaders in 1796.

The first political movement of which Djugashvili became a member, at the age of nineteen, was Georgian—a group of moderate Socialists, *Messame Dassy*. Expelled from the theological seminary in 1899 for not attending examinations, Djugashvili obtained a post as a clerk in the local Observatory. A police raid on his room there in March 1901 marks the beginning of his sixteen clandestine years. "Koba," as he now became known to his colleagues, was elected a member of the Tiflis Social Democratic Committee in November 1901. In April of the following year he was arrested and imprisoned for the first time, then condemned to three years' deportation to Siberia; but by the beginning of 1904 he had escaped and was back in Tiflis. By the end of that year he became an active Bolshevik, taking Lenin's side in the first rift to split the new Russian Social Democratic Workers Party—the famous schism* between Bolsheviks (the "majority" men) and Mensheviks (the men of the minority). In December 1905 the two men met for the first time, at a Bolshevik conference held at Tammerfors in Finland. Following the Vth Party Congress, held in London in 1907, which Stalin also attended, he was elected a member of the Party's committee in Baku, now an industrial city with a population of over a hundred thousand, which had begun the nineteenth century as the fortress town of a minor Turkish Khanate. (It was at the London Congress that he first met Leon Trotsky.) From this time onwards Stalin wrote in Russian, although he continued to speak it with a strong Georgian accent until the end of his life.†

The fact that the Bolsheviks were able to hold conferences at Tammerfors (then Russian territory) in 1905 and 1906 is some indication of the political sea-change that had swept over the Russian Empire after the first Russian Revolution, in January 1905, which was followed by the conclusion of peace with Japan in August, after a disastrous war. In

---

*Well described by Leonard Shapiro in Chapter 2 of his *The Communist Party of the Soviet Union*.
†Many of the early Bolsheviks assumed names that remained for the rest of their lives. Thus Lev Bronstein became Leon Trotsky, Ulyanov became Lenin, Skryabin became Molotov and Djugashvili became Stalin (*molot* is the Russian for "hammer" and *stal'* is the Russian for "steel").

October the beleaguered Tsar Nicholas II issued a manifesto promising constitutional freedoms and an elected parliament (the *Duma*), thereby ushering in one of the rare liberal interludes in Russian imperial history.[36] By the time the Vth Party Congress assembled in London, sixty-five Socialist deputies had been elected to the *Duma*. During the ten years that separated the London Congress from the Second (October) Revolution, Koba became first Koba-Stalin and finally Stalin.

These were years of repeated imprisonment, banishment and escape: the period that gave the future General Secretary a special underground preparation for his future role. This preparation was not confined to the qualities for which he afterwards became famous: secretiveness, endurance and the ability to go it alone. Stalin had the advantage of being one of the few senior 1917 revolutionaries who observed his country from within. And paradoxically, his escapes from banishment also enabled him to travel abroad, notably to Kraków and Vienna in 1912–13, when he wrote his *Marxism and the National Question* (published in Russia over the signature K. Stalin), which earned him Lenin's immediate praise as the "wonderful Georgian"[37] and, after the Revolution, his appointment as Minister for the Nationalities.* His short stay in southern Poland—then the Austro-Hungarian province of Galicia—also gave him first-hand knowledge of the country whose destiny was to loom so large in the Second World War.

In February 1913, Stalin was finally condemned to deportation to Siberia. Life for a Russian political prisoner of that epoch was very different from that of prisoners under Stalin's own regime: harshness tempered by incompetence and sometimes indulgence. Stalin, for example, received parcels—most important of all, of books—from the father of his future wife, a fellow Bolshevik, Sergo Alliluev, whose daughter Nadezhda he married in 1918. (Stalin's first wife, Ekaterina

---

*During the period covered by this book, members of the Soviet Council of Ministers were in fact called "People's Commissars" (*Narkom* for short), but it seems preferable to use western terminology. It should also be noted that until the Revolution of 25 October 1917 the old Russian calendar was in use (twelve days behind the western calendar in the nineteenth century and thirteen days in the twentieth).

Svanidze, a Georgian whom he married in church in 1905, had died in 1907.)[38] Stalin did not escape from Siberia until the collapse of the Tsarist regime at the end of February 1917, when Nicholas II abdicated and a Provisional Government was formed by moderate progressive members of the *Duma*.

When Stalin returned to Petrograd in March 1917, he held the reins of Party command for three weeks until Lenin himself reached the capital on 3 April. He then withdrew to the sidelines. In spite of his seniority in the Party leadership—and the renaming of the city of Tsaritsyn as Stalingrad notwithstanding—Stalin's role in the early years of the Revolution was not particularly illustrious. The astounding process whereby a handful of Bolsheviks, of little apparent significance at the beginning of 1917, succeeded on 25 October in seizing power in Petrograd by force of arms, was the achievement of Lenin and Trotsky, not Stalin, who at first advocated co-operation with the Provisional Government, and later, caution. In particular, he took no part in the Military Revolutionary Committee set up by the Petrograd Soviet, under Trotsky's direction, nor—from August to October 1917—in the Bolshevik Military Organisation.

As well as some of the personal characteristics that provoked the celebrated warning at the very end of Lenin's life, Stalin also showed another facet to his convoluted character: a certain degree of common sense, at any rate so far as foreign policy was concerned. As Political Commissar of the south-western group of armies in the Civil War,* for example, his was the decision not to allow reinforcements to be sent from the Lvov front to help Mikhail Tukhachevsky,[39] then advancing on Warsaw. This campaign ended with the successful Polish counter-attack, leading ultimately in 1921 to the Treaty of Riga, by which the Soviet Union was obliged to cede to Poland the western provinces of the Ukraine and Belorussia, whose recovery would prove a major factor in European politics from 1939 to 1945. Neither Stalin nor

---

*The 1917 Revolution was followed in 1918 by the outbreak of a savage civil war, in which the Bolsheviks were not finally victorious until the end of 1920.

Tukhachevsky ever forgot their disagreement. Yet, in the circumstances of the time, it is arguable that Stalin's decision was prudent. Fighting Polish forces on ethnically Polish soil was unwise; and in any case the south-western army group had other responsibilities.

Soon after Lenin's death, Stalin's launching of the policy of "Socialism in one country"—a kind of Soviet governmental isolationism, tempered by the activities of the Comintern—can be seen equally as a recognition of practical necessity: in this case, the need to halt the original Bolshevik ambition of "permanent revolution." Stalin had indeed suggested as early as 1917 that it might be that Russia would be the country that blazed the trail to socialism, although in 1924 he was careful to ascribe the suggestion to Lenin. Trotsky, whose personal contribution to Marxist thought before 1917 had been the concept of permanent revolution across the world, and Stalin stood at opposite poles. It was never probable that the inner Soviet leadership could find room for two men as different in almost every respect; with Lenin dead, a quarrel between them was inevitable, as Lenin himself had foreshadowed in his letter to the Party in December 1922. In January 1925 Stalin's chief adversary in the Communist Party resigned his office as Minister of War; in October of the following year he was expelled from the Politburo and in November 1927 from the Party. In January 1929 he was deported from the Soviet Union.* Trotsky's defeat opened the gate through which Stalin entered on supreme power.

At the end of the 1920s, Stalin initiated a quarter of a century in Soviet history so tragic that it would make Lenin's warning appear an understatement. By 1927, on the eve of these terrible events, the Soviet economy had sufficiently recovered from the ravages of war to regain roughly the level of production of 1913. That new policies were then needed to develop Soviet industry and to modernise Soviet agriculture was not in dispute. In January 1930, however, the Party became committed to a policy of enforced collectivisation of agriculture. Since

---

*Via Turkey and Norway, Trotsky finally found refuge in Mexico in 1937. He was murdered there by an NKVD agent in August 1940.

nearly three quarters of the Soviet population then lived on the land, this policy was well described by one of its principal opponents, Nikolai Bukharin, as the Third Revolution. The horrific results of a crash programme of collectivisation—undertaken at a time when the world price of grain had slumped, while Soviet grain exports were still maintained at a high level—were wistfully described by Stalin twelve years later, during one of his first talks with Churchill, as "very bad and difficult—but necessary."[40] In 1933, however, when preparations for the XVIIth Party Congress were under way, there seemed some hope that saner counsels might still prevail. The worst of the famine was over by the second half of the year. The successive waves of Stalinist terror still lay beyond the Soviet political horizon.

For Stalin himself the winter of 1932–33 was also a turning point in his life. On 8 November 1932 his wife shot herself in her bedroom in the Kremlin, after what her daughter Svetlana has described as a minor quarrel with Stalin during a banquet held in honour of the fifteenth anniversary of the Revolution.[41] It has been suggested that Allilueva's suicide was politically motivated, in the sense that, as a student in the Industrial Academy, she might well have heard accurate accounts of the terrible sufferings inflicted on the Soviet peasantry.[42] This is conceivable, but her daughter has also recorded that the Alliluev family was "plagued" by "schizophrenia."[43] What is beyond reasonable doubt is that Stalin was profoundly affected by his young wife's death. Exactly in what way, no one can say for certain. But the record of his daughter, even though she was born only in 1926, cannot lightly be disregarded.

> My mother's death was a dreadful, crushing blow, and it destroyed his faith in his friends and people in general. He had always considered my mother his closest and most faithful friend. He viewed her death as a betrayal and a stab in the back. He was embittered by it. . . .[44]

3

THE INTERNATIONAL

SETTING, 1933-38

Nos ex-ennemis sont entrés dans la Société des
Nations, chacun avec sa clientèle. Les ex-alliés
sont dissociés. Les Etats-Unis sont présents à la
Conférence, avec le désir évident de désarmer
l'Europe mais de réserver tous leurs privilèges.
La Tour de Babel . . . voilà mon impression
d'arrivée. . . . L'abstraction peut seule réunir des
éléments si divers. Toute réalité les divise.*

—*Edouard Herriot, French Prime Minister, on the eve of
the events described in Chapter 3*

The League of Nations

At the beginning of this decade each of the three
countries that would become allies in the 1940s was still conducting its
external policy within the parameters of the rickety political structure
of world power which two of them, together with France, had put
together in 1919 at Versailles, out of the wreckage left behind by the

---

*Our former enemies have entered the League of Nations, each with his own clientele. The former
allies have split up. The United States is present at the Conference [of World Disarmament], with
the obvious wish to disarm Europe, but to reserve all its privileges. The Tower of Babel . . . that is
my impression on first arrival. . . . Only abstractions can reunite such disparate elements. Any reality
divides them.

First World War. This structure was intended to preserve a peace settlement whose terms were both deeply resented by the vanquished and questioned by some penetrating critics in the countries of the victors. (John Maynard Keynes lambasted the Treaty in his *Economic Consequences of the Peace,* a book published in the year in which the Treaty was signed and soon translated into many languages, including Russian.) The Versailles settlement was also an artificial construction. From the outset the Soviet Union, torn apart by civil war, played no part in it. Far worse, on 19 March 1920, after months of debate, the U.S. Senate finally refused, by ten votes, to ratify the Treaty signed on 28 June 1919 at Versailles, whose first twenty-six articles consisted of the Covenant of the League of Nations. Woodrow Wilson, the President who had inspired the drafting of the Covenant, failed to persuade his fellow countrymen that it was right for the United States to join the League. Had he succeeded, the first meeting of the League Assembly and of the League Council would have been summoned, under the terms of the Treaty, by the President of the United States; and the U.S. Government would have been legally bound not only by the articles of the Covenant, but also by the crucially important Agreement Between the United States and France, linked to the Treaty Between the British Empire and France, which together constituted the keystone of the post-war military arch: an Anglo-American guarantee of the Franco-German frontier.[1] The keystone was irreplaceable. For the next twenty years the United States appeared on the world stage only when American interests were judged to be directly affected, although these appearances were often supplemented by promptings offered to the other actors from the wings.

Thus the League of Nations, intended as the guardian of world peace, was crippled from its inception. With both the world's greatest industrial power (which had now become its greatest international creditor) and continental Europe's largest military power absent from the League's councils, decision-making in Geneva could not be expected to be effective in the long run. For the time being, however, the League of Nations became an essential instrument of foreign policy for the other two major victorious powers, Britain and France, who virtu-

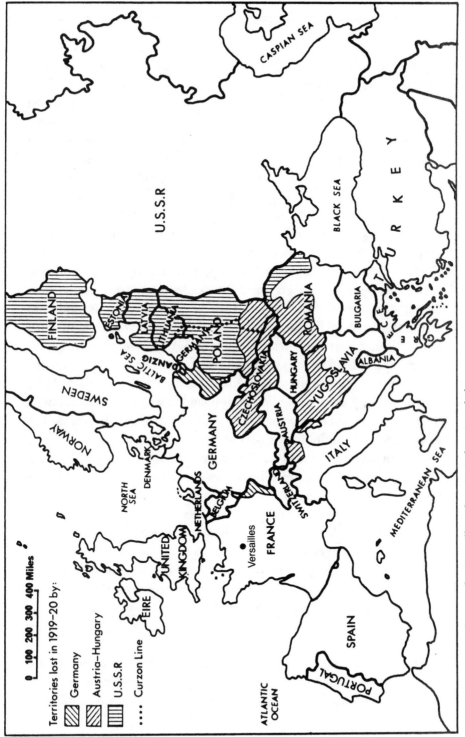

1. The European settlement after Versailles: The principal territorial changes

ally ran it. For all its faults, the League was more than that. In spite of the American defection, the concept of the League continued to exert a powerful intellectual and emotional appeal. This appeal was strongest in Britain, where the League of Nations Union, inspired by the leadership of the two "civic monks of the Anglo-Saxon world"[2]—Robert Cecil and Gilbert Murray—and with two former prime ministers as honorary presidents, had nearly a million members in 1933. The strength of this appeal, by no means confined to the Left in Britain, stemmed in part from a revulsion against the European system of heavily armed alliances held by many to have been responsible for the outbreak of the First World War, and partly also from a belief in the efficacy of economic sanctions, the subject of Article 16 of the League Covenant, for which the economic blockade of Germany during (and indeed after) the war had provided a kind of precedent. Beyond both these considerations lay the broader belief that what would, in the final analysis, deter aggression was the sheer weight of world public opinion. As one of the League's principal advocates, Cecil, had put it when the House of Commons debated the Treaty of Versailles in 1919: "What we rely upon is public opinion, and if we are wrong about it, then the whole thing is wrong. I believe we are right. If you do not rely upon public opinion, the decision of the assemblies ceases to be of the first importance."[3] And Cecil was speaking for a wide cross-section of public opinion, not only in his own country, when he told the League of Nations General Assembly twelve years later:

> I do not think that there is the slightest prospect of any war. I
> know . . . how rash it is to prophesy as to the future of interna-
> tional affairs; but, nevertheless, I do not believe that there is
> anyone in this room who will contradict me when I say that there
> has scarcely ever been a period in the world's history when war
> seemed less likely than it does at the present.[4]

Others were less inclined to self-deception, especially in France, the country (other than the Soviet Union) that had suffered most from the war. One year after Cecil's speech to the General Assembly, Edouard

Herriot, then French Prime Minister, offered the trenchant analysis of
the real state of international affairs quoted in the epigraph to this
chapter. Describing Geneva as a Tower of Babel, "any reality," wrote
Herriot, was divisive.[5] It was not only Europeans still suffering from
the aftermath of the First World War* who found it hard to face
reality at the beginning of the 1930s. (In the United States, President
Herbert Hoover was one of many who at first refused to recognise the
Great Depression for what it was: not just the end of the Jazz Age, but
a national and international disaster of the first magnitude.) Even after
Hitler's ascent to power, many—perhaps most—people on both sides
of the Atlantic took refuge from the *réalité* of Europe in what Herriot
called *"l'abstraction."* That nothing was the same after 30 January 1933
is self-evident today. Those who realised this at the time were few. In
part this was because the countries most affected were immersed in an
economic morass. But there was a further, confusing factor. The first
major challenge to the authority of the League of Nations was offered
not by Germany but by Japan, in a region where Britain, the Soviet
Union and the United States all had large interests, but, in the case of
Britain and the United States, few armed forces to protect them on the
spot.

On the night of 18 September 1931 the Japanese Kwantung Army,[6]
stationed on the mainland, had used a trumped-up incident at Muk-
den† to justify its invasion of Manchuria. Japanese forces had no difficulty in overrunning and occupying this vast territory, where the
central Chinese Government's writ had not run far even before the
invasion, and where Japanese military rights dated from 1905. At the
turn of the year 1932–33 the League of Nations Special Assembly met
to consider the report submitted by the commission sent by the League
to examine what was happening in Manchuria. This report, which

---

*This war cost the participants losses estimated between twenty and twenty-four million, including
non-births, during the four years 1914–18. The influenza epidemic that followed the war is estimated to have killed almost as many people as the war itself.
†Today, Shenyang.

avoided an explicit statement that Japan had broken the League Covenant by invading Manchuria, recommended the establishment of a largely autonomous Manchuria under Chinese sovereignty; a non-aggression pact between China and Japan; and recognition of Japanese rights in Manchuria, coupled with non-recognition of the state of Manchukuo, which the Japanese had set up, under a Manchu puppet Regent, in March 1932. The League Assembly approved these recommendations. Japan left the League in March 1933.

For two very different men, one a member of the British Tory Establishment and the other an American East Coast Republican, both of whom were closely concerned with what happened at the time, Japanese defiance of the League's disapproval seemed, with the hindsight of several years, to be the first beginning of all that followed in the rest of the decade. In Cecil's words, written in 1941, this had "brought us step by step to the present grave position"; while for Henry Stimson, "the road to World War II" was "clearly visible . . . from the railway tracks near Mukden to the operations of the bombers over Hiroshima and Nagasaki."[7] Neither of these views is tenable today. Cecil's ardent belief in the League was undimmed by its successive failures. Stimson, though a man of integrity, had a personal reason for holding his view: he had been U.S. Secretary of State during the Manchurian crisis and Secretary of War when the two atomic bombs were dropped on Japan. Moreover, he regarded his government's decision to withhold diplomatic recognition of the Japanese regime in Manchuria, and his personal success in persuading the League of Nations to follow suit, as "perhaps the greatest constructive achievement of his public life."[8]

As for the Left, what happened in China in 1931–33 also came to be perceived as the first in a chain of fascist acts of aggression during the decade. Some colour was lent to this view by the fact that in due course Japan became the ally of Germany and Italy. But at the time of the Manchurian crisis, this development lay far ahead; indeed it was not until 1938 that Hitler began to court Japan; and Germany recognised Manchukuo only in May of that year. The strength of the military within the Japanese governmental machine gave Japan in the 1930s militaristic affinities with European fascism. That, however, was about as far as the parallel went. The roots of Japanese nationalism were much older; and the abundant documentary evidence now available from all sources tells a different, far more complex, story of the evolution of Japanese policy in the ten years from 1931 onwards.[9]

The Manchurian episode as such was brought to an end[10] by a Sino-Japanese truce signed in May 1933.* Transferred to the European context, the argument about the lessons to be drawn from the proven inadequacy of the League as a peacekeeping instrument lasted for most of the rest of the decade. Short of rearmament, there were three broad options. First, conciliation. If the Japanese had a case, so too, in the eyes of some people, had the Germans. (From this line of thought Chamberlain would derive his policy of European "appeasement.") By contrast, others argued that Article 16 of the League Covenant should have been invoked against Japan: a policy of economic sanctions that would be attempted against Italy—half-heartedly—three years later. Thirdly, there was still widespread belief in the power of global exhortation, typified by the Stimsonian attitude of moral disapproval, even after the Manchurian Affair had exposed its limitations. In the main, during the years that followed, foreign policy on both sides of the Atlantic (including the Soviet Union) veered between these three options. But whereas Japan was a disappointed victor in the First World War, German aspirations from 1933 onwards were far more perilous, for they were fired by the bitterness of defeat.[11]

1933

On the morning of 30 January 1933 (Roosevelt's fifty-first birthday) the man whom, at their first meeting only a few months earlier, the German President Paul von Hindenburg had described as an odd fellow who would, at most, make a Minister of Posts,[12] was summoned by the President in order to be appointed Chancellor of Germany. Adolf

---

*The Sino-Japanese War proper did not break out until over four years later; see Chapter 4.

Hitler was not yet forty-four years old. He was not a member of the Reichstag—the "Bohemian corporal" had renounced his Austrian citizenship in 1925 and he had become a German citizen only in 1932. Out of a total of eleven portfolios in the Cabinet that he formed, only three, including his own, were held by members of the Nazi Party. If Hitler was underestimated by the non-Nazi majority in Germany during the early weeks of 1933,* it is hardly surprising that Germany's wartime enemies were slow to realise the full significance of what was happening in Berlin. And even if they had, these were precisely the weeks in which the ravages of the Great Depression loomed largest in the public mind and in political debate. There were fifteen million unemployed in the United States and three million in Britain, to cite the most obvious statistic (by comparison, the German figure was six million); and even the autarkic economy of the Soviet Union was not immune to the collapse of world prices of primary products (a 60 per cent fall between 1929 and 1934), although the Soviet famine of the winter of 1932–33 was a self-inflicted wound.

In so far as the task of grappling with their economic problems at home left governments a margin of attention free for international affairs, this was then focused on two multilateral conferences: the Disarmament Conference and the World Economic Conference. And, at one remove from the issues with which these conferences attempted to deal, relations between the governments of Britain, France and the United States were still plagued by the question of post-war debts and reparations. The issue of post-war debt formed the backdrop to the general economic malaise. In the first place, it was undeniable that, as Calvin Coolidge put it, "they hired the money, didn't they?" The major debtor to the United States at the end of the First World War—a total of over $4 billion—was Britain, the country that had been, in 1914, the world's greatest creditor; nearly half the total of the Liberty Loans, which constituted the principal wartime instrument for American financial flows to the Allied Powers, were held by the British

*Even in the general election held in March 1933 the Nazi Party won fewer than half the votes cast.

in 1918.[13] When Europe was overwhelmed by the 1931 crisis of international finance, Hoover promoted a one-year moratorium on debt repayment. At the end of 1932, when the British Government paid its instalment to the United States in full, it specified this payment as exceptional; the French attempt to make a similar conditional payment brought the government down in the Chamber of Deputies in December 1932. A final, token payment was made by Britain in mid-1933. Thereafter the British, like the French, were in default. Their source of balancing payments—German war reparations—had dried up. But in American eyes, Europeans who could afford expensive armaments could also afford to pay their debts.

It was against this inauspicious background, but with high hopes, that the Disarmament Conference was convened in Geneva and, a year later, the World Economic Conference in London. Both ended in fiasco in 1933. The Disarmament Conference lasted effectively until the autumn of that year, even though it remained formally in existence until April 1934. This conference, at which Archbishop William Temple preached an opening sermon, well deserved Herriot's description: "the Tower of Babel." The Soviet Union proposed total disarmament all round; the United States proposed a one-third reduction of land forces, including the abolition of tanks and bombers, together with a substantial reduction of naval forces; while Britain countered the American proposal with a complicated compromise, partly reflecting the fact that at this juncture the British Government's defence policy was contradictory. Secretly, the Cabinet had accepted the Chiefs of Staff's recommendation that the "ten-year rule" was no longer valid and had even instructed the Chiefs to make recommendations for filling the worst gaps in Britain's run-down defences.* Publicly, the Prime Minister, Ramsay Macdonald, was committed to the cause of

---

*The rolling ten-year rule (for whose adoption Churchill, of all people, had been responsible, as Chancellor of the Exchequer in 1928) was the British assumption, for planning purposes, that no great war need be expected for ten years. The Chiefs of Staff took nearly two years to present their recommendations, however.

disarmament; and his Chancellor of the Exchequer, Neville Chamberlain, had just introduced the lowest British defence estimates of the entire inter-war period. The German delegation announced after five months of discussion that it would cease to take part in the Geneva Conference until the German claim to equal rights with other countries—essentially, France—was granted. In vain the French, pressed by the British to agree to disarm, sought to obtain a British guarantee of their security. The problem was, in a way, solved in the following year, when Germany rejected a French offer—of equality in armaments after a trial period of four years; and Germany finally withdrew altogether both from the Disarmament Conference and from the League of Nations in October 1933.

The World Economic Conference, held in London, was even more chaotic. Today, it is clear that the attempt at currency stabilisation, on which the conference at once embarked, was a forlorn hope at a moment when the world's major currencies were still at sixes and sevens, in the wake of the financial crisis of 1931. Eventually, in 1936, Britain, France and the United States would succeed in reaching agreement on a kind of gold standard, which lasted until the outbreak of war; but a concerted attack on the whole range of problems of international economic order had to wait another ten years, until the Bretton Woods system was agreed in 1944. Meanwhile the failure of the World Economic Conference, which broke up in August 1933, after the delivery of Roosevelt's "bombshell" message, left a bitter taste in most British mouths.*

Adolf Hitler

While these multilateral efforts to secure a firmer foundation, both political and economic, for international order ground to a halt, Hitler consolidated, with dazzling speed, the power base from which he

---

*For the "bombshell" message, and for the attitude towards both these world conferences taken by Churchill and Roosevelt, see Chapter 4.

would soon launch his assault on the settlement of Versailles. Less than a month after he became Chancellor, the Reichstag in Berlin was burned down in mysterious circumstances, on the night of 27 February 1933. Hitler chose the day after the fire to promulgate the Decree for the Protection of the People and the State, which—among other things—suspended the Weimar Republic's guarantees of individual liberty. After the general election held in March, the National Socialist Party, in alliance with the Nationalist deputies, commanded a simple majority in the Reichstag. It required only the arrest or proscription of the Communist deputies to convert this into a clear Nazi majority. To amend the constitution, however, a two-thirds parliamentary majority was needed. This was forthcoming on 23 March, when, by 441 votes to 94, the deputies passed the bill that enabled Hitler to legislate for four years without the Reichstag.

In July 1933, the Nazi Party was proclaimed the only political party in Germany. In March 1934, large increases in the German military budget were announced; and one year later the existence of the *Luftwaffe* was made public, as was Hitler's intention to re-introduce conscription and to form an army of thirty-six divisions. On the night of 29–30 June 1934 Hitler had Ernst Röhm, Chief of Staff of the Brownshirted *Sturm Abteilung,* and some four hundred others, murdered— most, but not all, of them members of the *SA,* a force then many times larger than the German Army. Finally, within an hour of President von Hindenburg's death on 2 August 1934, it was announced that the office of President would be merged with that of Chancellor; Hitler became both President of Germany and Supreme Commander of the Armed Forces of the Reich. In just over eighteen months he had swept the board.

The numbers killed in Germany during the last weekend of June 1934 were trivial by comparison with the genocide that would follow in the ensuing years; and it is Hitler's responsibility for this crime that will ensure him a permanent place in the history of horror. Given Hitler's hatred of the Jews—"perhaps the most sincere emotion of which he was capable"[14]—it is difficult to separate his racial ideas from the main body of his political beliefs, which were a ragbag of ideas picked up in pre-First War Vienna. If, however, by some miracle anti-Semitism had been left out of this ragbag, what might history's verdict on Hitler as a political leader have been? The answer to this question must be paradoxical.

Intellectually, the mixture of ignorance and arrogance displayed by Hitler's *Table Talk* would have marked him out as one of the most boring conversationalists of the twentieth century. He knew little about any country outside Europe; Asia was a closed book; and the United States was for him "half Judaized, half negrified."[15] On the other hand, his skill as a tactician would have commanded respect. For a man who had travelled so little outside his own country and who spoke no language but his own, his political instinct was uncannily accurate, always provided that it was exercised within the confines of European affairs. His powers of persuasion, in private as well as in public, were extraordinary. Again and again in the years from 1936 onwards, his senior advisers, men of far wider experience than Hitler's, sought to hold him back, and repeatedly they were proved wrong. His assessment of France's internal weakness was right; it is hard to deny that his contempt for the members of the British governments of the 1930s was well founded; and his great adventure against the Soviet Union, though it was eventually his undoing, came within an ace of success. As the 1930s went forward, the world increasingly danced to his tune. Even the United States could not altogether escape the effects of his policies. In a sense, this dismal decade* was Hitler's own.

The arrival at the pinnacle of German power of a man who less than ten years earlier had made public in writing his view that "Destiny itself" pointed the way for Germany "towards Russia and the border states subject to her . . . a colossal empire in the east . . . ripe for dissolution,"[16] meant that sooner or later the Soviet Union would be drawn back into the European political arena, where its previous foreign policy had failed. The next chapter will examine the circumstances in which, in December 1933, Stalin decided to adopt a policy of

---

*"Dismal" politically. But in other fields—above all that of the arts—it was a period of consummate achievement.

collective security. In September 1934 the Soviet Union was elected to a permanent seat on the Council of the League of Nations, and in May of the follówing year the French Foreign Minister travelled to Moscow. The Franco-Soviet Pact, which he signed there, committed the two countries to come to each other's assistance if either became the object of unprovoked attack; and the circle was rounded off by the simultaneous conclusion of a similar agreement between the Soviet Union and Czechoslovakia, which was already the ally of France. Moreover, in April 1935 the governments of Britain, France and Italy had closed ranks at Stresa, where their prime ministers met and issued a renewed declaration of the independence of Austria, whose Chancellor, Engelbert Dollfuss, had been assassinated by Austrian Nazis— though probably without Hitler's foreknowledge—in July 1934.

On paper, these developments should have given Hitler pause. Yet he never lost the initiative. There was widespread distrust of the Soviet Union both in Britain and in France; the Franco-Soviet Pact was never complemented by a military convention; and the French Senate did not ratify the pact until March 1936. Hitler had shrewdly reinsured to the east himself, by means of a ten-year Pact of Non-Aggression concluded with Poland in January 1934. And—worst of all—in June 1935 he sent Joachim von Ribbentrop (then not yet Foreign Minister) to London, where he succeeded in persuading the British Government to conclude a naval pact. This agreement, about which Britain consulted neither France nor Italy, was a public slap in the face for both of them. Among other provisions, it allowed Germany the right to build submarines up to a hundred per cent of the combined submarine strength of the British Commonwealth. Hardly had this private deal run a coach and horses through the naval provisions of the Versailles Treaty than the British Government, now headed by Stanley Baldwin, lurched in the opposite direction.

Since the middle of March 1935, the League of Nations had had before it an appeal against Italy submitted by Abyssinia, a country where Benito Mussolini (*Duce* of Italy since 1922) aspired to a position that he regarded as similar to the one enjoyed by Britain in Egypt. On 11 September the British Foreign Secretary took the lead against Italy in Geneva; and when Italian forces attacked Abyssinia three weeks later, the League applied sanctions. Oil, however, was not included. There were repeated attempts at political compromise (notably the so-called Hoare-Laval Pact in December 1935, abandoned when it was greeted with a storm of public indignation in Britain) until sanctions were finally withdrawn in June 1936, after Chamberlain had ridiculed their continuation as "the very midsummer of madness." The effects of this imbroglio were twofold. The League of Nations failed the test of a conflict between two of its members for the second time; its authority was now irretrievably damaged. Secondly, the British-led attempt to counter Italian designs on Abyssinia—one of the few major Western European initiatives in foreign policy during the 1930s—ended by offering Hitler's diplomacy a golden opportunity outside the confines of Central Europe. Although Hitler avoided involvement in the Abyssinian issue itself, a year later the Rome-Berlin partnership was in place: the "axis," as Mussolini called it, an expression that became a catch-phrase famous in world politics for the next seven years.[17]

Well before the Italo-German Protocols were signed in October 1936 in Berlin, Hitler had already brought off the first masterstroke of his foreign policy, the remilitarisation of the Rhineland: a *casus foederis* under the 1925 Locarno Treaty, for Italy as well as for Britain and France. Article 43 of the Treaty of Versailles, moreover, was categorical: if Germany violated the provisions for the demilitarisation of the Rhineland laid down in the Treaty, this would be regarded as a "hostile act" committed against the signatories of the Treaty and "calculated to disturb the peace of the World." This critical operation was carried out with a force inadequate to resist opposition, had the British and the French been willing to fulfil their obligations under the provisions both of the Versailles Treaty and of the Locarno Pact. Were they unwilling or unable? There is room for argument, but what is beyond dispute is the size of the German force that was greeted with flowers by the crowds in the Rhineland on 7 March 1936: about one division east of the river and only three battalions west of it. Hitler was justified in claiming, as he later did, that what had saved him at this turning point of his career was his "unshakable obstinacy" and "amazing aplomb."[18] *The Times* headed its leader "A Chance to Rebuild." In default of a lead from the British and French governments, the nearest approach to an adverse reaction came from the East: Poland and the Soviet Union. The former briefly offered, on 9 March, to bring its alliance with France into operation; the latter proposed the imposition of sanctions by the League of Nations. Neither suggestion prospered.

The Downhill Slope

From March 1936 it was downhill all the way to the conclusion of the Munich Agreement on the last night of September 1938. Unlike the confused perceptions of the time, this Gadarene descent is clear today. What is still an open question is which of several intermediate points during these two and a half years should be identified as the most significant. In chronological order, four present themselves as candidates: the outbreak of the Spanish Civil War; the conclusion of the Anti-Comintern Pact; Edward Halifax's visit to Berchtesgaden; and the Austrian *Anschluss*.

The first of these events, which began on 16 July 1936, was unforeseen, nor did anyone expect the Spanish Civil War to last nearly three years. Although the struggle that developed in Spain, which claimed at least half a million dead from all causes, was soon afterwards dwarfed in scale by the Second World War, at the time it inflamed and divided Europe, especially Britain, where—only four months earlier—the German reoccupation of the Rhineland had left most of public opinion cold. For the Right in general, and especially for the Roman Catholic Church, the insurgent general, Francisco Franco, was fighting the extremes of socialism, anarchism and communism. For the Left as a whole—and indeed for much of public opinion left of centre, on both sides of the Atlantic—the civil war swiftly became a symbol; and, for the volunteers who fought for the Republicans in the international brigades, it was a crusade*—a precursor of global resistance to fascism. Nothing between the two world wars moved opinion in the West with such emotional force. Monuments to the power of its im-

---

*Five hundred British members of the international brigades lost their lives in Spain; 120 Americans in the Abraham Lincoln Battalion were killed.

pact have been left by poets (García Lorca, Auden), novelists (Hemingway, Malraux) and painters. Of all these the most poignant memorial is now at last in the Casón del Buen Retiro in Madrid: Picasso's mural painting of the German bombing[19] of the Basque town of Guernica, left under the terms of his will to the Spanish people, which is probably the most exhaustively documented work by any painter in the twentieth century.

Today, the massive Spanish archives that have at last been thrown open have both fuelled some fresh controversy and demolished some myths about this war.[20] One of the myths that has been eliminated is that the revolt was inspired or organised from without. There were indeed issues at stake whose significance went beyond the frontiers of the Spanish Republic; and part of the outcome of the war was that Spain did not re-enter the democratic community for nearly forty years. But the evidence shows that in its origins this conflict was accurately called the Spanish Civil War. Few, however, would dispute the facts that it was as the result of Hitler's personal decision[21] that Franco was able to use the Junkers air bridge in order to transport his troops from Morocco to Spain at the end of July 1936; that, numerically, the largest foreign force engaged in combat in Spain was Italian;[22] and that the Soviet decision to intervene, though taken after that of the two Fascist dictators, led to large shipments of arms to the Republican side.[23]

Exactly how the balance of the German, Italian and Soviet interventions—taken in conjunction with the international brigades and the quantities of armaments purchased by both sides in several countries (including France), and calculated against the background of the charade of non-intervention, directed by the British and French governments—weighed[24] in the scales of battle between the two sides in the civil war will long be debated. What is certain is that the belief, current in the 1930s, that Franco would, on ideological grounds, inevitably ally his country with the Axis once his mastery of Spain had been assured, was not borne out in the Second World War. True, Spanish soldiers fought side by side with the German Army in the Russian campaign. But earlier, at a critical moment of the war—23 October

1940—a nine-hour meeting with Hitler at the Franco-Spanish frontier town of Hendaye broke up in deadlock. At this meeting Franco stuck to Spanish national interests with a stubbornness summed up by Hitler himself in his remark that he "would prefer to have three or four teeth taken out" rather than go through the experience of negotiating with Franco again.[25] And paradoxically, one of the (unintended) side effects of the Munich Agreement in 1938 was to eliminate the possibility that the Spanish Civil War would—as the Republican leaders had hoped— be subsumed in a wider European conflict; had Britain and France gone to war one year earlier than they did, this might indeed have happened. At the time that the civil war was being waged, however, its gravest effect—with hindsight—was to distract western public opinion from the fascist danger on the doorstep: Nazi Germany.*

The German-Japanese Anti-Comintern Pact, signed in Tokyo in October 1936, was Ribbentrop's second personal diplomatic success; he negotiated it independently of the German Foreign Office. The Japanese motive for signature was fear of Soviet military power in Siberia and of Soviet influence in China. For his part, Ribbentrop left no doubt that his government was looking for more signatures; Mussolini added his during his state visit to Germany in November 1937. But the wording of the Pact was loose. Even its Secret Protocol only obliged each party, in the event of an unprovoked attack by the Soviet Union, to "take no measures which would tend to ease the situation of the USSR."[27] However, it contained the germ of the Tripartite Pact between Germany, Japan and Italy, concluded nearly three years later— an agreement whose signature was to prove of major significance in the Second World War.

Legend has dealt kindly with Edward Halifax, perhaps because of his earlier record as Viceroy of India and his later years as Ambassador in Washington; and the way in which he overcame his physical dis-

---

*Arguably, it also confused most people about the nature of modern warfare. Militarily speaking, the Spanish Civil War was more like the last act of the First World War than the first act of the Second.[26]

ability[28] also commands respect. His tenure of the Foreign Office, where he—albeit reluctantly—succeeded Anthony Eden in February 1938, was inglorious; and what he said to Hitler during his visit to Germany in November 1937 was indefensible, even if allowance is made for the fact that he was acting as the spokesman of a Prime Minister who was committed to a policy of appeasement. The auspices under which he undertook this visit were poor. Invited by Hermann Göring to visit a hunting exhibition in Berlin, Halifax (then holding the portfolio of Lord President in the British Cabinet)[29] was authorised by Chamberlain to see Hitler, who would not come to Berlin but received him in Berchtesgaden, in order to find out what the German Chancellor had in mind. According to all three records[30] of this unhappy conversation, Halifax did not confine himself to this. Even his own record shows Halifax, off his own bat, raising Danzig, Austria and Czechoslovakia as examples of "questions arising out of the Versailles settlement which seemed to us [the British Government] capable of causing trouble if they were unwisely handled." On all of these issues, the British Government was "not necessarily concerned to stand for the status quo as today"; its concern was "to avoid such treatment of them as would be likely to cause trouble"; and "if reasonable settlements could be reached with free assent and goodwill of those primarily concerned," the government "certainly had no desire to block. . . ." The language of the German record is less woolly. Danzig, Austria and Czechoslovakia are cited, in Halifax's mouth, as examples of "the category of possible alterations in the European order which might be destined to come about with the passage of time," and the British interest is defined as seeing that "any alterations should come through the course of peaceful evolution and that methods should be avoided which might cause far-reaching disturbances." As far as Czechoslovakia and Austria were concerned, "a settlement could be reached given a reasonable attitude."

The terms in which Halifax reported on his visit to his colleagues on his return to London, and the course of the Cabinet discussion, suggest that what was uppermost in his mind was not the future of Central Europe, about which he seems to have returned with a remarkably sanguine assessment, but the chances of achieving an Anglo-German colonial settlement. Be that as it may, Hitler could hardly have been given a greener light from London at that stage. In his diary, Chamberlain recorded his belief that Halifax's visit had been "a great success because it achieved its object, that of creating an atmosphere in which it is possible to discuss with Germany the practical questions involved in a European settlement."[31]

Of the three territories mentioned by Halifax in November 1937, the first to be "altered," four months later, was Austria. The Austrian Chancellor, Kurt von Schuschnigg, bullied by Hitler at a meeting at Berchtesgaden on 11 February 1938, had already conceded far-reaching German demands when, on 9 March, he announced that a plebiscite would be held four days later to determine the future of Austria. Hitler responded with preparations for invasion, at the same time taking the precaution of sending a personal emissary to Rome to reassure Mussolini.* Neither the cancellation of the plebiscite nor Schuschnigg's resignation was enough to stave off military occupation. German troops began crossing the frontier at dawn on 13 March, unopposed; Hitler crossed it himself that afternoon; and on the next day he laid a wreath on his parents' grave. There is no reason to doubt his word: the *Anschluss* was the proudest moment of his life. *Grossdeutschland* was indeed a prize that even Bismarck had not sought. Although Austria's incorporation in Germany was expressly forbidden by the Versailles Treaty, the British Government acquiesced on the grounds, as Chamberlain put it to the House of Commons on 14 March, that "nothing could have arrested what actually has happened" short of the use of force. And when the Soviet Government suggested the immediate convening of a conference of peace-loving countries (in practice, Britain, Czechoslovakia, France and the Soviet Union) to discuss

---

*Mussolini "accepted the whole thing in a very friendly manner." Hitler's reply, by telephone, confirmed by telegram, was that he "would never forget": gratitude which reflected the contrast between Mussolini's acquiescence in 1938 and his reaction to Dollfuss' assassination four years earlier, when he had sent troops to the Brenner Pass.[32]

means of preventing further aggression and "the removal of the growing danger of a new world war," the Prime Minister declined, on the grounds that this would increase the division of Europe into two blocs.[33]

Munich

The presence of over three million Germans within the borders of the Czechoslovak state established by the Treaty of Versailles—the ancient frontiers of Bohemia—coupled with the strategic need to cover Germany's southern flank before any eastward move could be contemplated, made it certain that this country would be Hitler's next target for "alteration." This time the British and French governments themselves tried to preempt Hitler by urging a policy of conciliation on the Czechoslovak Government; and in July 1938 an undistinguished British Cabinet minister[34] was sent to Prague to mediate between President Edvard Beneš and the Sudeten Germans. The climax of the tortuous course of the negotiations that followed was reached in the middle of September. The Czechoslovak Government then imposed martial law; the leader of the Sudeten Germans fled to Germany; and the divided French Government lost its nerve. Chamberlain then flew to Berchtesgaden—the first of his three visits to Germany. At this meeting he offered Hitler, on a personal basis, the peaceful incorporation within the Reich of the Sudeten Germans. At his second meeting, at Godesberg on 22 September, he offered not only this concession, to which both French and Czechoslovak agreement had been secured in the interval, but the dissolution of the Czechoslovak alliances with France and the Soviet Union, thrown in as well. As in the case of Austria, although Hitler's demands of Czechoslovakia appeared to have been met in full, he refused to be satisfied. Chamberlain, therefore, returned to London empty-handed, with Hitler's deadline for military occupation of the Sudetenland set at 1 October.

Even for the British Cabinet, this was too much. For six febrile days war seemed virtually inevitable. But on 28 September almost the entire House of Commons gave Chamberlain a standing ovation[35] when he announced that just at that moment—Mussolini's message was handed to him along the government benches—he had received an invitation to attend a four-power conference at Munich. The only official whom Chamberlain took with him was Horace Wilson, nominally his Chief Industrial Adviser.* Chamberlain, Edouard Daladier (the French Prime Minister), Hitler and Mussolini met the following day and signed the Munich Agreement in the early hours of 30 September.[36] The Czechoslovak Foreign Minister was informed of the agreement at 6:15 A.M. by the German Chargé d'Affaires in Prague, who transmitted the Munich decision, "invited" Czechoslovak representatives to be in Berlin at 5:00 P.M. and expressed his personal opinion that there was "no difference between Berchtesgaden and Godesberg."[37] (The Czechs were to receive their copy of the new map from the British Minister in Prague.) Hitler's deadline was met; German troops began their march into the Sudetenland on the following day; but as a concession to Chamberlain, it was agreed that the occupation of the Sudetenland should be carried out by stages in October.

The meeting at Munich had in fact originated not in an Italian, but in a British suggestion. (Hitler's decision to attend may, however, have been influenced by Mussolini, who played a practical though minor part in the proceedings, because he was the only one of the four leaders who could speak foreign languages.) No proper record appears to have been taken.[38] In a brief account, written from memory, Wilson spoke of "the chaos that ruled for the last five hours"; and after the war the official British historians were unable to find a signed copy of the Munich Agreement in the Foreign Office archives.[39] The terms of the agreement did indeed not differ substantially from the Godesberg pro-

---

*Wilson became, in addition, Permanent Secretary of the Treasury and head of the Civil Service in 1939. As such, he should have had no responsibility for advising on foreign affairs. In 1938, however, Chamberlain arranged for Robert Vansittart, regarded as Germanophobe, to be replaced by Alexander Cadogan as Permanent Under-Secretary at the Foreign Office, Vansittart receiving instead the largely honorific title of Chief Diplomatic Adviser. Wilson rapidly became Chamberlain's grey eminence in the execution of his appeasement policy: just how grey may be judged from the documents collected in the Dirksen Papers (Herbert von Dirksen was German Ambassador in London from April 1938 until the outbreak of war; his papers were captured in 1945). To cite only one example of Wilson's nefarious conduct, see the letter of 1 September 1938 to Dirksen from the German Chargé d'Affaires in London—Dirksen Papers, Document 7.

posals. The new frontiers were more strategic than ethnic, still leaving a quarter of a million Germans in Czechoslovakia and consigning eight hundred thousand Czechs to Germany. Both the Poles and the Hungarians lost no time in taking their own slices of the Czechoslovak cake. Within a month Beneš had gone into exile in London, the alliance with the Soviet Union had been denounced, and the Czech Ambassador in London, Jan Masaryk, broke down and wept, exclaiming to Ivan Maisky: "They have sold us into German slavery, as they used to sell negroes into slavery in America."[40]

The reactions of Churchill, Roosevelt and Stalin to this, the most traumatic event between the two world wars, will be described in the next chapter; but perhaps the most remarkable reaction of all to Munich was Hitler's. His pleasure in his success was qualified. He wanted what in America is known as "cream on his strawberry shortcake," and for this—the occupation of Prague—he had to wait another six months. By contrast, Chamberlain returned in triumph, comparing his own return from Munich to that of Disraeli from the Congress of Berlin and even embroidering the phrase that Disraeli had used in 1878—that he had brought back "peace with honour"—with the additional words: "I believe it is peace in our time."[41] As proof, he waved at the airport on his return a curious document that he and Hitler had signed at Munich, which coupled the Munich Agreement and the Anglo-German Naval Agreement (signed three years earlier) as "symbolic of the desire of our two peoples never to go to war with one another again," and recorded the two leaders' resolution that "the method of consultation shall be the method adopted to deal with any other questions that may concern our two countries." It was to this Joint Declaration, which had been a British draft, that *The Times* gave its centre-page headlines on 1 October. Its leading article, entitled "A New Dawn," opened with the words: "No conqueror returning from the battlefield has come home adorned with nobler laurels than Mr Chamberlain from Munich yesterday." On the following Sunday, prayers of thanksgiving were offered in British churches "for the sudden uplifting of the cloud which for the last weeks has darkened and oppressed our life."[42]

4

CHURCHILL,

ROOSEVELT AND

STALIN IN THE

GATHERING STORM

I believe it is peace in our time.

—*Neville Chamberlain, October 1938*

National Socialist Germany will never go to
Canossa!* If the rest of the world obstinately
bars the way to recognition of our rights by
the way of negotiation, then there should be no
surprise that we secure for ourselves our rights
in another way.

—*Adolf Hitler, November 1938*

EUROPE

Churchill

Of the three men whom the Second World War would throw together in the following decade, it is Churchill whose reaction to what

---

*Hitler was echoing the words used by Bismarck in a speech in the Reichstag in 1872, *Nach Canossa werden wir nicht gehen.* Because Canossa was the scene of the penance performed by the Holy Roman Emperor before the Pope in the eleventh century, the "road to Canossa" is the German metaphorical equivalent of publicly eating humble pie.

he called the Gathering Storm of the 1930s that has best withstood the test of time. Even so, Churchill's record is subject to some important qualifications. Because he was more often correct in his assessment of the current of world affairs in the 1930s than his contemporaries were, his mistakes are easily overlooked. Examples are his attack on the Indian reforms enacted by Parliament in 1935 (already mentioned), his initial misjudgment of the Spanish Civil War, and—above all—his persistent underestimation of Japan. Militarily speaking, his ideas were a blend of old and new. Thus he was a late convert to the new concept of armoured warfare; and in naval matters he now belonged to the old-fashioned battleship school of thought (a strange aberration by Churchill, considering the encouragement that he had given to the pioneers of air warfare at sea a quarter of a century earlier).[1] Moreover, his reputation as, above all, an orator in the 1930s meant that the public, recalling the extravagance of the language of his indictment of the India Act (phrases like "the vast pillage of a derelict Empire"), did not pay heed to his increasingly dire warnings about the danger in Europe until the decade was almost over. One of the reasons why Churchill's philippics in these years, which look so cogent on paper today, failed to convince most of his fellow countrymen at the time when they were delivered was that he had himself debased the coinage of warning. All this said, nothing can alter the salient fact: on the central issue of the 1930s Churchill was—to borrow words used to describe Roosevelt in a different context*—magnificently right. (Nor, however, is anything likely to dissuade revisionist historians from persisting in their efforts to prove him mistaken.)[2]

Churchill has left his own account of how he spent the first half of the 1930s: not very often in the House of Commons, for much of the time at Chartwell Manor in Kent, where he "never had a dull moment from morning till midnight," writing—or rather, dictating—thousands of words, bricklaying and painting: "I . . . dwelt at peace within my habitation."[3] This idyll was not continuous. On his own reckon-

---

*See p. 94.

ing, apart from his public anxieties (to which the same passage of his memoirs also refers), the early months of 1932 had been "the hardest time I have ever had in my life."[4] Knocked down by a motorcar on Fifth Avenue, New York, shortly after entering his fifty-eighth year, he was lucky not to be killed; characteristically, after only six weeks' convalescence, he fulfilled forty public engagements across the United States, lying on his back in a railway carriage by day, lecturing in the evening.

A backbencher in Parliament, outside the House of Commons Churchill was well served by a broad network of friends. Together, they provided him with the information that formed the background to his speeches and articles: in scientific matters, Frederick Lindemann, in secret intelligence, Desmond Morton, and at the head of the Central Department in the Foreign Office itself, Ralph Wigram, until his death in December 1936. From April 1935 onwards, moreover, both Churchill and Lindemann were members of the Air Research Sub-Committee of the Committee of Imperial Defence. Churchill took care to keep in close touch with successive French governments; and from 1936 onwards, with the Soviet Ambassador in London, Maisky.

It will be recalled from the preceding chapter that at the beginning of 1933 the British Government was still urging on the French the need to reach agreement with the German delegation at the Disarmament Conference in Geneva. Ironically, on the same day that the Reichstag voted to give Hitler supreme power for four years, Ramsay Mac-Donald was defending his proposals for comprehensive disarmament in the House of Commons. Churchill attacked both these proposals and the conference itself ("a solemn and prolonged farce"); his remark, "Thank God for the French Army," provoked "looks of pain and aversion"; and from the government benches, Eden—then Under-Secretary at the Foreign Office—replied that without French disarmament, Britain could not secure for Europe "that period of appeasement which is needed."[5] Three weeks later Churchill reminded the House that France was the "guarantor and protector of the whole crescent of small states which runs right round from Belgium to Yugoslavia and Romania"; the rise of Germany to full military equality with her neighbours would, he said, lead "within a measurable distance of the renewal of general European war." On 28 November 1934 he delivered a broadside in the House of Commons—he challenged Baldwin to "confirm, contradict or deny" three statements about the strength of the *Luftwaffe,* the first of which was that it was already approaching parity with the Royal Air Force.[6] Baldwin responded with a denial. The figures of German air strength that the Prime Minister had given the House in this debate were retracted only six months later,[7] by which time the British Government had published a White Paper entitled *Statement relating to Defence.* This document finally committed Britain to rearm.

The controversy about the front-line strength and the size of the reserves of the *Luftwaffe* continued in Whitehall for years after this opening public exchange, and it would not be resolved until well after Churchill had become Prime Minister.[8] Even if Churchill (like the British Chiefs of Staff) may at first have exaggerated the size of German defence expenditure, British rearmament, following years of neglect of the armed services, began perilously late and proceeded at a leisurely pace compared with that of Germany—so slow that it could not mop up unemployment, which still stood at over one million as late as May 1940. Within the tardily increased British defence estimates in the second half of the 1930s, the lion's share went to the RAF and to defence against the aerial bombardment of Britain (above all, of London and other major cities), because it was this which was generally perceived as the primary danger to the country in the event of war: the so-called "knock-out blow" that would cripple Britain from the outset of hostilities. The sheer force of Churchill's eloquence about the *Luftwaffe* made its own special contribution to the consequent neglect of the equally vital need to modernise both the small Army and the minuscule Fleet Air Arm. But at least he did not share the delusion, to which most of the Cabinet (and above all Chamberlain, who held the key post of Chancellor of the Exchequer for five and a half years before becoming Prime Minister) succumbed: namely, that air power offered an easy way of escaping commitment to British participation in another Western Front campaign and thus justified treating the Army as the Cinderella of the armed services—which it therefore remained up to the eve of the Second World War, with disastrous consequences for British arms in almost every land campaign fought during the first three years of the war.

After the first major test of Anglo-French resolution was miserably failed, in March 1936 (when Hitler reoccupied the Rhineland), it was left to Churchill to foretell, as he did in the House of Commons on 26 March, that once the western frontier of Germany had been fortified, it would become "a barrier across Germany's front door which will leave her free to sally out eastwards and southwards by the other doors." In the months that followed, the nucleus of something like a national defence consensus seemed to be forming around Churchill. Opposed to Baldwin's faltering leadership and committed both to large-scale rearmament and to collective security within the League of Nations, its supporters drawn from a broad spectrum outside as well as inside Parliament, this movement was called "Arms and the Covenant" by Churchill. But Churchill himself put paid to whatever chances of success it might have had by the romantic but self-destructive gesture which he made on King Edward VIII's behalf in the House of Commons, on 7 December 1936, on the eve of the abdication. The King abdicated after a reign of less than eleven months, in order to marry Wallis Simpson, an American, whose (second) divorce had received its decree nisi on 27 October 1936. In the interval the British and all the Dominion governments had united in opposition to this marriage. When Churchill pleaded in the House of Commons for delay, he was shouted down, for the one and only time in his parliamentary career.[9]

In 1937, as Churchill later recorded in his memoirs, almost everyone believed that his political life was at last ended. At the time, Churchill himself wrote of his life (in a letter to his wife) as "probably in its closing decade"; and his daughter has described him as suffering from "feelings of almost fatalistic depression."[10] It is therefore not surprising that 1937 was, politically, an indifferent year for Churchill. It was not only that he was isolated in Parliament, where his supporters could be counted on less than the fingers of one hand. His political judgement overall seems to have been shaken by what had happened in the preceding December. On the dominant issue in foreign affairs at this time—the Spanish Civil War—he was content to support the British Government's lame policy of non-intervention (only in April of the following year did he voice alarm at the possible consequences of German support for Franco's victory). He described himself as having been an alarmist earlier in the decade; and he even found some aspects of Hitler's achievement deserving of a measure of praise.[11] Something of Churchill's emotional state comes through his description of the sleepless night that he passed after Eden's resignation from the Foreign Office in February 1938: "I watched the daylight slowly creep in through the windows and saw before me in mental gaze the vision of Death."[12] And in the spring—a period of renewed recession in the United States—a crisis in his personal finances even obliged him to put Chartwell (briefly) on the market.[13]

As 1938, the year of appeasement, developed, its two landmarks—the Austrian *Anschluss* in March and the Munich Agreement in September—also marked the beginning of a change in Churchill's political fortunes. Chamberlain, who had succeeded Baldwin as Prime Minister in May of the previous year, became more and more personally identified with the policy of appeasement, to which Churchill remained the opposite pole. Had Chamberlain been content to present appeasement as no more than a practical recognition of necessity, required to allow time for British rearmament to gather pace, the defence of this policy might have been more effective. He went much further than that in public, however. And what he said privately was even more revealing: his impression of Hitler was that "here was a man who could be relied upon when he had given his word."*[14] For Churchill, the *Anschluss* confronted Europe with "a programme of aggression, nicely calculated

---

*True, appeasement reflected the mood of Parliament in 1938. On the afternoon of 28 September, in the chaotic scene in the House of Commons that followed Chamberlain's announcement of his departure for Munich, only Churchill, Eden, Leopold Amery, Harold Nicolson and the Communist MP William Gallacher would remain in their seats, and even in the debate after the signature of the Munich Agreement, only thirty members of the Conservative Party would abstain; none of them voted against the government.

and timed, unfolding stage by stage"; it had isolated Czechoslovakia, and a "wedge" had been "driven into the heart of what is called the Little Entente."[15] In order to protect Czechoslovakia, Churchill advocated the formation of what he described as a Grand Alliance composed of the same three countries that had faced the central powers in 1914—Britain, France and Russia—a proposal that he put to Maisky over lunch on 23 March 1938. In the course of this lunchtime conversation, which Maisky reported in an immediate telegram on the following day, Churchill suggested that now was the moment for the Soviet Government to make a "solemn and absolutely firm declaration that it would render serious help to Czechoslovakia in the event of aggression against her." Maisky's reply was that the Soviet Government "always fulfilled its promises." This long talk is also noteworthy for the frankness with which, according to Maisky's record, Churchill defined his personal attitude towards the Soviet Union:

> Twenty years ago I strove with all the energy in my power against Communism, because at that time I considered Communism, with its idea of world revolution, the greatest danger to the British Empire. Now Communism does not present such a danger to the Empire. On the contrary, nowadays German Nazism, with its idea of the world hegemony of Berlin, constitutes the greatest danger for the British Empire. Therefore, at the present time I strive against Hitler with all the energy in my power. If the danger for the British Empire from the side of Fascism were to disappear and the danger from the side of Communism were to rise again, I—I say this absolutely frankly—would begin to strive against you again. But for the immediate future, and certainly until the end of my life (Churchill is now sixty-three), I do not foresee such a situation. For this period of time we and you share the same path. This is the reason why I am in favour of close co-operation between England, France and the USSR.[16]

During the long weeks of the Munich crisis that followed the *Anschluss,* the British Government behaved almost as though the Soviet Union did not exist and as if the Franco-Soviet Treaty had been no more than a temporary aberration on the part of the French Government. At the height of the crisis, on 21 September, Churchill went so far as to issue a press statement warning, in devastating prose, of the consequences that would follow a partition of Czechoslovakia brought about under Anglo–French pressure. He did this nearly three weeks after he had taken the unusual step of writing Halifax a long letter, setting out the Soviet Government's position as described to him by Maisky (accurately, as we know from the telegram that Litvinov sent to the Soviet Ambassador in Prague on 2 September). He received a courteous brush-off in reply.

To the Munich Agreement itself he responded with a speech in the House of Commons that was at once trenchant, witty and prophetic. The agreement, a "disaster of the first magnitude", was a "total and unmitigated defeat." He epitomised Chamberlain's shuttle diplomacy in these words: "£1 was demanded at the pistol's point. When it was given, £2 were demanded at the pistol's point. Finally, the Dictator consented to take £1.17s.6d and the rest in promises of goodwill for the future." As for the future, this was "only the first sip, the first foretaste of a bitter cup." Czechoslovakia would be "engulfed in the Nazi regime." Although Churchill's oratory failed, once again, to shake the ranks of the Conservative phalanx in the House of Commons,* outside Parliament it struck a chord which did not fall silent.[17]

Chamberlain kept Churchill out of government as long as he was able, but in the prophetic words of an observer of the British scene in the spring of 1938, Maisky:

> . . . Churchill is a major and forceful figure, whereas the other members of the cabinet are colourless mediocrities, fearful of letting the wolf into the sheepfold; Churchill can crush all of

---

*In the general election of 1935 the Conservative Party won a landslide victory, which gave it 432 seats in the House of Commons and reduced the Labour Party's to 154. It was therefore largely with his own party that Churchill was at odds, over foreign and defence policy, in the 1930s. The Labour Party opposed rearmament until the middle of 1937; thereafter, its attitude was equivocal.

them especially in the event of some kind of crisis. Churchill will come to power when the critical moment in England's fortunes arrives. Does the leadership of the Conservative Party, in particular Chamberlain, consider that such a moment has already arrived? I doubt it. . . . We shall see.[18]

Once Churchill was "back,"* it was the memory of the stand that he had taken in the 1930s, culminating in 1938, which made him the only possible Prime Minister in the national emergency that developed in 1940. Churchill's political career may therefore be said to have been saved by the outbreak of war. Much the same, though for quite different reasons, may be said of Roosevelt. Had Europe not been at war in 1940, it is hard to believe that he would then have been elected President of the United States for a third term. By contrast, when the war finally engulfed the Soviet Union, in the summer of 1941, Stalin (and his country) came close to the brink of disaster.

Roosevelt

International affairs had played little or no part in the electoral campaign that brought Roosevelt to the White House at the beginning of 1933. Roosevelt never forgot the cold douche poured on his advocacy of the League of Nations in the electoral campaign of 1920, so that when, twelve years later, William Randolph Hearst (then supporting Roosevelt's candidacy) pressed him to make his position on this issue crystal clear, Roosevelt had no difficulty in declaring that the League was no longer the League conceived by Wilson; he therefore did not favour American participation. It was not just a matter of satisfying campaign backers. Opinion polls began to become politically significant in the 1930s. By the end of the decade, by which time polling of public opinion was conducted in a reasonably scientific manner, the

---

*"Winston is back" was the signal sent out by the Admiralty when he was appointed First Lord, for the second time in his career, after the outbreak of war in September 1939.

first wartime Roper Poll, published by *Fortune* Magazine, showed almost one in three Americans wishing to "have nothing to do with any warring country . . . even trade . . . on a cash-and-carry basis." This percentage remained more or less constant in the early months of the Second World War.[19] To such findings Roosevelt paid close attention.

American isolationism was not a policy but a state of mind, comprising several different strands of thought. Historically, the main frontier of the United States had for nearly three centuries been internal, gradually pushed further and further west. Among the men to whom Roosevelt may well have listened at Harvard was Frederick Jackson Turner, arguably the first academic to justify an American world view of politics. The essence of Turner's thesis was that, as he put it in an article written at the turn of the century, "having completed the conquest of the wilderness, and having consolidated our interests, we are beginning to consider the relations of democracy and empire." The American nation had therefore "turned . . . to deal with the Far East, to engage in the world politics of the Pacific Ocean," and had in this process "become an imperial republic with dependencies and protectorates."[20] In other words, the western frontiers of the United States had been thrust still further west, across the Pacific, while its eastern frontier remained firmly on the Atlantic seaboard. Towards Europe, which so many Americans had left in order to escape at best, poverty, and at worst, oppression, there was an atavistic distrust, which had only temporarily been overcome in 1917–18 and soon returned after the First World War had been won. American revulsion against the Treaty of Versailles, much of which had been Wilson's brainchild, was reinforced in the 1930s by the Europeans' failure to repay their debts to the United States.

The spectrum of isolationist sentiment in the 1930s was extremely broad. Even the lunatic fringe, whose most celebrated representative was the "radio priest" Charles Coughlin, carried enough domestic political weight to oblige the White House to pay it some attention. As in Britain, there was the pacifist movement—men and women disgusted by the experience of the First World War. There were ethnic groups, notably the Irish, who had special reasons for dislike of the countries which had ruled their ancestors. There were members of the progressive wing of the Republican Party, for whom the solution of American domestic problems must come first, an influential group which led the isolationists in Congress. And there were the many Americans for whom, again in Turner's words, "the age of the Pacific Ocean" had begun, "mysterious and unfathomable for our future."[21] If the foreign policy of the United States was to be focused, it must be on the Far East, not on Europe. And it is significant that when the United States finally abandoned its neutrality at the end of 1941, what compelled it to do so was a blow received in the Pacific Ocean.

In no country were the effects of the Great Depression more dramatic than in the United States, where it began. The first signal of impending economic disaster, strenuously denied for months afterwards by almost everyone who mattered, including President Hoover, was the collapse of the New York stock market in the autumn of 1929. In a period of under two months, on the Dow Jones Industrial Average the market fell from 386 in late September to 196 in November; and in spite of later rallies, it went on falling until June 1932, when it hit rock bottom at a figure of 41, a fall of 89 per cent from the peak of 1929. At one point, early on in the crash, the announcement was made that Rockefellers, Morgans and Mellons had agreed to form a large pool of money in order to support the market. For a moment the Stock Exchange stood still, but then one of the leading bear speculators, Michael Meaghan, roared:

> All the money of the Rockefellers, Mellons and Morgans and other millionaires will not stop the flood of shares which the great American public is going to pour onto the market. Sell five thousand steel![22]

In the Depression that followed it was not only that there was no longer any work for some fifteen million Americans, only one in four of whom were receiving any kind of relief. The fall in the price of primary products across the world reduced the American farmer's net income by more than two thirds between 1929 and 1932; farmers took out their shotguns in an attempt to prevent mortgage foreclosures. In the cities there were queues of unemployed and men peddled apples on the corners of New York streets.

The international capital market also collapsed once the fountain of American money, which had financed the world economy in the 1920s, dried up. The economic earthquake rolled outwards from the United States, not only to Europe, which suffered a financial collapse in 1931, but to Japan, where farmers were reduced to near starvation (selling their daughters into prostitution) by the disappearance of the American market for silk and the collapse of the price of rice. The outgoing President, Hoover, saw the solution to all these problems, including those of the American economy, as primarily international (hence the World Economic Conference, already being discussed at the beginning of 1933). It was Roosevelt's great service to his country—and arguably to the world as a whole—that he realised the need to begin with drastic measures taken within the boundaries of the American economy. By the time he took office on 4 March 1933, the emergency that had overwhelmed the American banking system had made this need compelling; that morning not a single bank in the United States had its doors open. Roosevelt's response was to draft an Emergency Banking Act and meanwhile to declare a four-day bank holiday, pending the passage of legislation. Congress, recalled in special session, passed the Banking Act on 9 March, in less than eight hours from the moment of introduction to presidential signature. This act was the first of fifteen passed by the 73rd Congress in one hundred days—the launching of the New Deal—or, in the language of Churchillian hyperbole: "Roosevelt is an explorer who has embarked on a voyage as uncertain as that of Columbus, and upon a quest which might conceivably be as important as the discovery of the New World."[23]

Two sentences in Roosevelt's inauguration speech set the guidelines for U.S. policy during the rest of 1933: "I favour as a practical policy the putting of first things first. I shall spare no effort to restore world trade by international economic adjustment, but the emergency at home cannot wait on that accomplishment."[24] And if international economic policy was to take second place, in logic this must apply *a fortiori* to foreign policy as a whole. In practice the conduct of U.S. external policy in 1933—and indeed for the rest of the decade—did not follow a strictly logical course. One of Roosevelt's most remarkable characteristics—often a strength, sometimes a weakness—was his ability to pursue two contradictory policies at one and the same time: hence his instruction to two of his advisers, holding diametrically opposed views on the tariff issue, when they were drafting a speech on tariff policy for him to deliver during the 1932 electoral campaign— "weave them together."[25] This explains much of what seemed, in foreign eyes, to be the ambivalence of his foreign policy at the beginning of his presidency: an ambivalence illustrated by Roosevelt's appointment of an internationalist, Cordell Hull, as Secretary of State, flanked by a nationalist Assistant Secretary, Raymond Moley, with responsibility, among other things, for the World Economic Conference.

Moreover, the hopes pinned on the new President by the leaders of other countries were pitched unrealistically high. These hopes received some initial encouragement from Roosevelt himself. His original idea had been to visit Europe during the interval between the election and his inauguration. He told the British Prime Minister so; and after he had abandoned the plan, invited him (and other political leaders) to visit the United States once he had been inaugurated. He even seems to have believed that, during MacDonald's visit, the issue of British war debt might be resolved. He offered support and encouragement for MacDonald's proposals at the Geneva Disarmament Conference. On 16 May 1933 he appealed to the heads of fifty-four states for "peace by disarmament" and "the end of economic chaos." And earlier in the same month, in his second radio Fireside Chat, he had told the American people that the World Economic Conference "must succeed."[26] To Henry Morgenthau, Jr. (his Secretary of the Treasury and a near neighbour at Hyde Park), he even said that he thought he had averted a war.[27]

The foreign visitors to Washington came and went, leaving bland communiqués behind them. On 12 June 1933 the World Economic Conference was opened in London by King George V, with MacDonald in the chair. The venue—without apparent irony—was the Geological Museum. Hull led the U.S. delegation, a coalition of conflicting views, which—in the words of the historian of the New Deal—"left Washington in a fog much denser than anything it might encounter in the Atlantic."[28] This fog thickened after the delegation had been joined in London on 28 June by Moley, hot foot from a meeting with Roosevelt, who was on his yacht off the Canadian coast. Moley gave his support to the conference's proposed declaration on currency stabilisation, but was then effectively disowned by Roosevelt, who torpedoed the conference with a harshly worded message, composed on board his yacht and written out in manuscript, that poured scorn on "old fetishes of international bankers."[29] Thanks to Hull's efforts, the conference did not break up at once; but although it dragged on for another three weeks, it achieved nothing.

Roosevelt's motive in sending to the conference on 3 July 1933 what has gone down to history as his "bombshell" message is clear enough: he was determined to agree to nothing that might have the effect of raising the international value of the dollar, which he had devalued in April. But the manner in which he secured this objective and the mismanagement of the U.S. delegation in London left a mark in Western Europe which took many years to erase. MacDonald never really recovered from the blow (he staggered on as Prime Minister until the summer of 1935), but the effect on Chamberlain and Baldwin should not be underestimated. In the House of Commons, however, Churchill ridiculed "anyone who could have imagined that Mr Roosevelt would tie up to gold out of love for France";* while in a newspaper article Keynes described Roosevelt as "magnificently right."[30]

In August 1933—two months before Germany left both the Disarmament Conference and the League of Nations—a message sent by Roosevelt to MacDonald expressed the not very helpful view that an "insane rush to further armaments in Continental Europe is infinitely more dangerous than any number of squabbles over gold or stabilisation or tariffs."[31] The economic squabbles took a turn for the worse on 19 October, when Roosevelt ordered the Reconstruction Finance Corporation to begin buying newly mined gold in the United States,[32] a

---

*France was the principal country in the so-called gold bloc.

phase of international monetary warfare that lasted until the end of January 1934, when the dollar was finally fixed at 59.06 per cent of its pre-1933 value. But the problem of European debt remained. In April 1934, Roosevelt signed a bill prohibiting the purchase of bonds from or the granting of loans to governments in default in their obligations to the United States, a measure that would loom large after the outbreak of the Second World War.[33]

Thus, so far as Western Europe was concerned, Roosevelt's beginning was not a happy one. On the one hand—in a speech delivered at the turn of the year to the Woodrow Wilson Foundation—Roosevelt reaffirmed his government's policy of continued co-operation with the League of Nations, which he praised, in the cause of disarmament and the prevention of war, even though this co-operation must be effected from outside the League. On the other, he was well aware that, however widespread in the United States resentment against Hitler's regime might become, this did not mean any greater willingness on the part of the American people to become involved in the political developments of Europe for the second time. Elsewhere, Roosevelt scored some successes, notably the launching of the "Good Neighbor" policy in Latin America (followed three years later by a triumphant presidential tour of the subcontinent) and the establishment of diplomatic relations with the Soviet Union in November 1933, for the first time since the October Revolution. In the short term the establishment of U.S.-Soviet relations proved to be of little consequence; in particular, the Soviet Union did not secure U.S. support against Japan. The United States did, however, make one immediate investment which later yielded a handsome dividend: the formation of a Russian-speaking cadre in the U.S. Foreign Service, including men who afterwards became famous, notably George Kennan.[34]

This was about as far as Roosevelt was able to go. By the turn of 1934–35 the President proved unable to command even the two-thirds majority in the Senate required for membership of the World Court, of which the United States was not yet a member. He sought approval from the Senate for membership on 16 January 1935; thirteen days later, deluged by telegrams from the Coughlin-Hearst lobbies, the Senate voted by only 52 votes to 36 in favour of admission. It was a

clear sign that the U.S. Government could not conduct a foreign policy
that ran against the isolationist mainstream of American national opinion. Seven months after this reverse, Congress passed the bill that
affected this policy more than any other piece of legislation in the
1930s: the Neutrality Act. On 21 August 1935, without even a vote of
record, the Senate approved a bill placing a mandatory embargo on
"arms, ammunition, or implements of war" to all belligerents, and
prohibiting American vessels from carrying munitions to belligerent
states. Through months of White House veering and tacking, which
lasted almost up to the last moment, Roosevelt, with Hull's help,
sought to muster support for a flexible embargo that would have given
the President much wider powers. As it was, after isolationist senators
had begun a filibuster on 20 August, the only powers that the bill
reserved to the President were to define what constituted an implement
of war and to decide when an embargo should come into effect. Passed
on the eve of the Italian invasion of Abyssinia, this bill was a temporary
measure. Though revised more than once, its essential provisions, contrary to Roosevelt's hopes, would remain the same.

The New Deal went into top gear around the turn of the year
1935–36. Although the American economy had by no means regained
the level of 1929, by comparison with the previous electoral year
(1932–33) all economic indicators were pointing upward—six million
new jobs, stock prices doubled, cash income of farmers almost doubled,
and the volume of industrial production doubled. Federal and other
relief agencies had provided more than $5 billion for work and relief
projects, while $4 billion had financed public works, some of which
constituted the beginning of the infrastructure of modern America.* And behind these statistics stood the dominant figure of the President. One of the things that distinguished the U.S. Government from
European governments, with few exceptions, in these years was the
fact that most of the men with whom Roosevelt surrounded himself
were exceedingly able, some of them young. Even though the mem-

---

*To cite only dams, apart from the Tennessee Valley Authority, the Public Works Administration
helped to build the Grand Coulee, the Bonneville, the Fort Peck and the Boulder Dam.

bers of his team were often at loggerheads with each other, Roosevelt delegated wide powers. The boundaries of delegated authority were deliberately blurred, however, and they overlapped. In the final resort, therefore, the vital decisions were Roosevelt's, often delayed until the last possible moment. The legendary charm of the "old smiler" could hinder as well as help; people would leave the White House mistakenly believing that the President agreed with all that they had said in his office. Charles de Gaulle, who had good reason to dislike Roosevelt, described him ten years after his first visit to the United States as *"cet artiste, ce séducteur"*—precisely the judgement of one of Roosevelt's closest collaborators: "he was a real artist in government."[35]

Roosevelt himself accurately described the electoral campaign of 1936: "I am the issue." In November, in William Allen White's words, he was "all but crowned by the people."[36] He won 523 out of 531 votes in the electoral college, the biggest majority since 1821, and he carried every state in the Union except Maine and Vermont. His inaugural address in January 1937, however, did not contain a word about foreign policy. So far as foreign affairs were concerned, he was in a congressional strait-jacket. Congress did, however, include the "cash-and-carry" provision when the Neutrality Act was revised in May—an advantage for any future belligerent whose navy commanded the Atlantic Ocean. Such as it was, Roosevelt's foreign policy from 1935 onwards was lack-lustre, though lit up by occasional flashes. In the Abyssinian War, it was Italy that benefited from the workings of the Neutrality Act; by the end of 1935, American oil exports to Italy were running at three times their normal level. In the Spanish Civil War, the U.S. Government went along with the Anglo-French policy of non-intervention. It was the Spanish Republicans, not their opponents, who suffered from the policy pursued by Roosevelt, who (though personally sympathetic to the Republicans) shied away from extending the arms embargo to Franco's backers, Germany and Italy; and here again, American oil companies did well. One of the flashes in the pan, Roosevelt's suggestion of a system of international "quarantine," which he put forward in a speech delivered in Chicago on 5 October 1937, was soon extinguished—he never attempted to explain what he meant by quarantine and the proposal was never pursued.[37]

The beginning of the following year saw a further flash: a presidential initiative, which Churchill, writing ten years later, described as the "last frail chance to save the world from tyranny otherwise than by war."[38] Roosevelt's secret proposal of 11 January 1938, which stemmed from an earlier idea of convening an international conference, was indeed his last real throw in foreign policy between then and the outbreak of war. It was only in 1982 that the record of the "amazing" telegraphic correspondence—as Alexander Cadogan, the Permanent Under-Secretary at the Foreign Office, described it at the time—between the U.S. President and the British Government was published in full.[39] What these papers illuminate is not so much what happened—as had long been well known, the initiative never left the ground—but rather the transatlantic implications of the manner of its failure.

In "utmost" secrecy, repeatedly emphasized by Sumner Welles, Roosevelt sought the British Government's "cordial approval and whole-hearted support" for his proposed invitation to nine governments to send representatives to Washington to negotiate an agreement on four basic principles, to which all governments would then be invited to subscribe. The President would not act until he received the British reply, which he asked for not later than 17 January. In Eden's absence on holiday in France—and without consulting him—Chamberlain replied two days after the receipt of the telegram from Washington. His telegram, though written in oleaginous Whitehall prose, was in substance a dusty answer. On 17 January Roosevelt, whose "disappointment was distinctly felt" by the British Ambassador, Ronald Lindsay, deferred his initiative "for a short while." A further telegram from London, sent this time by Eden (who broke off his holiday), was an attempt to limit the damage already done; and on 21 January Chamberlain himself telegraphed to Washington that he did not feel justified in asking the President to delay the announcement of his scheme any longer. Although in mid-February Roosevelt's purpose was still "to launch his plan substantially in its present form very soon," by the 25th he had decided to hold it in abeyance. Across his copy of the Washington telegram reporting this decision Chamberlain wrote: "This is excellent."

Roosevelt had made it clear from the outset that his proposal was "designed" to work "parallel to [the] effort which His Majesty's Government in the United Kingdom are making with the Central Powers," and to lend that effort "powerful support." Chamberlain, by contrast, believed that it was "likely to excite the derision of Germany and Italy." No doubt Hitler and Mussolini would have been unimpressed by the news that the governments of Sweden, the Netherlands, Belgium, Switzerland, Hungary, Yugoslavia, and three South American republics had been invited to send representatives to Washington in order to draft an agreement expressing Roosevelt's Four Points (as they would have become known to history).* His proposal was certainly not of a kind to stand up well to the scrutiny of a diplomatic microscope. His record, moreover, in so far as international conferences were concerned, was not a happy one in the 1930s. For Chamberlain, therefore, as for Baldwin, it was "always best and safest to count on nothing from the Americans but words."[40] But others saw the real point at once in January 1938. From the beginning of this episode Lindsay recommended "quick and very cordial acceptance"; Cadogan agreed; and Eden (alerted in France by Cadogan) recorded his view in writing to Chamberlain on his return, that the minuses in Roosevelt's message were "of minor importance against the significant fact that President Roosevelt, with all the authority of his position which is unique in the world, wishes to help to avert a general war."

He gives twice over who gives quickly—in the words of the old Latin tag—but this was rather a case of he refuses twice over who refuses quickly. Chamberlain's reaction was consistent with his blinkered view both of the United States and of the Soviet Union. Eden, although he realised that it would be "the greatest mistake" if President Roosevelt was deterred from making his appeal, lacked the political

---

*They comprised the essential and fundamental principles to be observed in international relations; the most effective methods for achieving the limitation and reduction of armaments; access for all peoples to raw materials; and, "in the unhappy event of war," the rights and obligations of governments.

will to force the issue; and when he did resign a month later, it was on a different issue (the modalities of Chamberlain's attempt at an Anglo-Italian *rapprochement*). In all these circumstances Roosevelt's decision to shelve his initiative is understandable. The question remains: was Churchill right in believing that the initiative offered a chance, however frail, of averting the cataclysm of 1939? At the beginning of 1938, whoever had been the occupant of 10 Downing Street, the U.S. Congress would have prevented any occupant of the White House from involving the United States in an effective international commitment. Roosevelt's proposal, though far from fantastic (Chamberlain's description of it in the privacy of his diary), was also far from clear cut; and Welles' memorandum laying out in advance the proposed "step by step" procedure to be followed (in his memorandum to Roosevelt dated 10 January) reads like a professional diplomat's nightmare.[41]

Nevertheless, had the British Government responded to Roosevelt's approach with some degree of political sensitivity, this might conceivably have marked the opening of a transatlantic dialogue. Where this might have led, once begun, is speculative. Instead, Chamberlain preferred to rebuff the President of the United States rather than run a "risk of cutting across" his own attempt "to bring about a measure of appeasement." In the months of crisis that followed in 1938, Roosevelt kept his doubts about Chamberlain's effort to himself. For the most part he was a silent observer. His last-minute public gestures, appealing for peace through negotiations, had no effect whatever. And when Chamberlain accepted the invitation to go to Munich at the end of September, the telegram that was sent to London (drafted in Roosevelt's own hand) said just two words: "Good man."*

Meanwhile, at home, Roosevelt's second presidential term, which had begun with every signal apparently set fair, followed a choppy course. For this Roosevelt's own preference for the secret, indirect approach to a political objective, followed by a dramatic assault (a preference that he shared with Stalin), was in part to blame. On 5

---

*A document that Harry Truman thought it inadvisable to make public as late as December 1950. [42]

February 1937 he suddenly announced a bill to give the President power to expand the membership of the Supreme Court, whose conservative rulings had, in 1935, already begun to threaten the institutions of the New Deal. Had the bill been passed, Roosevelt would have had the power to appoint six new justices in sympathy with the New Deal. In the political conflict that developed the opposing sides became no longer the President versus the Court, but the White House versus Congress. By midsummer it was clear that, less than a year after the greatest presidential victory for over a century, Roosevelt could not command the votes. Paradoxically, without any packing by the President, the Supreme Court handed down important decisions that favoured the New Deal during the remainder of Roosevelt's second term. Nevertheless, in 1937, he made the first big mistake and lost the first great battle of his presidency.

Congress passed the last major New Deal measure in April 1938; in the mid-term elections that autumn the Republican Party made significant gains; and from then onwards Roosevelt faced in Congress what amounted to a conservative coalition between Republicans and Democratic opponents of the New Deal. In the winter of 1937–38, moreover, there was a severe recession in the United States, during which business indices fell by one third. The reflationary measures which, after six months of hesitation, Roosevelt put before Congress in April 1938 were only partly successful; although business improved, two years later the number of unemployed still stood at over seven million. By the end of the decade—and indeed for some months beyond— Roosevelt was in such low water that it looked far from certain that he could win from his own party convention the unanimous draft on which his chances of a third-term victory in the presidential election seemed to depend. Even George Washington had been content to serve two terms; and the feeling against a third presidential term was by no means confined to the Republican Party.* "Lame duck" is not a term

---

*After the war, Congress passed a constitutional amendment making a third term impossible (as all American readers, but not all British, will be aware).

of art that sits well on a President of Roosevelt's calibre, but up to a late hour in his second term it was a more appropriate title than that of "Dr. Win the War" which his next four years at the White House would, as it turned out, enable him to claim.[43]

Thus the man who had been the cynosure of his country and of the democratic world at the outset of his presidency, now found himself at loggerheads with Congress at home and little more than an observer, often ambivalent, of events abroad. About his political future he kept his own counsel, his inner self enigmatic behind his smile, his ebullience and his repartee. Even those closest to him in Washington found him secretive.[44] Just how baffling foreigners found him in the 1930s is illustrated by observations made about him by three very different Europeans. In the eyes of a Marxist, Leon Trotsky, Roosevelt could be dismissed as a man who "abhors 'systems' and 'generalities' "; and the American "philosophic method" was "even more antiquated" than the "economic system" that Roosevelt was seeking to revive. To Keynes, he resembled "an Americanised Sir Edward Grey."* Of the three, only Carl Jung got close to the truth, when he described Roosevelt as "a man of superior but impenetrable mind, but perfectly ruthless, a highly versatile mind which you cannot foresee"—words that might well have been written to describe Stalin.[45]

Stalin

By 1933 Stalin was acknowledged as the national *Vozhd'*—"the Boss"—as *Pravda* had called him in its issue celebrating his fiftieth birthday on 21 December 1929. The "Third Revolution," which he had launched, was almost completed. The simultaneous combination of the industrialising process in the cities, pressed on at the ruthless pace of a forced march, and the chaotic and murderous collectivisation of the

---

*An odd comparison, perhaps. Grey was British Foreign Secretary from 1905 to 1916, remembered for his remark, in August 1914, that "the lamps are going out all over Europe; we shall not see them lit again in our lifetime."

countryside, together transformed the Soviet Union even more than the October Revolution had transformed Russia a decade earlier. In order to bring about these fundamental changes in Soviet society, what amounted almost to a second civil war had been waged: this time between the Communist Party on the one hand and the mass of the Soviet people—the peasantry—on the other. By violent means, the Party won. (It was for this reason that the XVIIth Party Congress, held in January 1934, was called the Congress of the Victors.) As has already been observed, in 1933 there were signs of a respite at last. The performance of the economy improved; the 1933 harvest was good; and both at the Congress and until late in 1934 it looked as though the advocates within the Politburo of a policy of compromise might carry the day. Instead, Stalin turned on the Party itself, which he systematically destroyed, refashioning it as the instrument of his personal rule. From then on—as a brilliant British Quaker doctor (who had worked in Russian villages during the Civil War) had foretold fifteen years earlier—Stalin allowed "only one kind of sin—disbelief in the complete correctness of its [the Kremlin's] system."[46]

The first spark of the fire that consumed the Soviet Communist Party was the murder of Sergei Kirov, shot in the back in Leningrad on 1 December 1934. The evidence that Stalin at least connived in the murder of his close Politburo colleague, who may have been one of the supporters of a milder policy, is strong. The case still essentially rests, however, with Khrushchev's statement, made over a quarter of a century later, in his speech to the XXIInd Party Congress in 1961 (three years before his fall), that a thoroughgoing enquiry was being made in order to find out who was really to blame, although *Pravda* in 1964 went further, observing that Kirov presented an obstacle to Stalin's ambitions. The conclusions of the Khrushchevian enquiry were never published and today a further enquiry is in progress.[47] However that may be, Kirov's death provided Stalin with the opportunity to embark on the great purges, executed first by Genrikh Yagoda and then by Nikolai Ezhov, a singularly repulsive, five-foot-high official, whose name was immortalised by the purges which are remembered in the Soviet Union as the *Ezhovshchina*. Ezhov was appointed Minister of

Internal Affairs, responsible for the Secret Police, in September 1936 as the result of a telegram that Stalin sent to Moscow from his holiday villa in Sochi, on the Black Sea:

> We consider it absolutely necessary and urgent to appoint Comrade Ezhov Commissar of Internal Affairs. Yagoda has obviously proved unequal to the task of exposing the Trotskyite-Zinoviev bloc. The OGPU [i.e., NKVD] is four years behind in this matter. . . .[48]

The terror, however, began well before Ezhov took over the NKVD. By mid-January 1935, Lev Kamenev and Gregorii Zinoviev, members of the Politburo since 1919 and 1921 respectively, both faced criminal charges; the first time that political opposition inside the Party had been publicly considered a criminal offence. Kamenev and Zinoviev were shot in 1936. Bukharin, who had been a member of the Politburo since 1924, was shot in 1938, having first made his wife learn by heart his political testament, addressed to "the future generation of party leaders." Half a century passed before his widow was able to fulfill his dying wish, direct to the Soviet public.*

In between these political trials, the Senior Deputy Defence Minister, Marshal Tukhachevsky was arrested on a charge trumped up with the aid of the German Secret Service. He was one of the first batch of military victims to be tried in secret and shot, in June 1937. Between then and the eve of the war, about half the Soviet officer corps was executed or imprisoned. In the successive waves of terror that followed—especially during Ezhov's two-year tenure of the highest re-

---

*On 4 February 1988 the Soviet Supreme Court ruled that twenty of the twenty-one condemned at the last great show trial in Moscow in March 1938, including Bukharin, had been the victims of falsified evidence, obtained by "unlawful means" and gross violations of socialist legality, and that their confessions had been obtained by "involuntary" methods. Their sentences were quashed (*Pravda,* 5 February 1988). For the similar quashing of Zinoviev and Kamenev's sentences, see *Izvestiya,* 13 June 1988. On 27 March 1988, *Pravda* announced Tukhachevsky's rehabilitation and the restoration of his Communist Party membership.

pressive office—the total number of executions of Soviet citizens of all kinds cannot even now be established with any degree of certainty: not less than half a million, perhaps as many as one million, with ten times as many incarcerated, in prison or in camps, at the end of 1938. On a single day at the end of that year Stalin approved the execution by firing squad of over three thousand of his compatriots; and among the many other statistics of his Great Terror, the list of the fate of ten members (women as well as men) of the families of his first and second wives makes grisly reading.[49] Whatever the exact figure of deaths in the purges, the number of those who perished during the years of forcible collectivisation was incomparably greater. Estimates of the total number of peasant deaths during these years, whether from famine or the terrible process of dispossession and deportation, vary enormously, but they all concur on one fact: that these deaths must be numbered in millions.[50] Moreover, it has now been publicly argued by a Soviet demographer that the total population of the Soviet Union, declared by the 1937 census to be 170 million—two million more than the figure announced by Stalin himself at the XVIIth Party Congress—had in reality declined during the previous four years.[51]

The terror eased off as suddenly as it had begun. In December 1938, Ezhov, who was probably executed in 1939 or 1940, was succeeded by Lavrentii Beria.* Stalin's own judgement of the purges was that, although "more mistakes than might have been expected" were made, the "results were, on the whole, beneficial"[52]—not unlike his summing up of the policy of collectivisation. They left him by the end of the decade in absolute control of his country, with virtually every member of its senior political echelons indebted to him for the position that he held. The cowed Soviet Communist Party was now his party.† In particular his nine colleagues in the Politburo after the XVIII Party

---

*A Georgian, the only one of Stalin's team whom Khrushchev and his colleagues found it necessary to execute, in 1953.

†In so far as practicable, foreign Communist parties were also extensively purged, notably that of Poland.

Congress in March 1939, with one exception, would remain at his side throughout the years of the Second World War.[53] Although the purges had ensured for Stalin the allegiance of the Communist Party and of the armed forces, the trauma that they had caused necessitated a period of convalescence for Soviet society—above all, the avoidance of war. They also contributed powerfully to the confusion about the Soviet Union that prevailed in the West during the 1930s.

This confusion was both intellectual and emotional. The secretiveness of Soviet society, coupled with the nature of Soviet statistics at this period, excuses some degree of western ignorance of the Soviet Union (Churchill, as we have seen, was a partial exception). The emotional confusion was even greater. For the hard Left, the ark of the covenant was still in the Kremlin even after August 1939. But for British and American left-of-centre opinion as a whole, until that date it was embarrassing to be regarded as anti-Communist. "Anti-anti-communism" has been described as a mentality "impelled by an impassioned longing to believe."[54] Keynes, a liberal, believed in 1931 that beneath the cruelty and the stupidity of New Russia some spark of the ideal might lie hid. Even to Henry Luce it then seemed that Russians thought like Americans. The American visitor to the Soviet Union after the Revolution who remarked that he had "seen the future, and it works," could, in 1929, describe the effort being made in the United States as "equal to that of Soviet Russia."[55] Many western observers turned a blind eye to what was happening, whether consciously or unconsciously (the Webbs are a notorious British example, the U.S. Ambassador in Moscow, Joseph Davies, an American one). Or, alternatively, they saw it, but drew the wrong deduction—that the Soviet Union had been so mauled by successive internal conflicts, culminating in the great purges, that it was incapable of the cohesive effort required for waging war.

For most people, on both sides of the Atlantic, it was not Czechoslovakia that was "a far away country . . . of whom we know nothing" (in the words of Chamberlain's notorious broadcast to the British people at the height of the Munich crisis), but the Soviet Union. Even Russian émigrés were not exempt from this ignorance: a Russian-language primer written by a White Russian living in Britain and published there immediately after the great Soviet famine included the following grotesque dialogue, imagined as taking place at a dinner party given in Moscow for two visitors from London.

> *A guest:* Champagne! We'd have to appear in tail-coats then! Thank goodness there is no such ceremony nowadays. I always hated having to dress for dinner.
>
> *The lady on Mr Stuart's right:* When they've made enough tractors and harvesters, we'll all have evening clothes.
>
> *Mr Stuart:* I was talking to a man yesterday, and he offered to bet me five pounds that in five years every peasant will possess a dinner-jacket in which to go to the theatre. I don't usually bet, but for the good cause I don't mind losing.
>
> *Mrs Stuart:* If he wins I'll be so overjoyed that I'll be willing to share your loss.[56]

Unlike Britain and France, where foreign ministers came and went in the 1930s, the Soviet Union had only two: Litvinov, who had been Georgii Chicherin's deputy at the Kuznetskii Most* until the latter's *de facto* retirement in 1928, becoming Foreign Minister in his own right two years later; and Vyacheslav Molotov, Chairman of the Council of Ministers, who replaced Litvinov as Foreign Minister in 1939. The difference between the two men says a good deal about the changes in Soviet foreign policy during the decade. Litvinov, Jewish, humorous, English-speaking (like Chicherin) and married to an English-born wife, became a member of the Communist Party Central Committee only in 1934, whereas Molotov, who had been a full member of the Politburo since 1926, spoke no foreign language, although he was a well-educated man (a nephew of the composer Alexander Skryabin); and he was so dour that, in the next decade, he would make the Russian word for "no" a part of the English vocabulary. Only once did

---

*Then the location of the Soviet Foreign Ministry.

Churchill succeed in evoking from him a "natural human reaction."*
It is, however, important to realise that both these foreign ministers
were the executants of a foreign policy determined by the Politburo of
the party: that is to say, in the late 1930s, by Stalin. The essence of the
Stalinist system of government was that, however much day-to-day
authority might be delegated, it always remained essential to "hand
down" *(spuskat')* the ultimate decisions. And perhaps the most significant difference between Molotov and Litvinov was the fact (noticed at
once by Djilas, on his first visit to the Kremlin) that Molotov and
Stalin addressed each other in the second-person singular. Stalin was
slower than Churchill and Roosevelt to come to terms with the significance of what happened in Berlin on 30 January 1933.

This was not only because in Moscow, as in other capitals, Hitler
was underestimated; indeed, to begin with, the Kremlin was more
concerned by the Nazi Party's Nationalist allies, such as the Vice-
Chancellor, Franz von Papen. It was also because, as the two principal
victims of the Versailles settlement, the Soviet Union and Germany
had got on well ever since their signature of the treaty dramatically
concluded between them at Rapallo on Easter Sunday, 1922 (followed
four years later by their Treaty of Neutrality and Non-Aggression,
which was renewed four months after Hitler came to power). Not only
did Germany become, as it had been before the First World War, the
Soviet Union's principal trading partner. The Rapallo Treaty, in itself
a breach of the Treaty of Versailles, led to a period of close co-operation between the two countries in the field of military technology,
training and defence procurement, with the result that the German
Army, thus enabled to escape from the restrictions imposed on it at
Versailles, and the Red Army grew to know each other well in the
next ten years.[58] As late as August 1933, Molotov was telling the
German Ambassador in Moscow that if Germany followed its former

---

*In 1942, at the garden gate of 10 Downing Street, Churchill gripped his arm and the two men
looked each other in the face. "Suddenly he appeared deeply moved. Inside the image there appeared
the man. He responded with an equal pressure. Silently we wrung each other's hands."[57]

policy, the Soviet Union would have no basis for altering its line; in his report to the Party's Central Executive Committee at the year's end, Litvinov said that "we maintain good relations with capitalist states of whatever regime, including fascist"; and in his speech to the XVIIth Party Congress in January 1934, Stalin said much the same thing about fascist regimes.[59] In the early 1930s Soviet policy towards Germany was a curious mixture. On the one hand, governmental relations were reasonably good—in Soviet diplomatic jargon, "businesslike." On the other, the ferocious opposition to all social-democratic parties (condemned as "Social-Fascists") that had been the Comintern's proclaimed policy since 1928 helped to smooth Hitler's rise to power, by splitting the Communist and Social-democratic opposition in the Reichstag. The Comintern's policy was based on the belief, which Moscow was slow to abandon in 1933, that since fascism was, according to the received doctrine, the final phase of capitalism, the logical consequence of a Nazi victory in Germany must be a proletarian revolution.

When—to use Marxist language—"life itself" demonstrated the bankruptcy of these theories, some senior officials in Moscow took refuge (as some did in other countries) in the hope that Hitler would become the prisoner of other, conservative forces in German society. Thus, as late as mid-1934, the Soviet Deputy Foreign Minister, Nikolai Krestinskii, speaking to the Italian Ambassador, Bernardo Attólico, after Hitler's June purge, suggested that Hitler could remain in power only by "becoming a kind of MacDonald."[60] It was not until the very end of 1933 that the first of the two U-turns in Soviet foreign policy during this decade received Kremlin approval, when the decision was taken to enter the League of Nations, "on certain conditions," and to pursue a policy of collective security in Europe. Only at the VIIth Congress of the Comintern, held eighteen months later,* did Stalin set

---

*It should be added that this long delay may partly have been caused by the illness of a crucial participant in the Congress, the Bulgarian Communist Georgii Dimitrov, who returned triumphantly to Moscow only in February 1934, having defied the Nazis at the Reichstag fire trial in the previous year.

his own stamp on a radically new policy to be followed by Communist parties the world over: the fight against "social fascism" was to be replaced by a united front, above all with Socialists (the former enemy), against fascism (the new enemy).[61] Well before this, the last, Congress of the Comintern was held, Stalin had set the governmental U-turn in motion, however. A new era of Soviet foreign policy seemed to open on 18 September 1934, when the Soviet Union took its seat in Geneva on the Council of the League of Nations. In April 1935, the Soviet pacts with France and with Czechoslovakia were signed in Moscow.

A year later—by comparison with the supine response of Britain and France to the German military occupation of the Rhineland—the Soviet Union did at least propose the imposition of sanctions, under Article 16 of the League Covenant. And although Stalin was cautious about expressing public support for the Republican Government in the Spanish Civil War, in 1936–37 substantial shipments of arms were delivered to the Republicans in Spain, to whom numerous Soviet advisers were also attached.* At the end of 1937, moreover, Halifax's deplorable journey to Berchtesgaden did not go unremarked. In an electoral speech delivered in Leningrad (where he was standing for the Supreme Soviet in November 1937), Litvinov caustically observed that there was a "division of labour in the international arena, whereby some states attack, and others make enquiries and await confirmation and clarification."[62]

As we have seen, in 1938, following Litvinov's report to the Politburo describing the *Anschluss*—in Churchillian language—as the most important "since the world war, fraught with dangers and not least for our Union," the Soviet Government put forward its proposal of an immediate conference to deter aggression.[63] This the British Govern-

---

*A more sinister Soviet export—that of NKVD officials—led to the slaughter of the Spanish anti-Stalinist Communist Party, the POUM, in Barcelona. George Orwell, who served with a POUM column, was a witness. His subsequent novels show how profoundly he was affected by this experience.

ment turned down, as it also rejected the later Soviet suggestion (which Churchill backed) of a Four-Power Declaration regarding Czechoslovakia; and the Soviet proposal in September for military staff talks between France, the Soviet Union and Czechoslovakia fared no better. Through the six months that intervened between the German occupation of Austria and the Munich Agreement, the basic position of the Soviet Union was repeatedly defined in the same terms as the Soviet Ambassador in Prague, acting on instructions, confirmed privately to Beneš on 20 September and as Litvinov declared publicly in Geneva on 21 September 1938: a firm commitment to honour its obligations under the terms of its treaties with France and Czechoslovakia.[64]

There were, however, two conditions, one spoken and the other tacit, on whose fulfilment the Soviet commitment depended. First, as the treaties themselves had specified, Soviet aid to Czechoslovakia, if attacked, was dependent on the French commitment to that country being honoured; and secondly, a route for Soviet troops to reach Czechoslovakia would have to be found. Even though Soviet aircraft might have been deployed (as a few were), it is hard to see, given Polish hatred of the Soviet Union and the Polish Government's determination to obtain part of Czechoslovak territory for itself, how this second condition could have been met; and in private conversations its importance was stressed by Litvinov at the time. Moreover, the Soviet Government had no illusions about the French Government's irresolution in the summer of 1938.[65] By 8 September Maisky was convinced that the British Government (on whose attitude that of the French Government depended) was "unwilling to do anything effective for the defence of Czechoslovakia," and that "no energetic actions of any kind" were to be expected of the government, short of the appearance of "some new, powerful factors capable of completely altering the situation."[66] During the few days later in the month when war began to look inevitable, some Soviet military preparations were undertaken,[67] but the agreement reached at Munich on the last day of September made the question of military aid to Czechoslovakia by any government academic. From this agreement the Soviet Union, like the United States, was excluded. Stalin was left to draw his own conclusions. As Maisky told Cadogan on 30 September, the Munich Agreement had opened the way for the unleashing of a new world war.[68]

Looking back, it is now clear that through these years Stalin kept two options open, so that if the first option (agreement with Britain and France), was closed off, the second (agreement with Germany) was still available as an alternative. No doubt there were in Moscow advocates both of the first policy, such as Litvinov, with whom it became personally identified in western eyes, and of the second, such as Molotov, who would later put his signature on the Nazi-Soviet Pact. But behind both of them stood the authority of the *Vozhd'*, Stalin. During the years of Soviet commitment to the policy of collective security and popular fronts, well before Chamberlain's arrival at 10 Downing Street, Stalin had reason not to put all his eggs in one basket. The Franco-Soviet Pact became embroiled in the internal conflict between Left and Right in France, so that instruments of ratification were not exchanged until the German action in the Rhineland finally convinced the French Parliament. Eden's visit to Moscow a year earlier can hardly have reassured the Kremlin. The reason why Eden went there was that the Foreign Secretary, John Simon, did not; both of them had been in Berlin talking to Hitler, for hours on end, immediately before Eden's visit to Moscow. Stalin flattered Eden (then only a junior Foreign Office Minister, responsible for League of Nations affairs) by receiving him in the Kremlin, where he took the line that the situation was now "fundamentally worse than in 1913." Some system of pacts was essential. It was "fatal to drift, since there was no time to lose if a check were to be placed on a potential aggressor." In Litvinov's words, "the real point of difference in the attitudes of His Majesty's Government and the Soviet Government was that the former did not believe in the aggressiveness of Germany policy." Eden demurred, but went on to admit that his government had not "hitherto wished to believe badly of German intentions."[69]

Following the signature of the Franco-Soviet Pact, in May 1935 Litvinov had a friendly talk with the German Ambassador, to whom he suggested that the way now lay open to the establishment of "more correct relations with Germany."[70] At the turn of that year the Soviet

Embassy in Berlin even floated the idea of a non-aggression treaty, after David Kandelaki, a member of Stalin's personal secretariat now appointed to the Berlin Embassy as Commercial Counsellor *(Torgpred)*, had—unsuccessfully—approached the Economics Minister, Hjalmar Schacht, to enquire about the potential for expanding the two countries' commercial relations. Kandelaki may well have been acting on Stalin's direct instructions; and it was through the *Torgpred* channel that Soviet feelers would later be put out in Berlin.[71] From these secret exchanges between Moscow and Berlin it was not a very far cry to Stalin's second U-turn in foreign policy, which would set off a shockwave whose repercussions echoed around the world, in August 1939.

THE FAR EAST

As the second half of the 1930s drew to a close, the eyes of the world, which at the outset of the decade had been turned inward, towards the ravages of the Great Depression within the borders of each country, were focused on one crucial part of the globe—Central Europe. By comparison with Europe, the Far East seemed to most people to have become almost a backwater. Earlier in the decade it had been the military intentions of Tokyo, rather than those of Berlin, that had been the major cause of anxiety in the field of defence shared by Britain, the Soviet Union and the United States. Now, however, the Far East barely evoked Churchill's interest; Roosevelt sought primarily to maintain a low profile in his dealings with Japan; and of the three future allies, only Stalin was actively involved[72]—with reason, since in 1938 there was a sharp frontier incident and in 1939 a substantial Soviet-Japanese battle in Outer Mongolia.* In reality, during the intervening years the Far Eastern political landscape had undergone a profound change.

Chapter 3 has described the League of Nations' failure to come to

---

*Then in effect a Soviet protectorate.

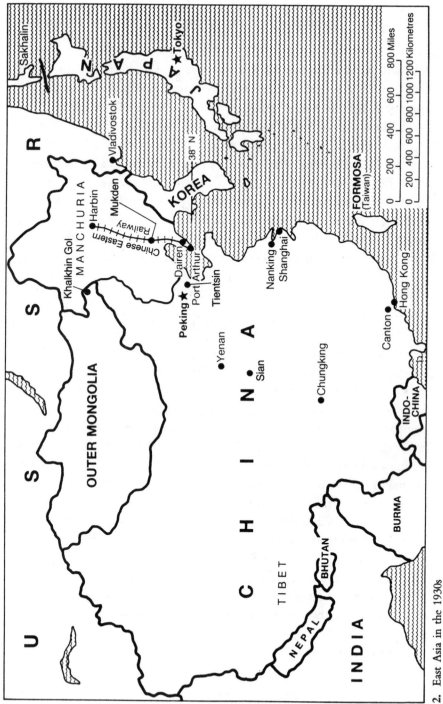

2. East Asia in the 1930s

grips with the Kwantung Army's occupation of Manchuria and the subsequent establishment of the puppet state of Manchukuo, which the Japanese Government formally recognised on 15 September 1932. Under the terms of the Sino-Japanese truce concluded (by military commanders on the spot) eight months later, the Japanese forces did not press home their military advantage beyond the Great Wall. This truce held for over four years, during which the Chinese Nationalist leader, Chiang Kai-shek, concentrated his efforts not against the Japanese but against the Chinese Communist forces, who by October 1935 had completed their Long March from Kiangsi to Yenan in the North Shensi Province. Meanwhile the major powers, in effect, waited to see what the Japanese would do next. This was not easy for outsiders to predict, partly because of the nature of Japanese society, and partly because in the 1930s there were widely differing schools of thought in Tokyo, especially within the senior ranks of the Japanese Army and Navy, even though most Japanese policy-makers, whether military or civilian, by now shared a perception of the 1920s as a decade of futile attempts at peaceful expansion through international cooperation—the so-called "Washington Conference system."[73]

At the outset of the Manchurian episode, the view from Washington remained relatively sanguine. General Douglas MacArthur, then Chief of the Army Staff (and himself an ardent "Pacific-firster"), saw "little likelihood of any belligerent outbreaks which might involve the United States in the Pacific"; Stimson, then Secretary of State, was—as we have already seen—convinced of the political power of moral reprobation;* and as late as the beginning of 1933 Joseph Grew, the U.S. Ambassador in Tokyo, was recording his private view that

> Japan will in all probability guarantee to Manchuria an administration of peace, safety and security which that unfortunate country has never before experienced . . . we must at least give her

---

*Yet even his efforts to mobilise world opinion against Japan raised American fears that they would lead to foreign entanglement of the United States.

credit for the fight she is putting up against communism which is now overwhelming China like a forest fire and would rapidly overrun Manchuria too if the Japanese hadn't taken a hand.[74]

One of the consequences of the Japanese alliance with the Manchukuo administration was the creation of a Japanese-Soviet frontier running the whole distance from the vital Soviet base at Vladivostok through Siberia and on westwards to Outer Mongolia. Many observers in Tokyo believed for some time that the next Japanese move would be against the Soviet Union; and Stalin attempted both reinsurance, by establishing diplomatic relations with the United States for the first time in 1933, and conciliation, by selling Soviet rights in the Chinese Eastern Railway, which included land and industrial property, to Manchukuo at a knock-down price, in 1935. Neither of these Soviet decision was enough to offset Japan's signature of the Anti-Comintern Pact in 1936. But Japanese membership of the Pact had little immediate effect. This grouping assumed major importance only after it became an alliance, in September 1940.

Stalin, moreover, had one invaluable asset in Japan. From 1933 to 1941 the *Frankfurter Allgemeine Zeitung*'s correspondent and the head of Soviet Military Intelligence in Tokyo were one and the same person: Richard Sorge, the most brilliant secret agent of any country engaged in the Second World War and arguably of the century, who achieved the feat of combining almost direct access to Prince Konoye Fumimaro, first appointed Japanese Prime Minister in June 1937, and close personal friendship with the German Ambassador (he and Sorge had served in the same division in the First World War). Twenty-two years after his execution by the Japanese, Sorge was declared a Hero of the Soviet Union. The quality of his reporting to Moscow speaks for itself, but many years later Sorge's Japanese interrogator said of him: "In my whole life I have never met anyone as great as he was."[75]

As it turned out, events took an altogether unexpected turn, not in Siberia but on the Chinese mainland: the bizarre Sian Incident of December 1936 and the fortuitous exchange of shots between Chinese and Japanese troops (engaged at the time in night manoeuvres) near the

Marco Polo Bridge outside Peking nearly seven months later. From 12 December until Christmas Day 1936, Chiang Kai-shek was held under arrest in Sian. His capture was organised by his own deputy, the so-called Young Marshal, Chang Hsueh-liang, who presented eight demands[76] to his chief, the first two of which were to reorganise his government in order to embrace representatives of all parties (including the Communist Party, therefore) and to put an immediate stop to the Chinese Civil War and fight the Japanese in China instead. Although these demands were met only in part, the civil war was halted; and when the clash occurred near the Marco Polo Bridge, an undeclared war between China and Japan followed. Peking and Tientsin were both occupied by Japanese forces a month later, fighting began in Shanghai on 13 August, and by the end of 1938 every major Chinese city was in Japanese hands. Politically, moreover, the publicly stated national objective of the Japanese Government had now become the establishment of a "new order" for ensuring permanent stability in East Asia.

The Chinese Government appealed to the League of Nations in November 1937. A Nine-Power Conference was convened in Brussels, but adjourned with only a weak statement of support for China, Roosevelt having vetoed the suggestions, made at Brussels, for the application of economic sanctions against Japan. From these developments the principal beneficiary was Stalin. A Sino-Soviet Treaty of Non-Aggression and Friendship was signed in August 1937; and from that date the flow of Soviet aid to Nanking (now the seat of the Chinese Government) was resumed. True, the potential Japanese threat to Siberia remained, and Japanese strategy continued to be based on the hypothesis of war with the Soviet Union even after the Japanese defeat in Outer Mongolia in 1939. Nevertheless, the Secret Protocol attached to the 1936 Anti-Comintern Pact absolved the signatories from assisting any one of them who became engaged in war with the Soviet Union. A Japanese Army numbering nearly a million men was now sunk in the morass of mainland China. And the long Sino-Japanese stalemate that followed the initial Japanese thrusts on the coast of China—with Chiang's government retreating south-westwards to

Chungking in mid-1938 and Mao secure in his Yenan fastness—suited the Soviet book in the Far East well enough.

As for Britain and the United States, although the "Open Door" concept had long been a cardinal point of American policy towards China, the principal American commercial interest in the Far East lay not in China, but in the United States' (predominant) share of trade with Japan; and the United States' chief defence commitment was in South-East Asia—the defence of the Philippines. The lion's share of investment in China, on the other hand, was British: Britain controlled the entrepôt trade of Hong Kong; in addition, the foreign exchange contributed by Malaya was of critical importance to the British balance of payments. Militarily, compared with Japan, both countries found themselves in a state of local inferiority in the Far East—pockets of troops scattered through the Chinese treaty ports,[77] a small British garrison in Hong Kong; the seaward defences of the Singapore naval base completed only in 1938; the U.S. Navy facing a distance of over six and a half thousand nautical miles from its home base in California to Guam and Manila (via Pearl Harbor);* and the Royal Navy separated from Singapore by five thousand miles from Alexandria. The conclusion of the British Chiefs of Staff surveying this scene in 1933 was that it was "about as bad as it could be."[78]

It was indeed. In London, the British ten-year defence planning rule was abolished by the end of 1933; and over the next five years the Treasury scraped together the money to pay for the completion of the Singapore base. In Washington, the U.S. naval planners tinkered with the so-called Plan *Orange;*[79] and, once appointed to the Philippines, MacArthur decided that this territory was defensible; nevertheless, the policy pursued by the two governments in the Far East for the rest of the decade boiled down essentially to that of Micawber, sometimes in humiliating circumstances. The Japanese sinking of the U.S. gunboat *Panay* on 12 December 1937 at first prompted Roosevelt to consider

---

*By contrast, the Japanese naval base at home was 1,318 nautical miles from Manila and under 3,000 from Singapore.

economic retaliation, but the strength of popular opinion against war prevailed; and the Japanese Government's apology and offer to pay damages, coupled with assurances about future conduct, were enough to bring the incident to a close. Eighteen months later, following Japanese troops' violation of the British concession area at Tientsin on 24 July 1939, the British Government formally acknowledged Japan's special position in China, including Japanese responsibility for law and order in Japanese-occupied territory in China.[80]

Towards the end of the decade public opinion, outraged by acts committed by Japanese troops in China, began to exert its influence in both capitals. In particular, American public opinion polls began to show a large majority in favour of an arms embargo against Japan and a boycott of Japanese goods. Roosevelt avoided both, but in July 1939 the U.S. Government (having just approved its first loan to China) now informed the Japanese Government of its intention to abandon the 1911 commercial treaty between the two countries: the first, hesitant step towards the economic confrontation between the United States and Japan two years later, against a background of growing public sympathy for what was increasingly seen as the resistance against fascism put up by Chinese democracy. The fact that Chinese Nationalist resistance to Japanese forces was, for the most part, little more than nominal was not generally recognised until a late stage of the Second World War. Roosevelt himself, however, enjoyed an advantage not shared by the British in assessing what was really going on in China: the reports that from 1937 onwards he began to receive from a U.S. Marine officer, Captain Evans Carlson, who had access to Mao's headquarters in Yenan.[81]

Of the three leaders of the future wartime alliance, only Stalin was seriously concerned at the prospect of a war on two fronts at the end of the 1930s. For Churchill, the threat that Japan would attempt to capture Singapore was "vain"[82] (a view that he did not alter after entering the government in September 1939). In Washington, Stimson (who would be brought back into government by Roosevelt as Secretary of War in 1940) had not altered the opinion that he held as Secretary of State at the beginning of the decade that Japan could be persuaded to "yield" to a clear expression of the United States' intention to "carry out a clear and affirmative policy in the Far East."[83]

Each of these two views—and not just with the benefit of hindsight—was absurd. And yet by the turn of the year 1941–42 the Far East would loom large for the leaders of all three countries. For Churchill, because in February 1942 the British Army suffered, at the hands of the Japanese, the greatest disaster in the entire history of British arms; for Roosevelt, because, had the Japanese not attacked Pearl Harbor before attacking British and Dutch possessions in South-East Asia, the U.S. Congress could hardly have been expected to vote as swiftly as it did on 8 December 1941 for the American declaration of war on Japan; and for Stalin, because his own decision to switch a substantial force from the Far East to the European front six months after the beginning of the German invasion depended above all on a Japanese decision—whether the Japanese armed forces should be launched against the Soviet Union or southwards against the Americans, the British, and the Dutch, as in the event they were in December 1941 (they could not undertake both these offensives). As Marshal Zhukov observed in his memoirs, with considerable understatement, the fresh units "which had fought in Mongolia . . . fought the Germans most effectively when moved to the Moscow area . . .,"[84] where they helped to inflict on Hitler's armed forces the first defeat that they had ever suffered on land.

To return to 1938—however ineffectively, Churchill, Roosevelt and Stalin had each been moving more or less in the same direction: against the tide. The immediate aftermath of the Munich Agreement left all three of them standing outside the mainstream of international events—Churchill, respected outside Parliament, but in the House of Commons only one of a handful of Conservative Party rebels; Roosevelt, admired throughout the democratic world, but in difficulties at home and facing a Congress that would have denied any President the votes needed for a dynamic foreign policy; and Stalin, in supreme command of the Kremlin, but still not finally committed to either of his two options abroad. The year 1938 having been largely that of Hitler and Chamberlain, 1939 would become the year of Hitler and Stalin. During that fateful summer, whereas both Churchill and Roosevelt remained powerless to prevent the curtain from rising on the first act of the drama of the Second World War, Stalin stepped onto the centre of the international stage for the first time.

5

THE ONSET OF WAR,

1939

My poor friend, what have you done? For us, I
can see no outcome other than a fourth
partition of Poland.

—*The Soviet Deputy Foreign Minister to the French
Ambassador in Moscow, 5 October 1938*

There is no question between the Baltic Sea
and the Black Sea that cannot be solved to the
complete satisfaction of both countries.

—*Joachim von Ribbentrop to the Soviet Foreign
Minister, August 1939*

Interlude

Paradoxically, with one infamous exception—the *Kristallnacht,* the pogrom of 9–10 November 1938—not a great deal happened in Europe during the first half of the eleven months that separated the events of October 1938 from the outbreak of the Second World War. In Britain, Munich deeply divided public[1]—as opposed to parliamentary—opinion. On the one hand, it had deprived Britain and France of the support of some thirty-five Czech divisions and of their line of fortifications in Central Europe, not to mention the Skoda armament production. The incorporation of the Sudeten Germans in *Grossdeutschland* (on top of nearly seven million incorporated through the Austrian *Anschluss* six months before) further increased the numer-

ical imbalance between the German and French armies; and the conclusion of the Munich Agreement dismayed Hitler's opponents in his own
country. To others, the Agreement seemed to have earned a respite that
could be used both for rearmament in Britain and, it was hoped, for
saner counsels to prevail in Germany. In the event, rearmament worked
both ways: the internal conflict between Left and Right in France was
still further intensified, and much of the hope for sanity in Berlin was
based on secret intelligence of poor quality or on wishful thinking, or
both. Unless it is recalled that on 10 March 1939 Samuel Hoare (then
Home Secretary, but an ex-Foreign Secretary, with an Intelligence
Service past) publicly expressed his hope for a five-year peace plan that
would in time lead to a "Golden Age,"[2] the following extract from the
novel *Brideshead Revisited* appears merely ludicrous:

> "They won't fight."
> "They can't fight. They haven't the money, they haven't the
> oil."
> "They haven't the wolfram; they haven't the men."
> "They haven't the guts."
> "They're afraid. . . ."
> "Of course it's a bluff. Where's their tungsten? Where's their
> manganese?"
> "Where's their chrome? . . ."
> "They haven't the steel."
> "They haven't the tools. They haven't the labour. They're half
> starving. They haven't the fats. The children have rickets."
> "The women are barren."
> "The men are impotent."
> "They haven't the doctors."
> "The doctors were Jewish."
> "Now they've got consumption."
> "Now they've got syphilis."
> "Goering told a friend of mine . . ."
> "Goebbels told a friend of mine . . ."
> "Ribbentrop told me that the army just kept Hitler in power

so long as he was able to get things for nothing. The moment anyone stands up to him, he's finished. The army will shoot him. . . ."

   "He'll scupper himself."

   "He'd do it now if it wasn't for Chamberlain."

   "If it wasn't for Halifax."

   "If it wasn't for Sir Samuel Hoare. . . ."[3]

This conversation was indeed imagined retrospectively by Evelyn Waugh as a satire, but until the middle of March 1939 it was what some people really thought; and there were those who still remained unconvinced* even by what happened on 15 March. Hitler spent that night in the palace on the Hradčany in Prague.

Prague Occupied—Poland Guaranteed

On 15 March, what was left of Czechoslovakia was dismembered. Unopposed—by a process that would thereafter be described as "indirect" reggression— German troops occupied the Czech lands, Bohemia and Moravia, which were declared a German protectorate; Hungary took the sub-Carpathian Ukraine; and Slovakia achieved a nominal independence. The Slovakian declaration of independence was used by the British Government as legal justification for claiming, in the House of Commons on the same day, that it was no longer bound by the obligation, assumed at Munich in 1938, to guarantee the frontiers of the post-Munich Czechoslovak state. "Do not," said Chamberlain, "let us . . . be deflected from our course." Forty-eight hours later, however, he changed course by what looked (and sounded—it was broadcast live) like a turn through 180 degrees. To a prepared speech, delivered in Birmingham, he added at the last moment an unexpected criticism of

---

*For nearly five months after this crucial event the *Daily Express,* for example, carried on its front page, day after day, the sentence: "There will be no major war in Europe this year or next year either."

Hitler, including the statement that any attempt to dominate the world by force was one which the democracies must resist. Almost simultaneously the German Government was reported—as it later turned out, incorrectly—to have delivered an ultimatum to Romania.[4] Decisions were then taken in London at breakneck, almost panic, speed. On 31 March, Chamberlain made his momentous declaration in the House of Commons, that the British Government had given the Polish Government an assurance that, if there were a threat to Polish independence which the Polish Government considered it vital to resist with all its national forces, the British Government would feel bound at once to lend the Polish Government all the support in its power.[5] The British Government's guarantee of Poland was followed, on 13 April, by guarantees to Romania and Greece.

Hitler was both surprised and enraged, above all by the guarantee given to Poland. On 3 April he issued a fresh directive to his commanders: the plan for the operation known as *Fall Weiss,* for the destruction of the Polish armed forces, was to be ready by 1 September. On 28 April he denounced both the German-Polish Non-Aggression Treaty and the Anglo-German Naval Treaty; a week later the German and Italian intention to enter into a treaty of alliance was announced; and and the so-called Pact of Steel was signed in Berlin on 22 May 1939. Churchill publicly admitted his surprise at the Polish guarantee, which he supported, however. He was not quite right in saying in the House of Commons soon afterwards that the British guarantee (matched by a French guarantee) had been given to Poland without the advice of the Chiefs of Staff.[6] The Chiefs, as we now know, were consulted, but it was not until 3 April that a military assessment of the "Implications of an Anglo-French Guarantee of Poland and Romania" began to work its way round Whitehall; this document pointed out the fact that neither Britain nor France could "render effective direct assistance to Poland."[7] Nevertheless, the guarantee given to Poland was the first step in the British approach march towards the Second World War. From then on, the general assumption among Whitehall defence planners was that the question was not whether, but when.

Yet the inner circle of British Cabinet ministers were reluctant to abandon the hope—right up to, and indeed well beyond, the last possi-

ble moment—that peace could somehow be preserved: a reluctance that is explained by the confused mixture of motives for which the Polish guarantee was given, which in turn partly explains the *ma non troppo* tempo imposed by the British Government on the diplomatic quadrille performed in European capitals during the next five months. This paradox (clearly illustrated by the 1939 reports from the German Embassy in London contained in the Dirksen Papers)[8] has been admirably summed up: a "neither . . . happy nor . . . edifying" spectacle, of "the British and French Cabinets, harried and hurried into guarantees that they could not or would not implement, into a system of deterrence they did not understand, and which left them in the last days of August desperately trying to avoid the realization that their policy had failed to deter. . . ."[9]

Negotiations with the Soviet Union

As earlier chapters have shown, the British Government had largely ignored the Soviet Government in 1938. The last days of March 1939, however, marked the beginning of a change. The alleged German ultimatum to Romania prompted the British Government to enquire whether the Soviet Union would help that country in the event of German aggression. Litvinov's response was to summon the British Ambassador in Moscow on 18 March, when he put to him his government's proposal that a conference should be immediately convened, at which Britain, France, Poland, Romania, the Soviet Union and Turkey* would be represented. Two days later the British Government, without rejecting the Soviet proposal, proposed a Four-Power Declaration: a brief joint statement by the governments of Britain, France, Poland and the Soviet Union, which would have committed them to consult together immediately on the steps needed to oppose actions constituting a threat to the political independence of any state. The Soviet reply, agreeing to subscribe to the declaration as soon as France and Poland agreed to do so, was given to the British Ambassador on 22

---

*Added three days later by Litvinov, who said that the omission of this country on 18 March had been accidental.

March. Internal Soviet documents, however, show that the Soviet Foreign Ministry remained sceptical both about the degree to which British foreign policy had really changed and about the likelihood of Polish acceptance of any agreement involving the Soviet Union.[10]

Whereas the French reply to the British was that an eastern front must include the Soviet Union, a view reiterated by the French delegation in the Anglo-French staff conversations held a month later ("the entry of Poland into a war on the side of Great Britain and France can only assume its full value if it brings about the constitution in the East of a long, solid and durable front"),[11] the Polish Government refused to sign anything but an Anglo-French agreement. Even though by now the German heat was turned full on against Warsaw,* the Polish Foreign Minister, Jósef Beck, continued to insist that there "were two things that it was impossible for Poland to do, namely to make her policy dependent upon either Berlin or Moscow"[12]—a dilemma from which the Anglo-French guarantee seemed to offer a way out for the Polish Government. As the events of September 1939 would prove, the military value of the guarantee, if invoked in practice, was minimal. But in the spring of that year its value as a deterrent was still an open question. Between two flicks of his cigarette, Beck accepted it.

At this point the British Government made an unfortunate mistake. Without clearance from Moscow, but relying on a fuzzy conversation with Maisky (whose first reaction to the proposed British guarantee was that it would be "a revolutionary change in British policy") and on the fact that the text of Chamberlain's declaration had been read out to him in the Foreign Office, albeit at the last moment, on 31 March, the declaration made in the House of Commons that afternoon included an expression of the British Government's belief that the Soviet Government "fully understood and approved" the principles on which

---

*As early as October 1938 Ribbentrop had asked Beck for the return to the Reich of the Free City of Danzig, which, under the terms of the Versailles settlement, was connected to Poland by the so-called Polish Corridor, a strip of territory that separated the rest of Germany from East Prussia. During his visit to Warsaw in January 1939, Beck turned him down flat. From the end of March 1939 onward (Germany having annexed Memel from Lithuania), the German request first became a demand and then began to sound increasingly like an ultimatum.

the British Government was acting.[13] Litvinov's reception of the British Ambassador, when he enquired, on 1 April, about the Soviet reaction to Chamberlain's statement, was—in Litvinov's own words—"very cold."[14] This was not a good beginning.

The Polish Government was tragically over-sanguine.[15] It continued to believe, long after the belief had any foundation in reality, that Germany needed Poland as an ally against the Soviet Union; it doubted the German Army's readiness for war in 1939; and what military plans existed in Warsaw at the beginning of that year were aimed rather at the country's traditional enemy—Russia, whose armed forces were underestimated by the Poles to an absurd degree. Faced with this dilemma, British public opinion was divided. Men who recalled the military lessons of the First World War, such as Churchill and Lloyd George, supported on this issue by Labour, urged that a Grand Alliance—Britain, France and the Soviet Union—was once again vital.[16] By contrast, Chamberlain from the outset confessed to "the most profound distrust of Russia" and to the conviction that "if bringing Russia in means their [Poland and Romania] running out," this change would be "a disastrous one"; nor—as he told his Cabinet colleagues as late as 19 July—could he "bring himself to believe that a real alliance between Russia and Germany was possible."[17] Given the Prime Minister's view, strongly held, as Chamberlain's opinions always were, the best endeavour that the British Government could manage was to saunter through a long summer of negotiations with the Soviet Government. Almost up to the last moment (when the French Prime Minister, losing patience with the British, intervened personally), this leisurely pace was maintained. At least one prescient telegram from the British Embassy in Moscow, sent as early as 13 April,[18] made no impact in London, nor did the prophetic advice of the Chiefs of Staff.* Little account, moreover, was taken of the implication of Stalin's own ambivalent but ominous warning to the western powers, included in his

---

*On 16 August 1939 the Chiefs of Staff said that, without effective Soviet assistance in the air and on land, "the less chance there would be of either Poland or Romania emerging at the end of it [the war] as independent states in anything like their original form."[19]

address to the XVIIIth Party Congress, held in Moscow five days before the German occupation of Prague. As the British Embassy did not fail to report at the time, Stalin said on this occasion that "business-like" contacts with all countries must be strengthened, and that the Soviet Union must "not . . . be drawn into conflicts by warmongers urging others to take the chestnuts out of the fire."[20] (literally translated, "to rake the fire with somebody else's hands").

On 17 April Litvinov made an offer which—in retrospect—was the swansong of the Soviet commitment to the policy of collective security: a tripartite alliance between Britain, France and the Soviet Union, to be supported by a military agreement. It took the British Government three weeks to send its reply,[21] which was essentially negative, but expressed in terms that did not exactly coincide with those of the French reply. Both the logic of the situation in Central Europe and the growing pressure of public opinion now began to propel the British Government in the direction of an alliance with the Soviet Union. Churchill, Eden and Lloyd George all spoke in favour of this fundamental realignment in the House of Commons on 19 May. The Soviet offer, said Churchill, was "a fair offer, and a better offer . . . than the terms which the Government seek to get for themselves; a more simple, a more direct and a more effective offer. Let it not be put aside and come to nothing. . . . Without Russia there can be no effective Eastern front."[22]

Reluctantly, the British Cabinet at last decided on 24 May to bite the bullet. Three days later the British and French ambassadors submitted to the Kremlin what seemed to them an historic proposal—the formation of a triple alliance. To their surprise, this proposal, which was hedged with significant conditions (including reference to the League of Nations, from past experience not a fair augury for the effectiveness of the proposed alliance), was not accepted by the Soviet Government.

By this time Litvinov, who resigned on 3 May, had been replaced by Molotov, the Soviet Prime Minister and Stalin's closest associate in the Politburo. Lamenting Litvinov's departure, the British Ambassador recalled that "talks with him were always stimulating, thanks to his knowledge of men and matters and to his efficient technique, the whole salted at times by a bracing bluntness . . . and lit up by a steely eye."[23] Although this change undoubtedly was of political significance, the tone of published telegrams to and from the Soviet Foreign Ministry does not reveal any noticeable variation following Molotov's takeover. And, as we now know, on 17 April—the very day of Litvinov's final offer—the Soviet Ambassador in Berlin, paying his first call on the head of the German Foreign Office, Ernst von Weizsäcker, for nearly a year, assured the State Secretary there that there was no reason why the Soviet Union should not live with Germany "on a normal footing," and "out of normal relations could grow increasingly improved relations." This Soviet feeler was repeated by the Soviet Chargé d'Affaires in Berlin on 5 May.[24] From then on the Anglo-French negotiations in Moscow overlapped with a series of Soviet-German exchanges. Stalin now had a foot in both camps.

Only one of the three leaders of the future wartime alliance was directly involved in these negotiations, whose outcome powerfully affected the outbreak of war and, in the longer term, bequeathed an enduring legacy of East-West mistrust. The rocks of substance which the political negotiations* hit are clear enough. To begin with (although this rock was eventually circumnavigated), there was the issue of reciprocity, on which the Soviet Government insisted from the outset; the precise definition of aggression (direct and indirect);† and above all, the refusal of other potential victims of German aggression to concede in advance their willingness to accept Soviet military aid. Although for a time the third issue was focused on the Baltic States, as time went on this vital question became concentrated on one country—Poland. It was never resolved.

What remains astounding to this day is not so much the substance of

---

*As opposed to the subsequent military negotiations, after the arrival of the British and French military missions in Moscow, in August 1939.

†"Indirect" aggression was the phrase used in these negotiations to mean the abandonment by a bordering country of its neutrality of its independence. In this context the Baltic states were particularly relevant.

these negotiations as the manner in which they were conducted. Issues
of such complexity could have been handled with despatch only if the
British and French foreign ministers* had gone to Moscow themselves. Halifax thought of doing so, but (never noted for his energy)
he felt that he was too busy at home; Eden offered to go, but his offer
was not accepted by Chamberlain; the British Ambassador in Moscow,
William Seeds, was a sick man; and on 14 June his Embassy was
reinforced by the head of the Foreign Office Central Department,
William Strang. Strang was a curious choice as political interlocutor
for Molotov, but—unlike the British Cabinet—he understood what a
Marxist would call the real correlationship of forces in the Moscow
negotiations, which he described on 20 July in these terms: ". . . a
humiliating experience. Time after time we have taken up a position
and a week later we have abandoned it . . . it is certain that if we want
an agreement with them [the Russians] we shall have to pay their price
or something very near it."[25] Strang's assessment was shrewd and accurate. The "humiliation," moreover, was not only metaphorical but
sometimes literal. On at least one occasion Molotov received the two
ambassadors without rising from his desk. Since this was situated on a
kind of dais, the ambassadors addressed him from a physically one-
down position.

By the time the Foreign Office received this letter, tempers were
becoming frayed, and not only in Moscow. Three weeks earlier, *Pravda*
had already published an article significantly entitled "Impasse," in
which a Politburo member, Andrei Zhdanov, had expressed his opinion (which he explicitly said was different from that of some of his
colleagues) that the Anglo-French aim was "an agreement in which the
Soviet Union would play the part of a hired labourer and bear the
whole weight of responsibility on its shoulders."[26] On 10 July Molotov was telling the two ambassadors that his government was "not
prepared to sign any political agreement" except simultaneously with

---

*The British were the lead negotiators, but successive moves had to be cleared between the Foreign
Office and the Quai d'Orsay.

"a military agreement which would form an organic whole with the political agreement"; otherwise the talks would have to be adjourned.[27] Under strong pressure from the French, the British Government gave way. On 28 July Molotov was informed by the two ambassadors that their governments agreed to the immediate opening of military conversations in Moscow.[28]

What took place from then on was farcical. As if to underscore the remoteness of what was happening in Moscow, Chamberlain insisted—against Churchill's protests—that the House of Commons should enjoy its customary two-month recess. Parliament therefore rose on 4 August; Chamberlain and Halifax left London, on holiday. Whereas the head of the French Military Mission was a member of the *Conseil Supérieur de Guerre,* General Joseph Edouard Doumenc (who, as the records of the missions' meetings in Moscow show, spoke with the authority of the French Chief of Staff), the head of the British Mission was Reginald Drax, an admiral then serving in his last appointment in the Royal Navy as Commander-in-Chief, The Nore.[29] The French wanted to get a move on, the British to delay; and Soviet historians have since found ready-made ammunition in the paragraph of the British Mission's instructions telling them to "go very slowly with the conversations" in Moscow.[30] Whereas the French were anxious to get their men to Moscow quickly,[31] the British insisted on travelling by sea—not in a cruiser, but in a chartered passenger ship, whose top speed was thirteen knots.

The missions reached Leningrad on 9–10 August; 10 August was spent sight-seeing in Leningrad, at the Hermitage and Tsarskoe Selo. They did not reach Moscow until the following day, and their first meeting (with the Soviet Defence Minister, Klimentii Voroshilov,) finally took place on 12 August. It was then discovered that Drax had arrived without letters of credence of any kind (these did not arrive from London until 21 August, by which time the meetings had been adjourned). At the fourth meeting, all of them attended by the Soviet Defence Minister and one of them notable for a long intervention by the Soviet Chief of Staff, Boris Shaposhnikov, Voroshilov put three pertinent questions. Would Soviet forces be allowed to:

(a) Move against East Prussia through Polish territory and, in particular, through the Vilno Gap?

(b) Advance through Polish Galicia in order to make contact with enemy troops?

(c) Use Romanian territory in the event of German aggression against that country?

The first two of these questions, put to the mission on 14 August and transmitted to Warsaw by the western ambassadors, received the same negative reply as before, at every level of the Polish Government, right up to 21 August. The Moscow talks were indefinitely adjourned on that day, therefore. Nevertheless, Doumenc made a last-ditch attempt. He saw Voroshilov alone (without Drax) on 23 August, acting on the personal instructions of the French Prime Minister. By then it was too late—indeed, it was probably already five minutes to midnight by the time the missions had their first meeting in Moscow. There was, however, a final meeting on 25 August, after which Voroshilov exclaimed, according to the record of the British Military Attaché, who was present: "Were we to have to conquer Poland in order to offer her our help, or were we to go on our knees and offer our help to Poland? The position was impossible for us."

The exact date in the summer of 1939 when Stalin took the final decision to make his second U-turn of the decade cannot, on the evidence at present available, be established with any degree of certainty. A recent western study of the relationship between Stalin and Hitler during 1939–41, and a recent Soviet account of Soviet foreign policy from 1936 to 1939, concur in placing Stalin's decision in August: the former specifically, at a meeting held in the Kremlin in the afternoon of 19 August, the latter more vaguely, in the middle of August, after the "fruitlessness" of the negotiations with the British and French had become "absolutely clear" and the German proposals "impossible to ignore."[32] The Soviet historian lays stress on three factors: that the British were also talking simultaneously with the Germans, that the Soviet Union faced the possibility of a war on two fronts, and that the Soviet Foreign Ministry had treated German advances to them that summer with extreme caution. About the first of these three, there is no doubt.[33] The second is also true: in the trial of strength which Japanese forces began on the Mongolian border in May 1939, the Khalkhin Gol battle ended only in the last ten days of August with a victory for the Soviet First Army Group (whose commander, Georgii Zhukov, would later win fame first as the defender of Moscow and then as the conqueror of Berlin).* The third factor is not in dispute, although the direction of negotiating traffic between Berlin and Moscow was by no means one-way.

The most probable timing, which cannot on present evidence be proved any more than any other, is that as soon as the enticing words "there is no question between the Baltic Sea and the Black Sea which cannot be solved to the complete satisfaction of both countries" began to be dangled before the Soviet Embassy in Berlin, coinciding, as they did, with the slapstick preparations then being made for the departure of the Anglo-French military missions for Moscow, Stalin can have had little doubt which of his two options would, sooner or later, prove preferable for Soviet interests. Whether he said as much to Voroshilov, whose instructions for the military talks he personally approved; whether he told only Molotov; or whether he kept his own counsel, is not a matter of great significance. (It is the view of the author of the latest study of Stalin that he made up his mind "earlier" than his colleagues.)[34] From the moment that Ribbentrop himself offered this bait to the Soviet Chargé d'Affaires in Berlin on 2 August—as his officials had already done a week earlier—all that Stalin needed to do was to pin Hitler down, not merely to the signature of a non-aggression pact (such agreements were two a penny in inter-war Europe), but also to the precise business of redrawing the map of Central and Eastern Europe implied by the phrase "between the Baltic Sea and the Black Sea."[35]

Had the political and strategic map of Europe still been as it was ten

---

*Soviet-Japanese hostilities were formally brought to an end by an agreement concluded on 15 September 1939.

months earlier, before the conclusion of the Munich Agreement, a
German offer couched in these terms would have looked different in
Moscow. As it was, however, it was not the German Government (as
Hitler maintained shortly after Munich) that had been obliged to take
the "road to Canossa" in 1938, but the British and the French.* In the
reduced political and strategic circumstances in which both governments found themselves in 1939, there was no offer to the Kremlin that
lay within their gift which could match—let alone outbid—the proposal eventually put to Stalin by Hitler in August of that year. His
offer amounted, in effect, to a chance for the Soviet Union to recover
the western territories of the Russian Empire lost after the First World
War. In the Soviet interest, it was essential for Stalin not to be in a
hurry—something that his innate caution would have dictated in any
case. Stalin's negotiating position at the turn of July–August 1939 was
a strong one. He could afford to move towards Hitler almost inch by
inch, weighing up every move, because it was Hitler who was now the
demandeur. Hitler had powerful military reasons—the imminence of
Operation *Fall Weiss*—for haste, whereas Stalin still held the military
negotiations with the British and French as a card in reserve.

The German-Soviet Pact

Voroshilov's three questions to the Anglo–French missions, quoted
above, still lay on the table unanswered on the evening of 15 August
when the German Ambassador, Friedrich von der Schulenburg, acting
on Ribbentrop's instructions to the letter (he read them out verbatim
to Molotov), proposed that Ribbentrop should visit Moscow in order
to expound Hitler's views personally to Stalin. Once again, there was
"no question between the Baltic Sea and the Black Sea" which could
not be "solved to the complete satisfaction of both countries." After
some to-ing and fro-ing, this move was pressed home by a personal
message from Hitler himself, asking Stalin to receive his Foreign Min-

---

*See epigraph to Chapter 4.

ister by 23 August at the latest: a date accepted by Stalin in a personal reply to Hitler on 21 August.[36]

In the early hours of 24 August the German–Soviet Non-Aggression Pact was signed in the Kremlin. What had eluded the British and their French allies through the entire summer, Ribbentrop had achieved in less than twenty-four hours. The terms of the German–Soviet Pact were unremarkable. What was critically important was the Secret Protocol (unknown until after the war), which divided Central and Eastern Europe into spheres of German and Soviet influence.[37] Its terms will be considered in the next chapter, partly because the Protocol did not come into effect until after the war had broken out and partly because one of its most significant provisions—that relating to Poland—was then modified. What must be noted at once, however, is that without the Protocol, the Pact would not have been signed by the Soviet negotiators. The accuracy of the text of the Protocol (reproduced in Appendix II) was for almost half a century denied in the Soviet Union. Nevertheless, in recent years there has been a gradual shift. A Soviet article on the German–Soviet Pact published in August 1988 stated flatly that "the majority of these materials are still not accessible for [Soviet] researchers"; and it described as "completely incomprehensible" the conclusion of the subsequent German–Soviet Treaty of 28 September 1939. On the fiftieth anniversary of the Pact, the text of the August Secret Protocol was published in the press of the Baltic republics of the Soviet Union. On 25 May 1989 *Pravda* published an article on the preliminary findings of the Soviet–Polish commission examining the events of 1939. According to this article, although "no original" of the August 1939 Protocol exists in the Soviet archives, "the subsequent development of events and diplomatic correspondence gives ground for concluding that agreement regarding the spheres of interest of the two countries was reached in some form or other in August 1939." Finally, on 24 December 1989, the Supreme Soviet formally acknowledged that the Secret Protocol had been "juridically invalid and inoperative from the moment of signature." [38]

In his memoirs nearly ten years afterwards, Churchill described the German–Soviet Pact as "cold-blooded," but "at the moment realistic in a high degree"—"sinister news" that "broke upon the world like an explosion."[39] Except for the few who had kept their eyes and ears open from the time of Munich onwards, it certainly did. Yet the eventual outcome that summer had been accurately foreseen by some western observers, notably Robert Coulondre, French Ambassador in Moscow in 1938 and Ambassador in Berlin by the time of Molotov's appointment in 1939. His despatches to the Quai d'Orsay of 4 October 1938 and 7 May 1939, both of which pointed towards a Soviet-German partition of Poland, make compelling reading today.[40] The State Department also received sound information from its Moscow Embassy, where in 1939 Charles Bohlen was kept informed by his opposite number in the German Embassy, Hans Heinrich Herwarth von Butenfeld (an anti-Nazi, serving as second secretary on Schulenburg's staff). By contrast, the Foreign Office could only lament—in the words of the departmental post-mortem held when it was all over—that they "were never told that the Germans and the Russians had started negotiations with each other—which was the one thing that mattered."*[41]

By concluding his agreement with Hitler in August 1939, Stalin—like Chamberlain in 1938—secured a respite, which in his case lasted for nearly two years. Even without public knowledge of the Secret Protocol, this agreement—followed by the German-Soviet Partition of Poland in September—incensed the Right. It caused dismay in Tokyo, where the Japanese Prime Minister, taken completely by surprise, issued a statement declaring that "inexplicable new conditions" had arisen in Europe; he then resigned. Above all, it obliged Communist parties and their friends throughout the world to perform a nonstop act of ideological acrobatics from which they were not released until June 1941. This feat they sought to justify on two main grounds.

---

*Even the telegram from the Washington Embassy to the Foreign Office, conveying the State Department's warning of the impending German-Soviet Pact, was delayed for four days by a pro-Soviet "mole" in the Foreign Office Communications Department, reaching the Central Department's desks four days after its despatch.[42]

First, Stalin's personal authority over the movement worldwide was such that it could not be questioned; he must be right. Secondly, most of the Right in Europe had made no secret of their belief that, however dangerous a man Hitler might be in other respects, he did at least offer a "bulwark against Bolshevism"—the phrase used, for example, by Halifax in his opening remarks to Hitler at Berchtesgaden in 1937. For those who believed this, the vision of a Four-Power Europe—Britain, France, Germany and Italy—opened up by the Munich Agreement had been a relief. For the Kremlin and its supporters abroad, on the other hand, it was correspondingly disturbing: an anxiety lest "German fascism, with Chamberlain's and Daladier's effective blessing, would continue its aggression eastwards,"[43] which was fed by the widespread public discussion of the future of the Ukraine in the months immediately after Munich (in 1918 Germany had signed a peace treaty with a separatist Ukrainian Government, and two years later Polish forces occupied Kiev).

It is not difficult to imagine Stalin's reaction to reports such as the one that Maisky wrote from London on 29 November 1938, following a lunch with Horace Wilson as his guest. One of the reasons that Wilson, Chamberlain's closest adviser, gave Maisky on this occasion for his belief that there would be no war in the immediate future in which Britain would take part was that Hitler's next line of attack would be "eastwards, towards the Ukraine."[44] In his speech in March 1939 Stalin had included the ironical remark: "One may surmise that they [Britain and France] gave the Germans the regions of Czechoslovakia as the price for the obligation to begin a war with the Soviet Union, but the Germans are now refusing to honour the bill."[45] Although, as we now know, Ribbentrop did throw the Ukranian fly over Beck—who did not rise to the suggestion that Poland might receive part of the Ukraine, in return for Danzig—by 1939 the idea had lost whatever substance it may have had in the closing months of 1938. When the moment of truth finally arrived for Stalin in the summer of 1939, the contrast between the dilatory, ambivalent diplomacy of the British Government (also of the French, though to a slightly lesser extent) and Hitler's eager overtures towards the Soviet Union were

enough, of themselves—seen from Moscow—to convince Stalin
which way his choice should go. What remains unexplained, perhaps
inexplicable, is the extent to which, for all his caution, he forgot the
need to beware of Greek gifts. Instead, like Chamberlain after Munich,
Stalin trusted Hitler to keep his word. The attitude of injured Soviet
innocence persisted down the years. In June 1941, Molotov observed to
the German Ambassador: "Surely we have not deserved that?"; in
Stalin's broadcast to the Soviet people on 3 July, he told them that "no
peace-loving state could have rejected such a pact with another country, even if rogues like Hitler and Ribbentrop were at its head"; and as
late as the summer of 1970, the walls of Moscow were adorned with
posters depicting a Nazi boot kicking through the Non-Aggression
Pact of August 1939.[46]

The Declaration of War

The agreement in Moscow was reached in good time for Hitler to beat
the deadline for the invasion of Poland laid down in his directive five
months earlier. The British Government responded on the following
day by signing its Treaty of Alliance, long delayed, with Poland (the
Danzig commitment was covered in a secret protocol attached to the
treaty)—the first major setback in a hitherto unbroken run of German
success.[47] On Hitler's last-minute orders, therefore, the invasion was
delayed by five days, to allow time for a frenetic round of negotiations
between Berlin, London, Paris and Warsaw. These negotiations continued even after the invasion had begun, at dawn on 1 September; it
was not until over forty-eight hours later that first the British Government (gloomily)* and then the French declared war on Germany. In
this final flurry neither Churchill nor Roosevelt nor Stalin played any
part. Stalin indeed had nothing more to say for the time being. He had

---

*A gloom that Chamberlain made no attempt to conceal. In the end he had either to send Hitler an
ultimatum or face a revolt not only in Parliament, where there was an angry scene on 2 September,
but in the Cabinet itself, where he found himself isolated on returning from the House of Commons.

said enough in the privacy of the Kremlin on the evening of 23 August, when—according to the German record—he proposed a toast to Hitler's health, remarking that he knew "how much the German people loves its Führer."[48] Whereas Stalin's remark was made behind closed doors, Molotov laid it on with a trowel in the Supreme Soviet, recommending to that body—in his capacity as Prime Minister as well as Minister of Foreign Affairs—ratification of the Non-Aggression Pact. He claimed that the Pact, which he described as a "milestone in the development of Europe" and "the turning point in the history of Europe, and not of Europe alone," had "brilliantly justified" the "historic prophecy" made by Stalin in his speech to the XVIIIth Party Congress.[49]

Churchill was invited to call at 10 Downing Street on 1 September. Chamberlain offered him a seat in the War Cabinet, which he accepted. He was not, however, appointed First Lord of the Admiralty until after war had been declared on 3 September. He spent the intervening forty-eight hours in a sort of political baulk. His repeated warnings of the previous years had been borne out. His efforts to win support for the formation of a Grand Alliance had been frustrated. During the scene in Parliament on 2 September, when Chamberlain found himself isolated, Churchill was the one man who, had he chosen to do so, might have brought him down. Instead he felt, in his own words, "a very strong sense of calm . . . a serenity of mind."[50]

For Roosevelt, by far the most significant effort, internationally speaking, that he undertook during the first half of 1939 was his attempt to amend the Neutrality Act. On 18 July he was finally obliged to admit defeat. As the Vice-President, John Garner, put it to him that evening: "Well, Captain, you haven't got the votes and that's all there is to it," and Roosevelt accurately told the press soon afterwards that he had "practically no power to make an American effort to prevent . . . a war from breaking out."[51] During the previous month he was host to King George VI—the first state visit to the United States in history of a reigning British monarch. This was counterbalanced by Roosevelt's unhappy appointment of Joseph Kennedy as Ambassador in London, a post in which he was not replaced until 1941—not a moment too soon.

Fortunately Kennedy's reports to Washington about the British will to resist were, in the event, outweighed by those of Edward Murrow, which reached a wider public in the United States.[52]

Roosevelt made several appeals to Hitler and Mussolini. One of these stands out: a personal message from the President to the Führer, which was broadcast on 15 April 1939, exactly one month after the German occupation of Prague, asked whether he would give assurances against aggression to some thirty, listed, countries. This ill-judged initiative evoked one of the most effective speeches of Hitler's whole career, delivered to the Reichstag on 28 April. Paragraph after paragraph apostrophised Roosevelt with withering scorn. Towards the end of this long passage, Hitler observed that the "conditions prevailing" in the United States were "on such a scale" that Roosevelt could "find time and leisure" to give his attention to "universal problems." Then he went on:

> Your concerns and suggestions, therefore, cover a much larger area than mine, because my world, Mr Roosevelt, in which Providence has placed me and for which I am therefore obliged to work, is unfortunately much smaller—although for me it is more precious than anything else, for it is limited to my people.
>
> I believe, however, that this is the way in which I can be of the most service to that for which we are all concerned, the justice, well-being, progress and peace of the whole human community.[53]

All Roosevelt's appeals were equally in vain. Shortly after war broke out, however, he wrote this letter to Churchill:

> It is because you and I occupied similar positions in the World War that I want you to know how glad I am that you are back again in the Admiralty. Your problems are, I realise, complicated

by new factors, but the essential is not very different. What I want you and the Prime Minister to know is that I shall at all times welcome it, if you will keep me in touch personally with anything you want me to know about. You can always send sealed letters through your pouch or my pouch.

I am glad you did the Marlboro volumes before this thing started—and I much enjoyed reading them.[54]

These three hundred-odd words provided the springboard from which, in the course of the next five and a half years, an extraordinary relationship would gradually develop.

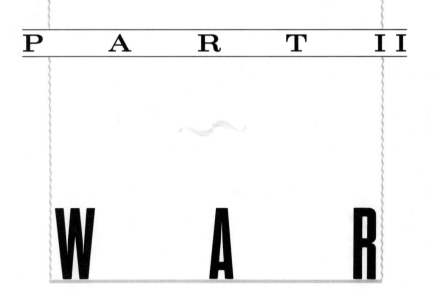

PART II

WAR

6

THE PHONEY WAR,

1939-40

> ... And, gentle, do not care to know,
> Where Poland draws her Eastern bow,
> What violence is done;
> Nor ask what doubtful act allows
> Our freedom in this English house,
> Our picnics in the sun.
>
> —W. H. Auden, *"Out on the Lawn I Lie in Bed"*

THE MILITARY SETTING

The opening months of the Second World War—from 1 September 1939* to 10 May 1940—soon became known as the "Phoney War" or, in France, as the *"drôle de guerre,"* and it is as such that they have gone down to history, although the war during these months was far from phoney for the population of Poland, the Finnish Army, the forces—

---

*With an uncharacteristic lack of magnanimity, in the first volume of his memoirs Churchill chose as the date for the outbreak of the Second World War 3 September 1939—the day on which first the British Government and then the French presented a reluctant ultimatum to the German Government. In a formal sense, this was the date on which the war began for Britain and France, rather than 1 September, the day on which the German invasion of Poland began.[1]

Norwegian and Allied—which resisted the German invasion of Norway and, in Britain, for those serving in the Royal Navy and the Merchant Marine (who were therefore actively engaged in from the war from its outset). During the long interval between the Anglo-French declaration of war on Germany and the launching of the German offensive in the following spring, however, the land and air forces of Britain and France undertook no offensive operations of any kind; the Royal Air Force dropped propaganda leaflets over Germany, and in September 1939 the French Army moved nine divisions into the Saar, towards—but without attacking—the German Siegfried Line five miles away from their own Maginot Line, to which these divisions were withdrawn a month later, after the Polish capitulation.

In Britain, the general mood was a curious mixture of gloom and complacency. The gloom stemmed partly from an accurate realisation—the opposite of August 1914—that this war would be a long one, partly from a mistaken calculation of the casualties that would be caused by German aerial bombardment, for which the destruction of defenceless and overcrowded Guernica two years earlier supplied the model in popular imagination.* On the other hand, the basis for complacency was the belief of Allied defence planners that time was on the side of Britain and France; hence the conclusion reached at the first meeting of the Anglo-French Supreme War Council, held at a moment when the Polish Army had almost ceased to exist as an organised force, that "there was no hurry."[2] This belief, like the fear of the effects of air attack on the civilian population, rested partly on fantasy of the kind satirised by Evelyn Waugh in the passage cited in the preceding chapter; partly on turning a blind eye to the Treasury's warnings of the effect that paying for a prolonged war must have on Britain's delicate balance of payments; but even more on the flawed assessment of the

---

*Nor was this imagination, fed by films like H. G. Wells' *The Shape of Things to Come,* only popular. British experts believed that the correct "multiplier" for each ton of bombs dropped was 50: a ton of bombs could be assumed to cause fifty casualties. In the event, the number of British deaths from German air attack during the entire war was sixty thousand (the number of German civilians killed from the air exceeded half a million, however).

state of the German economy in 1939 and of the cumulative impact on it which—the massive deliveries to Germany of Soviet raw materials notwithstanding—the Allied naval blockade would gradually exert. Even after the resignation of Chamberlain, for whom blockade was the principal weapon of war, Whitehall's belief in the effectiveness of economic warfare persisted for another year. In the event, Britain would become a country far more blockaded than Germany, whose economy was not fully mobilised for war until 1943.

Poland

At dawn on 1 September 1939 the German Army attacked across all the German-Polish frontiers. Unlike subsequent campaigns, in this one— once it had been launched—Hitler left his generals to win. The Polish Army resisted, but although the Polish capital did not fall until the 27th, the German armies, superior both in numbers and in equipment—above all in aircraft and armour—ably led and with the advantage of geography, had succeeded in surrounding Warsaw by the end of the first two weeks of a new kind of offensive warfare, the *Blitzkrieg*. [3] Ten days before the surrender of Warsaw, the Fourth Partition of Poland had begun. Those who carried out this partition cannot be excused by the fact that, even without a world war, the Second Polish Republic might have fallen apart, so great were the centrifugal forces at work within its 1921 frontiers; barely two thirds of its population— according to the 1931 census—were ethnically Polish. This said, the ordeal of Poland, which lasted for nearly six years, beggars description.

On 17 September 1939 the Red Army crossed the Soviet-Polish frontier in a strength of about forty divisions. It met with minimal Polish resistance. Nor did the German Army, whose advance had in some places taken it more than a hundred miles east of the line of rivers—the Narew, the Vistula and the San—named in the Secret Protocol of 23 August[4] as the approximate boundary of German and Soviet spheres of interest in Poland, make any difficulty about withdrawing to the river line. On the contrary, the two armies met jovially, almost as though nothing had ever happened to mar the spirit of the

Treaty of Rapallo. Moreover, in the ironically named "Frontier and Friendship" Treaty, signed in Moscow by Ribbentrop and Molotov on 28 September, the two governments reached a "definitive" division of the "territory of the former Polish state" between them.[5] Unlike the terms of the August Protocol, this new division gave Germany more or less that part of inter-war Poland which had lain west of the Curzon Line,* although this was not the terminology used in 1939. In return the Soviet Union received, as part of its sphere of interest, almost the whole of Lithuania, which had formed part of the German sphere of interest in the Protocol, in addition to the other two Baltic States, for whose incorporation in the Soviet sphere the Protocol already provided.

Poland, the immediate cause of the outbreak of the Second World War, having disappeared from the map of Europe, Hitler delivered a speech in the Reichstag offering peace to Britain and France. Even before receiving the British refusal, on 9 October, he wrote in a memorandum for his commanders-in-chief that his primary aim was the total destruction of the western armed forces.[6] Hitler's principal gain, though by no means the only one, from the German-Soviet agreements of August and September 1939 was the free hand that they gave him in the West. When the German attack on France and the Low Countries, after repeated delays, was finally delivered in May 1940, only seven German divisions would be left to cover the Eastern Front.

Militarily speaking, the partition of Poland was accomplished in the course of ten days. In political terms, for the Soviet Union it was a

---

*The Curzon Line, named after the British Foreign Secretary in 1920, was the line then advocated at the Paris Peace Conference as the eastern boundary of Poland. Following the Poles' victory over Tukhachevsky's army (see Chapter 2), the Polish Government was able to insist, in the Treaty of the Riga signed in 1921, on a Polish-Soviet frontier lying much further east, thereby incorporating within the newly established Polish state substantial minorities, most of whom were Ukrainians (about five million) and Belorussians, whose ethnic allegiance remained with the populations of the Soviet Republics of Ukraine and Belorussia. The Curzon Line—whether intentionally or through a clerical error—left to the east the largely Polish city of Lvov. This line would loom large in the discussion of Poland at the Yalta Conference, which cannot be understood except against the historical background of 1920–21 and 1939.

relatively simple matter to re-incorporate the western Ukraine and western Belorussia, now Soviet-occupied, into the Ukrainian and Belorussian Republics of the Soviet Union.[7] The Germans, on the other hand, having incorporated the western provinces of their share of Poland into the Reich, were left with the problem of the rump that remained. This was solved by creating a territory called the *General-Gouvernement,* ruled under Hans Frank, who, as Governor-General, installed himself in the Wawel (the ancient palace of the kings of Poland) in Kraków, where Archbishop Adam Sapieha is said to have served him Polish rations on gold plate. Frank's task in this territory was not only to exploit it to the utmost, by forced labour, but also to carry out the *Ausserordentliche Befriedigungsaktion* (Extraordinary Pacification Action), ironically named, since the object of this pro-gramme was to liquidate the Polish educated class. Simultaneously Himmler began the transportation to the *General Gouvernement* of the inhabitants of the annexed Polish provinces: 1.5 million in the first year, including 300,000 Jews. The gates of the Warsaw Ghetto were closed in November 1940, and it became a centre for collecting Jews from all over Poland, who from July 1942 onwards were deported from the ghetto to concentration camps. The camps in the *General Gouvernement* included, among others, the one still preserved as a mon-ument to this day at Oświęcim (Auschwitz).

As for the Soviet side of the new frontier, the number of Polish citizens deported to the Soviet Union has never been exactly estab-lished: roughly 1,500,000 of whom perhaps half survived until they were saved by the Soviet-Polish *rapprochement* that followed the Ger-man invasion of the Soviet Union two years later. Thus in Poland in 1939, the governments of Germany and the Soviet Union between them "made a desert and called it peace."[8] In the worst area of this desert—the *General Gouvernement,* or (as it was ironically called) the *Gangster-Gau*—Hitler made one significant exception to the overall policy directive of murderous exploitation given to Frank. On 17 October 1939 he said to the Chief of the OKW, Wilhelm Keitel: "The territory is important to us from a military point of view as an ad-vanced jumping-off point and can be used for the strategic concentration of troops. To that end the railroads, roads and lines of communication are to be kept in order."[9]

Finland

At the time of the German invasion of Poland, no one could have predicted that by the end of the year the only country in Europe that would be the scene of heavy fighting[10] would be Finland—the so-called Winter War. Poland once dealt with, the turn of the Baltic States came next. In the course of a single fortnight, between 28 September and 10 October, so-called mutual assistance agreements were signed in Moscow successively by the foreign ministers of Estonia, Latvia and Lithuania, providing for the stationing of contingents of Soviet troops in each country—a total of 100,000, of which 75,000 were in Lithuania (and thus adjacent to East Prussia). All three Baltic governments agreed to these arrangements with little or no demur. By contrast, the Finnish Foreign Minister refused Molotov's invitation to visit Moscow, sending there instead as his representative Juho Kusti Passikivi, the man who had led the Finnish delegation nearly twenty years earlier in the negotiations that led to the signature of the Treaty of Tartu. Under the terms of that treaty the Soviet Government—in the middle of a civil war as well as a war with Poland—had then made major territorial concessions to the newly independent Finland.[11] Now, in the altered circumstances of 1939, it became Soviet policy to claw back what had been conceded at Tartu—Finnish possession of Petsamo and of the islands in the Gulf of Finland commanding the seaward approaches to Leningrad and Kronstadt; and a demarcation of the border on the Karelian Isthmus that for the past twenty years had left the nearest point of the Soviet-Finnish frontier less than twenty miles from Leningrad. In 1939 the Finnish Government's reply was in effect: "What we have, we hold."

Unlike the brief talks with the three Baltic foreign ministers, the Soviet-Finnish discussions in Moscow lasted off and on for four weeks. The Finns were as determined as the Poles had been three months earlier; like the Poles, they too were invaded, but at first the outcome of their intransigence was very different. The Finnish Army was well led—its commander, Marshal Carl Gustav von Mannerheim, was an ex-Tsarist cavalry officer—and well equipped (for example, with skis) for the extreme conditions of Arctic and sub-Arctic warfare. The Red Army lumbered into battle on a broad front, relying on its numerical superiority. In the first phase of the campaign, which lasted from 30 November 1939 until the beginning of January 1940, the Red Army was beaten back in the north and south and suffered heavy casualties on the central sector. The plan that led to this fiasco was prepared not by the Chief of the General Staff but by the HQ and Staff of the Leningrad Military District: an indication of the fact that the Red Army expected a walk-over.

After changes in the Soviet command—General S. K. Timoshenko was appointed Commander-in-Chief of Soviet forces on the Finnish front—and this time according to a plan prepared by the General Staff, the Red Army, now massively reinforced, opened a fresh offensive on 11 February 1940. After further fierce fighting, the Finns bowed to the inevitable. The war was brought to an end on 11 March by the Finnish Prime Minister, Rysto Riti, accepting a treaty that imposed far more onerous conditions* on his country than those that had been demanded by the Soviet Government in November 1939. Strategically, the Soviet aim—the protection of the country's northern flank at highly sensitive points including Leningrad—was successfully achieved. But the price paid was heavy: the loss of thousands of Soviet soldiers and the public demonstration of the Red Army's deficiencies (it was its performance in this campaign,[12] undertaken by deliberate choice, rather than Zhukov's victory over the Japanese at Khalkhin Gol six months earlier, which left a lasting impression on most foreign observers). Moreover, the outcome of the Winter War had made virtually certain that, in the event of a future war between the Soviet Union and Germany, the Finns would be counted among the Germans' most reliable allies.

---

*In effect, a return to the frontier between Russia and Sweden in the eighteenth century. The Finns lost Viipuri, their second largest city; the Rybachi peninsula (above Petsamo); the Karelian isthmus; and the port of Hanko.

Norway

Meanwhile, the Winter War had important repercussions in London and Paris. Within a month of the outbreak of the Second World War both sides had begun, neither of them at first very seriously, to turn their attention towards Norway. The strategic importance of this country for the German war effort lay in the fact that, in winter, when the route southwards from the port of Lulea through the Gulf of Bothnia was frozen, the only route for supplies of Swedish iron ore (which then accounted for three quarters of Germany's consumption of ore) was down the west coast of Norway, by rail from the port of Narvik. For Britain, the only way of stopping these supplies from travelling during the winter months was to use its sea power: to mine the Norwegian "Leads" (as the territorial waters along the country's west coast were called) and to dominate Narvik. For Germany, the only way to forestall such an operation was to use the power of its army: to occupy Norway. And if German bases could be secured in Norway, the exercise of the British naval blockade of northern waters would be rendered much more difficult, being pushed back from the line between Shetland and northern Norway to the line Shetland–Faroes–Iceland.

For a time nothing happened either in London or in Berlin, but the outbreak of the Winter War in Finland gave a new twist to deliberations in both capitals. Finnish resistance was applauded throughout the democratic world. Even the League of Nations, in limbo since its failure to deal with Japan, Italy or Germany, summoned up a vote for the expulsion of the Soviet Union. On 5 February 1940 the Allied Supreme War Council decided in Paris on a plan to prepare an expeditionary force to be sent to Finland, via Narvik and Lulea, thus intending at a single stroke both to help the Finns and to cut off from Germany the Norwegian supply route for iron ore. Although this Anglo–French decision looked almost like common sense by comparison with the French Government's initial plan to bomb Soviet oil fields at Baku, it never squarely addressed the problem of Norwegian and Swedish neutrality, which it was Alled policy to respect. The hope—it can hardly be called a plan—was that British mine-laying in the Leads would evoke a German military reaction, to preempt which Allied troops could then be landed, in anticipation of a German attack, in order to assist both the Norwegians and the Finns. But it was never made clear how the Third Reich could be challenged, let alone defeated, by launching an attack on the Soviet Union first. Meanwhile Hitler, untroubled by considerations of Scandinavian neutrality, had already instructed an inter-service staff to plan the invasion both of Norway and of Denmark; and he appointed the commander of the operation on 20 February 1940.[13]

The Finnish decision to give way to Soviet demands in March removed the original basis for the Anglo–French decision of 5 February. But discussion of Scandinavian operations dithered onwards between the two capitals, in a manner that made the planning of the Gallipoli campaign, a quarter of a century earlier, a model of professional competence by comparison. In the end, the Leads were mined by four British destroyers at first light on 8 April, off the entrance to the fiord leading into the port of Narvik. (But for an eleventh-hour delay, the Royal Navy would have begun its mining operation three days earlier.) On the afternoon of the same day German warships were sighted moving northwards off the Norwegian coast. The German campaign was well planned and swiftly executed; it was also helped by good German cryptography and by bad British intelligence.* Denmark was occupied without resistance and the principal ports of Norway captured at a stroke, including Narvik, which was occupied by a force of some six thousand men.

In the Norwegian campaign that followed, Anglo–French forces, which attempted to oust the invaders, suffered from the classic sequence of order, counter-order and disorder. This even included, in its early

---

*So bad was it that, on the evening of the 7th, the fleet sailed out of the naval base at Scapa Flow in the wrong direction, ignoring the one sound piece of intelligence received (from the Copenhagen Embassy), with the result that the forces that should have prevented the German landings were on the wrong side of the North Sea the following day.[14]

stage, a quarrel between the British admiral and the British general off Narvik, the former eager to attack, the latter (rightly) refusing to do so. Narvik itself was finally captured by the Allies on 28 May, but evacuated ten days later; while the attempt to capture Trondheim was a total failure. Churchill, the principal advocate of mining the Leads and the British Cabinet Minister chiefly responsible for the direction of the Norwegian operations (which was at first exercised entirely from London), admitted in his memoirs that the British had been "completely outwitted" on their own doorstep in this "ramshackle" campaign.[15]

Of the principal results of the Norwegian campaign, the immediate consequence was entirely favourable for Germany. The Norwegian iron ore route was secured; the line of the British naval blockade was thrust far to the north-west; and thus the double German strategic arm was attained in full. Each of the other results was—in its own way— critical, and one of them was paradoxical as well. First, although the German fleet was boldly deployed in the Norwegian campaign, the losses suffered and the damage incurred were on such a scale that, when it came to mounting Operation *Sealion*—the invasion of Britain—at the end of June, its effective strength had been reduced for the time being to seven surface ships.[16] Secondly, it was not Churchill but Chamberlain who was brought down in the House of Commons by the misconduct of the Norwegian campaign.[17]

Churchill

Throughout the months of the Phoney War the future leaders of the Grand Alliance—each of them still operating in his separate compartment—scarcely interacted with one another at all. Roosevelt remained a detached observer of the darkening scene; Stalin's primary international relationship was now with Hitler; while Churchill, First Lord of the Admiralty and a member of the War Cabinet, but not an *ex officio* member[18] of the Anglo-French Supreme War Council, strove both to extract what encouragement he could from the course of events on the continent of Europe and to stir his colleagues from their perilous inertia—neither with much success. The gas-masks once distributed and the evacuation from the cities of about a million and a half primary schoolchildren and their mothers once accomplished, life in Britain resumed the even tenor of its way. Until night fell with the accompanying blackout, it was hard to realise in the autumn of 1939 and the spring of 1940 that this was a country at war. At the prime ministerial country residence, Chequers, the only telephone was in the butler's pantry. Chamberlain disliked being disturbed at weekends or even at Downing Street after dinner.[19]

Eighteen months before the Phoney War began (as will be recalled from Chapter 4), the Soviet Ambassador in London had prophesied that Churchill would come to power "when the critical moment in England's fortunes arrives." Maisky was proved right when the crisis did arrive, in May 1940. He was also right in regarding the members of Chamberlain's Cabinet in 1938 as "colourless mediocrities"—the only major exception being Chamberlain himself. (When he became Prime Minister, Chamberlain's qualities—integrity, firmness and determination—were at first welcomed in most of Whitehall as a refreshing change from the faltering leadership of his two predecessors; and in Cabinet he ran a tight ship right up to the end, even though its course was set straight for the rocks.) The part of Maisky's forecast that requires an important qualification, in the light of what happened in London in 1939–40, in his belief that, once admitted to the Cabinet, Churchill would "crush all his colleagues, especially in the event of a crisis." This he did not do, either when he first re-entered the Cabinet in September 1939, or when he finally became Prime Minister the following May. Throughout the months of the Phoney War Churchill was a loyal colleague to Chamberlain; when Chamberlain died in November 1940, Churchill paid a moving tribute to him in the House of Commons; and he was a pall-bearer at his funeral. What he could not restrain himself from doing from the moment he entered the government, however, was to bombard his colleagues with memoranda on various aspects of the conduct of the war.[20] At the age of sixty-five, Churchill's ideas bubbled and overflowed as swiftly as they had when he had last sat in the Admiralty and in the War Cabinet a quarter of a century earlier.

All that Churchill asked, he once observed of himself, was the compliance of others with his wishes, "after reasonable discussion."[21] Such were his energy, his power of persuasion and his method of working far into the night—a capacity which he owed to his habit of an afternoon sleep—that what he needed above all in wartime was a military staff of exceptional calibre and stamina. Only in this way could his ideas be assessed in depth and convincing proof be offered to him whenever a proposal that he was advocating at the time was either unworkable or disadvantageous. A highly effective military machine would eventually be assembled round Churchill after he had become both Prime Minister and Minister of Defence; but in 1939 this did not yet exist. Even in 1940 it took some time to shake down. For the first seven months of the war, the Ministry of Co-ordination of Defence, which had originally been conceived as essentially a peacetime[22] function, still existed. When the post was abolished in April 1940, Churchill, as the senior Service Minister, became successively Chairman of the Cabinet's Military Co-ordination Committee and then the Prime Minister's deputy in that Committee. But, as he pointed out to Chamberlain at the time,[23] this meant responsibility without power. Nevertheless, in the midst of the bureaucratic muddle in Whitehall exposed by the Norwegian campaign, one of Churchill's most valuable wartime relationships began: on 1 May Major-General Hastings Ismay was appointed senior staff officer in charge of the central staff of the War Cabinet and "placed at the disposal of the First Lord."[24]

During the period of the Phoney War, the quality of the output of Churchill's fertile brain was uneven. For example, he had not been back at the Admiralty as First Lord for more than four days when he asked the Naval Staff to prepare a plan for forcing a passage into the Baltic—an operation which the Admiralty thwarted by delaying tactics—and in November he first suggested feeding large numbers of floating mines into the Rhine—a proposal accepted by the French Government only after Paul Reynaud had become Prime Minister, by which time it was too late. On the other hand, his proposal to repeat the 1918 operation of laying a minefield in Norwegian territorial waters, with the object of preventing the transportation of Swedish iron ore to Germany in the winter months from the port of Narvik, which Churchill rapidly identified as a strategically key point, was of a different order. First mooted in Cabinet by Churchill as early as 19 September 1939, and repeatedly discussed in London and Paris thereafter, it did not receive final approval until 3 April 1940, when—as we have already seen—the operation was forestalled by the German invasion of Norway. Churchill's part in the conduct of the Norwegian campaign, once the German invasion had begun, was not his finest hour; but it is hard to disagree with the overall verdict offered in his memoirs:

> *He who will not when he may,*
> *When he will, he shall have Nay.*[25]

Churchill's responsibility for naval affairs and his increasing attention to the grand strategy of the war did not prevent him from thinking, with an eye on the future, about the British relationship both with Roosevelt and Stalin. Neither prospered during these first months. As Churchill later recalled, writing to President Eisenhower one year before the publication of the final volume of his history of the Second World War:

> I am most anxious that nothing should be published which might seem to others to threaten our current relations in our public duties or impair the sympathy and understanding which exist between our two countries. I have therefore gone over the book again in the last few months and have taken great pains to ensure that it contains nothing which might imply that there was in those days any controversy or lack of confidence between us.[26]

Whatever amendments Churchill may have made to his memoirs, his laconic summary of the state of Anglo-American relations during the Phoney War is objective and it was, therefore, presumably left untouched: "The United States was cooler than in any other period. I persevered in my correspondence with the President, but with little response."[27] There is now abundant archival evidence of the mistrust at this time between London and Washington, which was not immediately dissipated even during the early months of Churchill's premiership; and on the eastern side of the Atlantic it was summed up by a British quip that those who lived in White Houses should not throw stones.[28]

Churchill's assessment of the Soviet role in the partition of Poland was given in his first broadcast of the war, on 1 October 1939:

> Russia has pursued a cold policy of self-interest. We could have wished that the Russian armies should be standing on their present line as the friends and allies of Poland instead of as invaders. But that the Russian armies should stand on this line, was clearly necessary for the safety of Russia against the Nazi menace. At any rate, the line is there, and an eastern front has been created which Nazi Germany does not dare assail . . .
>
> I cannot forecast to you the action of Russia. It is a riddle wrapped in a mystery inside an enigma; but perhaps there is a key. That key is Russian national interest. It cannot be in accordance with the interest or the safety of Russia that Germany should plant itself upon the shores of the Black Sea, or that it should overrun the Balkan States and subjugate the Slavonic peoples of south-eastern Europe. That would be contrary to the historic life-interests of Russia.[29]

Churchill's concern for these Soviet "life-interests" across the Baltic was less clear than it was in relation to the Black Sea. As a participant, albeit a silent one, at the critical meeting of the Supreme Allied War Council on 5 February 1940, and still more as a member of the British War Cabinet, Churchill bore his share of responsibility for the Cloud-Cuckoo-Land strategy that was the Anglo-French response to the Winter War: a responsibility that he fully accepted in Parliament at the time and afterwards acknowledged in his memoirs. Whereas his initial reaction to the Soviet pressure put on Finland in 1939 was that it was not in the British interest to oppose Soviet claims for bases in the

Baltic, he later changed his mind; and at the end of March 1940 the agenda of the Supreme Allied War Council even included an item entitled "The case for and against going to war with Russia";[30] but from first to last the main strategic prize for Churchill was the port of Narvik, whose importance to the Germans is well attested by the lengths to which they went to forestall British action there.

As the minister primarily answerable to Parliament for the failure of the Norwegian campaign as a whole, and in particular for British naval losses, which—like the German Navy's—were heavy, it was Churchill who made the concluding speech on the government's behalf, on 8 May, the second day of a highly charged debate in the House of Commons, held at the Opposition's request.* By an unhappy coincidence, a month before this debate Chamberlain had claimed, in a speech delivered to a Conservative Party gathering in London, that "Hitler missed the bus."[31] These words were fresh in everyone's minds, because they had been reported on every newspaper placard in London on the day of his speech, and they were now jeeringly quoted back at him by members of Parliament. In the debate he went on to compound his error: in accepting the Opposition's challenge to a vote—in effect, though not formally, a vote of censure—he appealed to his "friends" to support him. In spite of the drama, the boredom of listening to a speech by Hoare (now Secretary of State for Air) in the afternoon drove most of them out of the chamber in search of tea. When Lloyd George's turn came to speak, however, they flooded back. The former Prime Minister's intervention was brief but devastating. He swept aside Churchill's acceptance of responsibility for everything that the Admiralty had done, with a warning that Churchill should not allow himself to be converted into "an air-raid shelter" for his colleagues. And he ended with these words:

> He [Chamberlain] has appealed for sacrifice . . . I say solemnly
> that the Prime Minister should give an example of sacrifice, be-

---

*No members of the Opposition—Labour and Liberal—parties joined the government when Chamberlain re-formed it in September 1939.

cause there is nothing which can contribute more to victory in this war than that he should sacrifice the seals of office.

Roger Keyes, a member of Parliament who was a First World War hero, wearing the uniform of an Admiral of the Fleet, lambasted the Admiralty. Leopold Amery quoted from Oliver Cromwell: "You have sat too long here for any good you have been doing. Depart, I say, and let us have done with you. In the name of God, go!"[32] When the House divided, the ranks of the Conservative Party phalanx broke at last. The government's majority, usually around the 240 mark in this Parliament, fell to 81.

Although not a formal defeat, this vote was a stinging rebuff. Yet Chamberlain did not give up. He tried to conciliate the Conservative rebels, about a hundred of whom had either voted against the government or abstained from voting on the previous day; he invited Labour Party leaders to join his government; and, failing all else, it was still open to him to advise the King to invite Halifax, who now briefly emerged as the Conservative Party's favourite son, to form a new government. At an historic meeting at 10 Downing Street on 9 May, Chamberlain conferred with Churchill, Halifax and the Conservative Chief Whip. When Chamberlain asked whether he would be willing to serve under Halifax, Churchill was, for once in his sixty-five years, silent. When Halifax broke the silence, saying that it would be difficult for a peer to be Prime Minister "in such a war as this,"* the die was effectively cast, although Chamberlain did not resign until the afternoon of 10 May, when he finally learned that Labour was prepared to serve only under a new Prime Minster. At six o'clock that evening Churchill was summoned to the Palace. Four hours later Churchill sent the King a list of the five members of his War Cabinet. By that time the Phoney War was already over: the Battle of France had begun.[33]

---

*An understatement. By 1939 it was already thirty-eight years since a British Prime Minister had sat in the House of Lords.

Stalin

As the year 1939 drew to a close, Hitler and Stalin exchanged fulsome greetings. The initial fiasco in Finland apart, Stalin had, in quick succession, taught the Japanese Army a sharp lesson, avoided Soviet involvement in the war between Germany and the western Allies, and secured Hitler's agreement to his recovery of the western territories of the Russian Empire that had been lost in the wake of the October Revolution and the Versailles settlement. The size of the Soviet garrisons installed in the Baltic States and Soviet insistence on recovering from Finland what had been conceded twenty years earlier both showed clearly which was the potential invader against whom Stalin was seeking to protect his country—Germany. But for the time being he, like almost everybody else, assumed that a long campaign in the West would keep Hitler's hands full.

It will be recalled that it was on Stalin's insistence that the German-Soviet Non-Aggression Pact of August 1939 was accompanied by the Secret Protocol, which was to serve as the grand design for the redrawing of the map of Central and Eastern Europe; the former would not have been signed in Moscow without the latter. It was also Stalin who took the initiative in proposing the major change in the provisions of the Protocol, which added Lithuania to the Soviet sphere of interest in the Baltic and effectively led to Poland's disappearance from the map altogether. Whereas Article 2 of the Protocol had left open the question whether or not the "maintenance of an independent Polish State" was "desirable" for both parties to the August agreement, on the evening of 25 September—only three days after the river line had been publicly announced[34] as the line of demarcation between the German and Soviet armies in Poland—the German Ambassador, Schulenburg, was summoned to the Kremlin. Stalin stated:

> In the final settlement of the Polish question anything that in the
> future might create friction between Germany and the Soviet
> Union must be avoided. From this point of view, he considered it
> wrong to leave an independent residual Poland. He proposed the

following: From the territory to the east of the demarcation line, all the Province of Lublin and that portion of the Province of Warsaw which extends to the Bug should be added to our share. In return we should waive our claim to Lithuania.[35]

This statement by Stalin did not quite come from a clear blue sky; as early as 20 September, Molotov had already hinted to Schulenberg that Stalin had changed his mind and was no longer inclined "to permit the existence of a residual Poland,"[36] although the Lithuanian exchange was not mentioned on that occasion. But when—on his second visit to Moscow—Ribbentrop arrived in the Kremlin at ten o'clock on the evening of 27 September, Stalin amicably but firmly left him in no doubt that this was his last word on the matter. (Just how firm Stalin could be was already clear to Ribbentrop from the Soviet response in mid-September to the strong objection that the German Government then raised to public mention by the Soviet Government of "the threat to Ukrainian and White Russian populations by Germany" as a ground for the Soviet occupation of eastern Poland—precisely the motivation that was offered by Molotov on 17 September in his broadcast explaining the Soviet invasion.)[37] Thus, when the final sesssion of this round of Soviet-German negotiations opened in the Kremlin at midnight, on 28 September, Ribbentrop received telephonic instructions from Hitler—a call that he took on Molotov's telephone—to give way.

To the Frontier and Friendship Treaty, signed in the early hours of the 28th, was appended yet another supplementary Protocol, delineating in detail the German-Soviet frontier "in the territory of the former Polish state." The map accompanying this treaty bears Stalin's signature as well as Ribbentrop's.[38] This last-minute bargain was reached at the high-water mark of German-Soviet collaboration: a joint declaration[39] signed in Moscow on 28 September by the foreign ministers of the two countries, expressing their conviction that "it would serve the interest of all peoples to put an end to the state of war existing at present between Germany . . . and England and France," and adding that if the war continued, this "would demonstrate the fact that England and

France are responsible for the continuation," in which case the German and Soviet governments would "engage in mutual consultations with regard to necessary measures." Moreover, a Secret Additional Protocol to the treaty consisted of two sinister sentences:

> Both parties will tolerate in their territories no Polish agitation which affects the territories of the other party. They will suppress in their territories all beginnings of such agitation and inform each other concerning suitable measures for this purpose.[40]

They did indeed. Although detailed evidence of the collaboration between the Gestapo and the NKVD that followed this agreement is hard to come by, the two Secret Police services must have conferred together. The probability is that they met at Zakopane (south of Kraków) in order to co-ordinate their policies in what had once been Poland.[41] Certainly they carried out a grim two-way traffic in political prisoners across the partition line.

Stalin also took a hand in the subsequent negotiations with the Baltic States and with Passikivi. In these he showed, by comparison with Molotov, a certain degree of flexibility. The initial Soviet demands presented to the Finns in 1939, moreover, were not unreasonable, measured against the Soviet need to protect the approaches to Kronstadt and Leningrad. The Finnish Government's refusal of these demands must be seen against the background partly of its hope that the worldwide sympathy for Finland, which even included Italy, would be translated into support; and partly of the Finnish assessment of what was by then happening on the ground in Poland. For this no knowledge of the agreements secretly concluded between the Soviet Union and Germany was needed; events spoke for themselves. Effective support for Finland proved to be minimal from all quarters. For the future, therefore, the Finns could look only to Germany.

In Moscow, to what extent Stalin, now turned sixty, learned the military lessons of the Winter War is not clear. According to Khrushchev, he had a blazing row with his Defence Minister. In the course of this quarrel Voroshilov picked up a dish with a roast sucking pig on it and smashed it on the table.[42] In May 1940 Timoshenko, promoted to the rank of marshal, took Voroshilov's place as Defence Minister*—a logical move—but what the *genshtabisty,* the members of the Soviet General Staff, found "incomprehensible"[43] was Stalin's subsequent decision to remove their chief, Shaposhnikov, from his post, although he too received a Marshal's baton (Stalin held Shaposhnikov, an ex-Tsarist officer, in high regard. He was the only officer whom Stalin allowed to smoke in his office. He always addressed him by his name and patronymic; and after the outbreak of war in 1941 he brought him back as Chief of the General Staff.) Timoshenko did institute some reforms. He also secured the release from prison camps of many officers, including one who would win fame in the Second World War.[44] But in the Red Army, as in most other armies (except the German), the general reaction to the Finnish Army's performance in the Winter War was that the power of the defensive had been proved once again.

Stalin's other preoccupation in the early weeks of 1940 was with the terms of the trade agreement to be signed with Germany. The exchange of Soviet raw materials for German industrial goods was an essential component of the German–Soviet deal concluded in August 1939. The questions now to be resolved were: how many of the former and what kind of the latter? It soon became apparent that the chief Soviet interest was in obtaining military supplies—so much so that in March 1940 Hitler instructed his own armed forces to take second place in the queue for delivery of military equipment. This was a measure of the importance in his mind both of Soviet raw materials, notably oil, grain and iron ore, and of the use of the Trans-Siberian Railway for the shipment to Germany of goods from the Far East, but perhaps above all of Soviet acquiescence while he attacked in the West. Although Molotov and Anastasas Mikoyan were the principal negotiators on the Soviet side, Stalin personally checked every detail of the trade agreement signed in Moscow on 11 February 1940, which—among other items

---

*Voroshilov, however, remained a member of the Politburo and Deputy Chairman of the Defence Committee. A survivor, he lived until 1970.

on the list—gave the Germans the promise of a million tons of grain and 900,000 tons of oil, and the Russians the hull of a German cruiser (to be completed in Leningrad shipyards), as well as drawings of the battleship *Bismarck* and of several modern types of aircraft.

One further Soviet territorial claim, included in the August Protocol, remained to be satisfied: in Romania. The relevant Article 3 of the Secret Protocol read: "With regard to South-Eastern Europe, the Soviet side emphasises its interest in Bessarabia. The German side declares complete political *désinteréssement* [disinterestedness] in these territories." The wording of these two sentences reflected the fact that, on the one hand, the north-eastern province of Bessarabia had formed part of the Russian Empire; on the other, Romanian oil was vital to Germany. On this unresolved question of Bessarabia, whose annexation had never been recognized by the Soviet Union, Molotov put down a public marker in his report to the Supreme Soviet on 29 March 1940, reminding Romania in the process that it was the only one of the Soviet Union's neighbours with whom the Soviet Union had no Non-Aggression Pact. The separate ways in which the Soviet and German governments solved the Romanian problem later in the year would become the first major bone of contention in the Soviet-German *rapprochement.*

Roosevelt

With one tremendous exception, nothing that Roosevelt did during the months of the Phoney War had any effect of lasting international significance. It was not only that the public opinion polls in September 1939 carried a clear warning that any show of willingness by the White House to assist the Allies at the risk of American involvement in the war would bring a backlash in the debate on revision of the Neutrality Act. The outbreak of war found Roosevelt within nine months of taking perhaps the most difficult domestic political decision of his life: whether or not to break the unwritten law and present himself as presidential candidate for a third term, in the summer of 1940. In these circumstances he moved with extreme caution. He issued the proclamation of neutrality that the Neutrality Act of 1937 required; he assured the American people in categorical terms that the nation would remain a neutral nation, although he added that he could not ask that every American should remain "neutral in thought as well."[45] At the same time he convened a special session of Congress, which he asked to repeal the embargo provisions of the existing neutrality legislation.

White House influence exerted behind the scenes in favour of revision had to be applied with the greatest circumspection. By the end of October Congress approved the revision of the Neutrality Law. Henceforward, arms could be supplied to belligerents on a cash-and-carry basis. Because of British naval superiority, this revision favoured the Allies. In practice, however, its initial results were not as great as might have been expected. At first the Allies did not place very large military orders in the United States—the flood of demand began only in 1940—and American legislation in effect prevented arms supplied from the United States from being carried to Europe in America shipping.[46] Nor were the dozen messages exchanged across the Atlantic between the President and the Naval Person of any great moment; only after the first long message from the Former Naval Person (as Churchill signed himself in his correspondence with the President after becoming Prime Minister) had been received at the White House early in the afternoon of 15 May would a new transatlantic relationship begin to evolve—and even then only very slowly indeed.[47]

In his dealings with the Soviet Government, Roosevelt also trod carefully. He refrained from designating the Soviet Union as a belligerent on 17 September 1939, under the terms of the Neutrality Law, and no protests were made to the Soviet Government about its treatment of the three Baltic States. Finland was another matter. Against Hull's advice, Roosevelt first sent a deprecatory telegram to the President of the Supreme Soviet about Soviet demands on Finland and later he made an offer of the United States' good offices in settling the dispute. Both received a dusty answer from Moscow. In spite of the depth of public feeling in the United States in favour of the Finnish cause, there was a wide gap between utterance and action: Congress finally approved a $20 million credit for non-military supplies to Finland after a prolonged debate, by which time the Winter War was almost over.

Confronted with apocalyptic reports in the autumn of 1939 from his ambassadors in London and Paris, and with considerations of domestic politics at least as much as of foreign policy in mind, at the beginning of 1940 (a moment when Roosevelt's fortunes had reached a low ebb) Welles was sent by the President on a peace mission to Rome, Berlin, Paris and London, in that order. The exact purpose of this mission is still a matter of debate. Welles' instructions were discreet, but they certainly focused on Mussolini, and they also included permission to revive the President's ill-fated proposal of April 1939.[48] Welles drew a predictable blank, reporting on his return to Washington at the end of March that there was not the slightest chance of any successful negotiations. By the spring of 1940 events in Europe were beginning to provide substance for Roosevelt's declaration, in the course of his State of the Union message on 3 January, that it was "not good for the ultimate health of ostriches to bury their heds in the sand."[49]

There was very little that any President could have done to persuade American ostriches to look up at what was coming. It was at the outset of the Second World War, however, that Roosevelt took a secret initiative that would ultimately have a profound effect not only on the outcome of the war but on the whole development of post-war history. Six months before the outbreak of war, the great Danish physicist Niels Bohr had published, in the *Physical Review,* an authoritative account of the recent discovery of nuclear fission. In August 1939 Albert Einstein signed a letter to Roosevelt. This was not sent to the President at once, but read out to him (together with an accompanying memorandum by the Hungarian physicist Leo Szilard) on 11 October by Alexander Sachs, an economist who combined a personal fascination with physics and easy access to the White House. Einstein's letter described "this new phenomenon" as such that "extremely powerful bombs of a new type may be constructed." Roosevelt's immediate response was that "this requires action." An advisory committee on uranium was set up. It achieved little, and another two years would pass before the decisive moves forward were made. Nonetheless it was from this modest beginning that a momentous undertaking afterwards developed: the Manhattan Project.[50]

7

CHURCHILL ALONE,

1940

How the British people held the fort alone till
those who hitherto had been half blind were
half ready.

*—Words chosen by Winston Churchill as the theme of
Volume II of his memoirs*[1]

O*n 13 May* 1940 Churchill, now Prime Minister of an all-party Coalition Government, received a unanimous vote of confidence from the House of Commons.[2] In spite of the disasters that befell Britain and its Allies in the rest of that month and in June, he became the personal symbol of their determination to continue the war. Yet, to begin with, he presided over a War Cabinet that was by no means single-minded; and he was answerable to a Parliament in which the overwhelming majority was still led by Chamberlain. From the other side of the Atlantic help did not immediately follow the change of government in London; the American writer who coined the phrase the "Common Law Alliance" for the new relationship between Britain and the United States rightly dated it as beginning only in 1941.[3] Moreover, Stalin's final attempt to preserve the Soviet-German *rap-*

prochement began in November 1940. An account of the second half of 1940 therefore becomes—Hitler apart—essentially a story of Churchill. What he had once observed of a British admiral[4] during the First World War—that he was the only Englishman who could lose the war in a single afternoon—now became true of Churchill himself.

THE MILITARY SETTING

France

The long-awaited offensive in Western Europe was the most brilliant campaign of Hitler's military career. (Thereafter none of his generals was able to question his authority—a crucial factor throughout his subsequent eastern campaign.) In 1940, Paris was captured almost as quickly as Warsaw had been in 1939. The numerical balance between the German Army and the sum of the forces facing them on land on 10 May 1940 was not greatly in the Germans' favour.[5] The French Army even had more tanks. The *Luftwaffe,* however, had air superiority, measured against the combined strength of the weak French Air Force and the RAF squadrons attached to the ten divisions of the British Expeditionary Force (BEF). In every other respect—strategic concept, tactical handling (above all, of tanks), chain of command and morale[6]—the German Army proved in this second *Blitzkrieg* campaign that it was the finest instrument of military power in Europe; and it swiftly expunged the memory of the German defeat of 1918. After only five days the French Prime Minister was convinced that the battle had already been lost.

Yet this battle, like the Polish campaign, had been lost even before it began. The essentially defensive strategy of the Supreme Allied Commander, the sixty-seven year-old General Maurice Gamelin, was based on the assessment that—the Maginot Line to the south being virtually impregnable—the main thrust of the German attack would be made through the Low Countries, into which the two best French armies (Seventh and First), with the BEF between them, moved forward as soon as the German attack had begun. This belief was fatally mistaken. Instead, the *Schwerpunkt** of the German attack hit the French immediately north of the Maginot Line, in the lightly defended Ardennes sector, where the thrust towards Sedan was led by two tank generals whose names from then on became famous in the Second World War: Heinz Guderian and Erwin Rommel. Three days after German forces had crossed the frontier, Guderian's panzer corps had already crossed the Meuse; and by 20 May his foremost troops had reached the Channel coast, beyond Abbeville—thus converting, in the language of the Germany military manuals, a break-in into a breakthrough, in the space of ten days.[7]

As we now know, the speed and extent of this breakthrough alarmed Guderian's superiors, all the way up the chain to Hitler himself, because of the long flanks that it exposed to the risk of an Allied counter-attack, particularly from the south. But it also mesmerised Gamelin, sitting at his headquarters in the fortress of Vincennes on the outskirts of Paris, until Reynaud replaced him as Commander-in-Chief by an even older General (summoned home from Syria), on the evening of 19 May.

The new Supreme Commander, General Maxime Weygand,[8] pitchforked into the fog of a war that was already beginning to take on the terrible aura of defeat,† was soon able to identify what ought to be done in theory. But in practice the Allied counter-attack hardly left the ground. After this failure Weygand issued an order of the day to the French Army urging it to hold the line of the rivers Somme and Aisne. He added the equivocal words, *"nous sommes au dernier quart d'heure."* Militarily, when the final German attack was launched on 5 June, the end of the battle for the French mainland was plainly in sight. Paris fell on 14 June. A week later, German and French plenipotentiaries met in the Forest of Compiègne, in the same railway carriage in which Mar-

---

*The nodal point of attack—literally, "centre of gravity."

†Anyone who has taken part in a prolonged retreat can recognise the fundamental difference between that fog and that aura.

shal Foch had received the German officers seeking an armistice in November 1918.

Hitler made his one and only mistake in the entire French campaign on 24 May, when he visited the headquarters of General Gerd von Rundstedt's army group, of which Guderian's corps formed a part. Instead of directing his panzer divisions northwards against the BEF[9] and the French forces now cut off on the coast—as Guderian, supported by other senior generals, was urging—he agreed with the cautious Rundstedt that his army group should regroup for the next phase of operations, directed against the bulk of the French Army, covering Paris; and he was persuaded by the arrogant Hermann Göring that the *Luftwaffe* could complete the destruction of the British and French forces on the coast. Paris was captured by the German Army for the second time in seventy years, but the BEF lived to fight another day.

The terms of the Franco-German Armistice in June 1940 were comparatively mild. While the northern half of France, including the capital, was (like the Low Countries) left under German occupation, the southern half remained under the French Government, which on 1 July installed itself at Vichy. Article 8 of the Armistice prescribed that the ships of the French fleet, which lay scattered among several ports, should be "collected in ports to be specified and there demobilised and disarmed under German or Italian supervision." Pétain's authority was acknowledged through almost the entire French Empire, although a junior and little known French general, Charles de Gaulle, flew to London, where—in a memorable appeal on 18 June—he reminded the few of his compatriots then prepared to listen to him that France had lost a battle, but had not lost the war.*

The fate of the French fleet was critical to the new calculus of naval power. The cruel dilemma now confronting the British and French governments was summed up by de Gaulle immediately after the event

---

*Words commemorated in French by a plaque on the wall of 4 Carlton Gardens, the London house where de Gaulle set up the headquarters of what became the Free French Movement: *La France a perdu une bataille. Mais elle n'a pas perdu la guerre.*

in two sentences—on the one hand, there was not a single Frenchman who had not "learned with sorrow and with anger that ships of the French Navy had been sunk by our allies"; on the other, there was "not the slightest doubt that, by principle and by necessity, the enemy would have used them one day either against Britain or against our own [the French] empire."[10] Late on the evening of 2 July 1940 the signal sent, at Churchill's request, to Vice-Admiral James Somerville at Gibraltar described what he had been ordered to do as "one of the most disagreeable and difficult tasks that a British Admiral has ever been faced with." This signal followed a detailed communication, to be transmitted to the French admiral commanding the powerful squadron at Oran, which offered three alternatives to scuttling his ships.[11] After a day spent in fruitless negotiation off Oran, just before six o'clock on the evening of 3 July the British bombardment of the French fleet in Mers-el-Kebir harbour began.

This engagement cost over a thousand French lives; three capital ships were destroyed or put out of action; and five days later the *Richelieu,* unfinished but carrying 15-inch guns, was attacked and disabled at Dakar.[12] At Alexandria—a harbour in British hands—the French fleet was, after some anxious moments, demobilised. All French vessels in Britain were taken under British control. Added to the mutual recrimination over the Dunkirk operation a month earlier, what happened at Mers-el-Kebir snapped the last link of the now fragile chain of the Anglo-French *entente.* * On 5 July the French Government broke off diplomatic relations with the British. By contrast, the U.S. Government continued to maintain diplomatic relations with Vichy, a difference between the political positions of Britain and the United States that would have significant consequences for Churchill and Roosevelt's relationship with each other later in the war, especially towards the end of 1942.

---

*Admiral Darlan's defence of his conduct, in a letter written to Churchill in December 1942, was printed in full by Churchill in his memoirs.[13]

Britain

On the same day that the Admiralty's signal was sent to Somerville, the first German directive for the planning of the invasion of Britain, Operation *Sealion,* was issued. In its final form, the plan called for an initial landing of thirteen divisions on the south-eastern coast of England, in the counties of Kent and Sussex. For this purpose a motley armada, consisting of some three thousand vessels of all kinds, was gradually assembled on the opposite coast. Given British naval superiority in the English Channel, however, a German victory had first to be won in the air. The Battle of Britain is generally regarded as lasting from mid-July until the end of October. It was primarily a battle fought by day. (The night raids that continued thereafter, though heavy and causing severe civilian casualties, could not secure the German aim of establishing air superiority over south-east England, which was essential for the success of the invasion.) And it was in August that the *Luftwaffe* began its critical attack, Operation *Adlerangriff.*

Some 620 Hurricanes and Spitfires, out of a total of 704 operational and serviceable aircraft in RAF Fighter Command, opposed a German fighter force of 980 and a bomber force of 1,480. British fighter aircraft, notably the Spitfire, were good, but the performance of the Messerschmidt 109 was in some respects better still, although it could operate over the southern outskirts of London—the furthest extent of its range—for only twenty minutes at a time. Outnumbered, Fighter Command nonetheless enjoyed some major advantages—a brilliant commander, Air Chief Marshal Hugh Dowding, the skill and the spirit of his pilots, a widely dispersed Observer Corps and a radar-based system of command and control—all against the background, as we now know, of the output of Bletchley Park (GCCS), where a brilliant group of cryptographers had—in May—succeeded in breaking the *Luftwaffe*'s cypher.[14] Both the concept and the conduct of this great air battle were Dowding's. It was he who had calculated—and during the French campaign, fought tooth and nail to maintain intact in Britain—the basic minimum number of fighter squadrons, which by August he had raised to a level just sufficient to defend the country against the main German assault. His judgement was proved right. Not an easy man, he was nonetheless revered by his pilots and respected by Churchill.*

The Battle of Britain,[16] like the Battle of Waterloo, was a close-run thing—and in its consequences no less decisive. In the first phase the *Luftwaffe* delivered co-ordinated attacks over a broad front, notably on 15 August. It suffered heavy losses: a total of 367 aircraft shot down in the ten days between 8 and 18 August.[17] In the next phase, from 24 August to 6 September, the *Luftwaffe* concentrated its attacks on the airfields of south-eastern England. But instead of persisting against these airfields—whose destruction, together with that of the radar chain, was the key to victory—the *Luftwaffe* switched to mass daylight raids on London, which began in the final phase on 7 September. On 15 September—the climax of the battle—RAF Fighter Command's reserves (above all, of experienced pilots, who numbered little more than twelve hundred at the outset of the Battle of Britain)† were exhausted; but seventy-six German aircraft were shot down on that day for the loss of thirty-two. By the end of the Battle of Britain, the *Luftwaffe* had lost 1,733 aircraft to the RAF's total of 1,163 from all three of its commands.

Towards the end of September Göring went over to night raids on cities.[18] Civilian morale held (as indeed it also did in Germany, under the impact of the vastly greater bombardment of cities carried out by the RAF and USAAF later in the war). Had the *Luftwaffe* adhered in the Battle of Britain to the *Schwerpunkt* principle, the issue might have been different. Instead, its commanders did just the opposite, and in 1940 Hitler was defeated for the first time. Two days after the major air battle of 15 September, Operation *Sealion,* first planned for that date,

---

*Nicknamed "Stuffy," he held no further command after winning this battle. Of the decoration (Grand Commander of the Order of the Bath) that he received after his victory, he wrote that he wished that he could "cut it up into a thousand pieces and distribute it to the fighter boys who are the ones who have really earned it."[15]

†Hence Churchill's tribute in the House of Commons: "never in the field of human conflict was so much owed by so many to so few."

was indefinitely postponed. On 12 October its date was formally altered to the following spring.

The Middle East

On 10 June 1940 Mussolini took the plunge and declared war on Britain and France. For Britain, this meant not only a radical change in the balance of naval power in the Mediterranean, but also the exposure of Egypt[19] to the threat of invasion by the numerically superior Italian forces in Libya. This invasion duly began on 13 September, but the Italian commander, Marshal Rodolfo Graziani, halted his advance two days later not far east of the frontier, at Sidi Barrani. Thanks to a decision taken by the British War Cabinet at the very height of the Battle of Britain to send reinforcements, including an armoured brigade, to Egypt, Graziani's troops were in turn attacked on 9 December by a British force—the equivalent of three divisions—ably commanded by General Richard O'Connor. So successful was this attack that, with General Archibald Wavell's backing, O'Connor extended it into Libyan territory; and by the time this campaign ended two months later, he had occupied the whole of Cyrenaica and destroyed some fourteen Italian divisions. The courage of the British decision to reinforce Egypt in August 1940 and the use to which O'Connor put these reinforcements in the Western Desert at the turn of the year were (as will be seen in Chapter 9) both wasted.* Instead of being exploited to its logical conclusion—the capture of Tripoli—which might well have brought the desert war to an end, O'Connor's victory marked only the beginning of a ding-dong conflict that lasted until May 1943.

During the next two years of warfare up and down the North African coast the size of the resources absorbed by these campaigns exercised a powerful influence on the pattern first of British and then of Anglo-American Grand Strategy. Many thousands of soldiers, coming

---

*Characteristically, Churchill wanted to send the reinforcements through the Mediterranean, but he was obliged to agree with the Admiralty that the slower but safer Cape route should be used instead.

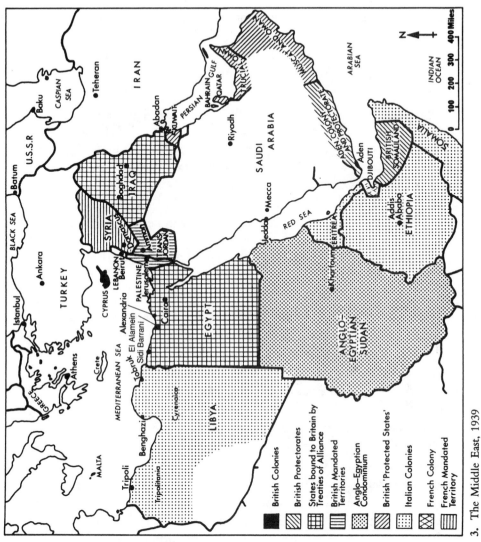

3. The Middle East, 1939

Legend:

- ■ British Colonies
- British Protectorates
- States bound to Britain by Treaties of Alliance
- British Mandated Territories
- Anglo-Egyptian Condominium
- British 'Protected States'
- Italian Colonies
- French Colony
- French Mandated Territory

from an extraordinary variety of nations—which, even before the arrival of the U.S. Army at the end of 1942, included Australia, Britain, Germany, India, Italy, France, Poland, New Zealand and South Africa—lost their lives in the Western Desert, which also proved to be the graveyard of the reputation of more than one British general. At the time when Churchill first visited Egypt, after the fall of Tobruk and the Eighth Army's retreat to El Alamein in 1942, the following story was circulating in the desert. Churchill's enquiries about the whereabouts of some officers, whom he knew personally, having received the answer, "In the bag," the Prime Minister was said to have retorted, "What is this expression that I hear—'in the bag'? Rather would I say, 'hounded into capitivity by incompetent generalship.' "[20]

Churchill, Prime Minister and Minister of Defence

In the middle of 1940 London suddenly found itself the epicentre of a geopolitical earthquake. The extent of the change of attitudes that this shock produced in Britain, by comparison with the atmosphere of the Phoney War, may be measured by a personal recollection of a small episode a few weeks before Churchill became Prime Minister. Across the table at a meal to which I had been invited by a Tory grandee—the descendant of the great Castlereagh, his family related by marriage to Churchill's—my host presented me with a copy of a book that he had written in defence of the policy of appeasement in 1938. Its Preface expressed the author's "particular gratitude to Herr Hitler, Field-Marshal Göring, Herr von Ribbentrop . . . for their repeated kindnesses and hospitality"; and its appendices contained letters of thanks for the book from, among others, Hitler. For the book's author, Charles Londonderry, neither its thesis—"a policy of friendship with Hitler and a better understanding of Germany's aims"[21]—nor the Nazi leader's reaction to it had apparently been outdated by several months of war. Although as recently as November 1935 he had been a Cabinet Minister, by 1940 he had become a faintly preposterous figure in British public life. Nevertheless, if Londonderry House and Cliveden[22]—the Astors' country house—were far from typical of British public opinion, their influence was not negligible, and the "Municheer" views that they notoriously represented did not, as this incident illustrates, change overnight after 3 September 1939. The Norwegian fiasco, followed almost immediately by the Germany invasion of France and the Low Countries, was enough to bring Churchill to power at the beginning of May 1940, but it took more than that to bring the entire British people to realise that the war on which they had embarked eight months earlier was a war of survival.

On a critical day during the time which he publicly described as Britain's "finest hour,"[23] Churchill summed up the new national mood in two short sentences. An instruction telegraphed to the British Ambassador in Washington, Philip Lothian, on 28 June, said: "Your mood should be bland and phlegmatic. No one is down-hearted here."[24] Both the qualities commended to Lothian in this telegram were needed in ample measure in face of the catastrophe that had overwhelmed most of Europe. Churchill's own response took the form of a series of inspired speeches in Parliament and on the radio, drawing on the deep consciousness of the national past to confront the present danger. These speeches not only provided a rallying cry in Britain itself, but also gradually exercised a growing influence across the Atlantic. From the U.S. Embassy in Grosvenor Square, the ambassador, a kind of honorary "Municheer," remained unconvinced of Britain's ability to survive right up to his return to the United States in the run-up to the presidential election—and indeed beyond*—by which time Kennedy's advice counted for little with either government. (His final letter of resignation to the President is dated 2 December 1940.)[25]

What did matter was the quality of the reports like those of Murrow, whether describing Churchill's performance in the House of Commons after the event, or speaking live on the steps of the church of St. Martin in the Fields, Trafalgar Square, during a night air raid. Murrow's broadcasts to CBS—delivered in a style that avoided any

---

*Kennedy was one of those who testified in Congress against the Lease-Lend Bill in 1941.

overstatement or unnecessary adjective, and always beginning with the three words, "This is . . . London"—were all the more potent because, as he himself later recorded, he had not been an anglophile at the time of his earlier visits to Britain before the war.[26]

In the first weeks after Churchill became Prime Minister, his political position was far from secure. His administration was formed with few acts of political reprisal. The Chamberlains continued to live at 10 Downing Street for another month, by Churchill's decision; he himself stayed on temporarily in the Admiralty House flat. Chamberlain, still the leader of the Conservative Party, took the office of Lord Privy Seal and retained his seat in the War Cabinet. Halifax, also still a member of the War Cabinet, stayed on at the Foreign Office, where Rab Butler[27] remained his deputy (and therefore the government's spokesman on foreign affairs in the House of Commons). Of the other principal appeasers, Simon was moved upwards, to the Woolsack in the House of Lords, and thus out of any direct contact with the direction of the war; Hoare was sent as Ambassador to Madrid, where he and Franco were well-matched interlocutors; and Wilson, Chamberlain's grey eminence for the past two years, was banished from the Prime Minister's office and relegated to the Treasury, the Department which was his natural habitat.[28]

In the War Cabinet, which now consisted of only five members, Churchill was at first uncomfortably flanked by the two architects of Munich on the one hand, and, on the other, by the two Labour Party leaders, Clement Attlee[29] and Arthur Greenwood. Later in the year this alignment was strengthened, first by the inclusion in the War Cabinet of the massive figure of Ernest Bevin, the Minister of Labour,[30] and then by fate: after Chamberlain's death[31] in November, Churchill became leader of the Conservative Party; and after Lothian died in Washington in the following month, he persuaded Halifax to transfer his daily wrestling with his convoluted conscience* to Lutyens' neo-Geor-

---

*These struggles sometimes took a bizarre form. According to a member of his Washington staff, when asked whether he had ever suffered from insomnia, Halifax said, yes, citing two examples. The

gian mansion on Massachusetts Avenue. There, after some initial gaffes, he became a respected ambassador.[33] In the summer of 1940, however, these developments were unforeseeable. Moreover, there was one still formidable political figure who, by his own choice, remained outside the government: Lloyd George. In spite of his age and his powerful intervention in the debate that brought Churchill to power, he cherished ambitions of succeeding Churchill, as a peace-making Prime Minister.[34]

These difficulties notwithstanding, Churchill succeeded in transforming the central direction of the war, almost at a stroke, by himself assuming the additional office—then new in British politics—of Minister of Defence. No new Department of State had to be formed, because the defence staff already existed: the military section of the secretariat of the War Cabinet, headed by General Ismay.* Within a fortnight, armed with this combined authority of Prime Minister and Minister of Defence, Churchill brought about a sea-change in Whitehall. Never had there "been such a rapid transformation of opinion in Whitehall and of the tempo at which business was conducted"—a testimony all the more convincing in that it came from the pen of one of his private secretaries, John Colville, who had served Chamberlain, whom he admired, in the same capacity.[35]

The pace set by Churchill—some of his minutes now flagged with the words "Action this day"—was such that not everybody could stand it. Some were unable to make the adjustment necessary to fit in with his unique temperament (Churchill could switch from tears to witicisms in a matter of minutes) and his idiosyncratic way of doing

---

first occasion was when he had to decide, as Viceroy of India, whether a death sentence should be commuted. After some wakeful hours, he decided to uphold the sentence. The second, which was a wholly sleepless night, was after John Simon had asked Halifax to call him "Jack."[32]

*The two officials on whom Churchill most depended from the outset, were Ismay and the Secretary of the War Cabinet, Edward Bridges, both of whom remained at his side throughout. The composition of the Chiefs of Staff did not assume its final form until September 1943 (when Admiral Dudley Pound resigned as First Sea Lord), but the decisive moment was when General Alan Brooke was appointed Chief of the Imperial General Staff (CIGS) at the turn of 1941–42.

business: an adjustment that was physical as well as psychological, since his closest staff and advisers often did not get to bed until the early hours of the morning.* Some of those who did relate well to his demanding personality still needed a diary as an exhaust valve for their frustrations. As for Whitehall opinion as a whole at the beginning of May 1940, it was summed up by the private secretary quoted above as "dubious of the choice [of Prime Minister] and . . . prepared to find its doubts justified," a summary that could be applied with equal force to the view of Churchill taken by the Washington Establishment at the time (Kennedy, among others, had passed on to Roosevelt the London tittle-tattle about Churchill's unorthodox way of running the Admiralty, his late nights and his use of alcohol).[37] These doubts were soon swept away in London, although in Washington they persisted for longer. Churchill drove everyone, not least himself, to the limit, however, and sometimes beyond—so much so that at one moment at the end of June his wife reminded him, in a perceptive letter, that he would not get the best results by "irascibility and rudeness."[38] The letter has to be read in its context. A month before Churchill received this advice from his wife (who at first tore up her letter and finally sent it only after several days' reflection), he had presided over the most fateful discussions held in London during the whole of the Second World War.

Formally speaking, the series of War Cabinet meetings spread over 26–28 May 1940 was prompted by consideration of an urgent proposal by the French Prime Minister for British participation in a joint approach to buy off Italy.[39] We now know, however, that the War Cabinet's prolonged debate during these three days ranged over a far wider field: in fact, the question of the possibility of a negotiated peace with Germany. At the time, the fate of the British Expeditionary Force was still uncertain; a service of Intercession and Prayer, attended by Churchill, was held in Westminster Abbey on Sunday 26 May; and in

---

*A prime example of a man for whom the personal chemistry with Churchill never worked at all was the first C–in–C, Middle East, General Wavell.[36]

the innermost councils of the British Government, the Munich syndrome recurred. As the records now available vividly show, this time the duel was fought not between Churchill and Chamberlain, but primarily between Churchill and Halifax. Churchill could look to the two Labour members of the War Cabinet for support, but—given the weakness of his personal position, at this early stage of his premiership, within the Conservative Party (still led by Chamberlain)—he had to carry Chamberlain and Halifax with him. Not only was he obliged to call in the leader of the Liberal Party[40] to attend the War Cabinet's discussions at an early stage; at the critical moment on the final day, he also took the pulse of the Cabinet as a whole.

Chamberlain veered to and fro during these three hectic days.[41] Halifax came close to resignation. Even before the War Cabinet began its deliberations, he had already told the Italian Ambassador that the British Government "would naturally be prepared to consider any proposals which might lead" to peace in Europe. Against Churchill's contention that "peace and security . . . under a German domination of Europe" could never be acceptable, Halifax argued, at the first meeting held on 26 May, that the War Cabinet "had to face the fact that it was not so much a question of imposing a defeat upon Germany but of safeguarding the independence of our Empire. . . ." At the second meeting on that day Halifax replayed the theme, familiar at the time of Munich, that Mussolini "would be anxious, if he could, to persuade Hitler to take a more reasonable attitude."[42]

On the second day the members of the War Cabinet had before them not only the French Government's original proposal (put personally to them on the 26th, when Reynaud flew to London), but also a request added "as a matter of great urgency" by the French Ambassador, on Reynaud's instructions, that the proposed joint approach to Mussolini should be given "geographical precision": that is to say, a "precise offer to Signor Mussolini of [territorial] concessions" by the two governments. Churchill, whose attitude had stiffened overnight (he had now received the Chiefs of Staff's considered reply[43] to his question whether Britain could fight on alone against Germany and probably Italy as well), pointed out that there was "a good deal of difference between making the approach ourselves and allowing one to be made by President Roosevelt ostensibly on his own initiative." A direct confrontation between Prime Minister and Foreign Secretary ensued. Halifax asked Churchill pointblank: "Suppose Herr Hitler, being anxious to end the war through knowledge of his own internal weaknesses, offered terms to France and England, would the Prime Minister be prepared to consider them?" Churchill replied that "he would not join with France in asking for terms; but if he were told what the terms offered were, he would be prepared to consider them."

Towards the end of a tense discussion on the afternoon of 28 May, the War Cabinet reached a position where Halifax was denying that anything "in his suggestion could even be remotely described as ultimate capitulation," whereas Churchill's calculation of "the chances of decent terms being offered at the present time" was "a thousand to one against." At 6:15 the War Cabinet adjourned. In the brief interval before they reconvened yet again, Churchill—never at his best as a party politician, but always a great parliamentarian—talked in his room in the House of Commons to the other (twenty-five) members of his Cabinet. Here, he "quite casually" remarked: "Of course, whatever happens at Dunkirk, we shall fight on."[44] What followed on the early evening of 28 May 1940 in Churchill's room was a personal ovation for Churchill from ministers belonging to all political parties—a display of emotion of a kind that makes his biographer's description of the scene, as "one of the most extraordinary . . . of the war," if anything an understatement.[45]

Thus fortified, on his return to the final round of War Cabinet discussions that began at seven o'clock, Churchill—now supported by Chamberlain—carried the day. To the specific question before the Cabinet—Reynaud's proposal of a joint approach to Mussolini—a robustly negative reply was unanimously agreed and sent, by telephone, to the British Embassy in Paris just before midnight. The full text of this telegram[46] now makes it clear, however, that what had really been decided was "to continue the war, if necessary for years, if necessary alone"—the words used by Churchill in his speech of 4 June 1940, which he concluded with the peroration: "We shall fight them on the beaches . . . we shall never surrender."

Yet even then the doubters were by no means convinced, as their diaries have since revealed.[47] When the possibility of Swedish mediation was in the air, Butler took a walk around St. James's Park with the Swedish Minister. On 25 June Churchill wrote an indignant letter to Halifax, describing Butler's language (of which he must have become aware through GCCS) during his stroll as "odd." Halifax replied defending his deputy, but whatever Butler said in the park—he made no record when he walked into the Foreign Office afterwards—it can hardly have been prudent; unlike Churchill, he was clearly then unaware of the cryptographic expertise of Bletchley Park.[48] Churchill was always ready to forgive errors committed, as he himself put it, "towards the enemy."[49] The reason why he pulled his punches to such an extent in the second volume of his memoirs was not only because at the time the volume was published, it was just three years since Halifax had left the Washington Embassy, but also because of the fifty- (now thirty-) year rule then governing the publication of British official records. As we can now see, it was not until the Battle of Britain had been won and a new transatlantic relationship was in the making that, fully master in his own house, Churchill could ignore the *sequelae* of Munich.

Churchill and the Fall of France

On 16 May, the day after Reynaud's first hopeless telephone call to London,* Churchill flew to Paris for the first time; there he attended a depressing meeting at the Quai d'Orsay, where files were already being burned in the garden. Churchill was "dumbfounded"[50] when Gamelin said—in reply to a direct question put to him by Churchill—that he had no reserves to face the German breakthrough at Sedan. Some semblance of a plan for a counter-attack was discussed, however; Churchill, who had left London with the War Cabinet's permission to offer the support of four additional RAF fighter squadrons, tele-

---

*To the French National Assembly Reynaud later declared: *"Seul un miracle peut sauver la France. Je crois en miracles"* ("Only a miracle can save France. I believe in miracles").

graphed recommending the despatch of six more. The Cabinet's agreement was telephoned to Paris shortly before midnight (Ismay took the call, in Hindustani); this news was then conveyed by Churchill, who drove straight to the French Prime Minister's flat, where he met Reynaud in his pyjamas.

Six days later Churchill was again in Paris, by which time Weygand had taken over from Gamelin. At the beginning of the desperate last week of May the two prime ministers decided to authorise the U.S. Government to let the Italian Government know of the British and French governments' willingness to consider at the end of the war any "reasonable" Italian claims, provided that this approach was "done on the President's own responsibility."[51] The American approach in Rome was categorically rebuffed. (Reynaud's flight to London on 26 May then led to the crucial series of War Cabinet meetings described above, at the end of which the British Government turned him down.) Meanwhile, on the ground, the Allied counter-attack finally approved by Weygand, such as it was, failed. On 27 May General John Gort, the British Commander-in-Chief, was ordered to evacuate as many men from Dunkirk as he could.

At first only a handful were expected to escape. What neither Churchill nor Gort then knew was what had been decided three days earlier during Hitler's visit to Rundstedt's headquarters. A furious air battle was fought in the skies above Dunkirk. The *Luftwaffe* was unable to fulfill Göring's assurance to Hitler. In just over a week, some 861 ships lifted a total of 338,226 men from the port of Dunkirk and the Dunkirk beaches and ferried them to Britain.* They arrived there with nothing, leaving behind most of their equipment; two thousand guns were abandoned. The great majority of the troops evacuated were British, in spite of the understanding[52] reached during Churchill's third flight to Paris, on 31 May, that the evacuation of British forces would proceed with the French, in Churchill's own words, *"bras dessus bras*

---

*This "Mosquito Armada" included, as well as warships, 372 small craft of every conceivable shape and size that were called into service from 27 May onwards.

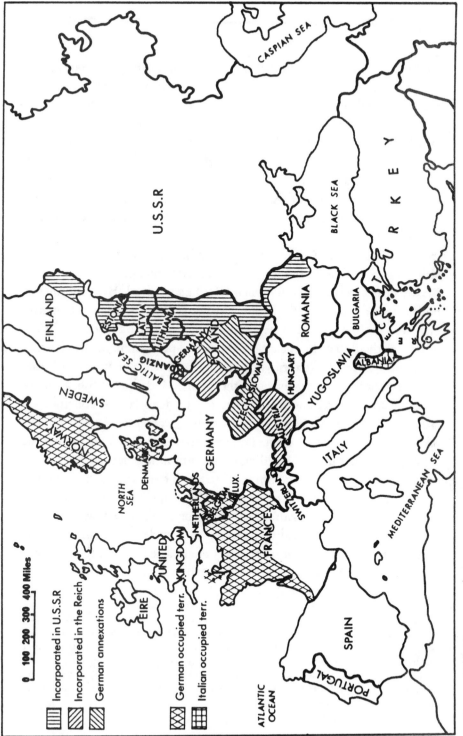

4. Europe, 1939–40

dessous" (arm-in-arm), and that the British would form the rearguard. In the event, the rearguard was largely formed by the French. In his report to Parliament on 4 June, Churchill warned the House not to "assign to this deliverance the attributes of victory."[53] By contemporary historians of the British Army Dunkirk is regarded as a humiliation.[54] The so-called "Dunkirk Spirit" afterwards developed into a part of British national mythology, however, and in this myth Dunkirk has taken on the attributes of the climax of the French campaign, whereas in reality the climax of the French tragedy was not reached for another two weeks.*

Two days before German troops marched down the Champs-Elysées, Churchill flew to France, for the fourth time, on this occasion to Briare, near Orléans, where French GHQ had moved. By this time the political stakes were of the highest order: would the French Government use its fine navy and its empire—in particular North and West Africa, with all that this meant for the Allied position in the Mediterranean and the South Atlantic—to continue the war, or would it break the obligation, assumed by both the French and the British governments less than three months earlier, not to negotiate or conclude an armistice or treaty of peace except by mutual agreement?[55] The French asked for RAF Fighter Command down to its last squadron. Churchill, resolved to keep intact Dowding's basic minimum needed for the air defence of Britain, confined himself to an undertaking to re-examine the whole question of air support; and he himself had to rest content for the time being with Admiral Darlan's oral assurance that to surrender the French fleet would be contrary to French naval traditions and honour. Except for a forlorn plan to defend a redoubt in the Brittany peninsula, nothing was agreed at the Briare meeting.

---

*True, without Dunkirk, the provision of a credible defence for Britain on land would have been far more difficult; and the fifty-five divisions which, at the outset of the war, the British Government had decided to raise, would have been an even harder target to attain had the original core of the British Army been lost in 1940. Forty-eight divisions were raised in Britain in the Second World War—fewer than in 1914–18, mainly because of the size of the RAF (over a million men), and also because of that of Anti-Aircraft Command.

It is against this sombre political background that Churchill's questionable decision to reinforce what was left of the BEF on French soil after Dunkirk, and to place it under French command on the flank of the westernmost French Army, must be assessed. Of its intended strength of three or four divisions, one—the 51st Highland—was soon cut off on the coast at St. Valéry and surrendered (to Rommel) on 12 June. That the rest of the British Army was able to leave France was in large measure due to the new force commander, General Brooke. His insistence on evacuation, on military grounds, met with equally firm opposition, on political grounds, from Churchill, to whom Brooke at one moment exclaimed, during a long telephone conversation, "You've lost one Scottish division. Do you want to lose another?" Brooke prevailed. Some 156,000 men (including 20,000 Poles who refused to surrender in France) were released from French command and evacuated in time, raising the total number of troops brought back to Britain from France in May–June to nearly half a million. This telephone conversation was the first time that these two men had ever spoken to each other—the beginning of another relationship that would later become of major importance for Churchill's conduct of the war.[56]

Churchill set foot on French soil for the last time for four years at Tours. Asked at this final meeting with Reynaud and his colleagues whether the British Government would, in the dire straits to which France had been reduced, agree to release the French Government from its solemn pledge, Churchill refused. The most that could be agreed before he flew back to London on 13 June was that the French would hold their hand until the outcome of an appeal (discussed below) made by Reynaud, with Churchill's support, to Roosevelt. By the afternoon of 16 June, the British Ambassador had been instructed to tell Reynaud that the British Government consented to the French Government asking what the German terms of an armistice for France would be, subject to one essential proviso: that, pending negotiations, the French fleet would sail at once for British harbours. Later that afternoon the last lines of the tragedy were spoken. They took a dramatic form: the draft of a Declaration of Union Between Britain and France.

This document proposed an "indissoluble union" between the countries, which would share "joint organs of defence, foreign, financial and economic policies," common citizenship and a single War Cabinet.[57] Approved by the British War Cabinet and telephoned from London to Reynaud by de Gaulle, this was followed by a telegram to Bordeaux, the temporary seat of the French Government, proposing a meeting in a cruiser off Brittany at noon on 17 June between representatives of the two governments. Churchill, accompanied by Chamberlain, the leaders of the Labour and Liberal parties and the Chiefs of Staff, was already on board the train at Waterloo Station that was to take him to Southampton when his private secretary brought him the telegram giving the first news of Reynaud's impending resignation. The aged hero of the First War defence of Verdun, Marshal Philippe Pétain,[58] succeeded Reynaud; France surrendered; although its army was in ruins, its fleet was intact; and the melancholy sequel, which took place on 3 July, has already been described.

The ideas on which the Declaration of Union was based had been widely discussed in Britain during the early months of the war. They stemmed from two interrelated concepts of the form that the political structure of the post-war world should take—the concept of a European federation, whose core would be Britain, France, and a democratic Germany; and the bilateral concept (in the words of a minute written by Orme Sargent, the Foreign Office Deputy Under-Secretary) of a "system of close and permanent co-operation between France and Great Britain, political, military and economic—as will for all intents and purposes make of the two countries a single unit in post-war Europe."[59] The supporters of the federal concept in Churchill's Cabinet included Attlee and Bevin; the bilateral concept led to the drafting of an Act of Perpetual Association between Britain and France, which had the support of Chamberlain and Halifax.[60] Thus it did not take long for Vansittart and Jean Monnet,[61] then head of the Anglo-French Co-ordinating Committee in London, to draft the Declaration of Union, nor for the War Cabinet to approve the draft on 16 June.

Although francophile, Churchill was initially sceptical about the feasibility of the proposals. Reynaud, who welcomed them, was beleaguered in Bordeaux, where he failed to persuade his colleagues to accept them. It was therefore Hitler's Germany that formed a united Europe, of a kind, in the 1940s. Despite the German occupation, however, the basic ideas underlying the draft Declaration of Union lived on: they would continue to exercise a powerful influence in continental Europe long after most people in Britain had forgotten them; and, once the war ended, they would re-emerge in the form that ultimately resulted in the signature of the Treaty of Rome in March 1957. As for Churchill, he persevered in his belief—not shared by Roosevelt—that France must be restored to its rightful place as a major European power. But the permanent association which from then on occupied the forefront of Churchill's mind, in thinking about the structure of the post-war world, was that of the English-speaking democracies.[62]

The Destroyer-Bases Deal

The French collapse exposed Britain to the danger of invasion for the first time for well over a hundred years. As Churchill at once recognized, the issue depended mainly, though not entirely, on the mastery of the air space over south-eastern England. The English Channel remained a powerful barrier to seaborne invasion, but any force that had succeeded in effecting a landing in June 1940 would have met an army either ill equipped or without any equipment at all. The fall of France and Italy's entry into the war vastly increased the Royal Navy's burden in the Mediterranean. And the Royal Navy was particularly short of destroyers.

Well before the fall of France, the loan of "forty or fifty of your older destroyers" already stood at the top of the list of requests that Churchill put to Roosevelt, in the first message that he addressed to him after becoming Prime Minister. Roosevelt's reply, though sent at once, on 16 May, was not particularly encouraging; and so far as destroyers were concerned, it was negative. In the messages that he sent to Roosevelt during the next four weeks (although these were primarily concerned with seeking American help in keeping France in the war), Churchill returned to the charge over destroyers repeatedly. This phase culminated in a long telegram sent on 15 June, which included the warning that, although he himself would "never fail to send the fleet across the Atlantic if resistance was beaten down here," the possibility of his being succeeded by "a pro-German government" could not be excluded. (A warning that he instructed Lothian to repeat—"never cease to impress on the President"—a fortnight later.) The last paragraph of the telegram to Roosevelt described the destroyer reinforcement "as a matter of life and death."[63] With one insignificant exception, a silence of six weeks between the two men followed. By the end of these six weeks Roosevelt had been nominated by the Democratic Party Convention in Chicago as presidential candidate for an unprecedented third term, the Battle of Britain had begun, and the Royal Navy had in effect removed the French Navy from the war—the first conclusive proof that Churchill's government was in deadly earnest.

Exactly four weeks after the action at Mers-el-Kebir, on the last day of July 1940, Churchill reopened his personal correspondence with Roosevelt. Once again the loan of destroyers was the kernel of his message, which included this sentence: "Mr. President, with great respect I must tell you that in the long history of the world, this is a thing to do now."[64] On 13 August Churchill received, for the first time in the war, a wholly positive response from Roosevelt. The President believed that it might be possible to "furnish to the British Government as immediate assistance at least fifty destroyers" in return for an "assurance on the part of the Prime Minister" about the future of the Royal Navy and an "agreement on the part of Great Britain that the British Government would authorise the use of Newfoundland, Bermuda, the Bahamas, Jamaica, St. Lucia, Trinidad and British Guiana as naval and air bases by the United States"[65]: an idea first conceived at the Century Association in New York.

Behind Roosevelt's decision lay not only the changes mentioned above, but also domestic developments in the United States. Whereas in the early summer Roosevelt would have been running an internal risk if he had responded strongly to Churchill, by August a reasonable margin of bi-partisan support was assured for presidential action, provided that the terms of the deal were demonstrably right. Even so, reaching agreement between the two governments was no simple matter. The legacy of transatlantic suspicion left behind by the 1930s was only gradually dissipated. There were eddies of opinion flowing back and forth both in London and in Washington. Churchill himself was one of many in London who had reservations about relying to this extent on the United States (for example, he delayed the departure to the United States of the Air Ministry's scientific adviser, Henry Tizard, until he was satisfied what Roosevelt's reply about the destroyers would be).

The haggling over the bargain ended only on 2 September. The agreements signed by the two governments on that day were explained differently in the two capitals. Roosevelt's concern was to be assured that the Royal Navy would never fall into enemy hands. Churchill, whose chief concern was the destroyers, was reluctant to add publicly to what he had already said in Parliament on 4 June (that, if Britain fell, "the British Fleet would carry on the struggle"), whatever he might have said privately to Roosevelt about the possibility of a Quisling government succeeding his own. The terms of the base leases were not settled until March 1941; and by the end of 1940 the total number of U.S. destroyers in service with the Royal Navy was nine.

Should the historical verdict be that Churchill's interpretation of the base leases in the House of Commons on 20 August 1940 was hyperbole? They meant, he said, that

> These two great organisations of the English-speaking democracies, the British Empire and the United States, will have to be somewhat mixed up together in some of their affairs for mutual and general advantage. For my own part, looking out upon the future, I do not view the process with any misgivings. I could not stop it if I wished; no one can stop it. Like the Mississippi, it just keeps rolling along. Let it roll. Let it roll on—full flood, inexorable, irresistible, benignant, to broader lands and better days.[66]

The answer comes from an unexpected source. Nearly twenty years earlier, Hitler had written these words in *Mein Kampf:*

> In consideration of the British Empire we too easily forget the Anglo-Saxon world as such. The position of England, if only because of her linguistic and cultural bond with the American Union, can be compared with no other state in Europe.[67]

In his later years Hitler disastrously underestimated the power of the United States, and his view of Roosevelt himself was absurd.[68] But the concept of the Anglo-Saxon world—or what Churchill called the English-speaking democracies—was one with which he had long been familiar. In 1940, confronted with this demonstration of the reality of the Anglo-Saxon world in the Atlantic, Hitler turned towards the Pacific. The outcome was the Tripartite Pact between Germany, Italy and Japan, negotiated in Tokyo, where Konoye was again Prime Minister, and signed on 27 September in Berlin. Simultaneously Japan established its forward base in South-East Asia, by occupying northern Indo-China, with the consent of the Vichy Government. Thus the stage began to be set for the great confrontation in the Pacific in the second half of 1941. In the words of the Japanese Foreign Minister, at a meeting held in the Emperor's presence a week before the signature of the Tripartite Pact, this agreement was a military alliance aimed at the United States. The normal Pacific station of the U.S. Navy was on the West Coast of the United States. In June 1940, however, Roosevelt, as Commander-in-Chief, took a major decision: to keep the Pacific Fleet in Hawaii.

Roosevelt

In the 1930s French society was deeply divided. When the French Government finally took the plunge—no less reluctantly than the British—in September 1939, it conducted the Phoney War under a slogan that was all the more ineffective for being untenable: *"nous vaincrons parceque nous sommes les plus forts."* Those, however, who expected the French Army to collapse as quickly and as completely as it did in 1940 were few and far between. And counted among the majority whom the fall of France took by surprise were Roosevelt and Stalin. The deductions that the two leaders drew from the French defeat were, however, diametrically opposite. For his part, Roosevelt began in August 1940 the gradual shift of policy which, by the time he broadcast his Fireside Chat to the American people at the year's end, would enable him to call the United States the great arsenal of democracy.

During the summer of 1940 Roosevelt, like Churchill—but for wholly different reasons—was vulnerable in domestic political terms. Roosevelt's caution in the matter of the destroyers needs no further emphasis. But, as well as the substance, the tone of his early messages to Churchill was also tepid: at a moment when the gravity of the German breakthrough in France was already apparent, Roosevelt's addition of half a dozen concluding words—"the best of luck to you"—to an otherwise largely negative message sent to Churchill on 16 May did not convey much personal encouragement. To begin with, Roosevelt, who did not know Churchill, could hardly be expected to ignore the doubts about him that were common currency in Whitehall in the early months of the war. Nor was it immediately clear that Britain would in practice be able to fulfil Churchill's commitment to fight on, given in the House of Commons on 4 June. In his messages to Roosevelt during this period, Churchill himself, as we have seen, was far from dismissing out of hand the possibility of his ultimate replacement by a Quisling government.

Roosevelt, however, had other grounds for caution that were at least equally compelling. In the early spring of 1940 his second term of office was still in low water. The performance of the American economy—with an unemployment level of seven to ten million—gave little sign of the surge in production that was soon to come. The whole American political landscape, moreover, was blurred by the impenetrable doubt that hung over Roosevelt's own intentions: would he run for an unprecedented third term, knowing that even within the ranks of his own party there was those who were opposed to it in principle and that, among Republicans, his own imperial style over the previous eight years had made this a burning issue? Whether he deliberately kept everyone, including potential rivals in his own party, guessing, or whether he himself was in two minds at any rate until the beginning of

July, or whether both were true, does not affect the present study. And even after the roar—"We want Roosevelt!"—began to spread among the Democratic Party delegates assembled in Chicago on the evening of 16 July, Roosevelt still had to face, in Wendell Willkie,* the most redoubtable Republican opponent that he ever encountered in his four presidential campaigns.

Thus the domestic political pressure on Roosevelt in the run-up, first to the Chicago convention and then to the presidential election itself, was heavy. Above all else, on the crucial issue of American involvement in war he could not afford to expose any flank at all. Hence his repeated refusal to be hustled by the increasingly agonised messages that he received from Reynaud, who ended by telegraphing Roosevelt on 15 June that, if France was to continue the war from overseas, the French Government must be assured that the United States would soon enter the war. This final French appeal was backed by Churchill, although he made it clear in his message that he was "not thinking in terms of an expeditionary force," but of the "tremendous moral effect" that such a decision by the U.S. Government would produce worldwide.[69]

Did Churchill really believe that the United States might enter the war at this juncture; or was he in this message to Roosevelt simply doing what he could to support Reynaud? Three weeks earlier Lothian had reported a conversation with the President, who had been "merely thinking aloud." On this occasion Roosevelt had gone so far as to tell the ambassador that, if the Royal Family had to leave Britain, he thought it would be better if the King went to Bermuda, rather than Canada, because of the adverse effect on public opinion (Latin American as well as Canadian) of "the monarchy being based on the American continent." And during this "curious" talk, as the ambassador—with justice—described it in his report, in answer to a

---

*A liberal, internationalist Republican businessman, who had called himself a Democrat until 1938, Willkie went along with the main lines of the New Deal, but attacked Roosevelt as a President seeking dictatorial power, while failing to restore the economy fully or to rearm the United States with sufficient speed.

direct question put to him by Lothian, Roosevelt had said that although the decision rested with Congress, he thought it "probable" that in the event of impending catastrophe, the United States would "be in the war on our side."[70]

In reality, the most that Roosevelt was in a position to offer in the summer of 1940 was material assistance. To give effect even to this offer, however, was far from straightforward. In spite of the great increases in defence appropriation, for which the President had at once asked on 16 May and which Congress rapidly approved, the needs of the United States' own armed services were also pressing. And at the very end of the presidential campaign, in his speech delivered in Boston on 30 October 1940, Roosevelt gave to the "mothers and fathers of America" his celebrated assurance: "I have said this before, but I shall say it again and again and again: your boys are not going to be sent into any foreign wars."[71]

Today we can see that just as the summer of 1940 was the turning point in Churchill's political career, so too it was the watershed of Roosevelt's long dominance. The controversial President now became the national Commander-in-Chief. And it was this role that he stressed in his speech accepting his party's nomination for a third presidential term. Nor did he do this only to make domestic political capital. Strategically, the immediate effect of the French collapse on the United States was that the assumptions on which its defence policy had long been based—in particular, British naval supremacy in the Atlantic— were called in question. All that the U.S. Navy then had stationed in the Atlantic was a weak squadron. The Regular Army numbered less than a quarter of a million men. Among the new dangers with which Washington defence planners had to contend was the German threat to South America. Exaggerated though we now know this threat to have been, hemispheric defence was taken with great seriousness in Washington at the time. For the United States, therefore—as for Britain— the fate of the French fleet was of cardinal importance. So too was the British Government's formal confirmation, as part of the September deal, of Churchill's statement in Parliament that the British fleet would never be allowed to fall into German hands.

In tracing the evolution of Roosevelt's foreign policy between May

and September 1940, there is one other significant signpost: the broad-
ening of his administration to include two leading members of the
Republican Party. Roosevelt's announcement, on 20 June 1940, that
Stimson would once again become Secretary of War and Frank Knox
would become Secretary of the Navy, was a shrewd domestic political
blow, timed before the Republican Party Convention. But Stimson
and Knox, as well as being senior Republicans, were also able men,
whose activist views on American involvement in the war would soon
reinforce those of Harold Ickes and Henry Morgenthau, Jr.[72] These
appointments and the destroyer-bases deal notwithstanding, Roosevelt's policy remained enigmatic until after his decisive victory over
Willkie on 5 November 1940. Even then he took his time. So did
Churchill. Having sent Roosevelt a courteous but brief message of
congratulation the day after his re-election,[73] he did not despatch the
crucial message of 1940 until 7 December, after much drafting and
re-drafting. In his letter Churchill set out at length the prospects for
1941 and Britain's principal needs, above all in the Atlantic, where he
foresaw that "the crunch of the whole war will be found." Only at the
very end of this message, which enclosed a detailed statement of shipping losses, did Churchill raise the crucial question of finance. He did
so in two paragraphs, the core of which was the simple sentence: "The
moment approaches when we shall no longer be able to pay cash for
shipping and other supplies."[74]

This letter, rightly regarded by Churchill as one of the most important that he ever wrote, was delivered to Roosevelt on board the
cruiser *Tuscaloosa* in the Caribbean. Although Roosevelt never sent a
direct reply, on his return to Washington he told the press at a news
conference held on 17 December that he wanted to get away from the
"silly, foolish old dollar sign"; and he went on to put forward his
famous analogy:

> Well, let me give you an illustration: suppose my neighbor's
> home catches on fire, and I have a length of garden hose four or
> five hundred feet away. If he can take my garden hose and con-
> nect it up with his hydrant, I may help him to put out his fire.

Now what do I do? I don't say to him before that operation, "Neighbor, my garden hose cost me $15; you have to pay me $15 for it." What is the transaction that goes on? I don't want $15—I want my garden hose back after the fire is over. All right. If it goes through the fire all right, intact, without any damage to it, he gives it back to me and thanks me very much for the use of it.[75]

Roosevelt's remarks, jauntily tossed to reporters who at once realised their importance, raised almost as many problems as they set out to solve. But he had, in his own inimitable manner, opened the way for a great debate on the draft bill which began three weeks later—Lend-Lease, the American cornerstone first of the Common Law Alliance and then of the Grand Alliance in 1941.

Stalin

By contrast, on 18 June—the day after Hitler received the former Emperor Wilhelm II's congratulations from his place of exile in Holland—the Soviet Foreign Minister summoned Schulenburg. He offered the ambassador the Soviet Government's warmest congratulations on the *Wehrmacht*'s "splendid success."[76] This was something that Molotov could not possibly have done without Stalin's approval; a week later Stalin ignored a skilfully worded message from Churchill;[77] and he went on to try to retrieve his flagging *rapprochement* with Hitler. At this point, therefore, he does not seem to have rated Churchill's chances very highly.

On the same day that Schulenburg was being congratulated in the Kremlin, Soviet troops marched into all three Baltic States, where new governments were formed and new elections held, under Soviet auspices, leading to their incorporation into the Soviet Union on 1 August 1940.* On 28 June the Red Army occupied not only Bessarabia, in

---

*With one exception—the so-called Suwalki Triangle, in south-west Lithuania—which the Soviet Union purchased from Germany on 1 January 1941 for $7.5 million, paid in gold.

accordance with the German-Soviet Protocol of 1939, but also the northern half of the province of Bukovina, of which the Protocol had made no mention. The entire province would have been taken, had it not been for German objections (*Volksdeutsche* formed a significant element in the Bukovina population). Molotov maintained that this was "the last remnant still missing from a unified Ukraine."[78] This was only the first stage in a running argument between Germany and the Soviet Union over Romania. Molotov protested at the so-called Vienna Award, as a breach of the 1939 agreement. By the terms of this award, handed down at a conference held in Vienna on 29–30 August, Germany and Italy imposed a territorial settlement on Romania—partitioning Transylvania between Hungary and Romania—whose remaining territory they then jointly guaranteed.[79] Three weeks later Romania was, in effect, occupied by German troops.

On 21 September, Molotov should have been informed that German troops were due to land in Finland the following morning (in order to cross overland to northern Norway). In the event, it seems that the German Government thought it better not to give the Soviet Government even this amount of advance warning; the text of the German-Finnish agreement was given to Molotov on 4 October, however.[80] The Finnish news was followed six days later by the signature of the Tripartite Pact in Tokyo. Although Article 5 of this agreement specifically preserved the existing German-Soviet relationship, it was hardly calculated to inspire Soviet confidence, especially since the Soviet Government was informed of it only at the very last moment.[81]

Thus by the autumn of 1940 the Soviet-German agreements signed in Moscow a year earlier were wearing thin. Hitler had already set in train the preliminary planning work for Operation *Barbarossa,* the invasion of the Soviet Union, on 31 July. Nevertheless, on 17 October the Soviet Prime Minister was handed a long letter—addressed to Stalin, signed by Ribbentrop, but probably dictated by Hitler—inviting Molotov to visit Berlin soon. The letter described the "historic mission of the four Powers—the Soviet Union, Italy, Japan and Germany—to adopt a long-range policy to direct the future development of their peoples into the right channels by delimitation of their interests

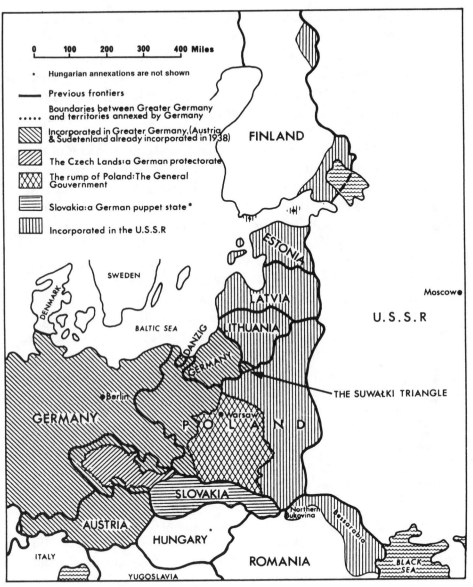

5. Central and Eastern Europe, 1939–40

for the ages."[82] Stalin was not the kind of man to be impressed by this sort of rhetoric, but it is a matter for speculation what, for example, he would have made of the detailed assessment of Britain's prospects offered to Roosevelt by Churchill in his message of 7 December 1940. The Soviet Union then having an insignificant navy, Stalin knew little about sea power, although the lessons of the air battle over Britain in the summer of 1940 could scarcely have escaped him. In the autumn of that year, as in 1939, Stalin was no doubt once again conscious of the danger of war on two fronts. As during the previous decade, moreover, he was perhaps confident of his ability to pursue two contradictory options right up to the last moment—a policy that had seemed to serve Soviet interests well in 1939. Be that as it may, five days after he had received Hitler's letter, Stalin wrote thanking him for his "confidence, as well as for the instructive analysis of recent events," and suggesting 10–12 November 1940 as the dates of Molotov's visit to Berlin.[83]

These forty-eight hours of German-Soviet negotiation in Berlin, in which Hitler took a personal part, have gone down to history chiefly because of a remark attributed to Molotov in an air-raid shelter to which he and Ribbentrop transferred their talk from the Soviet Embassy, where Molotov had been entertaining Ribbentrop to dinner. To Ribbentrop's claim that Britain was finished, Molotov retorted: "If that is so, why are we in this shelter, and whose are these bombs which fall?"* The negotiations, however, were an attempt by both governments to reconcile their differences. On the German side, this took the form of an invitation to the Soviet Union to join the Tripartite Pact. Once again there was to be a Secret Protocol, this time defining the four powers' spheres of influence, which in the Soviet case were to be centered "south of the national territory of the USSR in the direction of the Indian Ocean."[85] Molotov's response to the German proposals in Berlin was characteristic: a series of specific counter-questions about German intentions, principally in Europe.†

---

*Or so Stalin claimed, in conversation with Churchill, nearly two years later.[84]

†German guarantees were requested in respect of Finland, the Soviet Union's Black Sea frontiers and the need for a Soviet base in the Bosphorus—Dardanelles region.

Although Molotov took home with him an oral invitation from Hitler to Stalin proposing a summit meeting,[86] his visit to Berlin ended without any meeting of minds. Nevertheless, what was in Stalin's mind at the end of November 1940 is a matter of record. A fortnight later he wrote Ribbentrop a letter accepting the proposal to join the Tripartite Pact, subject only to certain conditions.[87] By anyone other than Hitler these conditions, mainly concerned with Eastern Europe, would have been interpreted as an opening bid. It is probable that this is what Stalin intended. Hitler thought otherwise. By his order, no reply was ever sent to Stalin—to the "astonishment" of the Soviet Government, expressed by Molotov to the German Ambassador on 17 January 1941.[88] Soviet writers, however, allude to a personal exchange of messages between Stalin and Hitler early in 1941: Stalin enquiring about the purpose of German troop concentrations in Poland and Hitler offering him reassurance.[89] There is no evidence of such an exchange in the German archives. Instead, on 18 December 1940, Hitler signed the most momentous military directive that he ever issued—No. 21, instructing the German armed forces to "be prepared to crush Soviet Russia in a quick campaign even before the conclusion of the war against England." Preparations were to be completed by 15 May 1941.[90]

8

THE COMMON LAW

ALLIANCE, 1941

An agreement between a man and a woman to
enter into the marriage relation without
ecclesiastical or civil ceremony, such agreement
being provable by the writings, declarations, or
conduct of the parties. In many jurisdictions it
is not recognized.

*—Webster's dictionary definition of common law
marriage, quoted by Robert Sherwood, who coined the
phrase "the Common Law Alliance"*

Hubris

The fateful year 1941 ended, as no one would have
predicted when it began, with the Grand Alliance in being. So far as
military operations were concerned, this year was for the most part
disastrous for the armed forces of the three countries which became
allies under the impact of these disasters. It had begun in comparative
calm, with the endorsement—by American, British and Canadian defence planners, during secret meetings lasting several weeks in Washington—of the fundamental principle of the Europe First strategy,
already recommended to Roosevelt by his Chief of Naval Operations,

Admiral Harold Stark, on 12 November 1940.* This principle jibed with the recommendation put forward by the British Chiefs of Staff two months earlier that, following a year of "attrition," in 1942 Britain should "re-establish a striking force on the Continent with which we can enter Germany. . . ."[1] The essential corollary of this offensive concept in Europe was that of the maintenance of a defensive strategy in the Pacific; and, taken together, the two concepts constituted the basic of the so-called *ABC-1* Plan. Neither Churchill nor Roosevelt formally endorsed this plan, but the fundamental principle—Europe first, the Pacific second—was common to both of them. Halfway through 1941, however, the war in Europe was suddenly changed— out of all recognition—by the German assault on the Soviet Union. And in the second week of December the war became a truly global conflict for the first time, as the result of two unexpected events that followed each other in quick succession: the Japanese attack on Pearl Harbor (to which the American response was to declare war on Japan) and, four days later, Hitler's declaration of war on the United States. When the Declaration of the United Nations[2] was issued in Washington on New Year's Day, 1942, every participant undertaking to co-operate with each other in the war and not to conclude a separate peace with their common enemies, its three principal signatories were Britain, the Soviet Union and the United States.

The fact that the leaders of these three countries proved capable, as early as the second half of 1942, of snatching the nucleus of ultimate victory from the jaws of initial defeat has lent colour to a bland interpretation of the history of 1941, best summed up in the words "so we had won after all!"—Churchill's verdict on what happened on 7 December. "We are all of us in the same boat with you and the people of the Empire" was Roosevelt's response. Five months earlier, during his broadcast to the Soviet people shortly after the German invasion, Stalin went out of his way to assure his listeners that "in this war of liberation we shall not be alone. In this great war we shall have true

---

*In "Plan Dog," as it was known, from its position in Paragraph D of Stark's assessment.

allies in the peoples of Europe and America."[3] All three of these state-ments in 1941 were, as we shall see, both right and wrong. The strident contention of revisionist historians—that Roosevelt virtually engi-neered the conjunction of events that, in December 1941, made Con-gress' declaration of war on Japan inevitable—is preposterous; but a far graver charge is the one quietly levelled against Roosevelt by his biographer, James Burns, who called it "The Miscalculated War"—a term that applied with even greater force to Stalin and to a lesser extent to Churchill in 1941.[4]

For the historian looking back at the triangular relationship that emerged from the events of 1941, that year is essentially one of hubris. Among the three Allied leaders, Stalin is the prime example, because he refused, right up to the last moment and in the teeth of the evidence, to believe that Hitler would run the risk of blunting the perfection of his military machine against an army which had been accurately assessed by the German General Staff as "a gigantic military instrument."[5] As the year went on, however, both Churchill and Roosevelt signally failed to realise the full extent of the danger from Japan; and in both London and Washington the Soviet power of resistance was at first underestimated. All three of them, moreover, ignored—to varying degrees—some of the plainest warning signs from intelligence that military leaders have ever received. Fortunately for them and for their peoples, the man whose hubris in 1941 was the greatest of all was Hitler. It was his decision, first, to invade the Soviet Union, and later, to declare war on the United States, that in the end brought down upon him the classical reward of all hubris—nemesis.* From this atti-tude, however, neither Churchill nor Roosevelt nor Stalin was im-mune in 1941. And it is this that supplies the common factor linking the kaleidoscopic sequence of events that transformed the course of the Second World War during the second half of 1941, in which whatever happened on one part of the globe reverberated round the rest of it.

---

*The codename *Barbarossa* was itself ominous—the nickname of the medieval Emperor Frederick I Hohenstaufen, who met a mysterious death in Asia Minor while leading the Third Crusade.

The Beginning of the Anglo-American Relationship

The phrase "Common Law Alliance," quoted in the epigraph to this chapter, describes more succinctly than any other the complex relationship that developed between Britain and the United States during this period, especially after the Lend-Lease Bill had become law. Nevertheless, information released many years after Sherwood wrote has revealed the transatlantic arguments, for example, that for the next two years bedevilled the first two items on the list of developments in the spring of 1941 with which he illustrated this relationship: the exchange of scientific (in particular, atomic) information and the pooling of secret intelligence.[6] Secondly, most common law alliances tend to become shaky under stress, and there was plenty of stress on both sides of the Atlantic in the first eleven months of 1941. In assessing transatlantic developments in 1941 in general the evolution of the Churchill-Roosevelt relationship in particular, it is important to recall how thin the texture of Anglo-American relations had been during the inter-war period.[7] (The remarkable fact that Churchill, a frequent visitor to the United States, and Roosevelt never met between the wars is only one example.) To Sherwood, therefore, writing only seven years after these events, the secret staff talks held in Washington during the opening weeks of 1941 seemed the most important element of all in the new Anglo-American relationship, although he rightly added that the conclusions reached by these staff officers bound nobody.[8] Today, with all the records of 1941 laid out before us, including the consequences of the *ABC* discussions on the war in the Pacific, the picture that they form has much more light and shade than was at first supposed.

By far the most important transatlantic events in the first half of 1941 were Harry Hopkins' visit to Britain, which lasted nearly six weeks from 9 January onwards, and the approval of Lend-Lease by the Senate on 8 March 1941. It was while Hopkins was in London that Roosevelt made one of the apparently unpremeditated[9] gestures of which he was a pastmaster. While talking in the White House to his recent electoral adversary, Willkie, on 19 January (the eve of Willkie's departure for London), Roosevelt took a sheet of his personal stationery and wrote on it, as a message for Willkie to take to Churchill, the five lines of Longfellow beginning "Sail on, O ship of state."* It was this message and Churchill's broadcast response ("What is the answer that I shall give . . . to this great man? . . . Give us the tools and we will finish the job") that hit the headlines and have—deservedly—been remembered by history.[10] But it was the long talks with Hopkins that helped to make history, laying the first solid foundation for the personal—as opposed to the political—relationship between Churchill and Roosevelt.

Born in 1890, the son of an Iowa harness-maker, Hopkins made his name as head of the Federal Emergency Relief and Civil Works Progress Administration in the New Deal years. He was appointed Secretary of Commerce in December 1938, but he was incapacitated by illness for most of the time that he held this office, which he resigned in August 1940. This was not Hopkins' first visit to Britain. In the summer of 1928 he had come to London, visiting places as different as Keats Walk in Hampstead and the East End. But until 1941, foreign affairs formed no part of his horizon. Then—suddenly—he found himself the President's "special representative," carrying not only Roosevelt's letters of introduction to all and sundry, but a personal letter to King George VI, and acting in his own words, as "a catalytic agent between these two prima donnas."[11] Almost from the start Churchill and Hopkins hit it off. Within a week of his arrival Hopkins wrote this, in manuscript,[12] to Roosevelt:

> *Churchill* is the gov't. in every sense of the word—he controls the grand strategy and often the details—labour trusts him—the army, navy, air force are behind him to a man. The politicians and upper crust pretend to like him. I cannot emphasize too strongly that he is the one and only person over here with whom you need to have a full meeting of minds.

---

*The original, framed, is at Chartwell.

Churchill wants to see you—the sooner the better—but I have told him of your problem until the bill is passed. I am convinced this meeting between you and Churchill is essential—and soon— for the battering continues and Hitler does not wait for Congress.

And, as Churchill put it in a telegram sent to Roosevelt on 28 January 1941, "Hopkins . . . has been a great comfort and encouragement to everyone he has met. One can easily see why he is so close to you."[13] For the next three years, Churchill was able to deal with Hopkins— who from mid-1940 until the autumn of 1943 worked in the White House (he lived in the Lincoln Room), as Roosevelt's *alter ego.* Churchill could do this—with good effect—not only because of Hopkins' unique position,* coupled with the fact that in April 1941 he was put in charge of Lend-Lease, but also because Churchill quickly appreciated the incisive qualities of Hopkins' mind, which prompted his witticism that if Hopkins were ever to become a member of the Upper House of the British Parliament, he should take as his title Lord Root of the Matter.

Lend-Lease

On 11 March 1941 Roosevelt signed the Lend-Lease Act into law and at once asked Congress for an appropriation of $7 billion to carry it out. (After a fortnight's debate this was approved.) Like the Marshall Plan six years later, the Lend-Lease Bill was drafted by a small group of men in Washington working at high speed. Presented to Congress on 10 January, barely three weeks after Roosevelt's "garden hose" press conference, it received resounding majorities in both Houses of Congress. But the great debate that preceded congressional approval was intense, raging up and down the whole country. Roosevelt himself

---

*Described thus by Roosevelt himself to Willkie in January 1941: ". . . some day . . . you'll learn what a lonely job this [President of the United States] is, and you'll discover the need for somebody like Harry Hopkins, who asks for nothing except to serve you."[14]

managed for most of the time to stay behind the scenes, where he was the final arbiter both of the form and of the philosophy of this vital measure, which the isolationism *Chicago Tribune* described as "a bill for the destruction of the American Republic . . . a brief for an unlimited dictatorship with power over the possessions and lives of the American people, with power to make war and alliances for ever."[15] Ranged against the isolationist America First Committee stood the nation-wide Committee to Defend America by Aiding the Allies and the New York-based interventionist Century Group. Roosevelt himself occupied the commanding middle ground of the debate by arguing that the purpose of the bill was not to lead the United States into the war, but the exact opposite: to keep his country out of it.[16] And—significantly—the title of the bill was "An Act to Promote the Defense of the United States."

The immediate results of the passage of Lend-Lease were slight—only $1 billion worth had been delivered to Britain (mostly food) by the end of the year—but as the war went on, they became immense. By 1944, Lend-Lease Aid represented 17 per cent of American war expenditure, valued in that year at $15 billion; and by that time the proportion of Lend-Lease deliveries to all countries by the United States consisting of munitions had risen to over 60 per cent. Most important of all, the war debt recrimination that had overhung transatlantic relations from 1918 onwards was avoided a quarter of a century later. Instead, the original principle of returning the garden hose was observed only as a formality. In practice, "most of the fire hose had been eaten up or shot away."[17] And by the final post-war settlement of December 1945, the slate was wiped virtually clean in both directions—over $26 billion in U.S. aid to Britain and about $6 billion in reverse Lend-Lease from Britain to the United States—even though in the parliamentary uproar over the terms of the U.S. post-war loan to Britain, the generosity of the Lend-Lease settlement was largely overlooked.[18]

Although the Act, hailed by Churchill on the following day in the House of Commons as "a monument of generous and far-seeing statesmanship," achieved its purpose, it was not quite as "unsordid" as he made out at the time.[19] Among the concessions made by Roosevelt to the bill's opponents during the congressional hearings was one announced in the Senate Foreign Relations Committee early on by the architect of the Lend-Lease legislation, Morgenthau himself, who excluded from the provisions of Lend-Lease all British orders already placed in the United States; and this was followed by an even more explicit statement by the Director of the Budget, in the House Appropriations Committee on 15 March—the day on which, as Churchill telegraphed to Halifax, "Morgenthau may have a bad time before his Committee, but Liverpool and Glasgow are having a bad time now."[20] One of the consequences was the forced sale of Courtaulds' American company, the American Viscose Corporation, for a mere $54 million.

The Lend-Lease Master Agreement, signed nearly a year later, after months of Anglo-American negotiation, contained in Article VII a significant British concession: a commitment to "the elimination of all forms of discriminatory treatment in international commerce, and to the reduction of tariffs and other trade barriers."[21] Since this clause directly affected the politically sensitive issue of British Imperial Preference, it was not easily agreed, and only after Churchill had received a long personal message from Roosevelt, who had himself to take account of his own Secretary of State's recent indictment of the Ottawa Agreements as "the greatest injury, in a commercial way, that has been inflicted on this country since I have been in public life." On the face of it, Churchill appears to have misunderstood[22] Roosevelt's assurance about the system of Imperial Preference, on a day when he was under extreme pressure (Singapore fell on 15 February). It is, however, also arguable that he simply turned a blind eye and that Churchill, who had called the preferential system agreed at Ottawa ten years earlier "Rottowa," remained a free-trader at heart.

For the management of the British economy, the most damaging condition added to Lend-Lease arose, four months after the bill became law, from the U.S. Government's insistence that Lend-Lease should not be used by British exporters in the manufacture of goods that competed with American exports. (The Latin American market was an area of particular concern.) Drafts of letters[23] not in fact sent by Roosevelt to Churchill in August 1941 show how acrimonious the dispute on this issue was. Although resolved on 10 September, by means of a unilateral statement issued by the British Government in the form of a White Paper,[24] this was an unhappy pendant to the great achievement of March 1941. U.S. pressure to keep British financial reserves down was rigorously exerted right up to the end of the war. Even as late as the Potsdam Conference in July 1945, Churchill received a memorandum from Truman alleging that British gold and foreign exchange reserves were higher than, in the U.S. Treasury view, they should have been.[25]

The Battle of the Atlantic

It will be recalled from the preceding chapter that the main thrust of Churchill's long message to Roosevelt of 7 December 1940 was his concern for the outcome of what soon came to be called the Battle of the Atlantic. The letter's enclosure gave exact figures of British, Allied, and neutral shipping lost by enemy action, week by week, from the beginning of June to the end of November 1940: a monthly average loss of 400,000 tons—in Churchill's words, "a scale about comparable to that of the worst years of the last war," which "would be fatal" were it to continue. His message offered, paragraph by paragraph, a range of solutions, including a suggestion that U.S. naval forces might "extend their sea control over the American side of the Atlantic." The final paragraph of this crucial letter expressed the belief that Roosevelt would regard it "not as an appeal for aid, but as a statement of minimum action necessary for our common purpose."[26] Once Roosevelt had launched the Lend-Lease Bill, it was tacitly agreed between the two leaders that the passage of this measure by Congress was paramount. As soon as it became law, however, the second problem remained to be solved: how to protect "the bridge of ships"[27] bringing supplies to Britain. By that time shipping losses had risen to half a million tons per month. "The Battle of the Atlantic is on," wrote *The New York Times* on 11 March 1941. On 1 April Roosevelt returned to Washington from another fishing trip in the Caribbean, but this time—unlike December 1940—without a solution for the main problem confronting both the American disciple of Alfred Mahan[28] and the British Former Naval Person.

As Roosevelt was well aware, he simply did not have enough butter to cover the bread. A two-ocean U.S. Navy had been approved in principle a year earlier, under the impact of the disasters in Europe and their effect on the world balance of naval power, but it had not yet been built. Through the spring of 1941, the drift to and fro of policy in the White House coincided with a series of British military reverses in the eastern Mediterranean and North Africa;* in particular, the unsuccessful defence of Crete in the last days of May cost the Royal Navy three battleships and an aircraft carrier damaged, three cruisers and six destroyers sunk, and six cruisers and seven destroyers damaged. Simultaneously, the most powerful battleship afloat, the *Bismarck*, accompanied by the cruiser *Prinz Eugen*, broke out from its Norwegian safe haven to raid shipping in the Atlantic. The *Bismarck* was sunk on 27 May, but not before blowing up the battle cruiser *Hood* and damaging the battleship *Prince of Wales*.

A major presidential address, delivered to the Pan American Union on the day of the sinking of the *Bismarck*, received widespread domestic approval. It declared an "unlimited emergency," but announced nothing more concrete to help the Battle of the Atlantic than "all additional measures necessary to deliver the goods" to Britain.[29] Two days later, however, Roosevelt at last made a move in that direction: the suggestion, put via the British Ambassador and welcomed by Churchill on 29 May, that U.S. troops should relieve the British garrison of Iceland.[30] Equally important, between mid-May and mid-June three battleships, four light cruisers and thirteen destroyers from the U.S. Pacific Fleet passed through the Panama Canal into the Atlantic. On 7 July the U.S. task force reached Reykjavik—the first American military expedition outside the western hemisphere since the First World War. By that time Roosevelt had authorized Admiral Stark to begin planning the escort of convoys in the western Atlantic.[31]

Roosevelt's stop-go decision-making during the spring and summer of 1941—a slowness which was as agonising for the interventionist members of his own team, such as Stimson, as it was for Churchill and

---

*Discussed, in their wider strategic context, in the next chapter.

his colleagues—reflected his innate preference for keeping his options open until the last possible moment, especially since Washington's assessment of the Japanese threat fluctuated, but even more his refusal, while seeking to carry domestic political opinion with him, to be seen leading it in the direction of war. This involved what, in British eyes, seemed a strange distinction: broadly speaking, whereas a limited number of U.S. naval casualties in the Atlantic was tolerable for American public opinion in 1941, anything that could be represented as inconsistent with Roosevelt's repeated promise not to send American soldiers into a foreign war was not. Hence the unpopularity of the draft, which—because Congress had authorised it in 1940, at a dramatic moment in the war and in the midst of the presidential election campaign, for only one year—came up for renewal in the summer. On 12 August 1941, following two powerful messages to Congress from Roosevelt and in spite of his declaration of a national emergency, the House extended the Selective Service Act by just one vote—and then only for eighteen months.[32] Without this narrow victory the U.S. Army could hardly have met the challenges with which it was confronted four months later. Few episodes illustrate more clearly Roosevelt's dilemma. And 12 August was the last day of his first meeting with Churchill in the Second World War.

The Atlantic Conference, 9–12 August 1941

Like the *ABC* Staff Conversations in Washington six months earlier, the Atlantic Conference was held in the strictest secrecy. Although the U.S. Government was now, unlike 1939–40, worthily represented in London by John Gilbert Winant as Ambassador and (more important) by Averell Harriman as the President's Special Representative and "Expediter" of Lend-Lease,* Hopkins was again sent to London in

---

*Winant, a former Governor of New Hampshire, was Ambassador in London for the rest of the war. Harriman, a millionaire by birth but also a successful banker in his own right, remained in London until 1943, when he was appointed Ambassador in Moscow. Both Winant and Harriman became close friends of the Churchill family.

order to prepare the way for the conference. He arrived there in mid-July, in the fourth week of the *Barbarossa* campaign. Two weeks later, after consultation with Churchill, he suggested to Roosevelt that he should fly to the Soviet Union to confer with Stalin; Roosevelt approved; and Hopkins returned to Britain just in time to sail to Newfoundland with Churchill. Thus when Churchill and Roosevelt met at Placentia Bay, Newfoundland, they had the advantage, not originally planned, of having with them a man whom both of them trusted, hot foot from long hours of discussion with Stalin. In parenthesis, the twenty-four-hour flights to and from Archangel in a Catalina flying-boat were a test of endurance even for a man in good health. For a man of Hopkins' physical frailty they were an ordeal, described afterwards in the pilot's report as "a noteworthy example of unparalleled devotion to duty."[33]

The instructions that Roosevelt gave Hopkins on 11 July, during a long talk in the White House study on the eve of his departure for London, were characteristically minimal. Hopkins took with him to London—and showed to Churchill on his arrival there—a small map of the Atlantic torn by Roosevelt from the *National Geographic Magazine,* with a pencilled line indicating the area west of which the U.S. Navy would, in due course, take over responsibility from the Royal Navy at sea and in the air.[34] Hopkins also wrote these notes as a kind of aide-mémoire for himself:

> Economic or territorial deals—NO.
> Harriman not policy.
> No talk about war.

The second of these notes need not concern us,[35] but the first and the third, coupled with the map, reveal clearly what was uppermost in Roosevelt's mind a month before his meeting with Churchill. They also show that at that time discussion of aid to the Soviet Union was not yet high on his agenda for Placentia Bay; Hopkins' visit to Moscow altered that, with major consequences. The question of "territorial deals," however, had Soviet overtones.

On 12 July, the British and Soviet governments had concluded, in Moscow, a two-clause agreement regarding "joint actions in the war against Germany." Although this agreement committed the two governments only to what the two clauses said—"mutual help and support of every kind,"[36] and not to engage, except by mutual agreement, in anything that could conceivably lead to an armistice or peace with Germany—in Washington, suspicions of secret covenants secretly arrived at, of the kind that had abounded in the First World War, were immediately aroused. Within forty-eight hours of the signature in Moscow, Roosevelt telegraphed to Churchill about "rumors regarding trades or deals which the British Government is alleged to be making with some of the occupied nations," and suggested that Churchill might make "an overall statement . . . making it clear that no post war peace commitments as to territories, populations or economies have been given"—a statement that Roosevelt himself would "back up in very strong terms."[37] This early reminder that the State Department's[38] conscience was as active in 1941 as Wilson's had been in 1918 had no immediate effect—there were no secret clauses in the Moscow Agreement, as Eden was able to tell the House of Commons—but as soon as the British and Soviet governments reached the point of negotiating a full-scale treaty, as they did at the very end of 1941, it was a different matter.

In the run-up to the Atlantic Conference there was another area of Anglo-American disagreement which must be mentioned at this stage, even though the disagreement was resolved at the time, because its wider implications for Grand Strategy would resurface later: the Middle East. The first day of May 1941 was a particularly unhappy one for Churchill. Following the German occupation of the Greek mainland, and with Rommel then delivering his first attack on the besieged garrison of Tobruk, the New Zealand commander in Crete, General Bernard Freyberg, had telegraphed his assessment that the forces at his disposal there were "totally inadequate to meet attack envisaged."[39] Churchill travelled that night to Plymouth, where he spent the whole of 2 May inspecting the damage done to the city, which had suffered heavy air raids for five nights in the course of just over a week. From this "scene of horror and desolation"[40] he drove to Chequers, where he arrived at midnight to find a long telegram from Roosevelt, praising the Greek campaign as "a wholly justified delaying action," but adding: "if you have to withdraw further in the Eastern Mediterranean . . . in the last analysis the Naval control of the Indian Ocean and the Atlantic Ocean will in time win the war."[41] "In worse gloom" than his private secretary had ever seen him, Churchill lost no time in sending Roosevelt a forceful reply on the significance of the Middle East. Beginning with the words, "We must not be too sure that the consequences of the loss of Egypt and the Middle East would not be grave,"* Churchill ended this part of his telegram:

> I adjure you, Mr. President, not to underrate the gravity of the consequences which may follow from a middle eastern collapse; in this war every post is a winning post and how many more are we going to lose?

In the midst of his harangue Churchill inserted an appeal (unique in his 1941 correspondence with Roosevelt) for direct U.S. military intervention "as a belligerent Power."[42] Roosevelt did not reply until 10 May. When he did, he ignored the appeal for direct U.S. intervention, but he was at pains to soften his previous remarks about the loss of the Middle East, while still adhering to his view that the outcome of the war would be decided in the Atlantic; "unless Hitler can win there, he cannot win anywhere in the world in the end."[43]

This exchange between Churchill and Roosevelt, which took place at the halfway point of the Common Law Alliance, has been quoted at some length for two reasons. First, it illustrates the difference, at this stage of the Second World War, between their two views of the war—Roosevelt's detached, long term and oceanic; Churchill's embattled, immediate and historically descended from Nelson's instruction to his captains before the Battle of Trafalgar: "No Captain can do very

---

*The earlier draft had the words "mortal (overwhelming)" in place of "grave."

wrong if he places his ship alongside that of an enemy." Secondly, there was at this time a view widely held in Washington that the British had bitten off more than they could chew in the Middle East.* To a logistics planner in Washington looking at a map of the world, it was the oil fields east of Suez that seemed vital to deny to the enemy, not Egypt, which for most of the British—and certainly for Churchill— was the political heart of British paramountcy in the Arab world as a whole and also militarily crucial, because of the naval importance of the base at Alexandria and of the Suez Canal. What most disturbed American critics was the fear that further commitment to the defence of the Middle East—and above all of Egypt—would fatally weaken the British effort in the Atlantic. This view even had its supporters in Whitehall, including the CIGS himself, General John Dill, who re- garded the loss of Egypt as a lesser sacrifice than the loss of Singapore (and told Churchill so).[45] This Anglo-American difference over the Middle East—the only theatre of war in which the British Army was engaged in action with the enemy at the time—was give a long airing at a meeting at 10 Downing Street, attended by Hopkins as well as military representatives of both sides, on 24 July 1941. Churchill's concept of the Middle East carried the day. Perhaps for this reason, the Middle East was not, in the event, a major item on the agenda at Placentia Bay.[46]

However the results of the Atlantic Conference may be assessed, it was an extraordinary occasion. Roosevelt, who had left South Dart- mouth, Massachusetts, in the presidential yacht *Potomac,* boarded Ad-

---

*One of the inputs to this view was the reporting of Colonel Bonner Fellers, U.S. Military Attaché in Cairo in October 1940–July 1942. In his subsequent citation for the Distinguished Service Medal, his reports were described as "models of clarity and accuracy." A frequent guest at XIII Corps Headquarters in the Western Desert, Fellers was told most of what was going on, often in advance, by the British. At least from January 1942, his voluminous messages sent from Cairo, encoded in the Washington Military Intelligence Division's "Black" Code, were in Rommel's hands, deciphered and translated, within hours of their transmission by radio to Washington. One of his last reports, sent shortly before he was transferred from Cairo, recorded his view (on 26 June 1942) that the Eighth Army had been "decisively beaten" and that this was a "suitable moment for Rommel to take the (Egyptian) Delta."[44]

miral Ernest King's flagship, the cruiser *Augusta,* off Martha's Vineyard on 5 August. Churchill travelled from Scapa Flow in the *Prince of Wales*—a journey by no means free of danger from U-boats. When the two groups of warships met, the peacetime spick and span of the U.S. naval vessels contrasted with the drab camouflage of the British; and the *Prince of Wales* still bore the marks of her recent encounter with the *Bismarck.* As the morning mist lifted on 9 August, Churchill was standing on the bridge of the battleship wearing the uniform of an Elder Brother of Trinity House.[47] This was the first real meeting between Churchill and Roosevelt (in 1918 in London they had done not much more than set eyes on each other), and it was a conference for which Roosevelt was at least as eager as Churchill.

The greatest achievement of the conference was the fact that from now on each of the two leaders had a clear mental picture of the other. Paradoxically, at this first summit meeting in August 1941, the extreme stereotypes (in American eyes) of European cunning and British phlegm were represented by a man who throughout his life took pains to choose just the right words to express exactly what he thought, who seldom sought to conceal what he felt and—the heir of a much earlier tradition of English soldier-statesman—did not fight back tears, whether of sorrow or of joy; whereas the stereotype of the opposite pole, the plain bluntness of the American homespun tradition, was represented there by a man so opaque that the subtlety of his political artistry was, as James Burns put it, Machiavellian.[48] During these four days, Churchill and Roosevelt met repeatedly; of the six meals that they ate together, five were on board the *Augusta;* and so they sized each other up. Without this preliminary meeting, it is difficult to believe either that the *Arcadia* Conference could have been mounted in Washington so quickly at the turn of the year or that the two men could have resisted the Allied reverses of 1942 in the comradely way that they did. The Atlantic Conference was, moreover, rich in symbols: both the very fact that it was held at sea and the carefully staged morning service held on the deck of the *Prince of Wales* on Sunday, 10 August, attended by the President and the Prime Minister—in Roosevelt's words at his subsequent press conference, one of the great historic services.

Publicly, what this conference presented to the world, as the basis of the two leaders' hopes for a better future, was the declaration of common principles that came to be known as the Atlantic Charter. The Charter, like the fact that the Atlantic Conference had taken place, was kept secret until it was simultaneously announced on both sides of the Atlantic on 14 August. Although it was Roosevelt for whom this document was important, mainly for reasons of American domestic politics, he preferred British prose to a document that Welles had already prepared. The ringing phrases of the Charter contained some carefully worded qualifications designed to protect the positions of both sides. Thus Article 4, on the freedom of international trade, included the seven words "with due respect for their existing obligations" (i.e., the Ottawa Agreements); and Article 3, pledging the two governments to "respect the right of all peoples to choose the form of government under which they will live," was interpreted by Churchill on his return to London as inapplicable to the territories of the British Empire, where prior obligations applied—a point that he would reiterate to Roosevelt in a telegram sent one year later, on the occasion of the first anniversary of the Atlantic Charter.[49]

As an exercise in public relations, the Charter did Roosevelt little good. The percentage of Americans opposed to involvement in the war was only one percentage point lower, according to a poll conducted immediately after the Atlantic Conference, than it had been before: 74 per cent instead of 75. Indeed, the capital where the Atlantic Charter had most immediate effect was Tokyo, where it was interpreted as aimed at maintaining an Anglo-American "system of world domination."[50] Nevertheless, the Charter was the first Anglo-American document to foresee the eventual[51] "establishment of a wider and permanent system of international security" after the war. Moreover, the Soviet Government adhered to the Charter (even accepting the inclusion of freedom of religion). And the Charter formed the basis of the Declaration of the United Nations at the year's end.

Behind the scenes, discussion between both the two leaders and their military advisers ranged over a wide field. On the latter talks, the entry written in his diary at the time by Lieutenant-Colonel Ian Jacob, Deputy Military Secretary to the War Cabinet, offers a shrewd assessment:

> The Americans have a long way to go before they can play any
> decisive part in the war. Their Navy is further ahead than their
> Army, both in thought and in resources. Both are standing like
> reluctant bathers on the brink, but the Navy are being forced to
> dip a toe at a time into the shark-infested water. Their ideas,
> however, have not got beyond how to avoid being bitten; they
> have not yet reached out to thoughts of how to get rid of the
> sharks. . . .

Jacob added in this entry that the American "sailors and soldiers only
hope that the moment [when the Germans could no longer disregard
American provocation] won't come before they can get together some
reasonably armed forces with which to fight."[52]

On the evening of 12 August Churchill left Placentia Bay in the
Prince of Wales, * escorted by U.S. destroyers as far as Iceland. He sent
this message from the ship: "God bless the President and the people of
the United States."[53] In his report to his colleagues in the War Cabinet
on 19 August, Churchill expressed his belief that Roosevelt "was obvi-
ously determined to come in" and "would look for an 'incident' which
would justify him in opening hostilities." Nevertheless, this euphoric
mood was short-lived. Only six days later the "wave of depression
through the Cabinet" was such that Churchill sent Hopkins a telegram
in terms which prompted Hopkins to warn Roosevelt that if the British "ever reached the conclusion" that the United States would not
ultimately "get into the war on some basis or other," that would be a
"very critical moment in the war and the British appeasers might have
some influence on Churchill."[54]

It has been well said of Roosevelt that he "eluded everyone who
tried to net the butterfly of his consent."[55] What exactly was in his
mind as he left Placentia Bay is not easy to establish from the records,
such as they are; second-hand accounts are not necessarily reliable; and
it is perhaps significant that in his report to Congress on the Atlantic

---

*The *Prince of Wales* was sunk by Japanese aircraft four months later.

Charter he never mentioned Churchill by name.[56] The Atlantic Conference did not, of itself, accelerate Roosevelt's military decisions. Not until after the clash between the destroyer *Greer* and a U-boat (the submarine fired two torpedoes at the destroyer, which dodged them) on 4 September, 125 miles south-west of Iceland, did he finally decide that the state of American public opinion was now such as to enable him to let the Royal Navy withdraw from the western Atlantic. A week after this clash he described "these Nazi submarines and raiders" in a broadcast as "the rattlesnakes of the Atlantic."[57] His order to the U.S. Navy came into effect on 16 September. Only after the loss of seven American seamen on board the destroyer *Kearney* on 17 October 1941, however, were the key sections of the Neutrality Act repealed; and even then convoys of armed U.S. merchant ships on the route to Britain did not follow at once.

With hindsight, the two questions discussed by Churchill and Roosevelt at their first summit meeting which mattered more than any others were aid for the Soviet Union and the problem of how to deal with Japan. (Also with hindsight, a notable exception from the two leaders' private agenda was the atomic bomb, whose future development had at that very moment reached a critical stage in the minds of the scientists of both countries.) In their joint message telegraphed to Stalin on 12 August 1941, Churchill and Roosevelt said:

> We realise how vitally important to the defeat of Hitlerism is the brave and steadfast resistance of the Soviet Union, and we feel therefore that we must not in any circumstance fail to act quickly and immediately in this matter of planning the programme for the future allocation of our joint resources.[58]

The result was the Beaverbrook-Harriman mission,* which—via Archangel—reached Moscow at the end of September for a series of

---

*Max Aitken, Lord Beaverbrook, Canadian-born, had raised the *Daily Express* to the highest circulation of any daily newspaper in Britain between the wars. A man of demonic energy, he was one of Churchill's oldest friends, although his political advice to Churchill was erratic.

meetings with Stalin. As for the Japanese issue, Churchill had—mindful of Munich—brought with him to the conference, in draft, stern notes of warning to the Japanese Government, to be delivered in parallel by the British and the U.S. governments. He left Placentia Bay believing that Roosevelt would not "tone down"[59] the British wording. The sequel, which ended at Pearl Harbor and Singapore, is the subject of the next chapter.

9

GLOBAL WAR:

THE BEGINNINGS OF

THE GRAND ALLIANCE

When Barbarossa begins, the world will hold
its breath.

—*Adolf Hitler, February 1941*

Throughout the world
Everywhere we are all brothers.
Why then do the winds and waves rage so
turbulently?

—*Verses quoted by the Emperor of Japan, at the Imperial
Conference held on
6 September 1941*

An account of the beginnings of the triangular relationship among the Big Three, as they would soon be called, starts in
1941, not with Churchill, Roosevelt and Stalin, but with Hitler: the
arbiter of the New European Order constructed on the basis of German
military power, and the man whose vision of his own destiny would
determine—more than any other single factor—the final outcome of
1941, which transformed the Second World War.

Hitler

Although Hitler declined both physically and mentally in the second
half of the war, at the moment when he decided to invade the Soviet
Union he was in his political prime and at the peak of his military

reputation—fifty-one years of age. He himself gave more than one reason for taking this momentous decision.[1] His visceral motive was never better expressed than in the last three sentences of the letter that he wrote to Mussolini on the eve of the German assault—Mussolini was woken up in the middle of the night to read it:

> Since I struggled through to this decision, I again feel spiritually free. The partnership with the Soviet Union, in spite of the complete sincerity of my efforts to bring about a final conciliation, was nevertheless often very irksome to me, for in some way or other it seemed to me to be a break with my whole origin, my concepts and my former obligations. I am happy now to be delivered from this torment.[2]

Hitler's original directive for Operation *Barbarossa* required preparations for the invasion to be completed by 15 May 1941. In the event, the operation was delayed by more than a month. The early morning on which the German Army, together with its Bulgarian, Finnish, and Romanian allies*—over three million strong—crossed the Soviet frontiers on a vast front (22 June 1941) was the anniversary of the very day on which Napoleon's *Grande Armée* had begun the disastrous Russian campaign one hundred and twenty-nine years before. So rigid, right up to the last moment, was Stalin's determination, both to observe the terms of his agreement with Hitler and to reject any evidence liable to shake confidence in his own mistaken strategic judgement, that the tactical surprise achieved by the invaders was total. Hitler's ultimate strategic line of defence in the East, grandiosely defined in his *Barbarossa* directive as running approximately from the Volga River to Archangel, might have been attained had two conditions been fulfilled—if the invasion had begun in May, as planned, and if a quarrel had not broken out between Hitler and his generals (including some of

---

*The Hungarians provided a token contingent, but did not become significant contributors to the war on the Eastern Front until the turn of the year.

the ablest, such as Guderian) over the vital question: what was the primary objective of the invasion?[3]

Neither of these conditions was fulfilled. Yet the invasion nearly succeeded. By the end of that year the Baltic States had been overrun, Leningrad was besieged and most of the Ukraine occupied. As for the Soviet capital, the monument (representing an anti-tank barrier) that every traveller between the centre of Moscow and its airport at Sheremet'evo sees at the side of the road today—twenty-three and a half kilometers from the Kremlin—is a reminder of just how close to victory the German Army came in December 1941.

The invasion of the Soviet Union was not postponed because of any lack of German preparedness. On the contrary, the transfer of forces eastwards and the accumulation of supplies in the East went steadily forward, accompanied by a campaign of disinformation[4] that partly accounted for the misreading of Hitler's real intention not only by Stalin, until the end, but also by British Military Intelligence in Whitehall, up to a very late date. The main reason for the delay was Hitler's personal decision to secure his right flank, in the Balkans and in the eastern Mediterranean, before *Barbarossa* was launched. As we now know, as late as the beginning of June 1941, Admiral Erich Raeder, a sceptic about the concept of *Barbarossa,* was urging Hitler to recognise that the invasion of the Soviet Union "must under no circumstances lead to the abandonment or reduction of plans, or to delay, in the conduct of the war in the eastern Mediterranean." Hitler rejected this advice. Had he been willing to allot even marginally larger forces than he did to this theatre of war, earlier described to him by Raeder as "more deadly to the British Empire than the capture of London,"[5] Churchill and Roosevelt's anxieties about the prospect of losing the Middle East altogether (discussed in the preceding chapter) would have been even greater than they were; and General Wavell's "Worst Possible Case" memorandum envisaging just that outcome might have become not just a hypothesis[6] but a reality.

Ideology apart, perhaps the greatest single difference between the Tripartite Pact and the Grand Alliance was the fact that the members of the former, contrary to what was widely believed at the time, never had any strategy agreed between them. The most striking example of this is Hitler's prolonged concealment from both Italy and Japan of his intention to invade the Soviet Union. Among the three Axis allies, however, there was already ample precedent for this duplicity, in 1940. Not only did Italy (whose strategic role, in German eyes, was to cover the Mediterranean flank and to invade Egypt) then bungle the invasion of Egypt, losing the whole of Cyrenaica early in 1941, but Mussolini also reneged on the assurance that he had just given to Hitler, by ordering the Italian Army in Albania[7] to invade Greece at the end of October 1940, allowing Hitler only four days' notice. The Greeks responded with their defiant *ochi*. *

These two Italian reverses obliged Hitler, first, to send the *Afrika Korps* to Tripoli, where its commander, General Rommel, arrived on 12 February,[8] and two months later to invade Greece. The German threat to Greece, which became apparent as soon as the Italian attack ran into difficulties, confronted Churchill with a dilemma, both political and military. How should the British guarantee, given to Greece by the Chamberlain government in the different circumstances of 1939, be honoured? Should military success—in Libya—be reinforced, or should an attempt be made to shore up what would otherwise be inevitable failure in Greece? (For the Greek Army on its own to repel an Italian invasion was a remarkable feat, but to withstand a German invasion defied any stretch of the imagination.)

On 24 February 1941 the British War Cabinet took its initial decision not to press home, up to Tripoli, the crushing victory recently won against the Italian Army, but instead to send three divisions to Greece. As Churchill's biographer has convincingly argued,[9] Churchill himself, in spite of his general tendency to chance his arm, on this occasion gave his advisers the opportunity to say no. Unfortunately, they—including Eden,[10] sent out to consult with Wavell and with the

---

*"No." (The Greek Government's refusal to accept the Italian ultimatum is annually commemorated on *Ochi* Day, 28 October.) The Greek Army not only repulsed the Italian invasion in 1940, but succeeded in advancing into Albania itself.

Greek Government—did not do so. On the contrary, partly because of the misreading of German intentions and capability by Wavell's intelligence staff in Cairo, and partly because of a sudden change of heart in Athens, they did just the opposite. Although the War Cabinet came close to reversing its decision to go into Greece on 6–7 March, in the end it was confirmed; and Churchill backed and subsequently defended it, with energy and eloquence. This was his first major failure since he became Prime Minister and Minister of Defence. Not only did British forces lose on land, both in Greece and in Libya, but the defence of Crete in particular cost the Royal Navy ships that were badly needed in the Atlantic and the Pacific Oceans.

What finally caused Hitler to postpone *Barbarossa* was not so much either the Libyan or the Greek operations, but his sudden, unpremeditated and emotional decision, taken at the end of March 1941, to "destroy Yugoslavia militarily and as a national unit."[11] Yugoslavia was swiftly overwhelmed, and the campaign in mainland Greece ended on 1 May; after a bitter, hand-to-hand fight, the British were—to Churchill's chagrin—unable to hold Crete, which was evacuated a month later. Meanwhile, by the middle of April Rommel, commanding a mixed Italo–German army, had driven the British Army occupying Cyrenaica[12] back to the frontier of Egypt,* only Tobruk remaining in British hands, besieged. It is against this rapidly darkening Balkan, Mediterranean and North African background that the Anglo-American misjudgment of where the real danger lay in the spring of 1941 must be assessed.

Churchill

On the face of it, Churchill was the only one of the Big Three who got it entirely right—witness his first wartime broadcast, made after the German–Soviet Partition of Poland (quoted in Chapter 6); his remark

---

*Where the failure of a British counter-attack on Rommel, launched by Wavell, urged on by Churchill, in June 1941 finally decided Churchill to replace Wavell by General Claude Auchinleck.

made to senior British commanders a year later that Germany would inevitably turn on Russia during 1941;[13] and above all his warning to Stalin in April 1941 (in oblique terms, because the source was an *Enigma* message decyphered at Bletchley Park) that the Soviet Union was in danger of being attacked by German forces in southern Poland.[14] The Soviet Ambassador in Washington, moreover, had already been warned by the State Department, on Roosevelt's instructions, acting on intelligence received from a different source.[15] In the third volume of his memoirs, Churchill afterwards described how, just before his warning to Stalin, "the whole Eastern scene" was "illuminated . . . in a lightning flash."[16] This statement now has to be taken in conjunction with the mass of other evidence, secret at the time when he was writing (and for twenty years afterwards), which is available today.[17] This shows clearly that, although Churchill was indeed often well ahead of his professional advisers, Whitehall's strategic assessment remained obstinately mistaken until the beginning of June 1941, and that it was only then that the British intelligence community at last came to terms with reality. In the weeks beforehand, Churchill had a great deal else on his mind. The account that follows concentrates on the performance of British intelligence, because it was British intelligence which then enjoyed the precious prerogative of the output of Bletchley Park, not yet at that time shared with their American opposite numbers. Moreover, the assessment was common to both Churchill's and Roosevelt's military advisers that if the Soviet Union were invaded by Germany, the campaign would end in German victory in a matter of weeks.

There are several strands in this immense miscalculation. Its influence on Anglo–American policy was not immediately dispelled by the news on 22 June 1941; and there was also a marked contrast between the conventional wisdom then prevailing and Churchill's own reaction to the outbreak of war between Germany and the Soviet Union. As he remarked to Colville, walking on the lawn at Chequers after dinner on the evening before the German invasion, if Hitler invaded Hell he would at least make a favourable reference to the Devil in the House of Commons.[18] It was not just that the proponents of the conventional wisdom about the Soviet Union refused to accept the stream of evidence—coming above all from Bletchley Park[19]—which was incompatible with their own assessment. The evidence in the spring of 1941 pointing towards an invasion of the Soviet Union was misread partly because earlier rumours of the German intention to attack eastwards had not been borne out. As early as January 1941, for example, the *Christian Science Monitor*'s correspondent in Berlin attended a gathering of military attachés at the home of a member of the U.S. Embassy staff. One by one, the attachés all spoke of the German military movement eastwards, and the last to speak, the Soviet Military Attaché, remarked that if the German Army attacked the Soviet Union, it would be *"kein Spaziergang"* ("no promenade").[20] Because nothing happened then on the Eastern Front—on the contrary, the next German thrust was into the Balkans—it was widely assumed that the rumours at the turn of the year had been ill founded.

So far as intelligence about the Soviet Union was concerned, the British in particular began from a very low baseline. An earlier chapter has examined the reasons for the general ignorance about the Soviet Union in the 1930s. A striking documentary example of the amateurishness of British intelligence about the Soviet Union has been preserved in the brief on the Red Army taken to Moscow by the British Military Mission[21] in August 1939. This brief not only assessed "any further increase" of Soviet aircraft production as "unlikely," but also contained the following statement:

> A further drawback is the indifferent state of the internal communications in Russia. The railways are already working to capacity and are incapable of taking any further strain. While they could play their part in the mobilisation of the Army in the first weeks of war, industry and other essential services would be more or less at a standstill. After two or three weeks military mobilisation might have to be suspended, or at least held up, to avoid a complete breakdown in industry and national life.[22]

The last two sentences would have been untrue even in the First World War, when the Russian railway system was able, at any rate for the first half of the war, to cope with massive movements of troops and supplies; and in the Second World War not only were groups of armies switched from one battle front to another, but during the Red Army's initial retreat, over 1,500 factories were dismantled and transferred, with their work forces, to the interior of the Soviet Union.

There were also other, more readily understandable, reasons for the attitude of Whitehall and Washington in 1941. Hitler had postponed Operation *Sealion* indefinitely in October 1940; and—as we now know—he was not prepared to consider it again until *Barbarossa* had succeeded. But Churchill and the British Chiefs of Staff had to plan for the direct threat, which for them was the invasion of Britain—not that of the Soviet Union. Even after the Soviet Union had been invaded, a state of maximum efficiency of British preparations to withstand invasion was ordered to be reached by 1 September—an order that was rescinded only in August 1941. On top of this, as we have seen in the previous chapter, there was the Battle of the Atlantic, which loomed particularly large in Churchill's and in Roosevelt's minds during the first half of the year. The historians of British Intelligence have, however, pointed out that whereas Military Intelligence remained hypnotised by *Sealion* until October 1940, thereafter its hypnosis "fastened on the Middle East." Indeed, this fixation had a basis in some solid military facts. It also corresponded with Churchill's own natural inclinations. He had never forgotten the role played by Turkey in the First World War, and he was determined that in the Second World War this strategically pivotal country should remain on the British side.

The British imperial position[23] in the Middle East was in large measure Churchill's personal creation, during the years immediately following the end of the First World War. Nevertheless, his conviction that it would be a catastrophe to lose the Middle East was in quite a different category from the hypnosis of Military Intelligence, which led to some ludicrous conclusions. Thus, three weeks before the invasion of the Soviet Union, the hard-pressed British Commanders-in-Chief, Middle East, received instructions from London to draw up plans for the seizure of Mosul (in Iraq) as a base from which to launch hypothetical attacks on Baku. The ground given for this grotesque instruction was that Stalin might be induced to resist German demands by the fear that, if he did not, the British would attack the Baku oil fields.[24]

By this time it had become an article of faith in Whitehall that, while it could not be doubted that Germany was making preparations for an attack on the Soviet Union, the German decision as to whether to attack was being deferred pending the outcome of Soviet-German political negotiations. These non-existent negotiations were a figment of what seems to have been the collective imagination of officials. Unfortunately, one of those who fell for the idea was the British Ambassador in Moscow, Stafford Cripps.[25] Cripps had earlier been a firm believer in a German invasion of the Soviet Union, but in the spring he began to wobble. In April he actually delayed the transmission of Churchill's personal warning to Stalin by over two weeks, obliging Churchill to send Eden a personal instruction conveying a direct order,[26] in response to which Cripps, in the end, handed the message not even to Molotov, but to the Soviet Deputy Foreign Minister.[27]

Whitehall gradually abandoned its dream world of political negotiations and a German "ultimatum," leading to an eventual agreement between Hitler and Stalin—still considered the "more likely" outcome by the Joint Intelligence Committee on 23 May 1941—and at the very end it laboriously arrived at the truth of what was about to happen. The final clincher—for those on the highly restricted distribution list of high-grade decrypts—was the telegram sent to Tokyo by the Japanese Ambassador in Berlin reporting his talk with Hitler on 4 June, which was deciphered by Bletchley Park on 12 June. The following day, after consulting Churchill, Eden told Maisky that the evidence of a German offensive was increasing and offered to send a Military Mission to Moscow. On 15 June Churchill telegraphed to Roosevelt that the invasion was imminent, ending his message with these words:

> I do not expect any class political reactions here and I trust a German-Russian conflict will not cause you any embarrassment.[28]

Roosevelt never answered this message, any more than Stalin responded to Churchill's warning in April 1941. Although Roosevelt sent Churchill some reassurance orally, through Winant,[29] in Washington he at first confined himself to approving a vapid statement about Soviet resistance, issued by the State Department; and in a press conference on 24 June he turned a question about whether defence of the Soviet Union was essential to that of the United States, replying: "Oh, ask me a different type of question—such as 'how old is Ann?' "[30]

Behind Roosevelt's caution lay not only the familiar problem of Congress, but also the belief, which survived after 22 June on both sides of the Atlantic, that the German Army would reach Moscow in three or four weeks.* One of the few who treated this estimate with the scepticism that it deserved was the former British cavalry officer, who had taken the trouble, between the wars, to study the Eastern Front campaigns of 1914–16.[31] On the evening of 22 June Churchill made a broadcast, deliberately consulting none of his Cabinet colleagues about the text in advance. Although he told the listening British people that he would "unsay no word" that he had spoken about communism over the past twenty-five years, he declared that Britain would "give whatever help we can to Russia and to the Russian people." And he concluded:

> The Russian danger is therefore our danger, and the danger of the United States, just as the cause of any Russian fighting for his hearth and home is the cause of free men and free peoples in every quarter of the globe. . . .[32]

Stalin

Few scenes in history are comparable with what happened in Moscow shortly before four o'clock on the morning of 22 June 1941. It was not

---

*Thereafter, so the British Joint Intelligence Committee calculated in mid-June 1941, an interval of four to six weeks would follow before Britain could be invaded.

long since Stalin had retired—unusually early—to sleep at his *dacha* at Kuntsevo, just outside Moscow. From the Kremlin, where the first reports of the German invasion were received not long after he had left, the Chief of the Soviet General Staff woke Stalin at Kuntsevo by telephone. Stalin's response to Zhukov's call was to order a meeting of the Politburo.[33] Perhaps there is a glimmer of a parallel in the news, brought to Wellington at the Duchess of Richmond's ball in Brussels on the eve of the Battle of Waterloo (also early on a June morning), that the thrust of the French Army's approach march through Belgium had outwitted him. Wellington's response,* before he left to take command on the battlefield, was "Napoleon has humbugged me, by God!"

By contrast, the military directive issued by the Politburo, after its meeting on the morning of 22 June, was still divorced from reality. Soviet ground troops were ordered to fight back, but not to cross the frontier without authority; while the Soviet Air Force (which on the 22nd alone had lost over a thousand aircraft, many of them destroyed on the ground) was allowed to attack targets up to 150 kilometers beyond the frontier. The tone of a message broadcast to the Soviet people at noon was more robust, recalling the Russian defeat of Napoleon. But it devoted many words to explaining Soviet loyalty to the German-Soviet agreements of 1939; and it was delivered not by Stalin (since 6 May, Soviet Prime Minister as well as General Secretary of the Soviet Communist Party), but by the Soviet Foreign Minister, Molotov.[34] This broadcast was followed on the evening of 22 June by a bombastic military directive. This time the invaders were to be surrounded and annihilated: a general counter-offensive that bore no relation to the reality of what was happening on the ground.

Four years after this, the supreme crisis in his long rule, speaking at a Kremlin banquet given in honour of his victorious commanders, Stalin would propose an historic toast: to the Russian people.† And in his

---

*Made in the Duke of Richmond's study, after he had been able to look at a map.

†At the time many in the West, including Churchill, used the word "Russian" when they really

speech at this banquet, he observed that any other people would have said in 1941, "Go away, we will set up another government."[35] After Stalin's death it was suggested not only that during the early days of the German invasion he suffered some kind of breakdown, but also that in October he panicked and temporarily left Moscow altogether.[36] On present evidence, what seems to have happened is that, convinced of and appalled by the true dimensions of the military disaster once the Germans captured Minsk on 28 June, Stalin withdrew to his *dacha,* from which he was virtually summoned back to the Kremlin by members of the Politburo. They came out to the *dacha* with what Stalin may well have thought at first to be a different purpose. *"Zachem Vy prishli?"* ("Why have you called?") is said to have been his initial reaction. Nevertheless, the "Brothers and Sisters" broadcast followed; and in the crisis of mid-October 1941, although Stalin initially intended to accompany the other members of the government to Kuibyshev (where the government and foreign missions then temporarily withdrew), he changed his mind and stayed, taking the salute as usual at the Red Army parade in Red Square on the anniversary of the Russian Revolution on 7 November 1941.[37]

As Stalin himself implied in his moment of candour at the banquet in May 1945, the Soviet people—and in particular the Red Army—had good cause for bewilderment[38] in June 1941. (Quite apart from the enormous casualties, nearly three million Soviet soldiers had been taken prisoner by the autumn of 1941; among those who did not survive the conditions of captivity in German camps was one of Stalin's sons, Jakov.) Only nine days before the Soviet Union was invaded, Moscow Radio had broadcast a Tass statement, dismissing as "false and provocative" the rumours of an impending war between the Soviet Union and Germany. This statement declared:

> Despite the obvious absurdity of these rumours, responsible circles in Moscow have thought it necessary, in view of the persist-

---

meant "Soviet." Stalin, however (a Georgian himself), was on this occasion, mindful of the Russian imperial past, deliberately playing to the *Russian* ethnic gallery.

ent spreading of these rumours, to authorise Tass to state that they are clumsily concocted propaganda measures by forces hostile to the Soviet Union and Germany, which are interested in a further extension and intensification of the war.[39]

It was not only Churchill's and Roosevelt's warnings that Stalin had ignored. A selection of documents in the KGB archives, recently quoted in *Pravda,*[40] shows that reports of German military intentions poured into the Kremlin. It has long been known that Stalin's intelligence agents in Japan and in Switzerland forecast the exact date of the invasion. German aerial reconnaissance on the Soviet side of the frontier from March 1941 onwards also pointed unmistakably to what was being planned; and on the eve of the invasion this was confirmed by German deserters. To make matters worse, Stalin had abandoned the Red Army's defence plan prepared in the previous year by his former Chief of General Staff, Shaposhnikov, who had based it on the fortifications of the pre-1939 Soviet frontiers; instead, he insisted on forward deployment behind the frontiers newly acquired in 1939–40. Yet literally up to midnight, Stalin continued to believe—or professed to believe—in the possibility of a gigantic act of German provocation.[41]

Writing nearly ten years afterwards, in the midst of the Cold War, Churchill described Stalin and his Politburo colleagues in mid-1941 as "the most completely out-witted bunglers of the Second World War."[42] From this verdict it has been, for some historians, a short step to the conclusion that Stalin alone was responsible for the Soviet errors of the first half of 1941. These errors were indeed of Himalayan proportions. Nevertheless, the mature judgement of the outstanding Soviet commander of the war, Zhukov, as recorded not in his memoirs but in private discussions twenty years later and published only in 1987,[43] deserves respect. Zhukov had a good claim to be regarded as unbiased. Not only was he *limogé* to the obscure command of the Odessa military district by Stalin after the war; his own military hero was the man whom Stalin had had executed in 1937—Tukhachevsky, whom Zhukov called "a giant of military thought" and "the star . . . in the pleiad of outstanding Red Army commanders."[44] In Zhukov's opinion, expressed with hindsight, others shared with Stalin the responsibility for the mistakes made in Moscow in 1941 (by which time he was himself Chief of the Soviet General Staff), "including his closest circle—Molotov, Malenkov and Kaganovich. . . . Part of the responsibility rests with Voroshilov . . . and part of the responsibility rests on us—the military." The Red Army's poor showing in the Finnish campaign had convinced Stalin that "a minimum of another two years in order to prepare for war was needed"; and in these later reflections Zhukov also spoke candidly both of the low state of the Red Army morale before the invasion and of the initially uneven performance of different Soviet divisions in battle after the Soviet Union was attacked.

Stalin's belief that the Red Army and the Soviet armaments industry still had some months' respite[45] in which to complete preparations certainly flew in the face of the evidence. But it also reflected the fact that the Red Army, although some of its equipment was excellent (notably a tank that would soon become famous, the T34), was for the most part trained to fight a war that was perceived as a mixture of the First World War and the Soviet Civil War. Even if the warnings that were ignored in the Kremlin in June 1941 had been heeded, the professional imbalance between the German Army, led by generals with the experience of a series of *Blitzkrieg* campaigns behind them, and the Red Army, lumbered with an unworkable dual system of command* and led by officers most of whom had not yet absorbed the real lessons of the Winter War, would still have remained. It took over a year's bitter fighting to convince Stalin that this dual system, which dated from the Civil War, must be scrapped; and until it was, the *bumazhnyie soldaty* ("paper soldiers"), as men like Voroshilov were called by the professional officer corps, wrought havoc in the Red Army.

Without further evidence we cannot be certain how candid the military advice offered to Stalin in 1941 really was. Zhukov's account suggests that Stalin was left in no doubt about German superiority (an

---

*The system whereby commanders were flanked by political commissars, themselves with military ranks. *Edinonachalie* was finally restored in October 1942—significantly, at the time of the Battle of Stalingrad.

interesting parallel with the depressing assessment offered to the British Government by their Chiefs of Staff in March 1938).[46] If so, Stalin would have had little difficulty with the Politburo in arguing the need to put off the evil day. But Stalin was not a man to do anything by halves. In the first months of 1941, he piled Pelion on Ossa, and the Soviet equivalent of Chamberlain's "peace in our time" of October 1938 was the preposterous Tass statement of 14 June 1941. Whatever the truth about June 1941 may in the end turn out to be, what happened from 3 July—the date of Stalin's "Brothers and Sisters" broadcast to the Soviet people[47]—onwards is well attested. Stalin, who had kept out of public view until then, became in rapid succession Chairman of the State Defence Committee (GKO), Defence Minister, Chairman of the *Stavka* of the Supreme Command and—on 8 August—Supreme Commander of the Armed Forces, by which time he once again had Shaposhnikov as his Chief of Staff.

In spite of Churchill's broadcast of 22 June, the initial dialogue between Moscow and London and between Moscow and Washington was tentative and non-committal. The chilly tone of Molotov's first telegram to Maisky, instructing him what to say in response to the British offer of help for the Soviet Union, on the opening day of the German invasion, speaks for itself.[48] The Soviet Ambassador in Washington (Konstantin Oumansky, who seems to have been personally disliked there—and not only by the President) did not succeed in being received by Roosevelt until 10 July: the first time that Roosevelt had spoken to any Soviet representative since the outbreak of war in 1939. Although this meeting, which lasted under an hour, went "somewhat better than expected"—as the ambassador put it in his telegram to Molotov[49]—it did not achieve a great deal. Nearly three weeks passed before the ice was broken, by Churchill, in a personal message to Stalin, which on this occasion Cripps delivered to Stalin himself on 8 July. Churchill's message[50] did not offer much beyond a general promise of help within the constraints of "time, geographical conditions and our growing resources," and a welcome to the arrival of the Soviet Military Mission in London.

In his talk with Stalin on that day (in which, incidentally, Stalin's

performance was about as unlike that of a broken man as it is possible
to imagine), Cripps was given a rough ride. According to the Soviet
record, Cripps resisted the conclusion of a "formal" Anglo-Soviet
agreement on mutual military assistance, coupled with a pledge not to
conclude a separate peace with Germany; and he argued instead in
favour of an exchange of notes. Stalin retorted that the British "slowness and exaggerated caution" recalled the negotiations in 1939; there
was, he said, "danger" in delay.[51] Churchill responded at once, on 10
July. Subject only to the agreement of the Dominion governments, the
British Government wholly approved of Stalin's proposal for an
Anglo-Soviet Declaration. Forty-eight hours later the agreement,
which embodied both the points discussed by Stalin with Cripps, was
signed in Moscow, by Cripps and Molotov.[52]

Stalin's next proposal fared less well. In a personal message to
Churchill on 18 July, he suggested, although it was not yet described as
such, the formation of a second front:* "a front against Hitler in the
West (Northern France) and in the North (the Arctic)." This request
for "active military aid to the Soviet Union" was repeated in a different form in Stalin's message of 13 September, when he even suggested
that "England could without risk land 25–30 divisions at Archangel or
transport them across Iran to the southern regions of the Soviet Union
for military co-operation with Soviet troops on the territory of the
Soviet Union."[53] These Soviet proposals and Churchill's refusal
marked the beginning of a long inter-Allied debate, which would not
be resolved until the Big Three met at Teheran over two years later.

By far the most important communication exchanged among the
Big Three between 22 June and the American entry into the war in
December 1941 was the message sent to Stalin by Churchill and Roosevelt, from Newfoundland, on 12 August. As the preceding chapter has
related, the question of aid to the Soviet Union, with all its implications both for American aid to Britain and for the equipment of the
U.S. armed forces, was one of the major issues agreed between Church-

---

*The term first appears in Stalin's message of 3 September 1941 to Churchill.

ill and Roosevelt at the Atlantic Conference. The outcome—the Bea-verbrook-Harriman mission to Moscow at the end of September 1941—started the great flow of military supplies to the Soviet Union from the United States. With hindsight, the agreement signed on 1 October, at the end of the mission to Moscow—or the Moscow Conference of Representatives of the USSR, the USA and Great Britain, as it is called in the Soviet archive[54]—may be regarded as the beginning of the Common Law Alliance between Britain, the Soviet Union and the United States. On 30 October 1941, with congressional approval, Roosevelt was able to inform Stalin that the U.S. Government would provide a billion dollars' worth of war supplies. One week earlier, at an Allied Conference held in London, the Soviet Government had declared its adherence to the "basic principles of the Atlantic Charter."[55] In mid-November, the Soviet Union became eligible for Lend-Lease.

Roosevelt

Japan was one of Roosevelt's great failures. Unlike Stalin—who was himself a native of an inter-continental frontier zone—Roosevelt, like Churchill, was at his worst where Asia was concerned.[56] As Churchill drew on his recollection of the India that he had known nearly half a century earlier, so Roosevelt recalled his family's connections with the China trade, to give him insight into the peoples then still commonly referred to by both Americans and British as "oriental." Of these, the most opaque, in western eyes, were the Japanese, whose language and largely closed society did indeed make theirs a difficult country for the outside world to interpret. But there were also racist overtones to this difficulty. Roosevelt's view of Asians—again like Churchill's—would today be generally regarded as repugnant or silly, or both. In the military field, moreover, those who accurately foresaw what daring and formidable opponents the Japanese would be, if war were to break out in the Pacific and South-East Asia, were few compared with the number of Americans and British who had realised in advance the full dimensions of the German military threat. In short, just as Hitler's personal hubris, combined with the professional quality of the German armed forces, blinded him to the true potential of the Red Army, so too there was a marked element of racial contempt in the general western assessment of the capability of the Japanese armed forces in 1941.

Roosevelt's handling of the Japanese issue in 1941 was complicated—as Churchill's was not—by the domestic impact of the China Lobby in the United States. The long tradition[57] of Sino-American ties was real enough. Moreover, from the conclusion of the Tripartite Pact in 1940 onwards, China was seen in Washington as a counterpoise to Japan and, once the United States had entered the war, as the eventual provider of bases for air attacks on Japan. Thus in the 1940s an explosion of enthusiasm for China swept through the United States.[58] The reports of those on the spot, who knew how corrupt and incompetent the Chinese Nationalist regime really was, could do little to soften the American paean of praise for Chinese democracy and Chinese resistance against Japan—both of them, at best, debatable concepts—which by 1942 reached a crescendo pitch. ("How many," the *Christian Science Monitor* asked its readers, "have considered what a different balance the world might have today were not the Generalissimo [Chiang Kai-shek] a Christian and his wife American-educated?")[59] It was not until Roosevelt met Chiang two years later that he seems to have begun to realise the kind of man he was dealing with. Towards the end of the war Roosevelt was working pragmatically with both the Nationalist and the Communist Chinese regimes, but in 1941 the leader of a country suffering from what amounted to a national hallucination about China could hardly find it easy to handle the country then occupying by far the most important part of the Chinese mainland.

The way in which the Japanese issue was managed in the White House in 1941 was also governed by time—the number of hours in any one day. The logical conclusion of the Europe First strategy was a defensive strategy in the Pacific. Almost inevitably, this meant that during the months between the conclusion of the *ABC* talks in March and the disasters of December 1941, Roosevelt and his team (like Churchill and his advisers) spent far more time thinking about the pressing problems of Europe, the Atlantic and the Mediterranean than they did about the potential problems of the Pacific and South-East Asia. In London, when Churchill was able to think about Far Eastern strategy (for which he went so far as to assume personal responsibility as Prime Minister and Minister of Defence, in a directive issued to the Chiefs of Staff in April 1941), he treated Japan as though it carried the same weight in Asia as Italy did in the Mediterranean; and he assured the First Sea Lord that they could settle how to fight the campaign against Japan afterwards.[60] In Washington, for the most part Roosevelt either did not think the problem through or left it to others, whom he did not supervise with the sustained attention that the problem demanded.

This simple lack of time is the most charitable explanation of the fact that, albeit with some important personal interventions, Roosevelt in the main allowed the State Department to conduct the American-Japanese negotiations which began in April and limped on into December 1941, covering the whole range of problems at issue between the two governments in East and South-East Asia and the future of the relationship between the two countries as Pacific powers. Roosevelt's distrust of the State Department—the "cookie-pushers"—was notorious. Cordell Hull, as a southern Democrat influential in Congress (of which he had been a member from 1907 to 1933), remained at Foggy Bottom from the beginning of Roosevelt's first administration until—excluded from participation in the Quebec Conference in September 1944—he threw in his hand. That Roosevelt was willing for most of the time to delegate responsibility for U.S.-Japanese negotiations to a man like Hull (whom, moreover, ill health kept away from the State Department for almost two months in the summer of 1941) says a great deal about the degree of priority that Japan received in the White House in the run-up to Pearl Harbor. And at the very end the danger that Roosevelt still believed he was facing was not a direct threat to the U.S. Navy in the Pacific and to the lives of Americans, whose Commander-in-Chief he was, but the apparently lesser, indirect, and yet (in terms of domestic American politics) awkward problem of Japanese aggression against the far-flung British and Dutch territories in South-East Asia.

Had Roosevelt realised that he had to contend with both threats, would he not have assumed continuous responsibility himself, at least from the beginning of July, or worked through a wholly trusted lieutenant, such as Hopkins? (In considering the answer to this particular question, it must also be remembered that Roosevelt had known personally Admiral Kichisaburo Nomura, the Japanese Ambassador appointed to Washington in February 1941, at the time when he had served there as Naval Attaché during the First World War.) Instead, following a pattern of administration that had served Roosevelt well in the different circumstances of the policies of the New Deal in the 1930s, he largely delegated in this crucial area of foreign policy in 1941: a year in which Washington was a capital still at peace, with little of the co-ordinating machinery required for running a war yet in place—and certainly no joint intelligence committee reporting to Joint Chiefs of Staff.

Anyone looking now at the records of the conduct of the U.S.-Japanese negotiations in 1941 (forty-five meetings held between Nomura and Hull, many of them in secret at Hull's apartment, six with Welles and nine with Roosevelt) must be struck both by the asymmetry between the mood of the two parties to the talks and by the parallel between the American attitude in these talks and that of the British in the Anglo-Soviet negotiations two years earlier.[61] On the Japanese side, the mood of increasing desperation becomes palpable as the weeks of talk go by, while on the American side there is little sense of urgency and more than a little complacency. This is all the more remarkable in that the 1941 negotiations in Washington were—or should have been—illuminated by a light that was lacking in London in 1939: sound advice from the Embassy on the spot and a steady flow of cryptographic intelligence. The State Department seems to have decided that it knew better than the U.S. Ambassador in Tokyo, Joseph Grew, who—like his British colleague, Robert Craigie—saw what was coming and said so forcefully. ("About the worst mistake," reported Craigie on 1 November, "that we and the Americans can make at this juncture is to under-estimate the strength and resolution of this country and its armed forces.")[62]

As for the *Magic* information derived from the decyphering of Japanese diplomatic messages, no intelligence, however good the raw material may be—and in this case it certainly was—can be of any real use to a commander unless it is properly assessed and co-ordinated. An example of the extent to which, remarkably late in the day, Roosevelt himself was completely misreading Japanese intentions, is his longhand letter written to Churchill, and brought back from Washington by Admiral Louis Mountbatten in the middle of October. In this letter Roosevelt said that he thought that the Japanese were now "headed North"[63]—that is to say, against the Soviet Union. Roosevelt wrote these words over two months after the Japanese Government had taken its formal decision not to attack in Siberia in 1941. By then Stalin, as we have seen, knew better—fortunately for the defence of Moscow.

So much for general observations. So far as the Common Law Alliance between Britain and the United States was concerned, the Japanese issue was the area of policy over which its writ ran at its weakest. In the purely military sphere, however, although there was fierce Anglo-American debate about Pacific strategy and naval deployment, there was also frankness on both sides. The British came to the *ABC* talks in Washington at the beginning of the year urging that the U.S. Pacific Fleet should be moved westwards from Hawaii, either to Singapore or to Manila. This suggestion was turned down flat, but in its final form the plan agreed between the two sides provided for a compromise, whereby the U.S. Navy would gradually reinforce the Atlantic, at the expense of the Pacific, and a British fleet would be sent to Singapore (as indeed prewar Admiralty plans had intended). The transfer of U.S. naval forces through the Panama Canal was duly completed during the summer; at the end of July, in a major reversal of policy, Roosevelt recalled Douglas MacArthur to the active service list and appointed him Commander-in-Chief of a combined U.S.-Filipino Army Command; and in September the first heavy U.S. bombers began to arrive in the Philippines, a territory hitherto regarded as indefensible by U.S. planners. For his part, in October Churchill overruled the caution of the Admiralty, who had intended gradually to put a balanced fleet in place at Singapore by the spring of 1942, insisting instead on the immediate despatch to Singapore of the *Prince of Wales* and a battle cruiser, accompanied by an aircraft carrier—a momentous decision, to which maximum publicity was given.[64]

On the diplomatic front, the records tell a different story. There was more than one occasion during the course of the negotiations when the British found themselves obliged to put up with American economy with the truth. Not until mid-May, when Japanese talks had been going on in Washington for over five weeks, did Hull let Halifax know of their existence—and then neither for a very friendly reason nor with the candour which might by that time have been expected between common law allies—so that Halifax at first remonstrated, Hull then took umbrage, and finally Eden poured oil on the troubled transatlantic waters.[65] At the outset, moreover, the negotiations began with a misunderstanding between Hull and Nomura—not perhaps surprisingly, given that they were initiated neither by the State Department nor by the Japanese Embassy, but by private individuals in both sides. And throughout they were quaintly described both to the future allies of the United States and to Japan as "informal and exploratory."[66] Two months after their unpromising beginning, a turning point was reached in Tokyo, where Konoye got rid of his foreign minister, Yosuka Matsuoka. Both Craigie and Grew were convinced that Matsuoka's fall offered a fresh chance of reaching agreement with Konoye, who did not want war with the United States. But by the end of July a Franco-Japanese agreement had been signed providing for the Japanese occupation of southern Indo-China.

At this juncture it becomes a debatable point—as between Washington and Tokyo—who exactly was reacting to whom. The American response to the Japanese move into southern Indo-China was to freeze all Japanese assets in the United States, a freeze that came into force on 26 July 1941. (As early at 16 June Ickes, in his capacity as Petroleum Co-ordinator for National Defence, had—off his own bat—already held up a shipment of petroleum from Philadelphia to Japan. For this he did indeed receive a rap over the knuckles from Roosevelt.)[67] Yet so loose was the machinery of government in Washington during the weeks following the July freeze (which preceded the Atlantic Conference) that instead of the partial deterrent, which Roosevelt himself had apparently at first intended,[68] and clean contrary to the advice and recommendation of the U.S. Navy,[69] what the U.S. bureaucracy worked out was, effectively, a total oil embargo.

After Roosevelt's return from his meeting with Churchill at Placentia Bay, this embargo became the policy of the U.S. Government, as it were by default; even after the event, Hull found it unnecessary to devote more than a single paragraph of his memoirs[70] to the freezing of Japanese assets. The British Government (like the Dutch) was kept in the dark for some weeks, but followed suit. There were, however, those in Whitehall who understood the danger of pushing Japanese backs against the wall, at a time when the Japanese Army had only twelve months' oil supplies in stock; and so concerned was the British Ambassador in Tokyo at the "form and tempo" in which the American-Japanese negotiations were being conducted that, in September 1941, Robert Craigie even took the remarkable step of seeking permission to spend a short leave in the United States, with the intention of putting forward in Washington a "specific plan for a compromise ... after consultation with Lord Halifax ... for the Japanese evacuation of Southern Indo-China."[71]

Through most of the eight months of the American-Japanese talks, Churchill stood on the sidelines, partly by design and partly because he had no other real option. His chief concern throughout was the danger of American "appeasement," based on a false analogy with the year of Munich and a failure to realise what the effect of a total oil embargo must, sooner or later, be on the Japanese. The major exception to this, at first sight, uncharacteristic passivity was at the Placentia Bay meeting, in August 1941. Here Churchill took the initiative. He strove to persuade Roosevelt of the need for the British, Dutch and U.S. governments to put the Japanese Government on formal notice, by means of parallel notes, that any further advance would evoke counter-measures that might lead to war. The wording of the proposed notes (in which Winant had taken a hand in London, in an attempt to take account of the congressional difficulty) was rejected by Roosevelt, who nonetheless gave Churchill grounds for believing that he would indeed warn Japan. Whether he really intended to do this, or whether Churchill, like other interlocutors of Roosevelt before him, heard Roosevelt say what he wanted to hear, is not certain. (Churchill's own report to his Cabinet colleagues on the commitment which he believed he had secured at Placentia Bay has been quoted at the end of the preceding chapter.)

In any case, whatever Roosevelt may have said on that occasion, it was soon submerged by events. On his return to Washington, he did hand Nomura a note of warning, but the warning was first "toned down" by Hull[72] and then overshadowed at this meeting by a further development: Konoye's proposal (received in Washington just before Roosevelt's departure) for a meeting with the President in the Pacific. Roosevelt began by saying yes. Then—against Grew's advice and in spite of an appeal made to him by Konoye in a personal letter as late as 27 August[73]—he was dissuaded by Hull, who thus became largely responsible for the conduct of the final round of negotiations. This he did, from the saddle of a high moral horse, in a manner that again recalls the Foreign Office's behaviour in the Anglo-Soviet negotiations of 1939. Every Japanese proposal was held up to the light in the State Department, to see whether it conformed to what Hull defined as the "fundamental principles" of American foreign policy. And if not, a lecture followed.

Given the fact that Japanese assets had already been frozen and that a total Allied oil embargo was in force against Japan by the beginning of September, it seems doubtful whether Churchill's proposal of parallel notes of warning in the second half of August would have made much difference to the eventual outcome. On 26 November, consulted by Roosevelt about the proposed *modus vivendi* (involving, among other points, Japanese withdrawal from southern Indo-China) then still under discussion with the Japanese, Churchill sent an unenthusiastic reply, in which he—for once—took shelter behind Chiang Kai-shek; and three days later he returned to the charge with his proposal of "a plain declaration, secret or public."[74] In the following week agreement was finally reached on the despatch of warning notes, but by the time they were ready, the Japanese had already declared war.

It is a moot point what a summit conference between two patrician leaders in the Pacific might have been able to achieve: Konoye, "an opaque, attractive figure, born a thousand years after his time,"[75] facing Roosevelt, equally opaque and no less attractive, but essentially a man of the twentieth century. In assessing what the prospects of such a meeting might have been, it must be remembered that, at the Imperial Conference held on 6 September, the Emperor delivered the oblique rebuke to his ministers—a quotation from a poem written by his grandfather[76]—which forms part of the epigraph to this chapter. Their response to the Emperor was interpreted by him and by Konoye as meaning war only as an unavoidable last resort, but for the military the policy guidelines approved at this momentous meeting meant preparing for war. Konoye held on for another six weeks, until on 16 October 1941 he resigned in despair. Thereafter, in spite of a flurry of proposals and counter-proposals, in which Roosevelt took some personal part,[77] it was in reality, as Grew put it in a personal letter to Roosevelt on 22 September, a matter of *facilis descensus Averno est:* "the road down to Hell is easy."[78] On 2 November, after a sixteen-hour meeting,[79] the Japanese leadership took its final decision: unless the Washington talks could at last be brought to a successful conclusion by midnight 30 November, war must follow in early December.

An eminent American historian has concluded that "had FDR been determined to avoid war with the Japanese if at all possible . . . he would have settled down to some hard and realistic dealings with the Japanese."[80] Considered simply as a problem of technical diplomacy, the gap between Washington and Tokyo in 1941 was not unbridgeable, although considered politically, the problem was very difficult for both sides. But what remains astounding with the hindsight of nearly half a century is not so much the political gap between the U.S. and Japanese governments as the dichotomy in Washington between the requirement of U.S. strategy in the Pacific, which was essentially to gain time for reinforcements to arrive—the USAAF in the Philippines, the balanced British fleet in Singapore—and the conduct of U.S. foreign policy, which (above all by the imposition of the total oil embargo) made anything more than a brief respite from July onwards ultimately unattainable. Almost up to the last moment Marshall and Stark[81] urged on Roosevelt the need to reach some kind of accommodation with the Japanese, simply in order to gain a little more time. Both the United States and its Western European Allies paid dearly for his failure to win a longer respite than he did. And, as will be seen in the next chapter, it was thanks to Hitler that the consequences of this mistake were compensated for by a wholly unconvenanted bonus.

10

THE CAESURA,

DECEMBER 1941

The threefold world divided . . .

—Shakespeare, *Julius Caesar, Act IV: Sc.1 (the Triumvir scene)*

The Big Three

The Grand Alliance[1] gradually took shape through the second half of 1941. The moment when it finally solidified can be pinpointed as the second week of December—the caesura of the Second World War. Arrogance had led Churchill, Roosevelt and Stalin into grievous error in 1941: Stalin's refusal to believe in *Barbarossa,* Roosevelt's nonchalance towards the Japanese issue overall and Churchill's myopia in the face of Japanese naval power. Unlike Hitler, however, whose two acts of supreme hubris in December 1941 conclude this chapter, all three leaders learned something from their mistakes, which they had committed at great human cost. The net result was the Grand Alliance, formed in the wake of common misfortune, at the turn of the year. Looking back at the war primarily through the lens of the Anglo-American relationship, some historians have questioned the concept of the Grand Alliance. They contrast, on the one hand, the intimacy of the Anglo-American partnership that developed during the war (in Marshall's words, "the most complete unification of military effort ever achieved by two Allied nations"),[2] based on the Combined Chiefs of Staff and the cluster of Joint Boards established in Washington and—as we now know—underpinned by the complete sharing of secret signals intelligence; and, on the other hand, what Churchill later described as the Soviet "far-distant, single, independent front," with which "there was neither need nor means of staff integration."[3] Moreover, except for Britain and the Soviet Union (from May 1942), the three partners in the Alliance were not formally bound by any treaty; and although they were the three principal signatories of the United Nations Declaration, this document was also signed on New Year's Day 1942 by the representatives of twenty-three other governments.[4]

Nevertheless, there are good reasons for thinking in terms of a Grand Alliance. For Churchill, who used this phrase throughout his memoirs of the Second World War, it echoed the Grand Alliance led by his ancestor, Marlborough, over two hundred years earlier. But the phrase had been widely used as the term for an anti-German coalition of European governments in the mid-1930s: a deterrent combination of which Churchill was himself one of the chief advocates, recognising the fact that Hitler could then be contained by nothing less than Britain, France and the Soviet Union acting in concert. By the turn of the year 1941–42—even taking full account of the vast industrial potential of the United States—the idea that Germany, Italy and Japan and their allies could be defeated by anything less than the joint efforts of the armed forces of Britain, the Soviet Union and the United States had been proved to be fanciful; and even so it was a task that—after further Allied defeats—took them almost four years of hard fighting to accomplish. The antagonisms of the Cold War subsequently blurred Soviet realisation of, for example, the grim nature of the prolonged

Battle of the Atlantic,* the appalling fate that hung over the PQ convoys carrying supplies along the exposed route to the ports of the Soviet Arctic, and the bitter battles of Iwo Jima and Okinawa; while, for the Americans and the British, it became easy to minimise the historical fact that, when their armies finally landed on the Normandy beaches in 1944, the German soldiers who fought them there belonged to a *Wehrmacht* whose back had been broken one year earlier on the Eastern Front, at the Battle of Kursk—a tank battle that was fought on a titanic scale. This difference in scale between the land battles on the Western and Eastern fronts was something of which, at the time, Churchill and Roosevelt were both aware and of which Stalin reminded them. For example, the German component of the force finally defeated by the Eighth Army at El Alamein in October 1942 consisted of only four divisions.

In fact the war developed not just into two "independent" theatres of operations, but into three. The war against Japan became in 1942 overwhelmingly an American theatre; the Eastern Front was always exclusively Soviet; and the campaigns, first in North Africa, then in Italy and finally in France, were Anglo-American.[5] Between these three there were, however, important logistic and strategic links—for example, the intense competition for landing craft between the U.S. Navy in the Pacific and the Anglo-American forces in Europe, which took on a major political dimension in the transatlantic strategic debate in 1943–44; the critical contribution to the Red Army made by Lend-Lease supplies; and, in the latter phase of the war, the timing of the delivery of simultaneous blows on all fronts.

From the turn of 1941–42 onwards, the reins of military and political power ran through the Map Rooms of Churchill, Roosevelt and Stalin. Their colleagues, advisers and commanders in the field played

---

*At first the American entry into the war made this battle not better, but far worse, for Allied shipping in the Atlantic. Thus in the first half of 1942 three million tons were sunk in the Atlantic for the loss of only fourteen U-boats (out of an operational total at any one time, of one hundred).

their parts, but the relationship between the war efforts of the three Allies was centered in and was epitomised by the triangular relationship between these three men. Within their process of decision-making Churchill at first occupied the pivotal position, but for the last eighteen months of his life this position was Roosevelt's. From the outset, moreover, they began among themselves the debate about the international settlement that would follow the war, once they had won it. For nearly four years the foreign ministers of the three countries became more like the chorus or the heralds in a Greek drama—pointing out lessons to be drawn, attempting to predict, bringing news—while the three protagonists were Churchill, Roosevelt and Stalin. It is the personal messages that they exchanged, often through channels that bypassed their colleagues and their officials, taken together with their discussions when they met each other, which demand the historian's attention. To adapt the words used by Hopkins of Churchill (reporting to Roosevelt on his first meetings with Churchill in the beginning of 1941), they "*were* the government." They were the Big Three.

The Battle for Moscow

In the first week of December 1941 two battles moved almost simultaneously towards a climax: the German-Soviet battle for Moscow and the battle of words between Japan and the United States. By the autumn, Hitler had at last been convinced that Moscow must be captured. This was to be achieved by means of one final, encircling operation, codenamed *Typhoon*. *Typhoon* was to ensure that "not a single Russian soldier, nor a single living being—man, woman or child—could leave (Moscow). Any attempt to get out must be crushed by force."[6] So sure had Hitler been that all that *Barbarossa* would consist of would be a short and sharp *Blitzkrieg* campaign, that he sought to derive no political advantage whatever from the disaffection of the inhabitants of the Baltic States and—even more important—the Ukraine, who had suffered greatly at Stalin's hands. On the contrary, his Commissioner for the East European Region, Alfred Rosenberg (who did attempt to develop some kind of policy in that direction), was completely out-gunned by the head of the *SS,* Heinrich Himmler, and by Göring, in his capacity as head of the German Four Year Economic Plan. For these two men, as for Hitler, the Slavs—let alone the Jews—were subhuman *Untermenschen.* Their fate was already being planned in Nazi memo-randa before the invasion. Of the victims who perished in the wake of the advancing German armies, those who were shot were fortunate; others were gassed or starved to death. Had Hitler's political aim been to unite the Soviet people behind Stalin in what soon became known as the Great Fatherland War, he could scarcely have done so in a more irrevocable manner.

Stalin was also greatly helped by the Japanese decision to advance southwards, instead of attacking the Soviet Union. Here again Hitler's conviction that *Barbarossa* was bound to succeed played an important part. When the Germanophile Japanese Foreign Minister, Matsuoka, visited Berlin in March 1941, it was Singapore that Hitler urged his government to make its goal. On his way home, Matsuoka signed a Non-Agression Pact in Moscow on 13 April. Such pacts had limited value, but in this case even less than usual, because Matsuoka's reaction to *Barbarossa* was to urge his colleagues to abrogate the Moscow pact and declare war on the Soviet Union at once.[7] Fortunately for Stalin, Matsuoka was so discredited in Tokyo by the German invasion of the Soviet Union, the news of which Hitler gave the Japanese Ambassador only at the last moment, that by 18 July he was no longer Foreign Minister; on 9 August, as we now know, the Japanese Government decided against undertaking operations in Siberia that year; and well before his arrest in Tokyo on 24 October 1941 Richard Sorge was able to confirm this crucial intelligence.[8] In consequence, Stalin was able to transfer between eight and ten divisions, together with one thousand tanks and as many aircraft, from the Far East to Moscow. Most of these fresh troops he kept as his reserve force, for use at the vital moment in December 1941.

By the time that the last spurt of Operation *Typhoon* petered out in the western outskirts of the Soviet capital on 2 December, deep winter had set in. Three days later Stalin unleashed the Soviet counter-offensive, led by Zhukov. The threat to Moscow was lifted, never to be repeated during the rest of the Second World War. On the Moscow front the German Army retreated[9] for the first time in the war; and on 19 December Hitler himself took over the post of Commander-in-Chief of the German Army from Walther von Brauchitsch, who had resigned. He had come within an ace of success. He therefore rejected his generals' advice that, *Barbarossa* having failed to reach the line laid down in his original directive, the German Army should now undertake a general withdrawal to a shorter and more easily defensible front. Instead, Hitler ordered the exact opposite: to "cling to every town and village, retreating not a step, fighting to the last round, to the last grenade."[10] This became the *leitmotiv* of every military directive that he issued during the rest of the war. It was entirely in character: an emotional response, in no way a decision reached after deliberation. And, in the crisis of December 1941, it worked; there was no Soviet breakthrough on the Moscow front.

Pearl Harbor

Meanwhile, the evidence from all sources of impending Japanese aggression became so compelling that on 1 December, at long last, Roosevelt gave the commitment that Churchill had sought from the Atlantic Conference onwards: if the Japanese attacked either the British or their Dutch allies in South-East Asia, the United States would give them armed support. Roosevelt gave this commitment not in any formal communication, but in an aside during a talk with Halifax—so vaguely indeed that even at this eleventh hour the British War Cabinet instructed the ambassador to "clinch the three points that the President had made."[11] This he did. In the event, neither this nor the parallel warnings to Japan that were finally approved (but could not be delivered in time) made any difference. Japanese forces landed not just in Siam, as had generally been expected, but also in Malaya and the Philippines. And early on the morning of Sunday 7 December they took Roosevelt, Churchill and the whole world by surprise,* by simultaneously launching an attack—at extreme range, from aircraft carriers—on the U.S. Pacific Fleet, lying at its moorings in Pearl Harbor. Of eight battleships, seven were sunk and the other seriously damaged. Ten hours later the heavy bombers that had been intended to transform American strategy in the Philippines were destroyed on the ground at Clark Field.[12] On 9 December both the *Prince of Wales* (in which the British Naval C-in-C was flying his flag) and the battle cruiser *Repulse* were caught without air cover and sunk. (The aircraft carrier that should have accompanied these two ships to the Far East had run aground in the Caribbean in November.) Land-based air cover was not summoned until too late. Thus by the end of 1941 not a single Allied capital ship was left afloat between Egypt and California.[13] As Churchill later put it in his memoirs, "in all the war" he "never received a more direct shock."[14] And much worse was to follow in 1942.

On the day after what Roosevelt called, in his address to Congress, "a day that will live in infamy,"† the two Houses voted to declare war on Japan, with only one dissenting vote.[16] The British declaration of war was quicker than the American; and on 9 December Churchill was already proposing to Roosevelt that he should again come to Washington—"the sooner, the better." After some discussion of Bermuda as a venue (for January)—Roosevelt at first expressed concern for Churchill's safety—the two leaders agreed on Washington forthwith.[17] The long *Arcadia* Conference followed, lasting well into the New Year (it is therefore described in the next chapter). Both Churchill and Roosevelt reacted to the Pacific disasters in a strikingly similar way. Roosevelt's wife later described him as having been "in a way more serene than he had appeared in a long time"; and Churchill's "so we had won after all!" was by no means a later afterthought. On the

---

*The U.S. Government had received what should have been ample warning from cryptography. But the long Japanese telegram to the Washington Embassy, including the declaration of war, did not reach Hull until almost an hour after Pearl Harbor had been attacked.

†A phrase that he added in his own hand, at the last moment, just before delivering the address.[15]

contrary, his telegram to Roosevelt on 12 December described his "enormous" relief at the "turn world events have taken." And even in his broadcast to the nation immediately after the surrender of Singapore two months later, he would describe the United States' entry into the war as "the first and greatest of events"—what he had "dreamed of, aimed at and worked for."[18]

On Churchill's side, recrimination was reserved not for the U.S. Government, but for the few such as Craigie, who, on his return from his mission in Tokyo, questioned American handling of the Japanese negotiations in 1941. It was not until nearly two years after Pearl Harbor that the Foreign Office sent Churchill his copy of Craigie's "Final Report on conclusion of his mission to Japan." In November 1942 Eden had warned Churchill that this long report was critical both of British and U.S. policy "prior to December last." In the interval Craigie "toned down" some passages in his report, which in September 1943 was given a strictly limited circulation—the King, the War Cabinet and within the Foreign Office—and was accompanied by an even longer memorandum "From the Burma Road Crisis to Pearl Harbour," prepared by the Foreign Office Far Eastern Department.

Churchill, who read Craigie's report while travelling back from the First Quebec Conference, was outraged. His subsequent minute to Eden reveals him as understanding Craigie's view as little as he did— on a different issue and on a far more serious level*—Niels Bohr's a year later. He wrote:

> This despatch throws the blame for the war between Japan and the United States on the failure of the United States to handle properly the compromise proposals of 20th November 1941. It is therefore a very strange document and one which should be kept most scrupulously secret. A more one-sided and pro-Japanese account of what occurred I have hardly ever read. The total lack of all sense of proportion as between British and American slips on

---

*See Chapter 16.

the one hand and the deliberate scheme of war eventuating in the outrage of Pearl Harbour on the other shows a detachment from events and from his country's fortunes. He also writes of the breach with Japan as it if were an unmitigated disaster.... It was, however, a blessing that Japan attacked the United States and thus brought America wholeheartedly and unitedly into the war. Greater good fortune has rarely happened to the British Empire than this event which has revealed our friends and foes in their true light, and may lead, through the merciless crushing of Japan, to a new relationship of immense benefit to the English-speaking countries and to the whole world. There should be no question of circulating this despatch to anyone....[19]

Eden replied to Churchill with a self-righteous minute, agreeing with his comments and drawing his attention to the departmental memorandum, which, he said, was designed to show

(a) that Japan was bent on our undoing;
(b) that no measure of appeasement would have averted this; and
(c) that our policy contributed to bring the British Empire, the United States and the Dutch into line in the Far East in time before Japan struck.

Craigie's report, although it contains some factual errors, is a well-argued and restrained document, which could be excoriated in terms such as those used by Churchill and Eden at the time only on the basis of their ignorance of Japan. The ambassador argued that, had a compromise agreement been reached "involving the withdrawal of Japanese troops from South Indo-China, war with Japan would not have been inevitable"; that the final American proposals in November 1941 could not have been expected to achieve a settlement "without recourse to arms"; that the U.S. Government should have known that there was no chance whatever of Japan yielding "without having first suffered defeat in the field"; and that "by the pursuit at this stage of a less uncompromising policy, the outbreak of war with Japan could at that time have been postponed for three months at the very least." He concluded:

> During the autumn of 1941 the United States Government must either have misread the Japanese situation or they must have decided that they were ready for war with Japan.

The interesting aspect of the departmental memorandum is not that it sought to redress the balance of argument against Craigie's thesis (which it did), but the fact that, in so doing, it nonetheless included several passages that reveal what Foreign Office officials must have felt at the time about the way in which the Japanese issue was handled in 1941. Thus, Hull's initial deviousness with Halifax gets a mention, as does Hull's long delay in giving Halifax a copy of his final memorandum of 26 November 1941 to the Japanese; and Hull's memorandum is plainly described as "a flat rejection of . . . all . . . Japanese proposals." Above all, the Foreign Office departmental memorandum establishes the vital point that the conversion of the freezing of Japanese assets, "which quietly assumed the character of a complete embargo, destroyed the margin for manoeuvre by either side without a fundamental change of front."

The documents published over the years that have passed since then lend more colour to Craigie's assessment than either Churchill or Roosevelt would ever have been prepared to admit. At the time Churchill did not have to contend—in public—with anything much more than an awkward debate in the House of Commons (which gave him a vote of confidence) and later a reconstruction of the government; there was no public enquiry, even after the surrender of Singapore.[20] In Washington, on the other hand, the reaction to what had happened in the Pacific was far more forceful.[21] The report of the thirty-nine-volume congressional enquiry, however, was not published until 1946. By then Roosevelt was dead.

The previous chapter has suggested some of the reasons for the drift into this series of military catastrophes. But, where great events are concerned, as in December 1941, the historian does well to distinguish between the micro- and the macro-aspects of history. On the former view, the American-Japanese negotiations of 1941 (like the Anglo-Soviet negotiations of 1939) now look as though they were conducted on the principle of Tennyson's Lady of Shallot: each side seeing the world refracted through a mirror. But if the outturn in the Far East in 1941 is looked at on the widest possible canvas, then Churchill's and Roosevelt's reactions to it become more understandable. This was the canvas on which, in Cabinet three weeks before Pearl Harbor, Churchill had drawn four broad possibilities:

1. U.S.A. in the war against Germany; Japan neutral
2. U.S.A. at war on the Allied side; Japan at war on the Axis side
3. U.S.A. and Japan both out of the war
4. U.S.A. out of the war; Japan in it.

Of these four, he said, the first was the best for Britain; the fourth was clearly the worst.[22] Churchill pinned his own hopes, initially against all rational hope, on American entry into the war. Being Churchill, he said so. Roosevelt being the man he was, did not. What he thought within himself remains a matter for endless speculation.

Meetings in Moscow

At the same time that Churchill was crossing the Atlantic westwards in the battleship *Duke of York,* heading for the *Arcadia* Conference, Eden was sailing eastwards to Murmansk, heading for Moscow. The Foreign Secretary's visit to Moscow in December 1941 was the outcome of a lively exchange of messages between Stalin and Churchill during the previous month, which is the more remarkable in that it took place while the German Operation *Typhoon* was still in progress outside Moscow. On 8 November Stalin had sent a personal message to Churchill agreeing with him on the need to introduce "clarity, which at present does not exist, in the mutual relations between the USSR and Great Britain"—the consequence, in Stalin's view, of the lack of "definite agreement between our countries on war aims and plans for post-war organisation" and "on mutual military assistance in Europe against Hitler." Churchill's response, a fortnight later, was to offer to send Eden to Moscow, accompanied by the Vice-Chief of the Imperial General Staff. His message making this offer suggested, in gentle language, that the first task was to win the war, after which the three principal participants would meet at the table of the Peace Conference. He added—and Stalin in his reply welcoming Eden's visit agreed— that the fact that the Soviet Union was a Communist state, while Britain and the United States were not, was no obstacle whatsoever in reaching agreement on the three countries' "mutual security and lawful interests." And by this time Churchill and Stalin had also reached the point of exchanging birthday greetings.[23]

Before the Moscow negotiations began, Churchill had regarded the most urgent question on the agenda as likely to be whether the Soviet Union should be asked to declare war on Japan. He and the Chiefs of Staff found it hard to make up their minds where the balance of advantage lay, but ended by giving Eden discretion to decide on the spot how far to press Stalin on this point. In the event, Eden's lengthy discussions with Stalin hardly touched it.[24] Instead, they concentrated primarily on the question of the Soviet Union's future frontiers in Europe. Throughout, Stalin insisted that it was "absolutely essential" that the "old frontiers, the frontiers of 1941" should be re-established. For Stalin, these frontiers meant the frontiers of the territories lost by the Soviet Union at the time of the Versailles settlement. For Eden, they meant new territories acquired by the Soviet Union as the fruit of the 1939 German-Soviet agreements. Eden took his stand on the principles of the Atlantic Charter and the British Government's need to consult with its other Allies—above all, the United States. Stalin ironically remarked that this gave the impression that the Atlantic Charter was "directed not against those people who were trying to establish world domination, but against the USSR," the country which was engaging almost the entire German Army in battle. A subsidiary discussion—about the possible location of a British force to be sent to the Soviet Union, either on the Leningrad or on the Ukrainian front, or alternatively, as part of a joint Soviet-British operation in the Arctic—

also got nowhere. Stiffened by telegrams sent by Churchill,[25] Eden dug in. The Anglo-Soviet Treaty, which should have been signed in Moscow, was shelved; and a meaningless communiqué was issued on 29 December 1941 instead.[26] There the matter of the treaty was left until the following spring.

These December conversations in Moscow set the stage for the Soviet debate with the British and U.S. governments that would take up much of Churchill's, Roosevelt's and Stalin's time in the years that followed. As things turned out later, the central territorial issue became that of Poland. Yet at the time when Stalin was talking to Eden, the Soviet record shows him as far less preoccupied with Poland than with other Soviet frontiers, above all in the Baltic. So far as Poland was concerned, Stalin offered to cover the matter in a separate letter to the Polish Prime Minister, General Władysław Sikorski,[27] which, he said, could even be published. (At this point Soviet-Polish relations were less hostile than they had been for many years. The discovery of the Katyn massacre still lay in the future.) Stalin, moreover, had had long talks with Sikorski in Moscow just before Eden arrived. Although Stalin left him in no doubt, as in his subsequent talks with Eden, that the Curzon Line must "form the basis" of the post-war Soviet-Polish frontier—in the words of Eden's formal report[28] written after the event—the Polish records also show him telling Sikorski that the time had come to "finish the brawl between Poles and Russians," who had fought each other again and again. Stalin said: "We should settle our common frontiers between ourselves and before the Peace Conference, as soon as the Polish Army* enters into action. We should stop talking on this subject. Don't worry, we will not harm you." Not surprisingly, Sikorski put Stalin on notice that he would return to the charge over this.[29] Nevertheless, comparison of all three records—British, Polish and Soviet—leaves the reader with the impression that, at this early stage, Stalin may have had a fairly open mind about the future form of the Soviet-Polish relationship.

---

*Then being formed from Poles deported to the Soviet Union from eastern Poland in 1939.

Hitler's Two Decisions

To return, finally, to Hitler—since his personal authority was by now incontestable, it is an academic question what Churchill, Roosevelt and, above all, Stalin would have done if the German Army, shivering in the uniforms in which they had begun what was planned as a summer campaign, but still a completely intact force, had been allowed to pull back all along the Russian front. (Might some kind of armed truce have followed? And, had the war somehow dragged on until 1945, might the target of the first atomic bomb have been Berlin?) A more realistic and perhaps more fascinating question is: what would have happened if Hitler had not taken, or had simply postponed, his second, extraordinary decision in December 1941—to declare war on the United States? His agreement with Japan did not oblige him to do this. His instructions to the German Navy to avoid any confrontation with the United States had, up to that point, been categorical. For four days, between the attack on Pearl Harbor and the vitriolic speech in which Hitler announced to the Reichstag the German declaration of war on 11 December, the world once again "held its breath." What it was that prompted him to embark on—as he called it in an extraordinary phrase—"a historical revision on a unique scale . . . imposed on us by the Creator"[30] will always remain a matter for debate, as will the related question: without Hitler's declaration of war, what would Roosevelt have done, as the President and Commander-in-Chief of a country at war with Japan, but not with Germany? What is beyond question is that on 11 December 1941 the unity of the Alliance between the Big Three was sealed.

11

THE ALLIANCE

CONFUSED: DECEMBER

1941–JULY 1942

With ruin upon ruin, rout on rout,
Confusion worse confounded . . .

—Milton, *Paradise Lost, Book II, l. 995*

Grand Strategy

In the middle of December 1941, while Eden was conferring with
Stalin and Molotov in Moscow, Churchill was zigzagging across the
Atlantic in the battleship *Duke of York,* her hatches battened down
against the heavy seas and maintaining radio silence for three days
because of the danger of U-boat attack. He landed at Hampton Roads
on 22 December and from there he flew to Washington, where he
spent most of the next three weeks* making, together with Roosevelt,

---

*Churchill did not spend all this time in Washington. As well as visiting Ottawa (where he
addressed the Canadian Parliament), he spent five days resting in Florida. While staying at the White

the first attempt at formulating a Grand Strategy: the *Arcadia* Conference.

By contrast, the three major partners of the Axis alliance never attempted to work out—still less to agree jointly—anything resembling a Grand Strategy. Between Berlin and Rome there had to be some co-ordination of military effort, if only because Rommel's *Panzerarmee Afrika* was a mixed Italo-German force, with its lines of communication stretching back through Libya and Italy; Italy, moreover, shared with Germany the military occupation of the Balkans; but the occasional summit meetings between Hitler and Mussolini consisted for the most part of monologues by Hitler.[1] Between Berlin and Tokyo there was no co-ordination whatever. At the turn of the year 1941–42 each of the three Axis partners went his own way, following paths down which smiling fortune still seemed to beckon them.

Between the leaders of the Grand Alliance, military co-ordination was, to begin with, largely Anglo-American; and it was only towards the end of 1942 that this began to bear fruit, although even then the grapes did not taste equally sweet to all three leaders of the Alliance. The strategic debate in 1942 reflected a paradox. In the Pacific and in South-East Asia, it was the Americans, the British and their allies who, dazed by the Japanese hammer-blows, now faced warfare of a kind that neither Churchill nor Roosevelt had previously envisaged in the Far Eastern theatre, where Stalin, whose country remained at peace with Japan, was able for the time being to lower his guard.* But in the European theatre (here broadly defined to include the Atlantic and the Mediterranean), Churchill and Roosevelt, with substantial forces uncommitted, enjoyed that margin of choice without which the term "Grand Strategy" is a meaningless concept; whereas for Stalin—outwitted in June 1941 and with the Red Army thereafter locked in a

---

House, he suffered his first (mild) attack of angina pectoris: a heart attack not made public at the time, but revealed a quarter of a century later.

*In April 1945, in accordance with the terms of the treaty, notice of termination of the Soviet-Japanese Non-Aggression Pact, of five years' duration, was correctly given by the Soviet Government.

solitary struggle along a vast front against the combined military strength of the *Wehrmacht* and the increasingly numerous forces of its allies[2]—the only option until almost the end of 1942 was simply "to suffer the slings and arrows of outrageous fortune." The German reverse outside Moscow at the turn of the year was not enough to prevent Hitler from mounting a second major offensive in the summer of 1942, which—once again—almost succeeded. Hence, on the one hand, the long and confused transatlantic debate on strategy through 1942, partly resolved at Casablanca in January 1943; and on the other hand, Stalin's continuous repetition of a single argument—the need for a second European front.

Churchill took advantage of the radio silence imposed on the *Duke of York* to dictate three papers[3] on the future course of the war, the complete text of which he reprinted in his memoirs. In spite of his mistaken belief in a strategy of multiple, dispersed landings on the continent, these papers, which Churchill gave copies of to Roosevelt on his arrival in Washington, remain a remarkable testament to the brilliance and breadth of Churchill's vision and also make clear the genesis of his Mediterranean strategy. In his mind, the invasion of Europe was an objective for 1943, not for 1942, when the "main offensive effort" should be the control of "the North and West African possessions of France" and of "the whole North African shore from Tunis to Egypt." The development of Churchill's strategic thinking during the war is—literally—an open book. By contrast, Roosevelt's "interior" was, in Sherwood's phrase, "heavily forested,"[4] and it has been well said of the American records of the Second World War: "All too often the historian who has struggled through mountains of paper finds the trail disappearing, at the crucial point of decision-making, somewhere in the direction of the White House."[5]

Today, through a wide variety of sources, we can see both how each of the Big Three fought his national corner and how their strategic thinking evolved and interacted. The commanding lead that the early publication of Churchill's memoirs established for him has long since been eroded. The immediate post-war concept of Roosevelt as a war leader who "on not more than two occasions"[6] overruled the unanimous decision of his own Chiefs of Staff no longer holds water. And although the gravity of Stalin's military blunders, by no means confined to June 1941, is common ground in both East and West, no historian can brush aside the verdict of the American who, perhaps more than anyone else in the Second World War, was able to observe the performance of the Big Three at close quarters—Averell Harriman, whose conclusion about Stalin, albeit "a murderous tyrant," was this:

> I found him better informed than Roosevelt, more realistic than Churchill, in some ways the most effective of the war leaders.[7]

The Arcadia Conference

This, the first Anglo-American conference held between Churchill and Roosevelt no longer as common law allies, but as belligerents against the common enemies of Britain and the United States, was their longest in the whole war. In spite of the appalling things that were happening in South-East Asia at the time, the codename *Arcadia* chosen for this conference proved somehow appropriate—witness their encounter in Churchill's bedroom, where Roosevelt sought him out, at a moment when Churchill was in the middle of dictating (to Patrick Kinna). Stark naked at the time, Churchill is said to have remarked: "The Prime Minister of Great Britain has nothing to conceal from the President of the United States."[8] On Christmas Eve, Churchill joined Roosevelt in lighting the Christmas Tree on the lawn of the White House. At this ceremony Roosevelt spoke of Churchill as "my associate, my old and good friend," and Churchill responded with "my illustrious friend, the President of the United States." On Christmas morning they sang hymns together at the Foundry Methodist Church. The following day Churchill included in his address to a joint session of Congress the reflection that, if his father had been American and his mother British, instead of the other way round, he might have got to Capitol Hill on his own. And on New Year's Day they signed the Declaration of the United Nations.

The specific military decision which at the time seemed the most important outcome of *Arcadia* was the appointment of General Wavell, at American suggestion, as Supreme Commander of the—as it turned out, still-born—ABDA (American-British-Dutch-Australian) Command, stretching from the Bay of Bengal to Australia, with his headquarters in the Dutch East Indies. The one result of this conference which did prove to be of high significance for the later direction of the war was the choice of Washington as the seat of a combined (Anglo-American) Chiefs of Staff: a development all the more remarkable in that the U.S. Joint Chiefs of Staff had not previously existed as a body. In a thoroughly Rooseveltian manner, the Joint Chiefs came into being without any presidential executive order;[9] they were responsible direct to the White House, as the American component of the Combined Chiefs; and the Combined Chiefs of Staff were a body whose creation never received the formal approval of either the President or the Prime Minister at *Arcadia*.

As the war developed, moreover, a panoply of Combined Boards followed, the first of which—the Combined Munitions Board—was formed during the *Arcadia* Conference, its location then being provisionally agreed as Washington. In the event, all these combined bodies were set up in Washington, where some nine thousand British officials gradually assembled. In this sense, the central direction of the Anglo-American war effort was from the outset exercised from Washington: a geographical advantage which did not embarrass Churchill so long as he continued to hold the highest military cards in his hand, but which would make itself keenly felt later in the war, after the military balance had swung to the other side of the Atlantic.

The Choice of Commanders

Few things mattered more in the Second World War for all three leaders of the Grand Alliance than their choice of military advisers and commanders, and these men once chosen, how they handled them. Churchill and Stalin both operated on the principle that a subordinate owed them total commitment, right down to the last ounce of his energy, which they ceaselessly, each in his own fashion, extracted; both had explosive tempers; and both were capable of showing, on occasion, flashes of personal consideration. On the other hand, Roosevelt's Olympian calm radiated a relaxed atmosphere, which usually encompassed people around him; he gave the appearance of delegating authority to the maximum extent in military policy (just as he had to those who helped him execute the policies of the New Deal); and yet he intervened decisively whenever he judged it necessary either for strategic or for political reasons.

Churchill was fortunate in Major-General Ismay's appointment as head of the military staff of the War Cabinet shortly before he became Prime Minister, but it was not until November 1941 that he invited General Brooke to succeed General Dill, who was no match for Churchill and was by then exhausted. Brooke—"simply the outstanding [British] soldier of his generation"—[10] became Chief of the Imperial General Staff (CIGS) on Christmas Day, and in March 1942 he was appointed Chairman of the British Chiefs of Staff,* both posts which he held for the rest of the war. He did not attend *Arcadia,* but just before Churchill left for Washington Brooke persuaded him, not without difficulty, to appoint Dill, whom Brooke respected and admired, head of the British Joint Services Mission in Washington. Dill therefore travelled with Churchill to this conference; and after it was over he became the senior British member of the newly formed Combined Chiefs of Staff. In this new office Dill became a superb military ambassador for his country and a close friend of the U.S. Army Chief of Staff, who described him, after his death, as "a dear friend unique in my lifetime, never to be out of my mind."[11] Since this was one of the most fruitful Anglo-American relationships of the entire war, Brooke looked back on his half hour's discussion with Churchill on 11 December 1941 as "one of my more important accomplishments";[12] and it is

---

*The naval and air members of this body were Admiral Dudley Pound (until his final illness obliged him to resign in 1943, when Admiral Andrew Cunningham replaced him) and Air Chief Marshal Charles Portal.

appropriate that Dill, a British Field-Marshal, should have been buried in Arlington National Cemetery in Washington, D.C., after his death in November 1944. His standing in Washington is comparable only with that of Oliver Franks, who—when British Ambassador six years later—established a unique relationship with the U.S. Secretary of State, as Dean Acheson recorded in his memoirs.[13]

Churchill's relationship with Brooke, which became central to the subsequent evolution of British strategy, was tempestuous, but the tension between the two men was usually creative. It is hard to imagine two more different characters. Churchill's ebullient, mercurial brilliance confronted in Brooke (an Ulsterman, born in France) a man whose internal sensitivity was masked by an armour of austerity—a defence reinforced by a Gallic gift of exegesis (his first language was French).[14] After less than a year, following a difficult passage between Prime Minister and CIGS, Churchill exclaimed to Ismay: "I cannot work with him. He hates me." Having first talked to Brooke, Ismay relayed to Churchill Brooke's response: that on the contrary, Brooke loved Churchill, but if Brooke ever told the Prime Minister that he agreed when he did not, Churchill must get rid of him. Churchill's eyes filled with tears as he murmured: *"Dear* Brooke!"[15]

Roosevelt was already familiar with the senior ranks of the U.S. Navy from his years as Assistant Secretary in the First World War, a personal knowledge which stood him in good stead when it came to making his crucial naval appointments as Commander-in-Chief. Notable examples are his choice of Chester Nimitz, a Texan of German stock, the architect of eventual American naval supremacy in the Pacific, to succeed Rear-Admiral Husband Kimmel as Commander-in-Chief, Pacific Fleet, after the disaster at Pearl Harbor; and his resolution of the awkward dividing line between the Chief of Naval Operations (Admiral Harold Stark) and the Commander-in-Chief, U.S. Fleet (Admiral Ernest King). Acting on Stark's advice, Roosevelt appointed Stark to command U.S. naval forces in Europe, giving both the CNO and the Commander-in-Chief, U.S. Fleet offices to King. Although Roosevelt knew the Army far less well than the Navy, he made a decisive choice over two years before the United States entered the war. On the day that Poland was invaded by Germany, an officer who one year earlier had been a brigadier-general took the oath as Chief of Staff, U.S. Army—George Marshall. He retained that post until the war ended. The contrast between Roosevelt's and Marshall's characters was not perhaps as great as that between Churchill and Brooke, but it was striking: the rocklike integrity of the reserved southerner[16] in the service of the political artistry of the Hudson Valley patrician who told Marshall, "I feel I could not sleep at night with you out of the country."[17] Marshall was the creator of the U.S. Army in the Second World War and one of the principal designers of the Grand Strategy that finally won it. And it was he who, in December 1941, brought to Washington, as deputy chief of the War Plans Division, a little known staff officer who had been a lieutenant-colonel at the outbreak of war, Dwight Eisenhower. Both of them had served on General John Pershing's staff in Washington between the wars.[18]

Roosevelt's immediate military circle was completed in July 1942 by the appointment, as White House Chief of Staff, of Admiral William Leahy, recalled from the U.S. Embassy in Vichy. A full admiral, Leahy was senior to the three Chiefs of Staff, but the function that he performed in Washington from then until the end of the war had much in common with Ismay's in London.[19] Thus by the middle of 1942 both Churchill and Roosevelt had established a framework of military advice that would stand the tests of global war. As is to be expected when strong men work together in a great endeavour, these advisers argued fiercely among themselves, on both sides of the Atlantic, and still more fiercely across the Atlantic. But, however much they disagreed, they commanded each other's respect.

Stalin achieved a similar result, but by a different route; and it took him longer. It will be recalled that the Red Army entered the war in June 1941 suffering from a dual (military and political) system of command; and the few senior officers who had survived the military purges of the late 1930s included those—for example, the moustachioed cavalryman Marshal S. M. Budenny—whose Civil War experience in no way qualified them to lead large groups of armies in conditions of modern warfare. The first few months of the war showed them up. At the time when the Soviet Union was invaded, the experienced Shaposhnikov had ceased to be Chief of the General Staff, a post briefly held by Zhukov. By August 1941, Shaposhnikov had been recalled (he remained Chief of Staff until his health gave way) and Zhukov had been given the first of the series of field commands which would make him the Soviet Union's foremost soldier of the Second World War (he also became Stalin's deputy in the latter's capacity as Supreme Commander). Nevertheless, another year passed before Stalin reinstated the single system of military command in the Red Army *(edinonachalie),* having gathered round him the small group of senior officers who would, under his leadership, win the series of battles which ended with the capture of Berlin.

The transmission belt between the interlocking directorate—the *Stavka* and the GKO[20]—through which the Supreme Commander-in-Chief, Stalin, ran the war and the several "fronts" into which the Red Army was divided, was the Soviet General Staff. In this transmission belt the vital links were the *predstaviteli Stavki* (representatives of the *Stavka*), among whom the outstanding general was Alexander Vasilevsky, the nearest Soviet equivalent to General Brooke.[21] Deputy Chief of the Military Operations Division of the Red Army General Staff at the outbreak of war, Vasilevsky was an admirer of Shaposhnikov, whom he succeeded as Chief of the General Staff in June 1942. Most of what Stalin gradually learned about the higher direction of military operations was absorbed from working with three former members of the Tsarist imperial army: Shaposhnikov, Vasilevsky and Zhukov. In an illuminating passage of his memoirs, Vasilevsky recorded a talk about Stalin with Voroshilov, which took place in March 1944. Asked by Vasilevsky how it was that Stalin now tolerated free discussion, in which he was open to argument, with members of the Politburo and of the *Stavka,* Voroshilov's reply was:

> Earlier Stalin was not like that. Probably the war has taught him a lot. Obviously he has understood that he can be mistaken and that his decisions cannot always be the best and that the knowledge and experience of others can also be valuable. And the years have

told on Stalin: before the war he was younger and more self-confident. . . .[22]

Vasilevsky's memoirs also offer two examples of the way in which Stalin behaved towards his closest military collaborators during the war. On one occasion, having ordered Vasilevsky to leave the Kremlin in order to get one good night's sleep at the former Yusupov country house near Moscow, Archangelskoe, immediately after he got there Stalin telephoned him in order to ask a completely trivial question. On the other, Stalin out of the blue insisted that Vasilevsky should make financial provision for his octogenarian father, from whom he had been estranged (for political reasons) since the October Revolution.[23]

For the reasons given in Chapter 9, Zhukov's mature judgment (as opposed to the opinion expressed in his censored memoirs) about Stalin has the ring of truth. Analysing Stalin's competence as Supreme Commander, he then distinguished three separate categories—strategy, operations, and tactics. Zhukov recalled Stalin as understanding strategic questions "from the very beginning of the war. Strategy was close to his accustomed sphere—politics, and the more direct the interaction that questions of strategy entered into with political questions, the surer he felt himself in them." Operationally, "at the beginning of the war his understanding was bad," but in the final phase of the Battle of Stalingrad Stalin began to "master operational questions"; and by the time of the Battle of Kursk he "felt completely confident in these questions as well." As for the third category—tactical questions—Stalin "strictly speaking, did not understand them right up to the very end"[24] (a judgment from which neither Churchill nor Roosevelt was immune).

Thus Stalin, supreme in every sense, learned to take professional advice, although he never gave up his punishing schedule of working to a large extent at night. Churchill—not being Commander-in-Chief—had to argue his view, case by case; and he did so over and over again, keeping his CIGS up into the small hours and harassing his field commanders by telegram, his exhortations to them often based on the evidence of the latest *Ultra* decrypts, which he studied raw. Roosevelt, a man who fell asleep the moment his head touched the pillow and who was, for most of the war, able to recharge his batteries by regularly spending several days at Hyde Park, contrived to keep the essential reins of military decision running through his hands; and although he was in a real (as well as constitutional) sense Commander-in-Chief, he also managed to maintain a breezy banter with almost all his commanders. Of the many examples of this, one will serve: on the bottom of the formal note submitted to Roosevelt by King, reminding the President that his sixty-fourth birthday—the date of mandatory retirement from the U.S. Navy—was approaching, Roosevelt scrawled: "So what, old top? I may send you a birthday present! FDR."[25]

Yet, in spite of these differences, which stemmed both from their individual temperaments and from the nature of the offices that each of the Big Three held, there remains one fundamental characteristic common to all of them. Unlike Hitler, the First War corporal and artist *manqué,* who despised the German officer class, once the leaders of the Grand Alliance had chosen their senior military advisers and field commanders by the end of 1942, they stuck to them: the first condition required to make a Grand Strategy possible.[26]

Europe First

It was at the *Arcadia* Conference that the Combined Chiefs of Staff made their first contribution to the prosecution of the war: a long memorandum, approved by Churchill and Roosevelt, known to history as *WWI* and entitled "Grand Strategy."[27] In this document much was left dangerously vague. Even though it contained the seeds of future controversy, however, its opening paragraphs unequivocally confirmed the earlier *ABC* agreement of February 1941 on "Europe First"—Germany was "the prime enemy and her defeat is the key to victory." Once Germany was defeated, therefore, "the defeat of Japan must follow"; and "it should be a cardinal principle . . . that only the minimum of force necessary for the safeguarding of vital interests in other theatres should be diverted from operations against Germany." What operations against Germany might entail was not clearly defined.

Subsequent paragraphs of the memorandum suggested that "the ring around Germany" might be strengthened and closed by "sustaining the Russian front, by arming and supporting Turkey, by increasing our strength in the Middle East and by gaining possession of the whole North African coast." The memorandum regarded any large-scale land offensive against Germany as unlikely in 1942 except on the Russian front (a 180-degree turn from estimates of Soviet capabilities six months earlier). Limited land offensives by Anglo-American forces were not excluded, however. Looking forward to 1943, the way might be "clear for a return to the Continent, across the Mediterranean, from Turkey into the Balkans, or by landings in Western Europe. Such operations must be the prelude to the final assault on Germany itself. . . ."

On the "Eastern Theatre," the final paragraph of the Chiefs' memorandum was both sanguine and enigmatic. The immediate objective was defined as being "to hold Hawaii and Alaska; Singapore, the East Indies Barrier and the Philippines; Rangoon and the route to China; the Maritime Provinces of Siberia." But the "minimum forces required" for the defence of these vast territories, of which all but the last were under immediate threat, was described only as having "to be a matter for mutual discussion." In other words, nobody knew.

Defeats

They soon did. In the course of the six months that followed Pearl Harbor the Americans and the British suffered a dire series of reverses on all fronts, which as time went on began to call in question the Europe First strategy; and on 28 June 1942 Hitler would launch his penultimate great offensive against the Red Army, directed this time not against the Central Front, but southward towards the Soviet trans-Caucasian oil fields, beyond which lay the British-controlled oil fields of the Middle East. The Anglo-American reverses were threefold. In the Battle of the Atlantic, where the German U-boat fleet could now be deployed along the eastern seaboard of the United States, 1942 became the worst year of the war. In these twelve months eight million tons of Allied shipping were sunk; and in the strategic debates of 1942 it was the availability of shipping which emerged again and again as the single most decisive factor in Anglo–American planning. In the Mediterranean, by the turn of the year 1941–42 the British fleet had been reduced to a strength of three cruisers and a few destroyers and submarines.[28] After defeating Rommel's army and relieving Tobruk in December 1941, the British force in the Western Desert—now called Eighth Army—was in turn pushed back by Rommel from the Cyrenaican–Tripolitanian border at the end of January 1942. For the next four months the two armies faced each other across the desert on a line running southwards from Tobruk (the so-called Gazala position), thus putting paid, for the time being, both to Churchill's hope of the conquest of Libya, linking up with Tunisia, and to the *Arcadian* concept of "gaining possession of the whole North African coast."

The worst blows fell in South-East Asia, where Wavell hardly had time to leave Delhi (he was Commander-in-Chief, India) and to set up the headquarters of his new command in Batavia before the Japanese overran, in quick succession, the Malayan Peninsula, Singapore, most of the Philippine archipelago and the Dutch East Indies. Manila was occupied by Japanese troops on 2 January 1942; on 15 February Singapore surrendered; and the surrender of Java followed three weeks later. The ABDA Command was dissolved. The fall of Singapore was followed by an ineffective defense of Burma; Rangoon fell at the beginning of March. On 12 March, on Roosevelt's orders, MacArthur, accompanied by his family and seventeen members of his staff, left the Philippine island fortress of Corregidor in patrol boats.* Three days later he was flown to Australia, where he established his headquarters as Commander-in-Chief, South-West Pacific. Such was the scale and speed of Japanese military success in the first half of 1942 that the

---

*Although it is MacArthur's histrionic promise to the people of the Philippines—that he would "return"—that has gone down to history, the last signal sent to Roosevelt by General Jonathan Wainwright from Corregidor on 5 May 1942—reporting that he was about to go forward to surrender "with bowed head"—is one of the most moving of the war.[29]

Greater East Asian Co-Prosperity Sphere, as it had originally been called, ballooned outwards into a huge expanse of Japanese-controlled sea and land in the western Pacific, extending southwards from Japan through China, Indo-China, Siam, Burma, Malaya and Singapore, then eastwards through the Dutch East Indies, Borneo, northern New Guinea and the Soloman Islands, and back northwards through the Gilberts, Marshall and Aleutian Islands to Japan.

Of all these defeats in 1942, by far the gravest was the loss of Singapore, the hinge of the entire British Far Eastern strategy, two months after the sinking of the *Prince of Wales* and the *Repulse* off the Malayan coast. In just over two months, 130,000 British troops[30] (including one division disastrously diverted, at Churchill's suggestion, at the last moment from its journey from Britain to the Middle East) were taken prisoner by a numerically inferior Japanese force—the "largest capitulation in British history."[31] These five words in Churchill's memoirs are accurate as far as they go. But an objective analysis of the causes, many of them avoidable, of this great national humiliation was beyond the powers of his pen even in retrospect, just as it was on 17 February 1942 in the House of Commons, where he made a statement, which was ill received, and then refused a debate, on the unconvincing ground that it would only contribute towards the "rattling" process, which "tends to give a feeling of insecurity."[32] Strategically, one of the immediate consequences of the fall of Singapore was to remove the British from the main direction of the war against Japan. This was largely in American hands from the spring of 1942 until the Japanese surrender on board the battleship *Missouri* in Tokyo Bay three and a half years later. Politically, the consequences were still greater. In the longer term, the British imperial position in the Far East and in Australasia could never be the same again. Immediately, the Japanese threat to India and the Indian Ocean evoked a wave of unrest throughout the subcontinent. Dutch and Australian resentment was bitter, particularly that of Australia, most of whose army was in the Middle East.

Churchill might stick to his guns—"if the Malay Peninsula has been starved for the sake of Libya and Russia," he said in one of his telegrams sent home from Washington during *Arcadia*, "no one is more responsible than I, and I would do the same again."[33] But the solemn commitment of the British Government given to the Australian Government in August 1940 was a matter of record: in the (as Churchill believed, unlikely) event of a Japanese invasion "on a large scale," the Prime Minister had "the explicit authority of [the] Cabinet to assure you [the Australian Government] that we should then cut our losses in the Mediterranean and proceed to your aid sacrificing every interest except only [the] defence position of this island on which all else depends."[34] Hence the signed article by the Australian Prime Minister, John Curtin, published in the *Melbourne Herald* on 27 December 1941, declaring that his government regarded the Pacific War as one in whose direction "the United States and Australia must have the fullest say," and that Australia was "now free of any pangs as to our traditional links with the United Kingdom," followed four weeks later by a telegram to Churchill (now back in London) saying that the evacuation of Malaya and Singapore would be regarded as "an inexcusable betrayal" of Australia.[35]

During these weeks of crisis, Roosevelt's serenity was undiminished, and in some memorable telegrams he sought to sustain Churchill. (On 30 January—Roosevelt's birthday—he replied to Churchill's good wishes with the words, "It is fun to be in the same decade with you"; and on 18 February he began a telegram by saying, "I know how the fall of Singapore has affected you . . . I want you to know that I think of you often," and ended this telegram: "Do let me hear from you.")[36] Those closest to Churchill realised that, both physically and emotionally, the opening weeks of 1942 severely taxed his strength.[37] On his return from the United States—travelling by flying-boat from Bermuda—his first thought was to pay an early visit to India, but the state of his health ruled this out. Nevertheless, Churchill, like Roosevelt, succeeded in retaining public confidence. He outfaced the House of Commons in a difficult mood, easily winning a vote of confidence on 29 January, and after the fall of Singapore he countered his critics by reconstructing his government. Meanwhile, Gallup polls in the United States, which in November 1941 had shown a positive answer in the low 70 percent range to the question, "Would you vote for Roosevelt today?", rose to 84 percent in early January and remained in the high seventies through the first half of 1942.[38]

The Strategic Debate

While the toll of shipping in the Battle of the Atlantic steadily mounted and the Middle East remained in a temporary stalemate, the Pacific theatre in Roosevelt's calculations* and India in Churchill's now loomed larger than had seemed possible at the time of the *Arcadia* Conference's categorical commitment to Europe First. And simultaneously both Churchill and Roosevelt now found themselves obliged to deal in earnest, for the first time, with Stalin's request for a second front. In the great debate that unfolded between the Big Three, there was one principal theme: assuming the continued validity of the basic assumption that Germany was the primary enemy not only of the Soviet Union (which was self-evident), but also of Britain and the United States, when and where should an Anglo-American invasion be launched, given the now inescapable demands of the Pacific War? But the debate was not nearly as clear-cut as that. It was not only that the course of the debate ebbed and flowed under the pressure of events in the various theatres of war. Its principal theme was subject to variation; and it was also intermingled, rather like a fugue, with others—for example, the question, fiercely argued within the British Chiefs of Staff Committee, whether Germany could best be brought to its knees not by invasion, but by the strategic bomber offensive.

On 14 February 1942 RAF Bomber Command received a momentous directive from the Chief of the Air Staff (not from the War Cabinet), in consultation with Churchill. This directive authorised Air Chief Marshal Arthur Harris, appointed Commander-in-Chief, Bomber Command, immediately afterwards, with direct access to

---

*The more so since MacArthur's requests for reinforcements made him, a dedicated Republican, a focus for former isolationists, who now became Pacific-firsters.

Churchill, to deploy his forces "without restriction . . . against the morale of the enemy civil population and, in particular, of industrial workers."[39] This subsidiary theme had major implications in terms of the diversion of RAF resources from other crying needs, notably that of anti-submarine warfare, and of the allocation of further industrial resources to the RAF, but it also served as a syren call for those in London who still believed that aerial bombardment would avoid altogether the need for Britain to take part in land warfare on the continent. On 30 May Harris, a convinced advocate of the primacy of the strategic air offensive, launched the first British attack of over one thousand bombers, on Cologne. Churchill sent Stalin regular telegrams reporting the tonnage of bombs dropped on Germany. It was not until much later in the war that Churchill (who on this issue was not helped by the calculations of his scientific adviser, Lindemann) was persuaded of the limitations of the effectiveness of an indiscriminate bombing policy of this kind.*

Of the central theme of the great strategic debate, the first half was Anglo-American, but the second—the question of the Second Front— was Soviet as well. Chapters 9 and 10 have shown how Stalin lost no time in asking first Churchill and later Roosevelt for a second front to be established in 1941. In 1942, it was Roosevelt who took the initiative. As early as 9 March he was proposing to Churchill that Britain and the United States should be jointly responsible for "definite plans for the establishment of a new front on the European continent," in which he was "becoming more and more interested," in the summer of 1942. Three days later he told Litvinov (now Soviet Ambassador in Washington) that he was "pressing the British with the object of establishing a second front," having prefaced the conversation with a remark that would recur in Roosevelt's thinking over the next three years: "It was hard to deal with the British and the Foreign Office and it was much easier for him to come to an agreement with Stalin and

---

*Harris was the only senior British commander not to be offered a peerage after the war.

with myself [Litvinov], since we both speak one and the same language." Litvinov's telegram ended with the reminder that on this occasion, as at almost every meeting with the President, Roosevelt had "repeated how much he would like to meet Stalin, with whom it would be easy to come to an arrangement, since they were both realists"—a belief which Roosevelt expressed directly to Churchill on 18 March:

> I know you will not mind my being brutally frank when I tell you I think I can personally handle Stalin better than your Foreign Office or my State Department. Stalin hates the guts of all your top people. He thinks he likes me better, and I hope he will continue to do so.

On 1 April, in a message drafted in his own hand, Roosevelt proposed sending Hopkins and Marshall to London, a visit which he hoped would be followed by a visit to Washington by Soviet representatives. Churchill having replied positively ("the sooner the better"), on 11 April Roosevelt sent Stalin a personal message, informing him of the purpose of the Hopkins-Marshall mission, which had reached London three days earlier, as the bearers of "an extremely important military proposal," connected with the deployment of "our armed forces in such a way as to relieve the critical situation on your eastern front." After airing the possibility of a bilateral meeting with Stalin in the coming summer near the American-Soviet frontier in Alaska, moreover, Roosevelt went on to invite Molotov and "a trusted general" to Washington in "the nearest possible future." Stalin agreed; Molotov would visit Washington not later than mid-May, calling in London on his way.[40]

Thus the stage was set for a misunderstanding between the Big Three, which might not have arisen, and need not have been so acute, if Grand Strategy had been discussed on a tripartite basis from the outset. An analysis of what followed is made easier if at this point the military codenames used for the operations under consideration in 1942 are listed. *Bolero* was the build-up in Britain of U.S. forces for subsequent operations in Europe; *Jupiter* * was a suggested operation against northern Norway; *Round-Up* was the major Allied invasion of Europe intended for 1943 (which in 1944 materialised as *Overlord*); *Sledgehammer* was the limited Allied invasion of Europe suggested for 1942; *Gymnast* was the original codename for operations to occupy French North Africa; and (after these operations had been decided on) *Torch* became the Anglo-American invasion of French North Africa.

The Anglo-American misunderstanding began at once, during Hopkins' and Marshall's visit to London. The Second Front plan that Marshall had brought with him was twofold: *Sledgehammer* in 1942, either if opportunity offered or if the plight of the Eastern Front required a "sacrificial" operation on the Western Front; and *Round-Up*, an invasion of Europe to be carried out by forty-eight divisions not later than 1 April 1943. At a meeting described by Churchill at the time as "memorable," the British Chiefs of Staff agreed that plans should be prepared on the lines of Marshall's proposals; and three days later the only qualification that Churchill added to his wholehearted agreement with the American "concept of concentration," expressed in a telegram to Roosevelt, was the need to "prevent a junction of the Japanese and the Germans."[41] Paradoxically, in April 1942 it was the British side who argued that the course of the Japanese war had now modified the *Arcadian* concept of "Europe First,"† whereas the essence of the American argument was that since shipping was so short, the Anglo-American effort must be concentrated on a narrow strip of water—the English Channel—and not be dispersed by a peripheral strategy in the Mediterranean. It is impossible to disagree with Ismay's subsequent conclusion:

> Our American friends went happily homewards under the mistaken impression that we had committed ourselves to both

---

*Over the next two years Churchill was virtually the only supporter of this operation, which his own Chiefs of Staff continuously rejected, with good reason.
†The threat to India and the political crisis that this produced there is discussed below.

Round-Up and *Sledgehammer*. . . . When we had to tell them
. . . that we were absolutely opposed to it [Sledgehammer], they
felt that we had broken faith with them. . . .[42]

The Molotov Mission

Molotov's visits left this confusion, if anything, worse confounded. So
far as Soviet territorial demands were concerned (which had largely
stultified Eden's conversations in the Kremlin during the previous December), in early March 1942 Churchill had veered towards the Foreign Office view that "the Atlantic Charter ought not to be construed
so as to deny Russia the frontiers she occupied when Germany attacked
her," and he even asked Roosevelt for "a free hand to sign the treaty
which Stalin desires as soon as possible."[43] Roosevelt's "realism," however, did not extend that far. In conformity with American opinion,
therefore, the Anglo-Soviet Treaty of Alliance, which was finally
signed in London on 26 May 1942, with a twenty-year duration,
omitted all territorial commitments—a Soviet concession for which
Churchill thanked Stalin warmly in a message sent on the following
day.[44] In the military discussions, in response to Molotov's request for a
second front capable of drawing off at least forty German divisions
from the Eastern Front, Churchill was vague.[45]

By contrast, Roosevelt, to whom Molotov repeated this request in
Washington, was not. This cannot have surprised Churchill, for in a
letter of 3 April (brought to London by Hopkins) Roosevelt had
written of Marshall's strategic plan that it "has all my heart and *mind* in
it."[46] The communiqué issued in Washington at the end of Molotov's
visit on 12 June included a sentence stating flatly: "Full agreement was
reached regarding the urgent tasks of establishing a second front in
Europe in 1942." The Soviet records[47] of these Washington talks show
Molotov accurately reporting both Roosevelt's determination to see a
second front opened in 1942 and Marshall's more cautious approach
(particularly his warning about the shortage of landing craft, at the
meeting in the White House on 30 May). They also reveal that, late on
the evening of the 29th, Hopkins came to Molotov's room in the

White House to advise him to "paint a black picture of the situation in the USSR," because the American generals did not agree with Roosevelt's view of the "acute necessity of a second front." Molotov did indeed argue the Soviet case with eloquence and skill. He was, however—again by Hopkins—left in no doubt that Roosevelt "could not give a definite reply about the Second Front without the British."

The fate of *Sledgehammer* had indeed been decided in London while Molotov was in Washington. On the evening of 27 May Churchill presided over a meeting of the Chiefs of Staff Committee, at which he concluded that "in view of the military arguments put forward, he was not prepared to give way to popular clamour for the opening of a second front in Europe in these circumstances" (i.e., in 1942). Unfortunately, the aide-mémoire which he gave to Molotov in London on 10 June fudged the issue: although the problem of landing craft made it impossible to say yet whether a continental landing could be carried out in 1942 and Britain could therefore "give no promise" (true), Britain would "not hesitate" to carry it out in August or September if this appeared "sound and sensible"[48] (by then, highly doubtful). Once again Molotov read between the lines. His summing up in a telegram sent to Stalin was this:

> Consequently the outcome is that the British Government does not accept an obligation upon itself to establish a second front this year; and declares, and that conditionally, that it is preparing some kind of experimental raiding operation.[49]

The June Conference—Hyde Park and Washington, 1942

Churchill travelled to the United States for this, his second wartime visit, in the same Boeing clipper flying-boat in which he had returned from Bermuda in January. By the time that the two leaders met on 19 June, at Hyde Park, hardly anything had gone right for Churchill since they had parted in Washington five months earlier; whereas for Roosevelt things were just beginning to go better. In the first week of June

1942 a great American victory had been won at sea, comparable in several respects with the British air victory won over England two years earlier. Both were battles sought by a numerically superior enemy; both were fought mainly by a small number of experienced pilots—in the Midway battle, operating from aircraft carriers;* both battles owed much to Allied use of cryptography and radar and to the quality of the Allied Commander-in-Chief (in this case, Admiral Nimitz); and both altered the course of the Second World War. This was Nimitz's battle; his opponent was the ablest Japanese naval commander, Admiral Isokuru Yamomoto; Nimitz's Letter of Instruction issued before the battle told his commanders that they would be governed by the principle of calculated risk; and this instruction they followed, destroying four Japanese aircraft carriers in a series of confused, hard-fought engagements. Had the Japanese fleet not been halted at the Battle of Midway, not only would Midway have been captured, but its capture would have opened the way for a further Japanese offensive in the Pacific, which might well have obliged Roosevelt to abandon his strategy of Europe First altogether. As it was, even though the full dimensions of this American victory were not immediately apparent, from then on it was the U.S. Navy that held the initiative in the Pacific. This did not mean that the Americans won every subsequent naval engagement. But on 7 August General Archer Vandegrift's Marines landed on Tulagi and Guadalcanal—the first of the series of amphibious operations on Pacific islands that characterised the American campaigns in this theatre for the next three years, of which the ferocious battles of Guadalcanal, Iwo Jima and Okinawa are only three examples.

The Battle of Midway, followed by the six months' battle for Guadalcanal, had other consequences for Grand Strategy. In spite of the agreed strategy of Europe First, the Pacific campaigns inevitably absorbed a far greater proportion of American resources than had at first been planned. One year after Pearl Harbor the number of U.S. Army

---

* No American aircraft carrier had been lost at Pearl Harbor. Fortunately they were all at sea at the time of the Japanese attack.

Churchill's birthday dinner party at the British Legation, Teheran, 30 November 1943.

David Low, "Rendezvous," 20 September 1939. (From *Years of Wrath* © 1946, 1973; Reprinted by permission of Simon & Schuster.)

"Now Supposing We All Try To Go Somewhere Together," David Low, 7 August 1942. (From *Years of Wrath* © 1946, 1973; Reprinted by permission of Simon & Schuster.)

Winston Churchill, by Max Beerbohm, circa 1900.

Roosevelt reviewing the fleet, July 1938. (AP/Wide World Photos.)

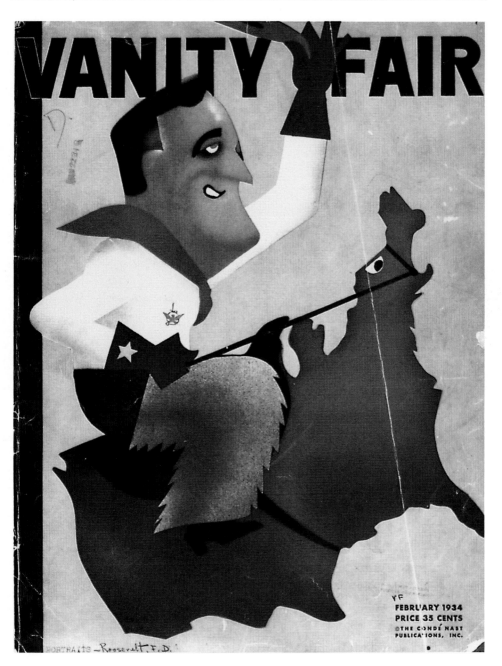

Franklin Roosevelt, by Leon Carlin, *Vanity Fair,* February 1934. (Courtesy of Vanity Fair, Condé Nast Publications, Inc.)

Stalin casting his vote in the Soviet election, 1937. (Sovfoto.)

Viktor Deni, "Stalin's Pipe," *Pravda,* 25 February 1930, p. 1. (Reproduced by courtesy of Dr. Stephen White.)

David Low, "What, no chair for me?" 30 September 1938. (From *Years of Wrath* © 1946, 1973; Reprinted by permission of Simon & Schuster.)

David Low, "Britain's New Defence," 5 October 1938. (From *Years of Wrath* © 1946, 1973; Reprinted by permission of Simon & Schuster.)

РОДИНА-МАТЬ ЗОВЕТ!

ВОЕННАЯ ПРИСЯГА

"The Motherland
—Mother Calls!"
Coloured lithograph
by I. M. Toidze, 1941.
(Reproduced by
courtesy of Dr.
Stephen White.)

"Women of Britain
Come into the
Factories," Second
World War British
poster, Imperial War
Museum.

WOMEN OF BRITAIN
COME INTO
THE FACTORIES
ASK AT ANY EMPLOYMENT EXCHANGE FOR ADVICE AND FULL DETAILS

"Triumph Over Tyranny—Buy War Bonds," Second World War American poster, *What's New,* 1943.

The Big Three on the porch of the Soviet Legation, Teheran, December 1943.
(AP/Wide World Photos.)

The Big Three outside the Livadia Palace, Yalta, February 1945.
(AP/Wide World Photos.)

Roosevelt's last address to Congress, 1 March 1945. (UPI/Bettman.)

Churchill making his victory broadcast in May 1945. (UPI/Bettman.)

Sec War

Reply to your 41011
suggestions approved
Release when ready
but not sooner than
August 2.

HST

Truman's final
instruction to Stimson
about the press release
regarding the atomic
bomb (written at
Potsdam). Courtesy of
George M. Elsey.

Attlee, Truman and Stalin at the Potsdam Conference, 1945. (Sovfoto.)

Stalin's funeral bier, March 1953. (Tass from Sovfoto.)

Churchill, aged 77, on board the *Williamsburg* with Truman, January 1952.

troops in the Pacific build-up exceeded by about 150,000 the total number projected for the area by the end of 1942 in the original *Bolero* planning. The greatest strategic consequence, however, concerned landing craft. The story of their production is a sorry one. Unlike Roosevelt, who shared the U.S. Navy's initial scepticism about landing craft, Churchill had seen and insisted on their crucial importance for European operations even in 1940; two years later the United States undertook a programme of mass production of LSTs (vessels carrying tanks ready for landing); but by the end of 1942 they had fallen to a low priority by comparison with other components of American shipping manufacture. Few, if any, military factors engendered so much acrimonious dispute in the strategic debate during the rest of the war as the question of how many landing craft could be used for any given operation and when; and the nub of this problem was the competing demands of the Pacific campaigns and the campaigns in Europe. As Churchill would remark in the spring of 1944, "history would never understand how the plans of two great empires should be so hamstrung and limited by a hundred or two of these particular vessels."[50]

To return to the June conference—when Churchill and Roosevelt met at Hyde Park, the U.S. Commander-in-Chief already had good cause for relief. Not so Churchill. Two months earlier he had urged on Roosevelt "the need to prevent a junction of the Japanese and the Germans"—an anxiety prompted by what was happening on the Burmese-Indian border, in the Indian Ocean and in India itself. Moreover, within days of his arrival in the United States this anxiety would be dwarfed by the prospect of another "junction" altogether—that of Italo-German forces sweeping through Egypt and joining hands with German forces overrunning the Caucasus. Until his arrival, however, the focus had been India. With hindsight, the Japanese military threat to India was exaggerated at the time, although the threat to Ceylon* was of a different order. But by the middle of May the Japanese, having conquered the whole of Burma, stood on the border of Assam. Politi-

---

*So much so that the British fleet scraped together after the collapse in South-East Asia (including some antiquated battleships) was withdrawn to Kalindi, on the coast of Kenya.

cally, as in the case of Australia, matters were made no easier by the fact that most operational divisions of the Indian Army were outside India. Pressure on Churchill to improve on the British Government's existing commitment—to grant Dominion status to India with the least possible delay after the war—mounted, not only in India and inside his own War Cabinet,[51] but also in Washington. In the White House the strategic significance of India was assessed both intrinsically and in relation to China as "a question of vital concern to our [American] military and naval interests in the Far East," a view for which there was also powerful support in the State Department, especially from Welles.[52]

The outcome was the mission to India led by Stafford Cripps (now a member of the War Cabinet), bearing an offer of somewhat improved British terms for Indian nationalism. The mission failed; and in August the Congress Party would begin a campaign of civil disobedience, to which the British reply was to imprison Mahatma Gandhi and the Congress Party leaders. Cripps may not have been the ideal man to carry out a task that was well-nigh impossible, given the political gulf not only among Indians but between Cripps, on the one hand, and the Viceroy, supported by Churchill and Amery, the Secretary of State for India, on the other. Roosevelt's simultaneous choice of Louis Johnson[53] as his personal representative in India was even worse, however. It was while these two men were in Delhi in the spring of 1942 (Johnson actively interfering in Cripps' negotiations) that Churchill and Roosevelt had a quarrel which, in one heated exchange,[54] led Churchill to hint that he might even contemplate resigning—a possibility which, if it ever existed, was publicly laid to rest six months later by his declaration in the Mansion House: "I have not been appointed the King's First Minister in order to preside over the liquidation of the British Empire."[55]

Again with hindsight, what Roosevelt privately suggested to Churchill on 10 March—the establishment of a "temporary" Dominion government in India, charged with the task of "setting up a body to consider a more permanent government for the whole country"—does not look very radical, especially in the light of the British decision to give independence to the Indian subcontinent five years afterwards. On

11 April, however, upon learning that Cripps was about to return to London, there being—in Cripps' own words—"no hope of agreement," Roosevelt sent Churchill a sharp message, laying the blame for the breakdown of the Indian negotiations squarely on the British Government.[56] Churchill's own ideas about India were nearly half a century out of date,[57] but this time Roosevelt overstepped the undeclared boundary of friendship. Fortunately the message was addressed to Hopkins for Churchill, with whom Hopkins was staying at Chequers at the time, so that it was Hopkins who took the full force of Churchill's initial fury. The first telegram that Churchill drafted in reply was never sent;[58] and by the time the second Anglo-American conference of 1942 convened in June, the Indian quarrel between the two leaders had faded into the background.

Nevertheless, the background as a whole was still inauspicious. Not only did this conference fail to inject clarity into the concept of Grand Strategy, but it was one of the occasions in the debate when the principal theme was submerged by another. Meeting straight away in Washington, the Combined Chiefs of Staff (including Brooke, who had travelled across the Atlantic with Churchill) reached agreement—each side for their own reasons—that the main thrust of the Anglo-American offensive should be in continental Europe as soon as conditions allowed, and that *Gymnast* should not be undertaken for the time being.[59] What emerged from the conference was something quite different, which had been agreed between Churchill and Roosevelt alone, at Hyde Park on 19 June, before they travelled to Washington to join their advisers there. Both men, again each for different reasons, saw the advantages of a North African operation in 1942. Churchill had long believed in it and—like his Chiefs of Staff—he did not believe in invading Europe in 1942. Roosevelt—in spite of his Chiefs of Staff—swung round to *Gymnast,* mainly because it would bring the U.S. Army to grips with the German Army quickly. The conference therefore ended with *Gymnast* revivified and *Sledgehammer* not yet formally buried.

The general who would have to live with this ambivalence was Eisenhower, appointed Commander of U.S. forces in Europe on the last day of the conference. The measure of Anglo–American agreement on strategy that was reached at this conference—it can hardly be described as more than that—was overshadowed by two specific decisions, one of which would remain secret until after the war: the oral, unrecorded agreement reached by Churchill and Roosevelt (which will find its place in Chapter 16) about the development of the atomic bomb. The other decision was Roosevelt's own, taken at Marshall's suggestion, on the afternoon of 21 June, after Marshall had brought into the President's room, where Churchill and Brooke were standing beside Roosevelt's desk talking to him, a telegram reporting the surrender of Tobruk. Churchill, who at first could not believe the news, never forgot Roosevelt's reaction: the offer of the immediate despatch of an American armoured division to Egypt. In the event three hundred Sherman tanks and a hundred self-propelled guns were sent instead; they arrived in time for the Battle of El Alamein.

July 1942

Between the end of June and the end of October 1942 Hitler came closer to winning the war in Europe and in the Middle East simultaneously—with the Battle of the Atlantic approaching its climax—than at any other time. For Churchill's personal leadership, July was a critical month. Cutting short his stay in Washington, he flew home on 27 June to confront a motion of censure in the House of Commons—that "this House has no confidence in the central direction of the war." Churchill was fortunate in that the proposer of this motion, a Conservative MP, included in his speech the ludicrous suggestion that the Duke of Gloucester* (who held a commission in the Army) should be appointed Commander-in-Chief of the British Army. After Churchill had defeated the motion—by 475 votes to 25—Roosevelt at once

---

*The Duke of Gloucester was one of the King's younger brothers. The practice whereby a member of the Royal Family held the office of C-in-C of the British Army had been discontinued in the nineteenth century.

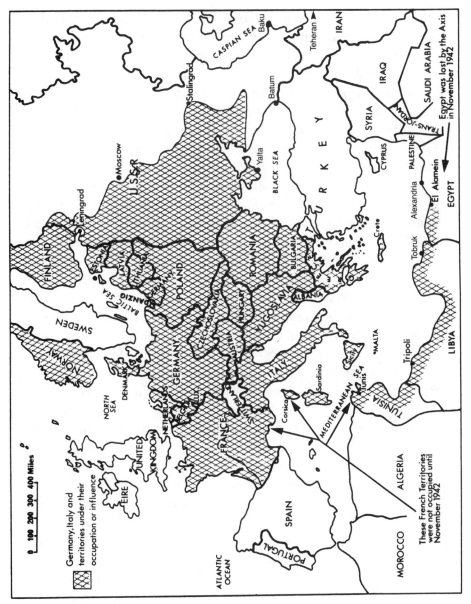

6. Europe and North Africa, 1942

telegraphed the three words "Good for you."[60] Nevertheless, both in the Middle East and in the southern Soviet Union—two areas not all that far removed from each other on the map—the military outlook now looked desperate.

On the day of Churchill's return to London, Rommel's forces were already deep into Egypt: the climax of a battle that had begun in Libya on 26 May between two armies of roughly comparable strength (the Germans had the best anti-tank weapons, while the British had more tanks). The Eighth Army, moreover, had one clear advantage over the *Panzerarmee Afrika:* a supply of "more information about more aspects of the enemy's operations than any forces enjoyed during any important campaign in the Second World War. . . ."[61] and arguably the best signals intelligence (Sigint) enjoyed by an army commander in any campaign since that fought in East Prussia in 1914.* This advantage was wasted. The surrender of Tobruk was bad enough in itself. But for the RAF's dominance in the air, however, the retreat from Gazala to El Alamein, only sixty miles from Alexandria—columns of vehicles moving slowly eastwards, bumper to bumper, along the narrow coastal road—might have become a rout. True, Hitler would probably have done better to rein in Rommel, who outran his supplies, and concentrate instead on the reduction of Malta. And Auchinleck, by assuming personal command of Eighth Army and reinforcing it with fresh divisions, was able to avert the immediate danger at Alamein. But the temporary stalemate that followed owed more to the exhaustion of both sides than to British generalship. The difference between the feeling of the opposing armies in Egypt at this moment may be illustrated by a simple comparison: while Eighth Army prepared a "worst possible case" contingency plan for further withdrawal, Rommel's "thrust line" at Alamein, if plotted on a map extending eastwards, ended exactly on the Giza pyramid.[63]

Meanwhile the German summer offensive in the southern Soviet

---

*When German Sigint gave Hindenburg the opportunity (which he seized) to win the Battle of Tannenberg against the invading Russian Army.[62]

Union began so successfully that by 28 July Stalin issued his famous order of the day, *ni shagu nazad* ("not one step backward").[64] But for disagreement between Hitler and his generals,* the *Wehrmacht* could then have captured Stalingrad. Even as it was, they succeeded in penetrating the heart of the city, where the most savage battle of the entire war soon developed, fought from house to house and from hand to hand; and early in August they reached the foothills of the Caucasus.

While the fate of the Alliance hung in the balance, the Anglo-American debate rumbled on. A fortnight after his return to London Churchill was telegraphing to Roosevelt his conviction that *Gymnast* was "by far the best chance for effecting relief of the Russian front in 1942 . . . the Second Front of 1942." "No responsible British General, Admiral or Air Marshal" was prepared, he said, to recommend *Sledgehammer* as a practicable operation in 1942; whereas soon after this the Joint Chiefs were putting their equally strong conviction, in a memorandum to the President, that *Gymnast* (the invasion of North Africa) "would be both indecisive and a heavy drain on our resources." In their view, therefore, unless the United States' adherence to "full *Bolero* plans" (that is to say, the build-up of forces in Britain for the purpose of invading France) was "forceful, unswerving," it should "turn to the Pacific and strike decisively against Japan."[65] This advice Roosevelt categorically rejected—one of his most decisive strategic interventions in the course of the war. In his own hand† he wrote:

> My first impression is that it is exactly what Germany hoped the United States would do after Pearl Harbor. Secondly it does not in fact provide use of American troops in fighting except in a lot of islands whose occupation will not affect the world situation this year or next. Third: it does not help Russia or the Near East. Therefore it is disapproved as of the present. Roosevelt C-in-C.

---

*As in 1941, the question at issue was the objective: this time, was it Stalingrad or was it the Caucasus? Hitler wanted both. He therefore got neither.

†The original is mounted, on display at the FDR Library, Hyde Park.

In consequence, Marshall, King and Hopkins travelled to London for yet another round of discussions with the British Chiefs of Staff. Their agreed conclusions sowed the seeds of further strategic dissension. Both Churchill and Roosevelt seem simply to have ignored this awkward fact. Instead, the telegrams that the two leaders exchanged on 27 July rejoiced at "the results of this strenuous week" (Churchill) and "the successful meeting of minds" (Roosevelt).[66] At a critical conference with the Joint Chiefs held in the White House on 30 July, Roosevelt—as Commander-in-Chief—ruled that Operation *Torch* (*Gymnast*'s new name) was to be undertaken at the earliest possible moment. This operation—to be commanded by General Eisenhower—was seen by Roosevelt as the "turning point of the whole war." Stalin, still not apprised of Anglo–American decisions taken since Molotov's visits to London and Washington, took a harsher view. A telegram sent to Churchill on 23 July ended with these words:

> I must declare in the most categorical manner that the Soviet Government cannot acquiesce in the postponement of the organisation of a Second Front until 1943.[67]

A week later Churchill proposed meeting Stalin himself in the southern Soviet Union. Stalin's reply[68] on the following day invited Churchill to visit Moscow for this, their first, meeting. Churchill at once accepted.

12

THE INVASION OF

NORTH AFRICA—

A SECOND FRONT?

We are no longer in the age of the
Renaissance, when one made use of the
myrmidons of Milan and the mercenaries of
Florence.

—*Charles de Gaulle's denunciation of the agreement
with Admiral François Darlan, 16 November 1942*[1]

$I_{n \ the \ summer}$ of 1942 Churchill and Roosevelt had
overridden the deliberations of their Chiefs of Staff by personally
deciding that French North Africa should be invaded—Operation
Gymnast, now called *Torch.* * Their decisions, as we shall now see, did
not of themselves settle the transatlantic strategic argument, because it
was one thing to decide to invade North Africa, but another matter to
agree what this invasion, in both the short and the longer term, was *for.*
By the end of July, however, one other bit of common ground between Churchill and Roosevelt was firm. The time had come when
Britain and the United States must do something more than they had

---

*A torch became the emblem worn on the arm badge of those serving at Allied Force Headquarters.

done so far to relieve the pressure on the Soviet Union; and they must do it soon. Why then did Churchill deliver, alone and in person,[2] the response to Stalin's categorical "declaration" about the Second Front? (In 1942 such journeys had to be made in an unheated bomber, equipped with oxygen masks.) Partly perhaps because Churchill was, throughout the war, ready to travel anywhere at the drop of a hat, and at the beginning of August 1942 a journey at any rate as far as Cairo had become imperative, in order to inject new blood into the British military leadership in Egypt. But an even stronger reason was that at this juncture he was the pivot of the Big Three's relationship. Stalin was well aware—certainly from the time of Molotov's visits to London and Washington onwards—that the final decision whether or not to invade continental Europe in 1942, Operation *Sledgehammer,* was primarily British, if only because most (probably all) of the divisions taking part in *Sledgehammer* would come from the British Army in the United Kingdom, which was in any case the only strategic base from which any assault on the continent, at whatever date, could be organised, launched and supplied.

The task that faced Churchill in Moscow was "a somewhat raw job," as he put it in a message to Roosevelt at the time.[3] Not only were the communiqués agreed with Molotov in London and Washington fresh in everyone's mind; the contrast between the recent surrender of Tobruk (where over thirty thousand men were taken prisoner by the *Afrika Korps* after a battle lasting just twenty-four hours) and the Soviet determination to defend the city of Stalingrad to the last man was painfully obvious; and—to make matters worse—the British War Cabinet had just decided to suspend convoys to the Soviet Arctic, following the disaster that befell the June convoy, PQ 17, when only eleven out of thirty-four merchant ships reached Archangel.

First, however, there was the urgent need to visit Cairo, which Churchill did twice—on the way to Moscow and again on his way back—accompanied by Brooke. At the time when Churchill first landed in Cairo early on the morning of 3 August 1942, the C-in-C, Middle East, Auchinleck, was still also commanding Eighth Army in the desert himself: a double command that could not be sustained.* The winning combination that finally emerged—General Harold Alexander at GHQ, Cairo, and General Bernard Montgomery as Eighth Army Commander—was the fruit of long discussions in Cairo during which, at different moments, Churchill offered Brooke first, the command of Eighth Army and later, the Middle East. Wisely and fortunately—he was the only senior British officer capable of dealing with Churchill as Chairman of the Chiefs of Staff—Brooke declined both these appointments. It was Brooke who throughout pressed on Churchill the case for Montgomery, who was not Churchill's first choice. On the other hand, Alexander had long been in Churchill's mind. As Churchill once remarked to Alexander, he was the kind of general Churchill would have liked to be himself, whereas Brooke was aware of Alexander's limitations.[5] As later events would show, in Alexander, the weaknesses were of intellect and decisiveness; in Montgomery, they were defects of character.

The first consequence of Churchill's decision[6] to appoint these generals in August 1942 to the commands of Eighth Army and of the Middle East was—just over two months later—the victory of El Alamein, the biggest battle, whether measured in numbers of troops, tanks or artillery, ever fought in North Africa during the Second World War. Even though this victory was not as vigorously exploited as had been hoped, it was nonetheless decisive. Two weeks of heavy fighting lifted the Axis threat from Egypt once and for all, two years after the initial Italian invasion, and from the whole of the Middle East. It also restored the British Army's confidence in itself battered by the experiences of the past two and a half years. For Churchill himself, moreover, it obliterated from the public memory the miserable record of the first half of 1942. From then on no one could say of him, as an opponent had done during the House of Commons' censure debate in July, that he won "debate after debate," but lost "battle after battle."[7]

---

*Churchill also spent a day in the Western Desert on each of his visits to Egypt in August 1942.[4]

The Moscow Conversations

From Cairo, Churchill flew to Moscow by way of Teheran. On the afternoon of 12 August 1942, when Churchill landed at Moscow airport—he was greeted there by Molotov before being installed in a state villa on the Lenin Hills—he could be certain neither of the victory soon to be won by the commanders whom he had just appointed, nor of the precise form that *Torch,* on which he and Roosevelt had agreed in principle only at the end of July, would take in practice. The summit meeting that took place in the Kremlin from 12 to 16 August ranks together with the Atlantic Conference a year earlier and with the Teheran Conference fourteen months later as the most extraordinary of the Second World War. All three were notable for bringing together men who had never met before: Churchill and Roosevelt at Placentia Bay, Churchill and Stalin in Moscow, Roosevelt and Stalin at Teheran. By August 1942 Britain, whose army had, twenty years earlier, only just withdrawn from Baku (occupied as part of British intervention in the Russian Civil War), was now bound by a twenty-year treaty of alliance with the Soviet Union, described by Stalin in a major speech as "an historic turning point in relations between our country and Britain."[8] In Moscow the greatest English parliamentarian of the twentieth century, now leading an embattled empire, faced a Georgian Marxist, the *Vozhd'* of the Soviet Union, vast tracts of which lay under the heel of the German Army, at that moment advancing still further east. The sparkling torrent of Churchillian eloquence was matched against the quiet thrust of Stalin's stiletto.*

Churchill and Stalin met four times in as many days,[9] the final meeting lasting until the small hours in Stalin's apartment in the Kremlin, where Churchill was introduced to his daughter, Svetlana. At dawn on 15 August, Churchill left Moscow believing that, as he put it in a telegram to Roosevelt, he had established "a personal relationship" with Stalin, and confident that "The disappointing news I brought

---

*Stalin was noted for his habit of speaking in a very low voice and for his economy with words.

could not have been imparted except by me personally without leading to really serious drifting apart. It was my duty to go. Now they know the worst. . . . Stalin is entirely convinced of the great advantages of *Torch*. . . ."[10]

To what extent was Churchill right to believe that, in such unpromising circumstances, he had achieved these two remarkable results? With one exception, when Churchill left his interpreter lost for words,[11] the British and the Soviet records of those talks between Churchill and Stalin do not reveal any major difference in their account of what the two leaders said to each other. Both records confirm that the talk between the two men was conducted with hammer and tongs—Stalin from time to time speaking insultingly as well as plainly. At their first meeting, held only two hours after Churchill's arrival, Churchill sought to deflect Stalin's reaction to knowing "the worst," first, by expounding the advantages of a massive *Round-Up* in 1943, by comparison with a catastrophic *Sledgehammer* in 1942 (he did not use these names in talking to Stalin, but he did tell Stalin about the code-name *Torch*), and secondly, by extolling the objectives of *Torch,* which he described to Stalin in some detail, using his much quoted analogy of the "soft underbelly of the crocodile" (which he drew for Stalin) and dangling before him the prospect that it "would open up additional routes for invading the European continent next year." So far as the military purpose of *Torch* was concerned, as Churchill wrote in his memoirs, Stalin "saw it all in a flash";[12] and his remark—"May God bless its execution"—is common to both sets of records.

When the two men met again on the following day, Stalin summed up the difference between Churchill's position and his own as: "Churchill considers this [the Russian] front secondary, but we consider it primary. Our allies are therefore giving their divisions to other places. There are differences of opinion between allies, and there is nothing tragic in this."[13] Stalin's view was, however, expressed far more bluntly in a memorandum handed to Churchill, which stated that the British Government's refusal to establish a second front in 1942 in Europe "struck a moral blow at the whole of Soviet society, which had counted on the establishment of a second front. . . ." To this, the essence of Churchill's reply on 14 August was its opening sentence: "The very best form of second front in 1942" was *Torch*. Any breach of promise was categorically denied—a denial supported in writing by Harriman.[14]

Armed with a new interpreter,[15] Churchill began his final meeting with Stalin on the evening of 15 August. At this meeting, which Stalin converted into a working dinner, the atmosphere improved.* It is according to the Soviet record that Stalin assured Churchill that

> He and Churchill had got to know and understand each other, and if there were differences of opinion between them, that was in the nature of things. . . . The fact that he and Churchill had met and got to know each other and had prepared the ground for future agreements, had great significance. He was inclined to look at the matter more optimistically.[16]

Thus the two leaders, so improbably thrown together, sized each other up, just as Churchill and Roosevelt had done one year earlier, at Placentia Bay. From August 1942 until August 1945 Churchill and Stalin had a mental picture of each other. This picture was not nearly as clear as that which Churchill and Roosevelt had formed of each other at their first meeting. Moreover, as at Placentia Bay (where his initial euphoria was soon followed by a wave of depression), Churchill may have persuaded himself rather more effectively than he persuaded his interlocutor.

Once again Colonel Ian Jacob, a participant at this meeting as he had been at Placentia Bay, recorded in his diary at the time an assessment on which it would be hard to improve:

> Looking back on the visit, I think it is very doubtful whether more could possibly have been achieved. Certainly, no-one but the Prime Minister could have got so far with Stalin. Neverthe-

---

*These changes of Stalin's mood—from fair to bad and back to better—were attributed at the time partly to negotiating tactics and partly to Stalin's need to refer back to colleagues even more hard-nosed than himself, a belief which the Americans also adopted later on. The myth of "Stalin, the prisoner of the Politburo," lasted for many years.

less, I am bound to say that I don't believe that it is possible to make friends with a man like Stalin, in the sense that we understand friendship. The thing that impressed me most about Stalin was his complete self-possession and detachment. He was absolute master of the situation at all times, and appeared to be cold and calculating. . . . I should say that to make friends with Stalin would be equivalent to making friends with a python. . . . The Prime Minister's relationship with Stalin would only be close and personal as long as Stalin thinks that his interests will be served thereby.[17]

This said, Stalin did not have to speak as he did on 15 August (in the passage of the Soviet record quoted above). What he said to Churchill then would be echoed nearly three years afterwards, at a tense moment of the relationship between the Big Three, in a telegram from Stalin to Churchill which included the two significant words *znaya Vas* ("knowing you").[18] And the fact that Churchill, then not far from his sixty-eighth birthday, should have undertaken this journey at all on top of the strains of the past eight months was in itself no small achievement. With hindsight, however, two other facts stand out. First, Stalin not only readily understood the military advantages of *Torch* (four[19] of which he himself at once enumerated, to Churchill's satisfaction), but he also put his finger on its principal weakness: the political planning of the operation. To this aspect he reverted more than once during his talks with Churchill, who brushed it aside; and at one moment Stalin suggested that de Gaulle ought to be included in *Torch.*[20] Secondly, what Churchill told Stalin about a future *Round-up*, without a hint of the need for further Anglo-American consultation, must have left Stalin with the impression that—at the very least—the invasion of Europe in 1943 was conceivable, even though an invasion, however limited, in 1942 was ruled out.* On the first of these two

---

*Through the autumn of 1942, however, there was much discussion of the possibility of sending an Anglo-American air force to support the Soviet defence of the Caucasus. It turned out to be unnecessary and the plan was dropped.

points, the course of events later in 1942 would prove Stalin right. The second left the debate on Grand Strategy even more confused than it had been before Churchill flew to Moscow. Little more than two months had passed since these conversations in Moscow when Stalin sent Maisky a furious telegram (doubtless influenced by what was happening at Stalingrad at that time) in which he said that everyone in Moscow had "the impression that Churchill is holding a course heading for the defeat of the USSR, in order thereafter to reach agreement with the Germany of Hitler or Brüning at the expense of our country." At the top of the list of reasons given by Stalin for this remarkable assumption was the question of a second front, but Stalin also threw in, as though for good measure, "the question of Hess."[21] (Rudolf Hess, Hitler's deputy, had flown to Scotland in May 1941. This dramatic episode, which had little practical effect at the time, was the sort of thing calculated to arouse Stalin's suspicions, even though in May 1941 he himself was in no position to criticise anything that was going on in Britain.)

On 27 November Stalin reminded Churchill of his "promise in Moscow to create a second front in Western Europe in 1943"; and by the beginning of December he was referring even more precisely to a second front "in the spring of 1943."[22] Shortly before these two telegrams were sent, Stalin had publicly reassured the Soviet people in these words: "People are asking: but will there still be a second front in Europe? Yes, there will be, sooner or later, but there will be."[23]

The Transatlantic Debate Continued

A good example of Dill's invaluable role as transatlantic interpreter is the warning telegraphed from Washington just before Churchill left for Cairo on 1 August—that "in the American mind" *Torch* in 1942 would make *Round-Up* improbable in 1943.[24] This was a tactful telegram, for it was not just the American Joint Chiefs, but the British Chiefs of Staff, whose minds Dill was representing to the Prime Minister; at their meeting held in London on 24 July the Combined Chiefs had agreed a memorandum *(CCS 94)* concluding, among other things, that a commitment to *Torch* "renders *Round-Up* in all probability impracticable of successful execution in 1943."[25] This was the memorandum which both the President and the Prime Minister had ignored. Their approval of *Torch* did not alter the fact that Marshall distrusted and King disliked the operation. Marshall's distrust stemmed from the fact that *Torch* looked to him—with good reason—like the beginning of a "peripheral" strategy for defeating Germany, whereas he was convinced that Germany could be defeated only by the concentration of the maximum of Allied military force against the territory nearest both to the invasion base (Britain) and to the invasion objective (Germany)—namely, northern France. King's dislike was simpler: *Torch* would make demands on the shipping needed for the great campaigns now beginning in the North-West Pacific. (Vandegrift's Marines landed on Guadalcanal on 7 August.) For both of them, *Torch,* which reversed the British commitment of the previous April, was acceptable only if it was regarded as no more than a part of "a defensive, encircling line of action for the continental European theatre" (to quote another phrase from the Combined Chiefs' unhappy memorandum *CCS 94*). Thus, a week after Dill sent his telegram to Churchill, he wrote to Marshall, in an equally tactful letter, that "at present our Chiefs of Staff quote *WWI** as *the* Bible, whereas some of your people, I think, look upon *CCS 94* as the Revised Version."[26]

From the intricate web of strategic negotiation[27] woven by military planners and Chiefs of Staff in London and in Washington during the months from August until the end of 1942, both the President and the Prime Minister managed to remain not exactly aloof, but at one remove. Both of them had their work cut out in deciding the immediate question: exactly how and when was North Africa to be invaded? And both of them were deeply concerned by what was happening in the Soviet Union. Churchill contested again and again his Chiefs of Staff's conviction that *Torch* did indeed rule out *Round-Up* in 1943.[28] He knew what a politically vulnerable hostage he had offered to fortune

---

*The memorandum laying down the "Europe First" strategy at the *Arcadia* Conference.

during his talks with Stalin in Moscow. Roosevelt was equally clear that the Russian front was "our greatest reliance."[29] All these transatlantic cross-currents of Grand Strategy would not flow into a single pool of argument, in which both the American and the British principals and their advisers were immersed, until the beginning of 1943.

The Execution of Torch

Meanwhile, after many twists and turns, the two leaders had reached agreement on *Torch* at the beginning of September 1942 in a memorable exchange of telegrams: Roosevelt's "Hurrah!" and Churchill's "Okay full blast."[30] Militarily speaking, the invasion began well. On 8 November the main U.S. forces landed successfully at Casablanca and Oran and an Anglo-American force landed at Algiers; three days later a British brigade landed one hundred miles further east; and even further east, a British parachute battalion captured Bone airfield on 12 November. Nevertheless, although French resistance lasted only three days,* the vital strategic objective—Tunis—was not captured for another six months. Victory in North Africa in 1942 was won not in Tunisia but in Egypt, where Rommel, defeated by Montgomery at Alamein, began the *Panzerarmee Afrika*'s long withdrawal towards Tunisia on 4 November. The paradoxical outcome was that Tunis fell only on 12 May 1943, after the two Allied armies had linked up in Tunisia in April. Thus Alexander (brought over from Cairo as Eisenhower's deputy to command the army group) was at last able to send Churchill this message: "We are masters of the North African shores." The number of Germans who then surrendered at Tunis—over 100,000—was larger than at Stalingrad three months earlier, and both battles were major turning points. But the two victories are hardly comparable. The ninety-odd thousand German soldiers whom Field-Marshal Friedrich von Paulus led into captivity from the ruins of Stalingrad were the

---

*French forces in North Africa, though ill equipped, were numerous—over a hundred thousand men.

haggard survivors of a German army most of whose soldiers had already either been killed or starved to death. The fall of Tunis, however (where even more Italians surrendered than Germans), was a mortal blow not for Hitler, but for Mussolini.

Had the *Torch* plan been accomplished on time, Tunis would have fallen before the end of December 1942. As it was, by mid-November the British advance eastwards from Algeria had reached Tabarka, some fifty miles from Tunis, when it was first checked by a scratch German force, hurriedly scraped together and flown into Tunis,* under the vigorous command of General Walther Nehring (previously the commander of the *Afrika Korps,* wounded on the Alamein front). This force was from then on rapidly built up and later united with the *Panzerarmee Afrika,* after the latter had been driven out of Libya by the Eighth Army. But at this early crisis of the Tunisian campaign the number of German medium tanks separating the British advance guard from its objective was sixteen. In the next six weeks Anglo-American forces got to within fifteen miles of Tunis, but by Christmas 1942 the way to Tunis was barred by General Jürgen von Arnim's Fifth *Panzerarmee.* The six months spent in taking Tunis had two major strategic consequences: the Mediterranean remained closed to Allied shipping just as the Battle of the Atlantic was reaching its climax. And the delay, as we shall see, finally destroyed all hope of opening a second front across the English Channel in 1943, with major implications for the Grand Strategy of the Big Three.

The factors responsible for the delay in completing the conquest of North Africa were at least as much political as military—an imbroglio, which might be described as a tragi-comedy if its tragic parts had not greatly outnumbered the comic. Within a few days of the Anglo-American landings, what was happening in Algiers† caused a political

---

*Ultimately, three divisions and a *Luftflotte.* Hitler also responded by occupying the whole of France.

†Algiers, as the capital of Algeria—a part of metropolitan France—was the political heart of French North Africa. The other two territories that made up North Africa—Tunisia and Morocco—had a completely different status.

uproar, which subjected the relationship between Churchill and Roosevelt to a strain potentially far greater than their disagreement about India, and which, had it continued, might even have led to a French civil war. France ranks together with China as Roosevelt's great political misconception in the Second World War. He once remarked to Frances Perkins, his Secretary of Labour, that he could tell a good Frenchman from a bad Frenchman. He could not. It was not just that he underrated and derided[31] de Gaulle. (So also did his Secretary of State, Hull, who had taken as a personal affront the Gaullist seizure of the St. Pierre and Miquelon Islands at Christmas 1941.) Moreover, although Churchill had a written agreement with de Gaulle dating from the dark days of 1940, when he had addressed him—at their brief meeting in Bordeaux—as *"l'homme du destin,"*[32] his attitude towards the general was ambivalent, reflecting the ups and downs of their difficult relationship. Whether or not, in a moment of exasperation, Churchill said that the heaviest cross he had to bear was his Cross of Lorraine—he later denied it—he certainly said some harsh things about de Gaulle to the House of Commons in secret session, on 10 December 1942.[33] At another moment, however, he had nothing but praise for the conduct of the Free French Brigade's defence of Bir Hacheim, the southernmost point of the Eighth Army's Gazala position in Libya, attacked by Rommel in May 1942.

Roosevelt's French policy at the turn of 1942–43 was based on a fundamental misunderstanding. Supported in this misapprehension by Admiral Leahy, who until his appointment as White House Chief of Staff had been U.S. Ambassador at Vichy (but spoke no French), Roosevelt believed that the American relationship with Vichy France was not only better than the British (which it undoubtedly was), but that it could serve as a foundation for the future of France. Acting on this assumption, he continued, long after *Torch,* to pursue a French policy which envisaged a post-war French state disarmed and deprived of much of the French Empire. In November 1942 this belief led logically to his insistence that de Gaulle, whose "certain idea of France" was totally different, should not be informed about *Torch* even a few hours before the operation was due to begin.[34] In this Churchill acquiesced. In his own words, he was "in the whole of *Torch,* military and political, your [Roosevelt's] Lieutenant."[35] But he declined to accept the American proposal that, in order to minimise French resistance, the initial landings should be all-American, apart from British naval and air support. The "Hurrah-Okay" exchange of telegrams between the two leaders was the end of a protracted haggle, at one point of which the Algiers landing—the only one in which British soldiers took part on 8 November—was to be excluded from the first phase of *Torch* altogether.[36]

This was not all, however. From April 1941, the senior American representative in Algiers was a member of the U.S. Foreign Service, Robert Murphy. (Before the invasion Roosevelt appointed him his personal representative.) Murphy was later criticised by Walter Lippmann as naive and gullible, and by de Gaulle as being influenced by the smart set in French circles. Certainly, the evidence shows him as a man boxing above his class. To be fair to Murphy, he was not helped by the fact that German intelligence initially read his (State Department) cypher. This decyphering of Murphy's telegrams in August 1941 led directly to the German insistence on the recall of General Weygand from North Africa by the Vichy Government,[37] which obliged Murphy to look for another French interlocutor in the run-up to the invasion. He was both overtly in touch with the French authorities on the spot and covertly with other Frenchmen in 1942. Towards the end his indirect contacts included two men who were destined to play key political roles once North Africa was invaded. One was General Henri Giraud, a distinguished soldier, then in unoccupied France, with no political following, who "had all the charm which General de Gaulle lacked, but . . . nothing else."[38] The other was Admiral François Darlan, now Commander-in-Chief of all (Vichy) French forces, essentially a man of Vichy, whose character was enigmatic in almost every respect save his anglophobia.

The United States' preferred instrument as leader of a French North Africa freed by American invasion was Giraud. On 1 November, however, Giraud (by now in Marseille) asked for three weeks' notice of the invasion—a request that Murphy (himself unaware of the date of the invasion until the eleventh hour) strongly supported in a telegram to Roosevelt, which received the immediate reply that this was "utterly impossible."[39] When Giraud finally arrived in Algiers (from Gibraltar, where he was brought by a British submarine from France) the day after the invasion, no Frenchman recognised his authority. The man who had arrived in Algiers three days before the invasion was Darlan. Churchill (followed in this unwitting misinterpretation by other historians) later described this as an "odd and formidable coincidence."* In fact, Darlan had arrived over a month earlier in Oran for a tour of inspection of French forces in North and West Africa. This tour, which included Algiers, lasted for most of October; and Murphy's recommendation that Darlan should be "encouraged" (via the intermediaries with whom Murphy was in touch) in order to secure his "eventual cooperation with Giraud" was made as early as 16 October.[40]

His tour completed, Darlan returned to France, but on 5 November he came back to Algiers for what was at first intended to be a brief visit. Two days later—on the eve of the invasion—he postponed his return. Thus it came about that, three days after the landings, agreement was reached in Algiers between Darlan and Eisenhower's deputy, Major-General Mark Clark, that Darlan should become the French supreme civil authority: an agreement accepted by Giraud, after a meeting with Darlan, in return for recognition of his own appointment as Commander-in-Chief, French forces in North Africa. Eisenhower, marooned in his headquarters in Gibraltar, recognised Darlan as French "High Commissioner." As he ruefully reported to the Combined Chiefs of Staff, "French sentiment in North Africa does not even remotely resemble prior calculations."[41] The Clark-Darlan agreement was formally signed at Algiers on 22nd November. Originally called a protocol, it became an agreement on Roosevelt's instructions.[42] By the first week of December it was announced in the Algiers press that

---

*The only real coincidence was that Darlan's son was, by the end of October, a victim of poliomyelitis. This led to a personal correspondence with Roosevelt about Warm Springs, Georgia (now in the FDR Library, Hyde Park), where Alain Darlan was in due course treated.

Darlan had established what he called a *Conseil Impérial,* thus assuming the prerogatives of head of the French state; Murphy had been given a copy of this document by Darlan on 30 November.

Churchill accepted Eisenhower's agreement to appoint Darlan as High Commissioner as an arrangement neither permanent nor healthy.[43] But western public opinion, especially in Britain, for whom the Atlantic Charter seemed to have been thrown out of the windows of the White House, was another matter. Seeking to bend with the wind, on 17 November Roosevelt tried to redeem his policy by himself issuing a statement declaring that the political arrangement made in North Africa was a "temporary expedient justifiable solely by the stress of battle" (the exact words used by Churchill in a message sent to Roosevelt on that day). This statement was initially welcomed by Churchill and pragmatically accepted by Stalin.[44] Nevertheless, it solved nothing in Algiers, where Darlan not only continued to maintain in force the policies of the existing Vichy administration (including its anti-*Résistance* and its anti-Semitism) in North Africa, but also failed to deliver to the Allies either of the two principal military advantages that might conceivably have justified their deal with him: the French fleet and Tunis. The French fleet remained at Toulon (where it was scuttled when the Germans occupied southern France) and—far worse—the French Resident-General in Tunisia, Admiral Jean-Pierre Estéva, did nothing whatever to oppose the German counter-invasion. Indeed, on 8 December French forces at the Bizerta naval base surrendered to German troops.

It is scarcely surprising that, forced to navigate as Supreme Commander in a stormy sea of unexpectedly high politics and physically far removed from the Tunisian front, Eisenhower had little time for conducting the battle there, whose success depended above all on speed of decision and hence on the forward troops feeling the imprint of personal leadership. The general, Kenneth Anderson, on whom this responsibility fell was British; and Montgomery's cruel judgment of his capacities as the opponent of Nehring and von Arnim—that he was "a good plain cook"—was not far out. Thus neither the military problem in North Africa nor the political problem—as Stalin had warned

Churchill in Moscow—was grasped with the firmness that both of them required.

Although Stalin took Darlan in his stride, he reacted forcefully to the Allies' lack of progress in Tunisia early in 1943.[45] For this indifferent outcome of a great expedition it is the Commander-in-Chief of the United States, Roosevelt—not the Allied Force Supreme Commander, Eisenhower—who bears the prime responsibility. Had it continued, he could have justified it only by arguments based on the same *raison d'état* as Stalin ruthlessly deployed about Poland from the summer of 1944 onwards. Even as it was, no one can say how much longer Churchill might have been able to tolerate it. Although his relationship with Roosevelt was paramount for Churchill, there were limits beyond which he could not expect some of his colleagues to go. (Eden could almost always be managed by Churchill, but not Bevin.)[46] And by early December 1942, Churchill and his colleagues had been left in no doubt by the British on the spot that something must be done. The senior Foreign Office representative in Algiers,* Henry Mack, head of the political section of Eisenhower's headquarters, summed up the position in a report containing these three short sentences:

> Darlan is Vichy and Vichy is representative of all those selfish interests which led to the downfall of France. There may be a civil war if Darlan remains. Darlan will have to go some time.[47]

Mack was a shrewd southern Irishman, who knew the French scene well and who could by no stretch of the imagination be regarded as a man of left-wing or radical sympathies.[48] On 9 December a message sent to Roosevelt by Churchill reflected some of the political background in Mack's assessment.[49]

On Christmas Day the BBC's first news bulletin opened with the words: "Good morning; a very happy Christmas to you all. Last night,

---

*It was not until later in the month that Churchill appointed a (then) little known conservative politician, Harold Macmillan, as British Minister Resident at AFHQ.

in Algiers, Admiral Darlan was assassinated." On the same day Berlin and Rome radio attributed Darlan's death to agents of the British Secret Service. According to the most recent work on this episode,[50] the young Frenchman who fired two shots into Admiral Darlan's stomach, Fernand Bonnier de la Chapelle, was a member of the commando *Corps Franc d'Afrique,* who had been attached to SOE after the landings; and he, together with others, was trained by SOE in the use of small arms and demolition first at Cap Matifou and later at the Club des Pins, near Algiers.* Bonnier was at once summarily tried and executed by the French civil authorities. For whom he was acting on 24 December 1942 and on whose orders is, at the time of writing, still a matter for speculation. For both de Gaulle and Churchill, however, who conferred at Chequers immediately after Darlan's assassination, it was a case of "for this relief, much thanks." For Roosevelt, it was "murder most foul." De Gaulle's visit (his first) to the United States was at the last moment postponed—as it turned out, until 1944.

Thus by the end of 1942 the Grand Alliance was no less confused than it had been earlier in the year. At the beginning of December Roosevelt suggested to Stalin that its three leaders should meet secretly about the middle of January 1943. Stalin's reply was that things were "so hot now" that he could not "be absent even for a single day."[51] By that time, the Red Army's counter-attack at Stalingrad, launched on 19 November 1942, had succeeded in encircling over 300,000 German troops. The German attempt to relieve von Paulus' army, now besieged by the Red Army in Stalingrad, failed. (The German army in the Caucasus escaped annihilation only by a timely withdrawal.) So it was that Churchill and Roosevelt conferred, again without Stalin, for the third time in thirteen months, at Casablanca. As Roosevelt put it to Churchill, "I prefer a comfortable oasis to the raft at Tilsit."[52]*

---

*SOE—Special Operations Executive—was the British secret organisation established in 1940, in Churchill's words," to set Europe ablaze." The corresponding American organisation formed part of the Office of Strategic Services (OSS), under Colonel William Donovan. Before the invasion SOE's North African operations were directed from Gibraltar and OSS's from Tangier.

*A reference to the historic meeting on the River Niemen between Napoleon and the Tsar Alexander I.

13

THE APPROACH

TO TEHERAN:

JANUARY-OCTOBER

1943

Frankly, his reason for desiring American
preponderance in force was to have the basis
for insisting upon an American commander
[for *Overlord*].

—*Franklin Roosevelt at a meeting held with the Joint
Chiefs of Staff at the White House, 10 August 1943*

It would be a terrible mistake if U.J. [Uncle
Joe = Stalin] thought we had ganged up on
him.

—*Franklin Roosevelt to Winston Churchill,
11 November 1943*

The change in the military balance during these ten
months of the Second World War was remarkable. The year had
begun with the Japanese in firm control of their far-flung conquests in
the Pacific and in South-East Asia; the *Wehrmacht* still holding the line
across the Soviet Union from which its 1942 offensive had been
launched, even though the army besieged in Stalingrad now faced
certain defeat; the Anglo-American Army bogged down in Tunisia;
and the British lifeline still at the mercy of the U-boats in the Battle of
the Atlantic. By mid-1943, the tide of the Battle of the Atlantic had

irreversibly turned; the whole of the North African seaboard was at last cleared; in the second half of the year Italy was invaded, Mussolini was brought down, and the Italian Government that succeeded him surrendered; in February the German army in Stalingrad surrendered; and in July 1943 the biggest tank battle in history was fought at Kursk, the scene of Hitler's last offensive against the Red Army, after which the *Wehrmacht* never again held the strategic initiative anywhere in Europe. Meanwhile, against Japan, the American "whip-saw"[1] offensive was by the end of 1943 beginning to approach the outer perimeter of the Japanese Empire.

The force of this contrast was evident at the time to both sides: witness, for example, the diaries of senior Allied participants, who could scarcely believe the extent of the change[2] that had come over the war, and the black pessimism of the song broadcast night after night by the German radio station in Belgrade—*Lili Marlene.* * Yet what also struck people at the time was that 1943 was as much a year of military conferences as it was of military operations. No less than six[3] of these conferences were attended by both Churchill and Roosevelt; in one of them Chiang Kai-shek took part; and in addition there was a meeting of the three Allied foreign ministers in Moscow. The questions at issue in these conferences, by far the most important of which were the first (Casablanca) and the last (Teheran), were essentially the same as in the previous year. When and where was France to be invaded? How did the needs of the European theatre relate to those of the Pacific and South-East Asia? And—as 1943 went forward—how should the developing Mediterranean campaign relate to the other two? (By the end of 1943 the size of American forces committed against Germany and against Japan—nearly two million in each theatre—was almost exactly equal.)[4] These questions were not resolved until the Big Three finally held their first tripartite summit meeting, where they reached definitive

---

*Ironically, the British Army in Africa, bored by the generally tedious English songs of the Second World War, often listened to this melancholy tune—so much so that in the end a sprightly English version had to be produced, which in turn found its way into the repertoires of dance bands in a form that disguised the fatalism of the German original.

agreement on their joint strategy for winning the war and also began to consider the political structure of the world to be established after the war was over: the Teheran Conference.

Between the Casablanca and the Teheran conferences there was a vast amount of argument across the Atlantic, punctuated by increasingly crisp interjections from Stalin. As before, much of the conduct of the argument was internal, within the two Chiefs of Staffs' organisations, as well as transatlantic and between the Big Three. On 11 November 1942, moreover, under the impact of *Torch*'s initial success, Roosevelt had been urging upon Churchill the need for "a survey of the possibilities including forward movements directed against Sardinia, Sicily, Italy, Greece and the other Balkan areas"[5]—precisely the Mediterranean strategy that Churchill had first outlined nearly a year earlier, but to which Marshall, anxious to close down Mediterranean operations once the North African coast had been secured, was resolutely opposed. As late as December, by which time the chances of an early capture of Tunis were already waning, Churchill had presented his Chiefs of Staff with a "target schedule" for the coming nine months, which opened with the completion of *Torch* by the "end of 1942" and closed with the completion of "all preparations for *Round-Up*" (the invasion of France) by the end of July 1943, followed by the words "August and September—Action."[6] And on 17 December Stalin's message to Roosevelt, finally declining the President's repeated invitation to a summit meeting (this time early in March), included this sentence:

> Allow me also to express the certainty that time is not passing to no purpose and that the promises regarding the opening of a second front in Europe, which were given by you, Mr. President, and by Mr. Churchill in respect of 1942 and now, in any case, in respect of the spring of 1943, will be fulfilled and that the second front in Europe will indeed by opened by the joint forces of Great Britain and the United States in the spring of next year.[7]

Churchill's "target schedule" was pulled to pieces by his Chiefs of Staff even before he left for Casablanca. Looking back, it is easy to see that they were right, and that Churchill was wrong in believing (right up to the spring of 1943, when Brooke finally convinced him to the contrary) that two "combined and concurrent operations"[8] could be undertaken in 1943, one from Britain and the other from North Africa. By the end of 1942 there were less than a hundred thousand American troops in Britain; and only if the Mediterranean campaign had been closed down as soon as Tunis had been captured could the U.S. Army in Britain have been built up to a force level large enough to make a cross-Channel invasion possible in 1943. In the event the further delay in the capture of Tunis, still unforeseen at the turn of the year, would probably have nullified this solution of the problem, even if the Battle of the Atlantic had been won in time to have allowed the American build-up and its subsequent maintenance across the ocean.

Casablanca

This conference was indeed held—in Roosevelt's words—at "a comfortable oasis": in the suburban villas of Anfa, where the first plenary meeting took place on 15 January 1943, both Churchill and Roosevelt having travelled to Casablanca by air. The conference lasted for nine days, after which the two men drove to Marrakesh, from where they were able to see the snow on the Atlas Mountains—a view familiar to Churchill from a visit that he had made there before the war. On the afternoon of the following day, after Roosevelt had begun his homeward flight and before Churchill set off for Turkey (in order to confer with the Turkish President), Churchill painted a picture of the Atlas Mountains—the only one that he painted throughout the war.

For Churchill and Roosevelt, when they met in the middle of January, there were two political imperatives of cardinal importance. The first they shared. Although it was Churchill who, in Moscow five months earlier, had given Stalin the commitment to a second front in 1943, Roosevelt never sought to dissociate himself from it; and even had he wished to do so on military grounds, it would have been politically impossible for him, given the overwhelming preponderance of the Eastern Front, in terms of the number of German divisions operationally engaged there at this stage of the war. For his part, Churchill had described his "supreme wish," in a message sent to Stalin just before the conference, as being "for the British and Americans to engage the enemy with the largest numbers in the shortest time."[9] The second imperative was more complex. At the beginning of 1943 Roosevelt, like most Americans, still regarded China as one of the linchpins of U.S. strategy for the defeat of Japan. The British must therefore be persuaded to do something militarily effective in northern Burma, in order to reopen the Burma Road—the supply route into southern China.[10] And within the presidential circle of advisers, King was determined that the Pacific theatre should be allotted a large enough share of resources—above all, of shipping—to make the American counter-offensive logistically feasible. This put the British on the spot. If they pressed too strongly at Casablanca the difficulty of mounting a cross-Channel invasion in 1943, this would have invited an American response that, in that case, U.S. resources would be put to better use in the coming months if they were diverted to the Pacific theatre instead of being concentrated in Britain (the *Bolero* build-up).

It remains a matter for speculation how the Casablanca Conference would have ended had Stalin attended it, as both Churchill and Roosevelt had wished in the first instance. In the event, the outcome of this intensive debate was an Anglo-American compromise. Apart from the directive on "The Bomber Offensive from the United Kingdom" issued to the British and U.S. Air Force commanders, defining their ultimate objective as being the point where the German people's capacity for resistance would be "fatally weakened,"[11] "Churchill and Roosevelt took two major military decisions at Casablanca, one of which was executed exactly on time. This was Operation *Husky,* the invasion of Sicily.* The second, Operation *Anakim,* a seaborne assault on Rangoon, was scheduled for the autumn of 1943 as part of the reconquest of Burma. (As it turned out, *Anakim* never got off the ground, and Burma was not reconquered until the final months of the

---

*The invasion of Sardinia was used as deception cover for *Husky.*

war.) Churchill and Roosevelt further agreed to establish forthwith a Combined Staff in London to prepare plans both for seizing and holding a bridgehead in the Cotentin Peninsula and for "a return to the Continent." Both these operations were subject to significant provisos: the bridgehead was to be exploited vigorously "if the state of German morale and resources permit," and the phrase "a return to the Continent" was immediately followed by the significant words "to take advantage of German disintegration." Finally, the Pacific-Europe conflict of resources was resolved by a formula in the Combined Chiefs' report of 23 January, whereby operations in the Pacific and the Far East were to be "kept within such limits as will not, in the opinion of the Combined Chiefs of Staff, jeopardise the capacity of the United Nations to take advantage of any favourable opportunity that may present itself for the decisive defeat of Germany in 1943."[12]

It was not until 27 January that Stalin received a joint message from Churchill and Roosevelt, two days after both men had left North Africa. Their message was so vaguely worded that Stalin's response on 30 January took this succinct form:

> On the understanding that the decisions you have taken in relation to Germany mean the task of destroying her by the opening of a second front in Europe in 1943, I would be grateful to be informed of the concrete operations planned in this sphere and of the intended timing of their execution.[13]

It took Churchill and Roosevelt no less than ten days to reply. Thus, it was four weeks after the two leaders had landed at Casablanca that Stalin finally received news of their plans both to seize Sicily and to prepare for a cross-Channel operation in August 1943. Even so, shipping and landing craft would, the joint message said, be "limiting factors"; and if the latter operation were delayed, it would be "prepared with stronger forces for September." The timing of the cross-Channel attack, however, was described as "dependent upon the condition of German defensive possibilities across the channel at the time."[14]

Predictably, Stalin did not take this tardy and qualified commitment kindly. In a message to both leaders on 16 February, after criticising the Tunisian delay at a moment when "the synchronisation of pressure on Hitler from our front and from your side in Tunisia would have great positive significance for our common cause," Stalin went on to insist that, in his view, it was "highly important that the blow from the West should not be postponed until the second half of the year, but should be delivered now, in the spring or at the beginning of the summer."[15] In other words, whereas Churchill had given a hostage to fortune in Moscow six months earlier, now both he and Roosevelt had done so. This time the two leaders replied separately* to Stalin, who sent another laconic reply to Churchill on 15 March. Although he welcomed the Sicilian operation, this could not "of itself replace a second front in France." He recognised the difficulties of Anglo-American operations there, but nonetheless further delay in opening a second front in France was "a grave danger." The final sentence concluded: "Therefore the vagueness of your statements regarding the planned Anglo-American offensive on the other side of the Channel arouses in me an anxiety, about which I cannot be silent."[16]

The news conference given by Churchill and Roosevelt on the last day of the Casablanca Conference, 24 January, was marked by two politically significant events—the formal public handshake finally contrived between de Gaulle and Giraud, and the enunciation by Roosevelt of the doctrine of unconditional surrender. A much longer shadow was cast on history, however, by the German news service's announcement seven weeks later: that a mass grave of thousands of Polish officers, all shot in the back of the neck, had been discovered in the Katyn Forest, near Smolensk. For many years past few historians have seriously doubted that these officers, deported from eastern Poland after the German-Soviet Partition, were victims of the NKVD: a fact that was finally admitted by the Soviet Government almost exactly fifty years later.[17] At the time, although the available evidence already

---

*Churchill was largely incapacitated by pneumonia for four weeks, from mid-February 1943.

pointed in this direction, Churchill tried to dissuade Sikorski from his natural reaction, which was to protest publicly and to imply that the responsibility for the massacre was not German, but Soviet. Stalin's response was to accuse the Polish Government-in-exile of collusion with the German Government and to break diplomatic relations between the two governments, which had been re-established only two years earlier. Churchill's emollient telegram of 24 April, assuring Stalin that the British Government would "energetically oppose any 'investigation' by the Red Cross or by any other organisation" on German-occupied territory, also reminded him of the extreme difficulty of Sikorski's position: far from being pro-German or in collusion with the Germans, he was "in danger of being overthrown by the Poles who consider that he had not stood up sufficiently against the Soviets."[18] By this time a Union of Polish Patriots had been formed in Moscow, from which in due course there emerged the Provisional Polish Government that would be recognised by the Soviet Government just before the Yalta Conference.

To return to the final day of the Casablanca Conference, before the assembled journalists and with the President and the Prime Minister as their smiling witnesses, Generals de Gaulle and Giraud shook hands. It was only with great difficulty that Churchill—acting as a sort of pig-in-the-middle between Roosevelt and de Gaulle—had persuaded de Gaulle to fly out to Algiers, where he talked to Giraud (who, as a senior general, addressed the acting brigadier-general with the words *"Bonjour, de Gaulle"*) and agreed with him the text of a statement, not as drafted by the Americans and the British, but consisting of no more than fifty-five delphic words.[19] It took another five months before de Gaulle and Giraud at last agreed to set up a French Committee of National Liberation in Algiers, under their joint presidency: an event that was preceded by a much quoted transatlantic exchange of jokes about the "bride," the "bridegroom" and "consummation," which today sounds neither very funny nor politically prescient. On 4 June 1943 Roosevelt wished Churchill "best of luck in getting rid of our mutual headache"; and four days later Churchill told the House of Commons that the formation of the National Committee "marked the end" of his relations with de Gaulle as defined by the letters earlier exchanged between them, dating from 1940, now subsumed in the British relationship with the National Committee.[20]

Caught between two stools, Churchill was over-sanguine. On the one hand, it quickly became clear that de Gaulle dominated the National Committee—and that he would equally dominate any conceivable members of the Committee in future—while Giraud, who had never been credible as a political leader, gradually receded into the background. On the other, Roosevelt's antipathy towards de Gaulle (shared by Hull and Leahy and with military overtones)* became almost pathological—so much so that in 1964 the American official historians of the *FRUS* bowdlerised the telegram that Roosevelt had sent to Churchill on 17 June 1943. Beginning with the words, "I am fed up with de Gaulle . . . there is no possibility of our working with him," this telegram went on to state: "we must divorce ourselves from de Gaulle."[21]

This was an issue on which Churchill's relationship with Roosevelt was bound, in the last resort, to take second place to the policy towards de Gaulle—clean contrary to Roosevelt's—advocated not only by Eden and Macmillan, but by virtually all members of the British War Cabinet, as Churchill candidly admitted to Roosevelt. True, at first Churchill went a long way towards accommodating Roosevelt over de Gaulle, whom he described in a long telegram to Roosevelt a month later as "a combination of Joan of Arc and Clemenceau."[22] Churchill's own political differences with de Gaulle, which were often acute (over Syria, for example), continued throughout the war. But as time went on, the deciding factor was not simply the fact that Churchill's colleagues could not be persuaded to swallow Roosevelt's idiosyncratic idea of de Gaulle (any more than his deal with Darlan). Churchill's concept of France itself was fundamentally different from Roosevelt's; and this gave to the relationship between Churchill and de Gaulle a

---

*Roosevelt was particularly interested in Dakar as a naval base; he also wanted to get the French out of their Bizerta naval base.

hard core which their quarrels over particular issues could not destroy. Whereas Roosevelt and de Gaulle went on exchanging snubs right up to the end,* almost as many Frenchmen greeted Churchill in Paris, which he visited as de Gaulle's guest in November 1944, as had thronged the Champs-Elysées when de Gaulle walked down from the Arc de Triomphe three months before. (Churchill's visit evoked a snide remark from Roosevelt, however.)[23] And the photograph given by de Gaulle to Churchill after the war, now at Chartwell, is inscribed with the three words *"à mon compagnon."*

The other significant event at the Casablanca press conference was Roosevelt's concluding statement, at once endorsed by Churchill, that "Peace can come to the world only by the total elimination of German and Japanese war power . . . [this] means the unconditional surrender by Germany, Japan and Italy. . . . This meeting may be called the "unconditional surrender" meeting." The text of this statement (which, in his memoirs, Churchill wrongly claimed took him by surprise)[24] was given to the press after the news conference had ended. Of its importance at the time there can be no doubt, both as reassurance for Stalin and as a sop to public opinion in the aftermath of the Darlan deal. Its significance in the subsequent history of the war in general, and in particular for the relationship between the Big Three, is debatable. The term "unconditional surrender" meant little in Germany early in May 1945, because by then there was no longer any real German Government in existence. When it came to the formal surrender of Japan, three months after the German disintegration, the formula of unconditionality was waived, in order to preserve the Emperor's position. In relation to the Italian Armistice terms, however, it had a grave effect in 1943.

---

*Having refused to let de Gaulle attend the Yalta Conference in February 1945, Roosevelt offered to meet him on his way home, at Algiers. De Gaulle—with public scorn—declined, although he offered to receive Roosevelt in Paris. Roosevelt declined.

The Beginning of the Italian Collapse

Ironically, Churchill's original intention at Casablanca had been to exclude Italy from the declaration of unconditional surrender, in order "to encourage a break up there," but the British War Cabinet, when consulted by telegram, replied to the Prime Minister, who accepted their view, that "knowledge of all rough stuff coming is surely more likely to have desired effect on Italian morale."[25] Eden's Italophobia was deep-seated and long-lasting. Three months after Casablanca, he mishandled[26] the approach made to the British Government by two distinguished anti-Fascists, Ugo La Malfa (a senior member of the Italian *Partito d'Azione*) and Prince Caracciolo, even though they were prepared to work with Marshal Badoglio and the Monarchist faction. (As late as 1954, when Eden was again Foreign Secretary, neither he nor any other British Minister attended the funeral of Alcide De Gasperi, the greatest Italian Prime Minister of the twentieth century.) On 4 February 1943—with the whole of the Italian Empire lost, the Italian Navy crippled in *mare nostrum* by lack of oil, and the Italian people more and more disgusted by the German alliance—Mussolini replaced Marshal Ugo Cavallero (Chief of the Italian General Staff for over two years, he was closely identified as a Germanophile officer)* by General Vittorio Ambrosio. Ambrosio's first strategic assessment submitted to Mussolini concluded that, short of the fulfillment by Italy's German allies of some highly improbable conditions, Italy would "no longer be obliged to follow them in their erroneous conduct of the war."[27] There were strikes in the industrial north of the country; after an inconclusive meeting with Hitler near Salzburg[28] in April, Mussolini gave his last address to the (artificially) assembled throng from the balcony of the Palazzo Venezia on 5 May. He then lapsed into a state of inertia (he was also suffering from a duodenal ulcer).

In the summer of 1943 King Victor Emmanuel III, the constitutional head of the Italian state, began a series of unobtrusive talks both

---

*He committed suicide on the day of Mussolini's arrest.

with the former leaders of the political parties that the Fascist order had replaced and with the retired Marshal Pietro Badoglio, the victor of the Italian campaign against the Austrian Army in the First World War, loyal to the House of Savoy and a fellow Piedmontese. On 2 June the elder statesman, Ivanoe Bonomi, who had been War Minister over twenty years earlier when Badoglio had been Deputy Chief of the Italian General Staff, offered to serve under Badoglio in a government which, once formed, would break the German alliance and include representation of all six democratic parties. When Badoglio himself recommended to the King the formation of a government of parliamentarians six weeks later, the King's comment—in Piedmontese—was "They are ghosts," to which Badoglio's reply, was "You and I, Your Majesty, are also spectres; but I see nothing else to be done."[29] His advice was not accepted. But when Mussolini was brought down by the Grand Council of his own Fascist Party in the early hours of the morning of 25 July, it was to Badoglio that the King turned. The government of officials that Badoglio then formed, although it in effect marked the end of the Fascist regime, nonetheless declared publicly *la guerra continua* ("the war goes on").

Trident

At two conferences in Washington and Quebec, which followed each other in quick succession in May and August 1943, Churchill and Roosevelt—without Stalin—reached preliminary agreement on the timing of the invasion of France in 1944. On the day before Stalin's peremptory message to Churchill (quoted above), the German Army had just succeeded in restablising its extended Eastern Front; Field-Marshal Erich von Manstein, now commanding the German Southern Army Group, recaptured Kharkov from the Red Army on 14 March. During the lull that followed the spring thaw Hitler issued the directive for what proved to be his last offensive against the Red Army—Operation *Zitadelle*. Although this operation was, by comparison with earlier German offensives, limited in scope—the objective was the elimination of the Soviet salient covering the town of Kursk, between

Orel and Kharkov—nearly two thousand German tanks were committed to *Zitadelle,* including some of the formidable Tiger and Panther models now coming off the production line. Initially planned for the beginning of May, it was described in Hitler's directive of 15 April as "a beacon-light for the world."[30] Nevertheless it was delayed for two months, giving Allied intelligence, Soviet as well as Anglo-American, ample warning.[31] Thus, when Churchill reached the White House on 11 May, he and Roosevelt were aware that this great battle was imminent (Hitler at first postponed the Kursk attack only until June).

By the time Churchill embarked on the Cunard liner *Queen Mary* on the Clyde on 5 May—his recent bout of pneumonia prevented him from flying—he had at last been convinced by Brooke that a cross-Channel invasion in 1943 was out of the question, if for no other reason than the shortage of landing craft (required in large numbers for the invasion of Sicily), which also ruled out amphibious operations in Burma in 1943. To Stalin, in a telegram sent from the *Queen Mary* in mid-Atlantic, he described the aim of his visit to Washington as being to decide the question of a "further blow in Europe" after the invasion of Sicily (Tunis fell while Churchill was at sea) and also to "discourage excessive bias towards the Pacific Ocean."[32]

As at Casablanca, the agreement reached at the *Trident* Conference, after a complicated fortnight's discussion between the British and the U.S. Chiefs of Staff, was a compromise.[33] The target date for the invasion of France—*Round-Up,* soon to be rechristened *Overlord*—was to be 1 May 1944, a date fixed by splitting the difference between the choice of 1 April (American) and 1 June (British). Meanwhile, once the invasion of Sicily—*Husky*—had been accomplished, "such operations in exploitation of *Husky*" were to be mounted as were "best calculated to eliminate Italy from the war and to contain the maximum number of German forces." Although the part of the agreement relating to Italy was made subject to certain conditions, notably that seven of the divisions then in the Mediterranean theatre should be held ready for withdrawal to Britain from 1 November, this seemed to be the beginning of a breakthrough for Churchill's Mediterranean strategy. Paradoxically, however, neither he nor Roosevelt appears to have seen any need to make plans in advance in order to deal swiftly with Italian overtures for peace; in the view of both leaders, "unconditional surrender" was good enough.[34] So far as the war against Japan was concerned, the *Anakim* operation, approved at Casablanca, was now rescinded. Churchill's personal preference for a different amphibious operation—a landing in northern Sumatra—found no favour among either his own advisers or the U.S. Joint Chiefs. But the alternative to both these operations, a land operation in northern Burma, sceptically regarded by all the British present at *Trident* (Churchill not least), nonetheless received the conference's approval, on Roosevelt's personal insistence.

Roosevelt's motive for this insistence was at least as much political as strategic, if not more so: the need to give visible support to Chiang Kai-shek. Looking back at this conference, the historian must be struck by the way in which both Roosevelt and Churchill, except for postponing the invasion of France (long since beyond their reach in that year) from 1943 to 1944, also avoided slamming any strategic doors in Europe; whereas their two senior advisers, Brooke and Marshall, though forcefully arguing opposite points of view, each accurately foresaw a major factor likely to have a radical effect on Allied Mediterranean strategy, which the two leaders ignored during *Trident*. For Brooke, this was the possibility that "we might be called upon by some political party other than the Fascists to enter Italy." For Marshall, it was the prospect that "a German decision to support Italy might make intended operations extremely difficult and time-consuming."[35] Subsequent events were to prove both generals right—Marshall over the course of the entire campaign of the Italian mainland from September 1943 onwards and Brooke within a matter of weeks.

The immediate problem that faced Churchill and Roosevelt, however, was Stalin's reaction to the news, which he received from Roosevelt (by hand of the U.S. Ambassador in Moscow) on 4 June, ten days after *Trident* was over,[36] that the invasion of France had been postponed for another year. Neither of them was surprised by a message from Stalin to Churchill on 11 June describing their joint decision as creating "exceptional difficulties for the Soviet Union," whose government "does not find it possible to associate itself with such a decision, taken moreover without its participation and without an attempt to consider jointly this important question, which may have grave consequences for the further course of the war."[37]

Equally Stalin himself cannot have been greatly surprised* by the *Trident* decision. Whether or not the way in which he reacted was intended to drive a wedge between Churchill and Roosevelt, each of the two men certainly responded differently to Stalin's "castigation," as Churchill described it to Roosevelt. In a lengthy reply to Stalin, Churchill suggested a summit meeting of the three leaders that summer at Scapa Flow (the British naval base in Orkney, Scotland). On the other hand, Roosevelt sent only a brief telegram, no doubt because he had already given Joseph Davies a letter to deliver personally to Stalin, inviting him to a bilateral meeting "either side of the Bering Straits," without the presence of Churchill. Davies, a businessman who had served as Ambassador in Moscow before the war, handed this letter to Stalin on 2 May. Stalin's initial reply, on 26 May, had been favourable, suggesting July or August.[39] Churchill did not learn the contents of the letter transmitted by Davies until Harriman told him a month later; the Prime Minister was distressed and said so to the President at once; and on 28 June Roosevelt replied to Churchill with a direct lie: "I did not suggest to U.J. [Stalin] that we meet alone. . . ." In the event, neither Roosevelt's separate Alaskan invitation nor Churchill's suggestion of Scapa Flow was accepted. Stalin made much of his visit "to the front" in August (it was the only time that he went to see his troops in the entire war). But he could not in fact have left the Soviet Union in July or August for a genuine reason: the Battle of Kursk, which the *Wehrmacht* finally launched on 5 July.[40]

---

*Not only was Maisky still Soviet Ambassador in London, but since 1942 the Soviet Embassy in Washington had had as its counsellor (later ambassador) one of the ablest members of Molotov's team of young diplomats, Andrei Gromyko. An early example of Gromyko's political judgment is provided by a long letter written by him to Molotov on 14 August 1942, analysing American opinion about the question of a second front.[38]

Quadrant

Almost simultaneously with the beginning of the Battle of Kursk, Sicily was invaded by Anglo-American forces: Operation *Husky*. The conquest of the island was completed by the middle of August. A fortnight after the landings Eisenhower sought permission to invade the Italian mainland as far north as air cover would permit: Operation *Avalanche,* south of Naples. This permission having been granted within twenty-four hours, it is reasonable to ask why Churchill and Roosevelt (Stalin having declined) found it necessary to meet again—this time in Quebec, where the conference was held in the Château Frontenac Hotel, above the St. Lawrence River, from 14 to 24 August. Churchill arrived in Quebec before the conference. He was thus able to meet the Canadian Cabinet there, on 11 August.

This was a conference to which few of the participants seem to have looked forward;[41] and, with one major exception—the secret atomic agreement signed at Quebec by Churchill and Roosevelt—its discussions broke no fresh ground. On the contrary, old ground was re-ploughed, although this wearisome process did succeed, for the time being, in restoring a measure of Anglo-American confidence in the strategic intentions of each side. And since Churchill himself remained in North America for over six weeks, he and Roosevelt were able, as it turned out, to confer together about the problems raised by the Italian surrender. For the persistence of this transatlantic distrust, the *Trident* agreements notwithstanding, there were two main reasons. At the level of the Chiefs of Staff, Brooke firmly believed, but could never convince Marshall, that the invasion of Italy and the invasion of France were strategically interdependent; a successful Italian campaign, if it was carried out with sufficient strength, would increase the chances of the success of *Overlord* in 1944. Marshall's scepticism was reinforced when, towards the end of July, the British Chiefs of Staff ordered a standstill on the dispersal of resources then in the Mediterranean—in the American view, a breach of the compromise agreed in Washington only two months earlier.

But the effect on Washington of this disagreement was compounded by Churchill. His restless imagination, stimulated by the prospect of Italy's removal from the war, was now beginning to range over a broad field of strategic options—an advance into the Po Valley, followed by an "attack westwards in the south of France or north-eastwards towards Vienna" and "the expulsion of the enemy from the Balkans and Greece." Although his talks with the Turkish President, Ismet Inönü, in January 1943 had achieved little or nothing, the advantages of capturing Rhodes and bringing Turkey into the war were seldom far from his mind; nor had he forgotten *Jupiter,* the Norwegian operation, of which he was the one and only advocate. On 19 July, moreover, he even put to the Chiefs of Staff the argument that, in the event that *Overlord* proved "beyond our strength in May" and had therefore to be "postponed until August 1944," *Jupiter* would be the alternative.[42] Unfortunately, this was no flash in the pan, nor did Churchill keep his doubts about *Overlord* to his own circle. Stimson, for example, after a visit to London in July, reported to Roosevelt his strongly held view that only an American commander could "overcome the natural difficulties of such an operation carried on in such an atmosphere of his [Churchill's] government."[43] One of the consequences of Churchill's doubts was that at Quebec, in deference to American views, he felt obliged to withdraw his offer of the supreme command of the *Overlord* operation to Brooke, which he had made as recently as 15 June—a bitter blow for Brooke, who nonetheless wrote these words in his diary the day after he got back to Britain: "He is quite the most difficult man to work with that I have ever struck, but I would not have missed the chance of working with him for anything on earth." No one who worked closely with Churchill ever wrote a more fitting summary of the experience than this.[44]

The outcome of *Quadrant* was to agree that "available resources" would be distributed between the two theatres—Italian and French—and employed "with the main object of ensuring the success of *Overlord.*" The British had to cancel their shipping standstill and to accept the continued need to transfer from the Mediterranean—in November—the seven divisions agreed at *Trident.* A Churchillian reference to *Jupiter,* as "a second string," was written into the Combined Chiefs of

Staff's report to the President and the Prime Minister, with no subsequent effect. An ambiguous formula left open the question how Burma was to be reconquered, but a new command was formed in South-East Asia. Mountbatten's appointment as Supreme Commander, South-East Asia (first suggested to Churchill by Amery), was approved by both Churchill and Roosevelt. Taken in conjunction with General William Slim's command of Fourteenth Army, this would later prove a winning combination, comparable to that of Alexander and Montgomery in 1942–43.[45]

The Italian Surrender

Although this, the First Quebec Conference, ended on 24 August, Churchill did not leave Canada—on board the battleship *Renown*—until 14 September, his six weeks' stay in North America being interspersed with visits to Washington and to Hyde Park. Thus he and Roosevelt were both at the White House on 8 September 1943. In the evening of that day the Italian surrender was announced by Badoglio on Rome Radio, only hours before Operation *Avalanche*—the Anglo-American landing near Salerno on the following morning. The Italian Armistice had in fact been secretly signed at Cassibile, in Sicily, five days earlier, by a senior member of General Ambrosio's staff, General Giuseppe Castellano. From the moment of his arrival in Madrid on 15 August, this officer, who spoke no English, became the man with whom the Americans and the British had to deal. The signature of the armistice agreement had been preceded by a whole month of discussions with a series of Italian emissaries, in Lisbon, in Tangier and finally in Sicily. Whereas in Algiers nine months earlier the deal had been struck with Darlan within seventy-two hours of the Allied landings, it took the British and the U.S. governments (the Soviet Government played no part) over a month to conclude an agreement with the administration formed on 25 July by Badoglio which, among its first measures, arrested and confined Mussolini and a week later began to put out feelers to the British and U.S. governments.

The man who at once foresaw the strategic implications of what happened in Rome on 25 July, in spite of the three words in the new Italian Government's pronouncement, *la guerra continua,* was Eisenhower. On 29 July Marshall sent Roosevelt a memorandum quoting an extract from a telegram just received from Eisenhower, who believed that "There might occur a vast but possibly fleeting opportunity to accomplish all that we are seeking in the Italian Peninsula." It was, Eisenhower continued, "of the utmost importance that the two Governments authorise me . . . to act decisively." Roosevelt agreed. But— unwisely—Churchill asked, on 30 July, for delay.[46] With hindsight, it seems self-evident that the speed with which the double invasion of the Italian mainland (first, across the Straits of Messina, and second, at Salerno), then in the final stage of preparation, could be exploited northwards might well depend on Italian co-operation; and that if the northward advance was slow, there was a risk not only of increasingly effective German military intervention, but also of an Italian civil war. Churchill, the main enthusiast for a Mediterranean strategy, never seems to have allowed his historical knowledge to lead him to reflect that the last time that Italy had been successfully conquered—up to just short of the Po Valley—by a general leapfrogging his army from Africa to Sicily and thence on to Rome was in the sixth century A.D.;* every other successful invasion had entered Italy from the north.

By comparison, Hitler's reaction to the fall of Mussolini and to the six weeks of uncertainty in Rome that followed was instant. Having committed only two divisions to help in the Italian defence of Sicily (where they fought stubbornly and conducted a skillful withdrawal to the mainland), he now at once prepared for the Italian defection, appointing Rommel to command a new army group, held ready to cross the Brenner: an operation which began in the middle of August. For Churchill and Roosevelt, a rapid Italian campaign—conducted in mountainous country by Anglo-American armies which, after the

---

*The great Byzantine general, Belisarius, recaptured Rome from the Goths and advanced as far as Ravenna. The historical parallel does not seem to have escaped the German General Staff; the German line of defence in the northern Apennines in 1944 was called the Gothic Line.

Salerno landing, only once used landing craft again and initially had no mountain units[47]—depended to a large extent on a swift political decision to conclude an Italian Armistice, which should at least have given them Rome. And indeed the original German strategy did not envisage the defence of southern Italy. (It was not until the beginning of October, just after the Allies at last captured Naples, that Hitler decided to hold the defensive line centered on Monte Cassino, which brought the Fifteenth Army Group's advance virtually to a halt until 1944.) Instead, in August 1943 the Italian Armistice negotiations[48] developed into a marathon—the exact opposite of the quick fix at Algiers in November 1942.

The reasons for this difference were both of form and of substance. At their outset these negotiations involved on the Allied side no less than four principal decision-making centres, as they would be called in today's jargon: AFHQ at Algiers, the Foreign Office in London, the Combined Chiefs of Staff in Washington and, after the Prime Minister's arrival for *Quadrant,* Churchill and Roosevelt in North America. During the first stage, when Churchill and Roosevelt were still on opposite sides of the Atlantic, they did not help by talking to each other indiscreetly on a telephone line intercepted by German intelligence.[49] Nor did the Italian Government help by operating through several different representatives; and—separately—the Vatican also represented to the two governments that Rome should be declared an open city.

The reasons of substance stemmed from a difference of approach towards post-Fascist Italy between Churchill and Roosevelt. This difference was already evident in their opening exchange of messages (before Churchill's departure from London) on 25 July. "We must be certain," Roosevelt telegraphed, "of the use of all Italian territory and transportation against the Germans in the North and against the whole Balkan peninsula, as well as the use of airfields of all kinds." He added, however, that "we should come as close as possible to unconditional surrender." While agreeing with Roosevelt's definition of the objectives, which they must be "certain" to secure, and expanding them to include the surrender both of the Italian fleet and of the Italian-garrisoned islands throughout the Mediterranean, Churchill also said:

"Now Mussolini is gone I would deal with any Non Fascist Italian Government which can deliver the goods."[50] Whereas Churchill's romantic feeling for the concept of monarchy in general made him comfortable with the prospect of dealing with the ancient House of Savoy, Roosevelt looked for the freedom of political choice within Italy which a policy of unconditional surrender by the Italian Government (which would then be suspended) seemed to offer him.

Both views were mistaken. Having acquiesced in the Fascist regime for over twenty years, King Victor Emmanuel had no hope of uniting Italians (had he been wise enough to abdicate at once, the outcome might have been different).* Equally, "unconditional surrender" was a formula scarcely calculated to inspire Italians of whatever political persuasion, even though most of them longed to see the back of the Germans and many wanted to fight alongside the Anglo-American forces. To make matters even worse, when Mussolini was arrested, Churchill and Roosevelt had no document agreed between them which Eisenhower could have been authorised to use at once as a basis for negotiation with the emissaries of the new Italian Government who soon began to make their appearance. Instead, there were soon two documents in the field: the so-called "Long Terms," a lengthy memorandum already drafted by the Foreign Office, which spelled out in Whitehall prose not just the arrangements for military surrender, but also the provisions for the disbandment of the Fascist regime and the demilitarisation of the Italian state, to be carried out by an Italian government under the directions of an Allied Commission. The Long Terms did not satisfy Washington, because they fell short of unconditional surrender and left an Italian Government in being. Meanwhile, from his headquarters in Algiers, where the Foreign Office draft had not yet been received, Eisenhower telegraphed to the Combined Chiefs of Staff a draft which came to be known as the "Short Terms," aimed exclusively at the fulfilment of his military requirements as Supreme

---

*In the end, he handed over to his son, the Crown Prince Umberto, as *Luogotenente* (roughly, in English, Regent) after the capture of Rome. Umberto abdicated on 9 August 1946, after a referendum had voted for a Republic.

Commander in the theatre, including "immediate acknowledgement" of his "overriding authority to establish Military Government" in Italy.[51] The ensuing exchanges between London and Washington, punctuated from 4 August onwards by reports of what the Italian emissaries had to say, continued until 17 August. At this point, nearly four weeks after the collapse of the Fascist regime, instructions agreed at Quebec by Churchill, Roosevelt and the Combined Chiefs of Staff, without securing agreement from London,[52] were at last telegraphed to Eisenhower: to present Castellano with the Short Terms* and to accept the Badoglio Government's offer to join in the fight against Germany.

These instructions once received, Eisenhower lost no time in sending his Chief of Staff and his chief intelligence officer,[53] in civilian clothes and with forged passports, to meet Castellano in Gibraltar. Thereafter almost everything that could go wrong did go wrong. By this time German troops were pouring across the Brenner Pass. As at Algiers nine months earlier, so now too the timing of the invasion could not be disclosed to the Italians, who made a disastrous guess.[54] The landing near Rome of the U.S. 81st Airborne Division, an operation added to the *Avalanche* landing by Eisenhower on 1 September at Castellano's express request, had to be cancelled literally at the eleventh hour, after Badoglio had refused to accept it and instead himself asked for the impossible—that the invasion should be postponed. (A British airborne division, embarked in warships, occupied Taranto on 9 September.) Late on the afternoon of 8 September—on the eve of *Avalanche*— Eisenhower broadcast the news of the armistice that had been earlier agreed. The consequence in Italy and for most of the Italian armed forces was chaos—an additional obstacle for the Allies and tragedy for the Italians. The King and Badoglio, taken by surprise, nonetheless honoured the armistice agreement, which Badoglio at once announced on Rome Radio. In the small hours they fled from Rome, leaving the

---

*The Long Terms, however, were not forgotten. Amended to include the words "unconditional surrender," they received final approval in Washington at the end of August; and they were signed by Badoglio himself just over a month later, under protest, on board H.M.S. *Nelson* in Valletta Harbour. On 13 October 1943 the Italian Government declared war on Germany.

Italian people without orders or guidance. Only the Italian Navy escaped German captivity.[55]

Rome was surrendered on 10 September to the German Army, which was thus enabled to meet the invasion on the Salerno beaches with no concern about the protection of its lines of communication. At the other end of the Mediterranean the Italian garrison of Rhodes surrendered to German forces. Within Italy, the political allegiance of the country now became divided between three poles—the King and the Badoglio Government, established at Brindisi; Mussolini (rescued from comfortable captivity in the Gran Sasso mountain range by German paratroopers) at Salò, in northern Italy, where he set up a puppet neo-Fascist government; and in Milan the clandestine Committee of National Liberation, in which all six democratic Italian political parties were represented, from 9 September 1943. For nearly two years northern Italy was effectively in a state of civil war.

Thus any hopes of a dashing advance up Italy and of setting the Balkans ablaze were, at any rate for 1943, destroyed. In the difficult circumstances of August–September 1943, Eisenhower might have been forgiven by history if he had failed to secure any Italian agreement at all before the Salerno landing. The fluctuating situation in Rome, the uncertain status of successive Italian emissaries and their lack of plenipotentiary powers, the need to refer to heads of government on the other side of the Atlantic (Churchill and Roosevelt were both moving about a good deal at the time, including picnics and a fishing expedition) and the speed of the German reaction—these were all factors loaded against him and Alexander. Nevertheless, the historian has only to pause to consider what might have happened if roles had been reversed—if, for example, Rommel had been in Alexander's position—in order to conclude that the failure to exploit the landings carried out by the two armies in southern Italy* was not inevitable.

---

*Five days before Clark's Fifth Army landed at Salerno, the Eighth Army, commanded by Montgomery, crossed the Straits into Calabria. Its laboriously slow advance northwards was hindered more by blown bridges than by direct enemy action. By the time it reached Salerno, the fiercely contested battle for the bridgehead there had already been won.

Be that as it may, there can be no doubt about Stalin's reaction to the political arrangements made in Italy with Churchill and Roosevelt's authority. Having begun by congratulating "the Anglo-American troops on the occasion of their most successful operations in Sicily," on 22 August he went on to complain to the two leaders, in a message sent jointly to both of them, that he had been left out of the Anglo-American discussions with the Italian Government (as "a passive third onlooker"). He therefore proposed the formation of "A military-political commission, composed of representatives of the three countries—the United States, Great Britain and the USSR—for the consideration of questions regarding negotiations with various governments breaking away from Germany." Stalin added that it was "impossible to tolerate such a situation any longer," and suggested that the proposed commission should be initially established in Sicily.[56] Although provision was later made for Soviet representation in Italy, the control of affairs in Italy remained essentially an Anglo-American preserve.[57] Stalin's reaction to this situation foreshadowed that of the Americans and the British to the Soviet Government's actions in territories occupied by the Red Army in Eastern Europe later in the war.

On 8 September Stalin finally agreed to a tripartite summit conference, suggesting Teheran as the venue, to be preceded by a meeting of the three foreign ministers in Moscow.[58] Although Roosevelt was at first reluctant to travel as far afield and much triangular correspondence followed, Teheran became the somewhat improbable setting for their first meeting, as a group, to which the Big Three in the end agreed on 11 November 1943.[59] By that time, following its crushing victory at Kursk in the summer, the Red Army had turned the *Wehrmacht* back along much of the Eastern Front; Kiev, the capital of the Ukraine, was recaptured on 6 November, after over two years of German occupation. Meanwhile, the Battle of the Atlantic had been won by September—in the last four months of the year the German Navy lost almost as many U-boats as they sank Allied ships.[60] In southern Italy, however, the Anglo-American advance had been brought to a halt: a disappointment from which Churchill and Roosevelt drew diametrically opposite conclusions. On 19 October Churchill directed the Chiefs of

Staff to conduct a review "in a most secret manner and on the assumption that commitments into which we have already entered with the Americans, particularly as regards *Overlord,* could be modified by agreement to meet the emergencies of a changing situation," which in his view included considering "a forward policy in the Balkans" and "the chance that may lie within our grasp to bring Turkey more actively on our side."[61] ("God knows where this may lead us with the Americans," wrote Brooke in his dairy the same day.)[62] To Roosevelt, a week later, Churchill insisted that the Italian campaign must not "degenerate into a deadlock . . . no matter what effect is produced on subsequent operations." These were views which he still defended ten years afterwards; he had, he wrote in his memoirs, been frustrated by "pedantic details in the minor sphere."[63]

Equally firmly, Roosevelt maintained that "no diversion of forces or equipment should prejudice *Overlord* as planned."[64] Churchill responded with a long expression of personal doubts about the planning of *Overlord:* "my dear friend, this is much the greatest thing we have ever attempted. . . . I desire an early conference."[65] Nor did Stalin, talking to Eden in Moscow on 21 and 23 October, show any sympathy for Churchill's mounting anxieties.[66] There was much for the Big Three to discuss at Teheran.

14

THE TEHERAN

CONFERENCE:

NOVEMBER–DECEMBER

1943

Never once in any of his statements did he
make any strategic error, nor did he ever fail to
appreciate all the implications of a situation
with a quick and unerring eye.

—*Field-Marshal Alanbrooke's reflection on Stalin's
performance at Teheran*[1]

The Teheran Conference was certainly the most significant Allied meeting of 1943 and—arguably—of the entire war. It
was the first occasion on which the two most powerful political leaders
in the world, Roosevelt and Stalin, met face to face; it was the last on
which Churchill was able to confer with them on equal terms and,
even so, he had to fight hard to maintain his position. Military historians—with justice—record this meeting as the moment when the decision to invade France, in 1944, finally became irreversible. But other
parts of the Teheran discussions were hardly less far-reaching, in particular the first look into the political future taken jointly by Churchill,
Roosevelt and Stalin. That the three leaders were able to do as much as
they did in the space of four days, by comparison with the weeks of
debate at earlier Anglo-American conferences, was partly because the

Soviet delegation, unlike the American and the British, did not include either the Chief or indeed any representatives of the Soviet General Staff; "Voroshilov and I will manage somehow," Stalin (who had now become a Marshal of the Soviet Union himself) ironically remarked[2]. It was also partly because some preliminary work had already been done both by the three foreign ministers in Moscow and by the Americans and the British in Cairo, immediately before their two delegations flew north to Teheran. Last, but not least, from 1941 onwards Churchill, Roosevelt and Stalin had already begun to exchange ideas about the political structure of the post-war world.

Early Exchanges

From the outset Stalin had insisted that the restoration of the "old" Soviet frontiers was "essential." Roosevelt then refused to enter into any territorial commitments, and he persuaded Churchill to exclude any mention of Soviet frontiers from the Anglo-Soviet Treaty signed in May 1942. Since then the problem of future frontiers in Eastern Europe had been exacerbated by the rupture of Soviet-Polish relations in April 1943.[3] As the Red Army's advance brought it nearer to the eastern frontier of inter-war Poland, the question could not be left off the agenda of the Big Three much longer; and beyond that lay the even greater problem of the future of Germany itself.

Roosevelt adopted an attitude towards European frontiers which, by comparison with that of Churchill and Stalin, was aloof. (It also stood in marked contrast to his clear-cut ideas about the future of territories in Africa, the Pacific and South-East Asia.) The post-war concept which engaged his attention most was the need to devise a mechanism for maintaining world order after the war that would avoid the defects of the League of Nations, would be capable of commanding congressional support, and would continue the co-operation of the three members of the Grand Alliance, with a fourth member added—China. We have seen how, as early as August 1941, the Atlantic Charter foresaw the eventual establishment of a permanent system of international security. Nine months later Roosevelt expounded his concept of the four policemen in his first talk with Molotov (then visiting Washington) at the White House: a conversation which warrants analysis both for the light that it throws on Roosevelt's thinking in mid-1942 and for Molotov's reaction to Roosevelt's opening offer of a continuing post-war U.S.-Soviet relationship. (Not that Roosevelt put his proposal only to Stalin; he spoke on similar lines to Eden when the Foreign Secretary visited Washington in March 1943.) According to the Soviet record, in his talk with Molotov Roosevelt even alleged that at Placentia Bay Churchill had been unable to suggest anything better than "an organisation of the community of nations, in other words, the League of Nations," adding that, if the United States and the Soviet Union were to insist on his (Roosevelt's) proposal, "Churchill would be obliged to accept it."*

In putting to Molotov this "important question," Roosevelt took as his premise that, in order to prevent the outbreak of war in the course of the next twenty-five to thirty years, it was essential to set up an international police force composed of three or four powers. Molotov at once agreed that in order to safeguard the peoples of the world from a new war, it was essential to unite the forces of "several dominant powers." Roosevelt went on to say that the police force must be formed by the United States, Britain, the USSR and China. The three victorious powers in the war (a category in which he does not seem at this point in the conversation to have included China) must maintain their armaments, whereas the aggressor states and the "associates of the aggressors—Germany, Japan, France, Italy, Romania and even, in addition, Poland and Czechoslovakia" must be disarmed and prevented from rearming in secret. If one of them began to rearm, the four policemen would declare a blockade against that country; and if that was not enough, they would bombard it.

The pertinent questions that Molotov then put to Roosevelt reflect

---

*Because it is important, for the purpose of the present study, to know exactly how Roosevelt's remarks on this occasion were reported to Stalin, this quotation, and the whole of the account given in the next two paragraphs, is taken from the Soviet record.

unease over two aspects of the President's proposal, which he at once undertook to report to Stalin, however. Had the Chinese Government been informed about Roosevelt's plan? And would France be "excluded from the number of participants in the proposed agreement"? To the first of these questions, Roosevelt answered no, adding that China's participation would depend on whether China would be able to form a central government. To the second question, his answer was yes (as his policy towards France later in 1942 would demonstrate). The United States, Britain and the Soviet Union might decide, however, that other countries, including France, could join "the common agreement."Molotov's concluding remark was that Roosevelt's plan was a great and important question, which the Soviet Union would treat with great attention. And Roosevelt's summing up was:

> The aim of the proposed union consists in preventing the Germans and the Japanese from attacking anybody. We hope that after twenty-five years the Germans and the Japanese will also understand that they must not fall upon their neighbors.[4]

Churchill, too, had thought about the shape of post-war security. Nine months before the Teheran Conference he had committed his thoughts to paper. Based on much the same premise as Roosevelt's proposal—that the renewal of acts of aggression must be prevented by the victorious powers, who would "continue fully armed," and that "the guilty nations" would be totally disarmed (although, in Churchill's view, their peoples should not be prevented from "leading a decent life")—the Prime Minister's "Morning Thoughts,"[5] as he entitled this note, warned against repeating the mistake made over reparations at Versailles and emphasised "economic reconstruction and rehabilitation" as the primary need "for a good many years" after the war. A "world organisation for the preservation of peace" would be created by "the Chiefs of the United Nations"; and as a part of this, "an instrument of European Government" would be established, which would "embody the spirit but not be subject to the weakness of the former League of Nations." Churchill saw this European body as composed of "a number of confederations formed among the smaller states"—Scandinavian, Danubian and Balkan. The "leading powers" would "prolong their honourable association" after winning the war; Britain would "do her utmost to organise a coalition resistance to any act of aggression"; and it was "believed" that the United States would "cooperate with her and even possibly take the lead of the world."

Churchill's personal thoughts were set out in much more detail in a memorandum[6] sent nearly four months later, on instructions, by Halifax to Roosevelt, in order to record a talk at a lunch in Washington attended by Churchill (but not Roosevelt) and a number of senior Americans, including the Chairman of the Senate Foreign Relations Committee, Tom Connally, during the *Trident* Conference. A "Supreme World Council" would be formed by Britain, the Soviet Union and the United States. If the United States wished China to be included, Churchill was "perfectly willing" for this, although China was "not comparable with the others." Subordinate to this Council, there would be three Regional Councils—one for Europe, (which would consist of some twelve "confederations"), one for the American Hemisphere and one for the Pacific. Representatives of these regional bodies should be elected to sit, in rotation, on the World Council.

Just as Churchill did not conceal his scepticism about China, so too he was candid about the importance of re-creating "a strong France, whatever we might think about French deserts or the probable difficulty of achieving our purpose." As for Germany, a Prussia divided from Germany would be "a manageable European unit." At the end of this memorandum Churchill is recorded as having added the "complementary" idea of a "fraternal association" between the United States and the British Commonwealth, including "the common use by their armed forces of bases for the common defence of common interests": a proposal to which he would revert nearly three years later, in his speech at Fulton, Missouri, famous for his advocacy of a "special relationship" between Britain and the United States.

The Moscow and Cairo Conferences, October–November 1943

Some of Churchill's and Roosevelt's thinking about post-war organisation found its way into the Four-Power Declaration on General Security that was signed in Moscow on 30 October. Although Roosevelt had himself suggested a declaration of this kind during the Quebec Conference, he does not seem to have expected much to come out of the Moscow Conference. This was indeed the only occasion during the war that he allowed Hull to attend a meeting of any significance abroad; and the reason that Hull had to be sent to this one was partly fortuitous.* At American insistence, opposed up to the last moment by the Soviet Government (which was not at war with Japan), the declaration was signed by the Chinese Ambassador, as well as by the three foreign ministers. In this declaration the four governments recognised "the necessity of establishing at the earliest practicable date a general international organisation, based on the principle of the sovereign equality of all peace-loving states . . . for the maintenance of international peace and security. . . ."

Far more significant than this declaration was the passage by the U.S. Senate, a week later, of the Connally Resolution, which recognised the necessity of establishing an international organisation for the maintenance of peace, which the United States should join. The voting in favour of this resolution was 85–5. So far as the Moscow Conference is concerned, however, we can now see that its most far-reaching decisions were taken almost in the margin of its main deliberations: the first step towards the dismemberment of *Grossdeutschland*. The three foreign ministers agreed in Moscow that Austria should be re-established as an independent state after Germany had been defeated. It was, moreover, at this conference that the European Advisory Commission was set

---

*In September 1943 Welles, with whom Roosevelt had always preferred to deal direct, had been obliged to leave the State Department. William Bullitt (who wanted Welles' job) had confronted Roosevelt with an affidavit, signed by a Southern Railway sleeping-car attendant, about Welles' homosexuality. Roosevelt never forgave Bullitt.[7]

up—the tripartite body which would in due course agree upon the zones of Allied military occupation in Germany.[8]

Consumed with anxiety about the fate of the Mediterranean campaign (not only in Italy itself, but also in the Aegean, where Churchill failed to convince either Roosevelt or Eisenhower's staff of the need to divert resources to capture Rhodes),[9] Churchill did all he could in a series of messages to persuade Roosevelt that the two of them should hold another conference before they met Stalin. Roosevelt was reluctant: a reluctance that would recur in 1945.[10] In the event, it was thanks—ironically—to a decision taken on 12 November by Stalin that Anglo-American bilateral discussions took place after all, because on that day Churchill received word from Stalin that "for certain reasons of a serious character, Molotov, to my regret, cannot go to Cairo." The second paragraph of Stalin's message makes it clear that the reason why Molotov would not be arriving in Cairo on 22 November—as Stalin had previously informed Roosevelt—was the fact that the Cairo Conference would be attended by Chiang Kai-shek.[11] At this stage of the war Stalin was not prepared to contemplate anything so publicly at variance with the Soviet-Japanese Treaty.

So it came about that from 23 to 26 November Churchill and Roosevelt (Churchill travelling in HMS *Renown* and Roosevelt in the U.S.S. *Iowa*) conferred yet again, this time almost in the shadow of the Pyramids, at the Mena House Hotel, requisitioned for the occasion. (The two men drove out together to visit the Sphinx before they left.) Militarily speaking, this, the first of the two Cairo meetings, between which the Teheran Conference was sandwiched, agreed on one thing and one thing only: Operation *Buccaneer,* an amphibious attack by the British on the Andaman Islands across the Bay of Bengal, timed to coincide with Chinese operations to be undertaken in northern Burma. This operation was agreed on in the first instance by Roosevelt and Chiang; Churchill and his Chiefs of Staff, conscious of what this commitment implied in terms of shipping, had either to take it or leave it. They accepted.

The Cairo Conference, at which Chiang was treated by Roosevelt as an equal, was the high-water mark of the Sino-American relationship during the Second World War. Of infinitely greater significance for history than the military planning at this conference was the political agreement, publicly announced in the communiqué issued in Cairo, after the conference had ended. This committed the Anglo-American-Chinese Allies, after the war, to strip Japan of all the islands in the Pacific which it had seized or occupied since the beginning of the First World War, and to restore to the Republic of China all territories "stolen from the Chinese, such as Manchuria, Formosa, [Taiwan] and the Pescadores"—[12]words that would cause a Sino-American crisis in the very different circumstances of East Asia in 1950.

Teheran, 27 November–1 December 1943

How the Big Three reached Teheran and how they spent their last evening there—at a dinner party at the British Legation, lasting into the small hours of 1 December—has already been described. The conference had a curious beginning. On the first evening Churchill, Roosevelt and Stalin dined separately; the dinner which had been planned for the three leaders together had to be called off because Churchill had almost completely lost his voice (he had left Britain with a fever). Nor did Churchill meet Roosevelt the following morning, as he had hoped; instead, Roosevelt and Stalin met for the first time on the afternoon of 28 November. That morning, according to the American record[13] of the conference, Roosevelt had decided to accept Stalin's invitation to move from the U.S. Legation, which was some distance away from the other two legations (then, as now, cheek by jowl), to the Soviet Legation compound. The reason for Stalin's invitation, which was conveyed through Harriman, was—again according to the American record—the possibility that "Axis sympathisers" in Teheran might cause "an unhappy incident to any of the Heads of State driving through the city to visit each other."

The Soviet record,[14] however, reminds us that it was in fact Roosevelt himself who first raised the question of security, in a telegram sent to Stalin from Cairo on 24 November, ending with the straight question: where, in Stalin's opinion, ought he and his staff to stay in Teheran? Since Beria was, as we now know, with Stalin at Teheran,[15] there is plenty of scope for speculation about the motive for the Soviet invitation and the use to which the presence of the U.S. delegation in the Soviet compound may have been put by the NKVD. What is relevant to the present study, however, is the degree of trust implied both by Roosevelt's telegram from Cairo and by the alacrity with which he and his advisers moved from the U.S. compound to the Soviet compound shortly before the first plenary session of the conference.

Considering the problems of interpretation, the differences between the three records of the Teheran Conference, like those of the other two wartime summit meetings, are remarkably small.* Of the historic first meeting between Roosevelt and Stalin, Charles Bohlen (who, as well as being Roosevelt's interpreter, was a career member of the Foreign Service) was the only American witness; Stalin was accompanied by Vladimir Pavlov, his interpreter. This meeting, which lasted about an hour, was something of an anti-climax. Initial courtesies were followed by a brief discussion of the state of operations on the Eastern Front, after which the discussion flitted over China, France, Indo-China and India. Roosevelt having described his recent talks with Chiang Kai-shek as very interesting, Stalin expressed disdain both for Chinese fighting abilities and for the Chinese leadership. Roosevelt's concurrence in Stalin's assessment of the former is included in the Soviet record, but omitted from the American. Roosevelt gave free rein to his dislike of de Gaulle; Stalin was careful to begin his remarks about France by saying that he did not know the general. (De Gaulle visited the Soviet Union a year later.) Roosevelt said that he did not share Churchill's view that France would soon become a great power again; and when Stalin turned the conversation towards Indo-China, which he thought could not return to a colonial regime once it was

---

*The accounts of the Teheran Conference in this chapter and of the Yalta and Potsdam Conferences in Chapters 17 and 18 are based mainly on the Bohlen Minutes in the *Foreign Relations of the United States* series, supplemented from time to time by the Soviet and British records.[16]

liberated, Roosevelt put forward his proposal that a body of three or four trustees should prepare Indo-China for self-government over a period of thirty to forty years—a proposal which, in his view, would be valid in relation to other colonies as well. This provided Roosevelt with the opportunity for another dig at Churchill, who, he said, was afraid of the need to apply this principle to British colonies—according to the Soviet record, which describes Stalin's reply as "Naturally, Churchill will not be pleased," whereas the American record describes Stalin as "completely" agreeing with Roosevelt's view on Indo-China. Finally, Roosevelt made scathing remarks about Churchill's view of India. Stalin observed that India was Churchill's "sore spot." And when Roosevelt suggested Indian reform "from the bottom, somewhat on the Soviet line," Stalin replied that this would mean going "along the path of revolution."

As for Grand Strategy, cards were laid face up on the table from the very beginning of the first plenary meeting of the Big Three, held on the same afternoon at the Soviet Legation immediately afterwards. Roosevelt, in the chair, began with an exposition of strategic plans for the defeat of Japan. He went on, first to recall the *Trident* adoption of 1 May 1944 as the date for *Overlord*, and then to raise the question how Allied forces in the Mediterranean theatre could best be used in order to "bring maximum aid to the Soviet armies" on the Eastern Front. As possible areas of operation for these forces he listed Italy, the Adriatic, the Aegean and Turkey, but he added that "some of these possibilities might involve a delay of two or three months" for *Overlord*.

Having confirmed at the beginning of his intervention that, once Germany had capitulated, the Soviet Union would be able to reinforce its forces in Siberia, after which there would be "a common front against Japan," Stalin gave a categorical reply to Roosevelt's Mediterranean questions. In the Soviet view, the great (in the Soviet record, "the only") value of the Italian campaign was freeing the Mediterranean for the passage of Allied shipping.[17] He did not believe that Italy was a suitable place from which to attack Germany (in the Soviet record, it "did not present any significance whatsoever in the sense of further operations against Germany"), because of the Alpine barrier.

He might have added, as he had remarked to Eden in Moscow shortly before, that if "he were Hitler, he would tie the British and the Americans to Italy, in order to give them battle in the Alpine mountain range."[18] Instead, Stalin concluded by saying that even an invasion through southern France would be better; if Turkey were willing to open the road to the Allies, the Balkans would still be nearer the heart of Germany (the Soviet record—the American record says "far from"); but Germany's weak spot was France.

Taking as his (sanguine) premise the capture of Rome in January 1944, Churchill maintained that Allied forces in the Mediterranean could not remain idle between that date and *Overlord*. True, some of the Mediterranean operations discussed might involve a delay "of some two months of *Overlord*," but there was no intention of advancing into the Po Valley or across the Alps. Once the Pisa-Rimini line was reached, forces would be free for other operations, perhaps in southern France or across the Adriatic. Churchill then described the advantages of Turkey's entry into the war. He concluded by asking whether the Soviet Government would be sufficiently interested in these operations (in the Soviet record, specifically "operations in the eastern part of the Mediterranean Sea") if they were perhaps to involve some delay in *Overlord*.

At this point, Roosevelt interposed his only remark during the Teheran Conference which suggested (as Churchill would remind him, clinging to this straw, during the major dispute about the Italian campaign that developed between them in the summer of 1944) that he had not closed his mind to the possibility of developing a Mediterranean-Balkan strategy of the kind that Churchill had secretly pressed on his Chiefs of Staff before leaving London. He had, the President now said, "thought of a possible operation at the head of the Adriatic to make a junction with the Partisans under Tito and then to operate northeast into Romania in conjunction with the Soviet advance." Churchill jumped at this, at once suggesting that a committee should be formed to study the question and to work out a detailed report. A bilateral debate between Churchill and Stalin ensued. Stalin dismissed Aegean operations as worthless unless Turkey entered the war; he was convinced (rightly) that Turkey would not do this. He questioned the wisdom of dispersing forces in the different Mediterranean operations suggested. Instead, he came down firmly in favour of *Overlord* as "the basis of all 1944 operations," with an invasion of southern France as a supporting operation. If necessary, he personally would even be in favour of going over to the defensive in Italy, postponing the capture of Rome. Towards the end of this exchange, Roosevelt made a decisive intervention: nothing should be done to delay the carrying out of *Overlord,* which might be necessary if any operations in the eastern Mediterranean were undertaken. And he proposed that a plan should be worked out on the following morning "for striking at southern France." Before the three leaders broke up, they agreed that Voroshilov and the Combined Chiefs of Staff should meet.

The three leaders themselves met for dinner that evening, with Roosevelt as host. Here they began to discuss the political future of Europe for the first time together, Stalin taking the lead. On the one hand, he was sceptical of the value of the principle of unconditional surrender in relation to Germany, whose people it merely served to unite. On the other, he believed that their ability and talents were so great that the German people "could easily revive within fifteen or twenty years and again become a threat to the world." He therefore insisted that the measures taken for the post-war control and disarmament of Germany must be rigorous. What specific measures he had in mind, according to Bohlen, was not clear, although he "appeared to favour the dismemberment of Germany." One particular point, however, he made crystal clear: the Polish western frontier should in future be on the River Oder, and the Soviet Union would help Poland to get this frontier.

Roosevelt, who was feeling unwell, went to bed after dinner, but Churchill and Stalin stayed on talking. It was Churchill who opened the Polish question. Speaking personally, he thought that "Poland might move westwards after the war, like soldiers at drill taking two steps left close. If Poland trod on some German toes, that could not be helped, but there must be a strong Poland. . . ." Later he illustrated what he had in mind with the help of three matches; and Eden explicitly said that "what Poland lost in the east [i.e., the territory east of the Curzon Line] she might gain in the west [territory taken from eastern Germany]." Although Churchill suggested that the three heads of government should see whether, at Teheran, they could "form some sort of policy which might be pressed upon the Poles [i.e., the Polish Government-in-exile in London] and which we could recommend to the Poles, and advise them to accept," Stalin's response was non–committal.[19]

Having declined Churchill's invitation to lunch with him before the second plenary session the following day, Roosevelt had a second private meeting with Stalin that afternoon, at which their principal topic was post-war international structure. Roosevelt outlined his proposal of a United Nations Organisation, upon which the organisation of the four policemen would be superimposed. Stalin repeatedly expressed scepticism about China; he also suggested that "a European state would probably resent China having the right to apply certain machinery to it"; and, as an alternative, he proposed setting up two organisations—one European (including the United States) and the other Far Eastern.* Roosevelt pointed out the similarity between Stalin's and Churchill's ideas in this respect, but he doubted whether the U.S. Congress would agree to the United States' participation in an exclusively European Committee. When Stalin observed that the President's own proposal, and in particular the four policemen, might also require American troops to be sent to Europe, Roosevelt's reply was that he had envisaged sending only aircraft and ships to Europe, where Britain and the Soviet Union would have to "handle the land armies in the event of any future threat to peace." He added, moreover, that "he doubted very much if it would have been possible to send any American forces to Europe" had the Japanese not attacked the United States in 1941. At the end of this talk, Stalin insisted that the post-war organisations proposed would not be enough to prevent aggression, primarily

---

*Towards the end of the conference, however, Stalin came round to support of a single, world organisation.

German, but also Japanese. The organisation must therefore "be able to occupy the most important strategic points . . . not only in Europe, but also in the Far East" (Soviet record). Roosevelt expressed "one hundred per cent" agreement. This bilateral meeting then came to an end, in order to allow Stalin to go and receive the Stalingrad sword, presented by Churchill on the King's behalf.

Although the morning military meeting reached no conclusions, it may have helped to clear the air, especially by leaving Voroshilov in no doubt about the crucial importance of landing craft, both for operations in the Mediterranean and for *Overlord* (Marshall remarked that, whereas before the war "he had never heard of any landing craft except a rubber boat," now he thought "about little else"). And in reply to a direct question from Voroshilov, for whom Mediterranean operations were "of secondary importance," Brooke said that although he too looked at them in this way, Mediterranean "operations were closely connected with the whole conduct of the war and, in particular, with the success of the operation in Northern France," which they would assist (Soviet record).

At the second plenary session, on 29 November, both Churchill and Stalin overplayed their hands. Having begun—correctly—by identifying the dilemma as shortage of landing craft to meet the competing demands of the Mediterranean, the Bay of Bengal, and *Overlord* (he tactfully did not mention the Pacific theatre), Churchill went on to spoil his case by talking at length about Turkey and operations in the Aegean, which he admitted might have the effect of delaying the date of *Overlord*. The arbiter of the dispute was Roosevelt. In another well-timed intervention, he said that he was in favour of adhering to the *Trident* date for *Overlord*—1 May. Churchill disagreed; but Stalin, for whom "Turkey, the Partisans and even the occupation of Rome were not really important operations," said that he did not mind when *Overlord* was undertaken, provided that it was in May. And towards the end of the session he asked Churchill pointblank whether the British "believe in Operation *Overlord,* or are they simply talking about it in order to reassure the Russians?" Churchill's reply was predictable. It was not a happy meeting.

The subsequent dinner at the Soviet Embassy did not go any better. Its "most notable feature," Bohlen recorded, was the attitude of Stalin, who "lost no opportunity to get a dig in at Mr. Churchill," whom he "apparently desired to put and keep . . . on the defensive." It was at this dinner that, as well as reiterating his insistence on the retention by the Allies of important strategic points in the world, Stalin made it a "condition" that between fifty and a hundred thousand German officers must be physically liquidated. When Roosevelt suggested a compromise of forty-nine thousand, Churchill left the table in disgust. As Churchill remarked in the passage of his memoirs describing this scene, Stalin had "a very captivating manner when he chooses to use it and I never saw him do so to such an extent as at this moment.[20] Stalin went out, clapped his hands on Churchill's shoulders "from behind" and persuaded him to return to the dining room.

On the morning of 30 November the Combined Chiefs of Staff succeeded in agreeing on everything but the question of operations in the Aegean—not a surprising exception, since Churchill's own advisers did not share his enthusiasm for these operations. Their agreement, reported to the third plenary session of the conference that afternoon, consisted of three points: a continuation of the advance in Italy to the Pisa-Rimini line (sixty-eight LSTs therefore being retained in the Mediterranean until 15 January 1944); an operation against the south of France, "for planning purposes" simultaneously with *Overlord* D-Day, "on the largest scale that is permitted by the landing craft available at the time"; and the launching of *Overlord* "during May," in conjunction with this "supporting operation" against southern France.[21] It took the Big Three less than an hour to give these recommendations the stamp of their approval. For his part, Stalin undertook to "organise a large-scale offensive against the Germans in several places" in May, and Roosevelt told his colleagues that his appointment of the Commander-in-Chief for *Overlord* would be made in three or four days' time.

That morning, Churchill, at his request, had met Stalin for an hour, alone with their interpreters. Churchill did most of the talking. He pointed out (with some justice, as the Second Cairo Conference would soon prove) that the choice was not only between operations in the

Mediterranean and *Overlord,* but also between operations in the Bay of Bengal and *Overlord.* Unfortunately, Chiang's presence in Cairo and Chinese affairs had taken up almost all the time at the recent conference there. Churchill went on to paint a glowing picture of the operations planned in Italy, including an amphibious attack delivered on the west coast. The importance of these operations lay not in the capture of Rome, but in the destruction of the German forces there—"a miniature Stalingrad."

In reply, Stalin reverted once again to the fact that the Red Army was counting on the execution of the landing in northern France. He was afraid that, if this operation did not take place in the month of May 1944, then it never would, because of worsening weather conditions. He then went on:

> If this operation does not take place, he must warn that this would provoke great disappointment and bad feelings. He feared that the absence of this operation could provoke a very bad feeling of isolation. Therefore he wanted to know whether operation *Overlord* would take place, or not. If it took place, that was good, but if not, he wished to know this in advance in order to be able to prevent the feelings which the absence of this operation might provoke. This was the most important question.[22]

Churchill gave Stalin a reply which, according to both the British and the Soviet records of this conversation, was qualified.[23] Stalin responded with the assurance, repeated shortly afterwards in plenary session, that the Red Army would mount an offensive on the Eastern Front simultaneously with *Overlord.*

The euphoria of the toasts exchanged that evening at Churchill's birthday dinner party would of themselves provide a fitting conclusion to the Teheran Conference. As well as the need to agree on a stirring communiqué, however, there were two further, highly significant meetings on 1 December: Roosevelt's third talk with Stalin and a tripartite meeting before dinner. At the first of these two meetings Roosevelt told Stalin, unasked, that he personally would like to see the eastern frontier of Poland moved further west and the western frontier moved "even to the River Oder," although reasons of domestic politics ("six to seven million Americans of Polish extraction") would during an electoral year prevent him from saying anything in public. He also put forward a muted plea on behalf of the peoples of the Baltic States, adding "jokingly" that when the Soviet armies reoccupied the areas, he did not intend to go to war with the Soviet Union on this point. Moreover, at the subsequent tripartite meeting, it was Roosevelt who introduced discussion of both the Polish and the German questions.

Although the discussion about Poland's future frontiers was inconclusive (and also interrupted at one point by a lengthy attempt to establish, on a map, exactly where the Curzon Line[24] ran), Roosevelt in effect confirmed Churchill's "three matches" suggestion when he asked Stalin whether, in his opinion, "East Prussia and the area between the old Polish frontier and the Oder was approximately equal to the former Polish territory acquired by the Soviet Union." The American record shows Stalin replying that "he did not know." (He undoubtedly did.) And at the very end of the meeting, in reply to Churchill's statement that the Polish question was urgent, Stalin said:

> If the Russians would be given the northern part of East Prussia, running along the left bank of the Niemen and include Tilsit and the City of Königsberg, he would be prepared to accept the Curzon Line as the frontier between the Soviet Union and Poland. He said the acquisition of that part of Eastern Prussia would not only afford the Soviet Union an ice-free port, but would also give to Russia a small piece of German territory which he felt was deserved.[25]

As for Germany, Roosevelt proposed its dismemberment and division into five self-governing parts; in addition, two crucial areas[26] would be placed under UN or "some form of international control." Churchill advanced his suggestion of a separate Prussia and the addition of southern Germany to a Danubian Confederation. Of these two proposals, Stalin preferred the former, but he also said that if it was decided to divide Germany, new units should not be created. "No measures existed capable of excluding the possibility of Germany uniting." Having got thus far, the three leaders decided to hand the problem over to the European Advisory Commission in London, for further study. Thus the Teheran Conference ended by taking the first tentative steps towards the third redrawing of the map of Central Europe in the span of one generation.

The Declaration of the Three Powers signed by Churchill, Roosevelt, and Stalin on 1 December 1943 and published a week later stated:

> We have concerted our plans for the destruction of the German forces . . . no power on earth can prevent our destroying the German armies by land, their U-boats by sea, and their war plants from the air.

The three leaders were sure that their concord would "make it an enduring peace." They looked forward to welcoming "all nations, large and small," into a "world family of democratic nations." And the declaration ended with these words:

> We came here with hope and determination. We leave here friends in fact, in spirit and in purpose.[27]

The Sequel, December 1943

The records of the Teheran Conference fully bear out Brooke's verdict (quoted in the epigraph to this chapter). In the sphere of Grand Strategy, Stalin at last achieved what he wanted. His political judgement was, moreover, also quickly proved right over the issue on which Churchill had poured out so many words at Teheran—Turkey. President Inönü accepted the invitation to confer with Churchill and Roosevelt in Cairo immediately after the Teheran Conference, but—even with Roosevelt's help—Churchill was no more able to persuade him to bring his country into the war than he had been when he met him at Adana eight months earlier. Remarkably, however, Churchill succeeded in getting from Roosevelt later in December what he had fought for at Teheran: enough landing craft in the Mediterranean to enable the flagging Italian campaign to be given a shot in the arm at the beginning of 1944. In Cairo, after much discussion between the Combined Chiefs of Staff, Roosevelt overruled his own Joint Chiefs and cancelled *Buccaneer*—the amphibious operation across the Bay of Bengal, on which he had insisted at the First Cairo Conference only a fortnight earlier. More than that, on 27 December 1943 Roosevelt telegraphed to Churchill his agreement that the departure from the Mediterranean of the LSTs required for *Overlord* should be delayed until February—long enough to enable Alexander to deliver an amphibious left hook at Anzio on 20 January: Operation *Shingle*. [28] As Dill had wisely remarked in a letter to Brooke before the Teheran Conference: "The American Chiefs of Staff have given way to our views a thousand times more than we have given way to them." But Dill added the prophetic warning that British "difficulties with the Americans" would "increase . . . with their growing strength and a Presidential Election approaching."[29]

15

THE ALLIANCE

DOMINANT

The history of warfare knows no other similar
undertaking in the breadth of its conception, in
its giant dimensions, and in the mastery of its
performance.... History will record this event
as an achievement of the highest order.

—*Joseph Stalin, 13 June 1944, describing the invasion
of Normandy*

The contrast between the Three-Power Declaration of
1 December 1943 and the confusion of 1942, followed by the debate
within the Grand Alliance through most of 1943, was manifest. The
declaration was received with enthusiastic acclaim in the capitals of all
three countries—nowhere more than in the Soviet Union, where in
addition to the paeans of press and radio, the significance of the declaration was explained at meetings specially convened in factories throughout the country. This time, the audiences at these meetings were told, it
was the real thing. One month after leaving Teheran, Stalin himself
described the conference in his New Year's Day speech to the Supreme
Soviet, in these words:

> The greatest event of our days, an historic landmark in the struggle against the German aggressor. . . . The leaders of the three

Great Powers reached full agreement on matters of war and peace. They agreed on exactly what the popular masses, suffering under the weight of the German boot in the occupied countries, are longing for.[1]

Stalin had solid grounds for satisfaction. So also did Churchill and Roosevelt. The strategic plan for the European theatre of war agreed by the three leaders at Teheran was carried out almost to the letter in 1944—the Anzio landing followed by the spring offensive, in Italy; the invasion of Normandy on 6 June, the great Soviet offensive in Belorussia four days later; and the invasion of southern France in August. Nor can the political paragraphs of the Teheran Declaration be dismissed as hot air. Before the conference, Churchill and Roosevelt had welcomed Stalin's decision to dissolve the Comintern. (In fact Stalin was glad to be rid of an organisation that had long ceased to serve any useful purpose for the conduct of Soviet policy.) After the conference, however, the way was open for the three powers to work together in planning the structure of the post-war world. This work was not just a matter of frontiers. The agreement establishing the United Nations Relief and Rehabilitation Administration (UNRRA), designed to deal with the emergency relief of liberated countries, had just been signed. And in 1944 the outlines of three major post-war international organisations would be worked out, with Soviet participation, at conferences held in the United States, at Dumbarton Oaks (the United Nations Organisation), and at Bretton Woods (the International Monetary Fund and the International Bank for Reconstruction and Development).[2]

Just over fourteen months separated the last day of the first meeting of the Big Three, at Teheran, and the first day of their second meeting, at Yalta. These fourteen months constitute a period—formative for the future configuration of Europe—that looks different according to which of several lenses the historian chooses in order to examine it, each of them focusing on one of a whole range of questions, all of which have to be answered for a comprehensive assessment of this period of the war. Thus, the military historian concentrates his lens on the deceptively simple question: how did it come about that, in spite of Allied command of the seas, numerical superiority on land and over-whelming mastery in the air, the war in Europe dragged on until May 1945? (By the time the three leaders left for their meeting in the Crimea, the *Wehrmacht* remained loyal to Hitler, who—after nar-rowly escaping assassination in July 1944—refused to admit defeat; and the frontiers of Germany remained more or less intact.) For the student of geopolitics, the most important decision—viewed in the longer term—is that taken by Churchill and Roosevelt in September 1944, that the first available atomic bomb should be dropped on Japan.[3] In the eyes of the historian of the Holocaust, these questions become secondary to the fact that, from mid-1944 onwards, the full horror of what was happening at Oświęcim (Auschwitz) at last became realised in the Alliance, although its leaders did very little about it.[4] And an account of the Resistance movements of occupied Europe turns the reader's gaze away from the main thrust of events, towards what hap-pened in one capital after another—Rome, Paris, Warsaw, Athens, Belgrade—as Allied forces drew near them, with quite different politi-cal results in each country. Nevertheless, important though all these questions are to a complete understanding both of this phase of the war and of what followed in Europe (and the list is not exhaustive), the student of the Big Three must follow his Ariadne's thread.[5]

The Big Three in 1944

In terms of the relationship between Churchill, Roosevelt and Stalin, the fourteen months between the Teheran and Yalta conferences repre-sent a high plateau, from which—with occasional hesitations—the three leaders refused to be deflected from their vision of the post-war peak towards which their Teheran Declaration had pointed. This was also a period during which the health, certainly of Churchill and Roosevelt, but probably of all three men, suffered. To take account of this fact in no way implies concurrence in the judgment pronounced twenty years afterwards by Churchill's self-appointed Boswell that "much that is otherwise inexplicable in the last year of the war—for instance, the deterioration in his [Churchill's] relations with Roosevelt" can be ascribed to Churchill's "exhaustion of mind and body."[6] Not only was Charles Moran seldom a first-hand witness of historic decisions at the time (although he was "quite often invited to dinner afterwards"), but the half-dozen members of Churchill's Whitehall team who combined to write a riposte to Moran's book recorded their collective view that his assessment of Churchill's "qualities as a statesman and leader of his country in war and peace" was "in some respects . . . incorrect and in others incomplete and on both counts misleading."[7] That the relative importance of Churchill's understanding and co-operation with Roosevelt declined in 1944 is undoubted, but the reasons for this were not medical.

This said, the historian cannot ignore the medical factor in assessing any of the leaders of the Grand Alliance (or for that matter Hitler) during 1944. In Stalin's case, the evidence at the time of writing is still scanty. Djilas, whose description of Stalin's appearance in early 1944 was quoted in Chapter 1, has also recorded the marked physical and mental change that had come over Stalin by the time the two men met four years later. There are other, unsubstantiated indications that, once victory was at last clearly in sight, the strain of the years 1941–42 began to take its toll. His sixty-fourth birthday followed one month after Churchill's sixty-ninth, celebrated at the three leaders' final dinner at Teheran.[8] Certainly from August 1944 onwards the candid common sense that marked Stalin's exchanges with his two allies during the previous three years begins to be tinged with a crude chauvinism.

On the other hand, we now know exactly both the severity of the illness suffered by Churchill in December 1943 and the nature of the mortal illness diagnosed by Roosevelt's doctors three months later. Churchill had made a remarkable recovery from his first attack of pneumonia earlier in 1943; he was not well when he left England in October, however, and once the stimulus of the three weeks spent conferring in Cairo, Teheran, and again in Cairo was removed, exhaustion took over. On 11 December he was subjected to a mismanaged flight. Starting at one o'clock in the morning from Cairo, he arrived in midwinter at the wrong airport in Tunis (where Eisenhower still had his headquarters), and after sleeping for a whole day, he collapsed with a fresh bout of pneumonia in the early hours of 12 December. This time his heart was affected—so much so that Moran summoned a cardiologist from Britain; and once the crisis was over, Churchill was persuaded to spend a fortnight's convalescence at Marrakesh (a long time for him, but in fact the bare minimum). He travelled home on board the battleship *King George V.* Within two hours of his return to London on 18 January 1944, he took his seat on the front bench of the House of Commons. After receiving a standing ovation, he answered parliamentary questions "as if he was the youngest Under-Secretary"; and at Buckingham Palace, when the King's private secretary met him at the door and offered him the use of the lift, Churchill's response was to run up the stairs two at a time.[9]

This was not, however, the end of the story. At the end of August Churchill had a recurrence of his pneumonia. Although this was minor, for most of 1944 the letters and diaries of those who observed Churchill at close quarters abound in references[10] to the visible signs of his damaged physical health. Probably for the first time in his life, Churchill experienced prolonged physical fatigue, and in private he even said so himself.[11] Nevertheless, his mental energy retained its extraordinary pitch—witness his sparks of brilliance, which could still illuminate the weaknesses of the collective wisdom of his advisers. (A notable example of this is the cogent memorandum, addressed to the Chiefs of Staff in early September 1944, questioning—with justice, as events soon proved—the confidence of the Joint Intelligence Committee that the war would be over by the end of the year.)[12] But the deployment of his energy also became increasingly dissipated. He spent hours discussing high policy—for example, the vexed question of the best form of British contribution to the war against Japan—arguments[13] which, though prolonged into the early morning, frequently ended by settling nothing.* His imaginative vision, moreover, which at its best served as

---

*The U.S. Navy was no longer interested in a British contribution towards the war in the Pacific, now regarded as an American preserve. Churchill and his Chiefs of Staff disagreed amongst them-

a gadfly to those less gifted than himself, now began to cling to enterprises which the colder calculations of men like Brooke accurately assessed as impossible of achievement.

In his seventieth year Churchill's reaction to physical illness coincided with his growing awareness that he, the founder member of the Grand Alliance, was no longer the hinge of the Alliance, in which during 1944 he gradually became the junior partner, especially once the invasion of Normandy had been carried out. Perhaps it was the combined effect of his resentment both of his physical fatigue and of his diminishing political and military power within the Alliance that caused him to drive himself harder than ever during the next twelve months. In spite of the state of his physical health, or perhaps because of it, Churchill spent much of 1944 shuttling to and fro. His many journeys included his second conference at Quebec with Roosevelt and his second conference in Moscow with Stalin. The other two leaders remained in their own countries.

Roosevelt left Cairo on 7 December 1943. After a stopover in Tunis, where he greeted Eisenhower with the remark that he had better start packing (in order to take command of Operation *Overlord*), Roosevelt returned home in the battleship *Iowa*. His entire Cabinet greeted him at the south entrance to the White House, where he had never looked—at any rate to one of his advisers—so satisfied and pleased.[14] Whether Roosevelt, who saw himself as a political realist, was fully convinced that he had succeeded in establishing a personal relationship with Stalin—as Churchill, by comparison with Roosevelt, a political romantic, believed that he had done in 1942—we cannot be certain. As usual, he spoke differently to different people. But what he said publicly in his broadcast from Hyde Park on Christmas Eve, where he spent Christmas with his family, including seven of his four-

---

selves about how and where British forces could most effectively be deployed in that theatre, assuming American objections could be overcome. And in addition Churchill himself was sceptical about the prospect of Slim's land offensive in Burma (which ultimately inflicted on the Japanese Army its biggest defeat on land of the whole war).

teen grandchildren, for the first time since the United States entered the war, is a matter of record:

> I may say that I "got along fine" with Marshal Stalin. He is a man who combines a tremendous relentless determination with a stalwart good humor. I believe he is truly representative of the heart and soul of Russia; and I believe that we are going to get along very well with him and the Russian people—very well indeed.[15]

In the New Year, Roosevelt's health began its decline. In January—he was sixty-two on the 30th—he had influenza. The after-effects of influenza, even though Roosevelt was a comparatively young man, lingered on, with morning tiredness, evening headaches and occasional dropping off in the middle of conversations—once even while signing his own name. Even so, it was not until almost the end of March, by which time he had also developed bronchitis, that a check-up for the President was arranged at Bethesda Hospital, Maryland, and—equally important—that Roosevelt was persuaded to go there. The young U.S. Naval consultant[16] who examined him at Bethesda was a brilliant cardiologist; a significant fact which does not seem to have interested Roosevelt in the least.

Amazingly, by the standards of today, no one seems to have told Roosevelt either the medical findings or the prognosis;* nor did he enquire what the digitalis (which the consultant insisted he should take from now on) was for. Thus it came about that the U.S. President and Commander-in-Chief, suffering in March 1944 from hypertension, hypertensive heart disease and cardiac failure—after a complete rest at Bernard Baruch's[17] house in South Carolina and with some reforms in his daily regime[18]—not only went on to complete the remainder of his third term of office, but also fought a fourth electoral campaign. In November 1944 Roosevelt was elected President once again, though

---

*Recent speculation has suggested that Roosevelt may also have been suffering from the early stage of cancer.

with a reduced popular majority.[19] The medication and the regime together helped to contain the immediate threat to his life.

The change in Roosevelt's appearance became obvious, although this was in part the result of a deliberate loss of weight. By September 1944 he struck more than one observer, including Churchill, as frail; by the time he reached Yalta, his looks were beginning to be alarming; and Churchill later recorded his impression that, at their final meeting (in Alexandria Harbour, after the Yalta Conference), the President had "a slender contact with life."[20] Like any man suffering from an illness of this gravity and carrying the burden that he did, Roosevelt clearly had good moments and bad as 1944 went forward, but there is nothing to substantiate the suggestion that at Yalta he did not realise what he was doing. The process of decision-making must have become more exacting for Roosevelt, as indeed it was even for Churchill's iron constitution. In general, however, as with the effects of poliomyelitis twenty-three years earlier, Roosevelt behaved as though the immense problem that he confronted simply did not exist.

Roosevelt and Stalin

During the fourteen-month interval between Teheran and Yalta, Stalin replaced Churchill as Roosevelt's principal partner in the Grand Alliance. In part this was the logical outcome of the shift in the balance of military and industrial power within the Alliance. By the middle of 1944 the British war effort had peaked. By then the number of U.S. divisions deployed exceeded those of Britain and the British Commonwealth; and indeed the main logistical problem in the European theatre of operations had become to find ports in continental Europe capable of handling the constant flow of fresh American troops arriving from the United States. Industrially speaking, moreover, although British manpower was mobilised for productive purposes more thoroughly than that of any other Allied country, in 1944 British arms production was not only dwarfed by that of the United States, but also equalled by that of the Soviet Union: in that year British industry and that of the British Commonwealth produced some thirty-one thousand aircraft for the one million-strong RAF, by comparison with American production of almost one hundred thousand aircraft and Soviet production of over forty thousand.[21]

In 1944, furthermore, American Grand Strategy for the defeat of Japan underwent a gradual but radical change. There were several different strands in this reformulation. In the first place, Roosevelt personally intervened in order to settle the dispute about Pacific strategy between Nimitz and MacArthur. The core of this was whether, as MacArthur insisted, the Philippines must be invaded, or whether, as Nimitz (initially backed by the U.S. Joint Chiefs of Staff) believed, it was Formosa (Taiwan) that should be the objective, the Philippines being by-passed. So critically important was this decision both on military grounds and for reasons of internal American politics— MacArthur left Roosevelt in no doubt that he would see to it that a decision against invading the Philippines would be used against Roosevelt by the Republican Party in the electoral campaign—that in July 1944 Roosevelt summoned Nimitz and MacArthur to meet him at Pearl Harbor. Roosevelt's opening remark to MacArthur, who (wearing his old khaki field-marshal's cap and leather flying jacket) arrived late, keeping his Commander-in-Chief waiting, is well known— "Hello, Douglas, what are you doing with that leather jacket on?"— but exactly what passed between the two men in the conference that followed is less certain. (No records were taken.)[22] MacArthur himself seems to have been surprised by the outcome: presidential approval for the invasion of the Philippines. Paradoxically, although Roosevelt's decision enabled MacArthur to fulfil his 1942 promise to "return" at the head of his army (and thus removed the danger of this becoming an American electoral issue), it also led to the greatest naval battle of the war—Leyte Gulf—in which the U.S. Navy destroyed the Japanese Navy irretrievably in October 1944.

The second major strand in the strategic change of 1944 in the Pacific theatre was the evolution of the administration's disillusionment with Chiang Kai-shek. The effect of the successful Japanese summer offensive against the Chinese, the growing strength of Mao Tse-tung in Yenan, and the corruption and incompetence of the

Chungking regime combined by the middle of the year to make Roosevelt himself, for the first time, doubtful whether China would hold together at all, let alone emerge at the end of the war as a great power. It was much too late for Roosevelt to abandon his concept of China as the fourth post-war policeman—even had he wanted to do so, the China Lobby in the United States was too powerful—but what was demonstrated beyond a peradventure was that the Chinese contribution to the defeat of Japan, other than obliging the Japanese to continue to retain an army of a million men on the Chinese mainland, would be minimal. Henceforward the principal ally on whom the United States counted for a major offensive contribution against Japan, once Germany had been defeated, was not China (nor for that matter Britain), but the Soviet Union.

Above and beyond these considerations stood Roosevelt's overall concept of the future relationship between the United States and the Soviet Union. It was not just that, as early as March 1942, Roosevelt believed that he was better fitted than Churchill to "handle" Stalin and had said so to Churchill, nor was this belief naive, as some have since maintained. Stalin was indeed the hardest nut to crack ever encountered by Roosevelt; but what Roosevelt had always excelled in—and he knew it—was precisely that: "handling" other people. The keystone to the American-Soviet arch, however, as Roosevelt saw it, was as much geopolitical as personal. Roosevelt's "cardinal" concept of the relationship between the two countries was the proposition that

> The interests of the United States were worldwide and not confined to North and South America and the Pacific Ocean . . . the Soviet Union had likewise worldwide interests and . . . the two countries could work out together any political or economic considerations at issue between them.[23]

The fact that this definition of Roosevelt's vision of the post-war world was expressed not in his own words, but in Hopkins'—during one of his last talks with Stalin, in Moscow—in no way lessens its force; if anything, perhaps the reverse. It was this cardinal concept that governed Roosevelt's dealings with Stalin from the Teheran Conference until he died (and indeed it remained in large measure the yardstick of U.S. policy towards the Soviet Union well after his death). Hence his repeated refusal in 1944–45 to become more than marginally involved in the increasingly central Soviet-Polish dispute. As late as November 1944, for example, after Churchill had spent days seeking to persuade the exiled Polish Prime Minister, Stanisław Mikołajczyk, to accept the Curzon Line as Poland's eastern frontier, the furthest that Roosevelt was prepared to go, in a letter to Mikołajczyk, was to state that if the Polish, Soviet and British governments were to reach a mutual agreement on Poland's frontiers, the U.S. Government would "offer no objection."[24] True, at Yalta he would be obliged to take a position, but in the weeks that followed that conference he distanced himself from the Polish problem as far as he could.

Churchill and Roosevelt

The relationship between Churchill and Roosevelt during the interval between the Teheran and the Crimean conferences may be looked at in one of two, apparently contradictory, ways. Both are founded in fact. On the one hand, because the relationship between Roosevelt and Stalin became paramount during these months, that between the President and the Prime Minister inevitably declined. The days of messages to each other in which the word "fun" occurs are over, and on both sides a new acerbic note now appears from time to time. On the other hand, although their disagreements multiplied during 1944 on a whole range of issues—political, military and commercial—it is also remarkable how far Roosevelt was still prepared to go, whenever he could, to give Churchill at least part—sometimes all—of what he wanted at any given moment.

A major concession made by Roosevelt to Churchill at the turn of the year 1943–44 has already been mentioned: the retention in the Mediterranean of the landing craft without which Operation *Shingle*— the Anglo-American landing at Anzio, south-east of Rome, on which Churchill had set his heart—could not have been carried out;

and, again on British insistence, the date for *Anvil* was put forward (so that it would now follow *Overlord*). On 22 January 1944 *Shingle*—the operation intended as a prelude to what Churchill had described to Stalin as "a miniature Stalingrad"—achieved complete surprise. But once again the bad luck that dogged Churchill's Mediterranean strategy in general, and the Italian campaign in particular, supervened. (Or, in this case, had generalship? The American corps commander at Anzio, Lieutenant-General John Lucas, has been blamed for an excess of caution, with reason, but Alexander's role is also open to criticism.)[25] In Churchill's own graphic words: "We hoped to land a wild cat that would tear out the bowels of the Boche. Instead we have stranded a vast whale with its tail flopping about in the water."[26]

What Churchill described in these two sentences was the fact that, once the Germans recovered from their initial surprise at Anzio and, relying on their superior lines of communication, counter-attacked the Allied bridgehead, it was only with great difficulty that the Americans and the British avoided being thrown back into the sea. A militarily ineffective and culturally inexcusable operation—the demolition of the historic Benedictine monastery on Monte Cassino by heavy bombers—followed, without denting the German defensive line.[27] When, in May 1944, Alexander finally concentrated the bulk of the forces of his army group west of the Apennines, he at last succeeded in forcing the Germans to withdraw from the Cassino position—in much better order than they should have done, however, thanks to General Mark Clark's exercise of his personal preference for occupying Rome rather than pursuing the German Fourteenth Army,[28] which was in full retreat at the time.

From this moment on the biggest strategic argument of the whole war between Churchill and Roosevelt began. The essential point at issue in the series of messages exchanged between London and Washington in June–July was this: now that Rome had at last fallen, nearly a year after the first Allied landing in Italy, should the divisions (most of them French) due to be withdrawn from Italy, in accordance with the agreement reached at Quebec in 1943, be deployed in the invasion of southern France *(Anvil,* agreed by the Big Three at Teheran as a supporting operation for *Overlord),* or should they be left in Italy after all, to enable Alexander* to exploit his recent success to the maximum? Subsumed in this bitter dispute between Churchill, who argued for the second of these two courses, and Roosevelt, who stuck to the first, were several themes that will be familiar to the reader of earlier chapters—the narrow margin of landing craft left over for the European theatre of operations from the Pacific; Churchill's belief in the flank attack on the "soft underbelly" versus Marshall's fear of the "suction pump" effect that a peripheral strategy would have on the resources required for *Overlord;* and the suspicion in Washington that Churchill's real aim was not so much military as political (a Balkan strategy designed to forestall the arrival of the Red Army in "east, middle and southern Europe").[29] Moreover, underlying all these factors there was perhaps also a specifically Churchillian anxiety not to see repeated in the Italian peninsula the dismal end of the Dardanelles campaign, where—nearly thirty years earlier—an imaginative strategic concept had been frustrated by the mistakes of inadequate commanders and, after great loss of life, operations had finally been called off just at the moment when they might still, with further perseverance, have been crowned with success.

Whereas Roosevelt had both his Joint Chiefs of Staff and Eisenhower solidly behind him in this dispute, Churchill did not enjoy his own team's wholehearted support. Before the capture of Rome, Wilson had recommended a landing in southern France in mid-August as the best of several options. Alexander's report immediately afterwards, however, suggested, again among other options, the possibility of the so-called "Vienna Alternative"—the development of the Italian campaign northeastwards through the Ljubljana Gap, in northwestern Yugoslavia. At first the Combined Chiefs of Staff had little difficulty in

---

*Eisenhower having left AFHQ in January 1944 in order to take command of *Overlord,* General Henry Maitland Wilson was then appointed Supreme Commander, Mediterranean, and General Alexander became Commander, Allied Forces in Italy, consisting of the Eighth (British) Army and the Fifth (U.S.) Army—both British officers. From then on the Mediterranean theatre was regarded as primarily a British responsibility.

agreeing that Alexander's advance—again as earlier agreed—should move quickly up to the Pisa-Rimini line, and that Operation *Anvil* (now confusingly rechristened *Dragoon*) should follow, either on the Riviera or in the Bay of Biscay. Brooke was from the outset sceptical about the Vienna Alternative—"wild hopes," not "based on any real study of the problem" by Alexander, of whose strategic judgement he never thought highly.[30] Not so Churchill. Particularly after *Ultra* had revealed the German determination once again to stand and fight in Italy further south than the Allies had expected,[31] Churchill seized on the Vienna Alternative, which by 19 June also commanded Wilson's support. Since this ambitious strategy could not be carried out without the ten divisions earmarked for *Anvil/Dragoon,* Anglo-American deadlock followed. On 28 June Churchill tried to break it by sending Roosevelt two telegrams—the first briefly letting the President know how "hardly" he took "the complete ruin of all our great affairs in the Mediterranean," and "earnestly" begging him to "examine the matter in detail" himself; the second containing the text of a long memorandum entitled "Operations in the European Theatres, Note by the Prime Minister and Minister of Defence," which poured cold water on the invasion of southern France and urged acceptance instead of the "project of an attack eastward across the Adriatic," with the aim of gaining possession of Trieste "by the end of September."[32]

Churchill's telegrams crossed a short one from Roosevelt, who played the ace of spades: Eisenhower (with Montgomery's agreement) was "definitely for *Anvil* . . . by August 30 and preferably earlier."[33] This was followed up next day by a longer, reasoned reply to Churchill's memorandum, drafted by the Joint Chiefs, but with the last paragraph added by Roosevelt himself. The telegram reminded Churchill of what had been agreed at Teheran and put him on notice that, should the two of them be unable to agree to direct Wilson by 1 July to launch *Anvil* at the earliest possible date, they "must communicate with Stalin immediately" (the Red Army's offensive in Belorussia had opened six days earlier and Minsk was recaptured by the end of the month). Roosevelt's own words in the final paragraph were candid: "For purely political considerations over here I would never survive even a slight setback in *Overlord* if it were known that fairly large forces had been diverted to the Balkans.[34]

Churchill's furious reply, drafted on 30 June—a day that he spent visiting defences against flying bombs (the V-1 pilotless weapon, whose attacks on London had begun in mid-June, causing nearly two thousand civilian deaths during the first fortnight)—offered to cross the Atlantic at once and even mentioned the possibility of resigning from office. The telegram was never sent. Instead, a longer telegram, both more formal and more moderate, was sent to Roosevelt on 1 July, declining the suggestion that Stalin should be jointly consulted and accepting Roosevelt's refusal—under "solemn protest" from the British Government—as soon as the President let him know that there was "no hope of reconsideration." This confirmation was at once forthcoming;[35] and in spite of further efforts by Churchill during July—this time to have the *Dragoon* landings diverted from the Riviera to Bordeaux—the invasion of southern France was accomplished at points between Toulon and Nice without difficulty on 15 August. Lyons was liberated on 3 September, and the link-up with Eisenhower's forces followed on 12 September 1944.

The removal of 40 per cent of the strength of the U.S. Fifth Army from Alexander's Italian command in July put paid to what Churchill had in his previous month regarded as the dazzling possibilities otherwise open to his favourite general ("gay, smiling, debonair," as Churchill described him in his memoirs).[36] Not that Churchill himself at once recognised this, whatever he had telegraphed to Roosevelt about it in the heat of the moments just described; at the end of August he was still telling Field-Marshal Jan Christian Smuts* of his hope of an "ultimate advance by Trieste and the Ljubljana Gap to Vienna."[37] In reality such an advance was by then a pipe dream. Whether it could in fact have been realised, had Alexander retained the divisions that he lost

---

*Having fought against the British in the Boer War, Smuts afterwards became South African Prime Minister and a member of the Imperial War Cabinet in the First World War. He was one of Churchill's oldest friends.

to *Dragoon,* remains a matter for speculation. (The German Army's ability to resist, in spite of Allied domination of the air, was generally underestimated right up to the last month of the Italian campaign, when—twenty-one months after the original landing in Sicily—Allied forces at last crossed the River Po.) What is certain is that the transatlantic dispute about the Italian campaign in the summer of 1944 marked the nadir of Churchill's relationship with Roosevelt.

The other disagreements between the two leaders during this period of the war covered a broad field. Politically speaking, Churchill's attitude towards the Italian Government had something in common with Roosevelt's towards de Gaulle. Whereas Roosevelt was in favour of supporting the programme of the six political parties and bringing them into the Italian Government as early as March 1944, on 10 June (almost a week after the fall of Rome, which was followed by the King's appointment of his son, the Crown Prince Umberto, as *Luogotenente*) Churchill was still telling Roosevelt that it was "a great disaster that Badoglio should be replaced by this group of aged and hungry politicians"—which is what then happened, Badoglio being succeeded as Prime Minister by "this wretched old" Bonomi.[38] Paradoxically, the Italian politician who became the principal target of Churchill's dislike was not the Communist Party leader, Palmiro Togliatti, who returned to Italy from Moscow[39] in March and on 1 April galvanised the Italian political scene by delivering a speech in Salerno announcing his party's readiness to enter a coalition led by Badoglio and to shelve the monarchist issue for the time being—the so-called *svolta di Salerno.* The man whom Churchill could not abide was an anti-fascist Liberal, Count Carlo Sforza[40]—so much so that in December 1944, when the Bonomi Government was being re-formed, the British Government announced a unilateral veto on Sforza either as Prime Minister or as Foreign Minister, thus provoking a public statement by the U.S. Government dissociating itself from the British veto. Much mud was flung across the Atlantic by the press of both countries until this altercation was patched up.[41]

On 6 June 1944 Operation *Overlord* was finally launched. De Gaulle was determined to prevent *"les Anglo-Saxons"* from producing a situation in France on Italian lines. His Committee of National Liberation proclaimed itself the Provisional Government of France, and he demanded its recognition as such. Churchill urged Roosevelt to invite de Gaulle to Washington at long last. Even at this late hour, Roosevelt declined "absolutely as head of the state to invite him to come over here"; de Gaulle had to ask if Roosevelt would see him.[42] This visit eventually took place at the beginning of July, eighteen months after it had originally been intended and one month after the invasion of Normandy. Grudgingly Roosevelt acceded to his own State Department's advice that *de facto* recognition should be given to de Gaulle (he could, by then, hardly have done less). Full recognition by both the British and the U.S. governments, in which the Soviet Government joined, was not granted until three months afterwards, however. The American decision to recognise them was taken in the wake of one of Roosevelt's sudden changes of mind, which "bewildered" Churchill, who like everybody else in London, was already convinced that this decision had become imperative.[43]

The two major commercial areas of Anglo-American difference which engaged Churchill's and Roosevelt's attention during 1944 were oil and civil aviation (the latter including the sensitive question of bases). Both were keenly contested issues and a foretaste of post-war rivalries between the two countries, but since neither question was then resolved,[44] they do no more than form part of the backdrop to this account of the ailing relationship between the two leaders in 1944. In September 1944, however, their relationship was, for the last time, briefly lit up—in Churchill's own words at the time—by a "blaze of friendship."[45] At the opening plenary session of the Second Quebec Conference on 13 September, Churchill observed that everything which they had touched had turned to gold: a reflection of the fact that on 25 July the Allied armies had broken their way out of the Normandy beachhead, entering Paris on 25 August and Brussels on 3 September. On the day on which this conference opened, American troops had just crossed the German frontier west of Aachen; the failure of the Anglo-American Airborne Army's attack in Holland was still a fortnight off; and under Soviet pressure, the first signs of German withdrawal from the Balkans were becoming apparent. The end of the war in Europe before Christmas did not look impossible.

Octagon

As in the previous year, Churchill travelled by sea to Halifax, whence a train journey of over twenty hours brought him to Quebec, on the morning of 11 September 1944. Roosevelt's train had just arrived. The two leaders drove together to the Citadel, where the conference meetings were held. The Second Quebec Conference, codenamed *Octagon,* was the last major bilateral meeting between Churchill and Roosevelt in the series of conferences that had begun at Placentia Bay three years earlier. Looking forward to it in August, Churchill described it as "the most necessary one" that he had "ever made since the very beginning," given the extent of Anglo-American differences.[46] In fact the differences were not only between London and Washington, but also between Churchill and his Chiefs of Staff. Brooke's relations with Churchill were now under severe strain. The discussions during the voyage across the Atlantic went so badly that, two days before their arrival at Halifax, Churchill remarked to the Chiefs of Staff that there was no single point on which he and they seemed to be in agreement (his own two main objectives, not shared by the Chiefs of Staff, were an advance on Vienna and the recapture of Singapore). And at the beginning of *Octagon* even Ismay handed his resignation to the Prime Minister, who refused it.[47] (There were extenuating factors. Churchill had not fully recovered from the relapse of pneumonia that he had suffered at the end of August; the weather in the Atlantic was oppressively hot and humid; and the first V-2 rockets* landed on London, while Churchill was at sea, on 8 September.) Yet, unexpectedly, at *Octagon* Churchill and Roosevelt achieved what, at the time, seemed a remarkable measure of agreement before going south to Hyde Park,

---

*The first guided missile in the history of warfare. Twenty-six of them fell in southern England in the week ending 18 September 1944, killing fifty-six civilians.

where Churchill and his wife (who—exceptionally—accompanied him at this conference) spent two days after the Quebec Conference. Churchill and Roosevelt both received honorary degrees from McGill University, whose academics travelled to Quebec for this purpose. At this ceremony, Churchill described his friendship with Roosevelt as having grown under the hammer-blows of war.

In just four days of discussion at Quebec—a strong contrast to the protracted debates of earlier Anglo-American conferences—issues which had hitherto occupied hours of heated argument were settled. Overruling King, his Chief of Naval Operations, Roosevelt accepted the British offer of a fleet in the Pacific. While General Slim was to press forward his offensive in Burma, the airborne and seaborne assault on Rangoon—Operation *Dracula*—would be carried out in 1945, if possible by March. Provided that the landing craft needed for *Dracula* were not thereby delayed in the Mediterranean, Alexander could mount an assault on Istria in the autumn; and no American troops would be withdrawn from Italy until the German Army there was defeated. Roosevelt also changed his mind on a matter on which he had long been adamant: the American zone of occupation in Germany, which he had not wanted to be dependent on France for its lines of communication. He now accepted the southern zone, provided that U.S. forces would also receive the ports of Bremen and Bremerhaven.

Potentially, however, the two most important agreements reached by Churchill and Roosevelt at Quebec were not military, but economic. Not only was Britain to receive, after the defeat of Germany, Lend-Lease aid during the continuing war against Japan, then estimated to last another eighteen months after the end of the war in Europe. (The detailed arrangements for this so-called Stage II aid—vital to the survival of the British economy—were agreed between the two governments in November 1944.)[48] In the absence of both their foreign secretaries,* Churchill and Roosevelt also endorsed a plan put forward

---

*Eden, who was horrified by the Morgenthau Plan, arrived at Quebec on 14 September. Hull, excluded from such conferences as usual, finally resigned in November 1944.

by Morgenthau, Secretary of the Treasury, over dinner on the opening day of the conference. Briefly known to history as the Morgenthau Plan, it provided for eliminating the "war-making industries in the Ruhr and in the Saar," and looked forward to "converting Germany into a country primarily agricultural and pastoral in its character." To his credit, Churchill's first instinctive reaction was adverse, but (influenced in part by Cherwell,[49] who urged the advantage to Britain of the elimination of German industrial competition) he went along with Roosevelt in this proposal, which was embodied in a memorandum jointly approved by the President and the Prime Minister—"OK, FDR, WSC"—on 15 September 1944. Economically preposterous in the longer term and—in the short term—a gift to Joseph Goebbels' propaganda machine, the Morgenthau Plan (which was leaked to the American press soon afterwards) was still-born.[50]

So too was much else agreed at Quebec. Lend-Lease was abruptly cut off by Truman a week after V-J Day. The British fleet did reach the Pacific, but neither *Dracula* nor the Istrian landing ever took place.[51] Roosevelt's reversal of his decision about the American occupation zone in southern Germany held, but his feud with de Gaulle, which had underlain his earlier reluctance in this matter, was pursued to the end. The dramatic outcome of the Hyde Park Aide-Mémoire on the atomic bomb, signed by Churchill and Roosevelt at the President's home on 19 September 1944,[52] would reverberate round the world after the atomic attacks on Hiroshima and Nagasaki in August 1945. At the time of its signature, Churchill reported to his colleagues in London that this agreement had been based on "indefinite collaboration in the post-war period subject to termination by joint agreement" or, as he put it to Attlee a year later, "a military understanding between us and the greatest and mightiest power in the world."[53] Although this cannot be proved either way from documentary evidence, Churchill's personal interpretation is unlikely to have been shared by Roosevelt at the time. In any event, atomic collaboration between the two countries was rapidly eroded after the war had come to an end.

Stalin and Churchill

Stalin left Teheran secure in the knowledge that Roosevelt would welcome the Soviet Union as the United States' principal ally against Japan, as soon as Germany had been defeated. Stalin's view of Chiang Kai-shek had long been realistic—a broken reed, Chiang was just the "best man under the circumstances."[54] And it only remained for Stalin to name the Soviet price for entry into the war against Japan, which he would do at Yalta. As for Central and Eastern Europe and the Balkans, what Roosevelt had said to Stalin at Teheran, especially about Poland and the Baltic States, left him in little doubt that—current electoral considerations apart—Roosevelt intended to keep a low profile on these issues, on which it was therefore with Churchill, not Roosevelt, that Stalin largely dealt in 1944. Churchill was his natural interlocutor for two main reasons. Temperamentally, the idea of leaving a difficult problem to sort itself out—often the Rooseveltian technique—was alien to Churchill, whose first instinct, when confronted with a problem, was to try to use this forceful powers of persuasion to solve it. In any case, so far as Poland was concerned—unlike Roosevelt—Churchill had to attempt to mediate between Stalin and the Polish Government, both because it was the Anglo-Polish Alliance that had obliged Britain to declare the war on Germany in September 1939 and because the seat of the Polish Government-in-exile was London. There was therefore no way in which the Polish problem could be ignored in London in 1944, especially after 10 January, when the Soviet Government publicly proposed the Curzon Line as the eastern frontier of post-war Poland.

Soviet responsibility for the crime of Katyn, horrible though it was, does not alter the fact that Stalin's reasons for insistence on the Curzon Line, with the exception of Lvov, were strong ones. Not only was it the British Foreign Secretary—as Stalin reminded Churchill and Roosevelt more than once—who had proposed this frontier for Poland as the most ethnically just, at the moment when the Polish state was being reconstituted (for the first time for over a hundred years) at the Paris Peace Conference a quarter of a century earlier. The inter-war

Polish regime of "The Colonels"[55] had seen the Second Polish Republic as the lineal descendant of the seventeenth-century Polish-Lithuanian Commonwealth stretching from the Baltic to the Black Sea, which Russia had only gradually replaced as the major power of Eastern Europe: a romantic concept of Polish nationalism which, though just possible to sustain so long as the Soviet Union was prostrate, had become Cloud-Cuckoo-Land in the 1940s. The one Pole who might perhaps have been able to do a deal with Stalin—Sikorski—was dead.

The attitudes both of the Government-in-exile and of the *AK* (the *Armja Krajowa,* the main Resistance movement in Poland) took little account of the fact that in 1944 it was unrealistic to hold out for Poland's inter-war frontiers, including as they had millions of Ukrainians and Belorussians and even the Lithuanian capital, Vilnius (Vilno), which the Poles had seized in 1920, and to which the Polish Government continued to lay claim well into 1944. Even Poles in London who realised that there would have to be a territorial accommodation between Poland and the Soviet Union to replace the outdated Treaty of Riga were inhibited by the fact that most of the Polish troops fighting the Germans under British command, and with great distinction, came from eastern Poland.

Into this confused conflict of ancient national rivalries[56] Churchill plunged within forty-eight hours of his return to London after his convalescence in Morocco. At this first meeting with the Poles in 1944 he got nowhere, Mikołajczyk even insisting on the retention—or rather, recovery—of Vilnius. On 28 January Churchill telegraphed a long report on his meeting to Stalin, saying that he had advised the Polish Government to accept the Curzon Line as a basis for discussion, with territorial compensation in the west, but also warning him of the dangers to the unity of the Grand Alliance that would be involved in "the creation in Warsaw of another Polish Government different from the one we have recognised up to the present."[57]

Through the next six months this argument went up and down. Thus on 5 February Churchill was able to tell Roosevelt of an "encouraging" talk which the British Ambassador had had with Stalin about Churchill's telegram sent a week before. Stalin had been reassuring on every point but one: three members of the London Polish Government must go. Churchill added his own view that Stalin would not deal with the government while these men remained in it—a point which Stalin confirmed in a telegram to Churchill on the following day.[58] After another fortnight the Polish Government, under Churchill's pressure and in a text agreed with the British Government, got as far as recognising that the Riga eastern frontier "no longer corresponds with realities," but subjected this recognition to a proviso: that a formal settlement should await the conference to be held "at the time of an armistice or peace." This proposal was turned down flat by Stalin on 28 February. Instead, he insisted on immediate recognition of the Curzon Line and reconstruction of the Polish Government without further delay. And on 23 March he followed up his rejection with an outraged telegram, in which he reminded Churchill of what had been said at Teheran and put him on notice that, if the Prime Minister himself were publicly to adopt the Polish formula—adding to it that the British Government could "recognise no forcible transferences of territory"— Stalin would consider this "an unjust act, unfriendly towards the Soviet Union."[59]

Thus Churchill's first attempt to reconcile Soviet-Polish differences failed. In June, the Red Army crossed the River Bug; in July, it recaptured Vilnius; and on 22 June, a Polish Committee of National Liberation was set up at Lublin. From then on Stalin dealt with the Lublin Committee, leaving Churchill to deal as best he could with the Polish Government in London. Nevertheless, as the Red Army approached Warsaw in July, Churchill persuaded Mikołajczyk to fly to Moscow. He also asked Roosevelt to send Mikołajczyk a telegram of encouragement. Roosevelt's response, sent to Mikołajczyk on 28 July, must be one of the most laconic messages that ever left the White House; it consisted of just one unhelpful sentence.[60] But Stalin sent Churchill a telegram on the following day, which Churchill described to Roosevelt as "the best ever received from U.J."[61] In any case, whatever hope there may have been of an agreed settlement at this juncture was suddenly wrecked by one of the most traumatic events of the Second World War.

The Warsaw Rising

On the day on which the Red Army reached the eastern outskirts of Warsaw, on the opposite bank of the River Vistula the *AK* rose against the Germans in Operation *Burza* ("Storm"). The Red Army's advance was halted at the Vistula; the units (Polish, operating with the Red Army) that succeeded in crossing the river were repulsed by the Germans. After fighting the German Army for two months, single-handed and with only small arms, the *AK* capitulated. Nearly 200,000 Poles (mostly civilians) were killed; the survivors were removed from the city, which the Germans systematically destroyed; and 150,000 were deported for forced labour. The telegrams sent to Stalin by Churchill in August and September 1944, urging him either to help Warsaw or to allow others to help it, were coolly received by Roosevelt and callously rejected by Stalin, who refused permission for aircraft of RAF Bomber Command to use Soviet airfields to drop supplies for the *AK*. [62] When the Red Army finally entered Warsaw in 1945, the city was in ruins, deserted by a population that had numbered almost a million people.

The judgment of the author of the relevant volume of the official British military history of the Second World War—published in 1956—was that from the Warsaw Rising onwards, "the Polish question . . . became the conscience of the West, and relations between Britain and Russia suffered a shock from which they never fully recovered."[63] This assessment, although understandable enough at the time when it was written, oversimplifies the events of 1944, which it telescopes with events that came later. In 1944, so far as the relationship between the Big Three was concerned, Churchill overcame his initial revulsion during the Rising quickly enough to be able to spend ten days with Stalin in October in Moscow, where he compelled Mikołajczyk, "under dire threats" (in Churchill's own words),[64] to confer with Stalin as well. By comparison with Churchill, Roosevelt remained unmoved throughout the Warsaw crisis of August–September, and in November he offered Mikołajczyk the cold comfort in the letter quoted earlier in this chapter. As for Stalin, his behaviour was as much

a political *bêtise* as it was a crime. Subsequent research suggests that the
Red Army's need for a pause of months—not just weeks—on the
Vistula, after an advance of four hundred miles, was genuine, as indeed
Stalin assured Churchill in Moscow (an assurance accepted absolutely
by Churchill at the time).[65] Be that as it may, what is certain is that the
only evidence that the *AK* commanders had at the end of July that the
Red Army's advance into Warsaw was imminent was the limited
observation of their own eyes—the long procession of German troops
withdrawing through the streets of the capital. The *AK* leaders in
Warsaw made no attempt to liaise with the Red Army, accepting
uncritically an exhortation to rise against the Germans broadcast in
Polish by their compatriots from a Soviet radio station. Much more
significant, however, is the fact that although the military aim of the
rising was directed against the Germans, the list of *Burza*'s objectives
telegraphed to London on 22 July (over a week before the Rising) by
the *AK* commander, General Tadeusz Bór Komorowsky, specifically
stated that, politically, the Rising was directed against the Soviet
Union.[66]

Once the Warsaw Rising had begun, it served no purpose whatsoever for Stalin to describe the *AK* to Churchill and Roosevelt as "a
bunch of criminals"—quite the contrary.[67] A temperate statement of
the military reasons[68] why the Red Army's summer offensive had
reached its limit, and why nothing could have saved Warsaw in August
1944, would have served Soviet interests far better. Instead, Stalin then
overplayed his hand. The simplest explanation of his conduct in this
crisis may be the best. The records of both sides left no doubt what had
been said at Teheran. In Stalin's eyes, under the influence of the "London" Poles, Churchill had increasingly broken ranks with Roosevelt
on this issue during the preceding six months; it was the Red Army
that had to suffer heavy casualties on Polish soil; and at no point after
the invasion of France did Stalin interfere with the conduct of Anglo-
American military operations in Europe. In August 1944 he lost his
temper—the first instance of this in his exchanges with the other two
leaders of the Grand Alliance.

The outcome of the Warsaw tragedy had two major consequences.

The Poles never forgot what had happened. In the longer term, so profound was the trauma suffered by the Polish people that right through the 1950s the inhabitants of Warsaw (by then largely rebuilt) were still accustomed to speak of past events not as happening before or after the war, but "before the Rising" or "since the Rising." In the short term, the Polish Government-in-exile no longer commanded the allegiance of any armed forces capable of exercising a direct influence on developments inside Poland—unlike the Lublin Committee, which had the support of a Polish Army, equipped by the Soviet Union, fighting side by side with the Red Army on Polish soil. From then on the members of the Polish Government in London found themselves in an increasingly weak position. Churchill having shot his bolt on their behalf in 1944, only Roosevelt's personal intervention might conceivably have helped their cause. It came, in the form of a strongly worded message to Stalin, far too late—on 30 December.[69] By that time it was three days since the final decision had been taken in Moscow to recognise the Lublin Polish National Committee as the Provisional Government of Poland: a decision publicly announced on 1 January 1945.

The Second Moscow Conference

Hardly had Churchill returned from his meetings with Roosevelt than he sent the President a "most especially secret" telegram, letting him know of his intention to visit Stalin, with "two great objects . . . first, to clinch his coming in against Japan and, secondly, to try to effect a friendly settlement with Poland." He added that there were "other points about Greece and Yugoslavia" that would also be discussed. Harriman's help would be welcome; and perhaps Roosevelt "could send Stettinius or Marshall."*[70] Roosevelt's response to Churchill was chilly, as Hopkins later made abundantly clear to the Soviet Ambassador in Washington. To send Stettinius or Marshall was neither practicable nor advantageous; Harriman could take part, but only as an

---

*Edward Stettinius, Jr., was appointed Secretary of State after Hull's resignation.

observer (a status which Roosevelt took the trouble to confirm to Stalin direct); Stalin's "intention to help us in the Orient" was a sensitive matter; and Roosevelt particularly asked Churchill not to raise the question of UN voting procedure, on which deadlock had been reached at the Dumbarton Oaks Conference.[71] There was, moreover, a background to Churchill's "other points" on his proposed Moscow agenda. At the end of June, against Hull's advice, Roosevelt had reluctantly agreed to Churchill's initiative (already put by the Foreign Office to the Soviet Ambassador in London at the end of May) that, for a trial period of three months and without establishing any "spheres of influence" (a bogey word in Washington), Britain should "take the lead" in Greek affairs and the Soviet Union in Romanian affairs. These three months were just up.[72]

A large part of the Moscow talks was, as intended, devoted to a final attempt to settle the Polish problem by agreement with the "London" Polish Government, Churchill himself having no less than seven meetings with Mikołajczyk (who flew to Moscow at Churchill's insistence). Once again the stumbling block was the immediate recognition of the Curzon Line as Poland's eastern frontier, and in particular, the future of Lvov. This time it was Churchill who lost his temper—with the Poles. In a report sent from Moscow to the King, he described "our lot from London" as "a decent but feeble lot of fools" and the Lublin Poles as "the greatest villains imaginable."[73] No agreement could be reached. Although the Polish Government in London continued to be recognised by both the British and the U.S. governments for another nine months, in effect it signed its own death warrant in Moscow in October 1944. Because Mikołajczyk (who resigned as Prime Minister a month later) and the colleagues who accompanied him to Moscow remained rooted in a position which none of the Big Three could accept, in the end the Polish question inevitably found itself near the top of the agenda of the next conference between Churchill, Roosevelt and Stalin: at Yalta, where of the three countries that went to war against Germany in 1939 only one—Britain—was represented.

In spite of the amount of time taken up at the Moscow Conference by the Polish question, what history has above all recalled from

Churchill's talks with Stalin on this occasion is what Churchill himself then called "the naughty document," which he handed to Stalin at their first meeting, held in the Kremlin late on the evening of 9 October. According to his memoirs, he suggested to Stalin that they should burn it, because it "might be thought rather cynical if it seemed we had disposed of these issues, so fateful to millions of people, in such an off-hand manner." Again according to Churchill's own account, Stalin's reply was: "No, you keep it." The relevant passage in the notes of this celebrated exchange kept by Churchill's interpreter has been preserved; the Cabinet Office record was bowdlerised by the officials concerned.[74]

What Churchill's "naughty document," which he seems to have written on the spur of the moment, proposed was a division of responsibility in the Balkans (broadly defined) between Britain and the Soviet Union, expressed in percentage terms: a range that extended from a Soviet 90 percent in Romania and a British 90 percent in Greece to 50–50 for both countries in Yugoslavia* and Hungary. Within forty-eight hours Churchill was himself doubtful enough about the wisdom of this document to write a letter of explanation to Stalin, which—on Harriman's recommendation—was never sent. In his memoirs, Harriman wondered "just what Churchill thought he was accomplishing by these percentages," which, he added, was "a question . . . never again raised" at Yalta.[75] Harriman's observation is fair comment in so far as—we now know—Stalin did not care for Resistance leaders, of whatever political complexion; the seeds of his great quarrel with Tito had already been sown; the leaders of the Greek Communist Party would soon learn that they were on their own; and Stalin's view of Togliatti, unlike Churchill's, was based on many years of personal experience ("a wise man, not an extremist", who "could tell Marshal

---

*For the preceding twelve months it was the British Government (the decision to back Josip Tito once taken) that played the major role in Yugoslav affairs. Tito had met Churchill near Naples in August and Stalin in Moscow a month later. The Red Army entered Belgrade on 15 October 1944.

Stalin to mind his own business"). Nevertheless, Churchill's "naughty" percentages were taken seriously enough in the Kremlin in October 1944 for Molotov to engage Eden in a haggle about the exact proportions of the division of responsibility proposed. Greece, Romania and Yugoslavia caused no dissent, but after discussion, the Bulgarian and Hungarian percentages ended at 80–20 in the Soviet favour.[76]

The real failure of this, the last, bilateral meeting between the two European members of the Big Three, was that they spent so little time during ten whole days—and that unprofitably—on the one question upon which the future of Europe above all depended: the future of Germany. On this, Churchill once again advanced his twin concept of a Germany divided into three and a confederation of Poland, Czechoslovakia and Hungary. Both Stalin and Molotov were opposed, Molotov making the pertinent criticism: "After the last war many new small states had been formed. Many of them had failed. It would be dangerous to go to the other extreme after this war and to force states to form groups."[77] So far as the future of Germany was concerned, with Roosevelt at Quebec Churchill had agreed on a solution which was nonsense; with Stalin in Moscow a month later he agreed on nothing at all.

Although an attack of fever kept Churchill in bed for one day during his stay in Moscow, and meetings at the Kremlin lasted almost until dawn, his report to the King leaves no doubt that in Moscow he enjoyed himself, in contrast to Teheran, where he had suffered from at least one wave of depression.[78] His description, in the telegram that on 10 October he and Stalin sent jointly to Roosevelt, of an "extraordinary atmosphere of goodwill"[79] was not altogether hyperbole. Not only did Stalin accompany Churchill to the Bolshoi Theatre; he came to lunch at the British Embassy (Stalin rarely visited foreign missions), and he saw Churchill off at the airport as well. Nevertheless, there was another, more significant, difference between this meeting of the two leaders and their first, just over two years earlier. This time it was Churchill who was in the position of *demandeur,* although he skilfully disguised this, ending his farewell letter to Stalin on 19 October:

My hopes for the future alliance of our peoples never stood so high. I hope you may long be spared to repair the ravages of war and lead All The Russians out of the years of storm into glorious sunshine.

Your friend and war-time comrade,
Winston S. Churchill[80]

The Athenian Postcript

Whereas Churchill had spent Christmas 1943 stranded by his pneumonia in the ruins of Carthage, he spent Christmas Day 1944 in Athens, in the midst of a Greek civil war. While he was in Moscow the German Army evacuated Athens; by the middle of October the British advance guard—the first regular British formations to set foot on Greek soil for over three years—reached Athens; and a Coalition Government representing the parties of both Right and Left, still without the controversial King George II, who remained in London, was established. On 29 November, however, the Greek Cabinet split. Its left-wing members left the government. Five days later a left-wing insurrection began in Athens. In the five weeks' fighting that followed, ELAS, the army of the Left, at one time held the whole of Greece but for the few square miles of Athens which remained in the hands of the small British force. The British Army (under whose operational command the Greek Prime Minister had placed all troops in Greece, by an agreement[81] reached immediately before the country was liberated) was powerfully reinforced from Italy and gradually gained the upper hand. The tide of battle was already flowing in their favour on Christmas Eve, when Churchill took the sudden decision to visit Athens himself.

So far as the civil war was concerned, by far the most important consequence of this visit was Churchill's abandonment of his previously held view that the Archbishop of Athens, Damaskinos—a massive man, of great height—was seeking the role of a "Dictator of the Left." Himself now persuaded of the contrary, on his return to London Churchill succeeded in persuading the King of Greece, after an all-night meeting, to agree to Damaskinos' appointment as Regent, and to announce that he himself would not return to Greece until he was "summoned by a free and fair expression of the national will." The Regent took the oath on the last day of 1944. A truce in Greece was signed on 11 January 1945, followed by an agreement in the following month between the government and the left-wing parties, which—for the time being—brought the civil war to a close, but not before Britain had shared with the Soviet Union the unhappy distinction of fighting against those who had themselves fought the Germans.[82]

The 1944 Greek crisis ended not a moment too soon for Churchill's relationship with Roosevelt. True, four months earlier Roosevelt had authorised "the use by General Wilson of American transport planes" for "a sufficient British force to preserve order in Greece when the German Forces evacuated that country." British military involvement in the subsequent civil war, however, not only elicited a public rebuke from the State Department; it also provoked a storm of public protest in Britain. The wording of Roosevelt's telegram to Churchill about Greece on 13 December was mild, but the message was unmistakable: the U.S. Government could not "take a stand with you in the present course of events in Greece."[83] What might have happened had the 1944 Greek crisis not been overcome in the last week of December is speculative (as indeed is the wider question whether it could have been avoided in the first place). Certainly Churchill did not forget what he regarded as Stalin's restraint in the matter. And by January 1945 the attention of all three leaders was focused on their forthcoming meeting in the Crimea.

16

THE HIDDEN

DIMENSION

"Pa, this requires action."

—*Franklin Roosevelt to General Edwin ("Pa") Watson,*
1939

"The balance has been destroyed. Provide the
bomb."

—*Joseph Stalin to Igor Kurchatov, 1945*

"What was gunpowder? Trivial. What was
electricity? Meaningless. This atomic bomb is
the Second Coming in Wrath."

—*Winston Churchill to Henry Stimson, 1945**

*A*mong the many remarkable features of the relationship established between Churchill and Roosevelt during the war,
none was more extraordinary or more far-reaching in its consequences
than the transatlantic interchange in the top secret sphere. This interchange applied above all to science and to signals intelligence (Sigint),†
although in the atomic field it became beset with problems, at first

---

*None of these remarks may have been made exactly as others later recorded them, but all three are
plausible.[1]

†A third aspect of the hidden dimension was that of the organisations set up successively by the
British Government (Special Operations Executive) and the U.S. Government (Office of Stategic
Services), in 1940 and 1942 respectively, in order to conduct covert operations and irregular warfare,
above all in support of Resistance movements in enemy-occupied countries. The very nature of the
tasks of these two organisations, however, precluded the degree of Anglo-American co-operation
that was attained in the other two fields.[2]

unforeseen, which were eventually overcome only with great difficulty. This top secret co-operation began even before the United States entered the war. As early as the *ABC* Staff Conversations, the "full and prompt exchange of pertinent information concerning war operations" between London and Washington was agreed upon; and the military missions established in the two capitals included intelligence staffs. With one major exception, however—the exchange of Japanese Sigint—the practical results of this agreement were slight during most of 1941. Information derived from *Ultra* (the British codeword for German high-grade cryptographic material) began to cross the Atlantic in the spring of that year; but it was not until the *Arcadia* Conference at the turn of the year that it was agreed between Churchill and Roosevelt that the "free exchange of intelligence" should "apply to all theatres" and that a Combined Intelligence Committee should be formed to prepare assessments for the Combined Chiefs of Staff, which the two leaders had established in Washington in January 1942. The translation of this agreement into practice still took over a year, although the first American cryptanalysts joined Bletchley Park in June 1942. From May 1943 onwards, however, while Bletchley concentrated on German and (for a few more months Italian) cyphers and the U.S. War Department concentrated on Japanese, there was a complete exchange of views and information at all levels of Anglo-American signals intelligence; and the actual product of Sigint (colloquially known in the British Army as BBR—"Burn before reading") was distributed to all commands in the European theatre of operations for the last two years of the war.[3]

Nothing resembling the intimacy of the Anglo-American exchange of intelligence existed in the two governments' relationship with the Soviet Government. Nevertheless, for the first year of the Russian campaign, a good deal of operational intelligence was sent via the British Military Mission in Moscow. Churchill's warning of the German invasion, sent to Stalin in April 1941, was based on *Ultra;* and in 1943 a major piece of *Ultra-* derived intelligence was communicated to Moscow before the Battle of Kursk. Little, if anything, passed in the opposite direction, although Soviet recollection of the disastrous experience of the Battle of Tannenberg in the First World War must have ensured that the Red Army gave a high priority both to signals intelligence and to signals security in the Second.

The Manhattan Project

Just over a month before the Crimean Conference of the Big Three convened at Yalta, Marshall received written confirmation from Major-General Leslie Groves, the director of the Manhattan Project, that he was "reasonably certain" that the first atomic bomb "should be ready . . . about 1 August 1945"[4]—an accurate forecast of the culmination of nearly four years of intense endeavour. Chapter 6 has described its point of departure—the reading of Einstein's letter to Roosevelt at the White House in October 1939—although at that time the only practical effect of this meeting was the appointment of a small committee, chaired by Lyman Briggs, an elderly scientific administrator. On 12 June 1940, however, a man whom Roosevelt had never met before, Vannevar Bush, president of the Carnegie Institution in Washington, D.C., had a brief meeting with the President, arranged through Hopkins' good offices. Three days later Bush was appointed chairman of a new body, the National Defense Research Committee, to which Roosevelt made the Briggs Committee subordinate.[5] Bush's closest colleague in the new organisation and eventual partner in the Manhattan Project was James Conant, president of Harvard. These two outstanding men were the prime movers, under Roosevelt, of the great leap forward towards the nuclear age that began almost exactly two years after Einstein's letter, again at a meeting in the White House, from which the launching of the Manhattan Project followed in 1942.

The scientific work done in the atomic field in Britain between 1939 and 1941 was critically important for Roosevelt's vital decision of 9 October 1941. (And when the Anglo-American scientific interchange in the atomic field broke down altogether soon after the war, it also paved the way for the eventual British decision to manufacture first an atomic bomb and later a hydrogen bomb.) Although there were other contributors to the brilliant success of the research effort in Britain during the first two years of the war, there is no question where it began: a paper written early in 1940 by two scientists, Otto Frisch and Rudolf Peierls, both of whom had taken refuge in Britain. This was the first memorandum written in any country—in Margaret Gowing's words, which have lost none of their force since she first wrote them a quarter of a century ago—"to foretell with scientific conviction the practical possibility of making a bomb and the horrors it would bring."

The Frisch-Peierls paper remained a strictly British secret, unknown in the United States, for over a year. During these, the darkest months of the war, their paper was studied by a committee of distinguished British scientists, working at speed and in secret, who took for themselves the codename MAUD—after a nurse in Kent who had worked for Niels Bohr's family, whose name has therefore gone down to history. The Maud Report was completed in July 1941 and submitted to Churchill in the following month.[6] This lapidary document—the first wartime milestone on the road towards the atomic explosion at Alamogordo, New Mexico, just four years later—reached the conclusions (described with British meiosis as "likely to suggest themselves to any capable physicist") that a uranium bomb was "practicable and likely to lead to decisive results in the war," and that the material for the first such bomb could be ready by the end of 1943. The report recommended that the highest priority should be given to work "necessary to obtain the bomb in the shortest possible time," and that "the present collaboration with America should be continued and extended especially in the region of experimental work."

The first of the many paradoxes in the chequered history of the atomic relationship between Britain and the United States now arose, at the very outset, in the autumn of 1941.[7] What happened on each side of the Atlantic during the next twelve months was in reality completely different. Yet, on the face of it, the initial reaction both of Churchill and of Roosevelt to the Maud Report was the same: to use an expression that occurs more than once in their correspondence on other matters during the war—full steam ahead. In his minute requesting the advice of the Chiefs of Staff, Churchill, although "personally . . . quite content with existing explosives," agreed with Cherwell's advice that the atomic project "must go forward."[8] At a meeting with Churchill on 3 September 1941, the Chiefs replied to the Prime Minister and Minister of Defence that the project should indeed be developed without sparing any "time, labour, materials or money"; and this should, in their view, be done "in Britain and not abroad."

In Washington, the impact of the Maud Report on the tight circle of American scientists advising Roosevelt was instantaneous. Even on the basis of the draft version of the report, which reached Vannevar Bush from his representative in London in July, he at once recognised (in his annual report on the work of his own committee) that "new knowledge . . . makes it probable that the production of a super-explosive may not be as remote a matter as previously appeared. This subject is now being intensively studied in England." By the time the chairman of the Maud Committee, Professor George Thomson, himself brought the report in its final form to Washington in October 1941, both Bush and Conant were convinced. At a meeting held at the White House on 9 October, attended only by Bush and Henry Wallace,[9] Roosevelt took the crucial decision. Of this there is no record. There is, however, no doubt that from then on—subject only to the President's ultimate yea or nay—the atomic project went ahead in earnest, under the guiding hands of six Americans: the President, Wallace, Bush, Conant, Stimson and Marshall. In practice, Roosevelt usually dealt on atomic matters direct with Bush, and it was "Bush, not Roosevelt, who was worried about loneliness.[10] Less than a month later Bush reported to Roosevelt the conclusion reached by a committee of American physicists that "if all possible effort" were spent on the project, fission bombs might be "available in significant quantity within three or four years." One week after Pearl Harbor, the U.S. War Department launched what rapidly became the Manhattan Project. As Roosevelt wrote to Bush on 11 March 1942, "time . . . is very much of the essence."

The other consequence of the meeting at the White House on 9 October 1941 was a letter of the 11th, drafted by Bush for Roosevelt (who crossed out "Mr. Churchill" and substituted "Winston"), the first sentence of which read:

It appears desirable that we should correspond or converse concerning the subject which is under study by your MAUD committee, and by Dr. Bush's organisation in this country, in order that any extended efforts may be coordinated or even jointly conducted.[11]

Churchill's reply, written in December 1941, assured Roosevelt of British readiness to collaborate with the U.S. administration in this matter.[12] But the two leaders did not discuss the atomic issue either at the Atlantic Conference or at the *Arcadia* Conference, nor did they do so at all until they were alone together at Hyde Park in June 1942. It will be recalled that it was at Hyde Park that Churchill and Roosevelt, away from their advisers, then agreed to invade North Africa: a decision that took their Chiefs of Staff by surprise. Whereas we know what followed that decision—the planning of Operation *Torch*—there is no record of their atomic discussion at Hyde Park. By the time they talked to each other there, although the two men do not seem to have acknowledged the fact, atomic matters had changed radically on each side of the Atlantic.

The fact that Churchill, the original architect of the Anglo-American relationship, should not have seized upon the offer of atomic partnership made to him in Roosevelt's letter of 11 October 1941—at any rate after Pearl Harbor had made the United States Britain's ally in the Second World War—is extraordinary. In 1941–42 there seem to have been two main reasons. The months during which, had Churchill so decided, this atomic partnership might have taken shape were also those in which British arms suffered one humiliating reverse after another. Indeed, the last in this grim series of defeats hit Churchill while he was in Washington in June 1942. He had much else on his mind, therefore, during this period, and what he needed from his advisers on the atomic issue was a firmly unanimous view. On the contrary, once the Maud Report reached the Cabinet's Scientific Advisory Committee and John Anderson,[13] whom Churchill had appointed the responsible minister, a split developed. On the one hand, there were those, including Cherwell, Professor James Chadwick[14] and the Chiefs of Staff, who wanted the atomic project to be undertaken in Britain. (As Cherwell put it, in a much quoted piece of advice tendered to Churchill, "However much I may trust my neighbour, and depend on him, I am very much averse to putting myself completely at his mercy and would therefore not press the Americans to undertake this work"). On the other hand, Anderson, backed by some scientists, believed that to build a plant of the size required in wartime Britain was impracticable; and moreover there was the risk that the plant might be bombed. Therefore, unlike the characteristically single-minded American decision in late 1941, to make "all possible effort" without more ado, the British decision was more tentative: to pursue atomic research and development as quickly as possible in Britain and, provided that the research and development fulfilled the Maud expectations, to have a plant built, not in Britain, but either in Canada or in the United States. On this British atomic programme only a sum of less than half a million pounds annually was being spent by early 1943.

Thus, when Churchill and Roosevelt met in mid-1942, whereas the Americans were already working against the clock in this field and regardless of what it might cost, the British were not. It was against this background that at Hyde Park Churchill and Roosevelt reached a purely oral understanding, which Churchill at least interpreted as agreement between them on a joint atomic undertaking; "everything," in his words, "was on the basis of fully sharing the results as equal partners." Whatever the two leaders may have thought that they had agreed in June, when the British concrete proposal—for a British pilot plant, to be built with American resources in the United States—was at last put forward in August 1942, one year after the Maud Report, it arrived in Washington at a moment when, in American eyes, it seemed an untimely diversion from the main task, which was the Manhattan Project, now surging forward with a massive budget. From the British standpoint, the negotiations[15] that ensued in Washington at the turn of 1942–43 proved a miserable sequel to what had been, in 1941, a head start; and they ended in a virtual interruption of atomic communication between Britain and the United States. As in all failures of communication, there was much fog on both sides. But the essence of the transatlantic difference during this eight-month deadlock was that, whereas the Americans perceived the British as seeking to cash in cheaply on an immense American enterprise, the British perceived the Americans as seeking to establish a military and industrial monopoly in the atomic field. This deadlock was not broken until the First Quebec Conference in 1943, almost two years after the Maud Report had made its great impact on both sides of the Atlantic.

Once he fully realised what had happened, Churchill made repeated attempts to break the deadlock. While not excluding what he described to Hopkins, in a message clearly intended for the President's eyes, as the "sombre decision" that the two countries should, in this one field, work separately after all—studies were at last put in hand for building a diffusion plant and a heavy-water plant and pile in Britain[16]—Churchill returned to the charge again and again, first at Casablanca in January, then in Washington in May and, perhaps most conclusively, on 22 July 1943 in London, where he, Anderson and Cherwell held a meeting with Bush, Stimson and Stimson's assistant, Harvey Bundy. Here much of the misunderstanding surrounding the atomic issue on both sides was cleared away and, for the first time, it was agreed that a paper should be prepared for signature by Churchill and Roosevelt. In fact, although none of the participants at this meeting could have been aware of it, two days earlier Hopkins had addressed this memorandum to Roosevelt: "I think you made a firm commitment to Churchill in regard to this when he was here and there is nothing to do but go through with it."

Churchill drafted the paper proposed at the London meeting; Anderson and Bush worked on his draft together in Washington; and it was signed in Quebec on 19 August 1943. So far as the practical consequences of this agreement are concerned, its signature restored "full and effective collaboration" between the two governments and their scientists in the atomic field, in which Britain was from now on represented in Washington by Chadwick, the discoverer of the neutron. Remarkably, he succeeded in developing a good relationship with Groves, the hardheaded general who directed the Manhattan Project. British scientists and engineers crossed the Atlantic to join the Manhattan Project. And it was the British who (after the Danish Resistance had smuggled Niels Bohr out of Copenhagen to Sweden in 1943) flew the greatest nuclear physicist in the world first to Britain and later to the United States. Even without taking account of the Maud Report, the British atomic contribution was significant, although estimates of the number of months that this contribution saved in the completion of the Manhattan Project vary greatly.[17]

On Roosevelt's side—apart from the removal of a major bone of transatlantic contention for the remainder of the war—the essence of the Quebec Agreement lay in the words: "to bring the Tube Alloys project to fruition at the earliest possible moment."* In a race against time, this was his overriding purpose. But the agreement also laid to rest both American suspicions that the British aim was not so much military atomic achievement as post-war commercial advantage in the field of atomic energy, and British suspicions that the Americans were seeking to evade the Churchill-Roosevelt understanding, which (in Roosevelt's own words to Bush) "encompasses the complete exchange of all information." For his part, Churchill said exactly what he thought of this agreement nine months later, in a minute to Cherwell:

> I am absolutely sure we cannot get any better terms by ourselves than are set forth in my secret Agreement with the President. It may be that in after years this may be judged to have been too confiding on our part. Only those who know the circumstances and moods prevailing beneath the Presidential level will be able to understand why I have made this Agreement. There is nothing more to do now but to carry on with it, and give the utmost possible aid. Our associations with the United States must be permanent, and I have no fear that they will maltreat us or cheat us.[18]

For those who had to cope, after the war, with the practical interpretation of the Quebec Agreement, together with Churchill and

---

*Tube Alloys was the British codename for the atomic bomb. It was also used in the United States, where another codename was S1.

Roosevelt's two subsequent (1944) atomic agreements—the Declaration of Trust and the Hyde Park Aide-Mémoire—it was a different matter.[19] It was not until May 1947 that the U.S. Secretary of State[20] felt able to give the Joint Congressional Committee on Atomic Energy, orally and in secret, a summary of the Quebec and the Hyde Park agreements.[21] And the senior British official concerned with post-war atomic negotiations between Britain and the United States has—with justice—described the wartime atomic agreements as "among the most bizarre diplomatic documents ever concluded."[22] Although these agreements (the text of the first and the third are printed in Appendix III and Appendix IV, respectively) were bilateral in form, they were trilateral (Anglo-American-Canadian)[23] in practice. Their continuing validity after the end of the war was, on a strict legal interpretation, open to question.[24] It did not, moreover, require much knowledge of the American Constitution to foresee that Article 2 of the Quebec Agreement, which in effect gave the British Government a right of veto over American use of the atomic bomb, would run into congressional opposition. In spite of this right of veto, such "mature consideration" as took place (in accordance with the terms of the Hyde Park Agreement) before the use of the bomb against Japan was in 1945 almost entirely confined to Washington; and the worldwide monopoly of supplies of uranium, which it was the purpose of the Combined Development Trust to secure for Anglo-American atomic purposes, proved after the war to be an illusion. If this were not enough, the single American copy of the Hyde Park Aide-Mémoire was lost and only discovered years later in the files of Roosevelt's naval aide; Churchill therefore had to send Truman a photocopy at Potsdam.[25] Finally, although knowledge of the Manhattan Project and of all questions relating to it was kept to a closely restricted circle in both countries—so much so that neither Truman nor Attlee had been initiated into the secret before succeeding Roosevelt and Churchill in 1945—and in spite of the two leaders' reaffirmation of the paramount need for secrecy in the Quebec Agreement and (still more) the Hyde Park Aide-Mémoire, we now know that by 1945 Soviet espionage was presenting Stalin with a picture of both the scientific and the political aspects of the Anglo-American atomic dimension.[26]

The Soviet Union

In all three countries of the Grand Alliance the initial thrust of atomic research and development was fuelled by the compelling fear that had inspired Einstein's letter in 1939: that German science and German industry might win the atomic race (and indeed, had the German war not ended when it did, the first atomic bomb might have been dropped not on Japan but on Germany). But, as it turned out, this fear of German skill and determination was unfounded—among other reasons, because the atomic bomb never captured the personal interest of Hitler, who, moreover, despised what he regarded as Jewish science. In the United States, therefore, by the end of 1944 the primary motive had become no longer to outstrip Germany, whose atomic scientists were by then known to be far from success and where in any case Allied victory was in sight, but to save lives—mainly American—in the war against Japan.

The Soviet Union shared the same impulse of the German threat, to begin with.[27] In the second half of 1942, however, when G. N. Flerov wrote his celebrated personal letter to Stalin appealing for the immediate establishment of a nuclear laboratory for the purpose of "building the uranium bomb," Stalin was also feeling the spur of Anglo-American competition in the atomic field.[28] The Soviet Union did not lack nuclear physicists—Igor Kurchatov, the Soviet equivalent of J. Robert Oppenheimer, and his young pupil, Flerov, are only two examples—but the pre-war team had been dispersed in the early part of the war; and—as in Britain—military defeats in the field were a powerful distraction. Thus it came about that the Soviet Union was a late starter. Only at the end of 1942 was the laboratory for which Flerov had pleaded established, and Kurchatov appointed its director. Kurchatov combined outstanding scientific competence with the ability to get on with Soviet politicians. Stalin does not seem to have held it against him that by the time the first atomic explosion took place at Alamogordo, Kurchatov had not progressed much beyond designing an industrial reactor for producing plutonium. It was not until after his return from Berlin in August 1945 that Stalin sent for him and said: "Request all that you need. Nothing will be refused."[29] It was not; four more years were enough for Kurchatov, with Stalin's backing.

In 1944, as the fear of a German atomic threat receded and as the success of the Manhattan Project became increasingly probable, so some of the best minds among those initiated in the Project turned to the question of the choice—as Stimson defined it in the last meeting that he ever had with Roosevelt—between "the secret close-in attempted control of the project" [i.e., the atomic bomb] by the United States and Britain and "international control based upon freedom both of science and of access."[30] We do not know how, if at all, Roosevelt reacted on this occasion; he died four weeks later. On the other side of the Atlantic, Cherwell had, a year earlier, told Churchill that "plans and preparations for the post-war world or even the peace conference are utterly illusory so long as this crucial factor is left out of account"; and in a manuscript letter written to Churchill on 15 June 1944, Smuts wrote: "If ever there was a matter for international control, this is one."[31] Churchill disagreed. For him the tablets of stone were the three categorical assurances that he and Roosevelt had already given each other at Quebec in 1943: never to use the atomic bomb against each other, not to use it against third parties without each other's consent and not to communicate any information about Tube Alloys to third parties except by mutual consent.

Roosevelt's opinion, on the other hand, fluctuated, as we now know from the story of Niels Bohr's intervention. On 10 July 1944 Felix Frankfurter[32] wrote Roosevelt a manuscript letter, enclosing a long memorandum typed by Bohr, which included the information that Bohr had been invited by a Soviet fellow scientist, Peter Kapitsa,[33] to visit Moscow. Unlike many others at that time, who regarded the atomic bomb as just another powerful weapon, Bohr described it as "a weapon of an unparalleled power . . . which will completely change all future conditions of warfare"; and he warned that "the terrifying prospect of a future competition between nations can only be avoided through a universal agreement in true confidence."[34] At the time when Frankfurter sent Bohr's remarkable memorandum to the White House, he had already himself had an hour and a half's talk, based on Bohr's anxiety about atomic energy, with Roosevelt, in February 1944. According to Frankfurter's own recollection, written down over a year later, Roosevelt had shown himself receptive and gravely concerned by the problem. In the interval between Frankfurter's visit to the White House and Roosevelt's receiving Bohr's memorandum, Bohr had a meeting on 16 May 1944 in London with Churchill. This meeting of two titanic but incompatible figures was an unmitigated disaster. Four months later Churchill went to the extreme length of telegraphing: "It seems to me that Bohr ought to be confined or at any rate made to see that he is very near the edge of mortal crimes."[35]

On 26 August Roosevelt in turn saw Bohr. Unlike Churchill, he treated Bohr in the manner that his eminence deserved. More important, he seems to have agreed that Stalin must be approached in this matter. Frankfurter followed this meeting up with another manuscript letter to Roosevelt, on 8 September, setting out three "solid" reasons why the Russians could not be kept in the dark. "The argument," he wrote, "is that appropriate candor would risk very little. Withholding, on the other hand, might have grave consequences." Making one of the sudden switches of policy to which Roosevelt was temperamentally inclined, ten days later the President signed, at his home, the three brief paragraphs recording his conversation with Churchill about the atomic bomb (Appendix IV).

Churchill's reasons for signing this fascinating document are clear from documentary evidence of his views on the subject, one example of which has already been quoted in this chapter. Roosevelt's are not; he discussed the Hyde Park Aide-Mémoire with nobody between the day on which he signed it and the day of his death. His motives were doubtless mixed, one of them—judging from what he had just signed at Quebec—being a wish to make up for some of the blows that Churchill suffered from him during the summer. For the time being, he agreed with Churchill against making an approach to Stalin about the bomb and about the future of atomic energy. At Yalta, five months later, the subject was never discussed. Nevertheless, Roosevelt being Roosevelt, this does not mean that at Potsdam, or earlier, he would not have gone his own way.

We shall never know. Although it cannot be proved that what

ought to have been the thought uppermost in the tired mind of this exhausted man, at the very end of his life, did indeed receive at least some of his attention, it is a fact that one of the last communications about the atomic bomb that Roosevelt received, on 25 March 1945, was written to him by Einstein. It was a letter introducing Leo Szilard to the President, because Einstein understood Szilard to be "greatly concerned about the lack of adequate contact between scientists who are doing this work and those members of your Cabinet who are responsible for formulating policy." Did Roosevelt conceivably have this concern in mind when he prepared the Jefferson Birthday Address, which death prevented him from delivering? Had he lived to give the address on 13 April 1945, it would have included this quotation from Jefferson:

> The brotherly spirit of Science, which unites into one family all of its votaries . . . however widely dispersed throughout the different quarters of the globe.[36]

PART III

WAR and

PEACE

17

THE CRIMEAN

CONFERENCE: YALTA,

4-11 FEBRUARY 1945

The Emperor insinuated that the question [of
Poland] could only end in one way, as he was
in possession. I observed that it was very true
His Imperial Majesty was in possession, and he
must know that no one was less disposed than
myself hostilely to dispute that possession; but I
was sure His Imperial Majesty would not be
satisfied to rest his pretensions on a title of
conquest in opposition to the general
sentiments of Europe.

—*Lord Castlereagh to the Tsar Alexander I, at the
Congress of Vienna*

"Point de reveries, messieurs!" ("No dreams,
gentlemen!")

—*The Tsar Alexander II, in Warsaw, May 1856*

The Approach to the Conference

The second meeting of the Big Three began its life in July 1944 briefly
with the codename *Eureka II,* the Teheran Conference having been
codenamed *Eureka.* Six months later, before leaving London for Yalta,
Churchill remarked that "if we had spent ten years on research, we
could not have found a worse place in the world"[1] in which to hold it.
Yet the first of the many venues considered for *Eureka II* was just as

improbable: Invergordon, on the Cromarty Firth* in Scotland—a conference to be held in September 1944. Churchill's leaping imagination at once foresaw King George VI entertaining Roosevelt and Stalin at Balmoral; Roosevelt was "rather keen about the idea of Invergordon or a spot on the west coast of Scotland"; but on 22 July Stalin replied that, for military reasons, he could not attend a conference at that time.[2] From September onwards triangular discussion of the venue began in earnest. Churchill and Roosevelt tried to persuade Stalin to meet them somewhere in the Mediterranean. Stalin, pleading medical advice (in fact he detested flying), stuck firmly to a Black Sea port. By the middle of November Roosevelt had decided that a conference held after his presidential inauguration (on 20 January 1945) was preferable and thus "destroyed" the "hope" which Churchill had "cherished," that Roosevelt would pay his "long-promised visit to Britain."[3] At the end of December, after further Mediterranean venues had been turned down by Stalin, Yalta was finally agreed on by all three.[4] There, on 3 February 1945, Churchill and Roosevelt, with a retinue of some seven hundred officials, arrived for deliberations whose outcome was at the time hailed as a triumph for the Grand Alliance. On 13 February 1945 *The Times* wrote of "unbounded satisfaction," "mutual confidence and unanimity of counsel"; and it described the Yalta "proposals for the settlement of the Polish question" as "one of the greatest achievements of the conference." In the words of *The New York Times* the same day, the Yalta agreements "justify and surpass most of the hopes placed on this fateful meeting." *Izvestiya* described the conference as "the greatest political event of current times."[5] Yet this last meeting of Churchill, Roosevelt and Stalin has since become one of the most controversial events in history.†

---

*The site of a British naval base.

†The more so when, thirty years afterwards, the full story of wartime and post-war repatriations to the Soviet Union became public knowledge. As Chapter 4 of Nikolai Tolstoy's book *Victims of Yalta* makes clear, however, the Yalta agreement on prisoners-of-war was a "ratification" of what the three governments had already agreed in the previous year. The first shiploads of Soviet citizens had left both the United States and Britain before the end of 1944.

Immediately before Yalta, concern among the well-informed in Britain and the United States was not about any appeasement of the Soviet Union that the conference might bring. On the contrary, the "policy of appeasement" to which *The Economist* devoted its New Year leading article was Churchill's policy, not towards the Soviet Union, but towards the United States, "which at [his] personal bidding, has been followed, with all the humiliation and abasements it has brought in its train, ever since Pearl Harbour removed the need for it"—an article of which the U.S. Secretary of State found of sufficient significance to warrant his sending a memorandum about it to Roosevelt on 2 January, saying that it "represents what is in the minds of millions of Englishmen . . . the underlying cause is the emotional difficulty which anyone, and especially any Englishman, has in adjusting himself to a secondary role after having always accepted a leading one as his national right."[6]

Once again, as before the Teheran Conference, Churchill had to pull out all the stops in order to persuade Roosevelt of the need for an Anglo-American meeting en route. As late as 6 January Roosevelt had told Churchill that such a meeting was impossible. Nevertheless, he relented. This time the bilateral conference took place at Malta, where the Chiefs of Staff of both countries and their two Secretaries of State met for the last two days of January; the Combined Chiefs of Staff had their last major row of the war; and at the two meetings between Churchill and Roosevelt on 2 February little or no business was done.[7] After dining together, they set off in their aeroplanes for the Crimea: a non-stop flight, followed by a five-hour road journey to Yalta from the airfield where they landed. The first plenary session of *Argonaut* (as the conference was finally codenamed, with a classical touch) opened at the Livadia Palace on 4 February. There the Big Three conferred for just over a week.

The photograph taken of the Big Three at this, the summer palace of the Tsars, on the day before the conference ended shows Churchill smoking his cigar, Roosevelt haggard—a cigarette in his left hand— and Stalin composed, his hands folded.[8] Stalin had sound reasons for composure even before the conference began. Whereas Eisenhower's forces had not yet crossed the Rhine and Alexander's final offensive in North Italy could not take place for another two months, the Red Army, under Zhukov's command, had undertaken an offensive in January, as—in Stalin's words—"a moral duty" to their American and British Allies, fulfilled in order to relieve the pressure exerted on Eisenhower's forces by the unexpected German counter-attack in the Ardennes just before Christmas: the Battle of the Bulge.* This Soviet offensive had not only captured Warsaw at last, but had reached the River Oder, where the westernmost tip of Zhukov's salient was, by the time Churchill, Roosevelt and Stalin sat down together on 4 February, less than forty miles from Berlin. Indeed, had the preliminary operational directive issued by Zhukov at the end of January received Stalin's approval, the final assault on Berlin would have begun while the Yalta Conference was in session.[10] As it was, almost the whole of pre-war Polish territory was now in Soviet hands.

Churchill's forebodings about the physical discomforts of the Crimean Conference were not fulfilled. Soviet hospitality was lavish. (He even paid a visit to the nineteenth-century Anglo-Russian battlefield of Balaclava before leaving the Soviet Union afterwards.) But his forecast of the meeting, in his telegram sent to Roosevelt on 8 January—"a fateful conference, coming at a moment when the great allies are divided"—[11]was nearer the mark, subject to one major qualification. At Yalta both the decisions taken by Churchill, Roosevelt and Stalin and the problems that they shelved proved "fateful" only so far as the future of Europe was concerned. In other areas of policy it was Roosevelt's conviction that "when the three of us get together,"[12] solutions would be found, which was borne out. As for Stalin, he would tell Churchill and Roosevelt on the third day of the Yalta

---

*Air Chief Marshal Tedder, Eisenhower's deputy, had been sent to Moscow in January 1945 in order to discuss the timing of operations on the Western and Eastern fronts, as the result of telegrams sent to Stalin by Churchill and Roosevelt. At his meeting with Stalin on 15 January, Stalin told Tedder that the Red Army's offensive had been launched "regardless of weather conditions"; and he undertook to "do everything within his power to keep them [the German Army] occupied on the eastern front."[9]

Conference, once the debate on Poland's future had been joined, that "the Polish question is a matter of life and death for the Soviet Union"; and "better let the war with the Germans continue a little longer still," he said, "but we must be in a position to compensate Poland in the west at Germany's expense."[13] Stimson (although he did not go to Yalta) hit the nail on the head in a memorandum sent to Roosevelt just before the President left Washington:

> Russia . . . will claim that, in the light of her bitter experience with Germany, her own self-defense as a guarantor of the peace of the world will depend on relations with buffer countries like Poland, Bulgaria, and Romania, which will be quite different from complete independence on the part of those countries.

Or, as Stalin would put it bluntly to the British Foreign Secretary (Ernest Bevin) in Moscow nearly a year later: "The United Kingdom had India and the Indian Ocean in her sphere of interest; the United States, China and Japan; the USSR had nothing."[14]

In these circumstances, how could Roosevelt say in January that he thought that "not more than five or six days" would be enough for the Yalta Conference? (As Churchill reminded him in response, "even the Almighty took seven" days.)[15] Perhaps Roosevelt felt himself a sick man, in a hurry. Perhaps he believed that five or six days would be long enough to secure his two principal objectives: agreement on the Far East and on the United Nations Organisation. More probably, he calculated that the high cards that he, alone of the Big Three, held in his hand would be better played at the later conference that was bound to be held once the war in Europe was over. In any event, what did he really make of a conference during which Stalin described Beria to him as "our Himmler"?[16]

The Conference

Roosevelt secured one of his objectives soon after the conference began and the other at the very end. On 7 February the deadlock on UN voting procedure (left unresolved at Dumbarton Oaks five months earlier) was settled, when Molotov conceded that the Soviet Union would not, after all, insist that permanent members of the Security Council should have the right of veto on procedural questions; and the number of Soviet republics which were to become members of the organisation was reduced from sixteen to "at least two"—in Roosevelt's words, "a great step forward," which would bring "joy and relief to the peoples of the world." The words just quoted were not exaggerated. The speed with which the names of the U.S. delegation, including the Republican leader Senator Arthur Vandenberg, were chosen to be invited to San Francisco for the inaugural conference of the United Nations is telling evidence of this. (The list of names[17] was agreed at once, even though the press release about the convening of the San Francisco Conference was not to be issued by the White House until the day after the conference communiqúe itself, in the middle of February.) The danger of a post-war relapse into American isolationism, which had wrecked the Versailles settlement of 1919, had finally been averted.

The secret agreement on the Far East,[18] signed on the last day of the Yalta Conference, was nominally trilateral, but Churchill was not consulted about the terms of this U.S.-Soviet deal by Roosevelt and Stalin. He overruled Eden and Cadogan, both of whom advised him not to endorse the agreement, on the ground that his signature was necessary in order to preserve an active role for Britain in Far Eastern affairs. Later, however, Churchill wrote in his memoirs that "to us the problem was remote and secondary."[19] The country vitally affected—China—was never consulted about its terms; indeed, the Chinese Government was not even aware of the existence of the agreement at the time. This agreement committed the Soviet Union to enter the war against Japan "in two or three months after Germany has surrendered," in return for three conditions that were to be "unquestionably fulfilled": the *status quo* in Outer Mongolia was to be preserved; "the former rights of Russia violated by the treacherous attack of Japan in 1904" were to be restored; and the Kurile Islands were to be handed over to the Soviet Union. A further clause of the agreement recognised that Chiang Kai-shek's concurrence in the fulfillment of the conditions relating to Outer Mongolia and Manchuria was required; the U.S. President was "to take measures to obtain this concurrence on advice from Marshal Stalin." Finally, the Soviet Union expressed its readiness to conclude a pact of friendship and alliance with the National Government of China (which it did on 14 August 1945). Although the Far Eastern part of Roosevelt's grand design received general applause on both sides of the Atlantic at the time when its terms became publicly known in August 1945, it was left to Mao, five years later, after he had taken power in Peking, to negotiate with the Soviet Union the reversal of all the concessions made at Yalta at China's expense, with the single exception of Mongolian independence.

Churchill's role at Yalta was Eurocentric. De Gaulle having been excluded from the conference, contrary to Churchill's suggestion, by Roosevelt, once the three leaders reached Yalta, Churchill argued strenuously—against opposition from both Roosevelt and Stalin—that France should both be given a zone of occupation in Germany and be made a member of the Allied Control Commission for Germany. At Roosevelt's first bilateral meeting with Stalin, he told him that the British wanted "to have their cake and eat it" over France; he himself thought that a French zone of occupation in Germany was "not a bad idea . . . but . . . only out of kindness." Nevertheless, on 10 February Roosevelt suddenly told his two colleagues that he had changed his mind, thus paving way for agreement on this issue, with significant consequences for France and for European politics as a whole after the war had ended.

At Yalta Churchill executed a 180-degree turn over Germany. Whereas at his meeting with Roosevelt at the Second Quebec Conference only four months earlier he had gone along with the American suggestion of the "pastoralisation" of Germany, which was to be stripped of its industry, Churchill now blocked the proposal (discussed by the Big Three at Teheran) for the dismemberment of Germany, which was referred to a tripartite committee, under Eden's chairmanship. He also offered a red rag to the Soviet bull by contesting Stalin's suggestion that the total amount of war reparations payable by Germany should be $20 billion, half of which should go to the Soviet Union, as the country devastated by the German occupation. Whereas Stalin and Roosevelt agreed at Yalta that the Tripartite Reparations Commission, one of the bodies established by the Yalta Conference, should "in its initial studies" take "as a basis for discussion" the Soviet figure of $20 billion, the protocol of the proceedings of the conference recorded the British view that no figure should be mentioned pending consideration by the Commission.

The European question which was by far the most pressing and by far the most far-reaching in its potential consequences for the whole of Europe in the longer run—Germany—was given scant attention at the Yalta Conference, whereas Poland received some eighteen thousand words of discussion. It is for this debate about Poland that the Yalta Conference has become famous. After a week of wrangling, it was agreed that a Polish Provisional Government of National Unity should be established, "which can be more broadly based than was possible before the recent liberation of Poland." The Provisional Government functioning in Poland "should therefore be reorganised on a broader democratic basis with the inclusion of democratic leaders from Poland itself and from Poles abroad." The Soviet Foreign Minister and the U.S. and British ambassadors were authorised by Churchill, Roosevelt and Stalin to act "as a Commission to consult in the first instance in Moscow with members of the present Provisional Government and with other Polish democratic leaders from within Poland and from abroad, with a view to the reorganisation of the present government along the above lines." "Free and unfettered" elections were to follow as soon as possible "on the basis of universal suffrage and secret ballot"; all "democratic and anti-Nazi parties" were to have the right to take part and put forward candidates.

As for the frontiers of this new Poland, after Roosevelt had put in a muted plea, which he did not press, for Polish retention of Lvov, it was agreed that the eastern frontier should follow the Curzon Line, with minor digressions. In the north and west, Poland "must receive substantial accessions of territory"; the "final delimitation" of the western frontier should await the Peace Conference. Although the adoption of the Curzon Line had been inevitable from the Teheran Conference onwards, the Yalta phraseology about the western frontier reflected disagreement about the Soviet proposal that this frontier should follow the River Oder and the *Western* River Neisse, thus incorporating in the new Polish state[20] the whole of Pomerania and Silesia—a diplomatic battle that was to be fought out at Potsdam. As we now know, over six months before the Yalta Conference Molotov had signed a Memorandum of Understanding with the head of the Lublin Committee. To the east, both parties to this agreement accepted the Curzon Line.[21] Article 4 of the agreement committed the Soviet government to "support the establishment of the Soviet-German frontier" along the line of the Oder-western Neisse.[22]

One of the factors that make the discussion about Poland at Yalta confusing to the present-day reader is that, although the debate was principally about the composition of the Provisional Government of Poland, it was also about the future frontiers of the new Polish state. The reason for this was that at the time of Yalta not even Mikołajczyk had publicly accepted the Curzon Line as Poland's eastern frontier—let alone the other members of the Polish Government-in-exile, from which he had resigned at the end of 1944. The other factor is that, although not directly related to the Polish question as such at Yalta, the Joint Declaration on Liberated Europe* issued there by the Big Three was in a sense superimposed upon the agreement over Poland, and subsequently the two became linked in the public mind. In fact, the original State Department drafters of this Wilsonian document almost certainly conceived it as aimed just as much at events in Greece, for which the British were responsible, as those in Poland. The declaration had little or no legal force as a binding commitment upon the signatories; and its implementation was made conditional—"where in their judgement conditions require." But it awakened hopes of a post-war

---

*The full text of this declaration, which looked forward to "the earliest possible establishment through free elections of governments responsive to the will of the people," is reproduced in Appendix V.

renaissance of democracy in countries, such as Greece and Poland itself, which before the war had been governed by regimes which could not have been described as democratic in a western sense. As Professor Arthur Schlesinger has pointed out in a recent study:

> Signing the Declaration was from the Soviet point of view a grave diplomatic blunder. This was not because the Declaration had any chance of stopping the Soviet Union from consolidating its position in Eastern Europe but because the Declaration laid down standards for Eastern Europe, and Stalin's subsequent violation of these standards exposed him, once the club was out of the closet, to persuasive charges of bad faith and of breaking the Yalta accords.[23]

To make matters worse, the loosely drafted wording of the agreement about the future Polish Government papered over so many cracks between the American, British and Soviet points of view at Yalta that it was virtually a foregone conclusion that, once Molotov sat down with Harriman and the British Ambassador, Archibald Clark Kerr, in order to determine which Polish leader was "democratic" and which was not, they were bound to run into difficulties. This is indeed what happened. The agreement reached on Poland at Yalta lasted little more than a month; Molotov made full use of the words "in the first instance in Moscow"; and at the end of March sixteen members of the Polish Resistance movement who had gone to Zhukov's headquarters under a Soviet guarantee of immunity disappeared. Only after a prolonged triangular argument between the three governments, which continued well after Roosevelt's death, was the Yalta agreement on Poland renegotiated—this time entirely through bilateral U.S.-Soviet discussions in Moscow—at the end of May 1945.*

---

*See Chapter 18.

The Sequel

Neither Churchill nor Roosevelt returned home direct, so that their accounts of Yalta to Parliament and to Congress were delayed—until 27 February and 1 March, respectively. Both of them included Egypt in their return journeys, so that it was in Alexandria Harbour that, on 15 February, Churchill and Roosevelt met for the last time, on board the U.S.S. *Quincy*. According to Churchill's own record, their principal topic of conversation was atomic: not a continuation of their discussion at Hyde Park five months earlier, but the prospect of Britain "going ahead with [its] own work on Tube Alloys," which Churchill raised with Roosevelt, in Hopkins' presence. "The President raised no objection of any kind" and "mentioned September for the first important trials."[24]

On 27 February, on his return to London, Churchill said to the House of Commons,

> The impression I brought back from the Crimea, and from all my other contacts, is that Marshal Stalin and the Soviet leaders wish to live in honourable friendship and equality with the Western democracies. I feel also that their word is their bond. I know of no Government which stands to its obligations, even in its own despite, more solidly than the Russian Soviet Government. I decline absolutely to embark here on a discussion about Russian good faith. It is quite evident that these matters touch the whole future of the world.[25]

Three days later, in his last address to Congress, Roosevelt described the Polish territorial decision at Yalta as "frankly, a compromise," but he added his conviction that "the agreement on Poland, under the circumstances," was "the most hopeful agreement possible for a free, independent and prosperous Polish state." He commended to "the Congress and the American people . . . the results of this Conference as the beginnings of a permanent structure of peace." The question whether his journey was entirely fruitful or not lay, he declared, "to a great extent in your hands."[26]

After making what turned out to be his last visit to his home at Hyde Park, on 29 March Roosevelt went to Warm Springs, Georgia, in an attempt to rest and recover his strength. During the final weeks of his life he was caught in a cross-fire of messages from Churchill and Stalin, primarily over Poland, but also about negotiations (secretly initiated in Switzerland in March by an *SS* general, Karl Wolff) for the surrender of German forces in Italy to Alexander. These negotiations, at which the Soviet Union was not represented, came to nothing, but not before they had given rise to the only furious exchange between Roosevelt and Stalin of the entire war. Stalin accused his two allies of trying to make a separate peace agreement, which Roosevelt rejected as a "vile" misrepresentation. In his last message to Stalin, however, Roosevelt described the episode as having "faded into the past."[27]

Poland was another matter. Just over a week after his defence of Yalta in Parliament, Churchill sent Roosevelt a long telegram enlisting his support for a message of protest to Stalin about the manner in which Molotov was in practice interpreting the agreement about the Polish Government laboriously worked out at Yalta, which Churchill now described as "The test case between us and the Russians of the meaning which is to be attached to such terms as Democracy, Sovereignty, Independence, Representative Government and free and unfettered elections."[28] This telegram not only marks the beginning of Churchill's decision to undertake one final stand on behalf of the "London" Poles, dictated in part by domestic political considerations,* but also the start of a U-turn away from his own percentages agreement, reached with Stalin in Moscow in October 1944. For—remarkably— the opening paragraphs of this telegram were concerned not with Poland, but with Soviet behaviour in two Balkan countries, Romania and Bulgaria, in which American and British interests were, by any standards, minimal—and this at a time when Churchill was fully aware

---

*Twenty-five members of Parliament voted against the government in the House of Commons on 1 March. Members of the Polish Government in London were able to lobby actively, in Parliament and elsewhere.

that, so far as Greece was concerned, he still needed Stalin's acquiescence in the execution of British policy there.[29]

By 13 March Churchill was seeking to convince Roosevelt that the three powers were "in the presence of a great failure and an utter breakdown of what was settled at Yalta." Roosevelt hesitated. It took three weeks before he finally sent Stalin a moderately worded expression (drafted by Leahy) of his "concern" at the "discouraging lack of progress in the carrying out ... of the political decisions ... reached at the Conference particularly those relating to the Polish question."[30] Stalin's reply was a categorical negative. After agreeing with Churchill and Roosevelt that the handling of the Polish question had indeed reached a dead end, Stalin went on to put the blame for this on the American and British members of the Commission established in Moscow by the Crimean Conference to deal with it. In particular, he said, Harriman and Clark Kerr had interpreted the "reconstruction of the Provisional Government" of Poland (i.e., the Warsaw Government) as "its liquidation and the creation of a completely new government." (According to Stalin, Harriman had gone so far as to state that it was possible that not a single member of the Provisional Government would become a member of the Polish Government of National Unity.) Whereas it had been agreed at Yalta—Stalin maintained—that the Commission should invite five Poles from Poland and three in London for consultations, it was now being suggested that each member of the Commission should be entitled to invite any number of Poles. By contrast, the Soviet position was that Poles invited for consultation must first, recognise the decisions of the Crimean Conference, including the Curzon Line, and secondly, seek in earnest to establish friendly relations between Poland and the Soviet Union, which had been invaded from Polish territory twice in the past twenty years. Stalin also insisted that consultation should "in the first instance" be carried out with representatives of the (Warsaw) Provisional Polish Government.[31]

Roosevelt's last word of advice to Churchill on the Polish question in a telegram sent on 11 April 1945 (and unlike most of his messages sent during his final weeks, drafted by himself) was to "minimise the general Soviet problem as much as possible" in Parliament.[32] On the following day he was reading papers while in the living room of his Warm Springs house, having a sketch made for his portrait. There was to be a barbecue in the late afternoon. Shortly after one o'clock Roosevelt spoke his last words—"I have a terrific headache." He suffered a massive stroke. Nearly three hours later his cardiologist, Commander Bruenn, pronounced the President dead.* The Grand Alliance, shaken first by the Polish controversy and now by Roosevelt's death, remained in being. But the triumvirate was over.

---

*Lucy Rutherfurd, with whom (after her husband's death) Roosevelt had resumed his earlier relationship, was with him. Eleanor Roosevelt, who was not present, only learned about this afterwards, to her chagrin.

18

THE ALLIANCE

VICTORIOUS

The question of a peace conference to settle the
European War . . . is knocking at the door.

—Joseph Stalin to Harry Hopkins, 26 May 1945

After a long war it is impossible to make a
quick peace.

*—Harold Nicolson, in the Introduction added to the
1943 edition of his book* Peacemaking 1919

*T*oday, *neither the* victors nor the vanquished can look
back with an untroubled conscience on the final months of the Second
World War. Except for the determination of the soldiers who won the
major battles, such as those for Berlin, Okinawa and Rangoon—to
name three of the most bitterly contested—they make ugly reading.
The fire-bombing of Dresden, a city crowded with refugees, in February, and that of Tokyo in March led on to the atomic climax at
Hiroshima and Nagasaki in August 1945 (Kyoto, General Groves'
preferred target, was spared only through Stimson's personal intervention).[1] The Red Army took its revenge in Germany; and throughout
Central Europe the NKVD showed that it had forgotten nothing and
learned nothing. Not only were the sixteen Polish Resistance officers
(arrested in the circumstances mentioned in the previous chapter) put
on trial and sentenced in Moscow, but in Budapest the NKVD arrested

and subsequently imprisoned the Swedish diplomat, Raoul Wallenberg,[2] who had, single-handed, prevented the Germans—whose work of extermination continued up to the very end—from transporting thousands of Jews to the concentration camps.

April–July 1945

During the run-up to Potsdam, although the high cards that Roosevelt had refrained from playing at Yalta remained in the hand of the new President of the United States, Stalin did not suffer from the domestic political disadvantages under which Churchill and Truman were operating. Churchill was increasingly distracted first by the prospect of and then by the campaign for the general election, the first to be held in Britain for ten years. A little over a month after Churchill's return to London, the editor of *The Economist* wrote that "the Coalition is growing more and more threadbare";[3] on 7 April Bevin, a strong supporter of the Coalition for nearly five years, said publicly that this had been neither a one-man government nor a one-man war; and on 20 May 1945 all the Labour Party ministers resigned from the government. Churchill then formed a government drawn from the Conservative and the National Liberal parties; and a general election was called for 6 July, the results of which were not to be announced until three weeks later, in order to allow time for the collection of all votes cast by those serving in the British armed forces round the world. Churchill's prophecy, in his first election broadcast on 4 June—that a Labour Government would introduce into Britain a kind of Gestapo, "no doubt humanely administered in the first instance"—probably did not exert much influence either way on the voters' choice[4] a month later: a landslide victory for the Labour Party. But it is evidence of the extent to which his political judgement was affected in the final weeks of the war. Nor is it an isolated example, as the record of his performance* at Potsdam also shows.

---

*All British eye-witnesses of this performance agree that it was poor—e.g., William Hayter, *The Kremlin and the Embassy,* pp. 29–30.

The man who took the presidential oath on 12 April 1945 on Capitol Hill, Harry Truman, had been chosen by Roosevelt to be his vice-presidential running mate in the 1944 election as the politician who would divide the Democratic Party ticket least—a sixty-year-old, middlewestern, middle-of-the-road senator. Truman had never been abroad except as an artillery officer in France in 1918; he knew little about international relations; and he knew nothing whatever about the most formidable problem confronting him—the atomic bomb—until Stimson and Groves (entering the White House by separate doors, as a security precaution)[5] gave him his first, preliminary briefing on 25 April. The two immediate problems that he had inherited a fortnight earlier, however, were the still unresolved Polish problem and the conduct of the final thrusts of the war against Germany.

The Polish problem was compounded by the question of how Poland was to be represented at the San Francisco founding conference of the United Nations. Since a Warsaw-led delegation was unacceptable to the U.S. and British governments, Stalin retaliated by deciding that Molotov should not attend the meeting—a decision which, after Roosevelt's death, he revoked on the eve of the conference as a personal gesture to the new President. Truman's initial response to this gesture was—by his own account—[6] to give Molotov a drubbing when he called on Truman in Washington on his way to San Francisco. The President followed this, however, by sending Hopkins to Moscow in May on a conciliatory mission, which led to the U.S.-Soviet renegotiation of the Yalta agreement on the formation of the Polish Government. In this bilateral negotiation Churchill played no part; indeed, Truman did not even consult him before deciding to send Hopkins to Moscow.[7] In the course of six meetings with Stalin, one of them alone, Hopkins resolved the problem of the composition of the Polish Government at last—a compromise (whereby five more Poles, including Mikołajczyk, joined the Polish Cabinet) grudgingly accepted by Churchill as "no advance on Yalta" but "an advance upon the deadlock";[8] whereas Harriman, though in no way starry-eyed about Stalin's intentions overall at the time, summed it up in the following words:

I believe that the stage is as well set as can be done at the present time and that if we continue to take a sympathetic interest in Polish affairs and are reasonably generous in our economic relations, there is a fair chance that things will work out satisfactorily from our standpoint.[9]

In consquence, a fortnight before the Potsdam Conference the British and U.S. governments finally recognised the Warsaw Government (of which Mikołajczyk had now become Deputy Prime Minister) as the Government of Poland.

At almost the same moment that Stalin was attacking Roosevelt about the secret negotiations conducted in Switzerland, Churchill had taken issue with Roosevelt over Eisenhower's declared intention (which he signalled direct to Stalin) of "driving eastward to join hands with the Russians or to attain [the] general line of [the] Elbe," urging instead that "from a political standpoint we should march as far east into Germany as possible," and "should Berlin be in our grasp we should certainly take it."[10] Eisenhower's strategy was upheld; Hitler committed suicide in the bunker below what was left of his monumental Reichschancellery, on 30 April; and a week later the European War ended* with the Red Army in control of Berlin, Prague and Vienna. Thwarted in this endeavour (later described by Marshall as "Monday morning quarter-backing"), Churchill nonetheless went on to urge upon Truman that, as a deliberate bargaining counter, there should be no western withdrawal from the areas held by their forces at the moment of the German surrender, well within the occupation zone allocated (by previous tripartite agreement) to the Soviet Union. On 11 June the President finally turned the Prime Minister down.[11] Only over Trieste, from which the (British) Eighth Army ejected Tito's troops, did he agree with Churchill. What followed in Germany was described nine months later by an unrepentant Churchill, in Truman's presence at Fulton, Missouri, as an Anglo-American withdrawal "to a

---

*The formal act of surrender was signed in Berlin on the morning of 8 May 1945.

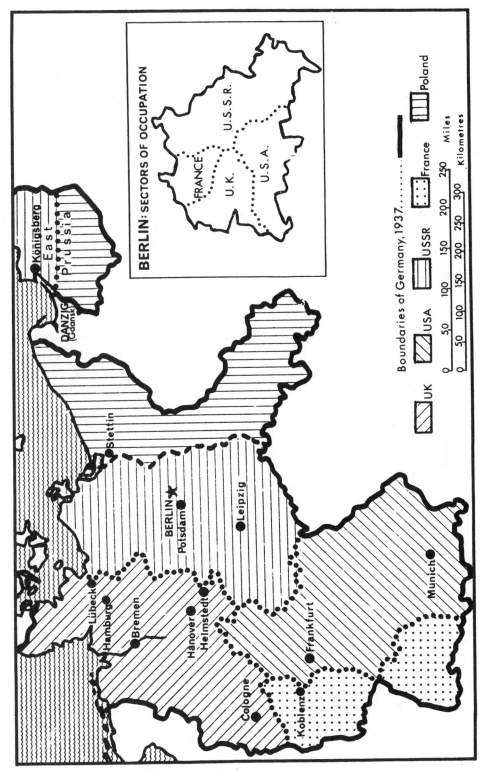

BERLIN: SECTORS OF OCCUPATION

FRANCE
U.S.S.R.
U.K.
U.S.A.

East Prussia
Königsberg

DANZIG
Gdansk

Stettin

BERLIN
Potsdam
Leipzig

Lübeck
Hamburg
Bremen
Hanover
Helmstedt
Cologne
Frankfurt
Koblenz
Munich

Boundaries of Germany, 1937 ....

UK
USA
USSR
France
Poland

0   50   100   150   200   250   Miles
0   50   100   150   200   250   300   Kilometres

7. Germany, July 1945

depth at some points of 120 miles on a front of nearly 400 miles to allow the Russians to occupy this vast expanse of territory which the Western democracies had conquered."[12]

Churchill's attempt to renege on the tripartite agreement on Allied zones of occupation in Germany has to be assessed against the background not only of his domestic preoccupations, but also of the chilly start to his personal relationship with Truman. After Truman had been at the White House for a month, Churchill sent him a dramatically worded telegram beginning with the words that "An iron curtain is being drawn down on their [the Russian] front" and ending: "This issue of a settlement with Russia before our strength has gone seems to me to dwarf all others."[13] What Churchill urged on Truman was the need for a showdown at a conference with Stalin—"the grave discussion on which the immediate future of the world depends"—and he invited the President to visit Britain on the way to the meeting. Truman refused this invitation, for a Rooseveltian reason—there should be no Anglo-Saxon "ganging-up"—and the British suggestion of a meeting of the Combined Chiefs of Staff in London was also turned down.[14] Matters were made worse by Truman's choice of Joseph Davies to give Churchill an oral message, which he delivered at Chequers, where the two men had an all-night session lasting eight hours. Churchill's detailed account of their argument does not square at all with Davies', but of one thing there is little doubt: this was the worst Anglo-American meeting held at Chequers throughout the war.[15]

The Prime Minister interpreted the President's message as meaning that there should first be a meeting between Truman and Stalin, which "representatives of His Majesty's Government should be invited to join a few days later." This hint of U.S.-Soviet condominium led Churchill to inform Truman on 31 May that he would "not be prepared to attend a meeting which was a continuation of a conference between yourself and Marshal Stalin . . . we should meet simultaneously and on equal terms." Churchill won this round. He was obliged to accept Truman's timing of the conference, however. (Hopkins had to assure Stalin that Truman really was proposing 15 July as the date for the conference—not 15 June, as suggested by Churchill.) Neither in its date, nor in its venue, nor in its purpose did this conference resemble the meeting that Churchill had originally proposed to Truman on 11 May.[16]

In Moscow, the agreement reached between Hopkins and Stalin was not confined to Poland. It covered a wide range: the date of the Red Army's readiness to invade Manchuria (8 August), agreement that Chinese Nationalist troops should enter Manchuria simultaneously, a joint effort to help to unify China under Chiang's leadership, final Soviet acceptance of the U.S. position on U.N. Security Council voting (thus averting a breakdown at San Francisco) and agreement on the holding of a summit meeting in Berlin in mid-July. Against Churchill's wish, Truman deliberately postponed the Berlin meeting to a date which would, if possible, make the first atomic test, at Alamogordo, New Mexico, precede it:[17] a link of which Churchill seems to have been strangely unaware during the run-up to Potsdam.

The Atomic Decision

Although Truman's first atomic briefing on 25 April lasted less than an hour, it had one immediate result: the formation, under Stimson's chairmanship, of an Interim Committee of advisers to the President. The main questions requiring decision were four, all of them predicated on a successful test at Alamogordo. Was the bomb to be dropped on Japan and when? Was the Japanese Government to be warned? Was the Soviet Government to be told about it in advance? Linked with this, there was the whole question of any future atomic relationship with the Soviet Union, which had been a controversial subject both in London and in Washington as early as the spring of 1944.

On 6 June this Committee, which had held its first meeting on 9 May, recommended to the President that the atomic bomb should be used against a Japanese "war plant surrounded by workers' homes," without warning, as soon as preparations could be made; the Soviet Government should not be informed about the weapon before it was used. In a memorandum which Stimson handed to the President, he added his own suggestion that the condition of a sharing of the secrets of the bomb with the Soviet Union should be either Soviet participation in an international control commission on atomic energy after the war, or a political accommodation in Eastern Europe. By 19 June, Stimson was describing the Interim Committee as "thinking in a vacuum" until the Soviet Union had been dealt with. In late June the Committee members changed their minds about warning the Soviet Union of the bomb's existence; they now recommended that the President should not wait until the bomb was used before informing the Soviet Government. Stimson conferred with the President on 2 and 3 July; and at the meeting of the Anglo-American Combined Policy Committee held on 4 July, he is recorded as saying:

> ... if nothing was said at this [the Berlin] meeting about the Tube Alloy weapon, its subsequent early use might have a serious effect on the relations of frankness between the three great Allies. He had therefore advised the President to watch the atmosphere at the meeting. If mutual frankness on other questions was found to be real and satisfactory, then the President might say that work was being done on the development of atomic fission for war purposes; that good progress had been made; and that an attempt to use a weapon would be made shortly, though it was not certain that it would succeed. If it did succeed, it would be necessary for a discussion to be held on the best method of handling the development in the interests of world peace and not for destruction. If Stalin pressed for immediate disclosure the President might say that he was not prepared to take the matter further at the present time. . . .[18]

In London, by contrast, ministerial discussion—as described when the relevant documents were examined nearly twenty years after the war by the official historian of the United Kingdom Atomic Energy Authority—was "cursory."[19] On 29 June 1945, the following minute was addressed to the Prime Minister by John Anderson:

> Lord Cherwell will have told you of the private manuscript letter which I have had from Field-Marshal Wilson reporting some

details which he had been given confidentially and unofficially of the outline plan for the first use of the weapon against the Japanese.

Field-Marshal Wilson has now reported that Mr Stimson proposed to raise this matter at a meeting of the Combined Policy Committee on 4th July, in order that the two Governments may record their decision on the use of the weapon, in accordance with the terms of the Quebec Agreement.

The Americans are now making their final plans and preparations for the use of the weapon. May I have your authority to instruct our representatives on the Combined Policy Committee to give their concurrence in the decision to use it?[20]

Churchill simply initialled this minute. Thereafter, Field-Marshal Wilson (Dill's successor in Washington) gave British consent to the use of the atomic bomb at the meeting of the Combined Policy Committee in Washington, adding only that the Prime Minister "might wish to discuss the matter with the President at the forthcoming meeting in Berlin."

The Potsdam Conference*

The Potsdam Conference was the last and the longest summit meeting of the Grand Alliance (and the last East-West summit for ten years). It also differed in two important respects from the two earlier meetings of the Big Three. First, the major negotiating role at Potsdam was played by the newly appointed U.S. Secretary of State, James Byrnes. Secondly, Churchill attended only the first week of the conference, leaving it—never to return—on 25 July. (Attlee, the leader of the victorious Labour Party, then took his place as Prime Minister). The

---

*The account given of the Potsdam Conference in this chapter does not differ significantly from that given in the author's book *Setting the Mould.* Unascribed references are derived from *FRUS, The Conference of Berlin (the Potsdam Conference).*

Protocol signed at Potsdam was the product of thirteen plenary sessions held in the neo-Tudor Schloss Cecilienhof, the former palace of the Crown Prince Wilhelm of Prussia. According to the communiqué of 2 August 1945, on that day the three leaders left the conference, which had "strengthened the ties between the three governments," with "renewed confidence that their governments and peoples, together with the United Nations, will ensure the creation of a just and enduring peace." This expression of triumphant accord was not simply intended for public consumption. As Attlee put it in a letter that he wrote to Churchill from Potsdam, the three leaders parted "in a good atmosphere,"[21] and at the final plenary session, held late in the evening of 1 August, when Truman said that he hoped there would soon be another meeting of the three leaders, Stalin's reply was (in the Soviet record), "May God grant it."[22]

Interspersed with the series of tripartite plenaries, preceded by meetings of the three foreign ministers, there was from first to last a shifting pattern of other meetings—internal, bilateral, and, on one day, even quadripartite—with ministers of the Polish government. Although the principal questions discussed by the three leaders and their foreign ministers jointly at Potsdam were the same as at Yalta—Central Europe (in which Germany itself at last become the dominant issue), the Far East and the establishment of peacemaking and consultative machinery—discussion of others ranged far and wide: Iran, Turkey, Italy, Romania, Bulgaria, Hungary and Finland. All these questions, though important, were secondary.

On the main issues that the leaders of the three countries discussed together, the communiqué which they issued, like their smiling photograph, gave a misleading impression of Allied unanimity. There were four cardinal differences between the reality and the appearance of Potsdam. First, the expression of tripartite solidarity masked the extent to which the outcome of the conference had depended on a U.S.-Soviet understanding, reached bilaterally between Byrnes and Molotov, regarding the critical questions of Poland and Germany—two questions which Byrnes linked deliberately and unequivocally. Secondly, the compromise agreed regarding these two questions at the very end of the conference (the last plenary session broke up just after midnight), while formally leaving the future of Germany open, in effect closed the options further. Thirdly, even the establishment of the five-power Council of Foreign Ministers, reassuringly sensible on paper, held the seeds of future controversy. Finally, only four days after the conference, a completely new factor was thrust into the equation of world power.

To begin with the first of these cardinal points—on the question of Central Europe, the three Allies had no difficulty in settling the Soviet Union's claim to its share of East Prussia (the remainder became Polish). But they resumed their argument over Poland's western frontier where they had left it at Yalta, subject to two differences: there was now a Polish Government which they all recognized, whose leaders came to Berlin to join in pressing the case for the adoption of the western River Neisse as Poland's western frontier; and, by now, the German population of the western territories claimed by Poland, with Soviet support, had been largely replaced by Poles. The argument in plenary began on 21 July; before leaving Berlin four days later (in order to learn the result of the British general election), Churchill declared at his last meeting with Truman and Stalin that if the conference ended with no agreement regarding the present state of affairs in Poland, with the Poles "practically admitted as a fifth occupational power" (of Germany), this "undoubtedly would mark a breakdown of the Conference"; the British and Soviet records soften this remark, using the word "failure" rather than "breakdown."

This deadlock continued, until Byrnes broke it on 30 July at his bilateral meeting with Molotov, who at once expressed his "gratification" in response. At this critical meeting, what the U.S. Government conceded was Polish administration of German territory up to the western Neisse, "pending the final determination of Poland's western frontier," which "should await the peace settlement." Byrnes expressly linked this major American concession to Soviet acceptance of the U.S. proposals regarding German reparations, put forward on the previous day at another bilateral U.S.-Soviet meeting (this time Truman was present). The essence of Byrnes' proposal on reparations was to get away from the Yalta concept of fixed sums, by establishing the principle that each occupying power would meet its claims to reparations from its own zone of occupation, although, as additional reparations, the Soviet Union would receive a percentage of industrial equipment, either from the Ruhr or from the three western zones taken together. The amount to be removed from the western zones was to be determined within six months; removals were to be completed within two years from the date of determination; and the "amount and character of the industrial equipment unnecessary for the German peace economy and therefore available for reparations" was to be determined by the Allied Control Council, with the participation of France, subject to the final approval of the commander of the zone concerned. (Austria was expressly exempted.)[23]

These two bilateral U.S.-Soviet meetings, on 29 and 30 July, were crucial to the outcome of the conference. Both of them stemmed from Byrnes' initiative. At the very end of the conference, Stalin had good reason to express his thanks to Byrnes, "who seemed to work harder than anyone else," and he added: "these sentiments, Secretary Byrnes, come from my heart." After Bevin (now Foreign Secretary) took over the British team, late on 28 July—Attlee himself hardly said a word— he held out until the afternoon of 31 July for the eastern River Neisse as Poland's western frontier, but in the end he accepted the U.S.-Soviet deal on both questions.[24] Churchill maintained, in his memoirs, that if he had returned to Berlin as Prime Minister, he and Eden would never have accepted the western Neisse as the Polish frontier, which not only ejected three million more German refugees into the western zones of occupation, but also deprived these zones of the benefits of Silesian coal.[25] It is hard to see what he could have done, beyond perhaps insisting that British dissatisfaction was recorded in the Protocol in some form of words that did not wreck the whole conference. It is also reasonable to conjecture why he did not raise the same degree of objection to the expulsion of almost as many Germans from Czecho-slovakia, which took place at the same time.

The political map of Central Europe began, in effect, to be redrawn at Potsdam; what was on paper provisional became permanent in prac-

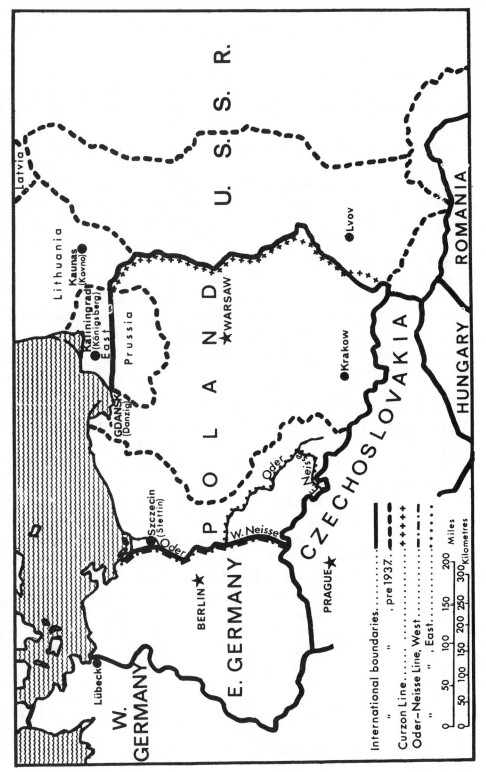

8. The Formation of Modern Poland

tice; and the Potsdam Agreement on German reparations also went, unintentionally, a long way towards the territorial reshaping of Germany. Molotov at once countered Byrnes' proposal on reparations by asking: "If reparations were not treated as a whole, what would happen to overall economic matters?" Byrnes insisted that his proposal did not affect the treatment of Germany as a single administrative and economic unit; and the "Economic Principles" of the Protocol of 2 August 1945 expressly stated that this was how the Allied Control Council would govern Germany. But Molotov's question was wholly to the point. And the memorandum written at the end of the conference by the senior British Treasury representative, David Waley,[26] is conclusive evidence that the British team were aware, as were some of the Americans at Potsdam, that the abstruse formula finally agreed regarding reparations was not unifying but divisive. As subsequent events were to prove, Section III* of the Potsdam Agreement lay close to the heart of the prolonged controversy that led ultimately to the division of Germany. Just how much trouble this section of the Protocol was storing up for the future becomes clear if three basic political and economic facts of Europe in the immediate aftermath of the war are recalled. These were the Soviet determination to milk Germany dry, the French insistence that the amputation of eastern Germany should be matched by a similar amputation in the west as "an essential condition for the security of Europe and the world,"[27] and the countervailing American and British refusal to allow the payment of reparations to be executed at the expense of feeding the German population in their zones of occupation—an expense which they foresaw would be their own, because both their zones had been historically dependent on food from the eastern part of Germany.

What looked at the time like the most solid achievement of the Grand Alliance at Potsdam was the creation of the Council of Foreign Ministers, an expansion of the consultative machinery established at Yalta. The compromise finally agreed about this at Potsdam provided

---

*Reproduced in full in Appendix VI.

for a membership of five (thereby including China as well as France); London was to be "the permanent seat of the joint Secretariat which the Council will form"; the first meeting was to be held there not later than 1 September 1945; the Council's immediate task was to draw up peace treaties with Italy, Romania, Bulgaria, Hungary, and Finland; and it was to be "utilised for the preparation of a peace settlement for Germany to be accepted by the Government of Germany when a government adequate for the purpose is established."*

The Atomic Attacks

Well before the Council could meet there had been dramatic developments, unforeseen in the agreements reached by the three heads of government at Potsdam. On 16 July Stimson received from Washington the first, brief report on the atomic explosion at Alamogordo, New Mexico, which had taken place at 0530 hours that morning. After lunching with Churchill on the following day, Stimson told him about the success of the test. Churchill was "strongly inclined against any disclosure" to Stalin, and Stimson argued against Churchill's view "at some length." On 18 July Truman asked Churchill what he "thought about telling the Russians. He [Truman] seemed determined to do this, but asked about the timing, and said that he thought that the end of the Conference would be best." Churchill's reply was twofold: it "might be better to hang it on the experiment, which was a new fact on which he and we had only just had knowledge"; and, "on behalf of His Majesty's Government," he "did not resist his [Truman's] proposed disclosure of the simple fact that we have this weapon."[28] In his diary four days later, Stimson described Churchill as "now not only . . . not

---

*The Protocol added this sentence: "For the discharge of these tasks the Council will be composed of members representing those States which were signatory to the terms of surrender imposed upon the enemy States concerned"; France was to be regarded as a signatory in the case of Italy. It was the strict Soviet interpretation of this procedural sentence that was the formal reason for the inauspicious breakdown of the first meeting of the Council of Foreign Ministers held in London two months later.

worried about giving the Russians information on the matter but . . . rather inclined to use it as an argument in our favour in negotiations." So far as final Anglo–American agreement on the atomic attack against Japan, required by the terms of the Churchill–Roosevelt agreements is concerned, the final stage was reached at Truman's meeting with Churchill (who had now read Groves' written report on the atomic test) on 22 July. Two days later, in a directive approved by Stimson, the commander of the U.S. Strategic Air Forces, General Carl Spaatz, was instructed to deliver the first atomic bomb "as soon as weather will permit visual bombing after about 3rd August 1945."[29]

On the same day after the plenary session had broken up, Truman "casually mentioned to Stalin that we had a new weapon of unusual destructive force." (He did not even hint that the weapon was atomic.) Stalin "showed no special interest. All he said was that he was glad to hear of it and hoped we would make 'good use of it against the Japanese.'" Churchill, who watched "the talk between these two potentates" from about five yards away, recorded in his memoirs ten years later his own certainty that at "that date Stalin had no special knowledge of the vast process" of Anglo–American research and of the "heroic gamble" of the United States' production of the bomb.[30] As we now know, Churchill and Truman were both wrong. But even if they had been right, Truman would not have damaged any Anglo–American interest had he handed Stalin a copy of the Smyth Report[31] which was due to be published in any case in August. (During the Interim Committee's earlier discussions in Washington, Marshall had even suggested that a Soviet observer should be invited to attend the explosion at Alamogordo.) Instead, on 26 July the ultimatum to Japan was published; on 30 July Stimson (by now back in Washington) informed the President that the "time schedule for Groves' project" was making such rapid progress that it was essential that the presidential statement to be released after the first atomic attack should be "available not later than Wednesday 1st August"; and, conscious that the conference was running late, Truman replied, "not sooner than August 2nd."[32]

On that day the Potsdam Conference ended. Thereafter the momentum of bureaucracy and the vagaries of the weather seem to have taken over. (The aircraft that dropped the atomic bomb on Hiroshima was, however, blessed by the USAAF chaplain before taking off from Tinian Field, in the Marianas.)[33] After the first bomb was dropped on 6 August, the timing of the second atomic attack, on Nagasaki, was purely military. In the seventy-two hours that separated the second attack from the first there was no review at political level, either in Washington or in London, or between the two capitals. Japan surrendered on 14 August 1945.*

So ended the Second World War, with no discussion of the fact that the world whose destiny the three leaders of the Grand Alliance were seeking to determine at Potsdam was at that very moment entering the nuclear age. And the dispositions regarding Germany which were agreed at the Conference of Berlin made it probable that Germany— quite apart from the territory lost to Poland—would be divided. In the event, no German Peace Conference was held. Instead, a *de facto* division of Germany gradually evolved in the years after Potsdam, the Soviet occupation zone emerging as the German Democratic Republic—the Prussian heartland, with parts of Saxony added to it—and the three western zones becoming the German Federal Republic. The frontiers of this divided Germany received general international recognition only in the 1970s—beginning with the Treaty of Moscow, concluded between the governments of the Federal German Republic and the Soviet Union in August 1970, and followed by other agreements, notably the Quadripartite Agreement on Berlin in 1971 and the Helsinki Final Act in 1975.[34] To these agreements and to the German Question the revolutionary events of the last two months of 1989 in Central and Eastern Europe added an entirely new political dimension, which will be considered in the chapter that follows.

---

*As previously agreed with the U.S. Government, the Soviet Union declared war on Japan on 8 August; the Red Army's invasion of Manchuria followed.

PART IV

THE LAST

ACT

19

THE BIG THREE:

INTO THE FUTURE

*They are ill discoverers that think there is no
land, when they can see nothing but sea.*

—*Francis Bacon (1605)*

Three Deaths

Churchill, Roosevelt and Stalin died in inverse order to their age. Of
the three members of this twentieth-century triumvirate, Roosevelt
died first, three months after he had begun his fourth term of office and
just before the war ended in Europe; only Stalin continued to rule, for
seven and a half years, after the end of the Second World War; and by
the time that Churchill, out of office for over six years, became Prime
Minister once again, Stalin had entered his final decline. In two of the
three countries the drama of the Grand Alliance was therefore played
out by understudies: Truman and Attlee.

·   ·   ·

At the time of death of the youngest of the Big Three, twelve years had passed since, in his first inaugural speech on Capitol Hill, Roosevelt had assured his fellow countrymen, paralysed by the impact of the Great Depression, that they had nothing to fear but fear itself. One of the principal consequences of the Second World War was that by the end the American people were "in the pleasant position of having to learn to live fifty percent better than they had ever lived before": a statement (made by the Secretary of the U.S. Treasury soon after Roosevelt's death)[1] which reflected the fact that the American gross national product had more than doubled in real terms during the war. The metropolitan territory of the United States (unlike that of its two partners in the Grand Alliance) was untouched by enemy action; and at home there were no civilians among the three hundred thousand American dead. Roosevelt was the American Commander-in-Chief; but within the United States he remained a controversial political figure to the very end. In the world at large, Roosevelt died at the height of his fame and power. In his presidential address on 8 December 1941, asking the U.S. Congress to declare war on Japan, Roosevelt had undertaken to wage war "through to absolute victory." Four months after his death, this promise would be climactically demonstrated, at Hiroshima and Nagasaki. But it had already been fulfilled by April 1945, when he died. Most of Berlin and Tokyo lay in ruins; victory in Europe was then imminent; and in the Pacific it was clearly in sight. By now all the main threads of international power—financial, nuclear and strategic—ran through a single pair of hands: those of the President of the United States of America.

When the first news flash—"WASHN-FDR DEAD"—reached London, Americans walking in the streets or travelling in buses suddenly found themselves offered sympathy by complete strangers. In Moscow, flags were flown at half-mast. In his tribute in the House of Commons, Churchill described Roosevelt as "the greatest American friend we have ever known."[2] In Stalin's words (in a message to Truman), "the American people and the United Nations have lost an outstanding world statesman and the herald of the organisation of peace and security after the war."[3] Yet, more than any of these tributes, what would have moved the man who had been denied a place in the Groton School roll of honour after the First World War would have been the Army-Navy Casualty List of 13 April 1945. The first of the "latest casualties in the military services, including next-of-kin," read: "ROOSEVELT, Franklin D., Commander in Chief, wife, Mrs Eleanor Roosevelt, the White House."[4] It was as a warrior—not only as a president—that Roosevelt's body was received in Washington. The funeral procession there, in which all the U.S. armed services (women as well as men) were represented, began on the morning of 14 April at Union Street Station and ended at the White House, where the coffin was laid in the East Room—the room in which Abraham Lincoln's body had lain exactly eighty years earlier. That evening it was returned to the presidential train, which reached Hyde Park on the following day, a Sunday. There the three volleys across the grave were fired by a funeral detachment of six hundred West Point cadets. Roosevelt's body was buried in the rose garden of the house where he had been born.

The second youngest of the triumvirs, Stalin, outlived Roosevelt by very nearly eight years. He thus ruled the Soviet Union for over a quarter of a century, leaving on Soviet society an imprint which—*glasnost'* and *perestroika* notwithstanding—will remain historically indelible, whether it is measured in terms of the millions of his fellow countrymen for whose death or bereavement he was responsible, or in terms of Soviet military, industrial and scientific achievements during the years of his supremacy in the Kremlin. Although the Soviet *sputnik* did not go into orbit until four years after Stalin's death, his country was well on the way to becoming a superpower before he died; the first Soviet atomic explosion—greeted with incredulity[5] for several weeks by many, both in Britain and the United States, at the time—took place in August 1949. For the first two and a half years after the end of the Second World War the triangular relationship between the three victorious governments continued, although it became less and less personal and increasingly fragile. And in July 1947 Stalin took one of the major decisions leading to the division of Europe: the Soviet refusal, extended to the Allies of the Soviet Union, to take part in the Marshall Plan.[6] As late as the summer of 1948, however, during the Soviet blockade of West Berlin, he could still refer to Britain, the Soviet Union and the United States as "allies," but by 1950—the pivotal year in the post-war period of history—the world was in the grip of the great schism* between East and West.

After the Great Fatherland War (as it was officially named in the Soviet Union) had been won, the soldiers who took part in the victory parade in Red Square threw down their captured standards as they marched past Stalin, just as the Imperial Army had done before the Tsar Alexander I after the Russian victory over Napoleon. Yet the windows that Stalin had allowed to be half opened in the Soviet Union during the war soon began to be closed again, one by one. Less than a year after the Red Army had captured Berlin, Stalin demanded from the Soviet people yet another gigantic effort, to reconstruct and to expand the Soviet industrial base, leaving the Soviet consumer to tighten his belt once again. The reflowering of Soviet arts, permitted during the war, was brought to a halt by a regime of drab conformism, presided over by Zhdanov, who silenced, among other Soviet writers, arguably the greatest Russian poet of the twentieth century, Anna Akhmatova, with a cheap jibe.[8] The sufferings endured by the Soviet people during the latter years of Stalin's rule were in a way even more senseless than those of the 1930s. For what was done in those terrible earlier years, some motive, however base, can usually be discerned. After the war this becomes increasingly difficult. Thousands of the Soviet soldiers who had somehow survived the conditions of German captivity found themselves, on their return to their own country, condemned to the *Gulag*. The technique of the political purge was resumed—there was

---

*Perhaps recalling the Great Schism that divided the western and eastern churches of Europe in the Middle Ages, Churchill (in his report to the House of Commons on Yalta) warned of the "sombre" danger that "some awful schism" might arise "between the Western democracies and the Russian Soviet Union."[7]

another Leningrad Affair, for example. And ominously, shortly before Stalin died, a Kremlin "doctors' plot" was revealed: but for his death, several of the doctors, many of them Jewish, normally attending members of the Politburo, would probably have faced the death sentence or the *Gulag* on trumped-up charges.* It is a measure of the pervasiveness of Stalin's system of government that, even though the head of his secret police, Beria, was executed soon after Stalin's death, it was not until February 1956 that Khrushchev dared to lift the veil on what was euphemistically called Stalin's "personality cult," in his report to the XXth Congress of the Soviet Communist Party—and then only in secret.

At the last Party Congress held in Stalin's lifetime, which opened on 5 October 1952, he was no longer capable of delivering the main report, of vast length as usual, which he had read himself at every Congress from 1924 onwards. (Instead, it was read in his presence by Georgii Malenkov, who at the time looked like Stalin's heir apparent and did indeed become Soviet Prime Minister, only to be ousted in 1955 by Khrushchev). Five months later Stalin died of a cerebral haemorrhage at his Kuntsevo *dacha,* where in 1941 he had received the news of the German invasion of his country and where he now lay speechless for four days after his stroke, no doctor being allowed near him by Beria for at least the first six hours.[10] Buried with pomp on 9 March 1953, Stalin's embalmed body was placed beside Lenin's in the Red Square mausoleum. It remained there for only eight years before being removed—on Khrushchev's orders—to take its place in the row of lesser Soviet Communist Party leaders behind.

---

*During the twilight period between Stalin's death and the delivery of Khrushchev's famous report on Stalin, Maisky (a Jewish ex-Menshevik), who had had the misfortune to be arrested on a charge of treason a few days before Stalin's death, was brought to trial, by which time the charge against him had been reduced to trivialities relating to his years at the London Embassy. His conviction was quashed on appeal and he was reinstated as a member of the Soviet Communist Party even before his appeal was heard. A member also of the Academy of Sciences, he died in comfortable retirement in 1975, aged over ninety.[9]

In Churchill's own words, early on the morning of 26 July 1945 he suddenly awoke "with a sharp stab of almost physical pain" and "a hitherto subconscious conviction" that he would lose the general election; and that "the power to shape the future would be denied" him.[11] Following his electoral defeat, once his initial reaction of Stygian gloom was overcome, and disregarding his wife's advice—that he should retire from political life after nearly half a century in Parliament—Churchill continued first as Leader of the Opposition for six and a half years, and then as Prime Minister for three and a half years from October 1951 onwards, until he resigned at the age of eighty.

In the early post-war years, Churchill's power of resilience showed itself once again. He resumed his painting. His beloved Chartwell (closed during the war) was reopened. Spared the disillusionment of conducting Britain's "financial Dunkirk" after the end of the war, he was, however, obliged to endure the galling experience of watching, from the Opposition front bench, a Labour Government gradually re-creating the special relationship with the United States which he had sought to establish during the war.[12] He contained his frustration on the whole, a notable exception being the occasion in December 1950 when he learnt for the first time that the Quebec Agreement on the atomic bomb, laboriously negotiated between himself and Roosevelt seven years earlier, had been abandoned. And his oratorical powers were undiminished—witness his celebrated "iron curtain" address to Westminster College at Fulton, Missouri, in March 1946 and his (much shorter and more remarkable) speech on European unity delivered in Zurich in September of that year.[13]

When Churchill was at last returned to office, having won the general election of 1951 by a narrow majority, his staff at 10 Downing Street, recalling the tempo of his wartime administration, put back the "Action this day" markers on the Prime Minister's desk. Aged almost seventy-seven, Churchill never used them again. The leadership that he exercised over his government in the 1950s was now mellow; and his failing energy was enough to enable him to concentrate only on a few issues, mainly of international policy. On the issues which did interest him, however, he still managed to show a greater measure of wisdom than most other people at that time. Thus, on 11 May 1953, two months after Stalin's death, without consulting Eisenhower (now President of the United States), he made this proposal:

> A conference on the highest level should take place between the leading Powers without long delay. This conference should not be overhung by a ponderous or rigid agenda, or led into mazes of technical details. The conference should be confined to the smallest number of Powers and persons possible. It should meet with a measure of informality and a still greater measure of privacy and seclusion. It might be that no hard-faced agreements would be reached, but there might be a general feeling among those gathered together that they might do something better than tear the human race, including themselves, into bits.[14]

Nothing came of Churchill's initiative, which was unwelcome in Washington and opposed by his own Foreign Secretary. Six weeks later he suffered a major stroke, which left his left side paralysed for a time. After an amazing recovery, in his last major speech in the House of Commons, delivered in March 1954—and (like all his speeches) written by himself—he included in a survey of world affairs lasting three quarters of an hour a far more sophisticated definition of strategic nuclear deterrence than the doctrine of "massive retaliation" which John Foster Dulles would shortly make famous. In Churchill's words: "It may well be that we shall, by a process of sublime irony, have reached a stage where safety will be the sturdy child of terror, and survival the twin brother of annihilation."[15]

Nevertheless, he could not go on. "More and more time was given to bezique [Churchill's favorite card game] and ever less to public business."[16] He was succeeded as Prime Minister by Eden, who had waited with mounting impatience to cross over from the Foreign Office on the south side of Downing Street to No. 10 on the opposite side. After the dinner party which Churchill gave on 4 April 1955, on the eve of his resignation—the Queen was his guest—Churchill's private secretary accompanied the Prime Minister up to his room, where he sat on his bed for several minutes in silence, still in full evening dress, wearing his Garter, knee breeches and Order of Merit. Then he exclaimed: "I don't believe Anthony can do it"—as the Suez crisis of 1956 would prove accurate up to the hilt.[17]

Until about the end of 1957 Churchill retained his extraordinary buoyancy.[18] Thereafter, a sad decline set in. Although he lived until the age of ninety, he became increasingly deaf, silent and withdrawn. Indeed, he might have said of himself what a much younger soldier-statesman, Simón Bolívar, said before he died: *"Sembré el mar"* ("I have sown the sea").[19] Long before this, in 1947—in a daydream conversation with his father, of which Churchill left a remarkable record[20]—he seems to have been unable to bring himself to tell his father that he had been Prime Minister, or even a member of Parliament. Instead, just at the moment when, in the dream, his father gives him an opening ("I really wonder you didn't go into politics"), their conversation comes to an end.

Churchill died peacefully at his house in London on 24 January 1965. The magnificence of his funeral can be compared only with that of the great Duke of Wellington, a century earlier. Before the funeral, Churchill's coffin lay in state in Westminster Hall, where over three hundred thousand people filed past the catafalque of the man now revered as a national hero. Among the three thousand who attended the funeral ceremony at St. Paul's Cathedral was Eisenhower, in his private capacity,[21] but the chief foreign mourner was de Gaulle, now President of France. He wrote these words about Churchill to the Queen: *"Dans ce grand drame, il fut le plus grand."*[22] Churchill was buried at Bladon, in Oxfordshire, less than a mile from where he had been born at Blenheim Palace.

PROBLEMS OF REASSESSMENT

Thus—to return to 1945—from 12 April onwards the student of the relationship between the Big Three begins to lose his Ariadne's thread. On that day death destroyed one of the triumvirs of the Grand Alliance; three and a half months later the second was removed by the ballot-box, a week before the Potsdam Conference ended; and by the end of July 1945 Stalin was the only member of the wartime triumvirate left in office. Even at a distance of nearly fifty years, although a reassessment of the three wartime leaders and their relationship with each other can answer some questions that were once obscure, it must still leave some questions unanswered and offer some answers that are tentative.

Immediately after Roosevelt's death the most senior and experienced member of Roosevelt's wartime administration, Henry Stimson, described him as "An ideal Commander in Chief . . . our greatest war President. And his courage . . . in times of great emergency won him the loyalty and affection of all who served under him." Yet, during Roosevelt's lifetime, Stimson's diary is full of entries such as "one-man government" and "this madhouse of Washington."[23] So long as Roosevelt lived, his individualistic system worked. Under this system the White House Map Room had for three and a half years been (with a very few exceptions)* the single nerve centre of American decision-making. In war, as in peace, Roosevelt was pastmaster of the art of multiple options. After pursuing two contradictory policies—often by appointing two men of opposed views with overlapping functions—when he finally concluded that one option must exclude the other (or the rest), his decision was not necessarily recorded; at most, an "OK, FDR" might eventually be forthcoming. In the first three months of 1945 he was beginning to change his mind on some questions—for example, France and Indo-China. How he would have handled the global issues of the second half of 1945, had he lived and had he retained the health to confront them, is what he himself would have called a very "iffy" question. So far as international relations are concerned, Roosevelt died politically intestate.

Churchill, on the other hand, almost completed the course; and the

---

*One such exception was Bretton Woods: the Final Act agreed at the 1944 Monetary and Financial Conference was the joint achievement of John Maynard Keynes and Harry Dexter White.[24]

record of his decisions during the war is abundantly documented. In the last volume of his memoirs, however—written long after the war, but when few official documents were accessible—Churchill gave other historians a powerful push towards acceptance of the interpretation of the events of the final months of the Second World War offered in that volume, entitled *Triumph and Tragedy,* which he published with political amendments and omissions dictated by considerations of the Cold War (as his letter to President Eisenhower, already quoted, makes clear).[25]

As for Stalin, although Soviet scholars are now beginning to have access to the Moscow archives,[26] there are still many *belye pyatna* (blank spots). By connecting pieces of evidence from a wide variety of sources, the historian can construct a mosaic of Stalin that may hang together at first sight. But intellectual rigour obliges him to add that there is much about this intensely contradictory man that remains speculative.

Attitudes

The political differences between Churchill, Roosevelt and Stalin were not confined to the obvious gulf of Marxist ideology. Had Roosevelt lived, he and Churchill would hardly have seen eye to eye about the role of the British Empire; in the press conference that he gave on board the U.S.S. *Quincy* on his way back from Yalta, Roosevelt publicly dismissed Churchill's view of colonial issues as "mid-Victorian."[27] During the war, moreover, none of the three men neglected his country's national interest; they began to discuss the territorial settlement that each of them wanted in different parts of the world, long before the tide of war had turned in favour of the Grand Alliance. Had Churchill, Roosevelt and Stalin been different kinds of men, their relationship might perhaps have remained simply what it was in origin: an "alliance" that had to be "combin'd" because they were all three "bay'd about with many enemies." Nevertheless, they also soon began to exchange ideas about the international structure to be established after the war, in order to preserve world peace, primarily by making future German and Japanese aggression impossible, and to ensure the rebuilding of the world economy.

The relative weight that each of the leaders gave to different aspects of the new world order varied, but one vital premise was shared by all of them: unless the three members of the Grand Alliance—the "Great Powers," as they were still called at the end of the war—continued to work together after the war, whatever new international structure they then agreed to establish could not be expected to work in practice. This lesson of Versailles was an experience still vividly recalled by Churchill, Roosevelt and Stalin[28]—and indeed by anyone who had experienced the tragic consequences of its failure. Thus, as the relationship between the Big Three grew more personal, the post-war aims of the Grand Alliance became increasingly far-reaching. Just as the triangular relationship was not static, but dynamic, so too the balance within the evolving relationship shifted as the war went on. The four-day meeting of the Big Three at Teheran was a turning point. By the time they met again at Yalta, Churchill had become the junior partner. And at Potsdam the conference was accurately described by a senior British participant as a meeting of the "Big Two and a Half."[29]

Roosevelt's attitude towards Stalin was, like all his policies, both domestic and foreign, always pragmatic, although it was conceptually based on his "cardinal" idea of the U.S.-Soviet relationship (described in Chapter 15). His attitude towards Churchill changed as the war developed. In 1940 it was still tentative; it was at its most intimate for a period of roughly two years, measured from their first meeting at the Atlantic Conference in August 1941; a gradual decline set in after the Teheran Conference; and yet it could still be lit up by occasional flashes.

By contrast, Churchill's attitude towards Stalin fluctuated. On the one hand, Churchill was impressed by Stalin's outstanding qualities—a computer-like memory (he never took a note at a summit conference); his lucidity in argument; and his ability suddenly to switch his mood and his negotiating technique from *grubost'* (to use Lenin's famous description of Stalin)[30] to charm. He was also a good host—something that appealed to Churchill. Thus at the beginning of 1944 Churchill remarked—of the Soviet-Polish dispute—that if only he could dine with Stalin once a week, "there would be no trouble at all"; and as late as Potsdam he could still repeatedly exclaim, "I like that man."[31] On the other hand, for an Englishman who had first held high office during the closing phase of the Concert of Europe—the international system that had kept the peace, tolerably well, during the hundred years that separated the Congress of Vienna from August 1914—the post-war balance of European continental power was a consideration of the first magnitude. And as the Second World War drew towards its close— the Anglo-Soviet Treaty of Alliance notwithstanding—the daunting prospect of Britain being "alone with the Bear" in Europe preyed increasingly on Churchill's mind. Something of his ambivalence towards Stalin may perhaps be reflected in Churchill's gesture—almost a personal farewell—at Potsdam, when in his own words: "I filled a small-sized claret glass with brandy for him and another for myself. I looked at him significantly. We both drained our glasses at a stroke and gazed approvingly at one another."[32]

Churchill himself remarked that he had wooed Stalin as a young man might woo a maid, and that no lover had ever studied every whim of his mistress as he had those of Roosevelt.[33] The style of the attitude that he adopted towards Stalin was indeed as nothing by comparison with the degree of deference that he practiced in almost all his exchanges with Roosevelt. This deference has often been explained by the suggestion that Churchill was conscious of the fact that Roosevelt, unlike himself, was a head of state. Although the difference in the constitutional status of the two leaders is undoubted (and it was also the reason why the U.S. President took the chair at all three tripartite conferences during the war), a difference between Churchill and Roosevelt which counted for more was the fact that in the 1940s Churchill, unlike Roosevelt, had not been elected head of the government by popular vote. It was the wish to be so elected that probably contributed more than any other factor to Churchill's decision not to retire from political life, as he could have done, loaded with the highest honours, after the end of the war. Be that as it may, Churchill was deliberate in his use of flattery in dealing with Roosevelt; "he had to play the role of courtier and seize opportunities as and when they arise."[34] There were, however, moments when Churchill's pursuit of an enduring personal relationship with Roosevelt suddenly erupted in a Churchillian explosion of a kind that was familiar to the Prime Minister's British advisers, but not to the President of the United States. A notable example was the occasion at the Second Quebec Conference, when he burst out to Roosevelt: "What do you want me to do? Get on my hind legs and beg like Fala?"*[35]

In order to illustrate the distinction that Stalin drew between his two partners in the Grand Alliance, his ironical quip is often quoted, to the effect that, although both needed careful watching, Roosevelt would take a rouble out of your pocket, whereas Churchill would even take a kopeck. Although this alleged comparison tells us something, there are other, more illuminating, recollections—for example, one by Andrei Gromyko in his memoirs, and the other by Stanisław Mikołajczyk in the memoirs that he wrote after he had left Poland.[36] The first of these recalls a question about Roosevelt put to Gromyko by Stalin, apparently out of the blue, during one of the intervals of the Yalta Conference. "Is he clever?" Stalin asked Gromyko. Gromyko's reply, readily accepted by Stalin at the time—that if not, Roosevelt could not have been elected President of the United States four times running—need not detain us.[37] What is interesting is that a man of Stalin's intelligence, with all the direct experience that he already had of Roosevelt, should have felt it necessary to ask this question at all in February 1945. What Mikołajczyk recalled is a remark made to him by Stalin, summing up Churchill late one evening at Potsdam: "Churchill did not trust us and in consequence we could not fully trust him either." Like most remarks made very late at night, this one might have required some qualification in the cold light of morning. The earlier stage of the Churchill-Stalin relationship was different; at least during the final months of the war, however, both parts of this remark were true.[38]

---

*Fala was Roosevelt's Scottish terrier.

Motivations

If this is the way in which the members of the twentieth-century triumvirate saw their relationship with each other, how did they see themselves? Of the three men, it is Roosevelt who still today, as he did when he was alive, eludes precise definition; even with all the resources of the Presidential Library at Hyde Park at their disposal, historians have the same problem in penetrating his "heavily forested interior" as his contemporaries did. Whatever the inner force that drove Roosevelt, it was something that gave him a sixth political sense, thanks to which he was able to persuade others that they could achieve the impossible: witness his much quoted injunction to his two New Deal advisers, holding opposite views, that they must "weave them together." It was the same combination of light-hearted self-confidence that enabled Roosevelt to look towards the second half of the twentieth century with a kind of intuitive certainty. Sometimes this intuition, because it was not always soundly based in fact, led him astray, as in the case of his policy towards France. And, although many years after his death events justified Roosevelt's belief that China would eventually emerge as a world power, he took an unconscionably long time to realise what Chiang Kai-shek and the *Kuomintang* movement were really like. Nevertheless, perhaps only an American who had, for a time during the 1930s, successfully played the role of President of all the people could believe that he could be equally successful in reconciling apparently irreconcilable forces on the stage of world politics.

The most powerful source of Churchill's motivation was the past. The son of a man who had defied his own political party in the nineteenth century and the descendant of a great soldier-statesman of the eighteenth century, he was steeped in history: the history of his family, of his country and of his country's role in the history of nations. Where Europe was concerned, this historical knowledge was often a sure guide—witness his belief in France's eventual recovery, firmly held even at the moment of deepest French humiliation, and his prophetic vision of Franco-German reconciliation, dramatically expressed in his speech delivered in Zurich only a year after the end of the

Second World War. Outside Europe and America, his knowledge was shakier; and in what he once described as "those wild lands"[39] of the Far East, he went grievously wrong. Nevertheless, just as de Gaulle had *une certaine idée de la France,* so Churchill had a concept of Britain, which stood him—and the world—in good stead in the summer of 1940.

To separate consideration of Stalin as statesman from that of the horrors of his system of personal rule is not easy, but the attempt must be made. Stalin was committed by the dialectical approach of Marxist theory to a long-term view of history. But he was also a Georgian, born in a marchland and therefore accustomed to the ferocity of the local loyalties and the sudden shifts of alliance that are characteristic of feuding peoples living on the frontier dividing great empires. Superimposed on this national heritage was the fact that Stalin was a Georgian turned Russian, who saw himself in the tradition of the greatest innovators in the history of his adopted country: Catherine the Great (herself a German), Peter the Great, and last but by no means least Ivan the Terrible. The well-attested interest that Stalin took in Eisenstein's script of his film of Ivan's life was no accident. Stalin was increasingly obsessed, during his own lifetime, by his position in history.[40]

A Balance Sheet

Much of the jargon of the Cold War lived on well after the Cold War itself was virtually over.[41] Today, however, it has become historically inadmissible to take as the basic premise of an assessment of the Big Three the political model that made up the conventional wisdom of the Cold War—in both West and East—and then to apply its assumptions retroactively to earlier events; in particular to what Churchill, Roosevelt and Stalin succeeded in doing together and to what they failed to do. (The application of a model, especially one couched in jargon, to any period of history seldom proves to be a useful tool; and the use of technical jargon is "always symptomatic of the fact that a model is at work.")[42] Instead, what is needed for a reassessment of the triangular relationship is to use the documentary evidence of the period that is now available in order to seek to re-create how the world, and the terrible events that shook it in the first half of the 1940s, looked at the time to the three principal actors and to the peoples of the countries that they were leading in alliance with each other.

Drawn up in this light, the collegiate balance sheet of the Big Three shows, I suggest, two great objectives achieved, set against two great issues left unresolved. These achievements and these omissions must both be assessed with full account taken of the fact that in these fateful years—as in all periods of history—what did not happen was just as important as what did happen. First and foremost, therefore, Hitler did not win the war. This is a prime example of something which, as the century draws towards its close, we tend to take increasingly for granted. Yet no expert knowledge of the military history of the Second World War is needed (a glance at some of the maps in this book is enough) to understand how close the Third Reich, with its allies— above all, Japan—came to winning it. The human carnage and the material destruction of 1939–45 were such that at this distance their nature and their scale are hard to grasp, perhaps even more for younger generations, grown accustomed to the televised horrors of subsequent warfare. The immense cost to civilisation of these six years of the Second World War was high enough as it was. But it pales into insignificance by comparison with the suffering that the world—above all, Europe—would have had to endure if the outcome of the war had left Hitler the victor. Any suggestion that in that event his adversaries in the war, let alone the millions whom he classified as *Untermenschen,* could have expected even relatively generous peace terms, flies in the face of the evidence not only of the Second, but also of the First World War.[43]

The primary condition of the victory of the Grand Alliance was that the Big Three should remain united. This they did. Soundings for separate negotiations there were, but they never got very far. Had one of the three broken ranks, some kind of armed truce might have resulted; a third round of world war might have followed later; but in any event the problem would not have been solved—only postponed. For Europe faced a double problem (and partly for that reason, the

European conflict cannot easily be compared with the conflict in the Pacific and South-East Asia). On one level, the Second World War may be regarded as the second phase of a thirty-year struggle for the control of Central Europe—the classical key to European hegemony—and, in this sense, a conflict of *Realpolitik*, even if the Second World War was distinguished from the First World War by its global reach and by its savagery. On another level, it was also seen by the men and women who took part in it and who lived through it as a war of ideas. The historian must not allow himself to be misled either by the similarity between the techniques of mass repression used both by Hitler and by Stalin, or by the dissimilarity of the reasons for which the three Great Powers entered the war one after the other. Once they were all three at war, their leaders were bound together not only because they were "at the stake," but also because they shared the belief that Hitler's brand of fascism—Nazism—must be eradicated.

The intensity of this belief varied from country to country—at its strongest in the one whose people suffered by far the most from German invasion and occupation, the Soviet Union—but it was common to all three countries of the Grand Alliance. By fascism, what most people, of whatever political persuasion themselves, understood was not the Fascist political system in its original form: the corporate state introduced in Italy by Mussolini in the immediate aftermath of the First World War and tempered by many specifically Italian factors (such as the continued existence in Italy of other powerful institutions, the easy-going national environment and the spread of venality and incompetence among the hierarchs of the Italian Fascist Party during nearly a quarter of a century of power). What they abhorred was Nazism: the system of personal power ruthlessly applied by Hitler, a decade after Mussolini's accession to power, first in Germany and Austria and then extended, as the racist domination of the *Herrenvolk*, imposed on the territories of Europe in which his "New European Order" was successively established from 1939 onwards. This, then, was the first and the greatest achievement of the Big Three: victory in Europe, which not only destroyed Hitler personally, but swept away Nazism—the ideological basis both of the Third Reich, which he had created, and of his supremacy over the tormented European continent.*

The second achievement of Churchill, Roosevelt and Stalin is one that has received general recognition over forty years afterwards. Until quite recently it was reasonable to take the view that the United Nations Organisation had declined to a point where its founding fathers would scarcely have been able to recognise it. Today, thanks mainly to the sea-change in the superpower relationship, the United Nations—and in particular the Security Council[44]—is at last beginning to play the role in the structure of world order envisaged nearly fifty years ago by Churchill, Roosevelt and Stalin. Whereas hardly any conceivable reform could have converted the League of Nations into a convincing international instrument, by comparison, the machinery of the United Nations Organisation, which the Big Three established in its place, was well designed. What it lacked for forty years was not a workable framework, but the political will of the major powers to use the organisation for the international purposes which Churchill, Roosevelt and Stalin originally intended it to serve. This will has now at the last been forthcoming, in particular since 7 December 1988, when Mikhail Gorbachev redefined the Soviet Union's attitude towards "the interdependence of the contemporary world" and—among other things—described the United Nations as blending "together the interests of different states" and being "the only organisation capable of merging into a single current their bilateral, regional and global efforts."[45]

Against those two principal achievements, the balance sheet must set the two great issues that the Big Three left unresolved. These were the impact on world strategy and politics of nuclear weaponry and the future of Central Europe, above all of Germany—respectively, the core of post-war geopolitics and the ancient heart of Europe. At Pots-

---

*Their parallel victory in Asia led on to a political settlement in the Indian subcontinent and to the renaissance of a new Japan—certainly not part of the collective design of the Big Three, but nonetheless indirect consequences (of far-reaching significance both in Asia and worldwide) which flowed from the defeat of Japan by the Allied powers.

dam the second of these two great issues became the subject of James Byrnes' botched deal, while the first—the core of post-war geopolitics—was never addressed either at Yalta or at Potsdam at all.

We can now see clearly that the smiling faces[46] of the three leaders at the end of the Berlin Conference had something in common with the enigmatic words that Shakespeare put in the mouth of one of the Roman triumvirs in *Julius Caesar*:

> *And some, that smile, have in their hearts, I fear,*
> *Millions of mischiefs.*

What Stalin was thinking while this photograph was taken at Potsdam is still largely guesswork. From the American archive, Truman's thoughts can be deduced (not very profound at that time—his moments as a remarkable President came much later). The initial shock with which Attlee reacted to his initiation into the atomic secret—although Deputy Prime Minister in the Coalition Government, he had not been included in the atomic inner circle of ministers—was eloquently recorded, immediately after the Potsdam Conference had ended, in a memorandum written in his own hand, which concluded with the words: "I can see no other course than that I should on behalf of the Government put the whole case to President Truman and propose that he and I and Stalin should forthwith take counsel together . . . I believe that only a bold course can save . . . civilisation."[47]

The historian can only conjecture what the Potsdam Conference might have been like, had the original Big Three conducted it—above all, if Roosevelt had been there, both alive and well. No one can say with any degree of plausibility, either "Had Roosevelt lived, things would have been better ordered," or "Roosevelt would have done no better than Truman and he might have done worse." All that seems probable is that things would have been different. Roosevelt might well have made another attempt to confer with Stalin alone in advance, without Churchill. But even had he at last succeeded in doing so, Churchill would probably have prevailed on him—once again—to confer with him before the trilateral encounter at Potsdam, which could not have been avoided. At Potsdam, it would surely have occurred to Roosevelt (as it did not to Byrnes and Truman), in negotiating the Central European settlement, to make some use of Stalin's request for an American loan for the reconstruction of his devastated country. And it is hard to imagine Roosevelt either addressing to Stalin the few laconic words that Truman used, on their way out of the plenary session of the conference on 24 July 1945,[48] or—had he done so—drawing the same facile conclusion about Soviet atomic ignorance from Stalin's enigmatic response. Whether or not Gromyko's recollection of Stalin's expression of his belief at the time of Potsdam—that there must be international agreement that "nuclear energy should be only allowed for peaceful purposes."[49]—is accurate, at least some kind of nuclear dialogue might have begun while the leaders of the three victorious powers were conferring together personally, for the last time. As it was, concealment on both sides fuelled suspicion still further: *omne ignotum pro magnifico.* * These questions are speculative, and the only remaining source of evidence that may help to suggest the answers lies in the Soviet, rather than in the American, archive.

The two achievements of the original Big Three are unlikely to be challenged by whatever fresh evidence may still be forthcoming, from whatever source. Of their two failures, their neglect of the nuclear issue is, with the hindsight of almost half a century, astounding. The nuclear genie was already irrevocably out of the bottle well before the time of Potsdam.[50] Even in the official American report on atomic energy published in the United States only six days after Hiroshima, Henry Smyth observed that the questions raised by future atomic developments "should be debated by the people and decisions made by the people through their representatives." Instead, during the decade that followed the two atomic attacks on Japan in 1945, "the relatively few ... privileged to work behind the atomic security barrier ... found

---

*Tacitus' epigram may be roughly paraphrased as "ignorance always intensifies awe."

themselves ever more isolated in a world their fellow citizens had never seen."[51] The barrier of secrecy is today no longer what it was during the first ten years after Hiroshima and Nagasaki. But we are all living with the geopolitical consequences of the failure in the summer of 1945 to debate even in secret, let alone in public, the great political and strategic issues raised by the development of nuclear weapons.

As for Central Europe, Harold Nicolson's warning—that after a long war it is impossible to make a quick peace—was borne out by what happened. The legacy of hatred left by the Second World War in the territories where it had begun in 1939 was so bitter that it would have been an extraordinary achievement if the Big Three at Yalta or those who took the decisions about this issue at Potsdam had succeeded in settling there problems whose solution had eluded earlier statesmen, with far more time spent deliberating at the conference tables of Vienna in 1814–15 and of Versailles in 1919. (There were some striking resemblances between Potsdam and the conferences of the past, however; what had been called the "transference of souls"[52] in 1815 became the mass migrations of 1945.) And the ink was scarcely dry on the Potsdam agreements when the new British Foreign Secretary, Ernest Bevin, wrote an accurate prophecy:

> The future too of the German people is going to be a constant source of insecurity, and every sort of political trick will be resorted to in order to control or eliminate this eventual reservoir of power. The French demands on the Ruhr and the Rhineland, and Russia's action in transferring Eastern Germany to Poland are already examples of this tendency, and when the German people recover consciousness we may be sure they themselves will soon be playing an active part in these highly dangerous manoeuvres.[53]

The *de facto* European settlement, which gradually evolved from Potsdam onwards, halted, though it did not eliminate for ever, the internecine nationalist quarrels that had bedevilled Central and Eastern Europe for over a century before the Second World War. (Almost all the European nationalist and irredentist problems that were familiar in the earlier twentieth century are now reappearing on the international stage.) Thus it brought order—of a kind—to the European continent at last. Western Europe was able to make use of this unaccustomed stability to surge forward on a wave of economic development on a scale beyond anything that Churchill, Roosevelt or Stalin could have conceived. Eastern Europe, on the other hand, paid for this stability a price that became increasingly heavy in economic (and also environmental) terms with the passage of the years, while in terms of human rights it was barely calculable.

A Second Chance

On 9 November 1989 the German Question itself at last returned to the international agenda, in the very heart of Europe: Berlin. The breaching of the Berlin Wall, followed by the decision to demolish it, is only the most dramatic of the succession of revolutionary changes which, in the course of 1989, called the post-war European settlement in question. The eventual outcome of these momentous events, which will include German unification, is at the moment of writing unforeseeable. Once again high hopes are being raised, comparable with those of forty-five years ago. Walter Lippmann's assessment then of the "prospect of a settled peace" found an echo in the observation made by Václaw Havel in the course of his memorable address "Words on Words," delivered (significantly, to a German audience) on 15 October 1989, over two months before he became President of Czechoslovakia—that it was a long time since there were so many grounds for hoping that everything would turn out well.[54]

Within a few years of Lippmann's remark, it had become the general assumption in both East and West, though for different reasons, that the Cold War was inevitable from the outset. True, hindsight suggests that it was a probable development from the outcome of the Second World War. But in human affairs, as Francis Bacon well understood, probability and inevitability must never be confused. As was suggested in the Preface, the great decisions of history tend to be reached by a hairsbreadth. In 1945 there was a chance, albeit a slender one, of an outcome different from the Cold War that followed. In the grim aftermath of the Second World War, this chance, that "concord" between the Big Three might lead "the world family of democratic nations" towards "enduring peace"—the vision of the Declaration of the Three Powers issued by Churchill, Roosevelt and Stalin on 1 December 1943, at the end of their first encounter—was missed.

Today, a second chance of "concord" is being offered to the leaders of the three centres of power on which the future of contemporary Europe, from the Atlantic to the Urals, depends: the two superpowers and a restored Europe, that will now include a united Germany.* To his expression of hope in the future in 1989, President Havel added this essential rider:

> At the same time, there have never been so many reasons for us to fear that if everything went wrong, the catastrophe would be final.

One catastrophe in the course of a century, during which the European continent has already endured a Thirty Years' War, is enough.

---

*Since this chapter was written, the two Germanies (to be united in October) and the Four Occupying Powers have concluded the Treaty on the Final Settlement with respect to Germany, in Moscow on 12 September 1990.

NOTE ON ABBREVIATIONS AND CODENAMES, NOMENCLATURE, TRANSLITERATION AND EXCHANGE RATES

Abbreviations and Codenames*

ABC	American–British–Canadian Staff Conversations, 1941
ABDA	American–British–Dutch–Australian Command, 1942
AK	Armja Krajowa (Home Army, the Polish Resistance)
AFHQ	Allied Force Headquarters
ANAKIM	Seaborne assault on Rangoon, planned for 1943
ARCADIA	First Washington Conference, 1941–42
ARGONAUT	Malta and Yalta Conferences, 1945
AVALANCHE	Salerno landing, 1944

---

*For a further list of abbreviations used in the Notes for sources to which frequent reference is made, see the Documentary Sources, pp. 499 ff. Codenames are italicized in the text of this book, although during the war, following military usage, they were spelled in capital letters.

ANVIL	Invasion of southern France, 1944
BARBAROSSA	German invasion of the Soviet Union, 1942
BEF	British Expeditionary Force
BOLERO	Build-up of U.S. forces in Britain, for subsequent operations in Europe
BUCCANEER	Proposal for operation against the Andaman Islands
BURZA	"Storm" (Polish codename for the Warsaw Rising, 1944)
CIGS	Chief of the Imperial General Staff
COMINTERN	The (Moscow-based) Third Communist International
CPSU	Communist Party of the Soviet Union
DRACULA	Proposed airborne and seaborne attack against Rangoon, 1945
DRAGOON	Later codename for *Anvil*
EAM/ELAS	Greek resistance movement and army
ENIGMA	High-grade German cypher
EUREKA	Teheran Conference
FALL WEISS	German invasion of Poland, 1939
GCCS	Government Communications and Cyphers School (Bletchley Park cryptographic centre)
GKO	(Soviet) State Defence Committee
GULAG	Soviet labour camp administration
GYMNAST	Invasion of North Africa, 1942
HUSKY	Invasion of Sicily, 1943
JUPITER	Proposal for the invasion of northern Norway
LST	Landing Ship, Tank (landing craft)
NKVD	(Soviet) National Committee of State Security (now the KGB, formerly *Cheka,* OGPU)
OCTAGON	Second Quebec Conference, 1944
OKW	*Oberkommando der Wehrmacht* (Supreme Command of the German Armed Forces)
OSS	Office of Stategic Services (U.S.)
OVERLORD	Invasion of northern France, 1944 (originally codenamed *Round-Up*)
POUM	*Partido Obrero de Unificación Marxista* (Spain)
QUADRANT	First Quebec Conference, 1943
ROUND-UP	Invasion of Europe, planned for 1943
SA	*Sturm Abteilung* (Stormtroopers, or Brownshirts)
SEALION	German plan for invasion of Britain
SHINGLE	Landing at Anzio, 1944
SIGINT	Anglo–American term for signals intelligence
SLEDGEHAMMER	(Limited) invasion of Europe, planned for 1942

SOE	Special Operations Executive (British)
SS	*Schutz Staffel*
SYMBOL	Casablanca Conference, 1943
TERMINAL	Potsdam Conference, 1945
TOLSTOY	Moscow Conference, October 1944
TORCH	Invasion of North Africa (originally codenamed Gymnast), 1942
TORGPRED	Head of Trade Department of Soviet missions abroad
TRIDENT	Washington Conference, 1943
TUBE ALLOYS	British codename for atomic bomb (the U.S. codename was D SI)
TYPHOON	Final German offensive against Moscow, 1941
ULTRA	Decyphering of high-grade German cypher
V-E DAY	Victory in Europe
V-J DAY	Victory in Japan
ZITADELLE	German offensive at Kursk, 1943

Nomenclature

First names are always given on first mention in the text (and occasionally thereafter), except in the case of some Russians, for whom the Russian practice of the initials of name and patronymic has been followed. Nicknames have been avoided in all languages. Titles, other than military, are generally omitted in the text, but they may be found in the Index (or sometimes in the Notes), as is also the case with second names.

Two apparently simple words present a problem during the period covered by this book: "Britain" and "British." By foreigners, the words "England" and "English" were then in general use (for example, in Russian sources). Churchill himself used "British Empire" to mean what, in correct usage, was the "British Empire and Commonwealth." And the British Army during the Second World War included, under British command, units from the United Kingdom, the Dominions, India and the Colonies (as well as units from Allied countries). Strictly speaking, therefore, a military historian seeks to distinguish between British, Imperial and British-controlled units; in the Eighth Army, for example, there were units of all three kinds; and to complicate matters further, a division of the Indian Army would consist of a mixture of British and Indian regiments. In the present study, however, the terms "Britain" and "British" have been used for the sake of simplicity even in some contexts where they are not entirely accurate.

Transliteration

For cyrillic, the system used by the journal *Soviet Studies* (published for Glasgow University by Carfax, Oxford) has been generally followed, with the important exception of the word *net,* which has become anglicised as *nyet.* For Chinese, rather than convert to pinyin the spelling in documents of the time, which used the older system of Chinese transliteration, and in maps relating to the period, the older system has been retained both in quotation and in the text. Similarly, Teheran has been preferred to the modern spelling, Tehran.

Exchange Rates

Although the word "billion" was not generally used in Britain during this period to mean a thousand million, it is so used throughout this book.

In order to convert to 1989 value amounts that are expressed (as they are in Parts II–III of this book) in prices current during the Second World War, it is necessary to multiply them by a factor to take into account inflation; there is a wide difference between the U.S. dollar and the pound sterling multiplier, and in any case the calculations involved can only be approximate. However, as a rough yardstick, an average dollar multiplier of 7.5 and an average pound sterling multiplier of 16 may be applied (Source—U.S. Department of Labor and the U.K. Department of Employment indices). The U.S.-U.K. exchange rate throughout the war was $4.03 to the pound sterling.

A SELECTIVE CHRONOLOGY
OF THE SECOND WORLD WAR

1939

1 September	German forces invade Poland
3 September	Great Britain and France declare war on Germany
11 October	Letter from Einstein read to Roosevelt about potential atomic bomb
17 September	Red Army invades Poland
27 September	German forces take Warsaw
28 September	**German-Soviet Frontier and Friendship Treaty signed in Moscow: Fourth Partition of Poland**
4 November	U.S. Neutrality Act passed; "cash and carry"
30 November	Red Army invades Finland

1940

12 March	**Finnish-Soviet Treaty signed in Moscow; major territorial concessions made to Soviet Union**

28 March	Anglo-French Supreme War Council agrees not to conclude peace or armistice without mutual consent
9 April	German forces occupy Denmark and invade Norway
9 April–7 June	Norwegian campaign; Anglo-French forces capture Narvik but later obliged to evacuate it
10 May	German forces invade Low Countries and France
10 May	**Churchill appointed Prime Minister and Minister of Defence; forms all-party Coalition Government**
15 May	Holland surrenders
27 May–4 June	Dunkirk evacuation
28 May	Belgium surrenders
June 1940–June 1943	Battle of the Atlantic*
10 June	Italy declares war on Great Britain and France
14 June	German forces take Paris
22 June	German-French Armistice signed; northern France under German military occupation
3 July	British bombardment of French fleet at Mers-el-Kebir
10 July–15 September	[Air] Battle of Britain; *Luftwaffe* defeated
2 September	Anglo-American "Destroyers-Bases" agreement signed
17 September	Hitler postpones invasion of Britain (Operation *Sealion*) indefinitely
23 September	British and Free French forces fail to take Dakar
27 September	**Tripartite Pact signed between Germany, Italy and Japan**
28 October	Italian forces invade Greece; subsequently driven back into Albania
5 November	**Roosevelt elected U.S. President for third term**
12–14 November	**Molotov's visit to Berlin; confers with Hitler**
9 December	British forces launch Western Desert offensive; fourteen Italian divisions destroyed
18 December	Hitler issues directive for invasion of Soviet Union (Operation *Barbarossa*)

1 9 4 1

22 January	British forces take Tobruk
12–14 February	General Rommel and *Deutsches Afrika Korps* arrive in Tripoli

---

*These dates mark the approximate beginning and end of the main Battle of the Atlantic.

7 March	British forces land in Greece
8 March	**U.S. Senate approves Lend-Lease Bill**
March–June	British forces capture Eritrea and Abyssinia
30 March	Axis forces launch first offensive in North Africa; take Benghazi, invest Tobruk and advance to Egyptian border
7 April	German forces invade Yugoslavia (capitulates 17 April) and Greece
10 April–1 May	Mainland Greek campaign; German victory
13 April	**Soviet-Japanese Non-Aggression Pact signed**
2 May	British forces invade Iraq; Iraqi uprising collapses (30 May)
6 May	**Stalin becomes Soviet Prime Minister**
20 May–1 June	Battle for Crete; German victory
8 June	British forces defeat Vichy French in Syria
22 June	German forces invade Soviet Union (Operation *Barbarossa*)
28 June	German forces take Minsk
7 July	U.S. forces arrive in Iceland
12 July	**Anglo-Soviet Mutual Assistance Agreement signed in Moscow**
25 July	Japanese forces occupy southern Indo-China; U.S. Government freezes Japanese assets
August–September	Konoye proposes summit meeting with Roosevelt; proposal declined
August	**Roosevelt and Churchill meet at Placentia Bay, Newfoundland; Atlantic Charter signed**
	Maud [atomic] Report submitted to Churchill
25 August	Anglo-Soviet forces occupy Iran
8 September	German forces invest Leningrad
19 September	German forces take Kiev
September–October	Beaverbrook-Harriman mission to Moscow
9 October	Roosevelt takes decision to proceed with atomic bomb; Manhattan Project follows in 1942
18 October	Tojo replaces Konoye as Japanese Prime Minister
24 October	**Lend-Lease extended to Soviet Union**
13 November	**U.S. Neutrality Act revised**
18 November	British forces launch Western Desert offensive; Tobruk relieved, 6th December
2 December	German offensive against Moscow (Operation *Typhoon*) stalls in outskirts of capital
6 December	Red Army launches counter-offensive outside Moscow

7 December	Japanese forces attack Pearl Harbor, Philippines, Hong Kong and Malaya
8 December	United States and Great Britain declare war on Japan
10 December	Japanese forces sink *Prince of Wales* and *Repulse* off Malaya
	Japanese forces take Guam
11 December	Germany and Italy declare war on United States and Great Britain
19 December	Hitler takes personal command of German Army
24 December	Japanese forces take Wake Island
25 December	Japanese forces take Hong Kong
December 1941–January 1942	**Churchill and Roosevelt meet at First Washington Conference** *(Arcadia)*

1942

January–May	Heavy Allied losses in the Battle of the Atlantic
21–28 January	Axis forces launch counter-offensive in Western Desert; retake Benghazi and drive British forces back to Gazala position
8 February	Rangoon surrenders; British forces evacuate, 7 March
15 February	Singapore surrenders
19 February	Japanese forces bomb Port Darwin, Australia
27–29 February	Battle of Java Sea; Japanese forces take Dutch East Indies
4–9 April	Japanese Navy obliges British fleet to withdraw to East Africa
9 April	Japanese forces take Bataan
6 May	Corregidor surrenders
20 May–10 June	**Molotov visits successively London, Washington and London; Anglo-Soviet Treaty of Alliance signed**
27 May	German battleship *Bismarck* sunk in the Atlantic
May–June	Gazala Battle; German victory; Egypt invaded
30 May	RAF launches first 1,000-bomber raid, on Cologne
June	**Churchill and Roosevelt meet at Second Washington Conference**
4–7 June	Battle of Midway Island: first major Japanese setback of Pacific War
21 June	Tobruk surrenders to Rommel

28 June	German forces launch major offensive in southern USSR
1 July	Axis forces launch unsuccessful offensive at El Alamein
7 August	U.S. Marines land on Guadalcanal
August	**Churchill and Stalin meet in Moscow**
16 September	Battle for Stalingrad begins
23 October–3 November	Battle of El Alamein; defeated Axis forces begin withdrawal to Tunisia
8 November	Anglo-American invasion of North Africa (Operation *Torch*); German forces occupy southern France, Corsica and Tunisia
December	German forces halt Anglo-American advance on Tunis

1943

January	**Churchill and Roosevelt meet at Casablanca Conference *(Symbol)***
23 January	British forces take Tripoli
2 February	German forces surrender at Stalingrad
April	British and American forces join up in Tunisia
16 April	First reports of Katyn Forest massacre; Soviet-Polish relations broken
May	**Churchill and Roosevelt meet at Third Washington Conference *(Trident)***
May	German U-boats withdrawn from North Atlantic
12 May	Axis forces surrender in Tunisia
July	Battle of Kursk; German attack halted, followed by Red Army's counter-offensive
10 July	Anglo-American forces invade Sicily
25 July	Dismissal and arrest of Mussolini; Badoglio Government puts out peace feelers
August–September	**Churchill and Roosevelt meet at First Quebec Conference *(Quadrant)* and Washington**
19 August	Quebec [atomic] Agreement signed
23 August	Red Army retakes Kharkov
3 September	Italian Armistice signed; announced on 8 September
September	Anglo-American landings at Salerno; German counter-attack repulsed; Naples taken (30 September)
October–November	Moscow Conference of Allied Foreign Ministers
13 October	Italy declares war on Germany
November	**Churchill, Roosevelt and Chiang Kai-shek meet at First Cairo Conference *(Sextant)***

6 November	Red Army retakes Kiev
November–December	**Churchill, Roosevelt and Stalin meet at Teheran Conference *(Eureka)***
December	Churchill and Roosevelt meet at Second Cairo Conference

1 9 4 4

22 January	Anglo-American forces land at Anzio
27 January	Red Army raises siege at Leningrad
18 March	German forces occupy Hungary
30 March	Red Army occupies Romania
10 April	Red Army retakes Odessa
11 May–4 June	Allied offensive in Italy; American forces enter Rome
6 June	Allied forces land in Normandy (Operation *Overlord*); battle won by mid-August
June	Red Army opens Belorussian offensive
12 June	First German V-1 hits London
13 June	Anglo-American [atomic] Combined Development Trust established
July	Bretton Woods Financial and Monetary Conference; Final Act signed (22 July)
3 July	Red Army retakes Minsk
4 July	Japanese forces defeated at Imphal
20 July	German officers attempt to assassinate Hitler
23 July	Polish Committee of Liberation established in Lublin
1 August	Warsaw Rising begins; Polish capitulation on 2 October
16 August	Invasion of southern France (Operation *Dragoon*)
21 August–29 September	Dumbarton Oaks Meeting (United Nations Organisation)
23 August	Romania surrenders
25 August	Paris liberated
31 August	Red Army takes Bucharest
September	**Churchill and Roosevelt meet at Second Quebec Conference *(Octagon)***
3 September	British forces take Brussels
8 September	First German V-2 hits London
September	Bulgaria surrenders; Finnish Armistice signed
19 September	**Churchill and Roosevelt sign (atomic) Hyde Park Aide-Mémoire**
25–26 September	Anglo-American airborne attack on Arnhem fails

October	**Churchill and Stalin meet in Moscow** *(Tolstoy)*
18 October	British forces land in Greece
20 October	Red Army enters Belgrade
	U.S. forces land in Philippines
23 October	British, Soviet and U.S. governments recognize de Gaulle's administration as Provisional Government of France
23–26 October	Battle of Leyte Gulf; destruction of Japanese fleet
7 November	**Roosevelt elected U.S. President for fourth term**
16 December	German forces launch Ardennes counter-offensive; halted, 25 December (The Battle of the Bulge)
December–January	British forces suppress left-wing insurrection in Greece
25–28 December	Churchill visits Athens; Greek Regency established (31 December); truce signed 15 January 1945

1945

9 January	U.S. forces land on Luzon
17 January	Red Army takes Warsaw and advances on River Oder
20 January	Hungary surrenders
January–February	**Churchill and Roosevelt meet at Malta Conference**
February	**Churchill, Roosevelt and Stalin meet at Crimean Conference, Yalta** *(Argonaut)*
4 February	U.S. forces take Manila
13 February	Red Army takes Budapest; fire-bombing of Dresden
7 March	U.S. forces cross Rhine near Remagen
9 March	U.S. B-29s fire-bomb Tokyo; over 80,000 dead
April–June	San Francisco Conference; Charter of United Nations Organisation signed 26 June
1 April	U.S. forces land on Okinawa
12 April	**Death of Roosevelt; Truman becomes U.S. President**
13 April	Red Army takes Vienna
19 April	U.S. forces take Leipzig
25 April	Soviet and American troops meet at Torgau
29 April	German forces in Italy surrender
30 April	Death of Hitler
2 May	Red Army takes Berlin
3 May	British forces retake Rangoon
8 May	**Formal German Act of Surrender signed in Berlin**
9 May	Red Army takes Prague
5 July	**General election in Great Britain—Labour Party victory (announced 26 July)**

July–August	**Berlin Conference, Potsdam *(Terminal)* Churchill, Stalin and Truman; Attlee replaces Churchill at conference on 29 July**
16 July	First atomic explosion at Alamogordo, New Mexico
6 August	U.S. Army Air Force launches atomic attack on Hiroshima
8 August	Soviet Union declares war on Japan; Red Army invades Manchuria
9 August	U.S. Army Air Force launches atomic attack on Nagasaki
14 August	**Japan capitulates: end of Second World War**

APPENDIX I:

PRINCIPAL BRITISH, SOVIET AND U.S. POLITICIANS MENTIONED IN THE TEXT

In Ramsay MacDonald's First National Government, August 1931

Prime Minister	Ramsay MacDonald
Lord President	Stanley Baldwin
Chancellor of the Exchequer	Philip Snowden
Foreign Secretary	Lord Reading
Secretary for India	Sir Samuel Hoare
Minister of Health	Neville Chamberlain

In MacDonald's Second National Government, November 1931

Prime Minister	Ramsay MacDonald
Lord President	Stanley Baldwin

Chancellor of the Exchequer	Neville Chamberlain
Foreign Secretary	Sir John Simon
Secretary for India	Sir Samuel Hoare
Secretary for War	Lord Hailsham
Secretary for Air	Lord Londonderry
Secretary for Scotland	Sir Archibald Sinclair
President of the Board of Trade	Walter Runciman

In Stanley Baldwin's National Government, June 1935

Prime Minister	Stanley Baldwin
Lord President	Ramsay MacDonald
Lord Privy Seal	Lord Londonderry
Chancellor of the Exchequer	Neville Chamberlain
Home Secretary	Sir John Simon
Foreign Secretary	Sir Samuel Hoare
Secretary for India	Lord Zetland
Secretary for War	Lord Halifax
Secretary for Air	Viscount Swinton
First Lord of the Admiralty	Viscount Monsell
President of the Board of Trade	Walter Runciman
Minister without portfolio for League of Nations Affairs	Anthony Eden

NOTE: In November 1935, Halifax succeeded Londonderry as Lord Privy Seal and was succeeded as Secretary for War by Alfred Duff Cooper. In December 1935 Eden succeeded Hoare as Foreign Secretary. In March 1936 Sir Thomas Inskip joined the Cabinet as Minister for the Coordination of Defence. In June 1936 Hoare became First Lord of the Admiralty.

In Neville Chamberlain's National Government, May 1937

Prime Minister	Neville Chamberlain
Lord President	Lord Halifax
Chancellor of the Exchequer	Sir John Simon
Home Secretary	Sir Samuel Hoare
Foreign Secretary	Anthony Eden (succeeded by Halifax, February 1938)
Secretary for India and Burma	Lord Zetland
Secretary for War	Leslie Hore-Belisha
Secretary for Air	Lord Swinton
First Lord of the Admiralty	Alfred Duff Cooper (resigned, October 1938)
President of the Board of Trade	Oliver Stanley
Minister for the Co-ordination of Defence	Sir Thomas Inskip

Chamberlain's War Cabinet, September 1939

Prime Minister	Neville Chamberlain
Lord Privy Seal	Sir Samuel Hoare
Chancellor of the Exchequer	Sir John Simon
Foreign Secretary	Lord Halifax
Secretary for War	Leslie Hore-Belisha
Secretary for Air	Sir Kingsley Wood
First Lord of the Admiralty	Winston Churchill
Minister for the Co-ordination of Defence	Admiral Lord Chatfield (until this post was abolished, April 1940)
Minister without portfolio	Lord Hankey

N O T E : In January 1940, Stanley succeeded Hore-Belisha, who resigned. Hoare and Wood changed places in April 1940.

Winston Churchill's War Cabinet, May 1940

Prime Minister and Minister of Defence	Winston Churchill
Lord President	Neville Chamberlain (resigned, October 1940)
Lord Privy Seal	Clement Attlee
Foreign Secretary	Lord Halifax
Minister without portfolio	Arthur Greenwood

N o t e :

August 1940	Lord Beaverbrook, Minister of Aircraft Production, joined the War Cabinet.
October 1940	Ernest Bevin, Minister of Labour, joined the War Cabinet, as did Sir Kingsley Wood, Chancellor of the Exchequer, and Sir John Anderson (first as Lord President, and then from September 1943 as Chancellor of the Exchequer, after the death of Kingsley Wood).
December 1940	Halifax was appointed Ambassador in Washington; Eden succeeded him as Foreign Secretary and became a member of the War Cabinet.
June 1941	Oliver Lyttelton entered the War Cabinet, on being appointed Minister of State in the Middle East.
February 1942	Beaverbrook resigned (by then, as Minister of War Production) and left the War Cabinet; Sir Stafford Cripps succeeded Attlee as Lord Privy Seal and became a member of the War Cabinet; Attlee, who became Deputy Prime Minister, remained in the War Cabinet; Greenwood and Wood left the War Cabinet.
March 1942	Richard Casey (a member of the Australian Parliament) was appointed Minister Resident in the Middle East and became a member of the War Cabinet. Lyttleton then became Minister of War Production.
October 1942	Cripps resigned as Lord Privy Seal and left the War Cabinet; Herbert Morrison (Home Secretary) entered the War Cabinet.
November 1943	Lord Woolton, Minister for Reconstruction, entered the War Cabinet.

Principal Members of Churchill's Caretaker Government, May–July 1945

Prime Minister and Minister of Defence	Winston Churchill

Lord President	Lord Woolton
Lord Privy Seal	Lord Beaverbrook
Chancellor of the Exchequer	Sir John Anderson
Foreign Secretary	Anthony Eden
Secretary for India and Burma	Leopold Amery (who held this office from May 1940, but was not previously a member of the War Cabinet)
Secretary for War	Sir James Grigg
Secretary for Air	Harold Macmillan
First Lord of the Admiralty	Brendan Bracken
President of the Board of Trade and Minister of Production	Oliver Lyttleton

Full Members of the Politburo of the Soviet Communist Party, 1941–1945 (the dates shown indicate the year in which they became full—as opposed to candidate—members)

J. V. Stalin*	1919
V. M. Molotov†	1926
M. I. Kalinin	1926
K. E. Voroshilov	1926
L. M. Kaganovich	1930
A. A. Andreyev	1932
A. I. Mikoyan	1935
N. S. Khrushchev	1939
A. A. Zhdanov	1939

---

*Prime Minister from May 1941; Defence Minister from August 1941.
†Foreign Minister from May 1939.

Some Members of the Roosevelt Administration, 1940–45

President	Franklin Delano Roosevelt
Vice-President	Henry A. Wallace (succeeded by Harry S. Truman, January 1945; Wallace became Secretary of Agriculture)
Secretary of Commerce	Harry Hopkins (resigned from the Cabinet, August 1940)
Secretary of the Interior	Harold L. Ickes
Secretary of Labour	Frances Perkins
Secretary of the Navy	Frank Knox
Secretary of State	Cordell Hull (succeeded by Edward R. Stettinius, Jr., previously Lend-Lease Administrator, in November 1944)
Secretary of the Treasury	Henry Morgenthau, Jr.
Secretary of War	Henry L. Stimson
and—from May 1942—	
James E. Byrnes	Head of the Office of War Mobilisation

NOTE: Given the special characteristics of Roosevelt's style of government, particularly during the war, this list is only an approximation. Hopkins' extensive wartime influence, for example, bore no relationship to the office that he held until August 1940. And no list of political (as opposed to military) figures closest to Roosevelt during the war is complete without his wife, Eleanor Roosevelt.

APPENDIX II:

SECRET ADDITIONAL PROTOCOL TO THE GERMAN-SOVIET PACT, 23 AUGUST 1939

On the occasion of the signature of the Non-Aggression Treaty between the German Reich and the Union of Soviet Socialist Republics, the undersigned plenipotentiaries of the two Parties discussed in strictly confidential conversations the question of the delimitation of their respective spheres of interest in Eastern Europe. These conversations led to the following result:

1. In the event of a territorial and political transformation in the territories belonging to the Baltic States (Finland, Estonia, Latvia, Lithuania), the northern frontier of Lithuania shall represent the frontier of the spheres of interest both of Germany and the USSR. In this connection the interest of Lithuania in the Vilna territory is recognized by both Parties.

2. In the event of a territorial and political transformation of the territories belonging to the Polish State, the spheres of interest of both Germany and the USSR shall be bounded approximately by the line of the rivers Narev, Vistula and San. The question whether the interests of both Parties make the maintenance of an independent Polish State appear desirable and how the frontiers of this State should be drawn can be definitely determined only in the course of further political developments. In any case both the Governments will resolve this question by means of a friendly understanding.

3. With regard to South-Eastern Europe, the Soviet side emphasises its interest in Bessarabia. The German side declares complete political *désintéressement* in these territories.

4. This Protocol will be treated by both parties as strictly secret.

Moscow, August 23, 1939.

For the Government of	With full power of the
the German Reich:	Government of the USSR:
v. RIBBENTROP	V. MOLOTOV

Author's Note: The text above is the English translation contained in *Documents on German Foreign Policy, 1918–1945, Series D,* Vol. VI. It is an accurate rendering of the German text in the archives of the Federal German Ministry of Foreign Affairs. Both the German and the Russian texts in the archives form part of a micro-film, made in 1943, of some 10,000 pages of files from the German Foreign Minister's office. The originals both of the 1939 German-Soviet Treaty and of the Secret Protocol, as also of the greater part of the material relating to the August and September treaties, were (deliberately) burned in the last days of the war in 1945. I am grateful to Dr. Maria Keipert, of the Federal German Foreign Ministry, for this clarification; and to Dr. Harold Shukman, of St. Antony's College, Oxford, for kindly letting me see his correspondence about this with Dr. Keipert. The text given in *DGFP* differs only in minor respects from the Russian text—for example, the French word *désintéressement* used in the German text is, in the Russian text, the Russian word *nezainteresovanie.*

APPENDIX III:

THE QUEBEC AGREEMENT, 19 AUGUST 1943

ARTICLES OF AGREEMENT Governing Collaboration Between the Authorities of the U.S.A. and the U.K. in the Matter of Tube Alloys

Whereas it is vital to our common safety in the present War to bring the Tube Alloys project to fruition at the earliest moment; and whereas this may be more speedily achieved if all available British and American brains and resources are pooled; and whereas owing to war conditions it would be an improvident use of war resources to duplicate plants on a large scale on both sides of the Atlantic and therefore a far greater expense has fallen upon the United States;

It is agreed between us

First, that we will never use this agency against each other.

Secondly, that we will not use it against third parties without each other's consent.

Thirdly, that we will not either of us communicate any information about Tube Alloys to third parties except by mutual consent.

Fourthly, that in view of the heavy burden of production falling upon the United States as the result of a wise division of war effort, the British Government recognize that any post-war advantages of an industrial or commercial character shall be dealt with as between the United States and Great Britain on terms to be specified by the President of the United States to the Prime Minister of Great Britain. The Prime Minister expressly disclaims any interest in these industrial and commercial aspects beyond what may be considered by the President of the United States to be fair and just and in harmony with the economic welfare of the world.

And Fifthly, that the following arrangements shall be made to ensure full and effective collaboration between the two countries in bringing the project to fruition:

(a) There shall be set up in Washington a Combined Policy Committee composed of:

The Secretary of War	(United States)
Dr. Vannevar Bush	(United States)
Dr. James B. Conant	(United States)
Field-Marshal Sir John Dill, G.C.B., C.M.G., D.S.O.	(United Kingdom)
Colonel the Right Hon. J. J. Llewellin C.B.E., M.C., M.P.	(United Kingdom)
The Honourable C. D. Bowe	(Canada)

The functions of this Committee, subject to the control of the respective Governments, will be:

(1) To agree from time to time upon the programme of work to be carried out in the two countries.

(2) To keep all sections of the project under constant review.

(3) To allocate materials apparatus and plant, in limited supply, in accordance with the requirements of the programme agreed by the Committee.

(4) To settle any questions which may arise on the interpretation or application of this Agreement.

(b) There shall be complete interchange of information and ideas on all sections of the project between members of the Policy Committee and their immediate technical advisers.

(c) In the field of scientific research and development there shall be full and effective interchange of information and ideas between those in the two countries engaged in the same sections of the field.

(d) In the field of design, construction and operation of large-scale plants, interchange of information and ideas shall be regulated by such *ad hoc* arrangements as may, in each section of the field, appear to be necessary or desirable if the project is to be brought to fruition at the earliest moment. Such *ad hoc* arrangements shall be subject to the approval of the Policy Committee.

Approved

19 August 1943

Franklin D. Roosevelt
Winston Churchill

APPENDIX IV:

AIDE-MÉMOIRE OF CONVERSATION BETWEEN THE PRESIDENT AND THE PRIME MINISTER AT HYDE PARK, 19 SEPTEMBER 1944

The suggestion that the world should be informed regarding tube alloys, with a view to an international agreement regarding its control and use, is not accepted. The matter should continue to be regarded as of the utmost secrecy; but when a "bomb" is finally available, it might perhaps, after mature consideration, be used against the Japanese, who should be warned that this bombardment will be repeated until they surrender.

2. Full collaboration between the United States and the British Government in developing tube alloys for military and commercial purposes should continue after the defeat of Japan unless and until terminated by joint agreement.

3. Enquiries should be made regarding the activities of Professor Bohr and steps taken to ensure that he is responsible for no leakage of information particularly to the Russians.

APPENDIX V:

THE DECLARATION ON LIBERATED EUROPE, 11 FEBRUARY 1945

We have drawn up and subscribed to a Declaration on liberated Europe. This Declaration provides for concerting the policies of the Three Powers and for joint action by them in meeting the political and economic problems of liberated Europe in accordance with democratic principles. The text of the Declaration is as follows:

The Premier of the Union of Soviet Socialist Republics, the Prime Minister of the United Kingdom, and the President of the United States of America have consulted with each other in the common interests of the peoples of their countries and those of liberated Europe. They jointly declare their mutual agreement to concert during the temporary period of instability in liberated Europe the policies of their three governments in assisting the peoples liberated from the domination of Nazi Germany and the peoples of the former Axis satellite states of Europe to solve by democratic means their pressing political and economic problems.

The establishment of order in Europe and the rebuilding of national economic life must be achieved by processes which will enable the liberated peoples to destroy the last vestiges of Nazism and Fascism and to creat[e] democratic institutions of their own choice. This is a principle of the Atlantic Charter—the right of all peoples to choose the form of government under which they will live—the restoration of sovereign rights and self-government to those peoples who have been forcibly deprived of them by the aggressor nations.

To foster the conditions in which the liberated peoples may exercise these rights, the three governments will jointly assist the people in any European liberated state or former Axis satellite state in Europe where in their judgment conditions require *(a)* to establish conditions of internal peace; *(b)* to carry out emergency measures for the relief of distressed people; *(c)* to form interim governmental authorities broadly representative of all democratic elements in the population and pledged to the earliest possible establishment through free elections of governments responsive to the will of the people; and *(d)* to facilitate where necessary the holding of such elections.

The three governments will consult the other United Nations and provisional authorities or other governments in Europe when matters of direct interest to them are under consideration.

When, in the opinion of the three governments, conditions in any European liberated state or any former Axis satellite state in Europe make such action necessary, they will immediately consult together on the measures necessary to discharge the joint responsibilities set forth in this declaration.

By this declaration we reaffirm our faith in the principles of the Atlantic Charter, our pledge in the Declaration by the United Nations, and our determination to build in cooperation with other peace-loving nations a world order under law, dedicated to peace, security, freedom and the general well-being of all mankind.

In issuing this declaration, the Three Powers express the hope that the Provisional Government of the French Republic may be associated with them in the procedure suggested.

APPENDIX VI:

SECTION III OF THE
POTSDAM PROTOCOL, 2 AUGUST 1945

Reparations from Germany

1. Reparation claims of the U.S.S.R. shall be met by removals from the zone of Germany occupied by the U.S.S.R., and from appropriate German external assets.

2. The U.S.S.R. undertakes to settle the reparation claims of Poland from its own share of reparations.

3. The reparations claims of the United States, the United Kingdom and other countries entitled to reparations shall be met from the Western Zones and from appropriate German external assets.

4. In addition to the reparations to be taken by the U.S.S.R. from its own zone of occupation, the U.S.S.R. shall receive additionally from the Western Zones:

(a) 15 per cent of such usable and complete industrial capital equipment, in the first place from the metallurgical, chemical and machine manufacturing industries, as is unnecessary for the German peace economy and should be removed from the Western Zones of Germany, in exchange for an equivalent value of food, coal, potash, zinc, timber, clay products, petroleum products, and such other commodities as may be agreed upon.

(b) 10 per cent of such industrial capital equipment as is unnecessary for the German peace economy and should be removed from the Western Zones, to be transferred to the Soviet Government on reparations account without payment or exchange of any kind in return.

Removals of equipment as provided in (a) and (b) above shall be made simultaneously.

5. The amount of equipment to be removed from the Western Zones on account of reparations must be determined within six months from now at the latest.

6. Removals of industrial capital equipment shall begin as soon as possible and shall be completed within two years from the determination specified in paragraph 5. The delivery of products covered by 4(a) above shall begin as soon as possible and shall be made by the U.S.S.R. in agreed instalments within five years of the date hereof. The determination of the amount and character of the industrial capital equipment unnecessary for the German peace economy and therefore available for reparations shall be made by the Control Council under policies fixed by the Allied Commission on reparations, with the participation of France, subject to the final approval of the Zone Commander in the Zone from which the equipment is to be removed.

7. Prior to the fixing of the total amount of such equipment subject to removal, advance deliveries shall be made in respect of such equipment as will be determined to be eligible for delivery in accordance with the procedure set forth in the last sentence of paragraph 6.

8. The Soviet Government renounces all claims in respect of reparations to shares of German enterprises which are located in the Western

Zones of occupation in Germany as well as to German foreign assets in all countries except those specified in paragraph 9 below.

9. The Governments of the United Kingdom and United States renounce all claims in respect of reparations to shares of German enterprises which are located in the Eastern Zone of occupation in Germany, as well as to German foreign assets in Bulgaria, Finland, Hungary, Roumania and Eastern Austria.

10. The Soviet Government makes no claims to gold captured by the Allied troops in Germany.

DOCUMENTARY SOURCES

At the time when the first studies of the relationship between Churchill, Roosevelt and Stalin were written, the historian was confined to sources consisting essentially of the memoirs of the principal actors of the Second World War, which began to appear in the late 1940s and early 1950s—notably those of Churchill himself, who won a head start over other historians—set against the background material of the speeches and the statements of the three wartime leaders; the published agreements that they reached together and the statements and White Papers issued by their governments during the war; the accounts and the discussion of the war in the press and on the radio of the countries principally involved; and the records of parliamentary and congressional debates. Forty years later the problem is the reverse of what it was in the early years after the war. Even for a study confined to the years of the war itself, let alone the longer period chosen as the time frame of the present book, the sky has now become the limit.*

Today, where is the historian to draw the line under his research, knowing that almost every file that he consults in—say—the Franklin D. Roosevelt Library or the British Public Record Office, in order to find a particular paper which he knows that he needs, will lead him on to read at least one other document that will turn out to be of equal interest? And once this line has been drawn, how can he best present the sources of his research to the reader, without plastering his text with notes? The Preface has given some indication at the outset of the way in which the problem is handled in the present book (a study, not of the military history of the Second World War, but of the development of the relationship between three men, to the exclusion therefore of other major figures)—the approach of the rifle, not of the scatter-gun. The three categories of sources determined by this approach offer a reasonably clear indication of where I have sought both information and ideas for this study of the relationship between Churchill, Roosevelt and Stalin; and they may also suggest where the reader's search may be directed, if he or she wishes.

I. THE HARD CORE—PRIMARY SOURCES

Apart from the background material mentioned above, which has lost none of its importance but is for the most part not listed here, lists being readily available elsewhere, the principal primary sources that form the basis of this book are:

Abbreviated in the Notes as:

Anglo-American

Warren F. Kimball, ed., *Churchill and Roosevelt:*   Kimball
the complete correspondence, 3 vols., Princeton
University Press, Princeton, N.J., 1984.

---

*To cite a major example, at the time of writing there are already more than a dozen documentary volumes that form the companion to Martin Gilbert's biography of Churchill.

Abbreviated in the Notes as:

American

The Roosevelt Papers, in the Franklin D.   FDR Library
Roosevelt Library, Hyde Park, N.Y.*

Foreign Relations of the United States, Diplomatic   *FRUS*
Papers, U.S. Government Printing Office,
Washington, D.C.

General Records of the Department of State,   *DSDF*
Decimal Files, National Archives, Washington,
D.C.

The Public Papers and Addresses of Franklin D.   *PPA*
Roosevelt, ed. Samuel I. Rosenman, 13 vols.,
Harper, New York, 1938–50.

British

Winston S. Churchill: his complete speeches,
1897–1963, ed. Robert Rhodes-James. Vols. VI
and VII, Chelsea House, New York, 1974.

Documents on British Foreign Policy, 1919–1939,   *DBFP*
Second and Third Series, ed. E. L. Woodward
and Rohan Butler, assisted by Margaret
Lambert, HMSO, London, 1949–50.†

Documents on British Policy Overseas, First   *DBPO*
Series,, ed. Rohan Butler, et al., Vol. 1, *1945,*
HMSO, London, 1954.

---

*This collection contains other important papers, including those of Harry Hopkins.
†The wartime gap in this series, up to July 1945, creates a lacuna that is peculiar to Britain; no fully documented British record of either the Teheran or the Yalta Conference has been published.

Abbreviated in the Notes as:

Cabinet Papers, Minutes, Conclusions and   CAB
Confidential Annexes, in the Public Record
Office (PRO), Kew, Richmond, Surrey.

Foreign Office General Political Papers, in the   FO 371 (there are also
Public Record Office.   a few references to
                                                    FO 800)

Papers of the Prime Minister's Office, in the   PREM
Public Record Office.

Margaret Gowing, *Britain and Atomic Energy,*
1939–1945 (the first volume of the official
History of the British Atomic Energy
Authority), Macmillan, London, 1964.

F. H. Hinsley, et al., *British Intelligence in the*   Hinsley, *British*
Second World War: its influence on strategy and   *Intelligence*
operations, 4 vols., HMSO, London, 1979–90.

French

Le Livre Jaune Français: Documents diplomatiques,
1938–1939, Ministère des Affaires Etrangères,
Imprimerie Nationale, Paris, 1939.

German

Documents on German Foreign Policy, 1918–1945,   *DGFP*
Series D, U.S. Government Printing Office,
Washington, D.C., 1949.

The Trial of the Major War Criminals Before the   *N.D., N.P.*
International Military Tribunal, Proceedings, Vols.
1–XXIII, and *Documents in Evidence,* Vols.
XXIV–XLII *Nuremberg, 1947–49,* (translations
of most of the relevant documents

published by the U.S. Government Printing
Office, Washington, D.C., 1946–48)

The Dirksen Papers, 1938–39
[See under Soviet section, *Dokumenty i materialy
kanuna vtoroi mirovoi voiny*]

Polish

Documents on Soviet-Polish Relations, 1939–45, 2
vols., The General Sikorsky Historical Institute,
Heinemann, London, 1961.

*Dokumenty i materialy do historii stosunków
polsko-radzieckich,* Vol. VIII, Warsaw, 1974.

Soviet

Dokumenty vneshnei politiki SSSR, Vols.   *DVPS*
XVI–XXI, Politizdat, Moscow, 1970–72.

SSSR v bor'be za mir nakanune vtoroi mirovoi   *Bor'ba za mir*
voiny 1938–1939: dokumenty i materialy.
Izdatel'stvo politicheskoi literatury, Moscow,
1971. (Translated as *Soviet Peace Efforts on the
Eve of World War II,* ed. V. M. Falin, et al.,
Novosti, Moscow, 1973.)

*Dokumenty i materialy kanuna vtoroi mirovoi
voiny, 1937–1939,* 2 vols., Politizdat, Moscow,
1981. (Translated, Foreign Languages Publishing
House, Moscow, 1948, as *Documents and
Materials Relating to the Eve of the Second World
War,* Vol. II of which consists of The Dirksen
Papers, 1938–1939.)

Sovetskii Soyuz na mezhdunarodnykh   *SSNMK*
konferentsiyakh perioda velikoi otechestvennoi voiny,

Abbreviated in the Notes as:

1941–1945 gg., Sbornik dokumentov, 6 vols.,
Izdatel'stvo politicheskoi literatury, Moscow,
1978–79.

Sovetsko-Angliiskie Otnosheniya vo vremya velikoi   *Sov.-Angl. O.*
otechestvennoi voiny, 1941–1945, 2 vols.,
Izdatel'stvo politicheskoi literatury, Moscow,
1983.

Sovetsko-Amerikanskie Otnosheniya vo vremya   *Sov.-Am. O.*
velikoi otechestvennoi voiny, 1941–1945, 2 vols.,
Izdatel'stvo politicheskoi literatury, Moscow,
1983.

Perepiska predsedatelya soveta ministrov SSSR s   *Perepiska*
prezidentami SShA i prem'er-ministrami
veliko-britanii vo vremya velikoi otechestvennoi
voiny, 1941–1945 gg., 2 vols., Izdatel'stvo
politicheskoi literatury, Moscow, 1986 (2nd
edn, 1989); an English translation was published
in Moscow, Foreign Languages Publishing
House, 1957.

LENIN, V. I.   *Polnoe sobranie sochinenii,* 5th edn, 55 vols., Izdatel'stvo politicheskoi
literatury, Moscow, 1958–65.

Abrreviated in the Notes as:
Lenin, *PSS*

STALIN, I. V.   *Sochineniya,* 16 vols., Vols. I–XIII, Gospolizdat, Moscow, 1947–53;
Vols. XIV–XVI, Hoover Institution, Stanford, Calif., 1967.

Abrreviated in the Notes as:
Stalin, *Sochineniya*

————   *O velikoi otechestvennoi voine Sovetskogo Soyuza,* Gospolizdat,
Moscow, 1947.

————   *The Problems of Leninism,* Foreign Languages Publishing House,
Moscow, 1947.

II. MEMOIRS AND DIARIES

Virtually all wartime memoirs have some bearing on the relationship between Churchill, Roosevelt and Stalin. So far as those written in English are concerned, the *embarrass de richesses* is vast. And there is an abundance of memoirs in Russian, although—where Stalin is concerned—these have to be used selectively and with care. (For example, Khrushchev's bias, although it does not rule his recollections out of court, has constantly to be borne in mind.) The many wartime diaries are important because they supply the emotional dimension that is usually missing from primary sources. For this very reason, they may either fill an historical gap or distort history. Eisenhower's warning is relevant here.*

ACHESON, Dean	*Present at the Creation: My years at the State Department* (New York: W. W. Norton, 1969).
ALANBROOKE, Field-Marshal Lord	The Alanbrooke Papers, deposited at King's College, London, including both his wartime diaries and his subsequent "Notes on my Life."
ALLILUEVA, Svetlana	*Twenty Letters to a Friend,* trans. Priscilla Johnson McMillan (New York: Harper & Row, 1967; Harmondsworth, Middlesex: Penguin Books, 1968; first published Hutchinson, 1967).
ATKINS, John B.	*Incidents and Reflections* (London: Christophers, 1947).
BALFOUR, John	*Not too correct an aureole* (London: Michael Russell, 1983).
BEREZHKOV, Valentin M.	*Tak delalas' istoriya* (Moscow, 1982), trans. as *History in the Making: memoirs of World War II diplomacy* (Moscow: Progress Publishers, 1983).
BOHLEN, Charles E., with PHELPS, Robert H.	*Witness to History 1929–1969* (New York: W. W. Norton, 1973).

---

*"I despise biographies [based on diaries] as showing real history. I don't believe they do."— *General Eisenhower on the Military Churchill: a conversation with Alistair Cooke,* ed. James Nelson, p. 64.

BLUM, John Morton — *From the Morgenthau Diaries,* Vol. III, *Years of War, 1941–1945* (Boston: Houghton Mifflin, 1967).

BUTLER, Lord — *The Art of the Possible: the memoirs of Lord Butler, K.G., C.H.* (London: Hamish Hamilton, 1971).

CADOGAN, Alexander — *The Diaries of Sir Alexander Cadogan,* ed. David Dilks (London: Cassell, 1971).

CASTELLANO, Giuseppe — *La Guerra Continva* (Milan: Rizzoli, revised edn, 1963).

CHURCHILL, Winston S. — *The Second World War,* 6 vols.(London: Cassell, 1948–54; Boston: Houghton Mifflin, 1948–53)—abbreviated in the Notes as Churchill.

——— — *My Early Life: a roving commission* (London: Collins, Fontana Paperback, 1959; first published Butterworth, 1930).

COLVILLE, John — *The Fringes of Power: Downing Street Diaries, 1939–1955* (London: Hodder & Stoughton, 1985; New York: W. W. Norton, 1987).

COOPER, Alfred Duff — *Old Men Forget: the autobiography of Duff Cooper* (London: Hart-Davis, 1954).

COULONDRE, Robert — *De Staline à Hitler: souvenirs de deux ambassades, 1936–1939* (Paris: Hachette, 1950).

DE GAULLE, Charles — *Mémoires de Guerre,* 3 vols. (Paris: Plon, 1954–59), trans. Richard Howard (New York: Da Capo Press, 1984).

DJILAS, Milovan — *Conversations with Stalin,* trans. Michael B. Petrovich (London: Hart-Davis, 1962; New York: Harcourt Brace Jovanovich, 1963).

EDEN, Anthony — *The Memoirs of Anthony Eden,* 3 vols. (London: Cassell, 1960–65; Boston: Houghton Mifflin, 1960–65).

EISENHOWER, Dwight D. — *Crusade in Europe* (Garden City, N.Y.: Doubleday, 1948).

FARLEY, James — *Behind the Ballots: the personal history of a politician* (New York: Harcourt, Brace, 1938).

GLADWYN, Lord — *The Memoirs of Lord Gladwyn* (London: Weidenfeld & Nicolson, 1972).

GNEDIN, Evgenii — *Iz istorii otnoshenii mezhdu SSSR i fashistkoi Germaniei* (New York: Khronika, 1977).

GROMYKO, Andrei A. — *Pamyatnoe,* 2 vols. (Moscow: Politizdat, 1988), trans. Harold Shukman as *Memories* (London: Hutchinson, 1989), and as *Memoirs* (Garden City, N.Y.: Doubleday, 1990).

HALIFAX, the Earl of — Lord Halifax's Secret Diary, at the Borthwick Institute of Historical Research, University of York.

HARRIMAN, W Averell, and ABEL, Elie — *Special Envoy to Churchill and Stalin, 1941–46* (New York: Random House, 1975).

HULL, Cordell — *The Memoirs of Cordell Hull,* 2 vols. (New York: Macmillan, 1948; London: Hodder & Stoughton, 1948).

HUNT, David — *A Don at War* (London: Frank Cass, revised n. 1990).

ICKES, Harold — *The Secret Diary of Harold L. Ickes,* 3 vols. (New York: Simon & Schuster, 1953–54; London: Weidenfeld & Nicolson, 1955).

JACOB, Lieutenant -General Sir Ian — The Jacob Diary, with the Jacob Papers at Woodbridge, Suffolk.

KENNAN, George F. — *Memoirs 1925–1950* (Boston: Little, Brown, 1967).

KHRUSHCHEV, Nikita — *Khrushchev Remembers,* 2 vols., trans. and ed. Strobe Talbott (Boston: Little, Brown, 1970–74).

von KLEMPERER, Klemens, ed. — *A Noble Combat: the letters of Sheila Grant Duff and Adam von Trotz zu Solz, 1932–1939* (Oxford: Clarendon Press, 1988).

MacARTHUR, Douglas — *Reminiscences* (London: Heinemann, 1964; New York: McGraw-Hill, 1964).

MIKOYAN, A. I. — "V sovete po evakvatsü," from unpublished manuscripts, *Voenno-istoricheskii zhurnal,* 3 (Moscow, 1989).

MIŁOSZ, Czesław — *Native Realm: a search for self-definition* (Harmondsworth, Middlesex: Penguin Books, 1988; first published Doubleday, New York, 1968).

MOLEY, Raymond

After Seven Years (New York and London: Harper, 1939; Lincoln, Nebr.: University of Nebraska Press, 1971).

MONNET, Jean

Mémoires (Paris: Fayard, 1967); trans. Richard Mayne (Garden City, N.Y.: Doubleday, 1978).

MONTGOMERY of ALAMEIN, Viscount

The Memoirs of Field-Marshal the Viscount Montgomery of Alamein (London: Collins, 1958).

MURPHY, Robert

Diplomat Among Warriors (Garden City, Doubleday, Doubleday, 1964).

NICOLSON, Harold

Diaries and Letters 1930–39, ed. Nigel Nicolson, (London: Fontana Books, 1969).

PERKINS, Frances

The Roosevelt I Knew (New York: Viking Press, 1946).

ROOSEVELT, Eleanor

This I Remember (New York: Harper & Brothers, 1949; London: Hutchinson, 1950).

SHERWOOD, Robert

The White House Papers of Harry L. Hopkins: an intimate history, 2 vols. (London: Eyre & Spottiswoode, 1948, 1949; rev. edn, New York: Harper & Brothers, 1950; first published as *Roosevelt and Hopkins: an intimate history,* Harper, 1948)—abbreviated in the Notes as Sherwood, *White House Papers*

SNOW, Helen Foster

My China Years (London: Harrop, 1984).

STIMSON, Henry L.

The Stimson Diary and Paper, at the Sterling Memorial Library, Yale University, New Haven.

———, and BUNDY, McGeorge

On Active Service in Peace and War (New York: Harper & Brothers, 1948; London: Hutchinson, 1949).

TRUMAN, Harry S.

Year of Decisions, 1945 (Garden City, N.Y.: Doubleday, 1955).

VASILEVSKY, A.M.

Delo vsei zhizni, 2nd, expanded edn (Moscow: Izdatel 'stvo politicheskoi literatury, 1975).

WASILIEWSKA, Wanda	*The Memoirs of Wanda Wasiliewska* (Warsaw: Archivum Ruchu Robotnichnego, 1982).
ZHUKOV, Georgii K.	*Vospominaniya i razmyshleniya* (Moscow: Novosti, 1969) trans. as *Reminiscences and Reflections,* 2 vols. (Moscow: Progress Publishers, 1985).

III. SECONDARY SOURCES

Although this enormous field includes some magisterial works, I have not attempted the invidious task of telling the reader which titles have contributed most effectively to my own learning curve, whether as signposts to areas of research, or as sources of ideas, or both; still less, which are "recommended for further study." This said, the present section lists virtually every book (and in a few cases, articles of particular relevance published in periodicals) that is referred to or quoted from in *The Big Three,* whether in the text or in the Notes. It also includes the books—whether or not they are cited or referred to—that have stood on the bookshelf nearest my desk, within arm's reach, during the past five years: a floating population that has usually numbered rather under a hundred volumes at any one time. Some of these have never left the shelf; some have remained there for a few weeks; some have made way for others, but returned later; while some have stayed only briefly, and a very few have been banished to outer darkness as quickly as possible (but even a negative reaction sometimes turns out to be stimulating).

From this list there are notable absentees, as there are from Section II above. Absence does not necessarily imply ignorance. There are other books, important in the context of this study, which I have read at one time or another, but unless they fall clearly into one of the categories defined above, their titles are not included here. A line has to be drawn somewhere, however arbitrary it may be.

ABBOTT, George C.	*International Indebtedness and the Developing Countries* (London: Croom Helm, 1979).
AKHMATOVA, Anna	*Selected Poems*, trans. Stanley Kunitz with Max Hayward (London: Collins Harvill, 1989).
ALLEN, Louis	*Singapore 1941–1942* (London: Davis-Poynter, 1977).

ALLISON, Graham *Essence of Decision: explaining the Cuban Missile Crisis* (Boston: Little, Brown, 1971).

ALSOP, Joseph *FDR, 1882–1945: a ceutenary remembrance* (London: Thames & Hudson, 1982; New York: Viking Press, 1982).

AMBROSE, Stephen E. *Eisenhower: the President* (London: Allen & Unwin, 1984; New York: Simon & Schuster, 1984).

———— *Eisenhower and Berlin, 1945: the decision to halt at the Elbe* (rev. edn. New York: W. W. Norton, 1986).

ANDREW, Christopher *Secret Service: the making of the British Intelligence community* (London: Heinemann, 1985).

BARNETT, Corelli *The Desert Generals* (London: William Kimber, 1960; new and enlarged edn, Allen & Unwin, 1983).

———— *The Collapse of British Power* (Gloucester, Engl.: Allan Sutton, 1984; first published 1972).

BEESLY, Patrick *Very Special Admiral: the life of Admiral J. H. Godfrey, CB* (London: Hamish Hamilton, 1980).

BELOFF, Max *The Foreign Policy of Soviet Russia, 1929–1941,* 2 vols. (London: Oxford University Press, 1966).

BERLIN, Isaiah *Concepts and Categories: philosophical essays,* ed. Henry Hardy (Oxford: Oxford University Press, 1980; first published Hogarth Press, 1978).

———— *Personal Impressions,* ed. Henry Hardy (London: Hogarth Press, 1981; New York: Viking Press, 1981).

———— *Washington Despatches, 1941–45,* ed. H. G. Nicholas (London: Weidenfeld & Nicholson, 1981).

BERTHOUD, Roger *Graham Sutherland: a biography* (London: Faber & Faber, 1982).

BIRKENHEAD, the Earl of *Halifax: the life of Lord Halifax* (London: Hamish Hamilton, 1965).

BLAKE, Robert

Disraeli (London: Methuen Paperback, 1969; first published Eyre & Spottiswoode, 1966).

BROWNELL, Will, and
BILLINGS, Richard N.

So Close to Greatness: the first biography of William C. Bullitt (New York and London: Macmillan, 1987).

BULLOCK, Alan

Hitler: a study in tyranny (completely revised edn London: Odhams Books, 1964; first published Odhams Press, 1952).

———

The Life and Times of Ernest Bevin, 3 vols. (London: Heinemann, 1967–83).

BUNDY, McGeorge

Danger and Survival: choices about the bomb in the first fifty years (New York: Random House, 1988).

BURNS, James
MacGregor

Roosevelt.: 2 vols., *The Lion and the Fox* (New York: Harcourt, Brace, 1956) and *The Soldier of Freedom* (New York: Harcourt Brace Jovanovich, 1970)—abbreviated in the notes as: Burns, *Roosevelt.*

BUTLER, J. R. M., ed.

Grand Strategy, 6 vols. (London: HMSO, 1956–76).*

CARR, Edward H.

Conditions of Peace (London: Macmillan, 1942).

CARR, Raymond, ed.

The Republic and the Civil War in Spain (London: Macmillan, 1971).

CARVER, Field-Marshal
Lord

Twentieth-Century Warriors: the development of the armed forces of the major military nations in the twentieth century (London: Weidenfeld & Nicolson, 1987).

CECIL, Lord Robert

A Great Experiment: an autobiography (London: Jonathan Cape, 1941).

CHARMLEY, John

Chamberlain and the Lost Peace (London: Hodder & Stoughton, Heinemann, 1989).

CHURCHILL, Randolph

Winston S. Churchill, Vol. I (London: Heinemann, 1966; Boston: Houston Mifflin, 1966).

CHURCHILL,
Winston S.

The World Crisis: the Eastern Front (London: Thornton Butterworth, 1931).

*See note at the end of Section III (p. 524).

———— *Marlborough: his life and times,* 4 vols. (London: Harrap, 1933–38).

———— *Great Contemporaries* (London: Macmillan, 1942; rev. edn Collins Fontana, 1965).

CIECHANOWSKI, J.M. *The Warsaw Rising of 1944* (Cambridge and New York: Cambridge University Press, 1974).

COLLECTIVE EDITORSHIP *Jalta wczoraj i dziś: wybor publicystiki, 1944–1985* (London: Polonia, 1985).

COLLECTIVE EDITORSHIP *Istoriya vneshnei politiki SSSR,* 2 vols. (Moscow: Nauka, 1982).

CONNELL, John *Wavell: scholar and soldier* (London: Collins, 1964).

CONQUEST, Robert *The Great Terror: Stalin's purge of the thirties* (London and New York: Macmillan, 1968).

COVERDALE, John F. *Italian Intervention in the Spanish Civil War* (Princeton, N.J.: Princeton University Press, 1975).

DALLEK, Robert *Franklin D. Roosevelt and American Foreign Policy 1932–45* (New York: Oxford University Press, paperback, 1981; first published 1979).

DAVIES, Norman *God's Playground: a history of Poland,* 2 vols. (Oxford: Clarendon Press, 1981; New York: Columbia University Press, 1982).

DAY, David *The Great Betrayal: Britain, Australia and the onset of the Pacific War, 1939–42* (New York: W. W. Norton, 1989).

DEAKIN, F. W., and STORRY, G. R. *The Case of Richard Sorge* (London: Chatto & Windus, 1966).

D'ESTE, Carlo *The Battle for Sicily, 1943* (London: Collins, 1988).

DEUTSCHER, Isaac *Stalin: a political biography* (Harmondsworth, Middlesex: Pelican Books, 1966; first published Oxford University Press, 1949).

DONOVAN, Robert J. *Conflict and Crisis: the presidency of Harry S. Truman, 1945–48* (New York: W. W. Norton, 1977).

EDMONDS, Robin

Setting the Mould: the United States and Britain, 1945–1950 (New York: W. W. Norton, 1986; Oxford: Clarendon Press, 1986).

EIZENSHTEIN,
Sergei M.

Ivan Groznyi, film script (Moscow: Gospolizdat, 1944).

ERICKSON, John

The Road to Stalingrad: Stalin's war with Germany, Vol. I (London: Weidenfeld & Nicolson, 1975; New York: Harper & Row, 1983).

———

The Road to Berlin: Stalin's war with Germany, Vol. II (London: Weidenfeld & Nicolson, 1983; Boulder, Colo.: Westview Press, 1983).

FEILING, Keith

The Life of Neville Chamberlain (London: Macmillan, 1946; Hamden, Conn., Shoe String Press, 1970).

FEIS, Herbert

Churchill Roosevelt Stalin: the war they waged and the peace they sought (London: Oxford University Press, 1957; Princeton, N.J.: Princeton University Press, 1957).

FLYNN, E. J.

You're the Boss (Westport, Conn.: Greenwood, 1983).

FOX, William T. R.

The Super-Powers: the United States, Britain and the Soviet Union—their responsibility for peace, Yale University Institute of International Studies (New York: Harcourt, Brace, 1944).

FRASER, David

Alanbrooke (Feltham, Middlesex: Hamlyn paperback, 1983; first published Collins, London, 1982).

———

And we shall shock them: the British Army in the Second World War (London: Sceptre edn, 1988; first published Hodder & Stoughton, 1983).

GAFENCU, Grigore

Prelude to the Russian Campaign, trans. Fletcher-Allen (London: Frederick Muller, 1945).

GILBERT, Martin

Winston S. Churchill, Vols. III–VIII (London: Heinemann, 1966–88)—abbreviated in the Notes to this book as Gilbert, *Churchill.*

GORER, Geoffrey, and RICKMAN, John — *The People of Greater Russia: a psychological study* (London: The Cresset Press, 1949).

GROSSMAN, Vasilii — *Life and Fate,* trans. R. H. Chandler (New York: Harper & Row, 1986; London: Fontana paperback, 1986; first published 1985).

HARBUTT, Frazer J., — *The Iron Curtain: Churchill, America, and the Origins of the Cold War* (New York and Oxford: Oxford University Press, 1986).

HARRIS, Kenneth — *Attlee* (London: Weidenfeld & Nicolson, 1982; New York: W. W. Norton, 1983).

HASLAM, Jonathan — *The Soviet Union and the Struggle for Collective Security in Europe, 1933–1939* (London: Macmillan, 1984; New York: St. Martin's Press, 1984).

HAYTER, William — *The Kremlin and the Embassy* (London: Hodder & Stoughton, 1966).

HEINRICHS, Waldo — *Threshold of War: Franklin D. Roosevelt and American entry into World War II* (New York: Oxford University Press, 1988).

HEWLETT, Richard, and ANDERSON, Oscar — *A History of the United States Atomic Energy Commission.* Vol. I, *The New World 1939/1946* (University Park, Pa.: Pennsylvania State University Press, 1962).

HILGER, Gustav, and MAYER, Alfred G. — *The Incompatible Allies: German–Soviet relations, 1918–1941* (New York: Macmillan, 1953).

HITLER, Adolf — *Hitler's Table Talk, 1941–44* (London: Weidenfeld & Nicolson, 1953.)

—— *My New Order,* Hitler's speeches ed. Raoul de Roussy de Sales (New York: Reynal & Hitchcock, 1941).

—— *Mein Kampf,* trans. James Murphy (London: Hurst & Blackett, 1939).

HOLLOWAY, David — *The Soviet Union and the Arms Race* (New Haven and London: Yale University Press, 1983).

IOIRYSH, A. I., MOROKHOV, I. D., and IVANOV, S. A. — *A-Bomba* (Moscow: Nauka, 1980).

IRIYE, Akira — *The Origins of the Second World War: Asia and the Pacific* (New York and London: Longman, 1987).

IRVING, David — *Churchill's War: the struggle for power* (Australia: Veritas, 1987).

JENKINS, Roy — *Asquith* (London: Collins, 1964).

KAHN, David — *The Codebreakers: the story of secret writing* (New York: Macmillan, 1967; London: Weidenfeld & Nicolson, 1974).

KARNOW, Stanley — *Mao and China: from Revolution to Revolution* (New York: Viking Press, 1972; London: Macmillan, 1973).

KEEBLE, Curtis — *Britain and the Soviet Union, 1917–1989* (London: Macmillan, 1990).

KELLY, Laurence — *Lermontov: tragedy in the Caucasus* (London: Robin Clark, 1983; first published Constable, 1977).

KENNEDY, Paul — *The Rise and Fall of the Great Powers: economic change and military conflict from 1500 to 2000* (New York: Random House, 1987; London: Unwin Hyman, 1988).

KEYNES, J. M. — *Essays in Persuasion* (London: Macmillan, 1931).

—— — *The Economic Consequences of the Peace* (London: Macmillan, 1920; New York: Harcourt, Brace & Howe, 1920).

KIRBY, S. Woodburn, et al. — *The War Against Japan* (London: HMSO, 1969).

KISSINGER, Henry A. — *A World Restored: Metternich, Castlereagh and the Problems of Peace, 1812–1822,* (London and New York: Gollancz and Houghton Mifflin. 1973.

LAMB, Richard — *The Ghosts of Peace, 1935–1945* (Salisbury, Wilts.: Michael Russell, 1987).

LAQUEUR, Walter, ed.   *Fascism: a reader's guide,* Juan J. Linz, et al. (London: Wildwood House, 1976).

LARKIN, Philip, ed.   *The Oxford Book of Twentieth-Century English Verse* (Oxford and New York: Oxford University Press, 1973).

LARRABEE, Eric   *Commander in Chief: Franklin Delano Roosevelt, his lieutenants and their war* (New York: Harper & Row, 1987; London: André Deutsch, 1987).

LARRAZÁBAL, Ramón Salas   *Historia del Ejército Popular de la República,* 4 vols. (Madrid: Editora Nacional, 1973).

LEVI, Primo   *If This Is a Man* and *The Truce,* trans. Stuart Woolf (London: Abacus, 1979; first published in Italian by Einaudi, 1958 and 1963, respectively).

LEWIN, Ronald   *Ultra Goes to War: the secret story* (London: Hutchinson, 1978; New York: Pocket Books, 1981).

LIPPMANN, Walter   *U.S. War Aims* (Boston: Little, Brown, 1944).

———   *Interpretations, 1933–1935,* ed. Allan Nevins (New York: Macmillan, 1936).

LONDONDERRY, the marquess of   *Ourselves and Germany* (Harmondsworth, Middlesex: Penguin Books, 1938; first published Robert Hale, 1938).

LOUIS, William Roger   *The British Empire in the Middle East, 1945–51: Arab nationalism, the United States, and postwar imperialism* (Oxford: Clarendon Press, 1984; New York: Oxford University Press, 1986).

———   *India, Africa and the Second World War, ethnic and racial studies* (London: Routledge & Kegan Paul, 1986).

MAHAN, Alfred T.   *The Influence of Sea Power upon History* (London: Methuen, 1965; Boston: Little, Brown, 1970).

———   *The Interest of America in Sea Power, Present and Future* (Port Washington and London: Kennikat Press, 1970).

MAKINS, Roger   "Britain's Nuclear Story, 1945–52: politics and
                               technology," review article, *Round Table,* 65 (1975).

MAL'KOV, Viktor L.   *Franklin Ruzvel't: problemy vnutrennei politiki i
                               diplomatii,* Russian edition (Moscow: Mysl', 1988).

MATLOFF, Maurice, and   *Strategic Planning for Coalition Warfare: 1943–1944: a*
SNELL, Edwin M.   volume in *The U.S. Army in the Second World War*
                               (Washington, D.C.: U.S. Department of Defense,
                               1953).

McNEAL, Robert H.   *Stalin: man and ruler* (New York: New York
                               University Press, 1988; London: Macmillan, 1988).

McNEILL, William H.   *America, Britain and Russia: their co-operation and conflict
                               1941–46* (London and New York: Oxford University
                               Press, 1953).

MEDVEDEV, Roy A.   *Let History Judge: the origins and consequences of
                               Stalinism* (London: Macmillan, 1972; New York:
                               Random House, 1973).

MITSCHERLICH,   *Die Unfähigkeit zu Trauern: Grundlagen kollektiven
Alexander and Margarete   Verhaltens* (Munich: R. Piper, 1968).

MONELLI, Paolo   *Roma 1943* (Milan: Mondadori, 1945).

MORAN, Charles   *Winston Churchill: the struggle for survival 1940–1965*
                               (London: Constable, 1966; Boston: Houghton Mifflin,
                               1966).

MORGAN, Kenneth O.   *Labour in Power: 1945–1951* (Oxford and New York:
                               Clarendon Press and Oxford University Press, 1984).

MORLEY, J. W., ed.   *Dilemmas of Growth in Pre-War Japan* (Princeton, N.J.:
                               Princeton University Press, 1971).

NASH, Charles, ed.   *History of the War in Afghanistan* (London: Thomas
                               Brooks, 1843).

NELSON, James, ed.   *General Eisenhower on the Military Churchill: a
                               conversation with Alistair Cooke* (New York: W. W.
                               Norton, 1970).

NICOLSON, Harold — *Peacemaking 1919* (London: Constable, 1943; Magnolia, Mass.: Peter Smith, 1954; first published 1933).

NISBET, Robert — *Roosevelt and Stalin: failed courtship* (Washington, D.C.: Regency Gateway, 1988).

NOBUTKA, Ike, ed. — *Japan's Decision for War* (Stanford, Calif.: Stanford University Press, 1967).

NORMANBROOK, Lord, and others — *Action This Day: working with Churchill* (London: Macmillan, 1968).

OKA, Yoshitake — *Konoye Fumimaro: a political biography* (Tokyo: University of Tokyo Press, 1983).

ORWELL, George — *The English People* (London: Collins, 1947; New York: Haskell House, 1984).

PARRISH, Thomas — *Roosevelt and Marshall: partners in politics and war—the personal story* (New York: William Morrow, 1989).

PAYNE, Stanley G. — *Franco's Spain* (London: Routledge & Kegan Paul, 1968).

PINDER, John — *The Federal Idea: a British contribution, Lord Lothian.* New Europe Papers, Round Table Issue No. 286 (London: Butterworth, 1983).

POGUE, Forrest C. — *George C. Marshall.* 4 vols. (New York: Viking Press, London: Macgibbon & Kee, 1963–87).

PRANGE, Gordon W. — *At Dawn We Slept* (New York: McGraw-Hill, 1981).

———, ed. — *Hitler's Words (Two Decades of National Socialism, 1922–43)* (Washington, D.C.: American Council on Public Affairs, 1944).

PRAZMOWSKA, Anita — *Britain, Poland and the Eastern Front, 1939* (Cambridge: The University Press, 1987).

READ, Anthony, and FISHER, David — *The Deadly Embrace: Hitler, Stalin and the Nazi-Soviet Pact, 1939–1941* (New York: W. W. Norton, 1988).

REYNAUD, Paul — *La France a sauvé l'Europe.* 2 vols. (Paris: Flammarion, 1947).

REYNOLDS, David

The Creation of the Anglo-American Alliance, 1937–41: a study in competitive cooperation (London: Europa Publications, 1981).

RICHARDS, Denis

Royal Air Force, 1939–45 (London: HMSO, 1974–75).

RHODES JAMES, Robert

Anthony Eden (London: Weidenfeld & Nicolson, 1987).

ROBERTS, Geoffrey

The Unholy Alliance: Stalin's Pact with Hitler (London: I. B. Tauris, 1989).

RYBAKOV, Anatoly

Children of the Arbat, trans. Harold Shukman (London: Hutchinson, 1988).

RZHESHEVSKY, O. A.

Istoriya vtorogo fronta: voina i diplomatiya (Moscow: Izdatel'stvo Znanie, 1988).

SCG—SOCIALIST CLARITY GROUP

The U.S.S.R.—its significance for the West (London: Victor Gollancz, 1942).

SCHAPIRO, Leonard

The Communist Party of the Soviet Union, 2nd edn (London: University Paperbacks, Methuen/Eyre & Spottiswoode, 1970; first published 1960).

SCHLESINGER, Arthur M., Jr.

The Age of Roosevelt, 3 vols.: *The Crisis of the Old Order, The Coming of the New Deal,* and *The Politics of Upheaval* (Boston: Houghton Mifflin, 1957, 1959, and 1960).

————

Roosevelt's Diplomacy at Yalta, Yalta: un mito che resiste (Rome: Edizioni dell' Ateneo, 1989).

SCHMIDT, Paul

Hitler's Interpreter (London: Heinemann, 1951).

SEMEONOFF, Anna

Brush Up Your Russian (London: J. M. Dent, 1933).

SETON-WATSON, Hugh

Eastern Europe Between the Wars, 1918–1941 (Cambridge: The University Press, 1946).

————

The Russian Empire, 1801–1917 (Oxford: Clarendon Press, 1967).

SHEPPERD, Alan

The Italian Campaign, 1943–45, a political and military reassessment (London: Arthur Barker, 1968; New York: Frederick Praeger, 1968).

SHTEMENKO, S. M.　*General'nyi shtab v gody voiny,* 2 vols. (Moscow: Voennoe Izdatel'stvo, 1981).

SIMONOV, K. M.　*"Zametki k biografii G. K. Zhukova"* published in instalments in "Voenno-istoricheskii zhurnal," (Moscow, 1987).

SIPOLS, Vilnis Ya.　*Diplomaticheskaya bor'ba nakanune vtoroi mirovoi voiny* (Moscow: Mezhdunarodnye Otnosheniya, 1979); trans. as *Diplomatic Battles Before World War II* (Moscow: Progress Publishers, 1982).

———　*Na puti k velikoi pobede: sovetskaya diplomatiya v 1941–1945 gg.* (Moscow: Politizdat, 1985).

———　*Vneshnyaya politika Sovetskogo Soyuza, 1936–1939 gg.* (Moscow: Nauka, 1987).

SLUSSER, Robert M.　*Stalin in October: the man who missed the Revolution* (Baltimore and London: Johns Hopkins Press, 1987).

SMYTH, H. D.　*Atomic Energy: general account of the development of methods of using atomic energy for military purposes under the auspices of the United States Government, 1940–1945* (Washington, D.C.: U.S. Government Printing Office, 1945; London: HMSO, 1945).

SNOW, Edgar　*Journey to the Beginning* (London: Victor Gollancz, 1959; New York: Random House, 1959).

SOAMES, Mary　*Clementine Churchill: the biography of a marriage* (London: Cassell, 1979; Boston: Houghton Mifflin, 1979; Harmondsworth, Middlesex: Penguin Books, 1981).

SOLZHENITSYN, Aleksandr　*Arkhipelag GULag, 1918–1956: opyt khudozhestvennogo issledovaniya,* 3 vols. (Paris: YMCA-Press, 1973–75); trans. Thomas P. Whitney as *The Gulag Archipelago: an experiment in literary investigation* (London: Collins/Fontana, 1974).

———　*August 1914,* trans. Michael Glenny (London: Bodley Head, 1972).

SORENSEN, Theodore C.　*Decision-making in the White House* (New York: Columbia University Press, 1963).

SOULIE, M.   *La vie politique d'Edouard Herriot* (Paris: Armand Colin, 1962).

STALIN, J. V.   *Dialectical and Historical Materialism* (Moscow: Foreign Languages Publishing House, 1951).

STERN, Fritz R., ed.   *The Varieties of History: from Voltaire to the present* (New York: Meridian Books, 1960).

STIMSON, Henry L.   *The Far Eastern Crisis: recollections and observations* (New York: Harper, for the Council on Foreign Relations, 1936).

SUVOROV, Viktor   *The Ice-Breaker: who started the Second World War?*, trans. Thomas Beattie (London: Hamish Hamilton, 1990).

TAYLOR, A. J. P.   *A History of England, 1914–1945* (Oxford: Clarendon Press, 1965).

————, et al.   *Churchill: four faces and the man* (London: Allen Lane, 1969), published in the U.S. as *Churchill Revised: a critical assessment* (New York: Dial Press, 1969).

TERRAINE, John   *The Right of the Line* (London: Hodder & Stoughton, 1985).

THOMAS, Hugh   *Armed Truce: the beginnings of the Cold War, 1945–46* (London: Hamish Hamilton, 1986; New York: Macmillan, 1987).

————   *The Spanish Civil War*, 3rd edn (Harmondsworth, Middlesex: Penguin Books, 1977; New York: Harper & Row, 1977; first published 1961).

THORNE, Christopher   *Allies of a Kind: the United States, Britain and the war against Japan* (New York: Oxford University Press, 1978; London: Hamish Hamilton, 1979).

THUCYDIDES   *History of the Peloponnesian War*, trans. Rex Warner (Harmondsworth, Middlesex: Penguin Books, 1954).

TOLSTOY, Nikolai   *Victims of Yalta* (London: Hodder & Stoughton, 1977).

TRENCH, Charles Chenevix   *Charley Gordon: an eminent Victorian reassessed* (London: Allen Lane, 1978).

TRILLING, Lionel — *The Middle of the Journey* (New York: Harcourt Brace Jovanovich, 1980; London: Secker & Warburg, 1947, 1975).

TRUKHANOVSKY, V. G. — *Uinston Cherchill*, 4th, expanded edition (Moscow: Mezhdunarodnye Otnosheniya, 1989; English trans., Moscow: Progress Publishers, 1978; first published 1968).

TUCKER, Robert C. — *Stalin as Revolutionary, 1879–1929: a study in history and personality* (New York: W. W. Norton, 1974; London: Chatto & Windus, 1977).

—— — *Stalin in Power: The Revolution from above 1928–1941* (New York: W.W. Norton, 1991).

—— — *The Soviet Political Mind: Stalinism and post-Stalin change* (New York: W. W. Norton, 1971; London: Allen & Unwin, 1972).

——, ed. — *Stalinism: essays in historical interpretation* (New York: W. W. Norton, 1977).

TUÑON DE LARA, Manuel, et al. — *La Guerra Civil Española, 50 años despues* (Barcelona: Editorial Labor, 1986).

TURNER, Frederick J. — *The Frontier in American History* (New York: Henry Holt, 1921).

ULAM, Adam B. — *Expansion and Coexistence: Soviet foreign policy, 1917–1973* (London: Secker & Warburg, 1968; 2nd edn, New York: Holt, Rinehart & Winston, 1974).

—— — *Stalin: the man and his era* (New York: Viking Press, 1973; London: Allen Lane, 1974).

VALEO, Francis — *The China White Paper*, a summary of the State Department volume *United States Relations with China, with special reference to the period 1944–1949,* 5 August 1949, prepared for the Library of Congress Legislative Reference Service, Washington, D.C., October 1949.

VAUSSARD, Maurice — *Histoire d'Italie contemporaine, 1870–1946* (Paris: Hachette, 1950).

VERRIER, Anthony — *Assassination in Algiers: Churchill, Roosevelt, De Gaulle and the murder of Admiral Darlan* (New York: W. W. Norton, 1990; London: Macmillan, 1990).

VIÑAS, Angel — *La Alemania y el 18 de julio* (Madrid: Alianza Editorial, 1974).

VINCIGUERRA, Mario — *I partiti italiani dal 1948 al 1955* (Rome: Centro Italiano dell' Osservatore, 1955).

VOLKOGONOV, Dmitrii A. — *I. V. Stalin: triumf i tragediya,* 2 vols. in 4 parts (Moscow: Izdatel'stvo Agenstva pechati Novosti, 1989)—abbreviated in the Notes as Volkogonov, *Stalin.*

WARD, Geoffrey — *A First-Class Temperament: the emergence of Franklin D. Roosevelt* (New York: Harper & Row, 1989).

WATT, Donald Cameron — *How War Came: the immediate origins of the Second World War, 1938–1939* (London: Heinemann, 1989).

——— — *Succeeding John Bull: America in Britain's place, 1900–1975* (Cambridge and New York: Cambridge University Press, 1984).

——— — "John Herbert King, a Soviet source in the Foreign Office," in *Intelligence and National Security,* Vol. 3, no. 4 (London: Frank Cass, 1988).

WAUGH, Evelyn — *Brideshead Revisited* (London: Chapman & Hall, 1945, 1960).

WHITE, Stephen — *The Origins of Detente: the Genoa Conference and Soviet-Western relations, 1921–22* (Cambridge: The University Press, 1985).

WILMOT, Chester — *The Struggle for Europe* (Westport, Conn.: Greenwood Press, 1952, 1972; London: Collins, 1959).

WILSON, Duncan — *Gilbert Murray, OM: 1866–1957* (Oxford: Clarendon Press, 1987).

WOODHOUSE, C. M. — *The Struggle for Greece, 1941–1949* (London: Hart-Davis, McGibbon, 1976; Woodstock, N.Y.: Beckman Publishers, 1979).

——— — *Apple of Discord: a survey of recent Greek politics in their international setting* (London: Hutchinson, 1948).

WOODWARD, E. L.   *British Foreign Policy on the Second World War*, 5 vols. (London: HMSO, 1970–76).*

ZAKHAROV, Marshal   *Finale* (Moscow: Progress Publishers, 1972).
M. V., ed.

---

*Both this history and *Grand Strategy* form part of the Official British History of the Second World War. As such, they (notably Michael Howard's brilliant Volume IV of *Grand Strategy*) are important works of scholarship. But—given the flood of wartime documents since released and also the revelation of the *Ultra* secret—neither can now be regarded as a primary source. Both are therefore listed here in Section III. Section I, however, includes the first volume of Margaret Gowing's official history of atomic energy, many of whose sources are now accessible, because she provides scholars with a detailed list of the exact references to the documentary sources used at the time when the book was written.

NOTES

Sources that recur repeatedly throughout the book (e.g., *FRUS—Foreign Relations of the United States*) are always quoted in a highly abbreviated form. Such abbreviations and acronyms will be found in the margin, in the Documentary Sources (pp. 499 ff.), opposite the full title of the source in each case. All other sources are quoted in full in the Notes on first occurrence. If they recur thereafter, a somewhat abbreviated (though readily intelligible) form is used.

PREFACE

1. The word "political" needs emphasis. The international economic structure of the modern world is another matter.
2. The phrase coined by Lord Carrington (former British Foreign Secretary and future Secretary-General of NATO) in his Alastair Buchan Memorial Address, delivered at the IISS, London, 21 April 1983.

3. E.g., W. H. McNeill, *America, Britain and Russia: their co-operation and conflict 1941–46* (London & New York: Oxford University Press, 1953; reprinted, New York: Johnson Reprint Corporation, 1970), and Herbert Feis, *Churchill Roosevelt Stalin: the war they waged and the peace they sought* (Princeton, N.J.: Princeton University Press, 1957).

4. In the twenty-one pages forming the conclusions of McNeill's *America, Britain and Russia,* the atomic bomb is nowhere mentioned.

5. The American release of wartime archives having shown the way, the British followed in 1972, when the documents for 1941–45 were released in one single operation (those for 1939–40 had already been made available).

6. And therefore the translations of many of the Soviet documents (both wartime and pre-war) quoted in the text are my own.

7. Cf. the observation (as recent as 1984) that the "Grand Alliance was primarily an Anglo-American partnership in which the Soviets . . . were included only so long as there was a common enemy"—Kimball, Vol. I, p. 5.

8. "You use the snaffle and the curb all right, / But where's the bloody horse?"—Roy Campbell, *Oxford Book of Twentieth Century English Verse* (Oxford: Oxford University Press, 1973), p. 338.

9. Paul Kennedy, *The Rise and Fall of the Great Powers: economic change and military conflict from 1500 to 2000* (London & Sydney, Unwin Hyman, 1988), p. 536. See also "the dynamic of technological change and military competitiveness," ibid., p. xvii.

10. John F. Kennedy, in the Foreword to Theodore C. Sorensen's *Decision-making in the White House* (New York: Columbia University Press, 1963), p. xi.

11. "Men of letters who have written history without taking part in public affairs . . . are always inclined to find general causes . . . politicians who have concerned themselves with producing events without thinking about them . . . are prone to imagine that everything is attributable to particular incidents, and that the wires that they pull are the same as those that move the world. It is to be presumed that both are equally deceived." I am indebted to Graham Allison for this quotation (on the flyleaf of his *Essence of Decision: explaining the Cuban Missile Crisis* (Boston: Little, Brown, 1971).

12. Leopold von Ranke, in *The Varieties of History from Voltaire to the Present,* ed. Fritz Stern (New York: Meridian Books, 1960), pp. 58–9.

CHAPTER 1

1. *FRUS, the Conferences at Cairo and Teheran, 1943,* p. 585, which is also the source of Roosevelt's remark about the rainbow in the epigraph to this chapter.

2. According to Stalin's interpreter, Valentin Berezhkov, he also dropped it; it was picked up by Voroshilov. The toast is described in ibid., p. 583.

3. Ibid., pp. 640–1.

4. On his way to the conference Stalin travelled by train as far as Baku. Then, of the two aircraft standing ready to make the journey to Teheran, he chose the one piloted by a relatively junior officer—a colonel—on the ground that he had more recent flying experience. In the event both aircraft arrived safely.

5. The *Manchester Guardian* war correspondent in South Africa was John Atkins, whose description of Churchill in 1899 is in his *Incidents and Reflections* (London: Christopher, 1947), p. 122.

6. Churchill did not smoke cigarettes or a pipe. For his drinking habits and his cigar-smoking, see Lieutenant-General Sir Ian Jacob's description in Lord Normanbrook, and others, *Action This Day: working with Churchill* (London: Macmillan, 1968), pp. 182–3. The photograph of Churchill referred to is the one in the Imperial War Museum, London, taken on the occasion of his victory broadcast on 8 May 1945, reproduced in the photo section.

7. Churchill's wartime dress varied enormously, ranging from formal parliamentary (short black coat and waistcoat with bow tie) through several uniforms to his siren suit, an example of which is preserved in the basement floor of Turnbull & Asser, Jermyn Street, London.

8. McIntyre used to examine Roosevelt about twice a week. For the diagnosis of Roosevelt in March 1944, see Chapter 15.

9. The archivist at Dunhill has confirmed the fact that Churchill sent General Ismay to Dunhill to buy pipes as a present for Stalin before his first visit to Moscow in August 1942.

10. Milovan Djilas, *Conversations with Stalin,* translated by Michael B. Petrovich (London: Hart-Davis, 1962), pp. 59–60.

11. John Erickson, *The Road to Stalingrad: Stalin's war with Germany* (London: Weidenfeld & Nicolson, 1975), Vol. I, p. 403. Stalin was also "quite sick for several months" soon after the end of the war—Svetlana Allilueva, *Twenty Letters to a Friend* (Harmondsworth, Middlesex: Penguin Books, 1968), p. 164.

12. At the opening plenary session of the Teheran Conference, 28 November 1943— *FRUS, the Conferences at Cairo and Teheran, 1943,* p. 487.

13. First used in G. W. Kaye's *History of the War in Afghanistan,* in 1843, this phrase became shorthand for Anglo-Russian rivalry in Asia.

14. For a recent example, see Hugh Thomas, *Armed Truce: the beginnings of the Cold War, 1945–46* (London: Hamish Hamilton, 1986).

15. Walter Lippmann, *U.S. War Aims* (Boston: Little, Brown, 1944), p. 132.

CHAPTER 2

1. Thucydides, *History of the Peloponnesian War,* II, 43.

2. The successive drafts of this speech are in the Speech File, 610–14, in the FDR Library, Hyde Park, N.Y.

3. Stalin, *Sochineniya* (Stanford edition), Vol. II, p. 1. The fact that the speech was poorly delivered (see Ivan Maisky in *Novy Mir,* December 1964, p. 165) does not detract from its remarkable form and substance.

4. A. J. P. Taylor, et al., *Churchill Revised: a critical assessment* (New York: Dial Press, 1969), p. 122. The friend was Desmond Morton; the story is related in this book by Robert Rhodes James. Like de Gaulle, Churchill spoke the language of the barrack room as well as of the eighteenth century.

5. Cited by E. T. Williams in his notice of Churchill in the *Dictionary of National Biography Supplement, 1961–1970* (Oxford: Oxford University Press, 1981), p. 214. Churchill's mother was the beautiful but prodigal Jennie Jerome.

6. "Hired out . . . like a conjuror"—see Churchill's letters to his mother of December 1900–January 1901 quoted in Randolph S. Churchill, *Winston S. Churchill* (London: Heinemann, 1966), Vol. I, pp. 543–5. The present chapter is indebted to this volume for its account of the first quarter century of Churchill's life.

7. Winston Churchill, *The World Crisis: the Eastern Front* (London: Thornton Butterworth, 1931), pp. 7 and 343ff.

8. In his broadcast on 1 October 1939, after the Soviet occupation of eastern Poland—see Churchill, Vol. I, p. 353.

9. Winston Churchill to his mother, 6 April 1897, quoted in Randolph S. Churchill, *Winston S. Churchill,* Vol I, p. 317.

10. Churchill's own account is *My Early Life: a roving commission* (London: Collins, Fontana, 1959).

11. Churchill to his brother, Jack, 2 December 1897, quoted by Randolph Churchill, *Winston S. Churchill,* Vol. I, p. 363.

12. There are differing accounts of Gordon's death. See Charles Chevenix Trench, *Charley Gordon: an eminent Victorian reassessed* (London: Allen Lane, 1978), pp. 290–1.

13. Cited by Williams, *DNB Supplement,* p. 194.

14. The Government of India Act, 1935, retained central power under the control of the British Viceroy, but conceded more or less democratic government at provincial level. For Churchill's role during the abdication crisis in 1936, see Chapter 4.

15. Churchill, Vol. I, p. 157. His words refer to one of a series of rebuts, on this occasion the government's decision not to appoint him Minister for the Co-ordination of Defence, in 1936.

16. Clementine Churchill to H. H. Asquith, then Prime Minister, May 1915, quoted in Roy Jenkins, *Asquith* (London: Collins, 1964), p. 361.

17. For Churchill's identification with his ancestor, see Winston S. Churchill, *Marlborough: his life and times* (London: Harrap, 1933–38), 4 vols., passim. His belief in "a specific world order" is well argued in Isaiah Berlin's essay on Churchill in his

Personal Impressions (London: Hogarth Press, 1981), p. 7. For the concept of "inherent sanity," see Taylor, et al., *Churchill Revised: a critical assessment*, pp. 136–7.

18. Quoted in Arthur M. Schlesinger, Jr., *The Age of Roosevelt*. Vol. I, *The Crisis of the Old Order, 1919–1933* (Boston: Houghton Mifflin, 1957), p. 350.

19. Kimball, Vol. I, p. 23.

20. On this relationship and its effect on the Roosevelts' marriage, see Joseph Alsop, *FDR, 1882–1945: a centenary remembrance* (New York: Viking Press, 1982), pp. 67 ff.

21. So recollected in a letter from Oliver Wendell Holmes to Harold Laski, 23 November 1932, cited in James MacGregor Burns, *Roosevelt: the Lion and the Fox* (New York: Harcourt Brace, 1956), Vol. I, p. 507.

22. Dr. George Draper, quoted in ibid., p. 88.

23. He spent much of his time at Warm Springs, Georgia, which—under Roosevelt's patronage—became a place of therapy for polio victims, including himself.

24. To Edward Flynn, in the gubernatorial library at Albany. E. J. Flynn, *You're the Boss* (Westport, Conn.: Greenwood Press, 1983), p. 84. And for Roosevelt's remark in 1928, see Schlesinger, *The Age of Roosevelt*, Vol. I, p. 355.

25. Winston S. Churchill, *Great Contemporaries* (London: Collins, Fontana, 1965), p. 303. (This essay was first published as an article in *Collier's*, 29 December 1934.) It was the Texas delegation's switch to Roosevelt that finally began the avalanche that secured his nomination.

26. Walter Lippmann, *Interpretations, 1933–1935*, ed. Allan Nevins (New York: Macmillan, 1936), pp. 261–2. See also *New York Herald Tribune*, 28 April 1932.

27. Quoted by Burns, *Roosevelt*, Vol. I, p. 157.

28. Kimball, Vol. I, p. 23.

29. Eleanor Roosevelt, *This I Remember* (London: 1950), (New York: Harper & Brothers, 1949), p. 63.

30. See, for example, Anthony Storr in A. J. P. Taylor, et al., *Churchill Revised*, pp. 229 ff.; and *Action This Day: working with Churchill*, memoirs by Lord Normanbrook and others, John Wheeler-Bennett's Introduction, p. 7. In Charles Moran's book, *Winston Churchill: the struggle for survival, 1940–1965* (London: Constable, 1966), his breach of the Hippocratic oath outraged the medical profession and its publication impelled several civil servants and a distinguished officer, all of whom had worked closely with Churchill throughout his years at Number 10, to combine to write *Action This Day*.

31. Sutherland's biographer's account is in Chapter 9 of Roger Berthoud, *Graham Sutherland* (London: Faber & Faber, 1982). The quotation, however, is from Mary Soames, *Clementine Churchill: the biography of a marriage* (Harmondsworth, Middlesex: Penguin Books, 1981), p. 713.

32. Volkogonov, *Stalin*, Vol. 1, Part 2, p. 303.

33. V. I. Lenin, *PSS.*, Vol. 45, pp. 345–6.

34. Quoted in Isaac Deutscher, *Stalin: a political biography,* revised edn (Harmonds-worth, Middlesex: Pelican Books, 1966), pp. 23–4.

35. This new date has been established (in Georgia) by Robert H. McNeal, *Stalin: man and ruler* (London: Macmillan, 1988), p. 336.

36. For an account, see, for example, Chapters XVII and XVIII of Hugh Seton-Wat-son, *The Russian Empire, 1801–1917* (Oxford: Clarendon Press, 1967).

37. In a letter to Maxim Gorky—of February 1913—Lenin, *PSS,* Vol. 48, p. 162.

38. For Svetlana Allilueva's account of the Svanidzes, see Chapters 3–8 of *Twenty Letters to a Friend.* The date—22 October 1907—of Ekatarina's death has been estab-lished from Georgian sources by McNeal, *Stalin,* p. 339.

39. For Tukhachevsky, see Chapter 4.

40. Churchill, Vol. IV, pp. 447–8. Deaths in the 1930s, both from collectivisation and the purges, are further discussed in Chapter 4.

41. Allilueva, *Twenty Letters,* p. 98.

42. Adam Ulam, *Stalin: the man and his era* (New York: Viking Press, 1973; London: Allen Lane, 1974), pp. 354–5.

43. Allilueva, *Twenty Letters,* p. 60.

44. Ibid., p. 121.

CHAPTER 3

1. Both the Agreement and the Treaty, "respecting Assistance to France in the event of Unprovoked Aggression by Germany," form part of *The Treaty of Peace between the Allied and Associated Powers and Germany,* Cmd. 153 (London: HMSO, 1920).

2. A remark made by Salvador de Madariaga in his autobiography, quoted by Duncan Wilson, *Gilbert Murray OM: 1866–1957* (Oxford: Clarendon Press, 1987), p. 293.

3. 118 House of Commons Debates (cited hereafter as H. C. Debs.), col. 992, 21 July 1919.

4. *League of Nations Official Journal,* Special Supplement 93 (Geneva, 1931), pp. 59–60.

5. Edouard Herriot, private papers, quoted in M. Soulié, *La vie politique d'Edouard Herriot* (Paris: Armand Colin, 1962), p. 377. I am indebted to Christopher Thorne, *The Limits of Foreign Policy: the West, the League and the Far Eastern Crisis of 1931–1933* (London: Hamish Hamilton, 1972), both for this quotation and for the two extracts from Cecil's speeches quoted above.

6. Officers and soldiers of the Kwantung Army, acting without the prior knowledge of its Commander-in-Chief (who, however, gave their action his speedy approval), used explosives to destroy less than one meter of the South Manchuria Railway, about five miles north of Mukden. A Japanese attack on Chinese forces in Mukden followed.

7. Robert Cecil, *A Great Experiment: an autobiography* (London: Cape, 1941), pp. 235–6,

and H. L. Stimson and M. Bundy, *On Active Service in Peace and War* (New York: Harper Brothers, 1948), p. 221. I am again indebted for these quotations to Thorne's *Limits of Foreign Policy.*

8. Stimson and Bundy, *On Active Service,* p. 262.

9. See, for example, the concise account offered in Akira Iriye, *The Origins of the Second World War: Asia and the Pacific* (London & New York: Longmans, 1987), passim.

10. Its transatlantic repercussions rumbled on, however. Anglo-American mutual re-crimination had never been far below the surface during the crisis, and in 1936 it erupted in Stimson's public accusation (he was by then out of office), that the British Government had thwarted his plan of halting Japan in its career of aggression. As we now know, western prevarication during the Manchurian crisis was fairly evenly balanced on each side of the Atlantic. For Stimson's accusation, see H. L. Stimson, *The Far Eastern Crisis: recollections and observations* (New York: Harper, for the Council on Foreign Relations, 1936), pp. 155 and 164.

11. Japanese disillusionment after the First World War (in which Japan was the ally of Britain, France and the United States) is further discussed in the second half of the next chapter. German and Austrian territorial losses as the result of the war are shown in map 1, "The European Settlement After Versailles."

12. Cited in Alan Bullock, *Hitler: a study in tyranny,* revised edn (London: Odhams Books, 1964), p. 187.

13. For a description of the profile of international indebtedness in the interwar period, see George C. Abbott, *International Indebtedness and the Developing Countries* (London: Croom Helm, 1979), pp. 16 ff.

14. Bullock, *Hitler,* p. 474.

15. Ibid., p. 672.

16. Adolf Hitler, *Mein Kampf,* translated by James Murphy (London: Hurst & Blackett, 1939), p. 553.

17. Mussolini's phrase was an "axis, round which all those European states which are animated by a desire for collaboration and peace may work together." In due course it became the "Rome-Berlin-Tokyo" Axis.

18. *Hitler's Table Talk, 1941–44* (London: Weidenfeld & Nicolson, 1953), pp. 258–9.

19. An important piece of contemporary evidence on this tragic episode is the letter written to the British Ambassador in Madrid, immediately after the bombing, by the British Consul in Bilbao, the full text of which forms Appendix 8 to Hugh Thomas' *The Spanish Civil War,* 3rd edn (Harmondsworth, Middlesex: Penguin Books, 1977). For a detailed examination by a military historian, formerly a Nationalist air force officer, see Ramón Salas Larrazábal, *Historia del Ejército Popular de la República,* Vol. II (Madrid: Editora Nacional, 1973), pp. 1384–92. No one knows for certain how many died in Guernica—one thousand, at a very rough guess.

20. See, for example, *The Republic and the Civil War in Spain,* ed. Raymond Carr (London: Macmillan, 1971). In his Preface to these essays, Carr states that he has not suppressed the contradictions between them.

21. Exhaustively analysed in Angel Viñas, *La Alemania y el 18 de julio* (Madrid: Alianza Editorial, 1974).

22. The first study to be based on a wide range of Italian documents is John F. Coverdale, *Italian Intervention in the Spanish Civil War* (Princeton, N.J.: Princeton University Press, 1975).

23. For Soviet supplies, see, for example, Jonathan Haslam, *The Soviet Union and the Struggle for Collective Security in Europe 1933–1939* (London: Macmillan, 1984), pp. 107 ff. They were paid for by the gradual transfer to Moscow of the Spanish Central Bank's reserves of gold.

24. Appendix 7 in Thomas' *The Spanish Civil War* assembles the evidence available at the time his book was written. For a contemporary analysis, see Larrazábal, *Historia,* Vol. II, pp. 2368 ff., and Angel Vinñas' contribution (pp. 123 ff.) in Manuel Tuñon de Lara, et al., *La Guerra Civil Española, 50 años despues,* 2nd edn (Barcelona: Editorial Labor, 1986).

25. Paul Schmidt, *Hitler's Interpreter* (London: Heinemann, 1951), p. 193.

26. Guernica was the major exception.

27. *DGFP,* Series D, Vol. I, Document 34, and Series C, Vol. V, Document 625.

28. Halifax's left arm was congenitally withered and handless.

29. A Cabinet minister, but without portfolio.

30. Halifax's own record is in *DBFP, 1919–1939,* Second Series, Vol. XIX, *1937–1938,* pp. 543–8 (FO file reference C 8161/270/18), and his report to the Cabinet is in pp. 572–5. Hitler's interpreter, Paul Schmidt, also made his notes available to the Foreign Office. The German record is in *DGFP,* Series D, Vol. I, pp. 55–67.

31. Keith Feiling, *The Life of Neville Chamberlain* (Hamden, Conn.: Shoe String Press, 1970), p. 332.

32. *N.D.,* 2929-PS.

33. This was the reason given by Chamberlain in the House of Commons. In the British note of refusal handed to Maisky by Cadogan on 24 March 1938, the British Government was said to have been willing to take part in a conference of all European powers, but considered that such a conference was impossible to arrange for the moment: *DVPS,* Vol. XXI, Document 102. The Soviet Government's proposal had been announced by Litvinov in a press conference on 17 March: ibid., Document 82 and *Izvestiya,* 18 March 1938.

34. Walter Runciman, who succeeded Halifax as Lord President of the Council.

35. The scene is well described in Harold Nicolson, *Diaries and Letters, 1930–1939,* ed. Nigel Nicolson (London: Collins, Fontana, 1969), p. 364.

36. The Munich Agreement, which bore the official date of 29 September 1938, was

published by HMSO as *Further Documents respecting Czechoslovakia,* Misc. No. 8, Cmd. 5848; and the Anglo-French "proposals" (in effect an ultimatum) to the Czechoslovak Government were published as Cmd. 5847 (London: HMSO, 1938), pp. 8–9.

37. See the record (in Czech) of this call made by the Secretary-General of the Czechoslovak Foreign Ministry, translated as Document 38 in *Dokumenty i materialy kanuna vtoroi mirovoi voiny, 1937–1939,* Vol. 1 (Moscow: Politizdat, 1981).

38. *DBFP, 1919–1939,* Third Series, Vol. II, p. 627.

39. Ibid., pp. 630 ff.

40. *DVPS,* Vol. XXI, Document 40, and *Bor'ba za mir,* Document 10.

41. Like Disraeli sixty years earlier, Chamberlain was addressing the crowds that welcomed him in Downing Street.

42. *The Times,* 3 October 1938.

CHAPTER 4

1. In his memoirs (Churchill, Vol. I, p. 325), Churchill acknowledged his mistake in believing that "an air attack upon British warships, armed and protected as they now are, will not prevent free exercise of their superior sea-power."

2. A recent example, which is unlikely to be the last, is John Charmley, *Chamberlain and the Lost Peace* (London: Hodder & Stoughton, Heinemann, 1989).

3. Churchill, Vol. I, p. 62.

4. Ibid., p. 61.

5. Eden's remark is quoted in Gilbert, *Churchill,* Vol. V, *1922–1939,* p. 461, and Churchill's in Churchill, Vol. I, pp. 59–60.

6. Churchill, Vol. I, loc. cit., and p. 93.

7. Ibid., p. 97.

8. See Hinsley, *British Intelligence,* Vol. I, pp. 298–302.

9. The debate in March 1936 is described in Churchill, Vol. I, p. 159. For "Arms and the Covenant" and for the effect on this movement—and on Churchill's political standing—of Churchill's intervention on the King's behalf on 7 December 1936, see ibid., pp. 170–1.

10. Churchill's letter, 2 February 1937, is quoted in Mary Soames, *Clementine Churchill,* p. 396, which is also the source of his daughter's description of his depression in early 1937.

11. Article in the *Evening Standard,* 17 September 1937.

12. Churchill, Vol. I, p. 201. The events leading up to Eden's quarrel with Chamberlain are discussed later in this chapter.

13. The American recession of 1937–38 left Churchill owing just over £18,000 to his stockbrokers. Chartwell was advertised for sale only briefly (in *The Times* of 2 April 1938) because Churchill's debt was paid by Sir Henry Strakosch on 23 March. For

purposes of comparison, Disraeli's debts, amounting to about £60,000, were taken over by Andrew Montagu in 1862, in return for a mortgage on Hughenden Manor and a minimal interest charge—Robert Blake, *Disraeli* (London: Methuen, 1969), p. 424.

14. Feiling, *The Life of Neville Chamberlain,* p. 367.
15. Churchill, Vol. I, pp. 212–13.
16. *DVPS,* Vol. XXI, Document 103. Five months later, in the course of an evening spent with Churchill, the latter—again according to Maisky's report—coined a new slogan: "Proletarians and freethinkers of all nations, unite against the fascist tyrants." Ibid., Document 321.
17. The text of Churchill's letter to Halifax, 3 September 1938, is in Churchill, Vol. I, pp. 229–30. Litvinov's telegram to the Soviet Ambassador in Prague is in *DVPS,* Vol. XXI, Document 324. For the October debate on the Munich Agreement, see Churchill, Vol. I, pp. 253. ff.
18. *DVPS,* Vol. XXI, Document 111.
19. 29.9 per cent in the Roper Poll of September 1939. For Roosevelt and Hearst in February 1932, see Schlesinger, *The Age of Roosevelt,* Vol. I, p. 297.
20. Frederick Jackson Turner, *The Frontier in American History* (New York: Henry Holt, 1921), pp. 246 and 315.
21. Ibid., pp. 296–7, written in 1914.
22. I am indebted to the long memory of a British merchant banker, the late Ivo Forde, for this personal recollection. From his own office across the street, Forde witnessed one of several suicides from the top of the Equitable Building committed by victims of the 1929 crash.
23. "While the World Watches," published in *Collier's,* 29 December 1934.
24. Speech File, 610–14, in the FDR Library, Hyde Park.
25. Raymond Moley, *After Seven Years* (Lincoln, Nebr.: University of Nebraska Press, 1971), pp. 47–52.
26. Speech File, 627, broadcast of 7 May 1933, in the FDR Library, Hyde Park.
27. Morgenthau Diary, quoted by Robert Dallek in *Franklin D. Roosevelt and American Foreign Policy 1932–1945* (New York: Oxford University Press, 1981), p. 58.
28. Schlesinger, *The Age of Roosevelt,* Vol. II (Boston: Houghton Mifflin, 1959), p. 209.
29. Speech File, 627, in the FDR Library, Hyde Park.
30. *Daily Mail,* 4 July 1933; and 280 H.C. Debs., cols. 787–8, 10 July 1933.
31. Quoted in Schlesinger, Vol. II, p. 232.
32. A decision which cost the resignation of one of the ablest of the younger members of the administration, Dean Acheson, Under-Secretary of the Treasury, who did not return to government until 1941.
33. *FRUS, 1934,* Vol. I, pp. 525–7.
34. Charles Bohlen and Llewellyn Thompson were also Russian linguists who had

distinguished careers in the U.S. Foreign Service. The British Diplomatic Service was much less far-sighted in this respect.

35. The old smiler was William Allen White's phrase, quoted (from the *Emporia Gazette*) in *Time,* 22 February 1943, p. 53; de Gaulle's description is in Charles de Gaulle, *Mémoires de Guerre,* 3 vols. (Paris: Plan, 1954–59), Vol.II, *L'Unité,* p.238; and Roosevelt was called an artist in government by Harold Smith, Director of the Budget, 1939–46, in an interview with Robert Sherwood after the war, quoted in *The White House Papers of Harry L. Hopkins: an intimate history* (London: Eyre & Spottiswoode, 1948), Vol. I, p. 73.

36. "I am the issue" is cited by Schlesinger, *The Age of Roosevelt,* Vol. III, *The Politics of Upheaval* (Boston: Houghton Mifflin, 1960), p. 578; White's remark is from *Time,* 19 November 1934.

37. This speech (vaguely indicating interest in American co-operation with other countries in "quarantining" those that were "creating a state of international anarchy and instability") is in *PPA: 1937,* pp. 406–11. Roosevelt's implication was "whom the cap fits . . . ," but he took it no further.

38. Churchill, Vol. I, p. 199.

39. The initiative is therefore described at some length in the next four paragraphs, in which all quotations (except where otherwise stated) are derived from the same source: *DBFP, 1919–1939,* Second Series, Vol. XIX, *1937–1938,* pp. 726 ff. (beginning with Washington telegram no. 38 to the Foreign Office—Document 422) and Appendix 1 (extracts from Chamberlain's diary). Cadogan's epithet "amazing" comes from his letter to Eden, 13 January 1938, which is included among these papers.

40. Feiling, *The Life of Neville Chamberlain,* p. 325.

41. *FRUS, 1938, General,* Vol. I, Sumner Welles' memorandum to the President, 10 January 1938.

42. I am indebted to the Director of the Harry S. Truman Library for letting me have copies of the papers from the Truman Confidential File relating to the subsequent history of Roosevelt's telegram to Chamberlain. Chamberlain's widow first enquired about this telegram through the U.S. Embassy in London in March 1948. Truman then refused to allow its release, because "it could be grossly misinterpreted during this coming year." In December 1950 Halifax asked for the message to be made public. On Dean Acheson's memorandum, reporting Halifax's request, Truman wrote: "I do not think it should be released." The manuscript original is in PSF Diplomatic Papers, Box 46, *Great Britain 1937–38,* at the FDR Library, Hyde Park.

43. Press and radio conference, 28 December 1943, Speech File, 1499, FDR Library, Hyde Park.

44. "You keep your cards close up against your belly. You never put them on the

table"—H. L. Ickes, *The Secret Diary of Harold L. Ickes,* 3 vols. (New York: Simon & Schuster, 1953–54), Vol. III, p. 659.

45. The sources of these three European assessments, in order, are Trotsky, "If America should go communist," *Liberty,* 23 March 1935; Keynes, after a not very successful teatime visit to the White House, quoted by Schlesinger, Vol. III, pp. 405–6; and Jung, writing in *The Observer,* 18 October 1936.

46. John Rickman published two articles in 1919 in *The Nation* (London) on the Russian attitude to "Truth and Guilt," the contents of which were reproduced thirty years later as Appendix III of *The People of Greater Russia* (London: The Cresset Press, 1949), p. 235.

47. *Pravda,* 7 February 1964 and 19 April 1988.

48. Quoted by Khrushchev in his speech to the XXth CPSU Congress, February 1956 (a secret speech, well known abroad but not published in the Soviet Union until 1989). OGPU is an earlier acronym for the NKVD, now the KGB.

49. 12 December 1938: Volkogonov, *Stalin,* Vol. I, Part 2, pp. 301 ff. For estimates of the number of purged victims, see Roy A. Medvedev, *Let History Judge: the origins and consequences of Stalinism* (New York: Knopf, 1971), p. 239, and Robert Conquest, *The Great Terror: Stalin's purge of the thirties* (London: Macmillan, 1968), Appendix A. Tukhachevsky, a former Tsarist officer, was Red Army Chief of Staff from 1925 to 1928, Deputy Defence Minister from 1934 to 1936, Marshal of the Soviet Union, 1935, and First Deputy Defence Minister from 1936. He was also a candidate member of the CPSU Central Committee from 1934 to 1937. For the framing of Tukhachevsky, see *Pravda,* 29 April 1988 and "O dele Tukhachevskogo," *Politicheskoe obrazovanie,* 5 (Moscow, 1989).

50. Estimates of the number of deaths from famine alone vary between 3 million (official Soviet historians) and 6 million (Medvedev), as of 1988. But the enormity of this tragedy is now officially recognised by the CPSU.

51. Article by Mark Tolts, published in *Ogonek,* and quoted by Rupert Cornwell in *The Independent,* 22 December 1987.

52. Stalin, *Sochineniya* (Stanford edition), Vol. I, pp.373–4.

53. The wartime membership of the Politburo of the CPSU is listed in Appendix I. The exception was Vlas Chubar, believed to have been shot in 1941.

54. Lionel Trilling, *The Middle of the Journey* (New York: Harcourt Brace Jovanovich 1980; London: Secker & Warburg, 1947 and 1975), pp. xix–xxi (in the Introduction to the 1975 edition).

55. Lincoln Steffens, cited in Schlesinger, *The Age of Roosevelt,* Vol. I, pp. 146–7.

56. Anna Semeonoff, *Brush Up Your Russian* (London: Dent, 1933), p. 64—a textbook still used at the London School of Slavonic Studies as late as 1940.

57. Churchill, Vol. I, p. 288. For Djilas' acute observation, see Djilas, *Conversations with Stalin,* p. 52.

58. On the Rapallo Treaty, see Stephen White, *The Origins of Detente: the Genoa Conference and Soviet-Western relations, 1921–22* (Cambridge: University Press, 1985), pp. 158 ff.

59. *DVPS*, Vol XVI, Document 266 and p. 792.

60. Attólico's report, 12 July 1934, is quoted by Jonathan Haslam, *The Soviet Union and the Struggle for Collective Security in Europe, 1933–1939*, p. 40.

61. Ibid., pp. 35 and 58. For the Soviet decision of 19 December 1933, see *DVPS*, Vol. XVI, pp. 876–7.

62. *Pravda*, 28 November 1937.

63. *Izvestiya*, 18 March 1938. See also *Istoriya vneshnei politiki SSSR*, Vol. I, pp.341–2.

64. *DVPS*, Vol. XXI, Documents 354 ff.

65. See, for example, ibid., Documents 197, 275 and 324.

66. Ibid., Document 338.

67. On 25 September 1938 the Soviet Defence Minister instructed his attaché in Paris to inform General Gamelin about these measures—ibid., Document 378. Cf. Volkogonov, *Stalin*, Vol. II, Part 1, p. 17.

68. A view that Maisky repeated at length, in a formal protest, to Halifax on 11 October 1938—ibid., Documents 396 and 414.

69. *DBFP, 1919–1939*, Second Series, Vol. XII, pp. 766 ff., and *DVPS*, Vol. XVIII, Document 178.

70. *DVPS*, Vol. XVIII, Document 215.

71. The range of sources about these early soundings taken in Berlin is wide: notably, *DGFP*, Series C, Vol. 4, Document 211, several documents in *DVPS* and—perhaps most significantly—Evgenii Gnedin's *Iz istorii otnoshenii mezhdu SSSR i fashistkoi Germaniei* (New York: Khronika, 1977), pp. 34–35. (Gnedin was Press Secretary at the Soviet Embassy at the time.)

72. The number of Far Eastern entries, including reports from Richard Sorge, in the 1939 volume of Soviet diplomatic documents is significant. The final document (no. 449) in this volume is the victorious Tass communiqué "on the liquidation of the remaining Japanese/Manchurian troops," dated 1 September 1939, published in *Pravda* on that day. See also Vilnis Ya. Sipols, *Vneshnyaya politika Sovetskogo Soyuza, 1936–1939 gg.* (Moscow: Nauka, 1987), pp. 301 ff.

73. This phrase was shorthand for the treaties signed by Japan after the First World War, notably the naval disarmament treaty of 1922. See Akira Iriye, *The Origins of the Second World War: Asia and the Pacific*, pp. 2 ff.

74. This entry in Grew's diary, 27 January–10 February 1933, like MacArthur's assessment, is quoted by Thorne in *The Limits of Foreign Policy*, p. 349. For MacArthur's view of the place of the Far East in American policy, see for example his *Reminiscences* (London: Heinemann, 1964), p. 32.

75. The tangled history of Sorge's career is unravelled by F. W. Deakin and G. R.

Storry, *The Case of Richard Sorge* (London: Chatto & Windus, 1966). The quotation is on p. 276.

76. Conveniently listed in Helen Foster Snow, *My China Years* (London: Harrap, 1984), p. 208.

77. Where western powers enjoyed extra-territorial rights, dating from the nineteenth century.

78. CAB 24/229, CP 104 (32).

79. The plan whereby the U.S. Navy was to cross the Pacific Ocean westwards in the event of war.

80. See *FRUS, Japan, 1931–41,* Vol. I, pp. 523 ff; and, for the Craigie-Arita agreement, *DBFP,* Third Series, Vol. IX, p. 313.

81. For the evolution of the Chinese Communist movement in the 1930s, see Edgar Snow, *Journey to the Beginning* (London: Gollancz, 1959), and Stanley Karnow, *Mao and China: from Revolution to Revolution* (New York: Viking Press, 1972).

82. PREM 1/345.

83. Quoted by Thorne, *Limits of Foreign Policy,* p. 3.

84. G. K. Zhukov, *Reminiscences and Reflections* (Moscow: Progress Publishers, 1985), Vol. I, pp. 202–3. Chapter 5 of this volume describes the Khalkin Gol campaign.

CHAPTER 5

1. As a hard-fought by-election held at Oxford immediately after the Munich Agreement, where it was the principal electoral issue, proved. Two future Conservative prime ministers, Edward Heath and Harold Macmillan, supported the anti-Chamberlain candidate (the Master of Balliol College) in this election.

2. See Churchill, Vol. I, pp. 267–8, for Hoare's speech and for the "wave of optimism" in Britain during early March 1939.

3. Evelyn Waugh, *Brideshead Revisited* (London: Chapman & Hall, 1960; first published 1945), pp. 322–3.

4. The alleged German ultimatum to his country was reported to Halifax by the Romanian Minister in London, Viorel Tilea, on 17 March: *DBFP,* Third Series, Vol. IV, Document 389.

5. The text of the declaration is in 345, H.C. Debs., col. 2415, 31 March 1939. For Chamberlain's earlier statement in the House of Commons and his Birmingham speech, see Churchill, Vol. I, pp. 268–70.

6. "God helping, we can do no other"—Churchill, Vol. I, pp. 270 and 293.

7. CAB 53/11, COS 288, 30 March 1939; and CAB 53/47, COS 872 (JP); February and April 1939.

8. For The Dirksen Papers, see p. 503.

9. Donald Cameron Watt, *How War Came: the immediate origins of the Second World War, 1938–1939* (London: Heinemann, 1989), p. 610.

10. The Soviet proposal of 18 March is in *Bor'ba za mir,* Document 162; the British counter-proposal of 20 March is in *DBFP,* Third Series, Vol. IV, Document 446; the Soviet reply thereto is in *Bor'ba za mir,* Document 178; and examples of Soviet scepticism are to be found in ibid., Documents 170 and 171 (last sentence).

11. CAB 29/160, 12th meeting, 26 April 1939.

12. As early as 24 March the Polish Ambassador was making this point clear to the Foreign Office (*DBFP,* Third Series, Vol. IV, Document 518) and it was rammed home by the Polish Foreign Minister when he came to London: see ibid., Vol. V, Document 1, recording Beck's conversation with Halifax on 4 April, from which this sentence is quoted.

13. 345 H.C. Debs, col. 2415, 31 March 1939.

14. The main Soviet documents relating to this episode are in *Bor'ba za mir,* pp. 284 ff. The Soviet account of Maisky's talk with Halifax, Document 200, does not agree with the British record (*DBFP,* Third Series, Vol. IV, Document 589) even on the time of day when it took place—1:00 P.M. according to Maisky. One thing is, however, common to both sets of documents: the cold wind blowing from the Kremlin after Chamberlain had spoken without prior consultation with Moscow, on 31 March: see *Bor'ba za mir,* Document 203 (last sentence), and the British Ambassador's report of this interview with Litvinov (*DBFP,* Third Series, Vol. IV, Document 597).

15. The British record of Beck's talks in London in the first week of April (the opening documents in *DBFP,* Third Series, Vol. V) shows him divorced from reality, although—perhaps because—he had been Polish Foreign Minister since 1932.

16. See, for example, Churchill, Vol. I, pp. 290 ff.

17. Chamberlain's letter of 21 May 1939 to his sister, Ida (NC 18/1/1100), and CAB 23/100, 38/39, 19 July 1939, are both quoted by Anita Prazmowska in *Britain, Poland and the Eastern Front* (Cambridge: Cambridge University Press, 1987), a study which shows the degree of Anglo-Polish misunderstanding during these months to have been little less than that between the British and Soviet governments described in the present chapter.

18. *DBFP,* Third Series, Vol. V, Document 52.

19. CAB 54/11, DCOS 179, 16 August 1939.

20. *Pravda,* 11 March 1939, and *DBFP,* Third Series, Vol. IV, Document 452.

21. *DBFP,* Third Series, Vol. V, Document 421—a "somewhat trying" interview with Molotov, whose own account is in *Bor'ba za mir,* Document 278.

22. 347 H.C. Debs., col. 1848, 19 May 1939.

23. *DBFP,* Third Series, Vol. V, Document 533.

24. *DBFP,* Series D, Vol. VI, Documents 215 and 332.

25. William Strang (who after the war became head of the British Foreign Service) in paragraphs 2 and 3 of his letter to Orme Sargent, Deputy Under-Secretary at the

Foreign Office, 20 July 1939—reproduced in *DBFP,* Third Series, Vol. V, Document 376. This volume of *DBFP* contains the British records of the "Strang round" of the Anglo-Soviet political negotiations as well as the run-up to the military round, including the British Mission's instructions, which are in Appendix V.

26. *Pravda,* 29 June 1939.

27. *DBFP,* Third Series, Vol. V, Document 281.

28. Ibid., Documents 357 and 473.

29. I.e., Portsmouth. The personal impression that he made seems to have varied. One of the author's contemporaries remembers him agreeably, although he appeared "dismal" to Rear-Admiral Sir Edmund Irving, who served under Drax as a midshipman in 1929–30. (I am indebted to Sir Edmund Irving for this recollection of Drax ten years before his mission to Moscow.) Drax—or to give him his full name, the Honourable Sir Reginald A. R. Plunkett-Ernle-Erle-Drax—certainly did not impress his Russian interlocutors.

30. The British record of the "Anglo-Franco-Russian Military Conversations" is in Appendix II of *DBFP,* Third Series, Vol. VII. The Soviet record is in *Bor'ba za mir,* pp. 543 ff. The "go-slow" paragraph is 8 in the British Mission's instructions (see note 25 above). The account given in this chapter draws on both records.

31. *DBFP,* Third Series, Vol. VI, Document 467.

32. The Soviet historian is V. Ya. Sipols, *Vneshnyaya politika Sovetskogo Soyuza, 1936–1939 gg.* pp.321 ff.The western study is Anthony Read and David Fisher, *The Deadly Embrace: Hitler, Stalin and the Nazi-Soviet Pact, 1939–1941* (New York: W. W. Norton, 1988). The evidence offered for the timing of Stalin's final decision in the latter book (p. 218) is purely circumstantial, however.

33. Apart from Neville Henderson's efforts at appeasement at the Berlin Embassy, the principal focus of Anglo-German discussion during these last weeks was the Wohltat and the Dahlerus talks. There was even a last-minute scheme to fly Göring to Britain.

34. Volkogonov, *Stalin,* Vol. II, Part 1, pp. 20 ff.

35. *DGFP,* Series D, Vol. VI, Documents 883–4. The offer a week earlier had been made over dinner in a Berlin restaurant—ibid., Document 847, and Read and Fisher, *The Deadly Embrace,* pp. 121–2.

36. *DGFP,* Series D, Vol. VII, Documents 56, 142 and 159.

37. Both the treaty and the Secret Protocol are in ibid., Documents 228 and 229.

38. A. S. Yakushevskii, Sovetsko-Germanskii Dogovor o Nenapadenii: vzglyad cherez gody, Voprosy Istorii KPSS, 8 (1988); *Sovetskaya Rossiya,* 24 August 1988, p. 4; and *Pravda,* 25 May and 28 December 1989.

39. Churchill, Vol. I, p. 307.

40. Robert Coulondre's despatch of 4 October 1938 is summarised in his *De Staline à Hitler: souvenirs de deux ambassades 1936–1939* (Paris: Hachette, 1950), pp. 165–8. His

despatch of 7 May 1939 is in *Le Livre Jaune Français. Documents diplomatiques, 1938–1939,* Ministère des Affaires Etrangères (Paris: Imprimerie Nationale, 1939), pp. 153 ff.

41. I am indebted to Christopher Andrew, *Secret Service: the making of the British Intelligence community* (London: Heinemann, 1985), p. 426, for this quotation from Orme Sargent's minute of 3 September 1939—FO 371/23686, N 4146. His book also throws searching light on the inadequacy of British sources of secret intelligence in 1939.

42. Ibid., p. 427. For the Soviet "mole" in the Foreign Office, see Donald Cameron Watt, "John Herbert King, a Soviet source in the Foreign Office," in *Intelligence and National Security,* Vol. 3, no. 4 (London: Frank Cass, 1988).

43. *Bor'ba za mir,* p. 5.

44. Ibid., Document 56 (cf. *DVPS,* Vol. XXI, Document 474).

45. Quoted in the Introduction to ibid., p. 7.

46. The text of Stalin's speech is in *Sochineniya* (Stanford edition), Vol. II, p. 3. Molotov's remark, accepted by Medvedev, *Let History Judge,* p. 452, is quoted by Gustav Hilger and Alfred G. Mayer in *The Incompatible Allies: German-Soviet relations, 1918–1941* (New York: Macmillan, 1953), p. 336.

47. Anita Prazmowska explains the reasons for this delay (the Anglo-Polish Financial Agreement was finally signed even later, after Poland had been invaded) in her book *Britain, Poland and the Eastern Front.* Appendix 4 in this book gives the text of the Political Agreement of 25 August 1939, including its Secret Protocol.

48. *DGFP,* Series D, Vol. VII, Document 213.

49. *Pravda,* 1 September 1939. For the "prophecy," see pp. 112–113.

50. Churchill, Vol. I, p. 320.

51. Both Garner's and Roosevelt's remarks are quoted in Robert Dallek, *Franklin D. Roosevelt and American Foreign Policy, 1932–1945,* p. 192.

52. Kennedy was anti-Semitic to boot. And by the beginning of 1941 Roosevelt was obliged to ask Hopkins (then on his first mission to London) to investigate the allegation that Kennedy had made a profit of half a million dollars, or even pounds, by financial speculations undertaken during the Czech crisis: see Roosevelt's letter to Hopkins, 15 January 1941, Hopkins Papers, Sherwood Collection, Box 304, in the FDR Library, Hyde Park (declassified in 1972).

53. Quoted in Bullock, *Hitler: a study in tyranny,* pp. 503–4. The text of Roosevelt's appeal of 15 April (which was no doubt primarily aimed at domestic opinion) is in *DBFP,* Third Series, Vol. V, Document 180, and in *PPA: 1939,* pp. 201–15.

54. Kimball, Vol. I, R–1x.

CHAPTER 6

1. In Churchill, Vol. I, Book 2. Churchill preferred the term "twilight war"—a phrase used in a private letter written at that time by Chamberlain—to "phoney war": see Feiling, *The Life of Neville Chamberlain*, p. 420.

2. There was "no hurry as time was on our side": meeting of the Anglo-French Supreme War Council, 13 September—CAB 65/1, War Cabinet 39/38, 20 September 1939.

3. "Lightning war"—in broad terms, the combined use of mechanised forces, especially tanks, and close-support aircraft in order to achieve a quick victory.

4. See Appendix II.

5. *DGFP*, Vol. VIII, Document 157.

6. *N.D.*, L-52. For Hitler's peace offer, see his speeches in *My New Order*, ed. Raoul de Roussy de Sales (New York: Reynal & Hitchcock, 1941), pp. 721–56.

7. A translation of the text of the Supreme Soviet decrees bringing these incorporations into force, 1 and 2 November 1939, is in *Documents on Soviet-Polish Relations, 1939–45,* The General Sikorsky Historical Institute (London: Heinemann, 1961), Vol. I, pp. 69–70.

8. Tacitus, *Agricola,* 30: *ubi solitudinem faciunt pacem appellant.*

9. *N.D.*, 864-PS.

10. Total Finnish casualties in the Winter War were just under 80,000. The estimate of Soviet casualties suggested by Khrushchev ("as many as a million lives") is absurd—Nikita Khrushchev, *Khrushchev Remembers,* translated and edited by Strobe Talbott (Boston: Little, Brown, 1970), Vol. I, p. 155. They may well have totalled 200,000, however.

11. Finland, previously part of Sweden, did not become part of the Russian Empire until 1809, when it became an Imperial Grand Duchy, enjoying a measure of local autonomy. It became an independent country for the first time after the Russian Revolution of 1917.

12. Afterwards described by a Soviet general who had good reason to know, from direct experience at the time, as insufficient knowledge of the special organisational features, the equipment and the tactical methods of the Finnish Army: A. M. Vasilevsky, *Delo vsei zhizni,* 2nd, expanded edn (Moscow: Izdatel'stvo politicheskoi literatury, 1975), pp. 95 ff. In other words, there was a complete failure of the Soviet military intelligence and planning.

13. General Nikolaus von Falkenhorst, who knew Finland from 1918.

14. For an analysis of this failure of British intelligence, see Patrick Beesly, *Very Special Admiral: the life of Admiral J. H. Godfrey, CB* (London: Hamish Hamilton, 1980), pp. 149 ff., and Hinsley, *British Intelligence,* Vol. I, pp. 121 ff.

15. See his minute to the First Sea Lord, 10 April 1940—Churchill, Vol. I, pp. 474, and, for the epithet "ramshackle," p. 480.

16. Three cruisers and four destroyers. Allied naval losses in the Norwegian campaign were also heavy: one aircraft carrier, two cruisers, nine destroyers and a sloop.

17. For a succinct summary of this campaign and of Churchill's part in it, see David Fraser, *And we shall shock them: the British Army in the Second World War* (London: Sceptre edition, 1988; first published Hodder & Stoughton, 1983), pp. 52–3.

18. Churchill attended a meeting of the Allied Supreme War Council for the first time in Paris in February 1940, at Chamberlain's invitation.

19. John Colville, *The Fringes of Power: Downing Street Diaries, 1933–1955,* Vol. I (London: Hodder & Stoughton, 1985), p. 39.

20. This bombardment began almost at once. Early examples are reproduced in Churchill, Vol. I, pp. 356–62.

21. Ibid., Vol. IV, p. 78.

22. To stand in, in peacetime, for the future War Cabinet.

23. Churchill, Vol. I, p. 505.

24. Ibid., p. 506. (But Ismay was called "Pug," never Hastings.)

25. Ibid., p. 458.

26. Kimball, Vol. I, p. 5, citing Churchill Papers 4/52.

27. Churchill, Vol. I, p. 435.

28. This mistrust is analysed in David Reynolds, *The Creation of the Anglo-American Alliance, 1937–41: a study in competitive co-operation* (London: Europa Publications, 1981), pp. 63–92, passim. See also Chapter 7 of the present book.

29. Quoted in Churchill, Vol. I, p. 353.

30. The agenda is paper 9/17 in FO 371/24298.

31. Few prime ministers have ever signed their own death warrants as effectively as Chamberlain did in this speech (quoted at length in Churchill, Vol I, p. 461). See also Preface, p. 19.

32. Leopold Amery, a former Conservative Cabinet Minister, re-entered the government under Churchill, as Secretary of State for India. He and Churchill had been contemporaries at Harrow School. Lloyd George had been Prime Minister, 1917–22.

33. There have been many accounts both of the emotional debate in the House of Commons and of the confused to-ings and fro-ings of the following forty-eight hours. Churchill's own account (Vol. I, Chapter XXXVIII) errs in giving the date of the decisive meeting with Chamberlain as 10 May, whereas in fact it took place on the 9th; he also does not mention the presence of David Margesson, the Chief Whip (see A. J. P. Taylor, *English History, 1914–1945* (Oxford: Clarendon Press, 1965), p. 473). But the one cardinal point is incontestable: at this meeting Churchill for once held his peace.

34. German-Soviet communiqué, Moscow, 22 September—*The Times,* 23 September 1939.

35. *DGFP,* Vol. VIII, Document 131.
36. Ibid., Document 104.
37. Text, translated from the Russian, in *Documents on Soviet-Polish Relations,* Vol. I, pp. 47–8.
38. This map forms Appendix VI to *DGFP,* Vol. VIII.
39. The declaration is in Ibid., Document 161.
40. Ibid., Document 160.
41. Communicated to the author from a confidential Polish source.
42. Khrushchev, *Khrushchev Remembers,* p. 154.
43. Vasilevsky, *Delo vsei zhizni,* p. 102.
44. The future marshal K. K. Rokossovsky. By contrast, the head of Soviet Military Intelligence was executed.
45. Speech File, 1240, FDR Library, Hyde Park.
46. The revised law obliged the President to designate "combat zones" which closed eight Atlantic and Baltic Sea routes to American shipping. In effect, this aided the German blockade, in the words of a commentator at the time (quoted in Dallek, *Franklin Roosevelt and American Foreign Policy, 1932–34,* p. 212) "as effectively as if all our ships had been torpedoed."
47. Kimball, Vol. I, pp. 25–35 and 37–8.
48. Described on p. 123. For the apocalyptic (notably Kennedy's) reporting, see Dallek, *Franklin Roosevelt,* pp. 213 ff.
49. *PPA: 1940,* pp. 1–6.
50. The Manhattan Project was the U.S. codename later adopted for the atomic bomb project; the British codename for atomic matters was Tube Alloys. For the 1939 beginning, see Atomic Energy File, folder 2, in the Hopkins Papers relating to Tube Alloys, FDR Library, Hyde Park; and the description given in Richard Hewlett and Oscar Anderson, Jr., *A History of the United States Atomic Energy Commission,* Vol. I, *The New World: 1939/1946* (University Park, Pa.: Pennsylvania State University Press, 1962), pp. 11 ff.

CHAPTER 7

1. In this sentence Churchill used the words "the British people" in its old, imperial sense. In 1940, as well as the British Government, the governments of Australia, Canada, India, New Zealand and South Africa continued to be at war with Germany and (from June onwards) Italy.
2. Following the speech described on p. 39.
3. The date of the passage by Congress of the Lend-Lease Bill was 8 March 1941. Robert Sherwood's definition of the Common Law Alliance between Britain and the United States that followed this turning point of the war (which forms the epigraph to Chapter 8) is in *The White House Papers of Harry L. Hopkins,* Vol. I, pp. 269–70.

4. John Jellicoe, Commander-in-Chief of the British Grand Fleet, 1914–16.

5. One hundred and thirty-six German divisions against ninety-four French and ten British, to which it was hoped to add a total of thirty-two Belgian and Dutch divisions.

6. For the state of the French Army's morale as early as November 1939, see Alanbrooke's "Notes for My Memoirs," cited in David Fraser, *Alanbrooke* (Feltham, Middlesex: Hamlyn Paperbacks, 1983, first published by William Collins, London, 1982), pp. 137–8. This accurate assessment of the demoralised state of the French Ninth Army (which later received the brunt of the German armoured attack) came from the pen of a francophile British general, whose first language was French.

7. The German military doctrine of 1940 was the opposite of the French belief in linear defence (a belief based on the obsolete experience of 1918). The object of a German attack, concentrated on a nodal point *(Schwerpunkt)*, was to force a break-in *(Einbruch)*, which was then to be converted into a breakthrough *(Durchbruch)*.

8. Weygand had been Foch's Chief of Staff in the First World War. Simultaneously with this appointment, Reynaud—disastrously—brought into his Cabinet, as Vice-Premier, Philippe Pétain, famous in 1917 as the defender of Verdun.

9. By the time the campaign began, the BEF consisted of I, II and III Corps. The French forces cut off consisted of the bulk of the First Army.

10. Charles de Gaulle, *Mémoires de Guerre* (Paris: Plon, 1954), Vol. I, p. 276.

11. Churchill, Vol. II, pp. 208–10. The three alternatives were continuing the war, sailing to British ports, and sailing to the French West Indies.

12. An Anglo-Free French expedition attempted to take Dakar, unsuccessfully, in August 1940.

13. Churchill, Vol. II, pp. 203–4.

14. The daily output of GCCS was available only to Dowding and his chief subordinate, Air Vice-Marshal Keith Park; but it was an invaluable adjunct in winning the Battle of Britain, during which, in specific combats, British fighter pilots though sometimes outnumbered by as much as twenty to one, still succeeded in shooting down two German aircraft for every British aircraft lost in battle.

15. This quotation is from a letter written by Dowding in answer to a letter of congratulation; the original, framed, hangs in Dowding's wartime office at Bentley Priory.

16. I am greatly indebted to Air Chief Marshal Sir John Aiken both for the assessment of the Battle of Britain that follows and for the quotation in the asterisked footnote to this page.

17. On 15 August alone, Britain was attacked by a total of 520 bombers and 1,270 fighters. German losses on that day—the crucial one in August—numbered seventy-six, over twice the losses of the RAF.

18. In the summer of 1940, the first beginnings of the aerial bombardment of cities in the Second World War, which would later acquire tremendous proportions, were to some extent accidental. A navigational error caused a German raid on the East

End of London; the RAF retaliated by raiding Berlin on 25 August; and the *Luft-waffe*'s first massive raid on London followed on 7 September.

19. British paramountcy in Egypt dated from the nineteenth century. The military base in the Suez Canal zone, however, rested on the Anglo-Egyptian Treaty of 1936. The Anglo-Egyptian Sudan, nominally a condominium, had effectively been a British colony since 1924.

20. British Army slang for prisoner-of-war was "in the bag." The story related may well be apocryphal, but it has a ring of truth.

21. The Marquess of Londonderry, *Ourselves and Germany,* published as a Penguin Special by Penguin Books in 1938 (first published by Robert Hale, London, 1938).

22. Londonderry House in Park Lane, London, was the Londonderrys' town house. Those who frequented Cliveden (in Buckinghamshire) at the time of Munich were known as "the Cliveden Set."

23. "If the British Empire and its Commonwealth last for a thousand years, men will still say 'This was their finest hour' "—Churchill in the House of Commons, 18 June 1940.

24. This important telegram—PREM 3/47610—is quoted in full in Churchill, Vol. II, p. 201. Philip Kerr (who succeeded to the marquessate of Lothian in 1930) had been Lloyd George's private secretary from 1917 to 1922.

25. Kennedy had in fact resigned a month earlier; see PSF, Box 53, *Great Britain— Joseph Kennedy,* FDR Library, Hyde Park. "Man of Munich" and "Municheer" were terms current at the time.

26. Murrow first visited Britain in 1930; he was posted to London by CBS in 1937. In his own words, Britain then seemed to him a "small, pleasant, historical, but relatively unimportant island off the coast of Europe," whose history he admired, but whose future he doubted—Edward R. Murrow, *A Reporter Remembers.* Vol. I, *The War Years,* recorded in February 1956 on Columbia 0ZL 332 OL 6187, side 1.

27. Richard Austen Butler: he was called "Rab" from an early age.

28. Simon was Lord Chancellor from 1940 to 1945. (Lloyd George once remarked of him that he had sat on the fence so long that the iron had entered his soul.) Hoare received a peerage in due course, becoming Lord Templewood. For Wilson, see p. 68.

29. Attlee, leader of the Labour Party, became Deputy Prime Minister in 1942. He was Prime Minister, 1945–51.

30. Bevin, the leader of the largest trade union in Britain, at first had no seat in the House of Commons. He was Foreign Secretary, 1945–51.

31. From July (when he was operated on for cancer) onwards, Chamberlain was a spent force.

32. This story was recounted to the author by a witness of the exchange.

33. Even after the Labour Government came to power after the general election of July

1945, he continued as ambassador until 1946. His early gaffes in Washington included riding to hounds in Virginia in hunting pink at a time when his compatriots in Britain were otherwise engaged.

34. See Reynolds, *Creation of the Anglo-American Alliance,* pp. 105–6. By a further stroke of good fortune, Lloyd George's doctors advised him not to accept the Washington Embassy, for which he was Churchill's first choice at the end of 1940.

35. This quotation comes from the chapter that Colville contributed to *Action This Day,* p. 49.

36. C-in-C, Middle East, until June 1941. Afterwards C-in-C, India, and later Viceroy. The contrast between Wavell's introverted, laconic Wykehamist manner and Churchill's exuberant personality was total.

37. "A fine two-handed drinker" was Kennedy's description of Churchill to Roosevelt, 10 July 1939: PSF, Box 53, *Great Britain—Joseph Kennedy,* in the FDR Library, Hyde Park. Kennedy was by no means the only American who reported on Churchill as a drunkard (for examples, see Reynolds, *Creation of the Anglo-American Alliance,* p. 144), a judgement that Roosevelt seems at first to have been inclined to accept.

38. This letter is cited in full in Soames, *Clementine Churchill,* pp. 419–20.

39. Reynaud's account of his visit to London in order to present this proposal is in his *La France a sauvé l'Europe* (Paris: Flammarion, 1947), Vol. II, pp. 200 ff.

40. Archibald Sinclair, Secretary of State for Air. He had been Churchill's regimental second-in-command on the Western Front in the First World War.

41. Those close to the events of those days (e.g., Cadogan and Colville) at the time were aware of what was going on, but it first came into the public domain when Halifax's diary was cited in the Earl of Birkenhead's *Halifax: the life of Lord Halifax* (London: Hamish Hamilton, 1965), p. 45.

42. The account given in these four paragraphs is, unless otherwise stated, derived from the records of the War Cabinet meetings of 26–28 May 1940 in CAB 65/13, beginning with WM(40), 139th Conclusions, Confidential Annex, 16 May.

43. Chiefs of Staff paper no. 168, 27 May 1940: a thirteen-paragraph memorandum reproduced in full in Churchill, Vol. II, pp. 79–9.

44. Churchill, Vol. IV, p. 88.

45. Gilbert, *Churchill,* Vol. VI, p. 419.

46. Foreign Office telegram no. 235 to Paris, 28 May 1940—text in CAB 65/13. Its final paragraph was clearly drafted by Churchill himself: "If we both stand out we may yet save ourselves from the fate of Denmark or Poland. Our success must depend first on our unity, then on our courage and endurance!"

47. For a convenient summary of diary evidence, see Reynolds, *Creation of the Anglo-American Alliance,* pp. 324–5.

48. By the time this book is published, more papers relating to the whole Swedish episode may be available in the PRO. In his autobiography, *The Art of the Possible:*

the memoirs of Lord Butler (London: Hamish Hamilton, 1971), p. 81, Butler denied giving the Swedish Minister ground for believing that "any of us had become less bellicose," citing Halifax's letter to Churchill (FO 800/322) of 27 June 1940 as proof of his loyalty. Butler was, however, removed from all contact with foreign affairs in 1941. Despite holding high office after the war, the premiership eluded him.

49. Churchill, Vol. II, p. 436.
50. Ibid., p. 42.
51. Foreign Office telegram no. 198 to Paris, 24 May 1940, in CAB 65/13.
52. For the Anglo–French understanding (although misunderstanding might be a better word to describe what happened on the ground), see Churchill, Vol. IV, p. 98.
53. Ibid., Vol. II, p. 102, records this warning, given to Parliament on 4 June 1940.
54. Including historians who themselves fought in the war and afterwards attained the highest ranks: e.g., Field–Marshal Lord Carver, *Twentieth-Century Warriors: the development of the armed forces of the major military nations in the twentieth century* (London: Weidenfeld & Nicolson, 1987), p. 29, and General Sir David Fraser, *And we shall shock them,* pp. 72, 79–80.
55. Signed on 29 March 1940; the text is in FO 371/24298.
56. Fraser, *Alanbrooke,* pp. 167–8, and Churchill, Vol. II, pp. 71–2. Churchill believed that he had spoken for only ten minutes. Brooke had previously been one of Gort's corps commanders.
57. Full text in Churchill, Vol. II, pp. 183–4.
58. He was Henri Philippe, but preferred his second Christian name.
59. Minute by Sargent of 28 February 1940, in FO 371/24298, C 4444/9/17, and the papers that follow in the same file.
60. I am indebted to John Pinder, both for drawing my attention to Sargent's minute and for his lucid summary of the background to the Declaration of Union. See Pinder, *The Federal Idea: a British Contribution, Lord Lothian.* New Europe Papers, Round Table issue no. 286 (London: Butterworth, 1983); pp. 10 ff.
61. For Vansittart, see p.68. Monnet became, after the war, the architect of the European Iron and Steel Community, which later developed into the European Economic Community (EEC).
62. As also in Lothian's thinking at the very end of his life, although he was a federalist. For Lothian's last speech, read for him in Baltimore on 11 December 1940, when he was on his deathbed, see Pinder, *The Federal Idea,* p. 12. For most British post-war policy-makers, the events of 1940 were a formative influence.
63. Kimball, Vol. I, C-9x, R-4x, C-17x and C-19x. The instruction to Lothian is in the telegram already quoted earlier (note 24).
64. Kimball, Vol. I, C-20x.
65. Ibid., R-8x.
66. 364 H.C. Debs, col. 1171, 20 August 1940.

67. Hitler, *Mein Kampf,* p. 139.
68. A creature in the hands of American Jewry was how Hitler depicted Roosevelt, for example, in his speech declaring war on the United States in December 1941.
69. Kimball, Vol. I, C-18x.
70. Washington telegram no. 834 to the Foreign Office, 26 May 1940, in CAB 65/13.
71. *PPA: 1940,* p. 517.
72. Henry Stimson, Secretary of State under Hoover and Secretary of War under Theodore Roosevelt, had commanded an artillery regiment in the First World War, and so he was often called "Colonel." (Of cryptography, he once remarked that "gentlemen do not read each other's mail.") Knox, a Chicago newspaper publisher, had been the Republican Party's vice-presidential candidate in 1936. Ickes was Secretary of the Interior—"the old curmudgeon."
73. Kimball, Vol. I, C-37x.
74. Ibid., Vol. I, C-43x, dated 8 December 1949 in PREM 3/486/1.
75. *PPA: 1940,* p. 607.
76. *DGFP,* Series D, Vol. IX, Documents 469 and 471.
77. Churchill, Vol. II, pp. 119–20.
78. *DGFP,* Series D. Vol. X, Documents 13 and 20.
79. Ibid., Document 413.
80. Ibid., Vol. XI, Documents 65, 142 and 148.
81. Ibid., Documents 118 (text of the pact) and 109.
82. Ibid., Document 176.
83. Ibid., Document 211.
84. Churchill, Vol. II, p. 518.
85. *DGFP,* Vol. XI, Document 309. The record of the final round of talks, conducted in the air-raid shelter, is in Document 329.
86. According to Molotov's interpreter, Valentin Berezhkov: on Soviet television, 12 May 1989, in the premier of "Eyewitness"—a programme made at the Ekran Studios.
87. *DGFP,* Vol. XI, Document 404.
88. Ibid., Document 669.
89. For example, K. M. Simonov, "Zametki k biografii G. K. Zhukova," published in *Voenno-istoricheskii zhurnal* (Moscow, 1987); and A. S. Yakushevskii, "Sovetsko-Germanskii dogovor o nepadenii: vzglyad cherez gody," published in *Voprosy Istorii KPSS,* 8 (Moscow, 1988).
90. *DGFP,* Vol. XI, Document 532. And on 10 January 1941 Hitler postponed *Sealion* for the last time, except in so far as it served as deception cover for *Barbarossa.*

CHAPTER 8

1. CAB 80/17, COS(40)683, 4 September 1940—"Future Strategy." This assessment, like the *ABC-1* Plan, rested on the unrealistic belief that Germany could be weakened

by a combination of blockade, aerial bombardment and subversion in occupied Europe to such an extent that "numerically inferior forces can be employed with good chance of success." For the *ABC* records, see CAB 99/5.

2. Originally drafted as a declaration by the "Allied and Associated Powers," it was at Roosevelt's suggestion that the term "United Nations" was used instead—a phrase which, as Churchill pointed out to him, appeared in Byron's *Childe Harold's Pilgrimage.* See Gilbert, *Churchill,* Vol. III, p. 35.

3. Churchill, Vol. III, pp. 538–9; Kimball, Vol. I, R-72x; and *Sov.-Angl. O.,* Vol. I, Document 10.

4. The title given by Burns to Part 1 of Vol. II of his *Roosevelt.*

5. Quoted by Robert Conquest in *The Great Terror: Stalin's purge of the thirties,* p. 487.

6. Neither of these crucial arguments was settled until 1943; a fact of which Sherwood could not have been aware when compiling his list.

7. Discussed, for example, in Robin Edmonds, *Setting the Mould: the United States and Britain, 1945–1950* (New York: W. W. Norton, and Oxford: Clarendon Press, 1986), Chapter 2.

8. Sherwood, *The White House Papers,* Vol. I, p. 271. His list of nine "developments, among others, in progress" by the spring of 1941 begins on p. 270.

9. Ibid., p. 235.

10. Broadcast on 9 February 1941.

11. Sherwood, *The White House Papers,* Vol. I, p. 237.

12. Ibid., p. 244; a photograph of the opening pages of this letter, written at Claridge's on 14 January 1941, is between pp. 248 and 249.

13. Kimball, Vol. I, C-58x. For the 1944 gap, caused partly by Hopkins' severe illness and partly by a temporary change in his relationship with Roosevelt, see Sherwood, *The White House Papers,* Vol. 1, pp. 805–6. Hopkins was sent to London by Roosevelt for the first time before the Atlantic Conference (which he attended). And after Roosevelt's death he made one last journey to Moscow, a mission of major importance.

14. Sherwood, *The White House Papers,* Vol. I, p. 4.

15. Quoted in Burns, *Roosevelt,* Vol. II, p. 45.

16. For the committees, pro and anti, see ibid., pp. 40 ff. Senator Wheeler's allegation that Lend-Lease would "plow under every fourth American boy" stung Roosevelt into a public response: "that really is the rottenest thing that has been said in public life in my generation"—*PPA: 1940,* pp. 711–12.

17. David Waley, in his comprehensive summary of Lend-Lease that forms Appendix II to McNeill, *America, Britain and Russia,* p. 773n.

18. See, for example, Edmonds, *Setting the Mould,* Chapter 8.

19. In the House of Commons on 12 March 1941 (the speech quoted) and in his message of gratitude sent to Roosevelt three days earlier—Kimball, Vol. I, C-65x.

20. PREM 4/17/2, a quotation for which I am indebted to Gilbert, *Churchill,* Vol. III, p. 1035.

21. *Agreement between the Governments of the United Kingdom and the United States of America on the Principles applying to Mutual Aid,* Cmd. 6341 (London: HMSO, 1942).

22. Kimball, Vol. I, R-105, and Reynolds, *Creation of the Anglo-American Alliance,* pp. 278 and 369–70. Hull's description of the Ottawa Agreements, which had established the Imperial Preference system in 1932, is in U.S. Congress, House Committee on Ways and Means, *Extension of Reciprocal Trade Agreements Act,* 76th Congress, 1st session (1940), Vol. I, p. 38.

23. Kimball, Vol. I, R-54x, drafts A and B.

24. *Correspondence respecting the Policy of His Majesty's Government in the United Kingdom in Connexion with the Use of Materials received under the Lend-Lease Act,* Cmd. 6311 (London: HMSO, 1941). Formally, it was a unilateral statement by the British Government, but it was treated by the U.S. Government as a contractual obligation.

25. *DBPO,* Vol. I, pp. 350–1. The British Treasury vigorously disagreed.

26. Kimball, Vol. I, C-A3x.

27. Ickes, *The Secret Diary of Harold L. Ickes,* Vol. II, p. 469.

28. Admiral Alfred T. Mahan, author of *The Influence of Sea Power on History* and *The Interest of America in Sea Power, Present and Future.*

29. *PPA: 1941,* Vol. 10, pp. 181–94.

30. Kimball, Vol. I, C-93x.

31. Probably on 1 July 1941. See Waldo Heinrichs, *Threshold of War: Franklin D. Roosevelt and American entry into World War II* (New York: Oxford University Press, 1988), p. 241.

32. *PPA: 1941,* pp. 272–7. The 1940 Selective Service Bill had been introduced in Congress just as the French Government signed the Armistice with Germany. Even so, it was not passed until mid-September 1940.

33. Sherwood, *The White House Papers,* Vol. I, p. 349. An account of Hopkins' discussions with Stalin may be found in ibid., pp. 325 ff, and *Sov.-Am. O.,* Vol. I, pp. 80 ff.

34. Sherwood, *The White House Papers,* p. 310; a photograph of the map faces p. 273.

35. It related to the overlap of responsibility between Winant and Harriman in London. See ibid., p. 312.

36. *Sov.-Angl. O.,* Vol. I, Document 21.

37. Kimball, Vol. I, R-50x.

38. In this particular case, mainly Adolf Berle's. See Heinrichs, *Threshold of War,* pp. 106 ff.

39. General Freyberg, a First World War VC, commanded the New Zealand Division throughout the Second World War. Shortly after sending this signal (quoted in Gilbert, *Churchill,* Vol. VI, p. 1076, from the Churchill Papers, 4/217), he was appointed commander of all troops in Crete. The New Zealand Division, a magnificent force, formed the backbone of the troops defending Crete.

40. John Colville, *The Fringes of Power,* pp. 381–2, which is also the source of his description of Churchill's mood in the next paragraph.

41. Kimball, Vol. I, R-38x.

42. Ibid., C-84x.
43. Ibid., R-39x.
44. Fellers' transfer from Cairo before doing further damage (some of which was—literally—lethal) seems likely to have been the result of British cryptography: see David Kahn, *The Codebreakers* (London: Weidenfeld & Nicolson, 1974), pp. 250 ff., and (more delicately worded) Hinsley, *British Intelligence,* Vol. II, pp. 331 and 389.
45. Dill also tried to shield Wavell from Churchill's increasing displeasure, for which Churchill had increasingly good reason as 1941 went on.
46. Although it was discussed by the American and British Chiefs of Staff at the conference; see the record in PREM 3/485/7, folios 74–80. The more important discussion in London is described in detail in Sherwood, *The White House Papers,* Vol. I, pp. 313 ff.
47. An exotic, quasi-naval uniform.
48. In the frontispiece to Vol. I of Burns' biography of Roosevelt.
49. The final text of the Atlantic Charter is the "Joint Declaration by the President and the Prime Minister"—in PREM 3/485/7. The first draft was Cadogan's; Churchill's own amendments can be seen in the photograph facing p. 394 of his memoirs, Vol. III. See also Gilbert, *Churchill,* Vol. VI, p. 1163, and Kimball, Vol. I, C-128.
50. *Asahi,* 16 August 1941.
51. "Eventual" needs stressing. At this stage Roosevelt insisted that the war should be followed by a transitional period of Anglo-American policing; the international machinery would be set up only after "that experimental period had passed." Sherwood, *The White House Papers,* Vol. I, pp. 349–50, and Churchill, Vol. II, pp. 366–9.
52. Lieutenant-General Sir Ian Jacob, Diary, 19 August 1941, in the Jacob Papers at Woodbridge, Suffolk.
53. Kimball, Vol. I, C-111x.
54. CAB 65/19, 19 and 25 August 1941, and Sherwood, *The White House Papers,* Vol. I, pp. 374–5.
55. Eric Larrabee, *Commander in Chief: Franklin Delano Roosevelt, his lieutenants and their war* (New York: Simon & Schuster, 1987), p. 13.
56. Speech File, 1377, Message to Congress, 21 August 1941, FDR Library, Hyde Park.
57. Speech File, 1381, broadcast of 11 September 1941, FDR Library, Hyde Park.
58. PREM 3/485/1, no. 22.
59. PREM 3/485/7.

CHAPTER 9

1. E.g., that the Red Army was on the point of attacking Germany (which the German Ambassador in Moscow assured Hitler was untrue) and—more credibly—that it would be harder for American aid to Britain to become militarily effective once the Soviet Union had been eliminated.

2. Cited in Bullock, *Hitler,* p. 65.

3. At the risk of oversimplification, the generals—on the whole—believed that it was to capture Moscow by compelling the Red Army to concentrate on the defence of the capital and thus to expose itself to a battle of annihilation as quickly as possible. On the other hand, Hitler believed that it was to capture as many Soviet soldiers as possible by means of encircling movements, in the opening weeks of the campaign, both on the southern and on the northern sectors of the front. In the end, Hitler wanted to attain all three objectives.

4. Designed to encourage the belief that the German strategic objectives in 1941 were first the Balkans and then Britain itself.

5. Cited in Bullock, *Hitler,* p. 638.

6. For the history of this document, first drafted by Wavell himself in June 1940, see Connell, *Wavell,* pp. 421–2. Unwisely, Wavell sent a copy of a revised version home in April 1941, when it was brought to the notice of Churchill, who was outraged at the idea that the C-in-C, Middle East, should remotely contemplate the possibility of evacuating Egypt, a prospect that would recur in July–August 1942.

7. Occupied by Italy in April 1939.

8. This corps, originally a small force, was later built up to a strength of four divisions, two of them armoured, which because the core of the Italo-GermanPanzerarmee. The principal events in these two German campaigns in the spring of 1941 will be found listed in the *Selective Chronology of the Second World War.*

9. See Gilbert, *Churchill,* Vol. VI, pp. 1012 ff.

10. Eden, who was accompanied by Dill, had until December 1940 been Secretary of State for War. They would have done better to follow the advice offered, in a personal letter to Dill before their departure, by Amery, who (though not a member of the War Cabinet) followed what was going on closely, cited at length in Connell, *Wavell,* pp. 321–4. Wavell began to recognise his mistake, too late: see Connell, *Wavell,* p. 388, and Hinsley, *British Intelligence,* Vol. I, p. 362.

11. *N.D.,* 1746-PS.

12. So greatly was the German threat underrated in Cairo that this force had been reduced by Wavell to a largely static command, with only two brigades at its disposal, quite inadequate to deal with an attack by a commander of Rommel's calibre.

13. Cited in Hinsley, *British Intelligence,* Vol. I, p. 432.

14. PREM 3/170/1, no. 1.

15. Either from a Japanese decrypt or directly from a source in contact with the U.S. Embassy in Berlin.

16. Churchill, Vol. III, p. 319.

17. This evidence is presented, forcefully and at length, in Chapter 14 of Hinsley, *British Intelligence,* Vol. I, from which the quotations in this and the subsequent six

paragraphs on this aspect of British official thinking in the run-up to *Barbarossa* are derived, unless otherwise stated.

18. Colville, *The Fringes of Power,* p. 404.

19. But an important collateral source was information received from Polish agents. See General Sikorski's letter of 23 May 1941 to Churchill, *Soviet-Polish Relations, 1939–1945,* Vol. I, Document 86.

20. I am indebted to the long memory of the correspondent in question, Mr. Joseph C. Harsch, for this personal recollection (*kein Spaziergang*—"no promenade").

21. For this mission, see Chapter 5.

22. *DBFP,* Third Series, 1938–9, Vol. VI, Appendix V, p. 766, C 10801/3356/18: a Foreign Office (Central Department) document, but one drawn up with "the full approval of the Chiefs of Staff."

23. Hardly any of this vast area was British sovereign territory, but Britain was the paramount power throughout: see William Roger Louis, *The British Empire in the Middle East, 1945–1951: Arab nationalism, the United States, and post-war imperialism* (Oxford: Clarendon Press, 1984), Parts I–III, *passim.*

24. Cited in Hinsley, *British Intelligence,* Vol. I, p. 482.

25. An able, wealthy, but austere maverick, Cripps (a barrister) was elected a Labour MP in 1931. Expelled, as a radical, from the party in 1939, he did not formally rejoin it until March 1945. His mission in Moscow was a failure, from which he was relieved, at his own request, in early 1942. In the post-war Labour Government, he became a respected president of the Board of Trade and (from 1947) Chancellor of the Exchequer.

26. Cited (from the Churchill Papers, 23/9) by Gilbert, *Churchill,* Vol. VI, pp. 1050–1.

27. Andrei Vyshinsky. Cripps was lucky to get away with this unprofessional behaviour. As late as 16 June, recalled to London for consultations, he was still talking to the Cabinet about a German "ultimatum"—see CAB 65/22.

28. Kimball, Vol. I, C-100x.

29. *Churchill,* Vol. III, p. 330.

30. Quoted in Dallek, *Franklin D. Roosevelt and American Foreign Policy,* p. 278.

31. See Chapter 2. For Churchill's scepticism about the advice that he received on the Soviet Union in 1941, see Churchill, Vol. III, p. 351.

32. Nicolson, *Diaries,* p. 174, described Churchill's broadcast of 22 June 1941 as a "masterpiece." Some of his Cabinet colleagues, however, including Eden, took a different view of the Soviet Union at that time. See Colville, *Fringes of Power,* pp. 405–6.

33. Zhukov, *Reminiscences and Reflections,* Vol. I, p. 281.

34. *Sov.-Angl. O.,* Vol. I, Document 1.

35. I. V. Stalin, *O velikoi otechestvennoi voine Sovetskogo Soyuza* (Moscow: Gospolizdat, 1947), pp. 196–7.

36. The prime mover was Khrushchev, whose account (he himself was not in Moscow

in 1941) was accepted uncritically by some western historians. See also Medvedev, *Let History Judge,* p. 458, who describes Stalin as "absent from his post" from 23 June. See also Volkogonov, *Stalin*, Vol. II, part 1, pp. 168–9.

37. Zhukov, *Reminiscences and Reflections,* Vol. I, p. 309, describes Stalin's reaction to the news of the fall of Minsk as "violent" on the two occasions when he visited the Defence Ministry and GHQ on 29 June. For Stalin's decision to stay on in Moscow, see A. I. Mikoyan, "Y sovete po evakuatsii," from unpublished manuscripts, *Voenno-istoricheskii zhurnal,* 3 (Moscow, 1980), pp. 33 ff.

38. Even Vasilevsky, who made as good a case for the Tass statement as he could muster in his memoirs, conceded that at the time, "the Tass statement at first evoked some surprise among . . . the General Staff, as also, naturally, among other Soviet people as well"—Vasilevsky, *Delo vsei zhizni,* pp. 118–19.

39. The English version of the Tass statement is reproduced in full in Churchill, Vol. III, pp. 326–7.

40. *Pravda,* 8 May 1989, a full-page article on p. 4.

41. Zhukov, *Reminiscences and Reflections,* Vol. 1, p. 277.

42. Churchill, Vol. III, p. 316.

43. K. M. Simonov, "Zametki k biographii G.K. Zhukova," in *Voenno-istoricheskii zhurnal* (Moscow, 1987), a series of articles "from unpublished manuscripts," from which the information and the quotations in this paragraph are derived.

44. For a posthumously published account of the circumstances in which Zhukov was relegated to the command of the Odessa Military District, see *Pravda,* 20 January 1989, "Korotko o Staline," by Mariya Zhukova, his daughter. And Zhukov's view of Tukhachevsky is quoted in the article *"O dele Tukhalhevskogo,"* by F. Sergeev, published in *Politicheskoe obrazovanie,* (1989), pp. 55–6.

45. Churchill, Vol. IV, p. 443, and *Sov.-Angl. O.,* Vol. I, p. 283.

46. CAB 27/627, FP (36) 57, COS 698.

47. An extract forms Document 10 in *Sov.-Angl. O.,* Vol. I.

48. Ibid., Document 3.

49. *Sov.-Am. O.,* Vol. I, Document 13.

50. Given pride of place in *Sov.-Angl. O.,* Vol. I, as Document 1.

51. Ibid., Document 15.

52. Ibid., Document 21.

53. *Perepiska,* Vol. I, Documents 3 and 12. A similar proposal was put to the United States.

54. *Sov.-Angl. O.,* Vol. I, Documents 47–49.

55. Ibid., Document 46.

56. The indebtedness of this paragraph to Christopher Thorne, *Allies of a Kind,* will be evident.

57. This tradition, as it seemed to the State Department looking back at the end of the

decade, was described at length in the "China White Paper," formally transmitted to President Truman by Dean Acheson on 30 July 1949.

58. Some of the British who should have known better—with the notable exception of Churchill—also went overboard for Chiang Kai-shek, but they came to their senses much sooner than the Americans.

59. *Christian Science Monitor,* 25 July 1942.

60. Admiral Dudley Pound, whose post—for American readers—was the equivalent of Chief of Naval Operations. Churchill's directive of 28 April 1941 is in PREM 3/156/6.

61. The account that follows does not attempt to cover these negotiations except in the broadest outline. Among recent studies of the U.S.-Japanese negotiations in 1941, Reynolds, *Creation of the Anglo-American Alliance,* Chapter 9, and Waldo Heinrichs, *Threshold of War,* passim, offer respectively a mainly British and a mainly American perspective. See also Eric Larrabee, *Commander in Chief,* pp. 1–95. The present chapter draws on all three accounts, as well as on the primary documents.

62. See Grew's telegram to Hull, 3 November 1941, *FRUS, Japan,* Vol. II, pp. 701–4, and Craigie's telegram no. 2186 to the Foreign Office, 1 November 1941, PREM 3/158/4.

63. Kimball, Vol. I, R-63x.

64. CAB 69/2 and 69/8, DC(0) (41), 65/1 and 66/1, 17 and 20 October 1941, respectively.

65. The only reason why Hull seems to have thought it necessary to say anything to Halifax at all at this stage was the fact that references to the talks cropped up in U.S. Army Intelligence reports received by the British. And he did not tell Halifax by any means the whole story.

66. At first they certainly were, if only because to begin with the two principals were James Drought, Vicar General of the (Catholic) Mary Knoll Missionary Society, and Ikawa Tadao, a Japanese (Christian) banker, who was close to Konoe.

67. Eric Larrabee, *Commander in Chief,* pp. 63–6, illuminates this "unilateral" declaration of war on Japan by Ickes.

68. Both the White House and the State Department press release of 1 August strongly suggest that at that point the embargo was intended to be flexible—see *FRUS, 1941, The Far East,* Vol. IV, pp. 836 ff.

69. The assessment of the Director of War Plans, Rear-Admiral Turner, on 19 July 1941 was that an oil "embargo would probably . . . involve the United States in early war in the Pacific"; Stark recommended against an embargo "at this time."

70. Cordell Hull, *The Memoirs of Cordell Hull,* Vol. II (New York: Macmillan, 1948), p. 1014.

71. See minute by Ashley Clarke, head of the Foreign Office Far Eastern Department,

10 July 1941 (FO 371/27663), which hit the nail on the head; and Final Report by Sir Robert Craigie, paragraphs 32–3—PREM 3/158/4.
72. Hull, *Memoirs,* p. 1018.
73. PSF Diplomatic File, Box no. 59, FDR Library, Hyde Park.
74. Kimball, Vol. I, R-69x, C-133x and C135x.
75. Cited in Deakin and Storry, *The Case of Richard Sorge,* p. 191.
76. Cited, for example (there is more than one version), in Ike Nobutka, ed., *Japan's Decision for War* (Stanford, Calif.: Stanford University Press, 1967), pp. 133 ff.
77. See, e.g., his message to Churchill of 24 November 1941—Kimball, Vol. I, R-69x.
78. Grew to Roosevelt, 22 September 1941, original letter in PSF Diplomatic File, Box no. 59, FDR Library, Hyde Park.
79. For an account of the arguments deployed for and against at this fateful meeting of the Japanese Liaison Conference, see Akira Iriye, *Origins of the Second World War: Asia and the Pacific,* pp. 172 ff.
80. George Kennan, "World War II: 30 years after," in *Survey,* Vol., 21 (Winter–Spring 1975), p. 30.
81. See Larrabee, *Commander in Chief,* p. 213.

CHAPTER 10

1. By 1950, however, when the third volume of Churchill's memoirs was published, it was becoming hard for most people in Britain and the United States to recall that, a few years earlier, the Soviet Union had been their ally. Churchill nonetheless used *The Grand Alliance* as the title of this volume.
2. In the Biennial Report submitted to the Secretary of War by the Chief of Staff of the U.S. Army, 1 July–30 June 1945.
3. Churchill, Vol. III, p. 609.
4. The list of signatories to this declaration included some improbable governments, such as that of Haiti.
5. South-East Asia Command, established in 1943, with Admiral Louis Mountbatten as Supreme Commander, though nominally a British responsibility, also became in practice Anglo-American. Until near the end of the war its impact on the overall strategy of the war was slight.
6. Quoted in Vasilevsky, *Delo vsei zhizni,* p. 149.
7. Matsuoka's foreign policy (not always clearly described in western sources) is analysed in Akira Iriye, *Origins of the Second World War: Asia and the Pacific,* Chapters 4 and 5.
8. Deakin and Storry, *The Case of Richard Sorge,* pp. 239 ff.
9. The battle on the Moscow front continued into the early months of 1942, by which

time the German Army had been pushed back for distances of up to two hundred miles, despite Hitler's directive.

10. Cited in Zhukov, *Reminiscences and Reflections,* Vol. II, p. 57.

11. For the U.S. commitment given to Halifax by Roosevelt on 1 December 1941, see the Secret Diary of Lord Halifax, 2 December 1941, p. 28, at the Borthwick Institute of Historical Research, University of York. (The entry for the previous day, on the same page, shows how uncertain Halifax then was that the commitment would be given.) Halifax reported his conversation with the President in Washington telegram no. 5519 to the Foreign Office. See the War Cabinet's discussion of "Far Eastern Policy," 2 December 1941, WP (41) 296—CAB 66/20—and the Defence Committee (Operations) meeting on the following day, DO (41) 71st Meeting—CAB 69/2.

12. Although the Japanese air attack was delivered many hours after the attack on Pearl Harbor, it was met by only four U.S. fighter aircraft. American air power in the Philippines was thus destroyed as effectively as its naval power in Hawaii. There was no public enquiry, however.

13. The U.S. Pacific Fleet withdrew to its base at San Diego.

14. Churchill, Vol. III, p. 55.

15. Speech file 1400, 8 December 1941, F.D.R. Library, Hyde Park.

16. That of Jeanette Rankin (Wyoming), who had voted against the 1917 declaration of war as well.

17. Kimball, Vol. I, C-138 and 139x.

18. Eleanor Roosevelt, *This I Remember* p. 186; Kimball, Vol. I, C-1412x; and final paragraph of Foreign Office Far Eastern Department Memorandum, 23 April 1943—PREM 3/158/4.

19. This quotation—and all others in this chapter relating to Craigie's Final Report—comes from the "Documents relating to the outbreak of war with Japan"—PREM 3/158/4. The normal practice would have been for a document such as Craigie's report to be given a broad distribution in the "Foreign Office and Whitehall" print series, which included circulation to posts abroad and to Dominion governments. Craigie appears to have written his report mainly from memory. Nor does he seem to have had access to *Magic* material. He does not, for example, highlight the crucial Imperial Conference held on 2 November 1941.

20. For the new War Cabinet, announced after the fall of Singapore, in February 1942, see Appendix I.

21. For the bitter American reaction to Pearl Harbor, see Gordon W. Prange, *At Dawn We Slept* (New York: McGraw-Hill, 1981).

22. CAB 65/24, WM 112 (41), Confidential Annex, 12 November 1941.

23. *Perepiska,* Vol. I, pp. 40–7.

24. Stalin took a sanguine view of Japan's inability to sustain a long campaign in the

Pacific, but he also declined to rule out the possibility of a Japanese attack on the Soviet Union—*Sov.-Angl. O.,* Vol. I, Document 76. For Churchill's changes of mind on this matter while he was at sea, see Churchill, Vol. III, pp. 557–8.

25. Churchill, Vol. III, pp. 559–60.
26. *Sov.-Angl. O,,* Vol. I, Document 78. The Soviet records of the Eden-Stalin negotiations are published in the same volume, pp. 184 ff., from which quotations in this paragraph and the next are derived, unless otherwise stated.
27. Władysław Sikorski, the outstanding member of the Polish Government-in-exile, was killed in an air crash in June 1943.
28. Dated 5 January 1942, it is cited at length in Churchill, Vol. III, pp. 558–9.
29. *Soviet-Polish Relations, 1939–1945,* Vol. I, Document 160.
30. *Hitler's Words (Two Decades of National Socialism, 1922–43),* ed. Gordon W. Prange (Washington, D.C.: American Council on Public Affairs, 1944), p. 97.

CHAPTER 11

1. At their meeting at the Berghof in January 1941, one of Hitler's speeches lasted two hours; and when he met Mussolini at the Brenner Pass on 2 June 1941 (less than three weeks before *Barbarossa*), Hitler mentioned the Soviet Union only in passing.
2. The Germans' original allies in the 1941 invasion of the Soviet Union were the Finns and the Romanians. They were later joined by divisions supplied by Hungary, Italy and Spain.
3. Churchill, Vol. III, pp. 574 ff.
4. Sherwood describes Roosevelt's "interior" as "heavily forested" in his *Roosevelt and Hopkins: an intimate history* (New York: Harper & Brothers, 1948), p. 9.
5. Maurice Matloff, *Mr. Roosevelt's Three Wars: FDR as War Leader,* Harmon Memorial Lecture 6, U.S. Air Force Academy, p. 3.
6. Sherwood, *The White House Papers,* Vol. I, p. 450.
7. W. Averell Harriman and Elie Abel, *Special Envoy to Churchill and Stalin, 1941–46* (New York: Random House, 1975), p. 536.
8. Churchill afterwards claimed (to Sherwood, *The White House Papers,* Vol. I, p. 446) that he never received Roosevelt in less than a bath towel; but see Gilbert, *Churchill,* Vol. VII, p. 28, note 2.
9. Three months later an "OK, FDR" was received from the White House, however; see Larrabee, *Commander in Chief,* p. 19.
10. This lapidary epitaph on Alanbrooke is Fraser's, in *Alanbrooke,* p. 538. For Ismay's appointment, see Chapter 6.
11. Cited in Thomas Parrish, *Roosevelt and Marshall: partners in policies and war—the personal story* (New York: William Morrow, 1989), p. 470.

12. Fraser, *Alanbrooke,* Alanbrooke Notes, pp. 229–20.

13. Dean Acheson, *Present at the Creation: my years at the State Department* (New York: W. W. Norton, 1969), p. 323.

14. Brooke's delivery in argument was characterised by the force of its logic and its machine-gun speed. His interventions would often began with the words "I flatly disagree."

15. Alanbrooke Papers, cited in Fraser, *Alanbrooke,* p. 295.

16. Although Marshall was born in Pennsylvania, his family was from the South, and he graduated from the Virginia Military Institute.

17. Marshall's account of what Roosevelt said to him on 5 December 1943, related to Sherwood, *White House Papers,* Vol. II, p. 793. The other two members of the Joint Chiefs—Admiral Ernest King and General Henry ("Hap") Arnold (USAAF)—also continued in that capacity until the end of the war.

18. Pershing had commanded the American Expeditionary Force in France in the First World War.

19. Though junior in rank to the three members of the British Chiefs of Staff, Ismay, in his capacity as Principal Staff Officer to the Minister of Defence, attended all meetings of the Chiefs of Staff Committee as of right. The chief function both of Ismay and of Leahy was to make rough ways smooth.

20. By August 1941 Stalin had assumed all three major military offices of the Soviet State, including that of Supreme Commander. The State Defence Committee (GKO) was composed entirely of civilians, whereas the membership of the *Stavka* (GHQ) was mainly military.

21. When Stalin reduced the size of the *Stavka* in February 1945, Vasilevsky became one of its members; subsequently he took command of the Far Eastern Front. A Marshal of the Soviet Union, he was appointed Defence Minister later in his career.

22. Vasilevsky, *Delo vsei zhizni,* pp. 549–50.

23. Vasilevsky's father was a village church choirmaster—ibid., pp. 548 and 104–5.

24. K.M. Simonov, "Zametki k biograffii G.K. Zhukova," p. 60.

25. Quoted in Larrabee, *Commander in Chief,* p. 25.

26. General Joseph Stilwell, whom Roosevelt treated shabbily, was a notable American exception. On the British side, Churchill was not able to rely on the military leadership in South-East Asia until the autumn of 1943, when Mountbatten was appointed Supreme Commander, South-East Asia Command, and Slim became Commander, Fourteenth Army.

27. Reproduced as Appendix I in Michael Howard, *Grand Strategy.* Vol. IV, *April 1942–September 1943* (London: HMSO, 1970), pp. 597 ff (from which the quotations that follow are derived).

28. On 18 December 1941 the last two battleships of the British Mediterranean Fleet were disabled in Alexandria Harbour by Italian Navy frogmen.

29. Cited in Burns, *Roosevelt,* Vol. II, p. 227.

30. For the definition of the term "British" in this context, see p. 460.

31. Churchill, Vol. IV, p. 81.

32. Cited in Gilbert, *Churchill,* Vol. VII, p. 61.

33. Ibid., p. 34.

34. CAB 65/14, Cabinet Conclusions, Confidential Annex, 8 August 1940, and *Documents on Australian Foreign Policy, 1927–49,* ed. R. G. Neale, et al. (Canberra, 1975–83), Vol. IV, Document 64—both cited in David Day, *The Great Betrayal: Britain, Australia and the onset of the Pacific War, 1939–42* (New York: W. W. Norton, 1989), pp. 72–3. Day's book illuminates the domestic dimension of Australian policy at the time, as well as the bitterness of the Australian Government. The Australian Government, for its part, had antagonised the British Government in 1941 by insisting on the relief of the Australian division besieged in Tobruk.

35. Gilbert, *Churchill,* Vol. VII, pp. 49–50, citing Churchill Papers, 20/69.

36. Kimball, Vol. I, R-78x and R-106.

37. See Gilbert, *Churchill,* Vol. VII, pp. 53 ff.

38. Burns, *Roosevelt,* Vol. II, p. 210.

39. Howard, *Grand Strategy,* Vol. IV, pp. 20 ff.

40. R-115, R-123/1 (letter), R-129 and C-63—in Kimball, Vol. I; *Sov.-Am. O.,* Vol. I, Documents 77 and 82; and *Sov.-Angl. O.,* Vol. I, Document 40.

41. Kimball, Vol. I, C-70.

42. Quoted in Forrest C. Pogue, *George C. Marshall,* 4 vols. (New York: Viking Press, 1963–87), Vol. II, pp. 318–19.

43. Kimball, Vol. I, C-40.

44. *Sov-Angl.-O.,* Vol. I, Document 110.

45. A full record of Churchill's meeting with Molotov on 22 May was telegraphed by him to Roosevelt on 28 May 1942—Kimball, Vol. I, C-92.

46. Ibid., R-131/1.

47. *Sov.-Am. O.,* Vol. I, Documents 96 ff., give a detailed account. Molotov's two private talks with Hopkins are nos. 98 and 101.

48. CAB 120/684, 10 June 1942, and *Sov.-Angl. O.,* Vol. I, Document 113.

49. *Sov.-Angl. O.,* Vol. I, Document 112.

50. Churchill to Marshall, 16 April 1944, telegram in Churchill Papers 20/162, cited in Gilbert, *Churchill,* Vol. VII, p. 741. Larrabee, *Commander in Chief,* pp. 444 ff., provides a summary of the landing craft argument. The comparison of U.S. Army strengths in the Pacific and European theatres is quoted from Maurice Matloff and Edwin Snell, *Strategic Planning for Coalition Warfare, 1941–1942* (Washington, D.C.: Office of the Chief of Military History, Department of the Army, 1953), pp. 359–61.

51. Notably on the part of Attlee, who knew India, and Bevin, who took a close interest in Indian (as in all international) affairs.

52. Welles to Roosevelt, 29 July 1942, cited in Thorne, *Allies of a Kind,* p. 241. For an account of the American apprehension about India in 1942, see William Roger Louis, *India, Africa and the Second World War: ethnic and racial studies* (London: Routledge & Kegan Paul, 1986), pp. 306 ff.

53. A former Assistant Secretary of War, "uniquely unsuited to deal with the British and the Indians," in the words of an American diplomat in India at the time, cited in ibid., p. 242.

54. Kimball, Vol. I, C-68.

55. At the Mansion House dinner in the City of London, on 10 November 1942.

56. Kimball, Vol. I, R-116 and 132.

57. For example, in discussing the communal composition of the Indian Army, he seems to have regarded Sikhs (its most important component) as Muslims.

58. Kimball, Vol. I, C-68, draft A, not sent.

59. This was Marshall's firm view throughout. On this occasion Brooke agreed with him, mainly because of the disaster that was already impending in the Western Desert. See Fraser, *Alanbrooke,* pp. 257 ff.

60. Kimball, Vol. I, R-160.

61. Hinsley, *British Intelligence,* Vol. II, p. 380 and Appendix 16. The sources of Eighth Army's intelligence were by no means confined to *Ultra.*

62. No reference to any work of military history is required to confirm this fact since the publication of Alexander Solzhenitsyn's *August 1914,* translated by Michael Glenny (London: Bodley Head, 1971), p. 115.

63. The *Stosslinie,* the main axis of a German advance, used by the German Army as a map reference system to enable forward units to report their positions in the simplest possible manner.

64. Reproduced in full in Vasilevsky, *Delo vsei zhizni,* pp. 231–2.

65. Kimball, Vol. I, C-107, and Larrabee, *Commander in Chief,* pp. 136–7.

66. Kimball, Vol. I, C-123 and R-170.

67. *Sov.-Angl. O.,* Vol. I, Document 123.

68. Ibid., Document 126.

CHAPTER 12

1. Extract from the French record of de Gaulle's meeting with Churchill and Eden, 16 November 1942—Charles de Gaulle, *Mémoires de Guerre,* Vol. II (Paris: Plon, 1956), p. 404.

2. At Churchill's request, however (at once granted by Roosevelt), Harriman accompanied him to Moscow.

3. Kimball, Vol. I, C-126a. Churchill's request to Roosevelt, telegraphed on 4 August from Cairo, is interesting in two respects. It determined Roosevelt to send Harriman, who had himself previously made the same suggestion, but was turned down;

and it is also one of the earliest examples of Stalin being referred to as "Joe" (or "Uncle Joe") in the correspondence between Churchill and Roosevelt.

4. Fraser, *Alanbrooke,* pp. 280 ff., gives a vivid account of Churchill's first Cairo visit (based on the Alanbrooke Papers), to which this paragraph is indebted.

5. For Churchill's remark to Alexander, see *General Eisenhower on the Military Churchill: a conversation with Alistair Cooke,* ed. James Nelson (New York: W. W. Norton, 1970), p. 79. For examples of Brooke's opinion of Alexander's abilities, see Fraser, *Alanbrooke,* pp. 334, 381, 390 and 429 ff.

6. Auchinleck, bitterly disappointed, declined the lesser command that Churchill offered him (Persia-Iraq), but later he again became C-in-C, India.

7. Aneurin Bevan, on 2 July 1942.

8. *Sov.-Angl. O.,* Vol. I, Document 151: extracts from a speech delivered in Moscow on 6 November 1942.

9. Three meetings and one state banquet. The British records of the Moscow talks are in PREM 3/76A/9 ff. and the Soviet are in *Sov.-Angl. O.,* Vol. I, pp. 265 ff.

10. Kimball, Vol. I, C-134—a copy of the report already sent by Churchill to the Cabinet.

11. According to British and American witnesses of the second meeting, at one point Churchill was so stung by Stalin's jibes about British unwillingness to fight Germans that he launched into a philippic. Stalin is said to have remarked that what Churchill was saying was not important; "what was vital was his spirit"—Gilbert, *Churchill,* Vol. VII, p. 186, citing Lieutenant-General Sir Ian Jacob and Averell Harriman, both of whom were present on this occasion. The Soviet records do not include this remark.

12. Churchill, Vol. IV, p. 434.

13. *Sov.-Angl. O.,* Vol. I, p. 273.

14. Ibid., Documents 132 and 133.

15. Major A. H. Birse, a member of the British Military Mission in Moscow, who interpreted for Churchill for the rest of the war. It was Jacob who suggested this bilingual officer to Churchill (who on his return to London requested Jacob's promotion).

16. *Sov.-Angl. O.,* Vol. I, p. 279.

17. Sir Ian Jacob's Diary, in Jacob Papers at Woodbridge, Suffolk, pp. 105 ff.

18. *Sov.-Angl. O.,* Vol. V, Document 244. Herbert Feis, *Churchill-Roosevelt-Stalin,* p. 614, regards Churchill's reaction to this in his memoirs as "ironical." Not necessarily so, I suggest.

19. Opening communications through the Mediterranean, securing bases for air attacks against Italy, posing a threat to Rommel's rear and blocking the Axis' way to Dakar—*Sov.-Angl-O.,* Vol. I, Document 130.

20. Ibid., Vol. I, p. 270.

21. Ibid., Document 147.
22. Ibid., Documents 161 and 163.
23. Ibid., p. 299.
24. Churchill Papers, cited in Gilbert, *Churchill,* Vol. VII, p. 160.
25. Subparagraph (c)(iv) of the memorandum then agreed, *CCS 94,* is quoted in full in Howard, *Grand Strategy,* Vol. IV, p. xxiii.
26. Cited ibid., p. 192.
27. Ibid., Chapter XI, "The Autumn Debates."
28. Loc. cit, and Fraser, *Alanbrooke,* pp. 263 ff.
29. Kimball, Vol. I, R-189.
30. Ibid., R-185 and C-145.
31. Frances Perkins, *The Roosevelt I Knew* (London: Hart Davis, 1946), p. 316. Roosevelt's "Joan of Arc" jibe about de Gaulle was based on a misunderstanding of a conversation between de Gaulle and Admiral King.
32. Churchill, Vol. I, p. 162.
33. The double-barred *Croix de Lorraine* was the symbol of the Free French. (Stalin also underrated de Gaulle until 1944.) For Churchill's secret speech, see Gilbert, *Churchill,* Vol. II, pp. 272 ff.
34. Kimball, Vol. I, R-186/1. The message was not in fact sent; but the first sentence of its second paragraph corresponds exactly with Roosevelt's view as known from other evidence.
35. Ibid., C-148.
36. Ibid., R-180 and C-142.
37. David Kahn, *The Codebreakers,* pp. 221–2.
38. Duff Cooper, *Old Men Forget: the autobiography of Duff Cooper* (London: Hart-Davis, 1954), p. 316. Duff Cooper was British Ambassador to France, 1944–47.
39. Map Room Files, Box 105, folder 3, FDR Library, Hyde Park, and *FRUS, 1942,* Vol. II, pp. 409 and 423.
40. *FRUS, 1942,* Vol. II, pp. 398 ff., and Map Room Files, Box 105, folder 3, FDR Library, Hyde Park. For Churchill's misinterpretation, see Churchill, Vol. IV, pp. 548 and 556.
41. Cited in Howard, *Grand Strategy,* Vol. IV, p. 174.
42. *FRUS, 1942,* Vol. II, pp. 453 ff.
43. Kimball, Vol. II, C-190.
44. Ibid., R-214 and C-198; *FRUS,* Vol. II, p. 445; and *Sov.-Angl. O.,* Vol. I, Document 161.
45. *Sov.-Angl. O.,* Vol. I, Documents 161, 184 and 1990.
46. Bevin was by this time widely acknowledged as the strongest member of the War Cabinet—with good reason.
47. CAB 66/WP42/565, 7 December 1942.

48. Henry ("Hal") Mack, who was serving at the Paris Embassy in 1940, then became head of the French Department in the Foreign Office. His Algiers appointment was followed by a series of senior posts, including Head of Mission in Vienna (1945–48), where the author was a member of his staff.
49. Kimball, Vol. II, C-227. Roosevelt did not accept its accuracy.
50. Anthony Verrier, *Assassination in Algiers* (New York: W. W. Norton, 1990). I am indebted to Anthony Verrier for drawing my attention to Mack's assessment quoted in the preceding paragraph.
51. *Perepiska,* Document 93.
52. Kimball, Vol. II, R-224.

CHAPTER 13

1. This description of a two-pronged counter-offensive simultaneously through the Central Pacific (Nimitz) and through New Guinea-the Philippines (MacArthur) was first proposed by King in February 1943. The subject of much intra-American rivalry and controversy, in the event this strategy worked well.
2. Brooke's diary entry of 1 January 1943 ("we start 1943 under conditions I would never had dared to hope for"), applies *a fortiori* to January 1944—Fraser, *Alanbrooke,* pp. 309–10.
3. The year 1943 was afterwards recalled as "the year of conferences" by Ismay (whose memoirs are cited in ibid., p. 308). The conferences attended by Churchill and Roosevelt were Casablanca, Washington *(Trident)*—Hyde Park, Quebec *(Quadrant)*—Hyde Park and Teheran *(Eureka), Eureka* being both preceded and followed by conferences held in Cairo—a grand total of six in all. In spite of being incapacitated by pneumonia in February–March, Churchill also made several other journeys, including one to Adana in January to meet the Turkish President and another to Algiers in June (accompanied by Marshall) to confer with Eisenhower.
4. John Ehrman, *Grand Strategy,* Vol. V, pp. 133–5.
5. Kimball, Vol. I, R-210.
6. Note by the Minister of Defence, 3 December 1942, quoted in full in Gilbert, *Churchill,* Vol. VII, pp. 270–1.
7. *Sov.-Am. O.,* Vol. I, Document 153; a translation was telegraphed by Roosevelt to Churchill three days later—Kimball, Vol. II, R-238.
8. Note by the Minister of Defence, 29 December 1942, cited in Gilbert, *Churchill,* Vol. VII, p. 285.
9. Ibid., p. 271.
10. The question of the importance of this route was a major source of Anglo-American military controversy in South-East Asia.
11. CCS 166/1/I, 21 January 1943 forms Appendix III (E) of Howard, *Grand Strategy,* Vol. IV.

12. Memorandum by the Combined Chiefs of Staff, "Conduct of the War in 1943," 19 January 1943, the text of which forms Appendix IV(D) of Howard, *Grand Strategy,* Vol. IV. The Combined Chiefs' report of 23 January, as approved by the President and the Prime Minister, forms Appendix IV(F) in this volume.

13. The final text of the joint message to Stalin, agreed by Churchill and Roosevelt and despatched on 9 February, is in Kimball, Vol. II, C-263. The Russian text is in *Sov.-Angl. O.,* Vol. I, Document 181. Stalin's request for concrete information is in ibid., Document 177.

14. Kimball, Vol. II, C-263, a message sent by Churchill to Stalin on both his and Roosevelt's behalf.

15. *Sov.-Angl. O.,* Vol I, Document 184. For the text of Churchill's message, to which this was the reply, see ibid., Document 196, and Kimball, Vol. II, C-271.

16. *Sov.-Angl. O.,* Vol. I, Document 199.

17. At Hyde Park on 13 August 1943, Churchill gave Roosevelt (to read and return) a copy of Owen O'Malley's "grim, well-written" despatch, dated 24 May, regarding the massacre—Kimball, Vol. II, C-412/2 ff. And See *Izvestiya,* 14 April 1990.

18. Churchill to Stalin, 24 April 1943. Stalin's telegram of 21 April, informing Churchill of the rupture of Soviet-Polish relations, is Document 210 in *Sov.-Angl. O.,* Vol. I. (Sikorski was killed in an air crash in June 1943.)

19. Translated in Howard, *Grand Strategy,* Vol. IV, p. 281.

20. Kimball, Vol. II, C-298, R-278, C-299, C-300 and C-325.

21. Ibid., p. 254 and R-288.

22. Ibid., C-373.

23. Kimball, Vol. III, R-648 (the last sentence).

24. Churchill, Vol. IV, p. 615.

25. CAB 65/37 and 120/79, 20 and 21 January 1943, respectively.

26. Arranged through SOE, this approach failed because Eden refused to allow La Malfa to be received at the Foreign Office, only at the War Office, as though he were not a political leader but an agent. La Malfa refused. See Richard Lamb, *The Ghosts of Peace, 1935–1945* (Salisbury, Wilts: Michael Russell, 1987), pp. 181–2.

27. Cited in Howard, *Grand Strategy,* Vol. IV, p. 341.

28. A final meeting in Italy (at Feltre), in mid-July, achieved even less.

29. Cited in Paolo Monelli, *Roma 1943* (Milan: Mondadori, 1945), p. 111—*"Ma i sun di revenant!"* and *"Anch' io e Lei, Maestà, siamo degli spettri; ma non vedo che ci sia altro da fare."* For Bonomi's 1943 talks with the King, see Maurice Vaussard, *Histoire de l'Italie contemporaine, 1870–1946* (Paris: Hachette, 1950), pp. 282 ff.

30. Cited in Howard, *Grand Strategy,* Vol. IV, p. 465.

31. As a general rule, the exchange of secret intelligence between the allies in Moscow was limited, but the German preparation for the Kursk battle was a notable exception. See Hinsley, *British Intelligence,* Vol. III, p. 624, and Appendix 22. It is also a matter for speculation whether all *Enigma* cypher machines and their operators escaped capture at Stalingrad.

32. Churchill to Stalin, 10 May 1943: Churchill Papers cited in Gilbert, *Churchill,* Vol. VII, p. 396, and full Russian text in *Sov.-Angl. O.,* Vol. I., Document 217.

33. Howard, *Grand Strategy,* Vol. IV, pp. 431 ff., cites the essential paragraph of the conclusions reached.

34. Ibid., p. 457.

35. Ibid., p. 431.

36. The Russian text is in *Sov.-Am. O.,* Vol. I, Document 196.

37. *Sov.-Anglo. O.,* Vol. I, Document 226.

38. *Sov.-Am. O.,* Vol. I, Document 131.

39. Kimball, Vol. II, C-309, C-310 and R-289; *Sov.-Am. O.,* Vol. I, Document 194; and *FRUS, the Teheran Conference,* pp. 3–4.

40. Kimball, Vol. II, C-328 and R-297; and *Sov.-Angl. O.,* Vol. I, Document 224.

41. Alanbrooke diary, 5 August 1943, cited in Fraser, *Alanbrooke,* p. 357.

42. Prime Minister's personal minute, 19 July 1943: Churchill Papers, cited in Gilbert, *Churchill,* pp. 444–5.

43. Cited in Howard, *Grand Strategy,* Vol. IV, p. 561.

44. Cited in Fraser, *Alanbrooke,* p. 361.

45. Howard, *Grand Strategy,* Vol. IV, Appendix VIII, contains the text of the *Final Report to the President and the Prime Minister at Quadrant,* 24 August 1943.

46. Map Room Files, Box 34, FDR Library, Hyde Park, Marshall to Roosevelt, 29 July; Roosevelt to Marshall, 30 July; and Churchill to Roosevelt, no. 339, 30 July 1943.

47. The only amphibious operation undertaken in the entire Italian campaign after Salerno was *Shingle* (see Chapter 15). By the spring of 1944 the only specifically mountain troops in Fifteenth Army Group were the Moroccan *goumier* regiments of the French Corps, which played a decisive role in the battle that outflanked Cassino in May–June 1944. All French troops were withdrawn after the capture of Rome, however. (The Gurkhas serving in the Indian divisions fighting in Italy were no strangers to mountains, but they could not accurately be described as mountain warfare units.)

48. The official British military historical record is Howard, *Grand Strategy,* Vol. IV, Chapter XXVII. From the Italian point of view, Monelli's *Roma 1943,* although written too soon after the war to make use of official sources, offers a vivid account. Since then there have been many others, based on the documentary evidence now publicly available—e.g. Giuseppe Castellano's *La guerra continua.*

49. Kimball, Vol. II, C-R/telephone 4.

50. Ibid., R-324 and C-383.

51. Cited in Howard, *Grand Strategy,* Vol. IV, p. 517.

52. Map Room Papers, Box 34, CCS telegram no. 50 to Eisenhower, 17 August 1943, FDR Library, Hyde Park. These instructions presented the British War Cabinet (Eden in particular still had reservations) with a *fait accompli*—Howard, *Grand Strategy,* Vol. IV, p. 524.

53. General Walter Bedell Smith and Brigadier Kenneth Strong (respectively, American and British).
54. 12 September 1943.
55. From its bases at Genoa and La Spezia, the Italian fleet, together with a squadron from Taranto, eventually reached Malta; on the way the battleship *Roma* was sunk by German aircraft, with great loss of life.
56. *Sov.-Am. O.,* Vol. I, Documents 219 and 220.
57. At the Moscow meeting of foreign ministers it was agreed to establish an Advisory Committee for Italy, on which the Soviet Government (but also the French, Greek and Yugoslav governments) was to be represented.
58. *Perepiska,* Vol. I, Document III.
59. Kimball, Vol. II, R–418.
60. Sixty-four U-boats lost in sinking sixty-seven Allied vessels.
61. Prime Minister's personal minute, 19 October 1943: Churchill Papers, cited in Gilbert, Churchill, Vol. VII, p. 533.
62. *Alanbrooke Diary,* 19 October 1943, cited in Ibid., p. 532.
63. Churchill, Vol. V, pp. 224–5.
64. Kimball, Vol. II, R–379.
65. Ibid., C–471.
66. *Sov.-Angl. O.,* Documents 294 and 295.

CHAPTER 14

1. Alanbrooke, Notes, cited in Fraser, *Alanbrooke,* p. 385.
2. *SSNMK,* Vol. II, p. 91. Whatever military decisions were taken at Teheran, Stalin was clearly determined to take them himself.
3. Following the discovery of the Katyn massacre.
4. *Sov.-Am. O.,* Vol. I, Document 96.
5. "Morning Thoughts, Note on Post War Security by the Prime Minister, 1 February 1943, full text in Howard, *Grand Strategy,* Vol. IV, Appendix V. This note was written in a strange location—the railway carriage at Adana, in which Churchill held his meetings with the Turkish President in January 1943.
6. Kimball, Vol. II, C–297/1, memorandum.
7. Will Brownell and Richard N. Billings, *So Close to Greatness: the first biography of William C. Bullitt* (New York: Macmillan, 1987), pp. 293 ff. Bullitt, who wanted Welles' job, went further than this in seeking to destroy Welles' reputation.
8. Russian text in *Sov.-Angl. O.,* Vol. I, Document 297.
9. The staff of AFHQ was Anglo-American. The Rhodes project never found much favour with the British Chiefs of Staff either, being part of Churchill's Aegean King Charles' head. The islands of Cos and Leros were occupied by British forces after the Italian surrender, but had been recaptured by the Germans by the time of the Teheran Conference.

10. In January 1945 Roosevelt resisted as long as he could Churchill's proposal of an Anglo-American meeting in Malta (en route for Yalta), and on 11 May 1945 Truman used the same phrase—"ganging-up"—in a message sent to Churchill.
11. *Sov.-Angl. O.,* Vol. I, Document 301.
12. Cited in McNeill, *America, Britain and Russia,* pp. 347–8.
13. *FRUS, the Teheran Conference,* p. 463.
14. *SSNMK,* Vol. II, Document 47.
15. This fact was recalled in 1989 by Valentin Berezhkov, in the televised programme already mentioned in Chapter 7, note 86.
16. The Bohlen Minutes of the Teheran meetings are in *FRUS, the Teheran Conference,* and the Soviet records are in *SSNMK,* Vol. II. There is no published British record of either the Teheran or the Yalta Conference. On Teheran, the principal PRO files are CAB 80/77, CAB 120/113, and PREM 3/136/10.
17. One million tons of shipping annually were saved by the opening of the Mediterranean, as a consequence of the invasion of Italy. The other major strategic gain, which Stalin must have been aware of but did not mention, was the capture of air bases in southern Italy.
18. *Sov.-Angl. O.,* Vol. I, p. 487.
19. CAB 120/113. See also Charles E. Bohlen, with Robert M. Phelps, *Witness to History, 1929–1969* (New York: W. W. Norton, 1973), pp. 144 ff.
20. Churchill, Vol. V, p. 330.
21. Combined Chiefs of Staff Minutes, JCS files, meeting at the British Legation, *FRUS, the Teheran Conference,* pp. 555 ff.
22. Soviet record, *SSNMK,* Vol. II, p. 124, translated into indirect speech. The British record—CAB 120/113—tallies with this, except that it also includes a remark by Stalin to the effect that it would be very difficult for the Russians, who were "war weary," to carry on if there were "no big change in 1944."
23. Churchill's proviso depended mainly on the number of German divisions opposing *Overlord.*
24. For the Curzon Line, see footnote on p. 129.
25. The Soviet record (*SSNMK,* Vol. II, p. 150) has the same formula, but puts it in Churchill's words, agreed to by Stalin.
26. Of these two areas, the first was the "Kiel Canal and the City of Hamburg"; the second was the "Ruhr and the Saar, the latter to be used for the benefit of all Europe."
27. *FRUS, the Teheran Conference,* pp. 640–1.
28. Kimball, Vol. II, C-521 and R-427.
29. Dill to Brooke, 16 October 1943, cited in Fraser, *Alanbrooke,* p. 374.

CHAPTER 15

1. *Sov.-Angl. O.,* Vol. II, Document 1.
2. The IBRD is today generally known as the World Bank.
3. In the Hyde Park Agreement, September 1944; see Appendix IV.
4. Churchill did at least instruct Eden "to get any thing out of the Air Force you can"—although without effect. See Gilbert, *Churchill,* Vol. VII, pp. 846–7.
5. See Preface, p. 18.
6. The remark quoted is in the Preface, p. 36, to Moran's book on Churchill (see Chapter 2, note 30).
7. *Action This Day: working with Churchill,* by Lord Normanbrook, and others, pp. 10–11. The ironical comment on Moran quoted here comes from John Colville's chapter in this book, p. 110. All royalties from the book were given by the six contributors to Churchill College, Cambridge.
8. Apart from Djilas' evidence *(Conversations with Stalin)* there is also the evidence of Stalin's daughter *(Twenty Letters to a Friend).* And there were several occasions during 1944 when Stalin referred to the state of his own health in his communications with his Allies.
9. Churchill's performance in the House of Commons and the episode at Buckingham Palace are both described in a letter from Harold Nicolson to his sons, cited in Gilbert, *Churchill,* Vol. VII, pp. 655–6.
10. See ibid., Chapters 38–50, passim.
11. E.g., *Alanbrooke Diary,* 7 May 1944, cited in ibid., p. 759.
12. Prime Minister's Personal Minute to General Ismay, for the Chiefs of Staff Committee, 8 September 1944, Churchill Papers 20/153, cited in Gilbert, *Churchill,* pp. 942–3.
13. Fraser, *Alanbrooke,* pp. 396 ff., cites many examples.
14. Arthur Rosenman; see Burns, *Roosevelt,* Vol. II, p. 416.
15. *PPA: 1943,* pp. 553–62.
16. Lieutenant-Commander Howard G. Bruenn.
17. Financier, philanthropist and personal friend both of Churchill and of Roosevelt, although Roosevelt once called Baruch 'that old pooh-bah'.
18. Including cutting down on cigarettes and alcohol, one hour's rest after meals, at least ten hours' sleep, no swimming in the pool and a low-fat diet of 2,600 calories.
19. Roosevelt's popular vote majority was 3.6 million, out of 48 million votes cast.
20. Churchill Papers 4/361, cited in Gilbert, *Churchill,* Vol. VII, p. 1223.
21. See Table 34—"Aircraft Production of the Powers, 1939–45"—in Paul Kennedy, *The Rise and Fall of the Great Powers,* p. 354.
22. For a summary of the evidence, see Larrabee, *Commander in Chief,* pp. 342 ff.
23. *FRUS: the Conference of Berlin (the Potsdam Conference), 1945,* Vol. I, p. 27.
24. *FRUS: the Conferences at Malta and Yalta, 1945,* pp. 209–10.
25. For an objective assessment, see Fraser, *Alanbrooke,* pp. 399 ff.

26. *Alanbrooke Diary,* 29 February 1944, cited in ibid, p. 403.
27. This operation was ineffective because the rubble caused by the bombing blocked the British troops' advance. It was also not always accurate; one stick of bombs landed, *east* of the Apennines, on Eighth Army Tactical HQ.
28. Clark's personal vanity was notorious, but—here again—the ultimate responsibility rested with Alexander.
29. Kimball, Vol. III, C-721.
30. *Alanbrooke Diary,* 22 and 23 June 1944, cited in Fraser, *Alanbrooke,* p. 429.
31. On 28 June, Bletchley Park decyphered Hitler's order that the "Apennine position" should be "the final blocking line," to prevent Allied "entry into the Po plain," which "would have incalculable consequences"—Special Intelligence Summary, 28 June 1944, cited in Gilbert, *Churchill,* Vol. VII, p. 822.
32. Kimball, Vol. III, C-717 and 718.
33. Ibid., R-573.
34. Ibid., R-574.
35. Ibid., C-721 (not sent) and C-721 (as sent). Roosevelt's definitive answer is R-577.
36. Churchill, Vol. VI, p. 105.
37. Prime Minister's Personal Telegram, 31 August 1944, cited in Gilbert, *Churchill,* Vol. VII, p. 931.
38. Prime Minister's Personal Minute, 10 June 1944, cited in ibid., p. 803.
39. Where (codenamed Ercole) he had worked for nearly twenty years at the Comintern; he had also taken part in the Spanish Civil War.
40. On the strength of a letter written by Sforza to the U.S. Assistant Secretary of State, Adolf Berle, on 23 September 1943 (text in Kimball, Vol. III, pp. 439–40), Churchill maintained that he had broken his promise to support King Victor Emmanuel. There was also no love lost between Sforza and Eden.
41. The State Department's statement, 5 December 1944 (which also took a side-swipe at British action in Greece), is in *FRUS, the Conferences at Malta and Yalta, 1945,* pp. 266–7.
42. Map Room Files, Box 31 FDR Library, Hyde Park, Roosevelt to Churchill, 31 May, 4 June and 9 June 1944.
43. Kimball, Vol. III, C-804.
44. An agreement was reached on Middle Eastern oil, but it was never ratified by Congress. For the exchange between Churchill and Roosevelt on civil aviation, see Kimball, Vol. III, C-836 and R-661.
45. Telegram "Gunfire" no. 112, sent by the Prime Minister, in Quebec, to the War Cabinet, 13 September 1944—CAB 120/152.
46. In a letter of 17 August 1944, written to his wife from Italy (where Churchill was visiting troops)—Spencer-Churchill Papers, cited in Gilbert, *Churchill,* Vol. VII, p. 936.

47. Fraser, *Alanbrooke,* p. 446.
48. For an analysis of the new arrangements, see McNeill, *America, Britain and Russia,* pp. 551 ff.
49. Professor Lindemann received a peerage during the war, becoming Lord Cherwell.
50. The full text of the memorandum is in McNeill, *America, Britain and Russia,* pp. 489–90. The subsequent press criticism in the United States covered a broad spectrum: the *New York Herald Tribune, The New York Times* and the *Chicago Daily News,* 27 September, 29 September and 2 October 1944, respectively. See also John Morton Blum, *From the Morgenthau Diaries,* Vol. III, *Years of War, 1941–1945* (Boston: Houghton Mifflin, 1967), pp. 369 ff.
51. Alexander's polyglot army group was now too short of trained manpower; and three divisions had to be sent to Greece.
52. This, together with the other atomic agreements concluded between Churchill and Roosevelt during the war, will be examined in the next chapter.
53. "Gunfire" telegram no. 293 from Quebec is in PREM 3/139/8A; and Churchill's (undated) letter of September 1945 to Attlee (by then Prime Minister) is in PREM 8/117, GEN 75/3, Annex II.
54. Harriman to Roosevelt, telegram of 11 June 1944, Map Room Files, Harriman-Roosevelt correspondence, Box 11, FDR Library, Hyde Park; and *FRUS, 1944,* Vol. VI, pp. 97 and 799–800.
55. The Polish regime of the 1930s was colloquially called "The Colonels" (Beck, the Foreign Minister, was one of them).
56. One of the best accounts of the inter-war ethnic make-up of this part of Europe is to be found in Czesław Miłosz, *Native Realm: A search for self-definition* (Harmondsworth, Middlesex: Penguin Books, 1988).
57. Prime Minister's Personal Telegram no. 227 to Moscow, 28 January 1944— Churchill Papers, 20/183, cited in Gilbert, *Churchill,* Vol. VII, p. 665.
58. Kimball, Vol. II, C-566.
59. *Perepiska,* Vol. I, Document 257.
60. Kimball, Vol. III, C-737 and R-592.
61. Ibid., C-740.
62. Ibid., pp. 282 ff., and *Perepiska,* Vol. I, pp. 285 ff.
63. John Ehrman, *Grand Strategy,* Vol. V, p. 376.
64. Churchill, Vol. VI, pp. 197 ff.
65. British Embassy, Moscow telegram no. 2819 to the Foreign Office, 12 October 1944.—Gilbert, *Churchill,* Vol VII, p. 1002.
66. The five objectives of Operation *Burza* are quoted in full in Jan Ciechanowski, *The Warsaw Rising of 1944* (Cambridge: University Press, 1974), the best account of the Rising, based mainly on Polish sources (pp. 217–18).
67. Stalin to Churchill and Roosevelt, 22 August 1944, *Perepiska,* Vol. I, Document 323.
68. See, for example, John Erickson, *The Road to Berlin,* pp. 269 ff.

69. Kimball, Vol. III, R–684.

70. Ibid., C–789.

71. Ibid., R–625 and 626; and (for Hopkins' talk over lunch with Gromyko on 13 October 1944) *Sov.-Angl. O.,* Vol. II, Document 135.

72. Map Room Files, Box 31, FDR Library, Hyde Park, messages exchanged between Churchill and Roosevelt, 31 May–23 June 1944.

73. British Embassy Moscow Telegram no. 2935 to the Foreign Office, 15 October 1944—Gilbert, *Churchill,* Vol. VII, p. 1010.

74. FO 800/302/227-35; CAB 120/158; and Churchill, Vol. VI, pp. 227–8.

75. Harriman and Abel, *Special Envoy to Churchill and Stalin, 1941–1946,* p. 358.

76. Stalin's remark about Togliatti is cited in Gilbert, *Churchill,* Vol. VII, p. 994. And see ibid., pp. 998 ff., for the "haggle."

77. PREM 3/434/4.

78. Moran's recollection of Churchill's depression on the evening of 29 November 1943 is cited in Gilbert, *Churchill,* Vol. VII, p. 581.

79. CAB 120/158.

80. Churchill Papers, 2/497, cited in Gilbert, *Churchill,* Vol. VII, p. 1031.

81. The so-called Caserta Agreement, concluded at Caserta (the site of AFHQ) on 26 September 1944; text in C. M. Woodhouse, *Apple of Discord: a survey of recent Greek politics in their international setting* (London: Hutchinson, 1948), Appendix H. See also ibid., p. 224, for the King of Greece's announcement of 30 December 1944.

82. Only in 1989 was legislation introduced in the Greek Parliament authorising payment of war pensions to former members of EAM/ELAS who resisted the Germans during their occupation of Greece.

83. Kimball, Vol. III, R–608 and R–673.

CHAPTER 16

1. For Roosevelt's remark to his military aide, General Edwin ("Pa") Watson, see Chapter 6, p. 000. For Stalin's instruction to Kurchatov, see A. Lavrent'eva, "Stroiteli novogo mira," *V mire knig,* 9 (Moscow, 1970), pp. 4–5 (and cf. British Embassy, Moscow telegram no. 5192 to the Foreign Office, 1945, in CAB 130/3). Churchill's remark is ascribed to him by Harvey H. Bundy, "Remembered Words," *The Atlantic* (March 1957), p. 57.

2. The OSS archive is open to scholars, at the National Archive, Washington, D.C. The SOE archive is not.

3. This paragraph and the one that immediately follows are based on Hinsley, *British Intelligence,* Vol. I, pp. 313 ff., and Vol. II, pp. 55 ff.

4. *FRUS, the Conference of Berlin,* Vol. I, p. 383.

5. Atomic Bomb File, folder 2, FDR Library, Hyde Park. Unascribed references to the Manhattan Project in the remainder of the present chapter are mainly based on

FDR Library Atomic Bomb file, but also on the relevant volumes of the two official histories: Margaret Gowing, *Britain and Atomic Energy, 1939–1945* (London: Macmillan, 1964), and Hewlett and Anderson, *History of the United States Atomic Energy Commission.* Vol. I, (see Chapter 6, note 50).

6. The text of the Maud Report and of the Frisch-Peierls paper both form appendices in Gowing, *Britain and Atomic Energy.*

7. For a summary of the post-war years of this sorry story, see Edmonds, *Setting the Mould,* Chapter 5. The atomic interchange was finally restored by the Anglo-American *Agreement on Cooperation on the uses of atomic energy for mutual defence purposes, 3rd July 1958,* Cmd. 537 (London: HMSO, 1958).

8. Frederick Lindemann ("the Prof."), created Lord Cherwell, was Churchill's personal scientific adviser.

9. Vice-President of the United States, but also a man with scientific understanding.

10. McGeorge Bundy, *Danger and Survival: choices about the bombs in the first fifty years* (New York: Random House, 1988), p. 46.

11. Kimball, Vol. I, R-62x.

12. Ibid., C-136x.

13. A member of the War Cabinet, who had been a scientist when young and a member of the British Civil Service for many years before the war, he was an able, sceptical Scot.

14. Discoverer of the neutron, a Nobel Prize-winner.

15. Mismanaged on the British side by William Akers, a director of Imperial Chemical Industries. For a summary of these negotiations, see Bundy, *Danger and Survival,* pp. 101–2.

16. Whether Churchill would have sanctioned the execution of this project, at this late stage and with its inevitable effect on other projects then being undertaken in Britain, is debatable, however.

17. They vary from two or three months to a whole year. As Bundy *(Danger and Survival)* remarks, even if the British contribution cut the Manhattan Project by six months, "there would have been no bomb in 1945 without the British" (p. 107).

18. Minute by the Prime Minister to the Paymaster-General (Cherwell), 27 May 1944—PREM 3/139/11A.

19. PREM 3/139/11A (entitled "1945—Explosives"), which is the key file in the Public Record Office on atomic energy, contains photocopies of the originals of all three wartime agreements.

20. Dean Acheson, who had some sympathy with the post-war British resentment: "a Government [of the U.S.], having made an agreement from which it had gained immeasurably, was not keeping its word and performing its obligations"—Dean Acheson, *Present at the Creation,* p. 164.

21. The British Government did not publish the Quebec Agreement as a White Paper (Cmd. 9123) until 1954, after Churchill, then again Prime Minister, had revealed its contents in Parliament.

22. Roger Makins (Lord Sherfield), "Britain's Nuclear Story, 1945–52: politics and technology," review article, *Round Table,* 65 (1975), p. 194.

23. Canadian involvement was the result partly of Canadian uranium resources and partly of the Anglo-Canadian heavy-water project in Canada, at Chalk River.

24. In spite of the wording both of the Hyde Park Aide-Mémoire and of the final clause of the Declaration of Trust.

25. On 18 July 1945—PREM 3/139/9. The codename "Tube Alloys" had misled whoever filed Roosevelt's copy into thinking that it had something to do with torpedoes.

26. Primarily through Klaus Fuchs scientifically and Donald Maclean politically. Fuchs worked at Los Alamos; Maclean became Joint Secretary of the (Anglo-American) Combined Policy Committee in mid-1945, although he had been dealing with atomic matters in the Washington Chancery since his arrival at the British Embassy in April 1944.

27. See, for example, the account given in "Kak delali bombu," *Pravda,* 22 July 1988.

28. See A. I. Ioirysh, I. D. Morokhov, and S. A. Ivanov, *A-Bomba* (Moscow: Nauka, 1980), pp. 390–1. Flerov, at that time a lieutenant in the Soviet Air Force, noticed that western scientific journals in the Voronezh Library no longer contained any mention of atomic matters; this acute observation prompted his letter to Stalin.

29. "Kak delali bombu," *Pravda,* 22 July, 1988.

30. Stimson, Diary, 15 March 1945, p. 2—Stimson Papers, Sterling Memorial Library, Yale University, New Haven.

31. PREM 3/139/11A.

32. Associate Justice of the U.S. Supreme Court, a close friend of Roosevelt.

33. Who had worked with Rutherford at his laboratory in Cambridge between the wars.

34. The original manuscripts of Frankfurter's letters, quoted in this and the succeeding paragraph, are in the Atomic Bomb File, folder 3, FDR Library, Hyde Park.

35. Prime Minister's telegram to Halifax (for Cherwell), 20 September 1944, sent to Washington by courier—PREM 3/139/8A-6698.

36. *PPA: 1944–45,* the (undelivered) Jefferson Birthday Address, 13 April 1945, p. 615.

CHAPTER 17

1. Kimball, Vol. III, C-894/1.

2. Ibid., C-732 and 733 and R-585.

3. Ibid., C-825.

4. Ibid., C-801; R-635, 641, 648, 650 and 676; and C-861.

5. *Izvestiya,* 13 February 1945.

6. *The Economist,* 30 December 1945, and Memorandum for the President from Edward R. Stettinius, 2 January 1945, *DSDF,* 711.41/1-245, National Archives.

7. The military argument concerned Eisenhower's plan for the forthcoming Rhine-

land offensive and the British proposal (not accepted) that Alexander should be appointed his deputy. See Sherwood, *The White House Papers,* Vol. II, p. 761.

8. This photograph is reproduced in the photo section.

9. Telegram of 16 January 1945 from the U.S. Military Mission, Moscow—Map Room File, Box 34, FDR Library, Hyde Park.

10. See John Erickson, *The Road to Berlin,* pp. 473 ff. and 741 ff.

11. Kimball, Vol. III, C–880.

12. Ibid., R–684 (copy of telegram sent to Stalin on 30 December 1944).

13. *SSNMK,* Vol. IV, pp. 100–1.

14. Memorandum from Stimson to the President, 23 January 1945, *FRUS, 1945: the Conference at Malta and Yalta,* p. 80. And Stalin's remark to Bevin, made on Christmas Eve 1945, is quoted in Alan Bullock, *The Life and Times of Ernest Bevin: Foreign Secretary 1945–1951* (New York: W. W. Norton, 1984), p. 210.

15. Kimball, Vol. III, R–696 and C–884.

16. Unless otherwise stated, quotations relating to the Yalta Conference in the rest of this chapter are derived from *FRUS, 1945: the Conferences at Malta and Yalta.* The Soviet record is in *SSNMK,* Vol. IV. The British papers are in CAB 120/170 and PREM 4/78/1.

17. The photograph of the list is reproduced in *FRUS, 1945,* p. 941.

18. The text is contained in the U.S. *China White Paper* (summarised by Francis Valeo for the Library of Congress in October 1949), pp. 113 ff.

19. Churchill, Vol. VI, p. 342, and Anthony Eden, *The Memoirs of Sir Anthony Eden* (London: Cassell, 1965), Vol. II, p. 513.

20. Although Polish sources offer some evidence for the belief that, at a still earlier stage, even Stalin was confused between the western and eastern Neisse, the territorial solution for Poland which he finally secured is a recognisable descendant of that proposed by the Tsarist Foreign Minister in 1914, Sazonow. See *The Memoirs of Wanda Wasiliewska* (Warsaw: Archivum Ruchu Robotnichnego, 1982), Vol. VIII, p. 394, recording a discussion of the frontier with Stalin "in the late spring or at the beginning of the summer of 1943." For a summary of Sazonow's proposals, see Norman Davies, *God's Playground: A history of Poland* (New York: Columbia University Press, 1982), Vol. II, p. 510.

21. Understanding between the Polish Committee of National Liberation and the Government of the USSR regarding the Polish-Soviet state frontier (signed by Molotov and Osóbka-Morawski), Moscow, 27 July 1944; Polish text published in *Dokumenty i materialy do historii stosunków polsko-radzieckich* (Warsaw, 1974), Vol. VIII.

22. The description of the line in this document is identical with that of the "Proposal of the Soviet Delegation regarding the western frontier of Poland" put forward at Potsdam on 20 July 1945—*SSNMK,* Vol. IV, p. 459.

23. Arthur M. Schlesinger, Jr., "Roosevelt's Diplomacy at Yalta," *Yalta: un mito che resiste* (Rome: Edizioni dell' Ateneo, 1989), p. 152. For the origin of the declaration in Washington and the British official reaction to it, see *FRUS, 1945: the Conferences at Malta and Yalta*, pp. 93 ff., especially John Hickerson's memorandum of 8 January 1945. See also Lord Gladwyn, *The Memoirs of Lord Gladwyn* (London: Weidenfeld & Nicolson, 1972), p. 156: "the general consensus [in London] was that nobody was committed very much" by the terms of the declaration.
24. PREM 3/139/11A.
25. 408 H.C. Debs., col. 1284, 27 February 1945.
26. *PPA: 1944–45,* pp. 570–86.
27. Kimball, Vol. III, p. 741. On the whole episode, see ibid., pp. 609 ff., and Charles Bohlen, *Witness to History,* p. 209.
28. Kimball, Vol. III, C-905
29. See, for example, Ibid., C-932.
30. Ibid., C-910 and R-730.
31. *Perepiska,* Vol. II, Document 289.
32. Kimball, Vol. III, R-742.

CHAPTER 18

1. The number of casualties in the Dresden raids (British by night, American by day) is still in dispute, but those killed in the Tokyo raid of 9/10 March 1945 certainly numbered over 84,000.
2. Wallenberg died in Soviet captivity: a crime publicly admitted by the Soviet Government in 1989. See the article by the Soviet Ambassador in Stockholm, Boris Pankin, published by *Moscow News,* 27 August 1989.
3. *The Economist,* 24 March 1945.
4. Churchill's preposterous statement was, however, condemned by moderate opinion at the time—e.g., *The Economist,* "pernicious nonsense," 9 June 1945.
5. Stimson Diary, 25 April 1945, Sterling Memorial Library, Yale University, New Haven.
6. Harry S. Truman, *Year of Decisions, 1945* (Garden City, N.Y.: Doubleday, 1955), p. 82. But this impression is not reflected in *Sov.-Am. O.*, Vol. II, Document 225.
7. *FRUS, 1945: the Conference of Berlin (the Potsdam Conference),* Vol. I, pp. 24 ff.
8. Churchill, Vol. VI, p. 506.
9. Harriman to the Secretary of State, 23 June 1945—*FRUS, 1945: the Conference of Berlin,* Vol. I, p. 728.
10. Kimball, Vol. III, C-931.
11. Churchill, Vol. VI, pp. 401–11, 441–51 and 525. For the "Monday morning quar-

ter-backing," see the Marshall tape in the George C. Marshall Library, Lexington, Va., quoted in James Nelson, ed., *General Eisenhower on the Military Churchill* (New York: W. W. Norton, 1970), pp. 58–9.

12. *St. Louis Post-Dispatch,* 6 March 1946.

13. Churchill to Truman, 10 May 1945, *FRUS, 1945: the Conference of Berlin,* Vol. I, pp. 8–9.

14. Churchill to Truman, 6 and 11 May, and Truman to Churchill, 11 May—ibid., pp. 3–8.

15. Ibid., pp. 64 ff. and 76, note 22; and Churchill, Vol. VI, pp. 502–5.

16. *FRUS, 1945: the Conference of Berlin,* Vol. I, pp. 53 and 89.

17. Richard Hewlett and Oscar Anderson, *History of the United States Atomic Energy Commission,* Vol. I, pp. 351 ff. Unascribed references in the paragraphs about the atomic bomb in this chapter are derived either from this source or from the *Stimson Papers,* Sterling Memorial Library, Yale University, New Haven.

18. *FRUS: 1945, the Conference of Berlin,* Vol. I, p. 221, contains a partial text of the Combined Policy Committee's meeting held on 4 July 1945.

19. Margaret Gowing, *Britain and Atomic Energy,* Vol. I, p. 363.

20. Minute by John Anderson to the Prime Minister, 29 June 1945—PREM 3/139/11A.

21. *DBPO,* Vol. I, p. 1143. This volume of *DBPO* contains the British record of the Potsdam Conference; the Soviet record is in *SSNMK,* Vol. VI.

22. *SSNMK,* Vol. VI, p. 299.

23. But the inclusion of a provision that "German external assets" in Austria were to be a source of German reparations for the Soviet Union was to bedevil the Austrian question for years to come.

24. The record of the British "staff conference" on 31 July *DBPO,* Vol. I, pp. 1052 ff.—at which Bevin decided to do this stands as a model of resigned realism, although before finally agreeing to the Western River Neisse, Bevin succeeded in extracting assurances from the Polish delegation about elections in Poland.

25. Churchill, Vol. VI, p. 581.

26. *DBPO,* Vol. I, pp. 1257 ff.

27. Memorandum by the French Delegation to the Council of Foreign Ministers, 13 September 1945—ibid., p. 150.

28. PREM 3/139/11A, and Churchill, Vol. VI, p. 554.

29. Truman, *Year of Decisions,* pp. 420–1, gives the complete text of the order to Spaatz.

30. Ibid., p. 416, and Churchill, Vol. VI, p. 580. There is a brief account in *SSNMK,* Vol. VI, p. 15.

31. *Atomic Energy: general account of the development of methods of using atomic energy for military purposes under the auspices of the United States Government, 1940–1945,* written by H. D. Smyth at the request of Major General L. R. Groves (Washington, D.C.:

Government Printing Office, 1945; reprinted London: HMSO, 1945), pp. 135–6; and Hewlett and Anderson, *History of the United States Atomic Energy Commission,* Vol. I, pp. xi–xii.

32. A photograph of Truman's manuscript instruction to Stimson, written at Potsdam, is reproduced in the photo section.

33. William Downey; his prayer is recorded on *I Can Hear It Now,* Columbia Masterworks, ML 4095, side 2.

34. For the text of these three agreements, see respectively *Pravda,* 13 August 1970 (translated in *Survival,* XII, 10 [October 1970]); *The Times,* 3 September 1971; and *The Conference on Security and Cooperation in Europe, Final Act,* Cmd. 6198 (London: HMSO, 1975).

CHAPTER 19

1. Fred Vinson, reported in *The Times,* 2 July 1945.

2. Churchill, Vol. VI, p. 417.

3. *Perepiska,* Vol. II, Document 291.

4. *The New York Post,* 13 April 1945.

5. Truman released the news of the Soviet explosion nearly a month after the event. The chief scientific adviser to the British Minister of Defence even believed that it was "quite possible" that the Russians had "managed to steal plutonium from the United States"—PREM 8/1101, minute by Henry Tizard, 26 September 1949.

6. For a summary of the critical events beginning in July 1947, see Edmonds, *Setting the Mould,* pp. 168–9.

7. For Stalin's remark, see *FRUS, 1948,* Vol. II, pp. 999–1006. Churchill's warning is in 408 H.C. Debs., col. 1284, 27 February 1945.

8. Akhmatova disliked the word "poetess." Practically none of her poetry could be published between 1923 and 1940; during the wartime relaxation, copies of her poems were passed from hand to hand by Soviet citizens of all kinds, including those serving in the Red Army; and after the war Zhdanov publicly denounced her as "half nun, half whore." When she died in 1966 five thousand people, mostly the young, attended her requiem mass in a Leningrad church.

9. *Survey,* XXII, 3–4 (1976), "The Arrest and Trial of I. M. Maisky," by Alexander Nekrich.

10. Volkogonov, *Stalin,* Vol. II, Part 2, pp. 193 ff.

11. Churchill, Vol. VI, p. 583.

12. "Financial Dunkirk" was the phrase used by Keynes in his memorandum, "Appreciation of our Overseas Financial Prospects," 13 August 1945 (CAB 129/1) eight days before Truman announced the end of Lend-Lease (described by Churchill at

the time as "a rough and harsh decision"—410 H.C. Debs, cols. 955–8, 29 August 1945).

13. The Fulton speech—over four thousand words—was carried in full by the *St. Louis Post-Dispatch*, 6 March 1946. For the speech at Zurich University, see *The Times*, 20 September 1946.

14. 515 H.C. Debs., col. 897, 11 May 1953.

15. Cited in Gilbert, *Churchill*, Vol. VIII, p. 1100. Dulles, appointed Secretary of State by President Eisenhower, used the phrase "massive retaliation" in his speech delivered on 12 June 1954.

16. Colville, *Fringes of Power*, pp. 704–7.

17. Ibid., p. 708.

18. Mary Soames, *Clementine Churchill*, p. 659.

19. "The Liberator"—the national hero of Venezuela, who died, a disillusioned man, in 1830, at half Churchill's age.

20. Gilbert, *Churchill*, Vol. VIII, Chapter 20, has the full text, which Churchill left in a locked box, discovered by his son twenty years later (first published by the *Sunday Telegraph*, 30 January 1966).

21. President Lyndon Johnson was represented by the U.S. Chief Justice.

22. *The Times*, 25 January 1965.

23. Stimson Diary, 15 March and 23 May 1944. His tribute to Roosevelt was paid in a letter to his widow, 16 April 1945—Stimson Papers, Sterling Memorial Library, Yale University, New Haven.

24. *United Nations Monetary and Financial Conference, Bretton Woods, New Hampshire, USA, July 1 to July 22, 1944 Final Act*, Cmd. 6546 (London: HMSO, 1944, reprinted 1945).

25. See p. 159.

26. Volkogonov's four-part study of Stalin is a recent example. Even he, however, is at pains to describe his work as "the sketch" of a political portrait.

27. *PPA: 1944–45*, Press Conference, 23 February 1945, p. 563.

28. *FRUS, 1945: the Conference of Berlin*, Vol. I, pp. 28–30.

29. *The Diaries of Sir Alexander Cadogan*, ed. David Dilks (London: Cassell, 1971), pp. 776–8.

30. See p. 50–1.

31. Memorandum by Colin Coote, 27 January 1944, cited in Gilbert, *Churchill*, Vol. VII, p. 664; and Eden Diary, 17 July 1945, cited in Robert Rhodes James, *Anthony Eden* (London: 1986), p. 307.

32. Churchill, Vol. VI, p. 579.

33. Colville, *Fringes of Power*, p. 624.

34. Eden Diary, 25 November 1943, in Anthony Eden, *The Memoirs of Anthony Eden*, 3 vols. (London: Cassell, 1960–65), Vol. II, p. 424.

35. Cited in Dallek, *Franklin D. Roosevelt and American Foreign Policy,* p. 470.

36. Mikołajczyk returned to Poland when he joined the Polish Government in Warsaw in 1945, as Deputy Prime Minister and Minister of Agriculture. He fled the country two years later.

37. Andrei Gromyko, *Memories,* translated by Harold Shukman (London: Hutchinson, 1989), pp. 89–90.

38. *FRUS, 1945: the Conference of Berlin,* Vol. II, p. 153: a memorandum by Mikołajczyk on a reception for the Polish Government given by Stalin on 27 July 1945. Mikołajczyk's notes form Appendix A to this volume.

39. Churchill to Eden, 21 October 1942, cited by Christopher Thorne, *Allies of a Kind,* p. 117.

40. See Volkogonov, *Stalin,* passim. The text of both parts of Sergei Eisenstein's *Ivan Groznyi* film script was published by Gospolizdat in Moscow in 1944; the second half was banned, however. For an account of Stalin's views of it, recorded by Eisenstein and Nikolai Cherkasov after a meeting with him on 25 February 1947, see *Moscow News,* 32 (1988), "Formidable Shadows of 1947: Stalin and the Tsar."

41. The date of the end of the Cold War, like the date of its beginning, is a matter of opinion. Brezhnev thought it had ended when he visited Washington in 1973. Once Reagan and Gorbachev began to meet in the mid-1980s it became an open question, which was finally closed at the Malta Summit by Bush and Gorbachev in December 1989.

42. Isaiah Berlin, *Concepts and Categories: philosophical essays,* ed. Henry Hardy (Oxford: Oxford University Press, 1980), p. 122.

43. For example, the peace terms imposed by Germany on Russia in the Treaty of Brest-Litovsk, in 1918.

44. And not only the Security Council. Among the instruments of post-war international order bequeathed to the world by the Grand Alliance, the International Monetary Fund and the World Bank, even though they are still themselves in a state of transition, both now have a major role to play in the reconstruction of the economies of the countries of Central and Eastern Europe.

45. Address by Mikhail Gorbachev to the 43rd Session of the UN General Assembly— full English translation in *Novosti* Press Agency release, 8 December 1989.

46. In the photograph section.

47. "The Atomic Bomb," Memorandum by the Prime Minister, 28 August 1945— CAB 130/3, GEN 75/1.

48. See p. 438.

49. Andrei Gromyko, *Memories,* p. 109.

50. By the time that the nuclear issue was first addressed, at the meeting of the Council of Foreign Ministers in Moscow at the very end of December 1945, it was already too late.

51. H. D. Smyth, *Atomic Energy (Chapter 18, note 31),* pp. 135–6, and Hewlett and Anderson, *History of the United States Atomic Energy Commission,* Vol. I, pp. xi–xii.

52. For the comparable Vienna concepts, see—for example—Harold Nicolson, *Peacemaking 1919* (London: Constable, 1943), pp. xvii and 25.

53. Top Secret Memorandum by the Secretary of State for Foreign Affairs (Ernest Bevin, who almost certainly drafted this document himself), 8 November 1945—in FO 800/478/MIS/45/14.

54. Text in *The New York Review of Books,* 18 January 1990, pp. 5 ff. Lippmann's forecast was quoted in the last sentence of Chapter 1.

INDEX